D1706360

From
New Babylon
to Eden

The Carolina Lowcountry and the Atlantic World

Sponsored by the Lowcountry and Atlantic Studies Program
of the College of Charleston

Money, Trade, and Power
Edited by Jack P. Greene, Rosemary Brana-Shute, and Randy J. Sparks

The Impact of the Haitian Revolution in the Atlantic World
Edited by David P. Geggus

London Booksellers and American Customers
James Raven

Memory and Identity
Edited by Bertrand Van Ruymbeke and Randy J. Sparks

This Remote Part of the World
Bradford J. Wood

The Final Victims
James A. McMillin

*The Atlantic Economy during the
Seventeenth and Eighteenth Centuries*
Edited by Peter A. Coclanis

From New Babylon to Eden
Bertrand Van Ruymbeke

From NEW BABYLON *to* EDEN

The Huguenots and Their Migration to Colonial South Carolina

BERTRAND VAN RUYMBEKE

University of South Carolina Press

© 2006 University of South Carolina

Published in Columbia, South Carolina,
by the University of South Carolina Press

Manufactured in the United States of America

10 09 08 07 06   5 4 3 2 1

Library of Congress Cataloging-in-Publication Data

Van Ruymbeke, Bertrand, 1962–
  From New Babylon to Eden : the Huguenots and their migration to colonial South Carolina /
Bertrand Van Ruymbeke.
      p. cm. — (The Carolina lowcountry and the Atlantic world)
  Includes bibliographical references and index.
  ISBN 1-57003-583-0 (alk. paper)
  1. Huguenots—South Carolina—History. 2. Huguenots—Migrations—History. 3. South
Carolina—History—Colonial period, ca. 1600–1775. 4. South Carolina—Ethnic relations.
5. South Carolina—Religious life and customs. I. Title. II. Series.
  F280.H9V36 2005
  975.7'02'0882845—dc22
        2005009664

Pour Bernard

CONTENTS

Illustrations

ACKNOWLEDGMENTS

This book was long in the making. The nucleus of the study is the dissertation I defended at the Université de la Sorbonne-Nouvelle in 1995. In the years that followed I continued my research in La Rochelle (fall 1996), London and Oxford (summer 1997), and Providence (fall 1998). In 1999 I began writing *From New Babylon to Eden,* a title from an exhibit that I curated in 1997 at the Charleston Museum, and I completed the manuscript in 2003. Thirteen years had passed since I first began my research, years during which I grew increasingly familiar with Charleston, the Carolina lowcountry, and—as much as is possible through the centuries—the few hundred Huguenots who settled in South Carolina. In a letter dated January 10, 1991, the late George C. Rogers Jr. told me that he wanted me to "write the big book on the S.C. Huguenots" and, with much generosity, offered to "do what I can over the years to assist you." To me this epitomizes the wonderful hospitality that I have received in South Carolina. I will never know if this volume is what he had in mind, but I am delighted to use these acknowledgments to express my gratitude to him and to the many people and institutions in the United States and Europe that have helped me to make this study as thorough as possible.

I would first like to thank Bernard Cottret, mentor and friend, who has taught me so much about history and encouraged me from very early on. My gratitude also goes to Jon Butler, who has generously shared his time and expertise in early American religious history with me since I first contacted him ten years ago. I would also like to thank Jack P. Greene for taking the time to read my two-volume French dissertation and advising me on how to best revise it. Many thanks also to Orest Ranum for his comments on chapter 1 and to my cyber-editors, Chuck Lesser and Lou Roper, who read and commented on the chapters I regularly e-mailed them from France or Charleston. We all need proofreaders, but especially when writing a book in a foreign language. Special thanks to Chuck for graciously answering many very detailed questions about proprietary South Carolina and guiding me through the maze of sources at the South Carolina Department of Archives and History in Columbia. My thanks also go to Alex Moore, fellow historian of proprietary South Carolina and acquisitions editor at the University of South Carolina Press, for his advice and, above all, his patience.

Various institutions and individuals have, financially and otherwise, helped me pursue and complete my research. In 1997 the College of Charleston Department of History offered me a Research & Development grant to work in the collections of the British Public Record Office (now the National Archives), the Fulham Palace Library, the Huguenot Society of Great Britain and Ireland Library, the French Church Archives, and the Bodleian. In fall 1998 Norman Fiering and the John Carter Brown Library welcomed me as a fellow, and in fall 2001 the Huguenot Society of America granted me a research stipend. The society has also helped me pay for the cost of some of the illustrations. Many thanks to its president, Robert Echauzier, and to Firth Fabend for making it possible. The College of Charleston Program in the Carolina Lowcountry and Atlantic World also offered me a fellowship in fall 2001 and 2002. I am grateful to Samuel Hines, dean of the School of Humanities and Social Sciences, and Marvin W. Dulaney, then chair of the Department of History, for their warm welcome.

Many others opened the doors of their libraries, offices, and even homes to me. Special thanks to Mike Philips, head of the Interlibrary Loan at the College of Charleston Library, for helping me acquire numerous books and articles, and to Gene Waddell, head of the Special Collections at the same institution, for sharing with me his thorough knowledge of Charleston history, architectural and otherwise, and for allowing me to use photographs of Charleston and the Carolina lowcountry from his impressive personal collection. I would also like to thank Randolph Vigne, editor of the *Huguenot Society of Great Britain and Ireland Proceedings,* and his wife, Gillian, for their London hospitality; Henry B. Hoff, of the New England Genealogical Society, for welcoming me in Boston; Olivier Fatio and Maria-Christina Pitassi for showing me Paul L'Escot's letters at the Bibliothèque Universitaire de Genève; Cheves Leland for making me feel at home at the Huguenot Society of South Carolina Library; and Ray Timmons for allowing me to use one of his photographs of the Middleburg Plantation. Scholars have also generously shared their unpublished research with me. Many thanks to Paula W. Carlo, Denis Vatinel, Michèle Magdelaine, Philippe Marty, and Jean-Luc Tulot.

I would also like to thank all the anonymous librarians at the College of Charleston, the Huguenot Society of South Carolina, the Huguenot Society of America, the Huguenot Society of Great Britain and Ireland, the South Carolina Room at the Charleston County Library, the Charleston Library Society, the Bodleian, the Bibliothèque Nationale de France, the Bibliothèque Municipale de La Rochelle, the John Carter Brown Library, the British Library and the archivists at the South Carolina Department of Archives and History, the British Public Record Office, the South Carolina Historical Society, and the Fulham Palace Library.

Last, but not least, I clearly do not see how I would have completed this book without the support and advice of my wife, Meredith, who has taught me so much about American culture.

INTRODUCTION

Following decades of legal harassment and of outright persecution, about two hundred thousand Huguenots, or French Calvinists, clandestinely left France between 1680 and 1710.[1] This emigration, traditionally known in French historiography as *le Refuge,* is one of the most dramatic dispersions in early modern Europe after the expulsions of the Jews in 1492 and the Moriscos in 1609 from Spain.[2] A small fraction of these Huguenots, about twenty-five hundred individuals, eventually crossed the Atlantic and settled in Massachusetts, Rhode Island, New York, Virginia, and South Carolina, where they founded a total of ten communities between 1680 and 1702.[3] In the history of the Huguenot settlement in early America, South Carolina occupies a particular place. In 1562 Jean Ribault founded Charlesfort near present-day Beaufort. About five hundred Huguenots arrived in the lowcountry at the time of the Revocation of the Edict of Nantes, and a few hundred more settled the Carolina backcountry in the 1760s and 1770s.[4] Today the state of South Carolina can boast one of the finest Huguenot architectural heritages in the United States and the largest American Huguenot Society. One of the many chapters of this history is the subject of this book.

New Babylon and Eden
France and South Carolina between Reality and Fantasy

From New Babylon to Eden describes the gradual marginalization of the Huguenots in France from the 1660s to the Revocation of the Edict of Nantes in 1685, their transatlantic migration to proprietary South Carolina by way of England, and their eventual integration into the religious, political, and socioeconomic fabric of this Restoration proprietary colony. The terms "New Babylon" and "Eden" purposefully refer to a simplistic dichotomy that contrasts an oppressive France to a paradisiacal Carolina and is inspired by proprietary promotional pamphlets and Huguenot accounts of the period. However, the book paradoxically argues that France was not for every refugee the hated and feared New Babylon and that Carolina was deceivingly Eden-like. Like many other transatlantic migrations of the time, the Huguenot migration to the lowcountry resulted from a series of intricately intertwined religious and economic factors, and Carolina, where land was cheap and plentiful and where everything had to be built, was certainly propitious for economic success. From New Babylon to Eden rather than Canaan, in other words, since the choice of such a faraway and unusual destination for Protestant subjects of Louis XIV was not devoid of practical economic considerations. Babylon and Eden thus embody the apparent contradiction inherent to a migration of religious refugees in search of a place to prosper.

The Huguenots were undeniably religious refugees who crossed the Atlantic to establish the conditions necessary for a peaceful spiritual existence away from the rigors of French royal policies. However, they all left France relatively early, at a time when an escape could be carefully planned, and the two recorded ships that brought refugees to the lowcountry, the *Richmond* and the *Margaret,* respectively arrived in Charleston in

April 1680 and March 1685, well before the actual Revocation of the Edict of Nantes. Clearly, although a few documented escapes relate dragooned homes, forced conversions, prison sentences, and nighttime flights and despite antiemigration laws enacted by the monarchy destined to compel Huguenots to remain in France and convert, many, if not most, Carolina Huguenots never personally lived the horror and captivity implied by the term "Babylon."

Similarly, if France was not a New Babylon for most refugees, neither was Carolina the Eden promised in the promotional pamphlets and fantasized by the migrants. The lowcountry, with its subtropical climate; its lush vegetation and somewhat exotic fauna, including the Edenic serpent; its large and hospitable harbors; its bountiful land and rivers, certainly evoked the long-sought Garden of Eden still believed by some chroniclers to be located in the Americas.[5] However, Eden is by definition metaphorically and physically unattainable. Unsurprisingly, life in the lowcountry, at least retrospectively, turned out to be particularly harsh and merciless. Judith Giton's brother, for example, who had left southern France with Carolina on his mind, died of a fever eighteen months after arriving in Charleston following a much-delayed and eventful voyage.[6] Epidemics, hurricanes, fires, Indian wars, Spanish and French raids, and even snakes took their toll. Outbreaks of malaria, smallpox, and the deadly yellow fever occurred in the lowcountry in 1684, 1698, 1699, 1706, 1711, and 1718; hurricanes hit the coast in 1686, 1700 (when the Charleston Huguenot Church was leveled), and 1712; and a fire broke out in Charleston in 1698. Also, the settlers were involved in military operations against the Spanish, the French, and hostile native groups in 1686, 1702, 1706, 1711, and 1715.

The 1699 yellow fever outbreak seems to have been particularly deadly. A contemporary report described its ravages in apocalyptic terms reminiscent of London accounts of the 1665 Great Plague: a "Terrible Tempest of Mortality" hit "our Charlestown," and "the destroying Anger slaughtered so furiously with his revenging Sword of Pestilence . . . 125 English . . . 37 French, 16 Indians, and 1 Negro."[7] The 37 French deaths, which included that of Élie Prioleau, pastor of the Huguenot Church, represent an incredible 22 percent of the 195 refugees settled in Charleston, according to a 1699 census. In other words, nearly a quarter of the French community perished of yellow fever in just two months, August and September 1699.[8] These figures confirmed the great vulnerability of the Huguenots to tropical diseases glimpsed in Giton's letter.[9] Actually, documented cases of sudden deaths among the refugees soon after landing in the colony are sprinkled over the probate records. In his 1709 will, Paul Bruneau de Rivedoux retrospectively deplored the deaths of Sieur Josias Marvilleau and two artisans who had accompanied him to Carolina soon after their arrival in the mid-1680s.[10] Pierre Bertrand, from Île de Ré, wrote his will "ill in his bed" and died at the early age of twenty-four in 1692.[11] For the entire proprietary period, Huguenot extant wills in which the testators mentioned their health show that 80 percent of them were ill. Following the title of a well-known study of mortality rates in lowcountry parishes, it can safely be stated that a large number of Huguenots actually died in paradise.[12]

Even when settlers were spared by epidemics, wars, and climatic disasters, life in proprietary Carolina was never easy. Land was easily available, in sharp contrast to what the refugees were used to in France, but turning a vacant wooded or marshy lot into a prosperous farm or a plantation demanded considerable energy, perseverance, and money. In a 1683 letter, Louis Thibou unambiguously and understatedly explained to his London correspondent that "Carolina is a good country for anyone who is not lazy."[13] Although the Huguenots were collectively successful and some of them even enjoyed spectacular prosperity, in the long run the necessity of acquiring significant capital to establish a slave-worked plantation or a successful trading company left many refugees on the wayside of the path to individual economic success.

The Carolina Huguenots in a Historiographic Perspective

The Huguenot immigration to British North America, and particularly to South Carolina, has been the subject of major scholarly investigations since the end of the nineteenth century. In 1885, the year of the tercentenary of the Revocation of the Edict of Nantes, the incorporation of the Huguenot Society of America, and the foundation of the Huguenot Society of South Carolina, Charles W. Baird published a monumental two-volume work entitled *History of the Huguenot Migration to America* in which he describes Huguenot involvement in the colonization of the Americas since the 1550s and partially accounted for the later migration of Huguenots to British America.[14] Regarding *le Refuge* in North America, Baird's book is a comprehensive, almost catalog-like, study of individual refugees based on extensive archival research; however, except for New England, it does not deal with the subsequent issue of integration. In 1925 the French literary historian Gilbert Chinard published his *Les réfugiés huguenots en Amérique,* which represents only a cursory and, in the case of South Carolina, somewhat erroneous overview of the Huguenot migration to North America simply enhanced by the author's pleasant style.[15] Three years later Arthur H. Hirsch wrote his *The Huguenots of Colonial South Carolina,* the only monograph entirely devoted to the South Carolina Huguenots, which was an expanded version of his 1915 University of Chicago dissertation.[16] Although Hirsch tackled the main issues of the Huguenot migration to Carolina (conformity to the Church of England, naturalization, and economic adaptation) with the historiographical means of his day, he placed too much emphasis on families and individuals at the expense of the group and failed to nuance the Huguenots' overall integration, somewhat naively turning it into a success story.

The new investigative methods and conceptual approaches in the fields of historical demography, immigration history, and cultural anthropology in the 1970s led to the emergence of two seminal works: Amy E. Friedlander's dissertation "Carolina Huguenots: A Study in Cultural Pluralism in the Low Country, 1679–1768"; and Jon Butler's book *The Huguenots in America: A Refugee People in New World Society.*[17] Friedlander's dissertation is a thorough study of the Carolina Huguenots over the long term. She reexamines Hirsch's thesis of successful assimilation in the light of the then relatively novel concept of ethnicity. She concludes that the Huguenots integrated rather than assimilated, retaining a diffuse cultural identity through successive generations. Butler's book is an overall study of the Huguenots in North America emphasizing the economic aspect of the migration, the Huguenots' incapacity to found permanent churches, and their rapid and complete assimilation, which he negatively characterizes as disintegration.[18] Butler also introduces the concept of "double-migration" through which the Huguenots who were refugees in England became economic migrants in the transatlantic migratory process.

From New Babylon to Eden is placed in historiographic continuity with these two works. I study the Huguenot migration to South Carolina in a comparative Atlantic context with the methods used by demographic and social historians. I also emphasize the socioeconomic and religious aspects of the migration and privilege the group over individuals and families. However, whereas Friedlander chose to examine four generations of Carolina Huguenots and Butler devoted one chapter to South Carolina in a larger work covering British North America, my book is entirely devoted to the migrating generation of Carolina Huguenots. This enables me to focus on the migration proper with more scrutiny. I use a detailed database of migrants based on a careful perusal of archival records (church, land, administrative, court, probate, and family) in England, France, Switzerland, and South Carolina, which follows each migrant through the migration and integration process. This also allows me to analyze the dynamics of the proprietary recruitment of Huguenots, which have never been studied in depth. Finally, my work benefits from recent studies published in the wake of the 1985 tercentenary of the Revocation of the Edict of Nantes and the 1998 quatercentenary of its promulgation, as well as the considerable development in the field of Atlantic history, especially with respect to migrations, and in the history of the colonial lower South.

All in all, I somewhat agree with Friedlander's thesis since my detailed study of the first generation shows that the Huguenot experience resembles a process of integration or even, as I argue, of acculturation and creolization rather than simply assimilation. The Huguenots undoubtedly retained a diffuse identity, which appeared, for example, in the formation of kinship alliances and, in turn, influenced the shaping of colonial Carolina society before blooming into the foundation of the Huguenot Society in 1885. However, my work, which is based on a significantly larger database drawn from a wider range of primary sources in North America and Europe, reaches deeper into the roots of the migration and describes in more detail and nuances the gradual transformation of the Huguenots from French refugees to South Carolina planters. Similarly, although indebted to Butler's book in terms of methodology and interpretive framework, my work reaches somewhat different conclusions than does *The Huguenots in America*. I argue that the Huguenot migration to Carolina belongs to a larger Atlantic Huguenot refugee world stretching from the British Isles to America, and that, even if disparities appear in the demographic profiles of the Huguenots who settled in Europe and those who crossed the Atlantic, the migratory process remains the same. I also believe that the Huguenots were adamant about creating their own churches. Conformity to the Church of England was imposed on the rest of the group by an Anglicized elite eager to carve out a niche within Anglo-Carolinian society. Additionally, conformity was more gradual than official records indicate at first sight. The Huguenots, in bishop-free Carolina, adapted insular Anglicanism to their continental Calvinism. Also, the exceptional economic success of the Huguenots, which Butler measured by the yardstick of slave ownership, materialized only in the 1730s and 1740s with the second generation. Finally, while a few Huguenot migrants undoubtedly experienced considerable prosperity, the majority of them, if they survived the harsh living conditions of colonial South Carolina, in essence worked hard for the benefit of their descendants.

Prologue

The Huguenots and the American Southeast before 1660

CAROLINA thus named in honour of Charles IX by the French who discovered it, took possession of it and settled it.

Guillaume De L'Isle, *Carte de la Louisiane* (1718)

From Charlesfort to Charleston
The Elusive Filiation

Twice during the period of their history before the Revocation of the Edict of Nantes, Huguenot leaders who wished to found a French Protestant settlement overseas turned their attention to the area that is now South Carolina. In the early 1560s Admiral Gaspard Coligny, in the wake of his failed attempt to establish a French settlement in Brazil, envisioned establishing a Huguenot colony in what was then called "La Florida."[1] In 1562 Jean Ribault, a Huguenot privateer turned explorer, led an expedition to explore the North American seaboard from the Saint John's River to Cape Fear.[2] Most likely on his own account unless it was a secret order, Ribault decided to found Charlesfort, named after King Charles IX of France, on the southern tip of Parris Island in Port Royal Bay before sailing back to France.[3] Ribault was unable to return to Charlesfort as promised because the Wars of Religion were then raging in France. He was involved in the defense of Dieppe, his hometown in Normandy, against the Catholic royal troops. The fall of Dieppe led Ribault to take refuge in England, where he wrote his *Whole and True Discoverye of Terra Florida* in 1563.[4] In the meantime, the thirty or so men left in Charlesfort sailed across the Atlantic on a makeshift boat and were rescued by fishermen off England's shores. Taking advantage of a period of internal peace the following year, Coligny sent another expedition to La Florida under the command of René de Laudonnière, a Huguenot sea captain from Poitou. Instead of rebuilding Charlesfort, which had been burned by the Spanish a few months earlier, Laudonnière founded Fort Caroline at the mouth of the River of May, the present-day Saint John's River.[5]

Eager to drive the French out of their zone of influence and determined to settle in the American Southeast permanently in order to discourage further incursions, the Spanish sent Pedro Menéndez de Avilés with a large number of settlers and troops to Florida. Menéndez arrived at the mouth of the River of May in September 1565 a few days after Ribault, who after his return from England had been sent by Coligny to Florida at the head of a large reinforcement fleet. The confrontation that took place in the following weeks led to the storming of Fort Caroline; the destruction of the French fleet; the execution of most of the French, including Ribault; and the founding of Saint Augustine.[6]

The fall of La Rochelle in 1628, which put an end to the last Huguenot rebellion, led to the migration of several notable French Protestant figures to England. One of them, Antoine Ridouet, Baron de Sancé, became involved with other Huguenot refugees in various English colonization schemes.[7] In spring 1629 Sancé first thought of founding a Huguenot settlement in Virginia "to plant vineyards and olive [trees], and make silk and salt."[8] With the help of another Huguenot courtier, he then proposed the migration of several hundred French Protestants to "Florida," meaning the land south of Virginia.[9] This "Florida" project, however, soon reached an impasse since Sancé and his Huguenot partners lacked a viable colonization plan and sufficient court influence. Consequently, in the spring of 1630 the same group of Huguenot *gentilshommes* led by Sancé joined Sir Robert Heath in a partnership to settle the newly granted "Carolana."[10]

Sancé's plan was to obtain the northern part of Carolana and to settle it with Huguenot salters who were to be recruited in La Rochelle if not available in England. These prospective colonists, whose "names and vocations were to be written in a book," were to "have certificates from their respective pastors in France."[11] This elaborate project, symptomatic of the unrealistic approach to colonization prevalent in the 1630s, proved to be impossible to implement. Sancé failed to send any Huguenot settlers to Carolana and even lost Heath's support. In April 1632, in an effort to exclude Huguenots from his overseas domain, Heath obtained a royal order stipulating that "no Strangers borne subjects to any prince or State out of our obeystance shall be willingly entertained into" Carolana and, since it was not enough to exclude Huguenots altogether, demanding that all prospective settlers conform to the Church of England.[12]

Do these early colonization ventures in the American Southeast constitute precedents to the Huguenot migration to proprietary South Carolina? Until recently the traditional historiographical view was to emphasize the continuity between Coligny's expeditions to La Florida, Sancé's colonization plans in Carolana, and later Huguenot migration to South Carolina. Charles Baird, Arthur Hirsch, and Gilbert Chinard all described these quite different historical phenomena as part of the same effort to seek a Huguenot refuge in the area.[13] The idea of making Carolina a destination for the Huguenots of the *premier* (1560s–1660s) and *second* (1670s–1710s) *Refuges,* as England and the Netherlands, for example, are in Europe, is attractive but anachronistic. Assuredly, both Coligny and Sancé wished to help their coreligionists by providing them with a place where they could escape royal persecution, but in neither project was the establishment of a religious haven a primary motive.[14] In the case of the La Florida expeditions, the military and economic motivations prevailed for two reasons. First, although Huguenots had individually migrated out of France since the 1530s, there was no actual need for places to accommodate massive waves of refugees before the Saint Bartholomew's Day Massacres (1572), to which, incidentally, Coligny was the first to succumb.[15] Second, when French Protestants fled France in the sixteenth century, they escaped to nearby locations and, so they hoped, for a short period of time. When, for example, Ribault fled to England after the surrender of Dieppe, he first stayed in Rye, a southern port just across the English Channel, in the hope of a prompt return.[16] Thus, although the settlement in La Florida was almost exclusively a Huguenot-led and Huguenot-manned enterprise, contrary to the religiously mixed Brazilian expeditions of a decade earlier, the idea of founding a Huguenot haven remained secondary in Coligny's mind. It was too early and too far. Coligny's motivations were essentially strategic and economic. The three expeditions to La Florida were part of an overall strategy meant to create a Huguenot Atlantic, home to navigators, explorers, fishermen, and privateers, for the benefit of France and at the expense of Spain. After attempting to found a permanent settlement in the Bay of Rio in the mid-1550s, Coligny chose to try again in Florida, perceived as a sound base from which to explore the interior of the North American continent in search of mineral deposits and to raid Spanish convoys on their way back from Havana. In short, Coligny's goal was to integrate the Huguenots into a national colonial policy that would enrich France and enhance its prestige while breaking the Iberian monopoly on the riches of the New World.

Although Sancé's plans in Carolana may represent "a distant echo of America as a Huguenot refuge first tried on [the same] coast seventy years before," his motivations were actually different from Coligny's.[17] The Carolana venture, which Paul Kopperman calls "one of the most spectacular fiascoes of this half-century [1600–1650]," was certainly ill planned, but from a Huguenot point of view its failure was due primarily to the individualistic nature of Sancé's interests and the French historical context.[18] First, Sancé was not acting for France or even for his coreligionists but rather for himself as a penniless refugee gentilhomme hoping to regain status and money through colonialization. Second, while it is reasonable to think that the failure of the last Huguenot rebellion and the costly fall of La Rochelle may have created a favorable context for the recruitment of French Protestant settlers, the fact is that it did not.[19] In the 1630s most French-speaking Calvinist refugees in England were Walloons, not Huguenots, since migration out of France was small.[20] Like Coligny in the 1560s, Sancé failed to trigger a significant Huguenot migration to the American Southeast. It was still too early.

There is no factual or consequential continuity between Coligny's attempt to settle La Florida or Sancé's involvement in the Carolana venture and later Huguenot migration to South Carolina, but both undeniably influenced subsequent developments and remain useful in our understanding of the Huguenot Refuge in North America and in the lowcountry in particular. Ironically, the Huguenots' failed colonization of the American Southeast benefited England, not France. Ribault's account was first published in English in a 1563 London edition and later included in Richard Hakluyt's *Divers Voyages* (1582).[21] Laudonnière's narrative, the 1586 first French edition of which was dedicated to Sir Walter Raleigh, was translated into English by Hakluyt and published under his sponsorship in 1587.[22] No doubt, as Loren Pennington points out, the opportune dedication to Raleigh was meant to bring public support for the Virginia voyages.[23] Jacques Le Moyne de Morgues, who, as the official cartographer on Laudonnière's 1564 expedition, drew a map of the Florida peninsula and sketches of the southeastern coastline and native life, took refuge in London at the time of the Saint Bartholomew's Day Massacres and died there in 1588.[24] While in London he met John White, on whom he had an undeniable influence.[25] Charlesfort survivors, who were rescued in 1563, were duly sent to Queen Elizabeth's court to be questioned on their American experience before being allowed to return to France.[26] Finally, while Ribault was in London, England prepared an expedition to take over Charlesfort, but the venture collapsed when Ribault attempted to flee to France with one of the ships.[27]

No doubt the English showed great interest in "French Florida," as John Hawkins's spying mission to Fort Caroline in the summer of 1565 makes clear.[28] In the 1560s the English collected from the Huguenots a lot of what might be called intelligence information about the American Southeast and the Spanish presence there. Thus, Hakluyt was sent to France in 1583 officially as the ambassador's chaplain but with the secret assignment to collect information on naval intelligence matters.[29] It is therefore fair to say that the English experience in North America was built, although not exclusively, on Coligny's aborted colonial policy.[30] As the English historian A. L. Rowse wrote, "the idea of American colonization came to us out of [the] Huguenot circle."[31] No doubt, as Hakluyt pointed out in the preface to his translation of Laudonnière's account, the history of the French colony could provide a useful lesson for the English. Thus, the bloody epilogue of Huguenot Florida, known as the Matanzas Massacres, which Frank Lestringant aptly called "la Saint-Barthélemy américaine" (the American Saint Bartholomew's Day) and which, incidentally, helped fuel the Protestant anti-Spanish *leyenda negra,* led the English judiciously to found a settlement at a safe distance from Spain's Florida in the 1580s.[32] The Spanish, who originally thought that England would attempt to settle in the vicinity of Santa Elena Sound where Charlesfort once stood, made only feeble attempts to seek out the colonists at Roanoke due to their limited resources and ill-planning.[33] The northern location of the settlement certainly made it appear less threatening than Charlesfort and Fort Caroline did in the 1560s, and its destruction, although regarded as necessary, did not constitute a foremost priority for the Spanish.[34]

The memory of Huguenot Florida lingered in England through the 1680s. In fact, concurring reports show that the Carolina coast was viewed, through a sort of Huguenot prism, as if the region had never been occupied by Europeans after the French had abandoned Charlesfort.[35] William Hilton, who was sent by the Barbadian Adventurers to reconnoiter the Carolina coast south of Cape Fear in 1663, sailed by Port Royal and noticed "the ruines of an old fort, compassing more than half an acre of land within the Trenches, which [he] supposed to be Charles's Fort, built and so called by the French in 1562."[36] Quite significantly, Hilton thought these ruins to be the remnants of Charlesfort and not of San Marcos (II), the last Spanish fort constructed on the site, while the French had remained in the area less than a year.[37] Similarly, when Robert Sandford sailed by the Edisto River in 1666, he wondered if it was not the "Gironde," following Ribault's fluvial nomenclature.[38] Then, when the Carolina proprietors decided to found a permanent settlement in their domain in 1669, undeniably influenced by the French enthusiastic description of the bay, they first thought of Port Royal as the ideal location.[39]

The memory of "Huguenot Florida" is also mentioned in two pamphlets published in the 1670s and 1680s. In *Description du Pays nommé Caroline,* one can read that Carolina "is part of a country once called Florida, first discovered by the Spanish, but later occupied by the French who have [since] abandoned it."[40] Although this reference is not actually intended as an argument to draw Huguenots to the colony, its presence in a promotional pamphlet indicates that sixteenth-century Huguenot involvement in Florida must have been known to the average French reader. This interest in Florida and more broadly in the American Southeast is confirmed by the publication of the *Histoire de la conquête de la Floride par les Espagnols sous Ferdinand de Soto* in 1685, the year when most Huguenots fled from France.[41] Instead of being used as a promotional argument, however, the reminiscence of Huguenot Florida was actually put forth in an adversarial pamphlet titled *Remarques sur la Nouvelle Relation de la Caroline, par un Gentilhomme François,* as a reason for French Calvinists to avoid settling in Carolina.[42] Alluding to the 1565 Matanzas Massacres, the anonymous pamphleteer thus warned Huguenot readers that whoever settled in Carolina could meet the same deadly fate.[43] Finally, in the eighteenth century when maps were used as means of propaganda in the Anglo-French rivalry in North America, the famed cartographer Guillaume De L'Isle would not hesitate to claim that Carolina not only had been named after Charles IX but also was settled by the French and that Charleston was formerly Charlesfort.[44]

Although lost in the annals of history, Huguenot involvement in the Carolana venture is also historically meaningful. By the 1630s the Huguenots, who had already been officially excluded from New France since 1627, were relegated to an increasingly peripheral role in France's colonial policy. Consequently, Huguenot would-be colonial entrepreneurs began to envision colonization projects within the nascent English empire in North America. Thus, whereas Ribault feigned to deliver Charlesfort to the English in the 1560s and deserted England to return to Florida to serve France, in the 1630s Sancé was willing to work for England. As a Huguenot gentilhomme-entrepreneur acting on his behalf within a larger English-sponsored colonial project, Sancé's plans set a precedent for later Huguenot initiatives, such as René Petit's and Jacob Guérard's *Richmond* expedition in 1679. Although unsuccessful, Sancé's venture was nonetheless visionary. Clearly, if the Huguenots were to immigrate to North America in significant numbers in the seventeenth century, it would be through individually sponsored projects within the frame of an aggressive English colonization policy.

Chapter 1

EAST OF EDEN

New Babylon

In ordinary speech, it is often said that toleration is always a relationship of inequality where the tolerated groups or individuals are cast in an inferior position. To tolerate someone else is an act of power; to be tolerated is an acceptance of weakness.

Michael Walzer, On Toleration (1997)

To be the restorer of the [Catholic] faith, the exterminator of heresy, these are . . . immortal titles, which will not only transcend time, but which will still remain when time shall cease.

D. de Cosnac, Bishop of Valence (July 14, 1685)

Everything about him [Louis XIV] was great, even his mistakes. This one [the Revocation of the Edict of Nantes] was immense.

Édouard Hervé, Discours à l'Académie Française (1887)

The Huguenots in Late Seventeenth-Century France

France during the second half of the seventeenth century was roughly the size of present-day France minus Lorraine, Corsica, Savoy, the Comté de Nice, and the Comtat Venaissin (Avignon). It had a population of slightly more than twenty million people, which made it the most populous country of Europe, well ahead of England, Spain, and even Russia.[1] France was essentially an agricultural nation, and the vast majority of Louis XIV's subjects lived in small communities. In 1700 fewer than four million of them, or less than 18 percent of the total population, resided in towns and cities of more than two thousand people.[2] This urban population lived predominantly in small towns as France had only twenty cities of more than thirty thousand people. Except for Paris, which with more than five hundred thousand people in 1700 was the most populous city in both France and Europe, the four largest cities—Lyon, Marseille, Rouen, and Lille—had a population of well under one hundred thousand each.[3]

This overwhelmingly rural population was also extremely diverse as France was then an intricate patchwork of regions and peoples with different languages, customs, systems of land tenure, and privileges that could be political, religious, or fiscal.[4] France was not then divided into *départements* of roughly equal sizes but into administrative regions called *généralités,* which more or less followed the contours of formerly independent territories that had been acquired through conquest and marriage by the French monarchy. In the 1680s there were thirty-two généralités. The powers of the intendant, the administrator in charge of the généralité, which were primarily fiscal and judicial, also varied enormously according to local customs and privileges as well as the size and status of the généralité.[5] In recently acquired provinces, for example, where the monarchy wanted to absorb the local population with tact, the intendant had to govern with moderation. Another factor that limited the power of the monarchy and its representatives was the presence of *parlements.* These provincial higher courts of justice exerted local fiscal and judicial prerogatives and could, at least in theory, refuse to register royal decrees.[6] A famous example is the refusal of the parlement of Rouen in Normandy to record the Edict of Nantes until 1609, or eleven years after its promulgation.[7]

The regions of France were diverse not only institutionally but also ethnically and linguistically. Basques, Picards, Bretons, Alsatians, and Catalans, for example, were of quite different ethnic origins and spoke mutually unintelligible languages. The last two had been French subjects for less than a generation.[8] In his linguistic study of seventeenth-century France, the Canadian historian Philippe Barbaud showed that only a minority of French subjects living in a zone comprising Île-de-France (the Paris basin), central, and west central France spoke French as a mother tongue. Elsewhere, while an increasing number of the king's subjects, especially in towns and cities, used the national language in everyday life, most spoke dialects or patois and regional languages of Celtic, Provençal, or Germanic origins, which were more or less understood by French speakers.[9]

The socioeconomic fabric of seventeenth-century France also defies modern conceptual frameworks in its complexity and archaism. Ancien regime French society was both a society of orders—with the nobility, the clergy, and the common people—in which social groups were defined by the dignity and importance of their occupation, and one of class based on inherited or produced wealth.[10] In other words, it was a society of orders whose internal dynamic was economic. The French population being predominantly agrarian, the ownership of land and the control of its yields, usually through taxes paid in money or in kind, was what primarily defined the elite, whether lay and ecclesiastical seigneurs, civil administrators, urban bourgeois, or simply rich landowning peasants.[11] Although France then led Europe in industrial production, manufacturing held a modest position in the French economy despite Colbert's vigorous mercantilist initiatives.[12] Except for a few urban textile centers such as Lille, Amiens, Nîmes, and Lyon, manufacturing was mainly a rural, part-time, and sometimes seasonal activity.[13] The textile industry, which included flax, wool, and silk, ranked first, followed by mining and metallurgy. French textiles, of average quality, were exported in great quantities to Antwerp, Amsterdam, and Cadiz, and from there they supplied the Iberian American market.[14] In sum, as one Englishman traveling through France in the 1680s observed, "it's certainly the most populous Country of its extent in Europe, and no less fertile and abounding in Corn, Wine, Olives, Almonds and Figs, which together with the Hemp, Flax, and Silk, have created a very considerable Commerce, greatly facilitated by diverse navigable Rivers, and Sea Ports commodiously seated for Traffick."[15]

Despite France's advantageous geographic location, topography, and economic wealth, its commerce was still comparatively small. One reason for this weakness is that even if practiced on a large scale, trade was regarded with disdain by the elite and therefore did not employ much human or financial capital. As an English observer satirically explained, "the merchants employ their money rather in buying offices than in exercising traffick, because officers' wives go before merchants' wives."[16] In 1686 the French merchant fleet numbered fewer than eight hundred vessels of one hundred tons or more, which was less than half the size of the Dutch fleet.[17] French commerce was mostly coastal along the Atlantic and Mediterranean shores since, except for the fisheries of the northern Atlantic, few French merchants were involved in transoceanic trade.

Notwithstanding its cultural diversity, the vast majority of the French population, apart from the Alsatian Lutherans, practiced *one* religion, which they shared with their monarch: Catholicism.[18] France had always played an influential role in what was once the unified western Christian church, a role that had given it the name "eldest daughter of the church" (*Fille aînée de l'Église*) and to its ruler the honorific title of "most Christian king" (*Roi très chrétien* or *Rex Christianissimus*).[19] In this Catholic France the Huguenots formed a small minority. Numbering roughly 730,000 in 1680, they represented less than 4 percent of the population. Since the turn of the seventeenth century, when it had been above the million mark, the Huguenot population had never ceased to decline until it leveled off after 1670. The reasons for this decrease are multiple: the rebellions of the 1620s; the restoration of Catholicism in Huguenot Béarn; epidemics; conversions; a lower birthrate in some traditionally Huguenot regions, such as the Cévennes in Languedoc and the Pays de Caux in Normandy; and the continuous immigration of surrounding Catholic peasants to Huguenot towns.[20]

This Huguenot population was unevenly distributed within France. According to American historian Philip Benedict's demographic study, in 1660 the northern provinces had 171 churches for 135,000 parishioners, whereas the southern provinces numbered 525 churches for 662,000 people. These figures indicate that 83 percent of the Huguenots lived in southern France and that the south to north ratio in churches and people was four to one.[21] The Protestant population tended to be more urban in the north (50 percent) than in the south (22 percent). Kingdomwide, with 26 percent, the urban rate of the Huguenot population was significantly higher than the national average of 18 percent.[22]

The social stratification of the Huguenot population also differed from its Catholic counterpart. After the conversion to Catholicism of Henri de La Tour d'Auvergne, Vicomte de Turenne, in 1668, the high nobility no longer counted a Calvinist in its ranks.[23] Similarly, the Huguenots who had bought or inherited high administrative offices, already few in numbers in the 1650s, gradually converted or resigned after 1660.[24] Consequently, the Huguenot elite was drawn from the lower provincial nobility and from the trade, banking, and industrial bourgeoisies. Provincial gentilshommes, who were removed from the splendor of Versailles and for whom conversion to Catholicism would not bring social promotion, maintained small churches, called *églises de fief,* on their estates.[25] Huguenots also tended to be numerous in manufacturing, banking, and especially commerce, not because of an alleged Calvinist penchant and aptitude for these professions but, as Janine Garrisson writes, "out of existential necessity."[26] Not all the

Huguenots were rich notables, though, as many of them were artisans—especially in the textile trades—retailers, seamen, and (in the south mostly) farmers.

Although Huguenots tended to be more urban, more artisanal, and more "bourgeois" than Catholics, as the French historian Élisabeth Labrousse stresses, they had more in common with them than is usually acknowledged. As she puts it, the Huguenots were before all "proud to be French" and considered foreigners with "tacit condescension."[27] They were also deeply involved in their communities and shared most of the lifeways of their Catholic social peers. Nonetheless, as Labrousse writes, they were "French in a peculiar way," as their civil and religious existence was guaranteed only by an edict that had been promulgated at the end of the Wars of Religion in 1598: the Edict of Nantes.[28]

The Crown and the Edict of Nantes
Strict Construction and Peaceful Conversions (1661–1679)

Promulgated by Henry IV, who had converted to Catholicism in order to ascend to the throne of France, the Edict of Nantes gave Huguenots civil, juridical, military, and religious rights.[29] According to its main clauses, the Huguenots were granted freedom of conscience, freedom of worship in cities and towns that they controlled in 1597, the right to build churches, complete access to education and offices, special bipartisan courts of justice called *chambres de l'Édit,* and the control of about 150 fortified towns.[30] The Edict of Nantes was a compromise, reached after months of intense negotiations between the Huguenot leadership and the monarchy, whose principal objective was peace rather than religious toleration. Despite the many privileges that it granted the Huguenots, it also contained clauses extremely favorable to the Catholic religion, and its structural weaknesses would be fatal to the Protestants.[31]

Catholicism was restored as the official religion of the kingdom and could be reestablished wherever it had been banned, sometimes for over forty years, by the Huguenots.[32] The Catholics thus enjoyed total freedom of worship, whereas that of the Huguenots was geographically limited to certain cities and seigneurial estates. Protestants were also required to pay the ecclesiastical tithe (*dîme*) and could not work during Catholic holidays.[33] Worse, two crucial privileges that were granted to them, the annual subsidy for the payment of pastors and the control of fortified towns manned by subsidized garrisons, were contained not in the edict itself but in two warrants. These warrants, or *brevets,* which did not need to be registered by the parlements to be enforced and which were explicitly meant to be temporary, were granted by the monarchy, who could choose not to renew them once they expired.[34] As Bernard Cottret writes, "what the king *can* give, he *can* also take away."[35] Not surprisingly, with the signing of the Peace of Alès at the end of the last Huguenot rebellion in 1629, the crown chose not to renew the brevets, therefore recognizing only the clauses contained in the edict proper. The Huguenots had then lost their political and military independence and no longer constituted "a state within the state."[36]

When Louis XIV took control of France at the death of Cardinal Mazarin in 1661 and chose to rule with the help of a smaller council and without a *principal ministre,* the Huguenots lived under the regime of an Edict of Nantes truncated by the Edict of Alès.[37] Until 1679, when intense persecution began, the monarchy alternately followed a policy of restrictions and of appeasement, depending on Louis XIV's views and on the international context. In his *Mémoires,* addressed to his son and written in the late 1660s, Louis XIV, while acknowledging that the "[Protestant] reformers obviously spoke the truth on many matters of fact," considered nonetheless that "the best means to reduce gradually the number of Huguenots in [his] kingdom was, in the first place, not to press them at all by any new rigor against them, to implement what they had obtained from [his] predecessors but to grant nothing further, and even to restrict its execution within the narrowest limits that justice and propriety would permit."[38] Consequently, in the 1660s and 1670s the monarchy's effort to reduce Protestantism and bring all French subjects under one religion was limited to a strict construction, or *interprétation à la rigueur,* of the Edict of Nantes. This policy materialized in two ways. First, French Protestantism was geographically circumscribed by verifying that new churches had not been erected outside the zone delineated by the edict. It was reported, for instance, that in Dauphiny alone 130 churches had been illegally built since 1597.[39] Second, anti-Protestant measures that were meant to explicitly outlaw what the edict did not allow and intended to make the life of the Huguenots difficult were consistently decreed.[40]

To lead the inquiry concerning the legitimacy of Huguenot congregations, a local team of two *commissaires* was appointed by the king. It was composed of a Huguenot, who was a member of the local gentry, and a Catholic, who usually was the intendant himself and thus of a higher rank than the local Protestant.[41] At first these commissions of inquiry were to be temporary, but in 1665 they became permanent. The procedure was the same in every province. The commissaires, responding to complaints from the local clergy about the alleged unlawful presence of a Huguenot church, demanded written proof from the congregation of its existence prior to 1598. These could be registers of baptisms or marriage as well as records of deliberations of the consistory.[42]

A Carolina-related illustration of this procedure and the ways Huguenots tried to defend themselves is provided by the legal actions taken against the Church of Pons, Saintonge, where Élie Prioleau, one of the first pastors of the Charleston congregation, and his father, Samuel, both officiated.[43] Following a first investigation the church was allowed to remain in 1664. In 1682 local Catholic authorities contested the 1664 decision on the grounds that the Pons Huguenots had shown incomplete documentation to the commissaires. The Pons congregation then submitted the original baptismal registers for the period 1575–92 and 1562–1606, consistory records covering the period 1584–97, and a 1600 royal decision confirming their right to worship in the town of Pons.[44] These types of documents, registers prior to 1597 and a decision confirming the existence of the congregation soon after the signing of the Edict of Nantes, are typical of what a church needed to preserve in order to survive. The Pons Huguenots won their case, which indicates that the procedure was conducted fairly or at least that documented Huguenot privileges were respected, but the amount of documentation that congregations had to provide shows how difficult it must have been for smaller or more rural churches to meet the test. Incidentally, the Pons case also shows that a legal victory in the 1660s did not prevent a second investigation twenty years later.

As expected, many churches could not gather such extensive documentation, sometimes simply because registers had been confiscated by the Catholic authorities at an earlier time, and were therefore disbanded and their temples razed.[45] The hardest-hit provinces were Languedoc, where more than a hundred temples were demolished; Poitou, where the number reached thirty; and Dauphiny, where half the temples were razed.[46] Throughout France, among the 650–700 Huguenot Church buildings in existence in 1661, more than 150, or over 20 percent, had been demolished by 1664.[47] The razing continued; John Locke, traveling in France in 1676, observed that "they [the Huguenots] have had within these 10 years 160 churches pulled down."[48]

In face of this new adversity, however, the Huguenots were not without defense or recourse. When the commissaires could not reach a decision immediately, a lengthy legal battle would follow, sometimes for more than a decade, during which the temple was still open. In some cases, when worship was banned and the temple confiscated or demolished, the congregation would meet in the chapel of a local seigneur or simply build another church in an area where they were authorized to do so. In other instances congregations would continue to meet at the locations of their former temples, and in some extreme cases Huguenots, sometimes women, would physically prevent the workers from razing their churches.[49]

In the 1660s and 1670s a series of measures, called *arrêts,* were also decreed by the monarchy against the Huguenots.[50] The crown's objectives were to isolate its Calvinist subjects politically and socially by restricting their civil and economic privileges, and to restrict their freedom of worship. All this was done, it was officially argued, without flouting the Edict of Nantes. As Bishop Gilbert Burnet comments in his *History of His Own Time,* "Many new edicts were coming out every day against them [the Huguenots], which contradicted the edict of Nantes in the most express words possible; And yet . . . the King did not intend by them to recall, nor to go against any article of the edict of Nantes."[51] In actuality, there were two types of arrêts: local and nationwide. The first were specific, as they were decreed against a congregation, school, cemetery, or individuals in response to complaints from local Catholics. These decrees were enforced swiftly and efficiently but were extended, by way of jurisprudence, to a province, and in some cases to the whole kingdom, only gradually. Between 1656 and 1682 two hundred such arrêts were enacted.[52] Arrêts of the other type, which were more general in their contents and applied to the entire Huguenot population, were not usually enforced, at least until 1680, as they were often deemed inapplicable or were simply ignored.[53] These nationwide arrêts numbered only twelve between 1661 and 1679.[54]

Politically, the crown tried to limit the influence of the Huguenots at the town level. The Déclaration of 1666 stipulated that in every Huguenot town the alderman and half of the councillors had to be Catholic.[55] This meant that Catholics would gain control of half the council even in overwhelmingly Huguenot towns and that the Protestants would necessarily lose councillors in the process. The town of Nîmes, Languedoc, for example, where the Huguenots formed a substantial majority, had, as Locke described, "2 Protestant and 2 Papist" councillors.[56] In some instances Huguenots could lose their political representation in the town council altogether and have their temples demolished. In his journal Locke mentions the case of the Languedoc town of Uzès where, in early 1676, the Huguenots were ordered "[by] the King to choose noe more consuls

[councillors] of the town of the [reformed] Religion" and had "their temple . . . puld down
. . . though three fourths of the town be Protestants."[57]

The monarchy also issued arrêts regulating the Huguenots' practice of certain trades
and professions in order to force them to convert to Catholicism or risk being socially
marginalized. In the 1660s and 1670s most of these arrêts, usually enacted by a parlement, were applicable only within the limits of a city or a province. In 1663 the parlement of Rouen issued a law stipulating that there could be only one Huguenot doctor
for fifteen Catholic doctors.[58] The following year the same parlement limited the number of Huguenot lawyers in the city of Rouen to ten, and in 1665 it set the ratio of silversmiths at one Huguenot for fifteen Catholic silversmiths.[59] Huguenot influence was also
curtailed within the guilds as, referring to an arrêt of 1667, Locke reported that in
Languedoc only "one third of any trade in any town suffered to pass masters, i.e. to set
up, [were] of the [Protestant] Religion."[60]

Not surprisingly, the bulk of the anti-Huguenot measures were meant to restrict their
freedom of worship and to make their religious life difficult. As some congregations
were too poor to have pastors or simply had no temples, it was common for Huguenot
churches to share ministers. A pastor's secondary church was then known as an *annexe*.
The crown attempted to restrict this practice by forbidding ministers to officiate where
they did not reside (1656), in open air or in annexes (1657), and eventually at more than
one church (1664).[61] The crown also intended to limit psalm singing, one of the most distinctive aspects of Huguenot religious practice. First, Huguenots could not sing psalms
in the privacy of their homes if they could be heard in the streets (1659). Then psalm
singing outside the temple was prohibited altogether in successive arrêts decreed in 1661,
1662, and 1663. Eventually, in 1664, it became illegal to sing psalms inside a church when
a Catholic procession was passing by.[62] Visiting the congregation of Guînes near Calais,
where the Charleston pastor Florent Trouillart's father officiated, White Kennet, future
bishop of Peterborough, England, recorded that it was "a custom for the protestants formerly at one mile distance from Calais to sing psalms in the severall boats till they came
to Guine, but of late forbidden by authority."[63] In 1663 daytime Huguenot funerals were
banned throughout the kingdom and processions were limited first to thirty and then, in
1664, to ten people.[64] The locations of Huguenot cemeteries, in which no monuments
could be erected, were also strictly regulated. After 1663 these had to be located outside
towns and villages and at least three hundred paces from a Catholic church.[65] Passing
through France on his return from Italy in 1665, the Englishman Philip Skippon noted that
in Nîmes "the protestants have a burying-place without the city, and bury their dead
either betimes in the morning or after sunset, the king of late years not suffering them to
accompany the corpse at any other time."[66]

In a period when education was permeated with religion, schools were rightfully perceived by the crown as an essential aspect of the Huguenots' religious life. Protestant
emphasis on knowledge of the Scriptures, the preponderance of Catholic religious orders
in French schools, and their exclusion from the universities led the Huguenots to set up
a separate educational system.[67] Throughout France they had a network of grammar
schools (*écoles*), Latin schools (*collèges*), and universities (*académies*). In the écoles masters taught a smattering of reading, writing, arithmetic, and catechism.[68] If both collèges

and académies offered classes in rhetorics, ancient languages, philosophy, and theology, the académies were specifically designed to train ministers.[69] In the mid-seventeenth century there were thirty Huguenot collèges and five académies.[70] In the 1660s, spurred by a Catholic clergy who, in vain, asked for the suppression of all the Huguenot collèges, the monarchy was determined to limit Protestant educational freedom within the strictest bounds of the Edict of Nantes. The crown's objectives were to limit the number of Huguenot educational institutions and professors and regulate their curricula. After 1662, as in the case of the temples, grammar schools and collèges could only remain where they had existed before 1598. When documented proof could not be submitted, the institutions became Catholic.[71] In 1663 an arrêt banned the teaching of catechism in the écoles, limiting the curriculum to reading, writing, and arithmetic, and in 1671 it was decided that they could hire only one master.[72] The crown's ultimate goal was to force Huguenot parents to send their children to Catholic schools and to keep Catholic children from attending Huguenot schools, as was often the case in small communities where the only école was Protestant.[73]

The 1660s ended with the unexpected Déclaration of 1669, which cancelled several previous anti-Huguenot decisions, especially those restricting their freedom of worship, and reiterated basic Huguenot civil and religious rights. Sometimes referred to as "a second Edict of Nantes," this *déclaration* seemed to reveal a change in the crown's objectives. In fact, it was more a change of strategy, partly caused by the international context of the war against the Calvinist Netherlands, than of goals.[74] The monarchy still wished to reunite its subjects under the Catholic religion, but a policy of appeasement and peaceful conversions was preferred to one of restrictions and coercion. In his *Mémoires*, Louis XIV explained that "out of kindness rather than out of bitterness," he had resolved not to grant the Huguenots "the graces that depended solely on [him] . . . so as to oblige them thereby to consider from time to time, by themselves and without constraint, if they had some good reason for depriving themselves voluntarily of the advantages that they could share with all [his] other subjects."[75] Aware that the hope of sharing his munificence with the rest of his subjects would not be attractive enough, Louis XIV nonetheless "resolved . . . to reward . . . those whom birth, education, and most often a zeal without knowledge hold in good faith to these pernicious errors."[76] This policy of subsidized conversions was not new as the Catholic Church had, since the promulgation of the Edict of Nantes, devoted part of its funds to convert and support Huguenots, especially pastors, who by the nature of their employment lost their revenues through conversion.[77] The clergy had also encouraged the organization of missions whose dual, and at times simultaneous, objectives were to educate the Catholic peasantry and convert Huguenots. Manned mainly by the Jesuit and Capuchin orders, these missions, called "apostolic expeditions," were short in duration and local in scope.[78]

The novelty of the 1670s was to make this conversion policy a national priority, extend it to all Huguenots, and set up a special fund for the sole purpose of financing conversions. Created in 1676, it was officially called the Caisse des Économats but was soon dubbed by the Huguenots "Caisse des Conversions" (the conversions treasury). Financed by revenues of vacant abbeys, this fund was managed by Paul Pellisson, a Huguenot convert and *académicien* who had come back into royal favor after spending a few years at the Bastille for his friendship with the disgraced Nicolas Fouquet. Ironically Pellisson eventually died as a Calvinist.[79] The *caisse* promised monetary compensations to Huguenot converts according to the gender, occupation, and status of the beneficiary. This procedure was justified by the Augustinian belief that one could manipulate an individual's greed to help him recognize the truth and by the fact that former Huguenots who had converted to Catholicism were most often ostracized by other Huguenots and thereby were at risk of losing their employment.[80] Although in theory a convert could receive from three to three hundred livres, the sums allotted per person remained small. In Aunis and Saintonge, for example, the highest award was forty-two livres and the most common was fifteen livres.[81] The results of this conversion policy were mediocre, to say the least. Between 1676 and 1679 the caisse converted only ten thousand Protestants nationwide, four thousand of whom were Waldensians from southeastern France. In regions with heavy concentrations of Huguenots the caisse experienced disastrous results. In Languedoc, for example, only five hundred people, or less than 1 percent of the total Huguenot population, converted through the works of the Caisse des Économats.[82] Additionally these converts, some of whom unscrupulously took advantage of the lack of coordination between dioceses and converted several times to collect successive rewards, were often people of loose morals and shaky faith whom the Huguenot churches were not desperate to keep.[83] Regardless of the numbers and of the poor motivation of the converts, this policy failed essentially because it opened the way for corruption as "converters" were substantially rewarded, it somewhat tarnished the noble objectives of the Catholic Church, and it led Huguenot consistories to create local counterfunds to retain their flocks.[84]

In 1679 the crown, dissatisfied with these mediocre results and having brought the war against the Netherlands to a successful conclusion with the Peace of Nijmegen, abandoned this policy of appeasement and peaceful conversion. Then and until the Revocation of the Edict of Nantes in October 1685, the monarchy, assisted by a Catholic clergy reinvigorated by this change of strategy, was determined to eradicate Protestantism and bring the Huguenots into the Catholic fold by all means, including physical violence if necessary.

Intense Persecution and the Revocation of the Edict of Nantes (1680–1685)

Bestowed in 1680 with the title of Louis le Grand by the City of Paris, Louis XIV, who was then at the pinnacle of his glory, could sit on the throne of France with confidence.[85] The successful peace of Nijmegen gave him the impression that he was the arbiter of European diplomacy, or as Voltaire emphatically put it, "his will was law throughout Europe."[86] This confidence led the French monarch, while Europe was at peace, to annex Franche-Comté, the principality of Luxembourg, territories along the Rhine River (Strasbourg was occupied in 1681), and parts of Savoy.[87] Fortified with these diplomatic and military successes, the monarchy became increasingly preoccupied with "the Huguenot problem," which it was determined to solve. Whereas it had decreed only twelve nationwide anti-Huguenot arrêts between 1661 and 1679, the number rocketed to eighty-five from 1680 to 1685.[88] Additionally, beginning in Poitou in 1681, the systematic billeting of troops in Huguenot homes, the infamous *dragonnades,* was resorted to in order to obtain rapid and massive conversions.[89] If the means to keep French Protestantism in check remained essentially the same, as even the dragonnades had previously been used if only sporadically, anti-Huguenot persecution suddenly intensified. This was a sign that the monarchy somehow seemed more determined to bring about religious uniformity. There is no doubt that after 1679, as the historian Émile Léonard wrote, the Huguenots "were hunted down in their religious, professional, familial, and personal lives."[90]

In 1679 the *chambres de l'Édit,* which had guaranteed the Huguenots some measure of judicial fairness, were all abolished.[91] Protestantism was also weakened in its ecclesiastical structure. Whereas the last national synod authorized to meet had convened in 1659 and the meeting of *colloques* (presbyteries) had been strictly regulated since 1657, the provincial synods, the last institution free to operate, could no longer meet after 1679 without the presence of a Catholic royal commissaire.[92] The destruction of "illegal" temples intensified with twenty-eight razed in 1681, forty-eight in 1682, and sixty-five in 1685.[93] In the town of Nanteuil-les-Meaux, Brie, home of the Carolina refugees Abel and Nicolas Bochet, a seigneur, representing royal authority locally, arrived on the site of the temple with a team of "masons, carpenters, locksmiths, and roofers" on October 20, 1685, or two days before the Edict of Revocation was officially registered. Starting with the roof, they literally took down the church building brick by brick in the space of three consecutive days and seized twenty-eight volumes of church records dating back to 1599.[94]

Arrêts excluding Huguenots from certain occupations and guilds were decreed at a faster pace. In 1680 Huguenot women were banned from midwifery so that sickly newborns would be baptized by Catholic midwives.[95] Huguenots were successively excluded from the guilds of hosiery dealers (1681), barbers and wig makers (1684), and printers and booksellers (1685).[96] Soon Huguenots could no longer be notaries, bailiffs, apothecaries, surgeons, doctors, or printers; nor could they have Catholic servants.[97] Starting in 1664 with Nîmes, by March 1685 the crown had ordered the closing of all the académies, which meant that Huguenot ministers could no longer be trained in France.[98]

A series of measures intended to restrict Huguenot worship was also decreed against pastors and congregations. After 1682 churches could no longer have services without pastors nor, after 1683, hire nonresident ministers. A 1682 decree prohibited ministers from living where worship had been abolished, and in 1684 they could no longer reside more than three years in the same community.[99] Huguenot services and pastors' sermons were also the objects of royal surveillance and censorship. In each temple specific pews had to be reserved for Catholics, lay or ecclesiastics, who were allowed to interrupt services and challenge the pastor if they deemed it necessary. In his memoirs Jaques Fontaine, a Huguenot minister who fled to the British Isles, explains that Capuchins and Jesuits came to listen to his father's sermons so regularly that "there was a bench especially marked for them in the temple . . . just opposite the minister's seat."[100] At times what was essentially spying led to formal investigations against ministers of the congregations. In 1684 Élie Prioleau, who was then pastor at Pons and whose father, Samuel, had already been banned from the Pons church for a year for "reading a sermon containing anti-Catholic assertions," became the object of such an investigation.[101] The purpose of this inquiry, led by one Du Vigier, a member of the parlement of Bordeaux, was to report any violation of the recent anti-Huguenot arrêts. With the assistance of two Franciscans who had attended Prioleau's services and copied down extracts of his sermons, Du Vigier compiled sixteen charges against him. In substance, Prioleau was accused of having preached at Pons before being appointed there by the provincial synod, christening a child who had already been baptized by a Catholic surgeon, and receiving children of recent converts in his church.[102] Despite Du Vigier's zeal, however, Prioleau was eventually acquitted for lack of tangible proof.

Although they were not enough to convict him, the charges brought against Prioleau, of which fourteen concerned preaching to children of Huguenots who had converted to Catholicism, demonstrate how much the crown was preoccupied with the question of conversions and "reconversions." Throughout the seventeenth century while Huguenots had abjured, Catholics had also, though in much smaller numbers, converted to Protestantism.[103] In La Rochelle, for example, between 1648 and 1680 annual Huguenot-Catholic conversions numbered between forty and fifty, and Catholic-Huguenot conversions seven.[104] Despite infinitesimal numbers nationwide, the monarchy was so concerned and displeased with the movement from Catholicism to Protestantism that an arrêt decreed in 1680 prohibited such conversions.[105] Knowing that quite a few recent Huguenot converts were actually former Huguenots who had temporarily converted to Catholicism to escape persecution, have access to social promotion, or simply for monetary gains, the crown issued a series of harsh measures against those it officially called, using a medical metaphor, *relaps*. After 1679 relaps and pastors who had encouraged them to recant their conversion to Catholicism were banished from France and had their possessions confiscated, and any temple that a relaps had entered had to be demolished.[106]

Conversely, Huguenots who had recently converted and remained Catholics were, in 1680, given three years to pay back their debts. As Élisabeth Labrousse stresses, beyond the fact that this could encourage abjurations, this was an astute decision since the creditors, most likely to be Huguenots, and not the monarchy would bear its cost.[107] The crown was also particularly sensitive to the question of children's conversions. Whereas after 1665 Huguenot boys and girls could convert at the ages of fourteen and twelve, respectively, an arrêt of 1681 lowered the age to seven for both.[108] In arguing that children at the age of seven were "able to see the paths of salvation," the monarchy's deliberate intention was actually to deprive Huguenots of their parental influence in religious matters.[109] Although this measure was never enforced, especially since in 1682 the official age to take vows was set at sixteen, it nonetheless profoundly disturbed Huguenot parents, who increasingly sent their children abroad despite royal prohibition.[110]

The decision to use military force systematically to obtain conversions remains the best-known aspect of Louis XIV's religious policy and one that made him known, in Huguenot circles, as the great persecutor, a new Nebuchadnezzar. As Jaques Fontaine asserts in his memoirs, "when Louis the Great sent his army against God's elect, his splendour crumbled."[111] Contrary to what the writing of Huguenot refugees such as Fontaine suggests though, dragonnades, or the billeting of troops in civilian homes, were not a novelty of the 1680s. The monarchy had used this type of repressive action in the 1620s and 1660s against rebellious Huguenot cities.[112] Nor was it imposed exclusively on Huguenots, as seditious Catholic peasants in Brittany who had violently opposed a new stamp tax in 1675 had also been dragooned.[113] The novelty was to use it against peaceful

Huguenot populations of entire provinces and with the sole objective of obtaining rapid and massive abjurations. Initiated by the intendant Marillac, with the backing of the Marquis de Louvois, Louis XIV's secretary for war, the dragonnades started in Poitou in 1681. From May to September about thirty-eight thousand Huguenots abjured.[114] Due to increased international pressure and perhaps Louis XIV's personal disapproval, the monarchy, despite the intendant's success, had Marillac and his dragoons recalled. However, the arrêt of 1680 against relaps guaranteed that these new converts could not legally return to Protestantism.[115] The crown quickly overcame its remorse, though, as a new dragonnade was launched on an even larger scale from July 1683 to October 1685. Often referred to as "the great dragonnade of the South," it ravaged the southern provinces of Dauphiny, Vivarais, Languedoc, and Béarn before moving west to Guyenne, Saintonge, Aunis, and Poitou. The South Carolina refugee Judith Giton, who then lived in the town of La Voulte, Vivarais, had her home dragooned before she decided to flee France. As she describes in her well-known letter, "we have suffered through eight months [of] exactions and quartering by the soldiery, for the religion with much evil."[116] By the fall 1685 officials had optimistically reported more than four hundred thousand abjurations.[117]

Aside from their cruelty and vulgarity, dragoons were an enormous financial burden for their Huguenot hosts simply because many were assigned to one home. Jaques Fontaine had to entertain eighteen of them, who "lived [in his home] until they had destroyed or sold everything, even the bolts on the doors."[118] Jean Migault, a Huguenot schoolteacher from Poitou who eventually fled to Amsterdam, wrote in his memoirs that he had to entertain fifteen dragoons, "who requested things impossible to find in the entire parish."[119] Similarly, traveling through Niort, Poitou, Locke met "a poor bookseller's wife" who told him "that there being last winter 1,200 soldiers quartrd in the towne, two were apointed for their share (for they were Protestants), which considering that they were to have 3 meales a day of flesh, breakfast, dinner & supper, besides a collation in the afternoon, all which was better to give them, & a 5th meale too if they desired it."[120] Having to support demanding and overbearing dragoons, these "half-priest and half-dragon monsters," as the Huguenot polemist Pierre Bayle dubbed them, was of course a lesser evil in relation to the cruelty that French Protestants had to endure if they refused to abjure.[121] Although the financial ruin of their hosts, through destruction of property, robbery, or exacting requests, was an essential element of the dragoons' strategy to obtain their conversions, instances of physical abuse occurred.[122] Instructed to obtain abjurations by all means short of rape and murder, these "booted missionaries," as the Huguenots called them, perpetrated numerous tortures, both physical and mental. They would deprive their coerced hosts of sleep for days, made them stand until they collapsed, played the drums in the house ceaselessly, and burned their feet with hot irons.[123]

The papers of Henry Compton, bishop of London and of the North American colonies, contains a fascinating letter addressed by another bookseller, also from Niort in Poitou, to his brother exiled in London that details the persecutions inflicted to his family by the dragoons in the most graphic and moving manner.[124] "As soon as the dragoons were in town," writes Thomas Bureau, "four were sent to our home. . . . They threw all the books on the floor . . . destroyed the carpentry work, the stacks, the windows with axes and hammers, brought their horses inside the shop, used the books as litter, then they climbed upstairs to our bedrooms and threw everything that was inside them into the streets as the mayor watched . . . filled with joy." Left alone with the dragoons, Thomas's mother and sister had to endure the abuse of their captain as they obstinately refused to abjure. Aggravated by their steadfast determination, the dragoons threatened "to hang them . . . or tie them to the harnesses of their horses and drag them through the streets like rabid dogs to serve as examples." As threats were not enough, four more dragoons were assigned to their home, and all the books were taken to a square in the town to be burned.[125]

Soon the cruelty of the dragoons was so well known that entire Huguenot communities converted en masse in the main Catholic church or nearest cathedral before the dragoons even reached the town.[126] In Rouen the arrival of three regiments of dragoons provoked the instant abjurations of more than 300 Huguenots.[127] In Mauzé, Aunis, the presence of the intendant with just a few soldiers, what the historian Yves Krumenacker humorously calls a "mini-dragonnade," led, nonetheless, the entire Huguenot population to abjure.[128] When the dragoons first occupied La Rochelle in September 1685, the rate of conversions reached 150 a day.[129] If the quality of these conversions, rightly dubbed "conversions by intimidation" by Krumenacker, remains doubtful, their sheer number could only satisfy a monarchy now dedicated to fully eradicating French Protestantism.[130]

Once safely in a Huguenot church outside of France, new converts had to recant their Catholicism in front of the consistory before being readmitted into the French Reformed community. These examinations, during which the new converts' sincerity and knowledge of the Reformed faith, rites, and discipline were literally being tested, were called reconnaissances since new converts admitted their error (reconnaissaient leur faute) while making amends for it. Several Carolina Huguenots did their reconnaissances before the London Threadneedle Street Church consistory prior to crossing the Atlantic. In January 1685 Pierre Bertrand, who died in Charleston in 1692, did his reconnaissance "for having gone to Mass." In September 1686 Benjamin Marion, Judith, Ester, and Madeleine Balluet, and Marie Nicolas appeared before the consistory for "having abjured [their] religion and having gone to Mass," and the church elders authorized them to do their public reconnaissances "after the sermon."[131] No doubt making amends publicly must have been uncomfortable for these refugees, but it left them at peace with themselves and proved their devotion to their Huguenot faith.

The Huguenot historian Daniel Ligou wrote: "The dragonnades made the Revocation inevitable."[132] Assuredly, once the monarchy took the decision to systematically ransack hundreds of Huguenot homes in entire regions and towns to obtain conversions through violence, the Revocation was in the making even if it was not yet in the minds of Louis XIV and his ministers. Indeed, the complex and paradoxical nature of the Revocation is that it appears to have been both the outcome of an anti-Huguenot policy that had been followed for more than two decades and a sudden decision. Edicts and arrêts decreed in the early months of 1685 show that the Revocation was not then on the royal agenda.[133] The Revocation was perhaps "inevitable," but the timing of the decision remains open to conjecture.

Conversely, the reasons behind the Revocation are well known to historians.[134] In hindsight it clearly appears that the Revocation was the result of multiple causes that are related to the intrinsic nature of the Edict of Nantes, to the domestic and international contexts of the 1680s, to Louis XIV's own religious aspirations, and to the political balance within the royal council.

In the preamble to the Edict of Fontainebleau, which revoked the Edict of Nantes in October 1685, two official reasons are given to justify the Revocation: religious reunification and the conversions of "the better and greater part of [the Protestant] subjects."[135] The authors of the new edict argued that the reunification of all the French people under the Catholic religion had been the ultimate objective of Louis XIV's royal predecessors, including Henry IV. Following this rationale, the Edict of Nantes was intended to be a temporary truce meant to be revoked as soon as the circumstances were favorable.[136] The crown undeniably interpreted the real nature of the Edict of Nantes with accuracy, but it also conveniently ignored the fact that the edict had remained in force more than eighty-five years, a duration that gave the *religion prétendue réformée* an inescapable legal and historical legitimacy. As for invoking the high number of abjurations as a justification for the Revocation, it was a clever attempt to prove that the Edict of Nantes had become pointless since, apparently, most Huguenots had converted.[137] The Edict of Nantes may indeed have become an empty shell by autumn 1685 since its most important clauses had been nullified by various arrêts, but it still guaranteed, de jure if not de facto, the right to profess a different religion than the king did to several hundred thousand of his subjects. As Élisabeth Labrousse stresses, the French Reformed churches had become almost invisible, but the Huguenots were still there.[138]

Assuredly, a close reading of the Edict of Nantes helps us understand the Revocation. As Pierre Chaunu once stressed, for the Revocation to be understood it is not so much the Edict of Fontainebleau but the Edict of Nantes that needs to be explained.[139] The Edict of Nantes, whose primary goals were peace and the restoration of Catholicism throughout the kingdom, resulted from difficult negotiations between the monarchy and the Huguenot party. It was the product of a *rapport de forces*. In 1685 the Huguenots no longer represented a threat to the political and religious unity of France and, as Emmanuel Le Roy Ladurie accurately points out, the monarchy possessed a formidable means of repression in its wartime army of three hundred thousand men.[140] Consequently, the Edict of Nantes had lost its raison d'être. Additionally, since its original goal of Catholic restoration seemed achieved in 1685, the Revocation just validated this new situation. As Cottret explains, "the Revocation often perceived as the negation of the Edict of Nantes was actually its logical result."[141] This being said, it can be argued that since the Huguenots, reduced to less than 4 percent of the population, no longer constituted a threat or a problem, there was actually no real need to revoke the Edict of Nantes. With time, Louis XIV's religious policy, what Le Roy Ladurie calls the "godly wonders of decalvinisation," would have yielded the expected results and reduced French Protestantism to isolated social and geographic pockets. In the 1680s the Huguenots, as Philippe Joutard writes, gave the impression of a group resigned to its disparition.[142] In his 1689 memorandum entitled *Mémoire pour le rappel des huguenots,* Maréchal de Vauban estimated than most Huguenots would have peacefully converted to Catholicism within twelve to fifteen years. Instead, he thought, brutal coercion reinvigorated their faith as "the blood of martyrs, in all religions, has always been . . . an infallible means to increase those that have been persecuted."[143] Quite inadvertently and ironically, the Revocation thus awakened among the Huguenots a spirit of resistance and revived a Protestant faith strengthened by martyrdom. The Revocation and the brutal persecution that preceded it, far from eradicating Protestantism, actually freed it from the inertia and the apathy that seemed to condemn it to a slow death.

The apparent success of the policy of "conversion by intimidation," embodied by the hundreds of thousands of abjurations obtained with the great dragonnade of 1685, gave the monarchy the illusory impression that only a few Huguenots remained in the country. Additionally, the exemption of taxes promised to those new converts was now becoming an increasingly heavy burden for the monarchy.[144] Revoking the Edict of Nantes would make these costly fiscal privileges unnecessary since there would be no need to reward voluntary conversions. Furthermore, the Assemblée du Clergé, the national convocation of the French prelates, became, after 1680, more pressing in its request for a forceful policy of religious reunification.[145] The extraordinary meeting of 1682, which gave Louis XIV full support in his effort to distance himself from the papacy, also drew up a formal warning toward the Huguenots entitled *Pastoral Admonishment of the Gallican Church Assembled in Paris . . . to Those of the Supposedly Reformed Religion, to Induce Them to Become Converted and Reconciled with the Church.*[146] With the legal and logistic support of the royal authorities, this declaration was read in all remaining Huguenot churches, which gave it the quasi-status of a royal edict. In substance, *Pastoral Admonishment* was an effort to convince the Huguenots that remaining outside the Gallican Church was an error. In this text the Huguenots were no longer referred to as heretics but as schismatics. This subtle lexical change meant in essence that the Huguenots were rebels against the Gallican Church and that the duty of bringing them back to the main Catholic fold was the responsibility of the king of France, not the pope.[147] Although it advocated peaceful and voluntary conversions, this declaration, which menacingly predicted for the Huguenots "evils incomparably more appalling and more harmful than all those which [their] rebellion and [their] schism had until now brought upon [them]," actually prepared the way for the Revocation.[148]

In the mid-1680s the international context also favored the Revocation as it seemed to invite an overconfident Louis XIV to prepare a *coup d'éclat.* The 1683 defeat of the Ottoman Turks at the battle of Kahlenberg near Vienna, achieved without active French participation, somewhat tarnished the image of Louis XIV, *Rex Christianissimus,* as the foremost defender of Christendom and made him look for a way to regain prestige. Additionally, apart from opening a period of peace with Spain and the Holy Empire, the 1684 Truce of Regensburg (Ratisbon), from a political and religious perspective, more importantly freed France from an awkward alliance with German Protestant states. This unnatural alliance had been justified by the French fear of a Habsburg hegemony over central Europe, which had for some time prevented Louis XIV from acting against the Huguenots with too much severity. After 1684 Louis could tackle the Huguenot problem without alienating the support of his Protestant allies. The following year the accession of the Catholic James II to the throne of England and his quelling of

Monmouth's insurrection in 1685 gave Louis XIV the illusory hope for a restoration of Catholicism across the English Channel, which would bring England within France's sphere of influence.[149] Louis XIV was, in the early 1680s, also experiencing difficulty with Pope Innocent XI, who disapproved of Louis's promotion of a Gallican Church that was less dependent on Rome and with whom he was fighting over control of the revenues of vacant French episcopal sees.[150] In sum, with the Revocation, Louis XIV was extirpating the Huguenot heresy in his kingdom and was, so he hoped, restoring his prominent position within Christendom and in the eyes of the pope. From this perspective, the Revocation was assuredly meant to satisfy Louis XIV's thirst for glory.

The timing of the Revocation can also be explained by Louis XIV's renewed piety and by a shift of influence within his council. Following the death of Queen Marie-Thérèse in 1683, Louis XIV, then under the growing influence of the pious Françoise de Maintenon, altered his somewhat carefree lifestyle and experienced a sort of conversion.[151] Mme de Maintenon described this change in her correspondence, noting in the early 1680s that "the king is beginning seriously to think about his own salvation and that of his subjects. If God preserves him for us, there will be no longer but one religion in the realm."[152] Louis XIV had become a *roi-prêtre* (king-priest) whose providential destiny was to achieve the religious reunification of his kingdom.[153] The Revocation was also the result of the taking over of the king's council by Le Tellier's clan over Colbert's. Since the disgrace of Fouquet in 1661, the council had been the object of a struggle of influence between Jean-Baptiste Colbert and Michel Le Tellier and their respective followers.[154] The Revocation unarguably confirmed that the Le Tellier clan, embodied by the powerful Marquis de Louvois, son of Michel Le Tellier, had held a predominant position within the council after Colbert's death in 1683.[155] Louvois, who as secretary of war had given his assent to and made his troops available for the dragonnades, had, along with his father, always been in favor of a harsh anti-Huguenot policy.[156] In autumn 1685 Louis XIV, then physically weakened by an extremely painful dental abscess and a fistula, leaned toward the Le Telliers and revoked the Edict of Nantes.[157]

The Revocation is inscribed in the politico-religious logic of the time. As Le Roy Ladurie explains, "[if] in terms of abstract morality, the Revocation proved reprehensible . . . it can [however] be vindicated if we stick to the requirements of Church, King and Country unity."[158] This unity, often referred to as one king, one faith, one law (*une foi, une loi, un roi*), or *cujus regio ejus religio,* had already served as a guiding principle for the elaboration of the religious peace settlements of Augsburg in 1555 and Westphalia in 1648.[159] This principle, also known as *jus reformandi,* gave the sovereign the right to determine the religion of his subjects.[160] In this respect, the France of the Edict of Nantes, with the legal existence of Protestantism, presented the unique situation of an absolute monarch implicitly agreeing to the existence of a numerically significant and socially prominent religious minority. The Edict of Nantes, as Chaunu reminds us, was "the fruit of very peculiar circumstances."[161] The Edict of Fontainebleau, however, was the result of an active process of religious and political normalization achieved in the wider context of the Catholic Reformation. The Huguenots were not the only minority to be discriminated against or persecuted in seventeenth-century Europe. Catholics in the British Isles and in the Scandinavian countries were also the victims of discriminatory laws and, at times, of outright repression.[162] What made the Revocation reprehensible was not its guiding principle or its objective but the fact that the Edict of Fontainebleau did not authorize the Huguenots to leave the kingdom and did not grant them, even temporarily, the right to private worship. In theory, the *jus reformandi* of the prince was to be compensated by the granting to the subjects of a different religion the *jus emigrandi,* or right to emigrate, and some sort of *devotio privata,* or right to worship individually, without religious structures.[163] According to the Edict of Fontainebleau, however, only the pastors were allowed to leave France, provided they did so within two weeks, and the privilege of private worship was granted to the Huguenots only deceitfully since new dragonnades forced the remaining Huguenots to convert.[164] The denial of these two universally acknowledged rights makes the Edict of Fontainebleau reprehensible and, ironically, created a new situation that was as unique as that of the Edict of Nantes.

The Revocation, as Élisabeth Labrousse puts it, proved to be "an appalling political mistake" since it created more problems that it actually solved.[165] It failed to bring France closer to the papacy. It provoked a diplomatic and military rapprochement between England and the United Provinces and also hardened the position of the Protestant states in Scandinavia and beyond the Rhine toward France. It failed to eradicate French Protestantism as several thousand Huguenots managed to preserve their faith and Protestant ways in the *églises du désert,* or underground churches, until they were granted civil rights again in 1787. The Revocation also led to de-Christianization in certain provinces as many new converts turned out to be poor churchgoers.[166] As the English historian Henry Phillips wrote, "in seeking to destroy the space of Protestantism the [Catholic] Church succeeded only in damaging its own."[167] Finally, the brutal repression of the early 1680s and the Revocation led to the exodus of close to two hundred thousand Huguenots throughout northern Europe and the North Atlantic basin—a migration that diffused French Protestantism to a hitherto unprecedented geographical scale and gave it a true international dimension.

Chapter 2

THE CAROLINA PROPRIETORS AND THE RECRUITMENT OF HUGUENOTS

Mercantilism and the Protestant Cause

> The Earl of *Shaft[e]sbury* [is] a Martyr for the *English* Liberties and the Protestant Religion.
>
> Andrew Marvell, *An Account of the Growth of Popery and Arbitrary Government* (1677)

> I am convinced that it is the spot of the earthly paradise, whither no one can go but by God's permission.
>
> Christopher Columbus, "Letter on the Third Voyage" (1494)

Restoration Imperialism and the Foundation of Carolina

With the 1651 Navigation Act, the 1652–54 Anglo-Dutch War, and the conquest of Jamaica from Spain in 1655, Oliver Cromwell launched an aggressive colonial and commercial expansionist policy, fueled by a strong anti-Dutch and anti-Spanish sentiment. This policy was not only pursued but also sharply intensified under Charles II after 1660.[1] For that reason the Restoration is no longer regarded as a watershed in British imperial history. This being said, the second half of the seventeenth century undeniably constitutes an unprecedented period of territorial and mercantile growth.[2] In the Caribbean, Charles II refused to return Jamaica to Spain and made Barbados and the Leeward Islands royal colonies by 1663.[3] In North America the English expanded south of Virginia into territories still formally claimed by Spain with the establishment of the Carolinas in 1663. The following year New Netherland, out of which the colonies of New York and New Jersey were carved, was conquered from the Dutch.

Commercially, two pieces of legislation, the 1660 Navigation Act and the 1663 Staple Act, completed Cromwell's regulation of the ever-expanding transoceanic trade. Simply put, these acts gave English merchants a monopoly over the trade of a list of enumerated commodities and turned England into an entrepôt through which goods imported from or exported to the colonies had to transit.[4] This commercial policy soon bore fruit as English transoceanic trade, while becoming increasingly diversified, grew tremendously at the expense of the traditional continental commerce.[5] England's trade had formerly been restricted to virtually one export, broadcloth, but by 1700 London, servicing both the

Atlantic and Indian trades, became an entrepôt rivaling Amsterdam.[6] By the end of the seventeenth century, trade with the American plantations and India had jumped from about 15 percent in 1634 to over 30 percent of imports and had reached 15 percent of exports.[7] This commercial expansion, as Nuala Zahedieh stresses, had innumerable repercussions for shipping, shipbuilding, port facilities, manufacturing, banking, insurance services, employment, and occupational and regional specialization and was a seminal factor in what became known as the English late seventeenth-century "Commercial Revolution."[8]

Institutionally, the Restoration marked the beginning of a growing realization of the need to control the empire through specific committees.[9] In 1660 the Council of Trade and the Council for Foreign Plantations were founded. They included, for the first time, members from outside the Privy Council, which had, since the time of the early Stuarts, handled colonial affairs somewhat diligently. The disruptions caused by the Great Plague in 1665, the Great Fire in 1666, and the 1665–67 Anglo-Dutch War led to the dispersal of these committees. For a brief two-year period beginning in 1668, the Privy Council resumed control of the colonies until the Council of Plantations, which Ian Steele calls "the first prototype of the Board of Trade," was created in 1670.[10]

The granting of the first Carolina charter in 1663, merely three years after the restoration of the Stuarts, is closely tied to these imperial and mercantile developments. Territorially, it marked England's expansion to the south at the expense of Spain. The new colony covered a great part of La Florida soon after Charles II challenged Spanish power by forming an alliance with Portugal in 1661.[11] In fact, "in an act that left the Spanish ambassador speechless," in 1665 Charles II granted a second Carolina charter that included Spanish Saint Augustine within its limits.[12] The bluff worked, and the Spanish answer to this provocative claim was to negotiate the Treaty of Madrid in 1670, which officially recognized England's effective occupation of the North American Atlantic coast from somewhere south of modern Charleston to Virginia.[13]

The Carolina venture was also a commercial endeavor in accordance with the mercantile aspirations of Restoration England. With its subtropical climate, Carolina seemed to offer the possibility of semitropical products whose export to England would improve its balance of trade and make it commercially less dependent on Spain and France. Politically, the Carolina grant is also illustrative of Restoration colonialism. Although the 1663 and 1665 charters contained clauses already included in Lord Baltimore's for Maryland and Sir Robert Heath's for Carolana, they nonetheless conferred unusually broad economic and institutional powers on their recipients. The latter, collectively called the Lords Proprietors, typically formed a small circle of influential men already involved in colonial affairs who, following the Restoration political logic, received their overseas domain from the crown in return for military, pecuniary, and political support.

A striking feature of the Carolina proprietorship is the remarkable social and political status of its eight original members. Edward Hyde, Earl of Clarendon and father-in-law of the future James II, headed Charles II's cabinet as lord chancellor from 1661 until his fall in 1667. George Monck, Duke of Albemarle, was lord of the treasury until 1670. Anthony Ashley Cooper (Earl of Shaftesbury after 1672) was successively chancellor of the exchequer (1671–72), lord chancellor (1672–73), and lord president (1679). Sir George

Carteret was treasurer of the navy from 1660 to 1667. William, Earl of Craven, and John, Lord Berkeley, both occupied high-ranking military positions. Sir William Berkeley, John's brother, was governor of Virginia from 1660 to 1676. Only Sir John Colleton, a wealthy planter from Barbados, moved in somewhat less influential circles.[14]

Although the commitment of these men to the Carolina venture varied greatly, each was more or less directly involved in colonial affairs. Most of them had financial interests in the New World, either in the form of shares in trading companies, such as the Hudson Bay Company (Ashley Cooper, George Monck, and George Carteret) or the Royal Africa Company (the same plus John Colleton and John Berkeley), or in West Caribbean plantations (Edward Hyde, John Colleton, and Ashley Cooper). Carteret and John Berkeley became proprietors of New Jersey in 1664, and William Berkeley was the chief executive officer in Virginia.[15] Six of the proprietors had participated in the elaboration of early Restoration imperial policies while sitting in the diverse councils for colonial affairs successively created in the 1660s.[16]

Even if a few of the proprietors had served the protectorate, such as, for example, Monck and Ashley, all had contributed in some way or another to the restoration of the Stuarts. Thus, the Carolina proprietorship, among other honors, was granted to them as a reward for their auspicious loyalty. Charles II, who "created more dukes during his reign than the total who lived in the previous century," bestowed Monck with a dukedom; Hyde, Craven, and Ashley with an earldom; and John Colleton with a baronetcy.[17]

Despite their initial enthusiasm, the proprietors failed to found a permanent settlement in Carolina until 1670. Historians no longer attribute this proprietary failure to incapacity and indifference, although the proprietorship at times may have suffered from both, but to a complex series of factors, some of which were quite beyond the proprietors' reach. A group of New Englanders settled along the Cape Fear River in 1665 but abandoned the settlement after a few months. That same year Barbadians established a settlement in present-day North Carolina (Clarendon County) and projected another in Port Royal, while Virginians moving south settled near Albemarle Sound. By 1667, however, only the Virginian settlement endured.[18] In the meantime the Great Plague, the London Fire, and the second Anglo-Dutch War monopolized the attention of the proprietors through 1667. Furthermore, the death of Colleton and the flight of Clarendon following his political disgrace, both events occurring in 1667, and the gradual withdrawal of Albemarle, who died in 1670, weakened the original proprietorship.[19]

Unsurprisingly, the late 1660s marked a turning point in the organization of the proprietorship and its management of Carolina affairs. By that time Ashley, the youngest of the eight original grantees, had for all practical purposes become the leading proprietor, and his conduct of proprietary business, until his own disgrace and flight in 1682, greatly influenced the early history of South Carolina. The Ashley-sponsored decision to finance a colonization expedition in 1669, which was originally bound for Port Royal but led to the foundation of the first permanent settlement along the Ashley (Kiawah) River, signaled two significant changes in proprietary policies.[20] First, the proprietors, or at least the most active among them—Ashley, Carteret, and Sir Peter Colleton—were no longer delegating their responsibilities to groups of settlers but assumed a direct role in recruiting and financing the passage and settlement of colonists.[21] Second, the proprietors abandoned their original plans to draw settlers from existing colonies, Barbados, New England, and Virginia and decided instead to recruit colonists in the British Isles and, to a lesser extent, from the Continent.[22] The year 1669 also saw the elaboration of the first version of the Ashley-sponsored Fundamental Constitutions, which was meant, in due time, to provide a socioeconomic, political, and religious framework for the colony. Ashley's leadership also gave early proprietary policies a Whiggish flavor, which decisively influenced the recruiting efforts of the 1680s aimed at English Dissenters, Scottish Covenanters, and Huguenots.

Mercantilism, Populationism, and Popery
The English Context of the Huguenot Migration to Carolina

The Huguenot migration to South Carolina did not unfold in a historical vacuum. Quite the contrary, it was the result of a proprietary recruiting policy that sprang out of the economic and political contexts of Restoration England. The prevailing economic belief of the time, commonly and retrospectively known as mercantilism, influenced the Carolina proprietors in their desire to recruit settlers able, at least in theory, to produce semitropical products whose trade would enrich England. Similarly, the predominant belief that England was suffering from underpopulation, known to historians as populationism, led the proprietors to recruit non-English settlers based on its postulate that the colonies potentially weakened England by draining away its population. Politically, the 1678 Popish Plot, the 1679–81 Exclusion Crisis, and the 1685 Revocation of the Edict of Nantes exacerbated anti-Catholic sentiment in England. Antipopery convinced the proprietors, especially Shaftesbury, to use Carolina in their struggle to support the Protestant cause. The Huguenots, Calvinist martyrs in Catholic absolutist France in search of a refuge and allegedly experts in Mediterranean products, ideally fitted the proprietary plans of the 1670s and 1680s. As opposed to the 1620s, when the Baron de Sancé failed to convince his coreligionists to settle in Sir Robert Heath's Carolana, the time was now ripe for a significant Huguenot migration to North America under English private sponsorship.[23]

Mercantilism, more appropriately referred to as balance of trade theory, was the prevailing economic strategy in preindustrial Europe. The term, unknown to contemporaries, does not correspond to a well-defined economic theory but refers to a composite of widely shared beliefs. Based on the idea that "the goods of a country are its natural wealth [but can] only create money when sold abroad," mercantilism argued that a beneficiary balance of trade increased the wealth of a nation, notably through the accumulation of specie.[24] As an economic writer stated in the mid-1670s, without an export surplus "out goes money and in comes poverty."[25] Mercantilism was not the equivalent of bullionism though, since the money generated through trade was to be used to produce more goods to be sold to other nations.[26] Enrichment through trade did not constitute a goal in itself either but was to facilitate national unification and confer on each nation prestige and power on the international stage.[27] Colonial expansion nicely fit this mercantilist view as long as the carrying trade and the home and colonial markets were protected from competitors, especially the omnipresent Dutch. Governmental intervention, whether legislative, economic, or military, was therefore necessary to make the system work. In the case of England, the Navigation Acts, which have been called "the culmination and the epitome of English mercantilist thought"; the conquest of Jamaica; the Anglo-Dutch Wars; and the establishment of new colonies in mainland North America all contributed to the elaboration of a coherent mercantilist policy.[28]

The mercantilist emphasis on foreign trade as a source of economic wealth and political as well as military power led to a general preoccupation with population. Restoration economic writers widely believed that England's national wealth depended on a large and growing population. More specifically, when they wrote that "people are the wealth of [a] nation" or "fewness of people are real poverty," *people* meant labor.[29] Labor was thus perceived as the necessary instrument of production without which the balance of trade was meaningless. As Daniel Statt explains, for the proponents of mercantilism, the process of acquiring wealth fell into three stages: "the existence of a pool of labor, the application of that labor to raw materials, and the sale of the resulting manufactured goods in foreign markets."[30]

The central role of labor in the mercantilist paradigm in turn led to a concern among economic theorists and statesmen about the size of England's population. Whereas in the sixteenth and early seventeenth centuries the fear of overpopulation, "the supernumerary of people," as it was then termed, dominated the economic and social debate, the opposite concern prevailed at the time of the Restoration.[31] This fear became particularly acute in the mid-1660s following the outbreak of the Great Plague, which was believed to have caused the death of several hundred thousand people in London alone.[32] Depopulation fears were based on impressions, not on actual figures, however, as seventeenth-century economists did not have the methodological and practical tools to accurately measure England's population. Yet, this concern was not purely imaginary. Demographic historians have recently estimated that the English population actually shrank between 1656 and 1661.[33] In the long term they have also found that it only increased by about one million from 1661 to 1761, as opposed to nearly three million between 1561 and 1661.[34]

Concerns about depopulation led to the elaboration and implementation of what historians call populationist theories and policies. Since a growing population was central to economic prosperity, it was believed that governments had to take measures to encourage immigration and limit emigration. As early as 1664 and 1667 proposals for general naturalization bills, motivated by the desire to increase England's population, were submitted to Parliament.[35] Although these projects could not overcome the traditional nativist fear of seeing England overwhelmed by hordes of foreigners, they initiated a seminal debate on immigration, population, and economic prosperity. In the same decade colonial emigration, which had once been regarded as the solution to England's overpopulation problem, was increasingly denounced as a contributing factor to its underpopulation crisis.[36] Englishmen, wrote a pamphleteer, are "decoyed away to New England and Virginia . . . unprofitable countries [that] help us not, but hinder us . . . and waste our people."[37]

If economically the late 1660s and 1670s were a period of growth due to renewed colonial and commercial expansion, politically these years were a time of instability and of crises fueled by an acute—at times hysterical—fear of Catholicism, significantly and somewhat derogatorily known as popery. As Mark Kishlansky explains, popery was "an essential element in the making of Protestant England, serving the purpose of the evil

God in a creation myth."[38] Popery, "everyone's worst nightmare," was a catalyst for real as well as imagined menaces to the English nation.[39] The Marian persecutions of the 1550s, the 1588 Great Armada, the 1605 Gunpowder Plot, and the Irish Rebellion of 1641 were collectively perceived as instances of how demoniac Catholic forces could threaten England's most vital interests. Although never far below the surface, English anti-Catholicism waned and waxed over the years. It also took on different forms as the nature and the origins of the threats varied through time. In the 1670s, to be sure, popery was only tangentially related to English Catholicism, whose practitioners numbered only sixty thousand, or barely 1.2 percent of the population.[40] As Geoffrey Holmes stresses, what most Englishmen feared was not *recusancy,* which was local and religious, but *popery,* which was international and political.[41]

In the late 1660s and 1670s the monarchy's views and policies diverged dangerously from the nation's aspirations.[42] Whereas Charles II and his cabinet continued to see the United Provinces as England's main economic and military rival and sought a French alliance to crush the Dutch, most Englishmen increasingly sensed that Catholic France constituted a far more considerable religious, economic, and military threat than did the Calvinist Netherlands. While even Charles II's political opponents were not particularly fond of the Dutch and recognized the potential economic threat of the United Provinces, they nonetheless believed that France was Spain's successor as a contender for European, and to some extent world, hegemony, which in the political parlance of the time was referred to as universal monarchy.[43] Concerned about Louis XIV's militaristic and expansionist policy of the 1660s and 1670s, political observers expressed their fears that the invasion of the Netherlands and the subjugation of England were elements in a global strategy to achieve universal dominion. As the English envoy to the Spanish Netherlands wrote, Louis XIV, whom the Whig poet Andrew Marvell called "the greatest Roman Catholic despot in Europe," sought "by division among his neighbors to pick up and bring them all at last under his dominion, as universal monarch over Christendom."[44]

The failure of the Franco-English land and naval assault on the Netherlands in 1672 eventually doomed Charles II's largely unpopular pro-French foreign policy. Meanwhile the 1670 Treaty of Dover, whose secret clauses provided for a formal toleration of English Catholics and for Charles II's public declaration of Catholicity in exchange for a French subsidy of £225,000; the 1672 Declaration of Indulgence, which permitted Catholics to worship privately; the 1672 Catholic marriage of James, Duke of York; the latter's public conversion to Catholicism the following year; and the growing suspicion that the king's ministers were crypto-Catholics all converged to arouse fears of a gigantic Franco-Catholic conspiracy to take over England.[45] As Kishlansky explains, almost everyone genuinely believed that "Britons were in imminent danger of being enslaved, that their lands would be occupied by the French, [and] their treasure shipped off to Rome."[46]

The "discovery" of the so-called Popish Plot in 1678 was the spark that provoked "the only significant crisis of [Charles II's] reign."[47] Detailed revelations about "a damnable and hellish plot . . . for the assassinating and murdering of the King . . . and rooting out and destroying the Protestant religion" raised antipopery fears to paroxysmal heights.[48] The nascent political opposition, alternatively called the Whig or country party, skillfully manipulated this collective and dual fear of Catholicism and absolutism to justify a bill to exclude Charles II's Catholic brother, James, from the throne of England.[49] From March 1679 to March 1681 English politics were thus totally dominated by the Exclusion Crisis. By the summer of 1681, however, Charles II's skillful political maneuvering had led to the defeat of the Exclusion movement, which had lost much of its vigor as anti-Catholic fears gradually subsided.

Shaftesbury, Locke, and the Huguenot-Whig Connection

The first Earl of Shaftesbury, whose increasing control of Carolina affairs was concomitant to his political ascension, played a key role in initiating a recruiting policy that led to the migration of several hundred Huguenots to the colony. Reputedly experts in making wine and silk as well as growing fruit, the Huguenots, from an economic perspective, were excellent potential colonists. Perhaps even more significantly in Shaftesbury's views, they were Protestants persecuted by a Catholic absolutist regime. Clearly, the recruitment of Huguenots not only served the economic interests of the proprietorship and of the colony but also met Shaftesbury's religious and political agenda. The Huguenot migration to Carolina is undeniably rooted in this concordance of economic, religious, and political interests within a wider European struggle between Catholic and Protestant forces.

From 1669 to the summer of 1682 Shaftesbury, for all practical purposes, headed the proprietorship, and no initiative was undertaken without his approval or at least his cognizance. During the same years Shaftesbury's eventful political career went through multiple stages. In the late 1660s he was Lord Ashley, Baron of Wimborne St. Giles, a hardworking and dedicated administrator without real political influence at court. In 1672, suddenly showered with royal favors, he became Charles II's lord chancellor in the wake of being granted an earldom. However, increasingly opposed to James, Duke of York, and distrusted by the king, Shaftesbury left the Privy Council in 1674 and gradually moved within opposition circles. Losing his first confrontation with the king and his main minister, Thomas Osborne, Earl of Danby, over parliamentary prerogatives, he was sent to the Tower in 1677, becoming, in the words of Andrew Marvell "a Martyr for the *English* Liberties and the Protestant Religion."[50] Released the following year, Shaftesbury surfed the anti-Catholic wave fueled by the "discovery" of the Popish Plot. By 1679 he was recognized as the leader of the opposition force, now known as the Whigs. Following the defeat of the Exclusion movement in 1681, in which he played a primary role, Shaftesbury was confined again to the Tower. On his release in 1682 he feared he would be brought before a grand jury made up of royal supporters. He went first into hiding and then into exile in Amsterdam, where he died in 1683.[51]

The year 1673 is clearly a watershed in Shaftesbury's career. His relationship with Charles II deteriorated as he learned about the secret Catholic clauses of the Treaty of Dover, unsuccessfully tried to convince the king to maintain his policy of religious toleration, and became increasingly opposed to the Duke of York, whose Catholicism and tendencies toward absolutism he feared. Shaftesbury's international views also changed. He had previously been instrumental in gaining parliamentary support for the third Anglo-Dutch War (1672–74), but by the mid-1670s he favored an anti-French foreign policy. Thus, if in his most famous prowar speech, *Delenda est Carthago* of 1672, "a spectacular piece of Hollandophobic rhetoric," Shaftesbury had claimed that "the States of Holland are England's eternal enemy both by interest and inclination," by 1675 the earl feared that the king of France might soon be the "perpetual Master of the Seas without dispute."[52]

Shaftesbury, whom the Puritan Richard Baxter regarded "as the chief political defender of the Protestant cause," became in the mid-1670s a staunch opponent to Catholicism and absolutism.[53] For a Whig, those threats defined France. The signing of the Treaty of Nijmegen in 1678 marked Louis XIV's preponderance in European affairs. Shaftesbury feared the existence of "a secret Catholic league" whose objective was "the utter extirpation of the Protestant religion out of the world."[54] As in the Whig slogan of "No Popery, No Slavery," Catholicism and absolutism were regarded as mutually reinforcing forces. A Catholic monarch on the throne of England would threaten the Protestant religion and the political liberties of the English people. France, with its absolutist Catholic regime and its persecuted Protestant minority, constituted a dangerously close illustration of the disastrous connection between popery and absolutism.[55] As one member of Parliament exclaimed in 1675, "Our jealousies of Popery, or an arbitrary government, are not from a few inconsiderable Papists here . . . but from the ill example we have from France."[56] Similarly, the author of the successful Whiggish pamphlet *Popery and Tyranny: or the Present State of France* exposed "the Tyranny the [Protestant] Subjects of France are under, being Enslaved by the two greatest Enemies to Reason, as well as to Christian or Human Liberty . . . *Popery* and *Arbitrary Power*."[57]

English public opinion was kept abreast of Louis XIV's expansionist and anti-Protestant policies through the press. The Whig newssheet *The True Protestant Mercury, or Occurrences Foreign and Domestick,* patronized by Shaftesbury, contained numerous sensational references to "the Persecutions of the Papists [carried] against the Protestants in France [that] increase daily."[58] In the earl's view, the English nation was to play a pivotal role in this struggle for the Protestant cause by resisting the advent of a Catholic king at home and by offering a refuge to persecuted Protestant minorities from the Continent. Clearly, welcoming Huguenots to England, from which some could be sent to the colonies, and excluding the Duke of York from the succession were two facets of the same struggle fought in the name of Protestantism.

Unsurprisingly, Shaftesbury's economic views supported his political and religious aspirations. "More keenly interested in matters of trade and overseas expansion than any other important politician of his day," Shaftesbury whole-heartedly believed that colonial expansion and trade surplus were the foundations of England's future economic growth.[59] In fact, it was solely on economic grounds that he supported the third Anglo-Dutch War because he then believed that the Netherlands threatened England's colonial and trade interests.[60] As an advocate of populationism, Shaftesbury also believed that colonial expansion should not be achieved at the demographic expense of England. Alluding to the economic slump of the late 1660s, he argued that "[economic] recovery must be [achieved] by using all rational and just ways to invite foreigners in, and stop the drain that carries natives away."[61] As a Whig, Shaftesbury was a proponent of generous naturalization laws that would encourage immigration to compensate for the loss of population allegedly made more acute by increasing emigration.[62] As a colonial proprietor in need of settlers and as an influential member of various colonial committees, Shaftesbury advocated the recruitment of colonists not only from already well-established colonies but also from the Continent.[63]

In view of his dominant role within the proprietorship from 1669 to 1682 and of the political context of the 1670s and early 1680s, the influence of Shaftesbury's Whig household and networks on the conduct of Carolina affairs comes as no surprise. The colonization of Carolina offered Shaftesbury an ideal opportunity to implement his political, religious, and economic ideas, especially through the recruitment of settlers, by far the most crucial aspect of a successful colonial enterprise.

Originally the proprietors tried to recruit colonists from the already established colonies of Virginia, New England, and Barbados. Apart from populationist considerations, proprietary objectives were to people their domain with experienced, or "seasoned," as it was then said, settlers and at a minimal cost. Accordingly, the various attempts at settling parts of the northern section of Carolina in the 1660s were all carried out by New Englanders, Virginians, and Barbadians. The proprietors were particularly interested in making Carolina an offshoot of Barbados, or, following Peter Wood's well-known phrase, "the dependent servant of an island master—in short the colony of a colony."[64] Several reasons account for this proprietary policy. First, with a white population of twenty-three thousand in 1655, it was thought in England that Barbados should play the role of "a nursery for planting Jamaica, Surinam, and other places."[65] Second, the expansion of large-scale sugar production in the 1650s and 1660s initiated a process of land concentration at the expense of the smaller planters, who increasingly sought land elsewhere. This white emigration reached three thousand in the 1660s and peaked at over four thousand between 1670 and 1675.[66] Although most of these planters did not move to Carolina, many did, as shown by the fact that a significant proportion of the people who settled along the Ashley River between 1670 and 1680 were Barbadians.[67] Third, the presence of the Colletons, an influential Barbadian family, within the proprietorship created a further incentive to use the island as a base for the demographic and economic development of Carolina.

Although Barbadians continued to immigrate to South Carolina, in the 1680s the British Isles and the Continent became the focus of a new proprietary recruiting effort. The proprietors were increasingly dissatisfied with what M. Eugene Sirmans called "a colony that returned neither profits nor obedience."[68] Some of the bones of contention were the control of the lucrative Indian trade, the insubordination of some officials, and the refusal of the colonists to pay their debts, to settle in towns, or to adopt Carolina's first constitution, the Fundamental Constitutions. Beyond these real but not incurable problems, however, the proprietors were particularly worried about the slow demographic progress of the colony, whose population had reached only one thousand by 1680, and the fact that no staple that could ensure the long-term prosperity of Carolina had yet been found.[69] The time had come to recruit a large number of settlers who possessed the necessary agricultural skills and the "right" political and religious inclinations.

Traditional South Carolina historiography has speculatively ascribed this recruitment initiative, which targeted English Nonconformists, Scottish Covenanters, and Huguenots, primarily to the proprietors' wish to offset the increasing influence of a disturbing antiproprietary faction led by a group of Barbadian Anglicans known as the "Goose Creek Men" after the area where most of them lived.[70] While it has recently been shown that this group of settlers was neither predominantly from Barbados nor consistently antiproprietary, it appears that the proprietors' recruiting strategy of the 1680s was not primarily determined by this faction's exaggerated influence.[71] Instead it was motivated more by the larger English, and to some extent European, religious and political context of the time rather than by the bickering atmosphere of Carolina's small political arena. In other words, Dissenters, Covenanters, and Huguenots were not recruited so much because the proprietors needed their presence in Carolina for local political support but rather because these persecuted religious groups needed a place to immigrate to and matched the inclinations of the leading proprietors. Along with the intention to develop agricultural products that would enrich the colony, such as wine and silk, the Whig-leaning and Ashley-led proprietary policy was therefore motivated by the desire to use Carolina in an effort to save the Protestant cause from the national and international dual menace of popery and absolutism.

In the late 1670s and early 1680s Shaftesbury's Whig household and social circles undoubtedly influenced the conduct of Carolina affairs. John Locke, who joined the earl's household in 1667 as a friend, doctor, and secretary, also served as the secretary of the proprietorship from 1668 to 1675.[72] In that position he kept up an active correspondence with the Carolina governors, coordinated proprietary initiatives, and assisted in drafting the original version of the Fundamental Constitutions. The Presbyterian Samuel Wilson, another member of Shaftesbury's household who remained loyal to his patron until the earl's death, was the proprietors' secretary from 1678 to 1683.[73] In that capacity, in 1682 he authored an influential promotional pamphlet, *An Account of the Province of Carolina in America,* which was translated into French for the Huguenot readership.[74] Robert Ferguson, a radical Scottish Whig and Shaftesbury's chaplain and agent, wrote another promotional pamphlet, *The Present State of Carolina with Advice to the Settlers,* which was also published in 1682.[75] Sir Peter Colleton, who served as the proprietors' treasurer and "man-of-all-business" from 1682 to 1694 and who had strong Nonconformist and Whig sympathies, played a crucial role in the recruitment of Scottish Covenanters and Huguenots.[76]

Among all these Whig sympathizers within Shaftesbury's orbit, Locke was the most actively involved in Huguenot circles in the 1670s. As a Whig and an opponent of popery and absolutism, Locke was concerned about the persecution of the French Protestants, among whom he had many friends.[77] For more than three years, from November 1675 to April 1679, Locke traveled through France and witnessed the daily harassment and legal privations from which the Huguenots increasingly suffered.[78] In every town he visited, Locke asked his Huguenot hosts about the size of their communities, their religious beliefs and practices, and the number of temples razed.[79] During his visit Locke, aware of his patron's interests in the making of olive oil, wine, and silk as well as fruit growing, also closely observed Huguenot viticultural, sericultural, and gardening techniques.[80] In a book entitled *Observations upon the Growth and Culture of Vines & Olives: The Production of Raw Silk & the Preservation of Fruits,* which he wrote and dedicated to Shaftesbury in 1679, Locke recorded a multitude of details concerning the tending of mulberry trees and silkworms as well as long lists of varieties of fruits, grapes, and olives.[81] While in France, however, Locke was not just a mere observer of Huguenot agricultural savoir faire and of their religious practices. There was an obvious political dimension to his sojourn, as his frequent meetings with Shaftesbury's agents testify. During his travels Locke maintained an assiduous correspondence with his patron and, although this is not documented, may very well have been one of Shaftesbury's informants on the secret dealings between the French and English courts.[82]

Although not specifically instructed to promote Carolina within Huguenot circles, Locke undoubtedly mentioned its existence and the proprietors' needs for settlers skilled in vine and silk production. In the 1670s Carolinians, in the hope of finding a lucrative staple, were experimenting with an extensive variety of crops following Shaftesbury's recommendations. Joseph Dalton, secretary to the proprietary government at the Ashley River settlement, wrote to Shaftesbury in 1672 that Carolina's "climate and Soyle" were particularly suited to the cultivation of "Wine, Oyle, and Silke," precisely what the Huguenots were reputedly experts at producing.[83] Locke, as former secretary to the Carolina proprietorship and as a witness to the anti-Protestant policy carried out in France, was obviously aware that recruiting Huguenots would serve the interests of both the proprietors and his increasingly beleaguered Huguenot friends. Actually, Locke's involvement in the recruitment of French Protestants was not limited to suggestions or thoughts. In 1684 he offered three thousand acres of Carolina land to his Parisian host, a then well-known Huguenot apothecary named Moyse Charas.[84]

Locke and Shaftesbury undoubtedly saw eye to eye on the Huguenot question. As Whigs, they wanted England to welcome these persecuted Protestants and favored a generous policy of naturalization. As colonial entrepreneurs, they believed that Huguenot refugees could be sent to the colonies to establish Mediterranean agricultural products that would enrich England by expanding its colonial trade and making it less dependent on its economic rivals, especially France. All this could be achieved without depleting England of its demographic resources since Huguenot colonists could be recruited either directly from the Continent or from the overcrowded eastern suburbs of London. Thus, their common involvement in the conduct of Carolina affairs in the 1670s led them to set the foundations of a recruiting policy geared toward the French Protestants, which would then be pursued by the proprietors, especially Sir Peter Colleton, through the mid-1680s.

The Recruiting Campaign of the 1680s

The proprietary campaign to recruit Huguenots began with negotiations that led to the sailing of the Carolina-bound *Richmond* with the first contingent of Huguenots on board in 1679. The campaign lasted until the publication of the last French promotional pamphlet in 1686. The variety of means employed and the level of energy displayed by the proprietors, Sir Peter Colleton in particular, and their agents in a relatively short period of time are striking. Pamphlets, including descriptive accounts, collections of letters, and lists of questions and answers, were written or translated into French and published in London, The Hague, and Geneva. French maps of Carolina were sold in the Netherlands by Dutch booksellers of Huguenot descent. Letters exchanged between Huguenots in Carolina and those in London were bought or seized in order to be published in pamphlets. Information about Carolina was supplied to Huguenot authors of geographic treatises. Articles describing the successful integration of the *Richmond* group were published in *The True Protestant Mercury*. Information concerning the colony and the specific advantages granted to Huguenot settlers was given to the consistory of the Threadneedle Huguenot Church in London. Some of the proprietors' agents were active among Huguenot circles in London and on the Continent ceaselessly promoting Carolina. To what extent this strong proprietary interest resulted from Whig-flavored political and religious considerations and the proprietors' sympathy for the Huguenot cause or simply from Shaftesbury's personal influence, which permeated the proprietorship long after his flight and death in the Netherlands, is unsure. What remains certain is that from 1679 to 1686 the recruitment of Huguenots constituted as much a proprietary priority as did the better-known recruitment of Scottish Covenanters, with which it shares many characteristics.

The timing of the tripartite negotiations between the proprietors, the Huguenot party, and the Lords of Trade and Plantations that preceded the departure of the HMS frigate *Richmond* in December 1679 is, from a proprietary perspective, far from coincidental.[85] Officially initiated by a Huguenot petition emanating from two seemingly noteworthy refugees from Normandy, René Petit and Jacob Guérard, the negotiations nonetheless corresponded to the return of Locke from France and Shaftesbury's successful return to the English political stage with the fall of Danby.[86]

Although no personal contact between the Huguenot undertakers and Locke or Shaftesbury is documented, they were most likely in touch in the weeks—perhaps months—preceding the official beginning of the negotiations, probably through common Huguenot friends. Having the Huguenots petition the English authorities instead of the proprietorship may have been a proprietary maneuver to obtain more from the crown. The proprietors, who claimed to have spent "seventeene or eighteene thousand pounds" to bring Carolina "to a prosperous condition," were reluctant to underwrite the expedition and, as part of a general policy, preferred to rely on intermediary entrepreneurs to finance the passage of settlers.[87]

The *Richmond* negotiations nicely fit the prevalent populationist and mercantilist paradigms. When they first reported on the Huguenot petition, the commissioners of customs objected to the plan, arguing that "it would be a good work to encourage them not to settle in Carolina" but to remain in England because "too many families already betake themselves to the Plantations and Ireland, and this tendency should be checked rather than encouraged." However, "if the families are not settled in England," the commissioners thought that "by all means they should be encouraged."[88] Consequently, the Lords of Trade and Plantations, on approving the project, recommended that the Huguenot settlers "shall be genuine arrivals from across the seas."[89] All parties also claimed that with time these settlers would be "a help and comfort to the rest of His Majesty's dominions by supplying them with silks, oils, wines and such other things which they are forced to purchase of foreign nations" and would "not only encrease the number of His Majesties Subjects but be most usefully plac'd for augmenting His Majesties Revenue & Customs."[90]

With Shaftesbury strategically sitting on the three committees, the proprietary board, the Council of Trade, and the Privy Council, all taking part in the negotiations, it is hard to imagine the project being turned down. The timing of the submission of the initial petition, which coincided with Shaftesbury's renewed influence, supports the view that this was not the spontaneous Huguenot request that the proprietors probably had wanted it to appear. Subsequent delays were simply due to the multiple administrative levels the project had to go through to gain royal sponsorship and, most important, to the proprietors' reluctance to underwrite the expedition. From the proprietors' financial point of view the negotiations were undeniably successful. The crown agreed to fit two ships and advance the sum of two thousand pounds sterling with the view that it would recoup this initial investment through an increase in customs revenues occasioned by trade in the commodities that the settlers would introduce in the colony.[91] It was also decided that the refugees were to provide for their own victuals. When the time came for the proprietors to pay their share, they collected only eight hundred of the fourteen hundred pounds agreed on![92]

The upcoming departure of the *Richmond* led to the publication of the first French Carolina promotional pamphlet, *Description du Pays nommé Caroline,* in late spring 1679. Likely authored by Petit and/or Guérard, this broadside of three pages duly informed the refugees of the imminent departure of the two Carolina-bound ships "generously granted by the king to carry them in considerable number."[93]

This first French Carolina publication initiated a pattern in the promotional argumentation that all subsequent authors followed. Although religious arguments were always present, authors preferably extolled the agricultural and trade potential of the colony along with the favorable political proprietary dispositions, which guaranteed each settler would be treated "according to his right . . . with all fairness and equity." Thus Carolina was depicted as undoubtedly "one [of] the most beautiful regions in the world," abounding in trees and plants of all sorts, enjoying a most healthy climate, and ideally located for the ever-expanding transoceanic trade. Epidemics were nonexistent, alligators small, and the rattlesnake, the famed "ringing grass snake" (*couleuvre sonnante*), had "bells at its end to warn of its approach." Through images of abundance, fertility, religious freedom, and political moderation the authors meticulously fabricated a transatlantic Eden in which even the serpent had its symbolic place.[94]

As in all promotional campaigns, the Carolina that the prospective settlers conjectured from reading the pamphlets, what historical geographers call the perceptual environment, mattered more than the actuality of the colony.[95] Following Jack Greene's phrase "selling a New World," it can be said that Carolina was for sale in the 1680s and consequently needed to be successfully advertised.[96] One can just imagine the impact that descriptions such as vines "whose stems are as big as a thigh" and a climate as good as "an everlasting spring" may have had on Huguenots who had never traveled beyond the limits of their parishes.[97]

Following the publication of *Description du Pays nommé Caroline,* seven other French Carolina pamphlets and promotional pieces were published between 1681 and 1686. Six of them appeared in Rotterdam, London, The Hague, and Geneva.[98] The first of these, entitled *Récit de l'Estat présent des célèbres colonies de la Virginie, de Marie-Land, de la Caroline* . . . and authored by Charles de Rochefort, is actually a forty-three-page opuscule on the North American colonies appended to the third French edition of the author's *Histoire naturelle et morale des îles Antilles.*[99] Rochefort was a Huguenot minister from La Rochelle with pastoral experience in the French West Indies. Mainly known for his *Histoire naturelle,* which went through successive French, Dutch, German, and English editions, Rochefort left France in the 1650s for Rotterdam, where he served the Huguenot Church until his retirement in 1681.[100] Rochefort's works, particularly *Récit de l'Estat présent,* were meant to provide prospective Huguenot colonists with information on transatlantic destinations. Although Rochefort borrowed from previous authors, he lived in the French Antilles and claimed to have visited the mainland colonies, which he collectively referred to as "Florida."[101]

Specifically and expressly intended to serve as a Huguenot emigrant guide, the forty-three-page *Récit* was most likely also available for sale independently from the main volume to which it was appended. This pamphlet contains a chapter on the southern colonies in which Carolina, praised as "an excellent colony," holds a prominent place. Significantly, a large section of the passage on Carolina emphasizes the favorable economic, political, and religious conditions offered to French Protestant refugees. Thus, for example, French settlers would receive land in perpetuity and free of rent for ten years. They would also benefit from the same economic and political "freedom and franchise" as the "naturels anglois" and would "profess under the same form of religion . . . as they are accustomed to in the countries whence they come."[102] Interestingly, Rochefort did not allude to the proprietors, stressing that the privileges granted to the prospective Huguenot settlers emanated from the king, and he even mentioned the presence of a royal governor in the colony! Although these errors could be the reflections of Rochefort's ignorance on the particulars of Carolina, they could also be due to a proprietary desire to remain in the background, thus echoing the famed letter addressed to Locke by Sir Peter Colleton in which the latter instructed the former "to draw a discourse . . . in the nature of a description such as might invite people without seeming to come from us."[103] If so, Rochefort's feigned ignorance was a proprietary stratagem to deceive Huguenots into believing that they would live under royal protection, which would appear more reliable and more permanent than proprietary patronage, in the then little-known Carolina.[104]

The promotional campaign reached a peak between 1684 and 1686 with the publication of six French pamphlets. Two of them were 1684 editions of a translation of Wilson's *An Account of the Province of Carolina,* simultaneously published under the title *Description de la Carolline Prés la Floride, ou La Nouvelle Angleterre en l'Amerique* in London and Geneva.[105] A follow-up of the Geneva edition, entitled *Suite de la Description de la Carolline,* subsequently appeared in the Swiss city in 1685.[106] A question-and-answer pamphlet, *Questions et Responses faites au sujet de la Caroline,* was also written that year.[107] Two other pamphlets appeared in The Hague in 1686. One was an account written by an alleged *gentilhomme françois,* entitled *Nouvelle Relation de la Caroline,* and the other, *Plan pour former un établissement en Caroline,* advertised the projected foundation of a Huguenot settlement.

Although substantially similar in contents, these pamphlets differ greatly in formats. The two *Description* publications are straightforward translations that, although not completely verbatim, stick fairly faithfully to Wilson's original. These translations are identical except for two letters, one by the Huguenot settler Louis Thibou and the other by the Dissenter Carolina governor Joseph Morton, which are appended to the Geneva edition. *Suite de la Description*, however, is a collection of short excerpts from Carolina Huguenot letters followed by "twenty and four questions and answers." *Questions et Responses faites au sujet de la Caroline* is a detailed pamphlet containing thirty-seven questions and answers. *Nouvelle Relation* is a long (more than thirty-five pages), laudatory, and most likely secondhand account of the province by an anonymous gentleman who, without any originality, claimed to have "returned from this new land" after spending "the spring and part of the summer of 85."[108] *Plan pour former un établissement* details the terms and requirements for the foundation of a prospective Huguenot settlement. Elaborate in its contents, this pamphlet provides guidelines to twelve would-be Huguenot investors concerning the number of acres to acquire, the internal organization of the settlement, the recruitment of settlers, and the privileges to be requested from the proprietors. Interested parties were supposed to form a corporation (*confédération*), collectively investing "15,600 French pounds or thereabouts," roughly 1,300 livres (£100) each, for the purchase of a twenty-four-thousand-acre tract to found a town.[109] The pamphlet also contained an opportune *prête-à-signer* (ready-to-sign) twenty-one-article convention to facilitate the prompt establishment of the corporation.

These pamphlets constituted the main thrust of the Carolina promotional campaign, but the proprietors, as innovative and determined as ever, resorted to other means to advertise for their colony. In 1681 and 1682, the *True Protestant Mercury* published articles describing the "hopeful and flourishing conditions of the province" and announcing the departures of Carolina-bound ships and the publication of pamphlets and maps about Carolina.[110] Other reports contained specific references to the "French Protestants . . . who went [to Carolina] about three years since," the "hopefulnes[s] of their Vintage," and "their having made Silk."[111]

In March 1682 an advertisement in the *True Protestant Mercury* announced the weekly meeting of the proprietors in the Carolina Coffee House.[112] The opening in London of this coffeehouse, where prospective settlers could obtain detailed practical information on the conditions of the transatlantic passage and settlement in Carolina, constituted a significant step in the proprietary effort to promote Carolina.[113] Soon its existence was made known to Huguenots through promotional pamphlets. The author of *Nouvelle Relation* informed his readers that they could repair to "le Café-hous de la Caroline," and *Questions et Responses faites au sujet de la Caroline* also mentions "[la] Carolina Coffe house in Burchinlane."[114] Ironically, those who wished to dissuade the Huguenots from settling in the colony also promoted the Carolina Coffee House and its role as a place where one could obtain reliable information about Carolina. The author of the adversarial pamphlet *Remarques sur la Nouvelle Relation*, expressly published to refute the arguments developed in *Nouvelle Relation*, sarcastically wrote that "this gentleman has gone too far in reporting only on hearsay, for the Coffee House to which he refers us in London might at least have procured him one friend of the Province who could have furnished him with an account as ample as that he gives us."[115] For the Huguenots, the proprietors could not have picked a more appropriate and convenient location. Birchin Lane was literally situated at a stone's throw from Threadneedle Street, where the largest London French Protestant church stood. One can easily picture Huguenot refugees stopping by the Carolina Coffee House to seek information about the colony on their way to or from a church service.

The Carolina proprietors, especially Shaftesbury, also made use of agents working across the English Channel in France and the Netherlands to promote their colony. More secretive and less prominent than William Penn's famous agent in the Netherlands, Benjamin Furly, Shaftesbury's envoys played a promotional role on the side of their political spying missions.[116] The obvious secret nature of their missions overseas and the fact that these were primarily political explain why their role as promotional agents is undocumented and therefore difficult to identify. Nonetheless, by piecing together different sources, historians can highlight the roles of some individuals and reconstruct plausible human promotional networks. As stated earlier, when visiting France, Locke, who was in contact with Shaftesbury's agents, also offered land to his Huguenot Parisian host, Moyse Charas. Peter Du Moulin II, an Englishman of Huguenot descent who acted as an English spy in the Netherlands in the 1670s, was also close to Shaftesbury.[117] He was so close that his nephew Peter Du Moulin III by 1682 settled in Carolina, where he and seven other prominent settlers, among whom were Daniel Axtell and James Colleton, were entrusted by Shaftesbury with the care of the earl's interests.[118] St. Julien Childs conjectured that the Huguenot squire Jacques Goulard de Vervant, who acquired fifteen thousand acres of Carolina land in 1686, may have been the proprietors' agent in Amsterdam or Rotterdam mentioned at the end of *Plan pour former un établissement en Caroline*.[119] This pamphlet, in which prospective Huguenot settlers were advised to contact individuals in London, Amsterdam, and Rotterdam, documents the fact that the proprietors had representatives in England and abroad instructed to inform all those who wished to remove themselves to Carolina. Whether those individuals and the proprietors' agents known to historians as operating on the Continent were the same people remains conjectural, yet it is likely, considering how intertwined personal, collective, officious, and official networks were at the time.

Carolina Fever, or the Impact of Promotion

No matter how imaginative and resourceful the Carolina proprietors were in their effort to promote their colony, printed materials, such as tracts, maps, and other items, carried the thrust of the campaign. In addition to the publication of eight pamphlets between 1679 and 1686, the Fundamental Constitutions were translated into French in 1683.[120] Two French maps of South Carolina, *Carte Générale de la Caroline* and *Carte Particulière de la Caroline,* were printed and sold in Amsterdam in 1696 by Pieter Mortier, a printer-bookseller, a descendant of Huguenots who had settled in the Netherlands in the early seventeenth century (see figures following page 96).[121] This extensive use of printed propaganda should come as no surprise since it was the least expensive and most effective way for the proprietors to reach prospective settlers simultaneously in England, the Netherlands, the Swiss cantons, and France.

A close look at the continental printers and booksellers hired by the Carolina proprietors to publish, sell, and circulate their pamphlets reveals a good knowledge and efficient use of existing distribution networks. The places of publication, London, The Hague, and Geneva, corresponded to cities to which Huguenot refugees had traditionally fled during periods of persecution. Despite all the risks entailed, there had long been Huguenot comings and goings between these urban centers and France that had created valuable channels of communication. In the 1680s the Carolina proprietors judiciously used them to disseminate information about their colony.

Reinier Leers, who published Rochefort's *Récit de l'Estat présent,* was a Rotterdam-based publisher with one of the most extensive international distribution networks of French books then available. Assisted by the erudite Huguenot Pierre Bayle as a publication consultant, Leers published a long list of Huguenot works, including Bayle's and Pierre Jurieu's.[122] Meindert Uytweft, who was to hold a prominent position in the book trade of The Hague, had recently become a master bookseller when he published *Nouvelle Relation* and *Plan pour former un établissement en Caroline* in 1686.[123] Although it cannot be documented, the fact that Uytwerf successively published two French Carolina tracts undeniably indicates that he had access to Huguenot distribution networks or that the proprietors believed he did. The case of the Swiss Jacques de Tournes, who published *Description de la Carolline* and *Suite de la Description* and about whom more is known, is a perfect illustration of the proprietors' use of these networks. Huguenot booksellers in Lyon since 1542, the de Tournes family settled in Geneva in 1585 during the Wars of Religion.[124] While in Switzerland, they remained in close contact with Huguenot communities, especially pastors, in Dauphiny and along the Rhône Valley, and from there they had access to French Protestant familial peddling networks throughout southeastern France.[125] The family regularly sent agents to London to collect the remittance of bills and information on recent publications, and was thus also part of a broader international book-selling network. A close look at their publication lists shows that the family had for generations been specialized in Huguenot and travel literature.[126]

By using these booksellers' distribution networks, which paralleled trade routes, the Carolina proprietors managed to circulate their promotional publications in the La Rochelle area from The Hague and London, and in Dauphiny and eastern Languedoc from Geneva. These two regions had the highest concentration of Huguenots in the 1680s except for the isolated Cévennes. Perhaps more significantly, they were the best-represented areas among the Carolina Huguenots. This observation leads to the crucial question of the impact of this promotional literature. In other words, did these pamphlets actually reach their intended public?

Several documents show that the Carolina promotional pamphlets were known in France, where they circulated clandestinely and raised a real interest among Huguenots that was mitigated only by a somewhat skeptical curiosity. The authors of the petition *Proposition en générale pour la Caroline,* who claimed to represent "many families who suffer for religion's sake from Poitou and Aunis," asked if "the account of Carolina that circulates in France is sincere."[127] The pamphlet *Questions et Responses faites au sujet de la Caroline* also contains a question about the authenticity of the Carolina promotional literature, thereby showing that the proprietors knew of the skepticism generated by their enchanted accounts.[128] Refugees' accounts also evidence similar interest and curiosity in these apparently well-known Carolina pamphlets. Durand de Dauphiné, author of *Voyages d'un François exilé pour la Religion,* mentioned printed tracts about Carolina that he had read in France and which had made him "obsessed with that land."[129] In the same vein, Judith Giton wrote about her elder brother who had "only Carolina on his mind," presumably because he had read promotional tracts.[130] In the La Rochelle area, fugitive lists compiled by French officials, which contain comments regarding refugees' intended destinations, often mention "parti à la Caroline" (gone to Carolina) next to a name, thereby showing that South Carolina was well known to local Huguenots as a potential retreat.[131] In fact, the circulation of these Carolina pamphlets much worried the La Rochelle intendant, who in a report written in December 1684 warned his superiors in Versailles that "for some time the English or those who have taken refuge in England circulate tracts containing an advantageous description of a land in America called Carolina where those who want to settle are promised great advantages."[132]

The anxiety transpiring in this report testifies to the proprietors' success in spreading an Edenic image of their colony across parts of France and Western Europe. Between 1684 and 1686, more than any other colony in British North America, Carolina was the object of particular attention on the part both of Huguenot refugees—literally gripped by Carolina fever—and also of other colonial landowners and proprietors, Huguenot church elders in London, and French officials on post in England.[133] Assuredly not all the refugees read the pamphlets, but many, and most of those who eventually settled in the lowcountry, had likely heard rumors about the colony before leaving Europe, if not France. This fragmented and idealized vision of South Carolina, which spread rapidly within refugee Huguenot communities, probably did more to promote the colony than did the printed propaganda that initiated it. These rumors in turn fueled a debate over the pros and cons of Carolina life and the opportuneness of immigrating there. This phenomenon, which reached a peak in 1685, was short lived since not only were no pamphlets published after 1686 but also most Carolina Huguenots had settled in the colony by 1687.

When Durand de Dauphiné arrived in London in 1686 with his hopes and his doubts, he immediately visited with two Huguenot pastors to ask them whether or not he should settle in Carolina. One tried to dissuade him and promised him that he would "use all his power to help him find an honest subsistence for two or three years," after which "it should be time to return to France." The other minister, whose advice Durand eventually followed, recommended going to Carolina since he had recently received a letter from a Huguenot merchant settled there that contained nothing but good news.[134] In his well-known 1683 letter Louis Thibou, one of the original *Richmond* settlers, twice implicitly mentions pro- and anti-Carolina discussions. First, obviously irritated, he flays a disappointed Huguenot in saying that "if he had worked instead of being lazy, no doubt he would be doing as well as me & would write about Carolina in good terms." Then in the postscript, alluding to a friend who chose to stay in England, he asserts with confidence that "he would have done better to come to this land."[135]

In his letter published in *Description de la Carolline,* Carolina governor Joseph Morton explained that whoever listened to "those who have some interest in Virginia, & Pennsylvania, & New England" would never settle in South Carolina, "for it is their interest to depict all the evils of this land."[136] This recommendation illustrates the needs felt by the proprietors to warn the Huguenot readership that their colony was the target of an aggressive counterpromotional campaign designed to dissuade them from immigrating there. Two extant French pamphlets, *Remarques sur la Nouvelle Relation* and Durand's *Voyages,* respectively published in 1686 and 1687, give us a taste of this counterpromotional literature.

Written out of "sympathy for the Protestant refugees of France," *Remarques* contains a point-by-point refutation of *Nouvelle Relation* and an unfavorable comparison of Carolina with other North American colonies.[137] The reader is informed, for example, that Carolina is located too far south to take part in the transatlantic trade, that its mild winter is not an advantage since cold purifies the air, that its sandy soil is not fertile, and that the lowcountry salty water is not drinkable. Conversely, the prospective emigrant is told that New England's soil is better suited for agriculture than Carolina's, that the livestock raised in New York is superior, and that horses are cheaper in Virginia, where "a simple planter" is worth more than "half-a-dozen [Carolina] caciques."[138] The anonymous pamphleteer also attacked the author of *Nouvelle Relation,* accusing him of "acting as a papist" in knowing Carolina only from hearsay and of making his the observations of others.[139] In doing so, we are to understand, he behaved like a gullible and deceptive Catholic. In what was intended as a deathblow, the author of *Remarques* used the reminiscence of Huguenot Florida as a reason for French Calvinists to avoid settling in Carolina. He bluntly warned the reader that "[he] who know[s] the sanguinary history between the Spanish and the French, in the same country, at the end of the last century, [should] not think the same things impossible whenever the strength or treachery of the Spaniards will furnish them a good occasion to renew them."[140] Although this warning had little effect on prospective Huguenot settlers, the author was not completely off the mark in light of the two destructive Spanish raids on the Port Royal Scottish Calvinist settlement of Stuart Town in 1686.[141] Had the Huguenots founded a town in the same location or settled among the Scots, as they were invited to do, they would undoubtedly have met the same fate.[142]

If *Remarques* is an undisguised frontal attack on Carolina, Durand's *Voyages* is a finely elaborated account born out of a promotional stratagem that understandably deceived contemporaries but has also puzzled historians since its publication in 1687.[143] With the benefit of hindsight and knowledge of Restoration promotional techniques, however, Durand's admittedly shrewd manipulation does not stand the test of a close reading. Durand first contended that he had read Carolina printed tracts that convinced him to settle in the colony. Because of a storm, however, the ship captain refused to sail into the Charleston bay and decided instead to go to Virginia, where Durand landed a week later. When the ship was ready to set sail for Carolina a few days later, Durand, suffering from an opportune fever, for which he later thanked "la providence" in a typically Calvinistic fashion, was unable to embark. The rest of the account is an apology of Virginia at the expense of Carolina, which, of course, Durand had never seen. In short, Durand expounded five reasons why Carolina did not stand the comparison: a climate too hot "to grow wheat" or "to raise sheep," the absence of tobacco, a limited trade, and the absence of "good waters" due to the flat Carolina topography.[144]

Although he reckoned that Virginia was "the most beautiful, the most pleasant & the most fertile land in all the West Indies," Durand did not stay but rather returned to Europe, where he had his account quickly published.[145] Beyond its incongruities and contradictions and the opportune presence of the Virginia land grant procedures at the end, this narrative reads like a promotional pamphlet. It contains a stereotypical apology of a colony (a pleasant climate, a fertile soil, the absence of diseases, a balanced government, and little taxation) developed at the expense of another, information on the departure of ships, and a set of guidelines on the acquisition of land, which had miraculously "fallen into the author's hands."[146] Durand's stratagem was simple. He deliberately emphasized an idealized perception of Carolina explicitly based on the reading of promotional pamphlets that circulated in France so as to better criticize Carolina and appear as a victim of its promotional literature. The episode during which he asked for pastoral advice while in London saves Durand from appearing too naive and idiotic. It may also have been an attack against the Nonconformist minister who encouraged him to go to Carolina since Virginia, which Durand promoted, was an Anglican colony. Durand then justified his problematic return by the hope to see "the religion" restored in France and, paradoxically, his altruistic desire to relieve "the faithful Huguenots [fleeing] from the Babylonian captivity," who surged into London, by "contributing to their settling in the most beautiful land [he] had ever seen."[147]

The likely story of Durand can be mapped out without much difficulty. Durand left the province of Dauphiny as it was about to be dragooned. A relatively well-off gentilhomme, he managed to reach England with a small amount of capital. Unprepared and unwilling to adjust to London city life, like many Huguenots of his condition, he decided to move on to South Carolina, where he hoped to establish a silk plantation. The vagaries of oceanic navigation led him to Virginia, where he met landowners eager to recruit skilled settlers among Huguenot refugees who were desperately idle amidst the urban crowds of London and The Hague. Soon disillusioned by Virginia and anxious to return to Europe, however, Durand most likely struck a deal with them. In exchange for a return passage and literary posterity, Durand agreed to write a promotional piece that would extol Virginia's advantages, especially the counties where his patrons owned land, at the expense of its growing southern neighbor.[148]

At one point in his narrative Durand claims that Virginia, as a royal colony, was at a disadvantage in this competition for settlers since "there were no proprietors" who could have promotional accounts printed "as in the case of Carolina and Pennsylvania."[149] Pennsylvania, with its energetic founder and its original emphasis on religious freedom, undeniably represented a potentially more serious threat than Virginia to the Carolina proprietors in their effort to recruit Huguenot refugees. Fortunately for the proprietors, despite his sympathy for the persecuted French Protestants, William Penn's promotional campaign was mainly aimed at Dutch and German Quakers and other Protestant groups.[150] Penn nonetheless had two French pamphlets, *Recüeil de Diverses Pièces concernant la Pennsylvanie* and *Instruction Très-Exacte pour ceux qui ont dessein de se transporter en Amerique, Et Principalement Pour Ceux qui sont intéressés dans la Province de Pennsylvanie,* published respectively in 1684 and 1686, during the peak of the Carolina campaign. These, however, in typical Quaker fashion, contain no hostile assertions toward Carolina.[151]

Both pamphlets were translations of earlier German and English pamphlets in the hand of Penn's polyglot and erudite agent on the Continent, the Anglo-Dutch Quaker merchant Benjamin Furly.[152] Sharing Shaftesbury's mercantilist and populationist views, Penn wished to recruit Huguenot refugees, especially wine growers, for his colony.[153] Having studied for a semester at the Saumur académie in Touraine in 1662, Penn was also well acquainted with French Protestantism and its increasingly precarious position in a Catholic absolutist state.[154] To promote his colony within refugee Huguenot circles, especially in the Netherlands, he could rely on Furly, who regularly mixed with eminent French Protestant theologians and writers, such as Pierre Bayle and Jacques Basnage, at the Lantern, a Rotterdam-based literary salon.[155] Like the Carolina proprietors, Penn also resorted to refugee Huguenot booksellers and their circulation networks. *Recüeil de Diverses Pièces,* for example, was printed and sold by Abraham Troyel, who also published and diffused the works of the Huguenot theologian Jurieu.[156] In addition Penn wrote a letter to the attention of the "poor French Protestants" promising free passage to Pennsylvania in exchange for a slightly higher quitrent to those who were without financial resources and objected to indenturing themselves.[157]

Documents show that for a brief period, between 1684 and 1686, the Huguenot refugees did not distinguish between Carolina and Pennsylvania as potential North American destinations. In June 1684 the Huguenot pastor Jean Claude, author of the influential and censured *Les plaintes des protestants cruellement opprimez dans le royaume de France,* translated as *A Short Account of the Complaints and Cruel Persecution of the Protestants in the Kingdom of France,* informed one of his correspondents of a project to send "a great number" of refugees to Carolina or Pennsylvania.[158] In February 1685 two elders were assigned by the Threadneedle Street Church consistory to go to "Sir Peter Colleton and Mr Penn" to ascertain what they were offering for Carolina and Pennsylvania. In the following months the same consistory attempted to raise funds to transport refugees "*either to Carolina or Pennsylvania*" (emphasis added).[159] In January 1686 a worried French official in England, most likely acting as a spy, reported about Huguenots "leaving Plymouth for Carolina and Pennsylvania."[160] Additionally, in his narrative Durand mentions reading pamphlets "about Carolina and Pennsylvania."[161]

Although these records substantiate that Pennsylvania was as well known as Carolina among Huguenot refugees, the fact is that few of them settled in the Quaker colony.[162] Thus, for example, only two Huguenots were among the first purchasers in Pennsylvania—Moyse Charas, the same apothecary to whom Locke had promised three thousand acres in Carolina, and the minister Pierre Daillé, who eventually settled in Boston.[163] This near absence of French Protestant settlers in Penn's colony, which Butler called "the Huguenot rejection of Pennsylvania," is a contrapuntal illustration of the success of the Carolina proprietors' campaign.[164] Over the long term South Carolina undeniably attracted far fewer colonists than did Pennsylvania, but it drew a fairly large contingent, possibly the largest in British North America, of Huguenots between 1685 and 1690.[165] This factual observation raises two crucial questions whose answers, unfortunately, remain speculative and, in some measure, elusive: how can this success be explained, and to what extent was this a success?

The number and variety of the French Carolina pamphlets alone constitute a manifest first explanation. Indeed, judging by the list of extant tracts, South Carolina was the most- and best-promoted North American colony among Huguenot refugees. The proprietors published seven French pamphlets, Penn two, and only one appeared for Virginia.[166] This profusion of French printed literature was, however, due more to promotional strategy than to determination, energy, or means since, contrary to Penn, the Carolina proprietors did not attempt to recruit German settlers before the early 1700s.[167] In the 1680s, however, with seven French pamphlets published to their attention out of a total of twelve tracts, the Huguenots undeniably constituted a recruiting priority for the Carolina proprietors.[168] The places of publication were efficiently chosen as these cities were areas of large Huguenot populations and also were strategically located along escape routes. The choice of these locations undoubtedly gave the proprietary recruiting campaign high visibility.

All the colonies offered more or less the same economic and, except for Virginia, religious advantages. The Carolina proprietors, however, intelligently put forth two arguments that may have particularly appealed to Huguenots: the presence of French settlers in the colony and easy naturalization. When Durand first decided to move to Carolina instead of Virginia, he explained that "since there were no French in Virginia, [he] could but be unhappy."[169] The author of *Description de la Carolline* did not fail to mention the presence of "fellow countrymen" in Charleston, and in *Suite de la Description* the Huguenot reader is informed of the ever growing Carolina population of "[French] reformed" settlers.[170] The successful settlement of the *Richmond* passengers, who arrived in Charleston in 1680, became an argument to lure more Huguenots. Rochefort, for instance, mentioned "the 80 families of foreign Protestants" sent to Carolina to establish "wheat, wine & olive oil" production and who "trade beyond England with the same liberty and franchise as the English naturals."[171]

The proprietors also knew that in the eyes of the Huguenot refugees naturalization was a sine qua non condition for the enjoyment of whatever political and economic privileges they were promised in the promotional literature. Thus, the proprietors astutely designed and subsequently promoted a free and easy naturalization procedure that required only the signing of the Fundamental Constitutions.[172] In fact, this procedure was so much perceived as giving Carolina the edge in the competitive search for Huguenot settlers that Furly did not fail to recommend that his patron, William Penn, insert a naturalization clause in his Frame of Government "as in the Carolina constitutions."[173]

More than the attractiveness of the specific advantages described in the tracts, however, the capacity of the proprietors to disseminate positive information about their colony within Huguenot circles proved decisive. From this perspective, the aura of Shaftesbury, the active involvement of Sir Peter Colleton in the campaign, and the proprietary capacity to effectively use Whig-Huguenot networks for the promotion of Carolina turned out to be essential. As an advocate of the immigration and naturalization of foreign Protestants and a champion of the Protestant cause in England and on the Continent, Shaftesbury enjoyed something close to the reputation of a protector among

Huguenots. Politically, a majority of Huguenots in England sided with the Whigs and consequently perceived Shaftesbury as a leader. As much as the Huguenot Whigs could count on Ashley Cooper to defend their rights, the earl could rely on their political loyalty in time of personal difficulty. When Shaftesbury was acquitted in the trial that followed the Exclusion Crisis in 1681, two prominent London Huguenot Whigs, Thomas Papillon and John Dubois, sat on the jury.[174] Two years later this Huguenot support for the Whig cause was aggressively denounced by Tory propaganda in the months following the announcement of a fake anti-Stuart conspiracy known as the Rye House Plot.[175] By then royal pressure was so intolerable that many Whig Huguenots, among them Papillon, followed Shaftesbury into his Dutch exile.[176] In sum, through a few influential and well-integrated second-generation Huguenots, Shaftesbury's political networks extended to the Threadneedle Street Church, the heart of the London French Protestant community. Whether utilized to gain anti-Stuart support or promote Carolina, those same Whig-Huguenot channels of communication proved immensely effective.

If Shaftesbury, with the help of Locke, initiated the drive to recruit Huguenots, Sir Peter Colleton, who began to run the affairs of the proprietorship after the earl fled to the Netherlands in 1682, actively and successfully pursued Shaftesbury's recruiting policy.[177] Although little discussed in Carolina Huguenot historiography, Colleton's pivotal role as a provider of information and a contact person in the later stage of the French campaign proved as crucial as Shaftesbury's influence had been earlier. In *Questions et Responses faites au sujet de la Caroline* readers seeking information about Carolina-bound ships and the purchase of land were instructed to contact "Mr le Chevalier Colleton in his house on Germanstreet," and throughout the pamphlet Colleton appears as the proprietary representative or spokesman.[178] In an effort to reassure his readers of the feasibility of growing vineyards in Carolina, the author of *Nouvelle Relation* claimed to have seen all sorts of vines in "Mr Colleton's estate."[179] Then, in the introduction to "Réponses à vint & quatre Questions touchant la Carolline," appended to *Suite de la Description,* the author is said to have obtained that tract from the hands of "Mr Colleton."[180] It was also Colleton who, in early 1685, contacted members of the consistory of the Threadneedle Street Church and provided them with information on Carolina.

Colleton's involvement in the promotion of Carolina, however, was not limited to recruiting Huguenots. In the early 1680s he was equally, and perhaps even more, involved in moving forward a projected settlement of Scottish Covenanters. In fact, beyond the personality and role of Colleton, the two recruiting campaigns had more in common than has usually been recognized. Covenanters, like the Huguenots, were Calvinists enduring increasingly intense pressure, which reached a peak in the mid-1680s during a period heroically, and somewhat hagiographically, known in Scottish Presbyterian history as the "Killing Times."[181] Covenanters caught taking part in conventicles, which resembled Huguenot illegal services, or *assemblées,* were fined, imprisoned, deported, or even executed, depending on their social ranks and obstinacy.[182]

An illuminating parallel can thus be drawn between the proprietary recruitment of these beleaguered Scots and that of the Huguenots in order to measure the success of the French campaign. Like the French refugees, the Scottish Covenanters, who could count on Whig support to defend their case in London, perceived Shaftesbury as a champion of the Protestant cause.[183] The earl most likely gave the impetus to the recruiting drive, but again Colleton was the Scots' favored contact among the Carolina proprietors before and after they settled in the colony.[184] The promotional pamphlet *A New and Most Exact Account of the Fertiles [sic] and Famous Colony of Carolina,* containing a "Journall from the River Clyd in the kingdom of Scotland to Port-Royal in Carolina," and a broadside advertising for a Carolina-bound ship "ready to set sail out of the River of Clyd" were also specifically published for the Scots in 1683 and 1684.[185] Clearly, the recruiting of the Covenanters and that of the Huguenots emerged from the same Whiggish political and religious preoccupations and were planned along similar lines.

Beyond these telling similarities, however, lie significant differences. Although prominent Huguenots, for example Papillon, followed Shaftesbury into exile in the wake of the Rye House Plot and the anti-Whig repression that followed, French Protestant immigration to Carolina had no political dimension.[186] Only Peter Du Moulin III may have settled in the earl's colony for political reasons. The proprietors were also more directly involved in the Scottish campaign because none of them had a firsthand knowledge of the French context and all relied on their agents and Locke for specific information. Moreover, although the negotiations between John Cochrane of Olchiltree and Sir George Campbell of Cessnock and the proprietors echo those preceding the departure of the *Richmond,* Petit and Guérard did not possess the stature of the two Scottish lords. Consequently, the Huguenots never enjoyed the leverage that enabled the Scots to convince the proprietors to revise the Fundamental Constitutions, obtain the control of a separate county, and have their leaders honored with the titles of landgrave and cacique.[187] Yet, whereas some 150 Scots settled unsuccessfully in the Port Royal area in 1684, several hundred Huguenots relocated in Carolina between 1680 and 1690.[188] In other words, the proprietors managed to trigger what for 1680 Carolina was a significant, albeit short-lived, migration and with a dynamic of its own.

Considering the limited logistical means of early modern Europe, the proprietors' Huguenot campaign undoubtedly appears successful. Its impact on the large pool of potential Huguenot settlers, however, remains small, to say the least. While in the 1680s an overwhelming number of Huguenots preferred Carolina to Pennsylvania, Virginia, and New England, the migration nonetheless remains statistically negligible in the perspective of the diaspora. The maximum estimate of six hundred individuals represents about 0.3 percent of the two hundred thousand Huguenots who fled France and only 1.0 percent of the fifty thousand who sought refuge in the British Isles. These infinitesimal proportions can be explained by dysfunction in a later stage of the proprietary campaign and by the more general reticence of most Huguenots to settle in distant colonies. Why did the Huguenot campaign abruptly cease in 1686, at a time when the Huguenot migration to England had not yet reached its peak?[189] Was it a proprietary decision to limit the cost of the campaign or was it simply mismanagement? Did the proprietors think enough had been done or spent to initiate a significant migration or did they suddenly lose interest? Their unwillingness to substantially finance the passage of large numbers of Huguenots and their exclusive reliance on individuals to recruit and arrange for the transportation of settlers also made it impossible for the migration to reach massive proportions. Yet, although the proprietors' lack of focus, means, and possibly coordination are significant factors to take into consideration, it was due to contextual factors inherent in the Huguenot diaspora that the Huguenot migration to Carolina would not become large and self-sustaining.

The Huguenot exodus was massive but sudden. Perhaps more importantly, it was caused by extraordinary circumstances that were therefore perceived by its victims as reversible. In the 1680s most Huguenots hoped for a restoration, if not of the Edict of Nantes, at least of some of their religious and civil rights. Durand's return to Europe, caused by a prophetic belief in the restoration of the Protestant religion in France before 1689, is in that respect ironically symptomatic.[190] Settling in Carolina necessarily implied a more distant and somewhat irrevocable exile that appeared neither attractive nor practical to most Huguenots. Those who settled in Carolina implicitly resigned themselves to never returning to France, recovering their confiscated estates, or being reunited with their siblings who remained behind and converted. No doubt this was a harrowing decision pregnant with far-reaching consequences. Furthermore, like most early modern Europeans, the Huguenots were reticent to confront the perils of a voyage across "the vast and furious ocean" when many other closer alternatives for relocation existed.[191] In this respect, the few Huguenots who opted for a transatlantic destination resembled the Palatines who migrated westward across the Atlantic instead of settling eastward along the Danube River. In other words, like the elector of Brandenburg-Prussia with whom they were in competition, the Carolina proprietors faced the difficult challenge of diverting part of the refugee flow away from its natural channels.[192] Considering these circumstances, the undeniable success of the proprietors was to convince a few hundred Huguenots to settle in a faraway and largely inhospitable land unknown to most of the refugees before the publication of the first pamphlet.

Chapter 3

FROM NEW BABYLON TO EDEN

The Saga of the South Carolina Huguenots

When I have named France, I have said all that is necessary to give you a complete idea of the blackest tyranny over men's consciences, persons, and estates.
Bishop Burnet, "A Sermon preached before the House of Peers" (1689)

We are happy that we have left this cursed Babylon, for we have not shared her plagues.
Jaques Fontaine, *Memoirs*

Papists have been the most bloody persecutors in the world; they have shed Rivers of Blood.
Increase Mather, *A Sermon wherein is shewed that the Church of God is Sometimes a Subject of Great Persecution* (1682)

To Remain and Endure
The Huguenot Ordeal in Post-Revocation France

Although excessive and politically biased, the Whig stereotyping of France as a country where absolutism and Catholicism ruled in terror was, from a Huguenot perspective, not far from the truth in the years immediately following the Revocation.[1] In the late 1680s Huguenots who refused to convert, who attended illegal services, or who were caught leaving the kingdom could be imprisoned, sentenced to the galleys, deported to the Caribbean, or sometimes even executed. Although the French Reformed Church somehow managed to survive into the eighteenth century, the Revocation was undoubtedly a traumatic experience that permanently changed the geographic and socioeconomic distribution as well as the religious nature of French Protestantism.

The Edict of Revocation was signed on October 18, 1685, and recorded by the parlement of Paris on October 22. This eagerness to make the new edict a law contrasted sharply with the circumstances surrounding the adoption of the Edict of Nantes when Henry IV had to overcome a determined parliamentary opposition. The Edict of Fontainebleau was undoubtedly a popular edict, and its adoption generated a true enthusiasm, not only among clergymen and courtiers but also among most of the French population. To celebrate its promulgation, poems and eulogies were composed, medals were coined, and paintings and statues were created.[2] In the funeral oration written in honor of Michel Le Tellier in January 1686, Bossuet, bishop of Meaux and unarguably the most prominent French prelate of the 1680s, referred to Louis XIV as "this new Constantine, this new

Theodosius . . . this new Charlemagne . . . who has exterminated the heretics."[3] A Catholic author similarly claimed in 1686 that the Edict of Fontainebleau was "an eternal monument to the zeal and piety of our invincible monarch Louis XIV."[4] Not surprisingly the same enthusiasm transpired from the king's entourage. A week after the Revocation, Madame de Sévigné asserted that "no king had ever achieved anything so memorable."[5] Even the Jansenists, who were also victims of Louis XIV's policy of religious normalization in the 1680s, praised the Revocation.[6]

In the rest of Europe, however, the Revocation did not raise any particular enthusiasm, even among France's Catholic allies, it reflected Louis XIV's overconfidence and seemed to announce the renewal of an aggressive foreign policy. Unsurprisingly, Protestant powers, led by the Netherlands, condemned the Revocation as a tyrannical act of Catholic absolutism. But if this reaction was to be expected and could be ignored by the French monarchy, the formation in July 1686 of a diplomatic and military coalition against France, known as the League of Augsburg, was an ill omen.[7] Comprising Catholic and Protestant states such as the Netherlands, Brandenburg, Sweden, Bavaria, Spain, and the Holy Roman Empire, this European-wide coalition shows to what extent the Revocation was a diplomatic miscalculation. Only James II, whose neutrality Louis XIV bought with ample subsidies, remained outside it. Even the papacy expressed only mild enthusiasm.[8] In November 1685 Pope Innocent XI sent Louis XIV a brief congratulating him, but only in the spring of 1686 was a Te Deum sung in Rome to celebrate the Edict of Fontainebleau.[9] This lack of papal euphoria was due to the fact that the Revocation in essence showed that the French monarchy was solely responsible for its domestic religious affairs. It was an assertion of Gallican autonomy, which did not please the papacy.

Contrary to the lengthy Edict of Nantes, the Edict of Fontainebleau, with only twelve articles, was amazingly brief for a document of that importance.[10] Article 1 "suppressed and revoked" the Edict of Nantes and ordered all remaining temples to be demolished. The second and third articles prohibited any kind of Huguenot worship, public or private. Article 4 expelled the pastors, who were given two weeks to leave. Article 5 promised financial rewards to those pastors who stayed and converted, and article 6 offered the former ministers the possibility of becoming attorneys. The seventh closed all Huguenot schools, and the eighth ordered Huguenot children to be baptized and reared as Catholics. Article 9 gave to the Huguenots who had already left the kingdom four months to return and "to re-enter in possession of their property" before it was confiscated. Article 10 prohibited Huguenots from leaving France "or transporting their goods there from under penalty, as respects for the men, of being sent to the galleys, and as respects for the women, of confiscation of body [imprisonment]." The eleventh article reiterated the arrêts decreed against relapsed Catholics. Article 12 most ambiguously granted the Huguenots the liberty to remain in France and "to continue their commerce, and to enjoy their possessions, without being subjected to molestation and hindrance, under pretext of the said R[*eligion*] P[*rétendue*] R[*éformée*]."[11] This last article, most likely inserted to appease France's German Protestant allies, remained a dead letter as new dragonnades ransacked Huguenot homes in regions and towns that had until then been spared.[12]

Although the Huguenots had been the victims of legal, civil, economic, and religious discrimination for more than two decades, and of brutal persecution since 1681, the Revocation created a new situation. French Protestantism was now legally banned. Officially there were no more Huguenots in the kingdom but only Catholics, by birth or by conversion. France, in the words of Pierre Bayle, had become "toute catholique" (all Catholic).[13] The seven hundred thousand or so Huguenots who then lived in France were all N.C.s, that is, *nouveaux catholiques* (new Catholics) or *nouveaux convertis* (new converts).[14] Until October 1685 the Huguenots could suffer discrimination and persecution and still hope for brighter days, but once the Edict of Nantes was revoked a point of no return seemed to have been reached. Since 1598 there had been enough royal declarations contradicting or annulling previous ones that it was not illusory to hope for another change of policy. However, the Edict of Fontainebleau somehow seemed more permanent and, ironically, more irrevocable.

The outlawing of their religion forced the Huguenots to take a position. They had the choice of converting, entering the underground church, or escaping from France—the last two at the risk of their lives. In the early 1760s Jean-Jacques Rousseau, himself a Genevan descendant of French Protestant refugees, described the fate of post-Revocation Huguenots with compassion while stressing the uniqueness of their situation in western history: "Once experience proved how greatly the revocation of the Edict of Nantes weakened the monarchy," he wrote, "there was a desire to retain in the Kingdom, along with the remainder of the persecuted sect, the only remaining source of subjects. Ever since then, these unfortunate, reduced to the most horrible situation in which any people has found itself since the world began, can neither stay or flee. They are allowed to be neither foreigners, nor citizens, nor men. The very rights of nature are taken from them. Marriage is forbidden; and divested all at once of fatherland, family, and goods, they are reduced to the status of beasts."[15]

The vast majority of the Huguenots (five hundred thousand or so) remained in France and at least nominally converted to Catholicism. Early on, when the ecclesiastical and civil authorities did not force them to practice their new religion but let them be "passive Catholics," these new converts could lead an existence based on practical compromises. Catholic baptism was recognized by Huguenot theologians. Marriages could be performed by a priest, who was then regarded as a civil official, as long as the new converts were not required to submit to Holy Communion before the ceremony. On the threshold of death, they could refuse the last rites and die claiming to be Calvinists.[16]

Very quickly, however, the monarchy initiated a policy of forced Catholicization that left no room for compromises. Weekly attendance at Mass was to be checked. In some cases recalcitrant Huguenots, called *opiniâtres* (obstinates), were even taken to Mass by dragoons and forced to take Holy Communion.[17] Huguenots who refused the last sacraments on their deathbeds were, if they survived, to be sentenced to life in prison (women) or in the galleys (men). Aware that coercion would not make true Catholics out of Huguenot adults, the crown soon started to emphasize the forced Catholicization of children through education. In 1698 the intendant of Languedoc well summarized the court's position, writing that "children who have not seen temples or ministers will be more disposed to the good impressions which we shall make on them."[18] That same year a royal decree stipulated mandatory Catholic schooling, catechization, and daily atten-dance at Mass for all Huguenot children.[19]

Yet this "educational crusade," as Phillips calls it, failed for several reasons.[20] First, there were not enough schools throughout the kingdom, and not enough money was allotted to build more of them. Second, in rural areas especially, Huguenot parents often successfully argued that children were needed at home to work. Third, parents efficiently corrected at home any Catholic "error" that their children had learned at school.[21] Élie Marion, one of the leaders of the early eighteenth-century Huguenot rebel-lion of the Cévennes, wrote about "the secret teaching that [he] received from [his] father and mother" that fueled his "aversion for idolatry and the errors of popery."[22]

This hardening of royal policy inevitably led to more resistance on the part of the new converts. Illegal outdoor meetings, called *assemblées du désert*, began to be held in several provinces. Lay members of former consistories, named *prédicants*, performed services in lieu of pastors by reading the liturgy or printed sermons. As expected, the crown reacted harshly to the emergence of this underground Huguenot religious life. As early as July 1686 a royal declaration sentenced Huguenots who attended these meetings to life in prison or in the galleys and the prédicants to death.[23] In the rural and mountainous Cévennes, Languedoc, Huguenots murdered an abbot in July 1702 and went on to open rebellion. These *camisards,* as they became known, resisted the royal troops until October 1704.[24]

Following the Revocation, thousands of Huguenots who challenged the crown by try-ing to leave the kingdom, attending underground church services, joining the camisard revolt, or stubbornly refusing to abjure were either sentenced to long terms in prison, convents, or in the king's galleys; transported to the West Indies; or executed. Due to fragmentary documentation and to the fact that the same individual could first be imprisoned and then sent to the galleys or to the West Indies, global estimates of sen-tenced Huguenots can only be speculative. Scholars have estimated their number at about ten thousand for the period 1685–1787, expressly specifying that this figure has to be regarded as a low estimate. The breakdown by gender and by types of sentences shows that nearly four thousand of these Huguenots were women and that most Huguenots (sixty-five hundred) were sentenced to prison terms.[25]

In his study of the galley slaves in France from 1680 to 1748, the historian André Zysberg recorded 1,550 "Huguenots" sentenced to life terms in the galleys, 60 of whom were actually Catholics who had helped Huguenots leave the kingdom.[26] Most of these sentences (1,419) were pronounced between 1685 and 1715, the peak years being 1686, 1688, and 1698.[27] More than half of the Huguenots who served in the king's galleys were charged with attending illegal assemblées and almost a fourth for attempting to leave France.[28] A few Huguenots who had already settled in foreign countries were also cap-tured by French privateers while traveling at sea and then sent to the galleys. This was the case of Elie Neau, a New York Huguenot merchant who, in 1692, was captured off the coast of Jamaica by French corsairs who took him back to Saint-Malo, Brittany, where he was summarily tried and convicted by an admiralty court despite his having acquired English citizenship in New York. Neau was then sent to the galleys, where he remained until his release, obtained through the intervention of the English ambassador to France, in 1698.[29] Huguenot convicts represented less than 5 percent of the total number of Louis

XIV's subjects sentenced to the galleys, most of the galley slaves being criminals, deserters, and smugglers. Zysberg explains this relatively small number of condemnations by the fact that the monarchy had plenty of convicts to man its galley ships without the Huguenots, and that therefore galley sentences for religion's sake were what he calls "'selective' repression."[30] These sentences were meant to be few and to appear as a particularly harsh and uncommon punishment.

Although some Huguenot women were imprisoned, most were sent to convents.[31] Without distinguishing confinement in prison or convent, scholars give an estimate of 3,250 Huguenot female prisoners for the period from 1685 to 1787.[32] As in the case of Huguenot men sent to the galleys, women confined to convents were mostly new converts reluctant to comply with their Catholic duties or Huguenots caught attempting to leave France. The order of the Ursulines, which emphasized education and had convents throughout France, received many of these women, as well as many girls whose parents had been arrested.[33] Other Huguenot women were confined to "prison-convents," as Garrisson calls them, expressly founded to train new Catholics.[34]

By and large, though, Mother Superiors rarely followed harsh royal instructions such as solitary confinement and head shaving. Numerous accounts described how nuns and abbesses sympathized with their Huguenot captives and sincerely tried to convert them without resorting to force.[35] Most of these women were of substantial means, and like the nuns, they were expected to pay for their board. Women of poor social condition were instead sent to *hôpitaux généraux,* the workhouses founded by Louis XIV where vagabonds, beggars, invalids, and mental patients were confined.

In 1686 the monarchy decided to release the more obstinate of the Huguenots from prisons and galleys and transport them to the West Indies. At first the authorities envisioned a massive transportation aimed at removing "all the peoples of the Cévennes," but the lack of determination and means as well as the practical unfeasibility of such a plan condemned it from the start.[36] Instead, fewer than 430 Huguenots were deported on five transport ships and two merchant ships in 1687 and 1688.[37] Living conditions on the transport ships were horrific, and the death rate averaged 25 percent, peaking at 37 percent on the first one.[38] Most convicts were men, but women represented a significant proportion. Of the 345 transported Huguenots identified by Gérard Lafleur, there were 252 men (75 percent) and 93 women (25 percent).[39]

The transportation sentence was pronounced against Huguenots of all social conditions who were caught fleeing the kingdom or attending illicit services and against those whose obstinate refusal to abjure made them, in the eyes of the monarchy, potential leaders.[40] Unlike regular convicts, who were to be sold as indentured servants to local planters, the Huguenots were to be given land and the means to establish themselves. The monarchy wanted to remove these Huguenots, hopelessly impervious to conversion, from France, not to make them martyrs. Therefore everything had to be done to induce them to stay permanently in the West Indies. Étienne Serres, a Huguenot from Montpellier who was deported to Martinique in March 1686, wrote in a letter to a friend that "in respect to their conscience, [Huguenot deportees] were entirely free as they were not pressured to change religion."[41] However, this policy failed entirely. The governor of Guadeloupe, in a document addressed to Versailles in 1687, reported that the Huguenots refused to be given land under the pretenses of being too weak as a result of the voyage, unaccustomed to farm work, or unable to get cash advances to live during the sowing season. This is exactly what Étienne Serres explained to his correspondent in saying that "prisoners have a difficult time making a living there [in Martinique] . . . especially those who are not used to tilling because there is nothing else to do there."[42]

In the face of this obstinate collective refusal, the governor chose to have them live among local settlers, usually new converts, until they became accustomed to the Caribbean climate and ready to take up land.[43] With the help of their hosts, however, Huguenot deportees set up escape networks quickly. The proximity of English and Dutch islands, with which Caribbean Huguenot settlers had steadily conducted an active illicit trade, and the incapacity of the local authorities to effectively patrol the coasts made escaping relatively easy. The islands that France ruled jointly or alternately with a Protestant power, such as Saint Christophe (Saint Kitts) with England or Saint Eustache (Saint Eustatius) with the Netherlands, were the Huguenot deportees' favorite escape destinations.[44] Once in an English or Dutch territory, they would find a ship to return to Europe with the help of Dutch, English, or naturalized Huguenot settlers who had escaped before the Revocation. Serres, for instance, first fled to Curaçao and then to Saint Eustatius before reaching Amsterdam, where "the hardest slavery turned into the happiest liberty."[45]

Thus, unlike Caribbean creole Huguenots, banished Huguenots did not flee to the English mainland colonies but returned to Europe in an attempt to be reunited with their relatives. The story of the gentilhomme Samuel de Pechels is another case in point. Originally from Montauban, Languedoc, Pechels was caught attempting to leave France and was imprisoned in Cahors. In September 1687, along with fifty-eight other Huguenots, he was transported to Saint Domingue, where he arrived in February 1688. Six months later he managed to escape by boarding an English sloop that was on her way to Jamaica. From there he sailed to England and reached London in October 1688. Two years later his wife, who had fled to Geneva while he was in the West Indies, joined him in London. They eventually settled in Dublin with a military pension in return for the time he served in William III's Huguenot regiments in Ireland.[46] Interestingly, in 1713 his eldest son, Jacob, married Carolina-born Jeanne-Élisabeth Boyd, daughter of Huguenot refugees Jean and Jeanne (Berchaud) Boyd.[47]

Despite the quelling of the Cévennes revolt and the sentencing of thousands of Huguenots to prison or to the galleys, all in all the royal repressive policy proved, like the Revocation, blatantly unsuccessful. In 1715 there were enough Huguenots and clandestine congregations for the meeting of an underground national synod.[48] In 1726 a seminary was opened in Lausanne, Switzerland, and by midcentury it had sent ninety pastors to serve the congregations in France.[49] By the first quarter of the eighteenth century the French Reformed Church was born again, and by 1760 France had a Calvinist population of about half a million.[50] By that time, however, roughly a fourth of the pre-Revocation Huguenot population, or about two hundred thousand individuals, had fled France and set roots throughout northwestern Europe and around the Atlantic basin.

Le Refuge, or the Flight out of New Babylon

The few hundred Huguenots who eventually settled in proprietary Carolina were part of a wider exodus traditionally known in French history as *le Refuge*.[51] This phenomenon was not new since migration out of France constituted a habitual means for Huguenots to escape persecution, but in contrast to previous migrations, the post-Revocation exodus was sudden, massive, and definitive.

Since the time of the first persecutions under the reigns of Francis I (1515–47) and of his son, Henry II (1547–59), Huguenots had taken refuge in neighboring Protestants cities, mainly Geneva and Strasbourg, and countries such as England, the Netherlands, and some Swiss cantons. This immigration, sometimes referred to as *le premier refuge,* reached a peak in the years following the 1572 Saint Bartholomew's Day Massacres. However, it was by nature small and occasional and, very often, led only to temporary exile.[52] The number of Huguenots who definitely left France from 1520 to 1660 did not exceed twenty thousand.[53] Furthermore, this emigration, which spanned more than a hundred years, was not continuous. Departures were occasioned by renewals of persecution and military conflicts and were interrupted by long periods of peace, such as the reign of Henry IV (1589–1610). Consequently, sixteenth- and early seventeenth-century Huguenot refugees often returned to France when the political and religious conditions were favorable to them. Until the 1660s Huguenot refugees, few in number, mingled with Walloons, French-speaking Calvinists from southern Netherlands, with whom they founded exile communities in which they represented small minorities.[54]

The exodus that centered around the period of the Revocation contrasted sharply with all previous Huguenot emigrations. It was sudden, brief, massive, and permanent. Historians estimate that about two hundred thousand Huguenots left France between 1679 and 1700.[55] The movement started with the intensification of the persecutions in 1679 and the first dragonnades of 1681, reached a peak between 1684 and 1687, and then dwindled in the 1690s, except for occasional outbreaks.[56] Thus, ten times more Huguenots left France in this 20-year period than did during the previous 150 years. Furthermore, contrary to their predecessors in exile, few of these Protestants ever returned to France. By the time the Edict of Toleration was enacted in 1787, third- and fourth-generation Huguenot refugees were, except perhaps in some areas in Germany, too thoroughly integrated into their host societies to consider moving back to their ancestral communities.[57]

The Huguenot diaspora was born out of a paradox. The French Protestants who wished to practice their Calvinism necessarily had to leave the kingdom, but they were not expelled. Except for pastors, who were authorized to leave within two weeks after the promulgation of the Edict of Revocation, and a few dignitaries who could obtain passports from Versailles, all were denied the *jus emigrandi*. In other words, Huguenots could only convert since emigration was not a legal alternative. This unique situation makes *le Refuge* distinct from the exodus of the Jews in 1492 and the expulsion of the Moriscos from Spain in 1609. While these religious minorities were granted a few months to leave, the Huguenots were compelled to remain and convert.[58]

Based on Maréchal de Vauban's *Mémoire pour le rappel des Huguenots* of 1689, in which he detailed the post-Revocation impoverishment of France and urged Versailles to take measures to lure back refugees, and until the 1960s, pamphleteers, philosophes, writers, and historians argued that the Huguenot exodus had plunged France into a fifty-year economic decline.[59] Since the publication of Warren Scoville's seminal and revisionist study of the impact of the Revocation on French economic development in 1960, however, the causes of France's late seventeenth-century economic decline have been reevaluated and religious factors have been minimized. It is now recognized that although the Huguenot dispersion globally weakened and, in some areas, ruined certain industries, the economic stagnation that affected France until the 1720s started before the 1680s and had multiple causes in addition to the Revocation, such as wars, famines, demographic decline, overtaxation, and official economic rigidity.[60]

The long-lived belief that France's economic decline was the inexorable consequence of horrid persecution perpetrated by a tyrannical monarchy spurred by a fanatic Catholic clergy was actually successfully propagated by Protestant—especially Huguenot—propagandists and by France's European enemies. In their writings economic decline was thus one of the plagues that supposedly afflicted France, *la nouvelle babylone*, as a sort of providential chastisement. In a typical Calvinist fashion Jaques Fontaine, who was "happy to have left this cursed Babylon" and "not to have shared her plagues," prophesied that "France, cruel France . . . will go from bad to worse, from misery to misery until [she] is destroyed or [she] turns from cruelty and idolatry."[61] Even across the Atlantic in Congregationalist New England, Cotton Mather, in a French pamphlet published in 1725, interpreted the 1720–22 plague epidemics that broke out in Marseille and Provence as a late divine punishment, the fruit of some sort of Protestant cosmic justice, in retribution for the "unjust and perfidious" persecution of the Huguenots.[62]

The pamphleteers and historians who asserted that the Revocation led France into a long-term economic and demographic decline contrapuntally argued that the Huguenot dispersion strengthened its main Protestant rivals, viz. England, the Netherlands, and Prussia, economically, militarily, demographically, and intellectually. Thus, for example, following the Revocation, England diversified and refined its textile industry, the Netherlands extended its commercial and intellectual influence in Northern Europe, and Prussia experienced a steady demographic growth.[63] While there is certainly some truth to that assertion, once again recent historiography has accurately minimized the role played by the Huguenot dispersion in the economic and demographic expansion of these nations. This being said, however, it remains unquestionable that the Revocation and the flight of thousands of Huguenots globally benefited France's Protestant rivals, especially England and Prussia, and isolated it diplomatically.

Although Versailles adopted a characteristically wavering and ambiguous strategy, alternately closing and opening the borders, the monarchy's objective over the last three decades of the seventeenth century was to limit the number of fugitives as much as possible by repeatedly enacting antiemigration arrêts whose severity was meant to be dissuasive.[64] A 1669 arrêt, which was enacted again in 1679, sentenced fugitives to the death penalty and confiscation of property. In 1685 the death penalty was converted to life confinement in the galleys.[65] Other arrêts condemned those who helped Huguenots escape from France, first to fines (1685), then to the galleys (1686), and ultimately to the death penalty (1687).[66] In addition, a decree enacted in 1686 encouraged informing.

Catholics who denounced Huguenots preparing their flight or who helped catch fugitives were to receive one-third of the victims' property, while the rest was distributed among the guards who made the arrests.[67]

Throughout the period the confiscation of property was an essential aspect of the crown's policy in its effort to dissuade Huguenots from escaping and entice refugees back to France. For a while, however, Huguenots easily avoided confiscation by selling their property before departing. Consequently, in 1682 the monarchy declared void all sales transacted within a year before sellers fled abroad.[68] An arrêt decreed in 1688 and confirmed the following year, however, allowed Catholic (that is, new converts) heirs to file claims to take possession of the confiscated property.[69] This measure was intended to relieve the royal administration, which was literally overwhelmed by the considerable number of confiscated estates, and draw refugees back to France. The law remained unchanged until 1699, when the crown eventually prohibited new converts from selling their property without the permission of the local authorities and no longer recognized the claims of Catholic heirs.[70]

Until 1688, when the confiscated properties of the fugitives were collectively joined to the king's domain, the intendants were responsible for their administration. As a rule, they leased the real property to administrators until successfully reclaimed by Catholic relatives and often auctioned off the personal property to pay for the administrative and judicial costs entailed by the confiscation procedure.[71] Among Carolina refugees, for example, Pierre de St. Julien who came from Vitré, Brittany, had his estate leased for a value of 3,400 livres (£260) and his furniture sold for 700 livres (£53).[72] Isaac Mazyck and Pierre Bontecou, both from Saint-Martin, Île-de-Ré (Aunis), and Élie Boudinot from Marans, Aunis, had their estates estimated at 3,100, 1,200, and 8,300 livres (£238, £92, and £645), respectively.[73] In some cases relatives of Carolina refugees successfully petitioned the intendants of their provinces to retain the familial property even before the 1688 arrêt. Gaspard France, father of the Arnaud France who arrived in South Carolina in 1685 on board the *Margaret,* recovered his son's estate in 1687.[74] The case of Jean Hubert Chastaigner, brother of Carolina Huguenots Henry Auguste and Alexandre Thésée Chastaigner, is unusually well documented. In December 1686 Jean-Hubert wrote the La Rochelle intendant, Arnoul, explaining that his two brothers had left France with all their furniture and silver plate and had sold the rest of their personal property. He requested the authorization to take possession of an estate that had jointly belonged to his brothers and that was now confiscated, claiming that it had been his as much as theirs. The intendant forwarded the request to Versailles, mentioning that the petitioner was an officer in the king's regiments and had converted to Catholicism long ago. The crown gave a favorable answer to Jean-Hubert's request, simply asking the intendant to verify how long Jean-Hubert had been a new Catholic.[75]

As noted by Intendant Arnoul in 1686, it was not in the interest of the crown to sell the fugitives' property since the possibility of recovering their estates was a strong incentive to return and convert.[76] Several arrêts thus authorized both fugitives who were caught at the borders and refugees to regain possession of their property on condition of conversion.[77] In 1698 the monarchy extended this measure to children of refugees, even if born abroad, provided that they returned to France within two years ensuing the enactment of the arrêt, abjured, and kept the property for six years.[78]

While fugitives were almost certain to lose their real property if no relatives remained behind to claim it, most attempted to turn their personal property into cash to cover the cost of their escape and settlement abroad. In this respect merchants involved in international commerce were in a privileged position as they could transfer their assets abroad through the disguise of a transaction. As Intendant Arnoul explained in a report addressed to Versailles in 1686, merchants would liquidate their assets by shipping their goods abroad and ask their clients to pay their agents, who then kept the funds. Then, knowing that they would have to leave their real property behind, they ran their businesses on credit and eventually left once their loans equaled the value of their estates.[79] Although this is not documented, it is possible that a few Charleston Huguenot merchants, such as Isaac Mazyck and Josias DuPré, used that stratagem to transfer part of their capital to England or the Netherlands and then on to South Carolina.[80] Similarly, Huguenots such as Jacques LeBas, Isaac LeGrand, and Jacques Nicolas, who purchased South Carolina land in London, had necessarily managed to move substantial amounts of money out of France.[81]

Although denying Huguenots the *jus emigrandi* certainly limited emigration, royal measures taken against the fugitives seem to have had little effect. Those who were determined to flee did so despite the risks and the losses involved. The decision to flee, however, as well as its timing, was conditioned by a complex series of contextual and personal factors. Therefore, as Élisabeth Labrousse has stressed, to regard the upholding of their faith as the sole reason that pushed many Huguenots beyond the borders of France is an overly simplistic interpretation of the dispersion.[82] Assuredly, fugitives fled primarily to preserve their Calvinism, but many other factors made escaping feasible, less dangerous, and easier to prepare, or conversely more difficult or even impossible.

The emigration rate tended to be inversely proportional to the density of the local Protestant population. Huguenots who resided in overwhelmingly Catholic provinces, such as Brittany, Burgundy, and Provence, were more prone to leave than those who lived in Languedoc or Béarn, where the concentration of Protestants made persecution somewhat less painful to bear and resistance easier to organize.[83] Geography also influenced departure rates, as well as destinations. Huguenots who lived near the coast or the borders could, for obvious reasons, escape at a lower cost and with fewer risks. Huguenots from Saintonge and Poitou escaped through La Rochelle and Île-de-Ré and those from Brittany through the Channel Island of Jersey, and from there they took a ship to England or the Netherlands. Huguenots from Dauphiny traversed the Alps to reach Geneva, and those living in the northern provinces of Flanders and Artois crossed the border to reach Frankfurt.[84] Huguenots who resided in urban environments along trade routes were more apt to flee than those who lived in remote rural areas. The timing and intensity of the persecution constituted another significant factor. Provinces and regions that were dragooned, such as Poitou and eastern Languedoc (Vivarais), and towns where temples were razed as a result of the commissaires' investigations lost a significant portion of their Huguenot population early on. Huguenots who held occupations that became legally limited to Catholics in the 1670s and 1680s had to leave or abjure simply to survive

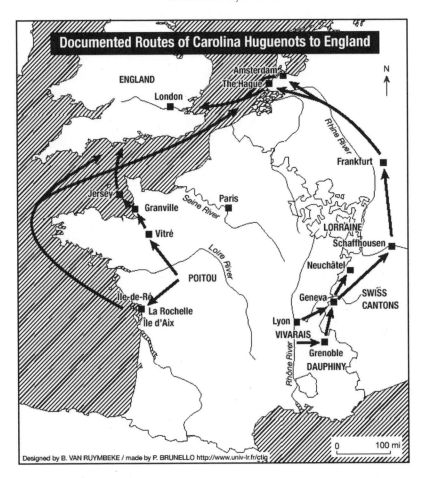

Designed by B. VAN RUYMBEKE / made by P. BRUNELLO http://www.univ-lr.fr/ctig

economically. The Carolina Huguenot Joseph Marbœuf, for example, left Vieillevigne, Brittany, for England in 1685 along with all the other local Huguenot apothecaries following the enactment of an edict prohibiting them from practicing their trade.[85]

The decision to flee was also determined by personal and familial factors. Families were often divided between those who chose to convert to preserve their careers, as seems to have been the case with the army officer Jean Hubert Chastaigner, or to inherit an estate and those who decided to leave. In 1686 Intendant Arnoul reported that "le Sieur D'Harriette," a newly converted La Rochelle merchant whose offspring eventually settled in New York City, petitioned for part of the familial property because his two children left him penniless out of "hatred for his recent conversion."[86] Members of some families could also volunteer or be designated by the parents to abjure and remain behind to hold the property in the hope of a future return. Age and education, too, were significant factors as older Huguenots were less likely than their younger relatives to cover miles of rugged terrain or marshland; Huguenots who had some sense of European geography and could read a map were also better equipped to escape.

The resolve to abandon relatives and friends as well as the comfort of a familiar environment known since birth was undoubtedly difficult, but making that decision was easy compared to surmounting the obstacles to carry it out successfully. Attempting to escape from France was a risky and costly enterprise that necessitated not only courage, perseverance, ingenuity, resourcefulness, and luck but also and above all money and contacts. Money was essential as it served to pay guides who knew how to reach the coast or the border safely and fishermen who provided a passage to an English or Dutch ship anchored off a French harbor. Fugitives also needed to buy maps with itineraries and lists of inns and homes where one could dine and rest. Whatever was left could be used to bribe venal coast and border guards in case of an unexpected encounter. In order to be successful, fugitives had to take time to plan their flights in secrecy and also had to be prepared to leave on short notice, usually at night. Huguenots most often escaped with groups of relatives and neighbors rather than alone. Thus, for example, the four Carolina-bound families of St. Julien, Ravenel, DuBourdieu, and De Farcy—all from Vitré—left their hometown together for England in late 1685.[87]

Itineraries captured along with the guides who helped fugitives pass across the French borders enable the historian to map familiar escape routes. A map acquired on the arrest of the guide Pierre Michaut (who confessed to obtaining it from a French domestic of the governor of Jersey), along with eight fugitives, in 1715 uncovered two common routes out of Poitou to Jersey through Brittany, Maine, and Normandy. One route crossed Brittany through Nantes and Vitré, and the other crossed Maine through Angers and Laval. Both joined at the port of Granville, on the southern cost of Normandy, where a boat could be taken to Jersey.[88] Located about thirty miles off the French shores, Jersey hosted a significant population of French speakers. It was a familiar stopover on the way to England, especially for Huguenots living in Brittany, lower Normandy, and Poitou. The Carolina refugees René Ravenel from Vitré and Ester LeCert and Louise Thoury from Rennes were all in Jersey in April 1686, according to a report addressed by the former pastor of the Rennes church to the bishop of London.[89] Although it is not documented, other Carolina Huguenots hailing from Poitou, Normandy, and Brittany likely took that route to escape from France. In fact, one of the fugitives arrested with Michaut in 1715, Marie Thoreau, age sixty-eight, mentioned a son living in "a [en] caroline."[90]

Michaut's arrest also provides the historian with information on the prices that guides charged the fugitives and confirms that attempting to escape was a risky business. The fugitives' depositions inform us that after asking for one hundred livres (eight pounds sterling) per person, Michaut had eventually settled for eighty livres (six pounds sterling). This was a comparatively low price, perhaps because it was for a party of eight, since the cost of an escape out of Brittany by way of Jersey usually ranged from two hundred to one thousand livres (fifteen to seventy-five pounds sterling).[91] Following a brief investigation, the men in the group were sentenced to serve in the galleys and the women to confinement in the *hôpital général* of Poitiers. All were fined a thousand livres (seventy-five pounds sterling), and Michaut was publicly hanged in the town of La Mothe-Saint-Héray, Poitou.[92]

Many fugitives from Poitou and most of those from Saintonge and Aunis chose to leave France by way of islands located a few miles off La Rochelle, such as Île-de-Ré or

Île d'Aix.[93] As described by Jaques Fontaine and Jean Migault in their escape narratives, they would first travel to the coast and then meet at night on a beach to board a small craft. The craft would then take them to one of these islands, where they could embark on an English or Dutch ship or meet that same ship in high waters.[94] This is the escape route likely traveled by most Carolina Huguenots since a large proportion of them hailed from the La Rochelle area, including Île-de-Ré. Huguenots living in southern France (Guyenne, Languedoc, Dauphiny, and Provence) escaped by way of a Spanish or Italian port such as San Sebastián, Barcelona, or Genoa, where they could board a ship bound for England or the Netherlands. Durand du Dauphiné, for example, first reached Marseille and then Livorno, Italy, where he found a ship that took him to London.[95] Others crossed the Alps to Geneva before going north along the Rhine River all the way to Amsterdam.[96]

Although unrepresentative of regular escape routes, Judith Giton's step-by-step account of her epical journey from her hometown of La Voulte, Vivarais, all the way to Charleston constitutes a unique source to understand the difficulty, cost, and risks involved in emigrating from southern France to South Carolina in the 1680s. Leaving the dragoons asleep in their beds, the Giton family (Judith; her mother, Madeleine Cottin; and two of her brothers, Pierre and Louis) left La Voulte sometime in the summer or early fall of 1684.[97] They first reached Romans, Dauphiny, where they hid for ten days "while search was made to find" them. Then they continued on to Lyon, Dijon, Langres, and Metz (in Lorraine), and from there they followed the Moselle and Rhine rivers through Treves, Kochem, Coblentz, and Cologne. From there they went to Wesel by coach and finally on to England by way of the Netherlands. In April 1685, three months after their arrival in London, they boarded a ship that took them to "a Portuguese island" (most likely the Azores) and then to Bermuda. There the vessel was seized because the captain "[had] committed certain rascalities." The Gitons having run out of money, Judith and Louis indentured themselves to pay their way to Carolina, which they eventually reached eight months later in late 1685 or early 1686.[98] The Gitons chose not to cross over to Geneva and follow the Swiss route. Instead they went up the Rhône River to Lyon and continued north to Lorraine. This choice is surprising since most refugees logically tended to take the shortest route out of France and then to continue on to their final destinations through more hospitable lands instead of prolonging the risk of an arrest by French troops. Although in her letter she does not mention why they chose this more dangerous route, the Gitons likely knew of places to stay along the way and were more comfortable with an itinerary that crossed France from south to north.[99] Once in the Duchy of Lorraine, of course, the Gitons were safely out of France.

The well-documented case of the Carolina Gaillard family represents another informative illustration of the obstacles inherent to leaving the kingdom and how refugees surmounted them. Although originally from Montpellier, Joachim Gaillard, a well-off and well-connected merchant, lived in Annonay, Vivarais, at the time of the Revocation. Early in October 1685 he decided to let his house for a period of three years for 100 livres (£8) a year and moved with his family into the home of one of his wife's (Ester Paparel) cousins. At about that time Joachim, Ester, and two of their sons, Barthélemy and Jean, who had just completed their apprenticeships respectively as an apothecary and a

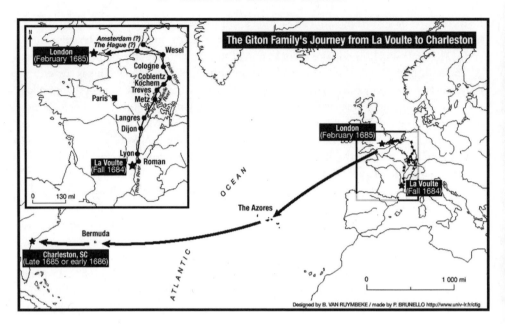

clothier, crossed the Rhône River in an attempt to escape to Switzerland. An apprentice cobbler whom they had hired to help them carry their belongings accompanied them. Two days after their departure, the three young men were arrested in an inn near Grenoble, Dauphiny, as they were looking for a guide to help them reach Geneva. The police report reveals that Barthélemy and Jean were not traveling lightly as their bags contained numerous fine pieces of clothing and precious objects made of silver and ivory as well as more than thirty books. A few days later Barthélemy and Jean were released and sent back to their home in Annonay, most likely under the promise of converting, which they did along with their parents. Soon afterward the whole family moved to Lyon, where Joachim and his sons served as guides to help new converts escape to Geneva. In December 1686 the Gaillard estate in Annonay, valued at 3,000 livres (£230), was seized, but the entire family—Joachim, Ester, Barthélemy, Jean, and Pierre—was then safely in Switzerland. They reached England by way of Schaffhosen, Frankfurt, and the Netherlands. In October 1687 in London, Joachim purchased six hundred acres of Carolina land, and he arrived in Charleston that same year.[100] The Gaillards, however, were not ready to abandon their estate in Annonay to the French authorities. In 1692 Barthélemy went back to France. Using his certificate of conversion, which he had signed in 1686, as a sort of a safe-conduct, he recovered his parents' property and sold it before returning to South Carolina.[101]

The choice of a destination, like the decision to leave France, was conditioned by a complex series of factors, among which geography was certainly one of the most decisive. Huguenots who lived in northwestern France, especially Normandy, fled massively to England.[102] Those who were from the Atlantic seaboard, Aunis, Saintonge, and lower Poitou, escaped either to England or the Netherlands following well-known maritime trade routes. The Charleston merchant Isaac Mazyck, from Saint-Martin, Île-de-Ré, left his hometown on November 1, 1685, and was in Rotterdam with his brother Étienne two weeks later.[103] Huguenots who resided in southern and eastern France usually took the Swiss route and followed the Rhine River to the Netherlands and, sometimes, crossed the English Channel, or settled somewhere in the German states. The Carolina refugees Jacques and Madeleine de Bourdeaux, from Grenoble, and André and Anne Rembert, from Pont-en-Royan (both in Dauphiny), first reached Frankfurt by way of Switzerland respectively in April 1686 and June 1687 before continuing on to England.[104] Refugees also tended to settle in cities where they knew they would find Huguenot churches and a well-established French community. Specific official state policies, such as the famed German *Édits d'accueil,* also influenced the Huguenots in their decisions since refugees settled where they were promised financial assistance, land, and/or employment. Subjective and elusive factors such as personal preferences, prior contacts in a foreign country through trade, or simply chance were, of course, also at play. Embarkment on a ship, either English or Dutch, off Île-de-Ré, for example, led refugees to England or the Netherlands regardless of whether they had originally planned to relocate there. Furthermore, some refugees never really chose to settle in one place or another but followed neighbors, friends, and relatives or simply wandered across northern Europe until they found a permanent home. In her letter Judith Giton explained that she followed her eldest brother, her "master," to Carolina because she had to do "all as he wished."[105] The Carolina refugee Louis Gourdin from Goncourt, Artois, stopped twice in Frankfurt, in September 1686 and October 1689, requesting financial assistance to go to the Netherlands.[106]

In many respects England appeared to the Huguenots as an attractive destination. Geographically close to France, England had since the sixteenth century welcomed Huguenot refugees. In the 1680s London could boast of a significant Huguenot population that maintained several congregations. Whether they reached England directly by sea or traversed the Alps to Switzerland and followed the Rhine River across parts of Germany and the Netherlands, all Carolina Huguenots sojourned in England, most of them in London, before crossing the Atlantic. England represented a necessary stopover where they could obtain information on the colony, collect funds to pay for their transatlantic passage, be naturalized, and join other Carolina-bound fellow refugees. More significantly, during their sometimes long stay across the English Channel, these exiled Huguenots became acquainted with the English political and religious culture. Some of them even acquired the legal and linguistic skills necessary to make sense of early Carolina politics.

England, or the New Goshen

The edict of July 5, 1681, which lowered the legal age for the conversion of Huguenot children to seven, raised considerable uproar in England.[107] In the wake of that measure and of the first dragonnades launched in Poitou a few months earlier, numerous pamphlets and petitions were published in 1681 to denounce the boundless horror of Louis XIV's government and of the French Catholic clergy.[108] Capitalizing on this renewed surge of pro-Huguenot sympathy and anti-Catholicism, officials of the Huguenot Church in London opportunely addressed a petition to Charles II through the Privy

Council soliciting a series of measures that would entice French Protestants to cross the English Channel. The petitioners recommended that the refugees be granted free denization, the right to practice their trades, equal access to education, and the removal of customs duty for their personal belongings, and they stressed the urgent need for the establishment of a fund to relieve refugees of their sudden poverty.[109] Charles II, who held himself "obliged in honour and conscience to comfort and support all such afflicted Protestant . . . who shall be forced to quit their native country," quickly reacted by issuing a generous proclamation on July 28, 1681, known as the Declaration of Hampton Court.[110] The English monarch granted the refugees virtually all the petitioners' requests except for the right to practice their occupations, instead letting the guilds admit Huguenots on an individual basis according to their own requirements. Despite this significant limitation, England's Huguenot community received the proclamation with true enthusiasm. In an official response that was published the following October, the French minister of the London conformist Church of the Savoy, David Primrose, on behalf of the refugees, characterized it as a "master-piece of Providence" and a "*Phoenomenon* that fills both the Church and the World with admiration." In a traditional Calvinist biblical analogy, Primrose also compared England, which he called "the true *Canaan*," to "Old *Rome*" because like "that famous City," it "[had] become the Refuge and habitation of all the Reformed World." The minister ended his harangue with an emphatic pledge of allegiance and pagan adoration toward Charles II, assuring him that the Huguenots loved him "as a God on Earth . . . like the *Romans* lov'd their *Trajan* or their *Scipio*, whom they called their Darlings."[111]

In proclaiming a generous declaration in favor of the persecuted Huguenots, Charles II was in harmony with most of his subjects, who, in the 1680s, welcomed the French refugees with open arms. In his narrative Jaques Fontaine reminisced that the "residents of Barnstaple [Devon]" treated him "with incredible kindness and friendship."[112] Similarly, in their 1679 petition the Carolina Huguenots Petit and Guérard alluded to the "charitable Josephs who have welcomed many of their brethren."[113] The generosity of the English population toward the refugees is best reflected in the massive amounts of money raised through the four national collections of 1681, 1686, 1688, and 1694. Nearly ninety thousand pounds sterling were thus collected to be distributed to exiled Huguenots.[114] With the ever-growing influx of refugees, however, the mood expectedly changed and the initial hearty welcome gave way to fits of Francophobic hostility.[115] The Huguenots, these "afflicted Protestants," were nonetheless French. As such they were by and large distrusted and in some cases despised, not just as foreigners but as "the worst of foreigners . . . the epitome of 'woggery.'"[116] What Malcolm Thorp has labeled "the Anti-Huguenot undercurrent" actually gushed out in various regions of England and took different forms.[117] While the City of Lincoln categorically refused to receive any refugees, anti-Huguenot riots erupted in Norwich and refugees were assaulted on their way to church in Rye.[118] In London guilds were by and large reluctant to admit Huguenot craftsmen on the grounds that they had not completed their apprenticeships in England and that they hired fellow refugees to the detriment of natives. They regularly addressed petitions against "unfair" domestic foreign competition to the Privy Council.[119]

A flurry of anti-Huguenot literature occasionally awakened an ever latent Francophobic sentiment, for example, denouncing in explicit terms the overwhelming presence of "Froglanders" taking "the bread out of the mouths of the natives" and "claim[ing] as much benefit of our [English] Laws and Customs, as if their Ancestors had at the expense of their blood . . . acquired the Magna Carta."[120] The authors of these hostile pamphlets and broadsides helped propagate rumors meant to depict Huguenots as "outlandish men" whose presence potentially threatened England's economic prosperity and political stability. The French refugees were thus accused of eating "cabbage and roots nourished from the sewers," of "robbing English orphans and widows of charity," and most con- tradictorily, of being "republicans" and "papists in disguise."[121]

In 1685 the accession of James II, with his ambiguous and wavering religious policy, his admiration of Louis XIV, and his own Catholicism, also somewhat altered the royal attitude toward the Huguenot refugees. Charles II's unequivocal compassion and sincere generosity gave way to thinly disguised distrust, reluctant assistance, and political manip- ulation. James ordered Claude's *Account of the Persecutions and Oppressions of the Protestants in France* to be publicly burned by the hangman and, in an effort to keep his Protestant subjects uninformed about Louis's anti-Huguenot policy, instructed that the *London Gazette,* the official newspaper, make no mention of events happening in France.[122] James also delayed as long as he possibly could the issuing of a brief for another collection to assist the refugees and imposed Anglican conformity as a necessary require- ment to receive financial assistance.[123] Despite royal procrastination and lack of enthusi- asm, this 1686 collection, which renewed in 1688, was enormously successful. Close to forty-three thousand pounds sterling, the largest sum for a seventeenth-century brief, were raised in three years.[124] This success, which as Sugiko Nishikawa writes, "reflected a sense of Protestant crisis among the English on the eve of the 'Glorious Revolution,'" can be explained by the impact on English popular opinion of the Revocation and of the increasing number of refugees crossing the English Channel, as well as, ironically, by growing popular opposition to James II.[125] Although his words were often at odds with his acts, historians agree that James, as a Catholic, disliked the Huguenots, whom he regarded as republican agitators. He nonetheless disapproved of the dragonnades specifically and of persecution in general. The Revocation placed James in an embar- rassing position as he had to satisfy a Protestant public opinion largely sympathetic to the Huguenot cause without angering the French monarch to whom he was financially and diplomatically tied.[126]

Financial Assistance and Migration to Carolina

The nationwide collections made during the reigns of Charles II and James II consti- tuted an essential aspect of the assistance provided by the English royal, ecclesiastical, and municipal authorities to the French refugees.[127] In the case of South Carolina Huguenots, this financial aid turned out to be crucial. Without it many would not have been able to pay for their transatlantic passages and in some cases would not even have contemplated settling in the colonies.

Collections were launched through the issuance of a letter patent or brief in which the monarch, as head of the Church of England, invoked the generosity of his subjects and outlined the procedure for the collection, administration, and distribution of the funds.[128] They were prefaced by introductions portraying in more (Charles II) or less (James II) moving terms the plight of the refugees.[129] The briefs, which were renewable, were in theory issued for one or two years, but money continued to be donated long after they expired.[130] With the churchwardens who went from door to door asking for contributions, the pastors who raised their parishioners' compassion by eloquently describing the sufferings endured by the refugees, and the bishops who transferred the funds to the City of London treasury (which served as a depositing bank)—every echelon of the Church of England was involved in these collections. In 1681 Charles II appointed a seven-member committee (the Lords Commissioners), who met weekly to supervise the distribution of the monies to needy refugees through Huguenot churches.[131] With the 1686 brief, however, James II significantly altered this procedure by appointing sixty Lords Commissioners.[132] The sheer size of the newly formed committee made it impossible for its members to play an active role in the management of the funds. This situation occasioned the creation of a new body, alternatively called the French Committee or Comité Français, whose function was to allocate the funds.[133]

This consequential shift of roles and responsibilities reflected the disengagement of the English government and, to some extent, the Anglican Church in the direct management of Huguenot relief. Except for a few of them who had personal interest in the Huguenot cause, the Lords Commissioners merely occupied prestigious honorary positions, while the Comité Français, composed exclusively of Huguenots, handled the vital task of distributing the monies to the refugees. Although the Lords Commissioners were instructed to examine their accounts, the French Committee operated without close supervision.[134] Consequently, the Comité Français was regularly accused of fraud. Several acrimonious petitions reached the Privy Council and the House of Commons complaining about the authoritarian practices of the Comité Français and denouncing specific cases of discrimination, double payment, neglect, and embezzlement.[135] While revealing errors and abuses for which they had to answer, the royal and parliamentary investigations and audits into the affairs and accounts of the French Committee, however, largely cleared them of these accusations. Rather than being objectively justified by the committee's mismanagement of the charity funds, the petitions appear to have reflected internecine rivalries between groups of Huguenots and the personal discontent and disillusion of some refugees.[136] Although knowing somebody on the committee may have helped fugitives to obtain more funds, historical records show that the committee performed its work with dedication and integrity within the discriminatory social constraints of the time, which, for example, favored ministers and members of the nobility over the rank and file refugees.[137] Thus, for instance, Élie Prioleau, "fils de ministre" (son of a minister), and Jacob Pirou, mariner, who both solicited financial assistance to settle in South Carolina, respectively received eight and two pounds sterling.[138] This discrepancy was not the expression of any favoritism toward Prioleau on the part of the Comité Français but of the social consideration attached to the recipients' occupations.

Although the bulk of the refugees who were assisted through the collections secured grants of money without restriction regarding its spending, many obtained monies to be used for specific purposes and even sometimes received aid in kind, usually clothes and tools. Funds were thus granted to purchase beds, shoes, looms, or medicine; to pay for the service of a doctor or a midwife; to rent a room; to provide a decent burial for a deceased relative; and, most important for this study, to secure a passage to the American colonies.[139] These forms of assistance were not mutually exclusive as some refugees obtained several kinds of aid at one time or on different occasions. In May 1687, for example, South Carolina Huguenots Élie Horry and Louis Perdriau respectively received £2.4 "for cloaths" and £10 "for supply" plus £5 and £10 for their transatlantic voyages.[140] Some refugees were so desperate that they applied for multiple grants. The anchor smith Charles Fauchereau, who once "wrought for the East India Company but [had] no more work," received sixteen grants for a total £10.2.6 in 1681 and 1682 to help him support his wife and three children, one of whom was "very sick," and to help him find employment before he eventually settled in South Carolina.[141]

The Comité Français and the London churches also allocated funds to needy refugees to encourage them to leave the overcrowded capital. If some Huguenots were sent "to the country to learn the language" or "for apprenticeship," implying a likely return, most received money for permanent relocation in Britain, Ireland, northern Europe, or North America. Extant relief records of the Comité Français, the Threadneedle Street Church, and the Church of the Savoy show that 442 refugees received assistance to settle out of London between 1685 and 1688.[142] Although a multitude of destinations in continental Europe (the Netherlands, Brandenburg, the Swiss cantons, and Denmark), Ireland, Scotland, and England (Bristol, Canterbury, Plymouth, Southampton, York, Newcastle, Exeter, for example) were recorded, nearly half (215, or 48 percent) of the assistees wished to settle in a North American colony. Eight other refugees receiving assistance for transatlantic relocation in 1681 and 1682 can be added to this number, making a total of 223.[143] Out of the 174 intended destinations appearing in the records, South Carolina (with 126 entries) is by far the transatlantic destination most often mentioned by the refugees, followed by the Chesapeake (25), New England (14), New York / New Jersey (5), and Pennsylvania (4) (table 1). The preeminence of South Carolina is another illustration of the success of the proprietors' promotional campaign that made the newly founded colony the most talked about North American destination within London Huguenot circles in the mid-1680s.[144] At this point, though, it is essential to note that these records deal only with intended destinations. Many refugees who wished to settle overseas actually never did. More than two-thirds of the potentially South Carolina–bound Huguenots do not appear in the colony's records. Some immigrated to another colony. Ambroise Sicard, his wife, and their five children received forty pounds sterling in August 1687 to go to Carolina but actually settled in New Rochelle, New York.[145] Others who had originally planned to cross the Atlantic instead opted to stay in Britain. Pierre-François Brisson, his wife, and their two children first wanted to settle in Carolina, for which they were to be granted fifteen pounds sterling, but instead chose to go to Canterbury and received ten pounds sterling to that end.[146] Similarly, Antoine Vautié, who was assigned forty pounds sterling to go to Carolina with his wife, Jeanne, and their "large family," decided instead to remain in England and enlist in the military (*entrer dans les troupes*), for which he received thirty pounds sterling. Some may have actually embarked for Carolina but died during the oceanic voyage or soon after arriving in Charleston, or chose to return to England before their presence in the colony could be recorded.[147]

Although Carolina-bound refugees also received material assistance in the form of tools and clothes, money to pay for the transatlantic voyage was what they essentially needed. A survey of the sums granted by the French Committee and the Threadneedle

Table 1.   *Intended North American destinations of Huguenots assisted in London, 1685–87*

Destinations	N	%
South Carolina	126	72.4
Chesapeake	25	14.4
New England	14	8.0
New York / New Jersey	5	2.9
Pennsylvania	4	2.3
Total	**174**	**100**

Street Church shows that Huguenots planning to settle in America received an average of about £8 per person, which was enough money to pay for a passage to Charleston, estimated at about £5 per adult passenger in the Carolina promotional literature.[148] This average, of course, masks significant disparities in the sums allotted by the committee based on social status, specific circumstances, and possibly previous assistance. Pierre de St. Julien, esquire, obtained £60 for himself, his wife, and their three children, but Daniel Jouet, sail maker, received £25 (less than half) for himself, his wife, and their two children.[149] Charlotte Joly, "demoiselle," was granted £15, whereas Louise Thoury, maid, received £1.10 and clothes. Unequal grants were assigned even among refugees of similar occupations, implying perhaps favoritism. Élie Prioleau and Daniel Bondet, for example, respectively received £8 and £25 to settle in Carolina although they were both pastors.[150] All in all, however, the Comité Français appears to have been fair and, to some extent, generous and definitely more unpredictable than discriminatory in its distribution of funds.

Compared to the total number of Huguenots who fled to England, the percentage of refugees requesting funds to relocate in North America seems quite low, especially since the nature of the records tends to overrepresent them simply because one would more likely need financial assistance to go to New England or South Carolina than to Southampton or Canterbury. Even if the claim by the French Committee to have granted funds to six hundred Huguenots to settle in America by 1688 is taken at face value, this high figure still represents an infinitesimal proportion, probably about 1 percent, of the refugees assisted in England.[151] This percentage corroborates the Huguenots' reluctance to settle far away from Europe and also reveals the absence of an effective and sustained royal policy to encourage relocation in North America under the late Stuarts. The crown-sponsored *Richmond* expedition was truly an exceptional undertaking whose inception and execution owed much to Shaftesbury's influence. Only in the early years of the eighteenth century did the crown attempt to adopt a definite policy to help Huguenots relocate in North America with the foundation of Manakintown, Virginia, under William III's sponsorship.[152]

Chapter 4

———➤–◦–◄———

THE SOUTH CAROLINA HUGUENOTS

A Migration Profile

To decide to go to America, one must travel among several families because
otherwise . . . one has to spend his life with people who do not always turn out
to be honest.

Suite de la Description de la Carolline (1685)

Passage to Eden
Estimates and Migratory Waves

Unfortunately, the exact number of Huguenots who settled in South Carolina will never
be known because the systematic records of arrivals in the colony have not survived
and because only three passenger lists are still extant.[1] Consequently, historians have to
reconstruct the Carolina refugee population from postmigratory records. These consist
of specific Huguenot sources such as the 1696 naturalization list and the 1699 census, as
well as the more general land, probate, and miscellaneous records.

The 1696 naturalization list, known as *Liste des François et Suisses,* is an essential
source in South Carolina Huguenot historiography and the obligatory starting point of
any demographic analysis of the colony's Francophone population.[2] The *Liste* enumerates the refugees by name with information about their parents and, if applicable, their
spouses and children. However, because it was compiled in 1696, sixteen years after the
arrival of the first Huguenots, it includes neither the refugees who died or left the colony
before that year nor those who arrived after 1696. It also fails to mention Huguenots who
happened to be temporarily absent from the colony at the time, such as, for example,
Barthélemy Gaillard. Surprisingly, a few refugees whose presence in Carolina at that
time is documented elsewhere were not listed either.[3] For these reasons, additional names
must be gleaned from all types of proprietary records to estimate the total number of
Carolina Huguenots. The *Liste* contains 356 refugees (200 adults and 156 children), the
Act of Naturalization of 1697 mentions 12 adults who are not in the *Liste,* and a systematic examination of the proprietary records yields the names of 135 other refugees.[4]
Adding these names together results in a total of 347 adult Huguenot migrants present
in the colony at some point between 1680 and 1712.[5]

The loss of arrival records makes it impossible to know exactly when all the Huguenots settled in the colony. However, one can still make a fairly accurate estimate of the
number of arrivals for most of them based on the three extant passenger lists, the land

warrants that contain dates of arrival, and the first dates of appearance in the records for refugees who are mentioned in neither previous source.[6]

In his pamphlet *Carolina, or a Description of the Present State of That Country,* Thomas Amy reported that in April 1680, "His Majesties Frigat the *Richmond,*" transporting "Forty Five French Protestants Passengers . . . the half of a greater Number design'd for that place," arrived in Charleston.[7] Tracing the history of the Huguenot immigration to Carolina in a September 1695 letter to Governor Archdale, Jacques Boyd evoked "the Richmond frigatt carrying 45 french refugees in 1680" who were the "first French that came in this country."[8] Contrary to what the historian Arthur Hirsch wrote, this contingent was the first group of Carolina-bound Huguenots, and the arrival of the *Richmond* marked the starting point of the migration.[9] Although the 1679 negotiations that resulted in the voyage of the *Richmond* arranged for the transport of eighty families on board two ships, records show that the *Richmond* brought over only twenty-five adults and that no ship followed.[10] With an entirely plausible adult/children ratio of 1.8, however, this total of twenty-five adults corresponds to the forty-five passengers mentioned by Amy and Boyd.[11]

The question remains as to what happened to the "second half." In his detailed study of the *Richmond* list, the historian St. Julien Childs conjectures that a second ship with another group of Huguenots arrived late in 1680. This assertion is based primarily on the land warrants of Henry Blanchard, who is recorded as settling in the colony in September 1680 but who transferred his head right to Abraham Fleury de La Plaine, a *Richmond* passenger, and of Marguerite Petit, whom Childs thought could be the wife of René Petit, one of the two promoters of the *Richmond* expedition.[12] Records in England show that René Petit appeared before the Threadneedle Street Church consistory to request financial assistance for his Carolina project in July 1680, three months after the *Richmond* arrived in Charleston. This reference reveals that neither Petit nor the second ship had yet left and also, worse, that Petit had lost official support for his expedition. The plan of sending two ships to Carolina under the auspices of the crown somehow derailed in the spring of 1680, perhaps for lack of funds and political backing or simply lack of proprietary interest. René Petit never surfaced in the Carolina records, which implies that he most likely did not settle in the colony. Margaret Petit, who took up her land in February 1680, that is, two months before the *Richmond* arrived, was therefore not likely related to René and perhaps not even French.[13] As for Blanchard, he may well have traveled on his own since not all Huguenots migrated in groups.

Another ship, the *Margaret,* an oceangoing pink, arrived in Charleston in late summer or early fall 1685 with fifty or so Huguenots on board.[14] That same summer a third ship was recorded as planning to leave England with allegedly "about two hundred French people" on board and bound for Carolina, but no passenger list has survived.[15] Hirsch mentions another contingent of "600 Huguenots" that would have arrived in Carolina in 1687, presumably led by Élie Prioleau.[16] The Huguenots tended to travel in clusters of families, often from the same town or province and under the guidance of a pastor. That fact and the 1685–87 peak in the number of arrivals make the sailing, in the wake of the *Margaret,* of two, possibly three, additional ships with significant—although certainly not as large as Hirsch conjectured—groups of Huguenots on board in 1685, 1686, and 1687 not only entirely possible but likely.[17] One may have been the June 1685 ship whose planned departure was possibly delayed in the wake of the Monmouth Rebellion; another may have carried the Vitré group, including the Ravenel, St. Julien, DuBourdieu, and De Farcy families, who arrived in Charleston in 1686 accompanied by the Rennes pastor Étienne Dusout; another in 1687 may have brought to Carolina a group led by Prioleau.[18]

In 1692 the *Loyal Jamaica* arrived in Charleston with the Huguenots François Blanchard and Daniel Horry on board. Because she was believed by the Charleston authorities to be "a privateer or a pyratt ship," Carolinians had to post bond for each passenger. Pierre LaSalle and Jean Thomas did so for François Blanchard and Isaac "Massique" (Mazyck) and Pierre Girrard did so for Daniel Horry.[19] Needless to say, the presence of these Huguenots on the *Loyal Jamaica,* which sailed from the Caribbean, is purely coincidental and does not correspond to any migratory trends. By 1692 the great majority of Huguenots were already settled in the colony.

Based on the passenger lists and the Carolina records, the annual number of arrivals shows two high peaks, 1680 and 1685–87, followed by a low period with few or no arrivals until it rises twice in the early 1700s (1701–4 and 1709–12). The 25 arrivals in 1680 correspond to the *Richmond* passengers, and it is possible that the three Huguenots who appear in the records in 1683 and 1684 were also on the same ship.[20] A total of 145 Huguenots arrived in Charleston in the three-year period 1685–87.[21] This figure, which represents 40 percent of the total, includes the *Margaret* passengers and, as has been noted above, strongly suggests the arrival of at least two and possibly three other ships.

Only thirteen Huguenots arrived in the colony in the 1690s. Those who did migrated by themselves and, except for the two *Loyal Jamaica* passengers, came from other North American colonies where they, or in some cases their parents, had settled in the mid-1680s. Marie Tauvron, for example, was in Narragansett Bay, Rhode Island, by 1688 and moved in 1691 to New York, where her husband Moyse Lebrun died. In 1694 or 1695 she settled in South Carolina, where she joined her brother Étienne.[22] Nearly forty Huguenots arrived between 1700 and 1712, most of them in the two periods, 1701–4 and 1709–12. These Huguenots either came from other North American colonies, mainly New York and Virginia, as did members of the Manakintown settlement who trickled down to Santee between 1709 and 1712, or were second-generation refugees, usually merchants, hailing from England or the Caribbean, such as Jacob Satur, Benjamin de La Conseillère, Benjamin Godin, and John-Abraham Motte.[23]

Thus the total number of arrivals, which includes 228 adult Huguenot migrants (65 percent) for whom a year of arrival (precise or ± six months) is known, shows that 181 of them (52 percent of the total) were in the colony before 1690, almost all of them (175) before 1688. If the Huguenots who first appear in the records during the 1696–97 naturalization process and for whom no dates of arrival are known are included, the number of refugees settling in Carolina before 1696 rises to 285 (82 percent of the total).

The absence of baptismal, marriage, and burial records prevents the historian from reconstructing the demographic composition of the Carolina Huguenot population with certainty. One can only compute a rough estimate of the total (adult and children) refugee population through hypothetical statistical calculations based on the *Liste des*

François et Suisses, which is the only document that contains precise and reliable demographic information on the Huguenot community at a given time. By applying the adult-to-child ratio calculated from the *Liste* to the number of Huguenots known to be in the colony and subtracting those for whom a date of death has been recorded, the Carolina Huguenot population can be sketched in five-year intervals: 56 (1680–84), 322 (1685–89), 359 (1690–94), 501 (1695–99), and 507 (1700–1704), and for a slightly longer period: 496 (1705–12).[24] These figures, which should be regarded as high estimates, show that the Huguenot population grew suddenly in 1685, the year of the Revocation and the arrival of the *Margaret;* then gradually rose from 300 to 400 between 1685 and 1695; and eventually leveled off at about 500 individuals from the early 1690s to the early 1710s. The apparent jump from 1690 to 1695 is a distortion due to the incorporation in the statistics of a large number of refugees who first appear in the records in the 1696 *Liste* but who must have been in the colony for a few years, possibly since the late 1680s. The progression was obviously more gradual than the records show, and the Huguenot population most certainly reached the 500 mark before 1695.

Rough as they may be, these figures compare favorably with available contemporary estimates. The pamphlet *Questions et Responses faites au sujet de la Caroline,* whose publication predates the 1685 influx of refugees in the colony, mentions "a hundred French people" settled in Carolina.[25] In a 1687 letter to the Marquis de Seigneulay, the French navy secretary, Intendant Arnoul of La Rochelle wrote that sailors coming from Saint Domingue estimated the Carolina Huguenot population at approximately 400.[26] Additionally, the 1696 *Liste* mentions 396 refugees and the 1699 census 438.[27] In proportion to the colony's white population, the Huguenots respectively represented 7 percent (56/800) in 1680, 15 percent (359/2,400) in 1690, and 15.5 percent (507/3,260) in 1700 (table 2).[28]

A Geographic and Sociological Profile of the Refugees

The geographic origins of the South Carolina Huguenots are quite varied since no fewer than fifteen different French provinces are represented (table 3).[29] This diversity, however, masks the importance of the western regions in general and the La Rochelle area in particular. The five provinces of Aunis, Saintonge, Poitou, Normandy, and Brittany account for nearly 60 percent of the refugees, with the three provinces of Aunis (which includes La Rochelle), Saintonge, and Poitou accounting for more than 45 percent.[30]

The predominance of Aunis, Saintonge, and Poitou is explained by the strong economic role La Rochelle played in the French Atlantic trade. In the decade that preceded the Revocation, La Rochelle concentrated on colonial trade, which the local intendant called its "great and principal commerce."[31] Although La Rochelle had only eighteen

TABLE 2. *South Carolina Huguenot population estimates and percentages of the colony's population, 1680–1700*

1680	1690	1700
56/800	389/2,400	507/3,260
(7%)	(15%)	(15.5%)

TABLE 3.   *Geographic origins of the South Carolina Huguenots*

French Provinces and Switzerland	N	%
Aunis	55	23.1
Poitou	28	11.7
Saintonge	26	10.9
Normandy	26	10.9
Île-de-France	18	7.5
Touraine	16	6.7
Languedoc	14	5.8
Dauphiny	12	5.0
Brittany	11	4.6
Berry	9	3.7
Picardy	8	3.3
Guyenne	5	2.1
Others (Artois, Lyonnais, Orléanais)	4	1.7
Pays de Vaud (Switzerland)	6	2.5
Total	**238**	**99.5**

one-hundred-ton ships in 1664, the number had risen to fifty by 1682 and to ninety-three by 1686. Similarly, from 1664 to 1682 the number of shipowners increased from thirty-seven to sixty.[32] The Atlantic trade, especially with the West Indies, whose traffic grew from ten ships a year in 1642 to fifty-five in 1686, was the main factor for this spectacular increase.[33] In the 1670s and 1680s La Rochelle served as a port of embarkation for its hinterland and as a western center for news about the Americas. This role as a regional center and point of contact with North America and the Caribbean became crucial when Huguenots living in the area began to flee the kingdom in the early 1680s. Jean Migault, a schoolteacher from Poitou who settled in the Netherlands, explained in his memoirs that many Huguenots from Poitou went to La Rochelle and "having found there foreign vessels . . . some fled to Holland, others to England, Ireland and a few to Carolina."[34] Not all Huguenots hailed from areas in contact with the Atlantic, however, as nearly 15 percent were from Île-de-France (the Paris basin) and the Loire Valley, and another 15 percent of the Carolina Huguenots came from southern France (Dauphiny, Languedoc, and Guyenne).[35] These percentages confirm the fact that, due to an efficient promotional campaign, going to South Carolina was not just an option available once the refugees reached London but a potential destination known to Huguenots wherever they lived in France.

Most Carolina refugees (65 percent) came from urban areas.[36] More than half (55 percent) were from cities proper (Paris, Tours, Caen, Montpellier, and Grenoble), 31 percent from large towns (Marennes in Saintonge, Vitré in Brittany, Saint-Lô in Normandy, and Loudun in Poitou), and 13.5 percent from market towns (Pons, La Tremblade, and Saint-Jean-d'Angély—all in Saintonge—and Saint-Martin de Ré in Aunis).[37] Nearly a

Origins of the Carolina Huguenots

Designed by B. VAN RUYMBEKE / made by P. BRUNELLO http://www.univ-lr.fr/ctig

third of these urban Huguenots came from the four western ports of Dieppe, Le Havre, La Rochelle, and Bordeaux, all of which had long been involved in the colonial Atlantic trade. Nonetheless, the migration to South Carolina departs significantly from general colonial transatlantic migratory patterns in that more than a third of the Huguenots were from villages such as Soubise in Saintonge and Cherveux in Poitou. This is a relatively high proportion, considering that these refugees were less informed about the colonies and less likely to travel long distances than their urban coreligionists were.

As unambiguously indicated by the title of the 1696 naturalization list, *Liste des François et Suisses,* a small fraction (2.5 percent) of the Carolina Francophone settlers hailed from the Swiss cantons. The Swiss presence among Huguenot refugees is a well-known phenomenon of the post-Revocation exodus that is referred to by Myriam Yardeni as the "helvetization of the Refuge" and is particularly noticeable in Brandenburg.[38] Swiss Calvinists were among the first South Carolina refugees, but the process of Helvetization culminated with the foundation of Purrysburgh, a mostly Swiss township, in 1732.[39] In the 1680s the few Swiss present in the colony were not religious refugees but economic migrants who had joined the flow of Huguenots traversing Swiss cantons on their way to the German states, the Netherlands, or England.[40] With the exception of the pastor Pierre Robert's wife, Jeanne Bayer, who was from Basel, most Carolina Swiss hailed from the French-speaking region known as the Pays de Vaud, which was then part of the Bern canton.[41] Jean-François Gignilliat and Honoré Michaud were from Vevey and its environs, Suzanne Horry from Neuchâtel, and Jean-Pierre Pelé from "le Païs de Vaud."[42]

Unsurprisingly, and despite the socioeconomic fluidity inherent to early colonial societies, the South Carolina Huguenots to a large extent brought with them the rigid social stratification of early modern Europe. At the top of the group, squires and merchants, who either managed to transfer funds to the colony or found in Carolina the opportunity to recoup the losses incurred by their flight from France, formed a landed and urban elite. These refugees maintained, and in some cases strengthened, their dominant role at first within the group and then in the lowcountry society at large through intermarriage with their British social peers. Below them stood the numerous artisans and landowning farmers, as well as a few surgeons, who materially and socially gained from the migration. Landless farmers and indentured servants, for whom the transatlantic road to material success proved to be illusory or arduous at best, constituted the lowest strata within the group.[43]

A striking social feature of the Huguenot migration to Carolina was the presence of a significant number of gentilshommes (10.6 percent) within the group (table 4).[44] Bearing the titles of écuyers (esquires), most of these refugees were members of the French lower provincial nobility. A few were even of ancient noble lineage.[45] The Bruneaus— Arnaud, Sieur de La Chabocière, and his son Paul, Sieur de Rivedoux, for example—were gentilshommes from Aunis whose family had held the fief of Rivedoux in Île-de-Ré since 1480.[46] The Chastaigner brothers, Alexandre Thésée and Henry Auguste, respectively Sieur de L'Isle and Sieur de Cramahé, who had owned the seigniory of Cramahé in Aunis since 1506, are other examples.[47] As for René Ravenel, Sieur de Boisteilleul, referred to as equitem in the Latin certificate of his Carolina marriage to Charlotte de St. Julien, his title of nobility was twice recognized before the Revocation, in 1677 and 1681.[48] Jacques Goulart, Marquis de Vervant, who appears in the Carolina records as "Chevalier Baronet," was by far the most prestigious of these Huguenot nobles.[49] Son of Jacques Goulart (or Goulard), Sieur de Breuil-Goulard, and Angélique Martel, he narrowly escaped France in 1685, leaving behind his wife, Marthe-Fabrice, and two daughters, who were all imprisoned in an Ursuline convent in Angoulême after being caught trying to leave the kingdom.[50] Jacques reached South Carolina in 1687 after purchasing estates of twelve thousand and three thousand acres for a sum of £675, or 8,100 livres.[51]

To attract these Huguenots of noble extraction, the proprietors successfully advertised in the French promotional pamphlets the possibility of acquiring manorial estates with judicial privileges at low prices or as outright gifts.[52] These manors turned out to be an efficient promotional device probably because the Huguenots were familiar with the seigneurial system that was prevalent in Quebec at the time. The promise of owning large estates overseas, with or without manorial privileges, looked attractive to these Huguenot rentiers also because they had little hope of acquiring land in England and did not have the desire or the entrepreneurial skills to turn to trade. The undeniable success of this promotional effort is illustrated by the extant land warrants of fifteen of these refugees, who collectively acquired twenty-four thousand acres, for an individual average of sixteen hundred acres.[53]

Merchants, who constituted the second-largest group after the artisans among the South Carolina Huguenots (20.8 percent), were at the time of the migration an elite class in the making. They did not share the prestige and high social status associated in France with land ownership and nobility, but as they successfully adapted to their new economic environment they built the foundations of family fortunes that eventually benefited their descendants. These merchants were local retailers who specialized in the Caribbean and intercolonial trades or, especially at turn of the eighteenth century, factors for London-based companies active in the transatlantic commerce. The former, by far the most numerous, were either refugees who succeeded in transferring funds to England before leaving France, and who were thus able to engage in trade shortly after their arrival, or, more likely, farmer-retailers who sold their production, usually silk, wine, and meat, locally. Josias Dupré, who was already actively exporting luxury items to Antigua barely three years after his arrival in the colony, is a good example of the former.[54] La Rochelle refugee Pierre Manigault well illustrates the Huguenot farmer-planters who, unable to bring capital to Carolina, first engaged in a multitude of activities before making their fortunes in trade. On his arrival in the colony, Pierre first worked as a cooper. He then acquired four hundred acres and moved out of Charleston. A few years later he sold his land, moved back to Charleston, opened a distillery, and began to export whiskey and rum to England.[55] Likewise, Jean Guérard, who appeared in the 1697 Naturalization Act as a weaver, cofounded a trading company with fellow refugees ten years later.[56]

At the turn of the eighteenth century, when trade in Carolina commodities soared, Huguenot factors representing the interests of English companies arrived in Charleston. These refugees were a generation younger than their predecessors. Benjamin de La Conseillère and Benjamin Godin, for example, were respectively one and eleven years old at the time of the Revocation.[57] Once in the colony, they first worked for London-based, and sometimes Huguenot-owned, companies and then after a few years went out on their own, made their fortunes, and settled permanently in the colony.[58] The highly successful career of Benjamin Godin is a case in point. Originally from Le Havre, he arrived in South Carolina sometime before 1707 as a factor for an English company. He soon became associated with fellow Normand refugees de La Conseillère and Guérard in a successful mercantile enterprise.[59] At his death Godin possessed thirty thousand Carolina pounds (four thousand pounds sterling), and owned an estate of over eleven thousand acres, a plantation in Goose Creek, a house in Charleston, and several hundred slaves.[60]

The geographic origins of these Carolina Huguenot merchants played a crucial role in their decision to migrate to North America. Of twenty-seven merchants whose places of origin are known, seventeen hailed from Aunis, Poitou, and Normandy and fifteen from maritime ports, seven of those from La Rochelle.[61] The Huguenot control of the La

TABLE 4.   *Status and occupations of the South Carolina Huguenots*

Status or Occupation	N	%
Artisans	53	28.3
Merchants	39	20.8
Indentured Servants	37	19.7
Yeomen ("planters")	25	13.3
Gentilshommes (*écuyers*)	20	10.6
Others (Surgeons, Apothecaries, Pastors)	13	6.9
Total	**187**	**99.6**

Rochelle trade and the involvement of Huguenot merchants in transatlantic routes explain the predominance of La Rochelle and its hinterland, a phenomenon even more pronounced for the merchants than for the entire Carolina Huguenot community. In the 1680s, when La Rochelle's colonial commerce was growing at a fast pace, twenty-one of its twenty-five wealthiest shipowners were Huguenot.[62] Several members of these families, such as the Manigaults, the Belins, and the Perdriaus, eventually settled in Charleston. In the case of the Manigaults, John Bosher has shown that they had pre-Revocation trade contacts with Newfoundland and the French West Indies.[63]

In the series of questions and answers included in the 1685 pamphlet *Suite de la Description de la Carolline,* the answer to the question "What kind of artisans are the most necessary there [in South Carolina]?" first mentioned "smiths, carpenters, [and] all those who work in the building trades." Similarly, the following year *Plan pour former un établissement en Caroline* advised investors to recruit metal and wood workers, all regarded as "absolutely necessary."[64] These pamphlets reflected the need for skilled artisans in the decade when Charleston was expanding on its new peninsular location. This need was well heeded by Huguenots. Most of the artisans, who represented almost a third (28.3 percent) of the Carolina Huguenots whose occupations could be identified, worked wood and metal. The large majority of them were coopers, followed by joiners and different types of smiths. Among these refugees were Jérémie Cothonneau, a cooper from Saint-Martin de Ré; Pierre Poinset [Poincet] Sr. and Pierre Poinset Jr., smiths; and Charles Faucheraud, anchor smith—all three from Soubise, Saintonge; Auguste Mémim, a gunsmith from La Forge-Nossay, Poitou; Moïse Carion, a joiner from Faugère, Languedoc; and Pierre LeChevalier, a carpenter from Saint-Lô, Normandy.[65] LeChevalier seemed to have been particularly successful and highly regarded since he acquired five town lots and was commissioned to "make a Balloting box with the Locks & hinges thereon fixt" that was used in the 1702 legislative elections.[66]

Much less in demand in the nascent South Carolina economy, the artisans who worked in the textile industry formed a homogeneous subgroup. Most of them were weavers, and many came from the same areas in France. Antoine Poitevin and Antoine Jr., Daniel Trézévant and Daniel Jr., and Pierre Dutartre, for example, were all weavers from the province of Beauce.[67] Unlike the tanners and shammy dressers sought by the Indian traders, weavers, if they could practice their trade, sold their production locally only, most likely to their neighbors.[68] In 1708 Pierre Dutartre and Daniel Trézévant Jr. wove and spun silk and wool into woofs, kerchiefs, and caps for their neighbor Nicolas de Longuemare Jr.[69] Most weavers acquired land and switched to farming but, for a while at least, kept weaving as a minor secondary activity. Jean Pétineau, at his death, owned a farm of a hundred acres, six slaves, fourteen heads of cattle, two geldings, and eleven sheep but also an "old weaver loom."[70] Jean Guérard, who petitioned for naturalization in 1697 as a weaver, by the turn of the century had turned to trade and become a successful Charleston merchant.[71]

If most weavers managed to adjust to their new economic environment or at least remained in the colony even though unable to survive solely by their weaving, conversely the few maritime artisans, who were mostly shipwrights, were singularly unsuccessful. Pierre and Isaac Dugué, both shipwrights from Bésance, Berry, a small town on the Loire River where they learned their trade, eventually left for Jamaica.[72] Similarly, Daniel Jouet, a sail maker from Île-de-Ré who arrived in South Carolina in 1695 by way of Narragansett Bay and New York, eventually moved to Elizabethtown, New Jersey, where he died in the early 1720s.[73]

Four Huguenot artisans who arrived in the colony before 1700 and worked in the luxury trade were Nicolas de Longuemare, a watchmaker; Nicolas de Longuemare Jr., a silversmith; and the goldsmiths Pierre-Jacob Guérard and Salomon Legaré. Nicolas de Longuemare Jr. was particularly successful, as his many-sided career illustrates.[74] Born in Dieppe in the 1670s, Nicolas arrived in South Carolina in 1685 with his father.[75] His account ledger for the years 1703–11 shows that, along with his trade in various fabrics, he catered to the lowcountry elite, repairing their watches and clocks and furnishing them with silver spoons, needles, buckles, and various articles of jewelry. His renown also earned him orders from the colonial government to make and engrave official seals for the Admiralty and the Indian Trade Commission as well as "a Copper Plate for makeing the Country Bills."[76]

Six Huguenots appear in the sources with the locally inflated title of doctor.[77] Jean Thomas's medical expertise was emphatically recognized by the Anglican commissary Gideon Johnston, who asserted that Thomas was "the only person that deserves the name of a Physician in this Place." Strictly speaking, however, these refugees, even Thomas, were not doctors.[78] Five of them were surgeon-barbers and the other was an apothecary. Technically, all had no or little theoretical knowledge of medicine and should therefore be regarded as artisans.[79] Isaac Porcher, for example, said to have been a graduate of the University of Paris, was nonetheless, in the will of fellow Huguenot Georges Baudoin, alluded to as "le chirurgien."[80] It is also highly unlikely that these "doctors" ever practiced their medical skills on a regular basis in the colony since most acquired land and established farms.[81] Thomas, who owned a lot in Charleston, also had a plantation outside the town where he raised cattle and registered his stock mark in 1702.[82] Porcher and Antoine Cordes acquired three thousand and eight hundred acres, respectively.[83] Joseph de La Brosse Marbœuf, who fled Viellevigne, Brittany, for England in 1681 when Huguenot apothecaries had to abjure or give up their practices, lived in Carolina as a farmer, acquiring six hundred acres, registering his stock mark, and owning at the time of his death twelve slaves, forty-two heads of cattle, and a few horses.[84] These refugees therefore practiced medicine only occasionally, if ever. Thomas, who tended Commissary Johnston and in 1692 performed the earliest autopsy recorded in the colony, may have been the most active medically.[85]

Even in the land of freedom and opportunity that Carolina represented for the Huguenots, economic success and social promotion were not accessible to all. A significant number of refugees with no marketable skills arrived in the colony penniless and, in some cases, unfree. Except for a few of them who eventually managed to acquire enough land for themselves and their offspring, these truly uprooted and displaced individuals failed to leave long-lasting marks in the Carolina historical records, succumbing to early deaths or deciding to return to England.

Nearly 15 percent of the Huguenots appear in the records as "planters." In proprietary South Carolina, the deceiving word "planter," unlike the term "esquire," referred to an occupation and not a status.[86] These planters were small landowning farmers at best, most of them being landless laborers.[87] Extant land records show that of the twelve Huguenot petitioners referred to as planters in the 1697 Act of Naturalization, ten had not yet acquired land and the other two owned only 150 acres each, the legal minimum granted to a family of three after 1682.[88] Landless Huguenot farmers settled on land owned by close relatives, as did Louis and René Juin when they worked on their brother George's farm, or were simply hired by other Huguenots. Landless or not, however, these farmers were generally of modest socioeconomic extraction and were free or indentured at the time of their migration. These refugees were not peasants but rather artisans who were unable to practice their trades and had, at least for a time, to work somebody else's land for a living.

Among the Huguenot men who petitioned for naturalization as planters and artisans, four of them came to Carolina as indentured servants: Charles Fromaget, Jacques Gallopin, Salomon Brémar, and Jean Carrière.[89] Their presence in the records as free individuals brings to light a little-known aspect of the migration. Huguenot servants have been either underestimated or ignored by historians, probably because none of them is mentioned in extant inventories and no contract of indenture has survived.[90] Huguenot servants appear only in the passenger lists of the *Richmond* and the *Margaret* and in a few wills and land warrants. These records show the presence of thirty-seven Huguenot servants who settled in Carolina between 1680 and 1690, twenty-five of whom are mentioned by name.[91] These thirty-seven servants represent nearly 20 percent of the Carolina Huguenots whose status or occupations are known. This significant percentage is corroborated by the passenger list of the *Margaret,* which enumerates nine servants out of forty-nine Huguenot migrants, or 18 percent.[92]

Huguenot servants were especially numerous in the first years of the migration. The vast majority of them (twenty-eight) arrived in the colony before 1687 and more than a third (fourteen) before 1685, a time when there were few slaves in the colony and when proprietary land policies made importing servants profitable. These servants were predominantly males; among those identified there were seventeen men and eight women. The occupations of the male indentured servants can only be determined retroactively when they surface again in the records as free settlers because during their servitude they appear in the sources either as servants or, in documents drawn in French, as *engagés.*[93]

Unfortunately, the occupations of only four former servants, three of the four above mentioned who petitioned for naturalization plus Gabriel Ribouteau, have been recorded. Jean Carrière and Gabriel Ribouleau were coopers, Jacques Gallopin a saddler, and Salomon Brémar a weaver.[94] Of the eight female servants three, Antoinette and Françoise (last names unknown) and a third mentioned anonymously, appear in the records as maids.[95] Although it is risky to generalize from three examples, Huguenot female servants seem most likely to have been employed as housemaids and possibly dairywomen.[96] At least three of them, Ester Madeleine Balluet, Marie Nicolas, and Marie Isambert, founded families after serving their time, respectively marrying the surgeon Antoine Cordes; Mathurin Guérin, a gardener; and Daniel Bonnel (occupation unknown).[97]

In his 1687 letter to the Marquis de Seigneulay, Intendant Arnoul reported that the Carolina Huguenots "were poor and that almost all of them had indentured themselves to the English for seven years, having squandered all the money that they had managed to carry out of France during their transatlantic voyages."[98] Although in the absence of extant contracts not much is known about the recruiting terms or the working conditions of the servants, the little information available in the records does not corroborate this intentionally pessimistic report. First, the recruitment was internal to the group as the thirty-seven French servants were indentured to fourteen Huguenot masters, an average of slightly fewer than three servants per master, with a range between one and six. Jacob Guérard, for example, arrived in Charleston in 1680 with six servants, whereas Antoine Boureau imported one in 1686.[99] Unsurprisingly, the socioeconomic profiles of the masters show that most of them, seven of the nine whose occupations or status are known, were merchants and squires.[100]

Second, all servants whose geographic origins are known came from the two western provinces of Normandy and Poitou, as did their owners. This is explained by the fact that Huguenots, both servants and masters, who lived in those provinces were in contact with the Atlantic world and therefore familiar with the institution of indentured servitude.[101] Yet, because the post-Revocation exodus was a time of rupture, recruitment was not, except in one case, as local as it might have been in normal circumstances.[102] Servants were most likely hired either during the flight from France, when groups of Huguenots from neighboring towns crossed the borders or the English Channel together, or in London, where they tended to regroup according to their provinces or towns of origin.

Third, records tend to show that Carolina Huguenot servants were not submitted to the brutal and anonymous treatment that awaited servants in the Chesapeake and in the French Caribbean, where they were reduced to simple commodities in a trade based on profit. Instead, in a context reminiscent of seventeenth-century Puritan New England and Quaker Pennsylvania, they seem to have been *domestiques* or valets brought over by their masters as members of their households or young adults who were entrusted by their parents to a guardian in the hope that the children would have better lives across the Atlantic.[103] In his will, François Macaire released his three servants, all of whom had two more years to serve, instead of bequeathing or selling them.[104] Jacques LeSade, who arrived in Carolina in 1685, had with him an eleven-year-old servant named Isaac Formé. LeSade knew Isaac's parents well since he had served as a witness at the christening of Isaac's brother Adam in 1677 at the London Threadneedle Street Church.[105] Louis Naudin, who came to Carolina indentured to Antoine Boureau, was actually Antoine's nephew.[106] In his 1683 letter Louis Thibou instructed his correspondent to reassure the mother of "the young boy" he had brought to Carolina about her son's well-being. This young boy was most likely one of the two servants who arrived in Charleston with Thibou in 1680.[107] The case of the female servant Ester Madeleine Balluet is also symptomatic of these ill-defined master-servant relationships, which at times seem to have been anything but what should be expected in such circumstances. Ester Madeleine arrived in Carolina as one of Benjamin Marion's servants. Yet her sister, Judith, was or became, once in the colony, Benjamin's wife. Did Marion marry down or is the term "servant," as used in the land warrant, devoid of any real social meaning or ambiguous at best?[108] As for Louis Naudin, not only did he mysteriously indenture himself to his uncle, but he did so while he had been granted five pounds sterling for his passage by the London French Committee.[109] Why did he not emigrate as a free settler?

The internal dynamics of Huguenot servitude are therefore difficult to delineate. Only a fine line separated servants from penniless free settlers, and the former were not necessarily of poorer social backgrounds than the latter. Servitude appears to have been a temporary solution to financial difficulties or the result of negotiations, devoid of any social stigma and certainly not an insurmountable obstacle to material success and social promotion. Salomon Brémar, one of Jacob Guérard's servants, after the expiration of his term acquired more than two thousand acres of land. He was in that respect much more successful ·than most free Huguenot migrants of modest origins.[110] Louise Thoury, from Rennes, described on the island of Jersey as a "poor girl [*pauvre fille*] who has spent all her savings for her passage" and in London as a "maid [*domestique*]," nonetheless emigrated as a free settler. Once in Carolina, in a most unconventional way that is illustrative of the social dislocation brought about by forced dispersal and a tight ethnic matrimonial market, she married the squire Samuel DuBourdieu.[111] Thoury was lucky enough to have her transatlantic passage paid for, perhaps by DuBourdieu, and thus avoided servitude. However, without her socially upward marriage she would have toiled as a maid in the colony.

Some of the Huguenot servants received wages. In his will, François Macaire instructed his executors to give Michel Antoine ten écus (two pounds sterling), a sum in line with the minimum annual wage for a New England servant, and Cézar Mozé in his will bequeathed his maid, Françoise, "five sterling pounds in goods or three in silver in lieu of payment."[112] Macaire's testament contains the only available indication of the cost of these servants. On his deathbed Macaire agreed to free Benoît Charron in return for the sum of forty-eight écus (nearly ten pounds sterling), which he said he had paid for a term of two years.[113]

As for the ages of the servants, evidence is again thin, but it seems that, as in the Chesapeake and the Caribbean, they were young adults. Except for the above-mentioned Isaac Formé, who was eleven when he arrived in Charleston, and Louis Naudin, who was under sixteen when he emigrated with Antoine Boureau, most Huguenot servants were above sixteen years of age, as shown in their masters' land warrants.[114] Perhaps this was not coincidental but reflected a knowledge of the rules regulating the land grant procedures by Huguenots who wished to obtain as much land as possible by importing older servants. The acquisition of larger acreage was certainly a crucial factor in making claim to servants, as Marie Isambert's case illustrates. Marie arrived in Carolina indentured to the Bontecou family on board the *Margaret* in 1685. The Bontecous moved on to New York by 1689, but Marie remained in Carolina where she married Daniel Bonnel. However, in early 1693 Isaac Caillabœuf, also a passenger on the *Margaret,* claimed Marie's arrival rights.[115] For the same reason, free Huguenot settlers may have chosen to transfer their head rights to others, perhaps in return for loans in the form of free passage or simply because they did not feel strong enough to clear land on their own and therefore agreed to be recorded as servants in the warrants of their "benefactors." Louis Naudin, or most likely his parents, may have agreed to give Antoine Boureau the five pounds sterling granted to Louis by the French Committee plus his arrival rights in exchange for taking him to Carolina and training him as an apprentice. The difficulty in determining the nature of the relationship between masters and servants, in a broader perspective, reflects the mutual closeness of the Huguenot migrants who came to Carolina within families, or clusters of families, often from the same towns or areas in France.

Kinship and the Carolina Huguenot Migration

On December 2, 1687, bedridden in the house of a fellow Huguenot from Dauphiny, Alexandre Pépin, and in the presence of a Jean Roux "master mariner," the Charleston merchant François Macaire dictated a nuncupative (oral) will in French to the refugee Nicolas Mayrant. In this testament Macaire gave instructions to his business partners, Huguenot Jacques Boyd and Swiss Jean-François Gignilliat, and declared that he wished to be buried in the graveyard of the city's French Reformed church.[116] As this scene suggests, in the years immediately following the migration, whether they were Santee squires, Orange Quarter artisans, or Charleston merchants, the Carolina Huguenots formed a close-knit community. Although not cut off from the rest of the colony's population, they stuck together for several reasons. First, many of them hailed from the same towns and areas, and especially in the 1670s when persecution intensified, their minority status as French Calvinists accentuated their common religious and cultural heritage at the expense of their social and parochial differences. Second, the experience of the flight out of France, usually shared by groups of refugees, created unexpected but strong ties between individuals who would not have socialized with one another in normal circumstances. Third, once in London, a large city in a foreign land, they immediately looked for fellow Huguenots, relatives and neighbors from their hometowns with whom they had temporarily lost contact because of the dispersal. Fourth, Huguenots rarely faced the dangers of a transatlantic passage or overcame the difficulties of settling in a faraway and in many ways inhospitable land, such as Carolina, alone but were usually accompanied by relatives and friends. Fifth, the small size of the Carolina settlements created, in the case of Charleston, an environment evocative of the typical market towns many of them hailed from and, in the case of Santee and Orange Quarter, situations similar to the isolated rural communities others had called home. In the seventeenth-century lowcountry, where everybody was everyone else's neighbor, this was even more the case for a few hundred out-of-place, odd-sounding French settlers. Thus, at least until the early 1700s, the Huguenots compensated the dual alienation of living in a transatlantic colony and in a foreign country by preserving old familial and peer networks and creating new ones whenever these had been unsuccessfully transplanted. They migrated to Carolina together, settled near each other, intermarried with one another, witnessed each other's transactions, and appointed one another as testamentary executors.

One of the letters published in the 1685 tract *Suite de la Description de la Carolline* recommended that "to decide to go to America, one must travel among several families because otherwise . . . one has to spend his life with people who do not always turn out to be honest."[117] The Huguenots heeded this recommendation, and the preservation of kinship ties proved to be a determining factor in their migration to Carolina. Lorri Glover's observation that "settling South Carolina was . . . a family affair" bears all the more truth in the case of an alien minority such as the Huguenots.[118] Of the 347 migrants identified, more than 40 percent (152) emigrated with one or several family members other than their spouses and their children. For nearly half of these (69), the relative was a sibling, and close to a third of these adult refugees arrived with at least one parent.[119] Examples of sibling migration are Gabriel and Pierre Manigault; Jacques, Jean, and Gabriel Boyd; Alexandre Thésée and Henry Auguste Chasteigner; and René, Georges, Louis, and Élisabeth Juin.[120] Examples of intergenerational migrations are Judith Giton, her brothers, Louis and Pierre, and their mother, Madeleine Cottin; Jean Postel and his mother, Marie Brugnet Postel; and Henry Bruneau, his uncle Paul Bruneau, and his grandfather Arnaud Bruneau, Sieur de La Chabocière.[121] The largest single family to migrate was that of the Dugués. Jacques Sr. arrived in Charleston with his six children, Jacques, Judith, Marie, Pierre, Isaac, and Élisabeth, the first three born to him by his first wife, the late Judith Soumin, and the last three by his second wife, Élisabeth Dupuy, who followed him to Carolina.[122]

A study of the passenger lists of the *Richmond* and *Margaret* further corroborates the familial dimension of the migration. Thirteen of the twenty-two Huguenots on board the *Richmond* were registered with their families, and the fifty French passengers of the *Margaret* made up a group of just eight families. Family sizes on both ships varied from two to eight members, but the majority of them included more than four people. Examples are Jacob Guérard, who traveled on the *Richmond* with his wife, Marguerite Nileson, and their six children, Pierre Jacob, Isaac, Jean, Joseph, Marguerite, and Élisabeth; and Daniel Garnier, who boarded the *Margaret* with his wife, Élisabeth Fanton, his sister-in-law Rachel, and his children Étienne, Rachel, Sarah, Marguerite, and Anne.[123]

A significant proportion of Carolina Huguenots also emigrated in clusters of families. Some, usually from the same areas in France, met in London and decided to continue on to Carolina from there. In other cases, related families from the same towns and socioeconomic milieus migrated together all the way to Carolina from France via England. Archetypal examples of these interfamilial clusters are found in the migrations of the LeSade-D'Amberbaut-Torquet-Formé-Guérard, the St. Julien–Ravenel–De Farcy–DuBourdieu, and the Poitevin-Dutartre-Trézévant groups.

Jacques LeSade, from Yerville, Normandy, arrived in Carolina with his wife Élisabeth D'Amberbaut, who was born in Amsterdam of a Huguenot family from Rouen and whom he had married in London in 1676; his mother-in-law, Marguerite LeMotteux-D'Amberbaut-Poitevin; and his servant Isaac Formé. While in London, Jacques and Élisabeth attended the christenings of Catherine Françoise, daughter of Jacques Torquet and Judith LeMotteux, Élisabeth's stepsister, and of Adam Formé, Isaac's brother. In 1686 Jacques Torquet, along with his two brothers, Paul and Omphroy (Humphrey), was in Carolina, where three years later Pierre LeSade, Jacques' brother, joined them. Furthermore, through their mother, Anne Guérard, the LeSade brothers were also related to Jacob Guérard, one of the two promoters of the *Richmond* expedition, who had been in Carolina with his wife and their six children since 1680. All these Carolina Huguenots belonged to a few closely related families from neighboring towns located in upper Normandy (Yerville, Dieppe, Fécamp, and Rouen). They managed not only to preserve but also to strengthen already established kinship ties through the dispersal and the transatlantic migration.[124]

In June 1686 Pierre de St. Julien, from Vitré, received twenty pounds sterling from the French Committee to transport himself, his wife, Jeanne Lefèvre, and their three children, Pierre Jr., Louis, and Charlotte, to Carolina. The following year in Carolina, in the Pompion (pronounced *pumpkin*) Hill chapel, Pierre attended the marriage of Charlotte to René Ravenel, another squire from Vitré. In 1690 Samuel DuBourdieu, also an écuyer from Vitré, signed a contract with Jacques Dugué Sr. to marry Jacques' daughter, Judith. DuBourdieu's witnesses were Jean and Suzanne De Farcy, also members of the Huguenot Vitré gentry. A 1687 letter written in London, in which a relative of Samuel's explained that "Samuel went to Carolina with Mr. [Pierre de St. Julien, Sieur] de Malacare and others," and research in the Vitré records confirm what could be inferred from these glimpses of early Carolina social life. These four gentry families, who had intermarried in Vitré for decades, not to say centuries, immigrated together to Carolina, where they preserved their mutual ties, which were not just ethnic and regional but eminently social.[125]

Antoine Poitevin was in London as early as 1681 with his wife, Gabrielle Bérou, and their three children, Antoine, Pierre, and Anne. Originally from Orsemont, a small community in Beauce, he received two pounds sterling from the Threadneedle Street Church. Four years later the Poitevin family landed in Charleston accompanied by the Trézévant family—Daniel, his wife, Suzanne Maulard, and their son, Daniel—and fellow refugee Pierre Dutartre, all also from the province of Beauce. Soon after their arrival in the colony, these three families settled in the community of Orange Quarter, along the Cooper River. A look at their juxtaposed entries in the *Liste des François et Suisses* shows that the Trévézants were related to the Poitevins through Gabrielle Bérou, who was the widow of Lubin Maulard before becoming Pierre Poitevin's wife and the mother of Daniel Trézévant Sr.'s wife. Daniel Jr. and Antoine Poitevin were born in the same town of Menthenon, Beauce, thereby indicating that the Poitevins and the Trézévants lived in the same community before their escape from France. Furthermore, in 1697, except for Pierre Poitevin who petitioned as a planter, Daniel Trézévant Sr., Daniel Jr., Antoine Poitevin Sr., Antoine Jr., and Pierre Dutartre were all registered as weavers.[126] As opposed to the Vitré squires, these Huguenot families of textile artisans did not immigrate to Carolina together in the hope of transplanting influential social networks but simply to re-create a communal environment that would help them surmount the innumerable difficulties associated with starting life anew in a strange and foreign land. Whatever their goals may have been, these different familial associations show that migrating to Carolina was for the Huguenots a family affair.

The 1696–1697 Naturalization List and Carolina Huguenot Demographics

The study of the refugees included in the *Liste des François et Suisses,* hereafter referred to as "the cohort," enables the historian to draw a fairly detailed demographic profile of the Carolina Huguenot community at a given time through a largely representative subgroup. Drawn in the mid-1690s, the *Liste* offers a unique opportunity to probe into the Carolina Huguenot community shortly after the migration of most of the refugees and before the mutual ethnic, religious, and provincial ties that bound the group together started to loosen.

The cohort contains 196 adults, including 118 (60 percent) men and 78 (40 percent) women (table 5).[127] These figures, which give a fairly balanced gender ratio of 1.51 to 1, show that single men did not dominate the Huguenot migration. Unsurprisingly, the majority of the refugees appearing on the list were married (138 of 196), a handful of them (15) being remarried widows and widowers, and cross-references show that 15 others were married shortly before the *Liste* was compiled. Only 43 refugees, all men except for Élisabeth Dugué, were still single.[128]

A study of the 74 couples for whom the place of marriage could be determined indicates that 34 (46 percent) of them were formed in Europe before the migration. Thus, almost one out of two cohort members migrated to Carolina with their spouses. Except for a minority of the refugees (less than 10 percent) who wed in England, most were married even before leaving France and Switzerland.

The same study shows that these refugees were young. Almost two-thirds of the couples formed in Europe had only one child at the time of the migration, which indicates that they had been married only for a few years before crossing the Atlantic. Those who married in Carolina in the late 1680s and early 1690s were either young adults who came with their parents or middle-aged individuals at the time of the migration. René Ravenel, for example, was thirty-one when he wedded nineteen-year-old Charlotte de St. Julien in Pompion Hill a year after their arrival in Carolina.[129]

This impression of youth is confirmed by the fact that nearly half (41 percent) of all the Carolina Huguenots for whom dates of birth are known and who were at least fifteen years old at the time of the Revocation (12 percent of the total) were less than twenty-five

TABLE 5. *A South Carolina Huguenot demographic profile, 1696–97 (N=352)*

Adults	Children	Male	Female	Gender Ratio	Married	Known Places of Marriage
196	156	118 (60%)	78 (40%)	1.51 : 1	138	40 (54%) SC
						34 (46%) Europe

years old in 1685 (born in the 1660s), and another 46 percent were in their thirties (born in the 1650s) and forties (born in the 1640s).[130] Of the few Huguenots whose exact ages at migration are known (27 migrants, or 8 percent of the total), more than half (14) were between twenty and thirty-four years old and nearly a third (8, or 29 percent) were between thirty-five and forty-five (table 6).[131] A breakdown of this data by gender shows that the 4 women whose ages at migration are known averaged twenty-two years of age and the average age of the 23 men was thirty-six, while the average age for all these migrants was thirty-four.[132] This figure is corroborated by the only Huguenot census in British North America that includes ages, that of New Rochelle, New York, from which an average age at migration of thirty-two can be inferred.[133]

This youth, however, must not hide the fact that the Carolina Huguenot migration was two-generational. In the cohort, a fourth of the refugees (49) had parents or adult children also petitioning for naturalization. Jean Postel, for example, was recorded with his widowed mother, Marye Brugnet Postel, and Damaris Élisabeth, Marianne, and Suzanne registered with their parents, Jacques and Élisabeth (Léger) LeSerrurier.[134] A handful of refugees were also well beyond their forties, such as Joachim Gaillard (sixty-two), Noé Royer Sr. (fifty-seven), Jacques de Bourdeaux (fifty-six), and Abraham (fifty-four) and Isaac Fleury (fifty-two), when they started life anew in faraway Carolina.[135]

A study of the 25 (of the 35) couples that were formed in Carolina and for which the provincial and social origins of the spouses could be determined enables the historian to observe to what extent the migration altered the high level of regional and social endogamies that characterized marriages in early modern France.[136] Statistics show that, when possible, Carolina Huguenots tried to preserve regional ties through marriage, but the unequal representation of the provinces among the group and the skewed gender ratio within groups of refugees from the same regions made regional exogamy inevitable. Among the 25 couples studied, only 3 were formed by refugees from the same province and 5 from the same region. Unsurprisingly these Huguenots were predominantly from well-represented provinces, such as Poitou, Saintonge, and Aunis. Examples of these intra- and interregional Carolina couples from western France are Philippe Normand and Élisabeth Juin, both from Poitou; Alexandre Thésée Chastaigner and Élisabeth Buretel from Aunis (La Rochelle); Élye Bisset and Jeanne Poinset from Saintonge; and Mathurin Guérin from Saintonge and Marie Nicolas from Poitou.[137]

Huguenots hailing from little-represented provinces, however, had to find matrimonial partners who came from regions far from their hometowns and where dialects and cultural lifeways were quite different from theirs. Although these French (French-speaking, in the case of the Swiss) Calvinist refugees living in a British environment shared common ethnic (that is, Francophone) and religious backgrounds, the largely different regional origins of these spouses must have caused an undeniable strain on their

TABLE 6.   *Ages at migration (N=27)*

20–34	35–45	Over 45
14 (51%)	8 (29%)	5 (18%)

family lives and necessarily forced them to go through a period of mutual cultural adaptation. Examples of matrimonial unions between cultural extremes are Pastor Florent Philippe Trouillart from the rural community of La Ferté-Vidam, upper Normandy, and Madeleine Maslet from Sète, a busy Mediterranean port in coastal Languedoc; Pierre Le Chevalier from Saint-Lô, lower Normandy, and Madeleine Garillon from Grenoble in Alpine Dauphiny; and Antoine Cordes, from Mazamet, a small town in mountainous Languedoc, and Ester Madeleine Balluet from La Chaume in coastal Poitou. A few transcultural marriages also occurred between Swiss and Huguenot settlers such as the Swiss Jean-François Gignilliat and Suzanne LeSerrurier from Saint-Quentin, Picardy; and Jacques Varin from Rouen, and Suzanne Horry from Neuchâtel, Switzerland.[138]

These unions, which would have seemed odd back in France, reflect the desire and necessity for the Huguenots to marry within the group while an inevitably restricted matrimonial market seriously limited their options.[139] It should be stressed that the relative lack of female partners also led some Huguenot males to remain single for long periods after the migration instead of choosing British spouses. François de Rousserye, from Montpellier, came to Carolina on board the *Richmond* with one servant and acquired more than a thousand acres by 1698. Whereas he could objectively claim to be an excellent match, he nonetheless remained single for twenty years, a remarkably long time for the seventeenth century, before marrying in the early 1700s.[140] Another example is Jean Girardeau, who married the young Anne LeSade, daughter of the immigrant Pierre LeSade, in 1703 at the unusual age of thirty-eight.[141] Charles Fromaget, who arrived in 1680, and Jacques Gallopin and Gabriel Ribouteau, both in the colony in 1685, were still single in 1696.[142] In a colony where land was plentiful and Francophone partners scarce, the promise of material security was therefore hardly an irresistible appeal, and as result Huguenot women, old and young, could well afford to be finicky. While the need to find Huguenot spouses and the tight matrimonial market undoubtedly led Huguenot men to marry much younger women, in one case it even stretched the limits of ethically permissible intrafamilial marital unions. Abraham Michaud, perhaps discouraged in his effort to find a suitable Huguenot spouse, decided to marry Ester Jaudon, daughter of his sister-in-law born of a prior marriage. Although Abraham and Ester were not consanguinely related, they were nonetheless members of the same extended family, and Ester was most likely significantly younger than Abraham.[143]

If regional exogamy, uncommon in France, was perceived as inevitable in Carolina and therefore accepted by the Huguenots, social exogamy remained exceptional, at least among the first generation. Of the thirteen couples for which the social status of both members could be ascertained, only two were exogamous. One was the most unusual union between the esquire Samuel DuBourdieu and the maidservant Louise Thoury, which would have been clearly perceived, perhaps even denounced, in France as a *mésalliance* and which could only have been formed in a time of social confusion brought about by the sudden dispersal.[144] The other socially exogamous marriage was between Antoine Poitevin, son of a weaver from Beauce, and Marguerite de Bourdeaux, daughter of the esquire Jacques de Bourdeaux from Grenoble.[145] The tight Carolina Huguenot matrimonial market and the physical proximity inherent to a small alien transatlantic community most likely explain these unions, involving younger refugees, more than the breaking down of social barriers caused by the migration. In both cases, however, decisive personal factors that transcended social rules and inherited customs were evidently at play.

Writing to his brother back in Switzerland in 1690 about his future marriage with "damoiselle [Suzanne] LeSerrurier," Jean-François Gignilliat, who thought that he was regarded "as the wealthiest foreigner [in Carolina] in great part due to his being Swiss because the English seem to very much like [his] Nation," claimed that "he could have found no better or more advantageous match" in the colony.[146] Unsurprisingly, the other eleven couples fit this established pattern of social endogamy. Refugees of modest social origins and Huguenots of high social status found spouses within their subgroups. Mathurin Guérin, a gardener, married Marie Nicolas, one of Benjamin Marion's servants; and Pierre de St. Julien, esquire, married Élisabeth LeSerrurier, daughter of the merchant and self-styled esquire Jacques LeSerrurier. The latter case shows that the Huguenot restricted matrimonial market certainly benefited socially ambitious families Their daughters' marriages enabled them to seal alliances in the nascent Carolina colony that would have been extremely difficult to form in France. This type of marriage typically paired an esquire with the daughter of a merchant. At a time when Carolina land was plentiful and cheap but hardly profitable, esquires could trade status for wealth in join-ing prosperous mercantile families. Merchants, in turn, acquired a sort of noble status in exchange for cash. The second marriage of Samuel DuBourdieu is a case in point. After the death of his first spouse, Louise Thoury, Samuel married Judith Dugué, daughter of the merchant Jacques Dugué, also a self-styled esquire. Their marriage contract entitled Judith to a third of Samuel's entire real estate not only "en Caroline Pays d'Amérique," but, more importantly in terms of social ascension from the perspective of first-genera-tion Carolina Huguenots, also "en Bretagne province de france," if, of course, "God allowed His elect to recover all their estates, which they were forced to abandon in France because of the persecution aroused against them."[147] This type of union, reminis-cent of French marriages that opened the doors of the *petite noblesse* to the bourgeoisie, is illustrative of the transfer of *mentalité* that occurred with the migration and took root in the Carolina transatlantic setting.

In some of these cases, especially among landowning esquire families, social endogamy reflected the continuation of familial strategies that the migration and the exile did not interrupt but, conversely, strengthened. The marital alliances of the St. Juliens and the Ravenels are illustrative of that trend. René Ravenel and Charlotte de St. Julien, who married in 1687, were both of provincial noble families from Vitré; their son, Daniel, married Élisabeth Damaris de St. Julien, daughter of Pierre de St. Julien and Élisabeth LeSerrurier; and one of their grandsons, also named Daniel, wed Sarah de St. Julien II, daughter of Pierre de St. Julien III and Sarah Godin, in 1757. In successive generations the Ravenels and the St. Juliens continued to intermarry well into the eighteenth century while their lines also merged with those of mercantile families such as the Mazycks, Godins, Le Serruriers, and LeNobles.[148]

These unions served to consolidate estates but were also the expression of an esprit de corps to which the merchants, and occasionally successful artisans, were admitted because of the limited number of Francophone families of gentry status living in Carolina and on the basis of their material wealth. When René Ravenel married Charlotte de St. Julien, the witnesses were Josias Dupré, son of the merchant Josias Dupré Sr.; the silversmith Nicolas de Longuemare; and Charlotte's two brothers, Pierre and Louis. Similarly, the esquires Henry LeNoble, Jean-François Gignilliat, and René Ravenel, and a merchant, Pierre LaSalle, witnessed Isaac Mazyck's wedding with Marianne LeSerrurier.[149]

In the first decades of the eighteenth century, however, members of the Huguenot elite began to intermarry with English settlers. The preservation of estates and status became more important than the preservation of their French identity. Viewed broadly this trend can be interpreted as a sign of an overall integration. From a local perspective, however, these ethnically exogamous unions were socially endogamous and represented more the merging of Huguenot and English landed and mercantile families. Such unions, for example, were formed between the Ravenels and the Broughtons, and the Dugués and the Wraggs.[150]

This being said, however, second-generation Huguenots continued to intermarry when possible. The marriage between Daniel Huger and Élisabeth Gendron, sealed by a contract drawn in French, is a well-documented illustration of the survival of regional and social endogamous marital strategies into the eighteenth century. On January 7, 1710, Daniel Huger, a merchant from Loudin, Poitou, and his wife Marguerite Perdriau, daughter of a La Rochelle merchant, drew an elaborate contract for the union of their son Daniel to Elisabeth, daughter of the widower and self-styled esquire Philippe Gendron of Marans, Aunis. Daniel Huger agreed to give his son half of his possessions, including "the plantation where he lives, [his] Negroe as well as Indian slaves, horses, oxen, cows, sheep & pigs with the exception of a young slave girl named Babet already given to damoiselle Huger his wife . . . the day following consummation of said future marriage," on condition that the young couple would live on the plantation. The profits accrued "through the work of the slaves and the sales of horses and other livestock" minus the running expenses of the estate, "such as the purchase of clothes for the slaves," were to be shared equally between Huger and his son annually. In return, Philippe Gendron agreed to give his daughter a dowry of "two hundred pounds of Carolina money" (£130) to be paid in three installments over the next three years on each first day of March.[151]

The Elusive Eden
Huguenot Returnees and Drifters

At the turn of the eighteenth century, after having married their daughters Suzanne, Catherine, Damaris Élisabeth, and Marianne respectively to Jean-François Gignilliat, Henry LeNoble, Pierre de St. Julien, and Isaac Mazyck, Jacques and Élisabeth LeSerrurier returned to England, probably happy to have secured their four daughters excellent matches.[152] In 1697, however, both had petitioned for naturalization in Carolina, allegedly to remain permanently in the colony.[153] In 1700 Pierre de St. Julien Sr. decided to move to Ireland after spending thirteen years in Carolina. Leaving behind his three children, Pierre, Louis, and Charlotte, he settled in Dublin, where he joined his granddaughter Jeanne Charlotte Ravenel. He died in the Irish capital in 1705 at the age of seventy.[154] Élie Boudinot, a merchant from Marans, arrived in Carolina in 1687. The following year, however, he was an elder of the Huguenot Church in New York City.[155]

These Huguenots are among the few (thirty-five) refugees who either returned to Great Britain or settled in another colony on the mainland or in the Caribbean, and whose motivations for leaving Carolina are as diverse as those that led them thither in the first place.

These returnees were either older refugees who left well-established children back in Carolina or Huguenots who seemed to have met financial difficulties or were simply disappointed with a colonial life that had not matched their expectations. In May 1705 Charleston merchant Jacques Nicholas (Nicolas), also known as Petitbois, wrote a letter of attorney to Jean Boisseau empowering him to dispose of as he saw fit his "Goods, Wares, Merchandizes, Effects, Chattel and Things whatsoever which [he] leaves behind [him] at [his] departure from this Province" and had his will recorded in preparation for a perilous oceanic voyage.[156] Was Jacques Nicholas dissatisfied with his Carolina existence? Did he wish to finish his life nearer to France, or did he return to Britain to join relatives and friends? Other cases of return migration are easier to explain. After residing in Carolina for nearly ten years, Jacques Goulart de Vervant sold his goods, lands, and slaves in 1696 and left the colony, presumably for England, most likely because a nobleman of his rank felt dissatisfied, perhaps out of place, in a nascent colonial society.[157]

Fleeting references to real estate left behind in France mentioned in Huguenot wills also show that until the early years of the eighteenth century the first-generation refugees encouraged their descendants to return to France. Unsurprisingly, this illusory hope was particularly strong among the landowning esquires, who had been unable to liquidate their assets before the flight. In his 1692 will, Arnaud Bruneau de La Chabocière instructed his son Paul to do everything he could to recover the family estate in Aunis. In 1709 Paul in turn bequeathed the estate to his nephew Henry and encouraged him to return to France "if the Protestant religion were to be restored."[158] Of all the Carolina Huguenots, however, only Barthélemy Gaillard seems to have managed to return to France during a period of administrative confusion in order to recover and sell the family property.[159]

Most Huguenots who left Carolina opted for relocation in another English colony instead of the British Isles. New York, with its more urban environment, healthier climate, and larger Francophone community, attracted more than two-thirds of them. Some were merchants, such as Élie Boudinot and Isaac Lenoir, who likely moved to New York City in the hope of finding a cosmopolitan environment more propitious for transoceanic trade.[160] Others, such as René and Anne (Courcier) Rézeau and Pierre and Marguerite Bontecou, left Carolina for New York City for no apparent reasons. All were literally birds of passage, as they did not linger in the colony more than two or three years. The Rézeaus, who arrived in Carolina in 1685, had settled in New York by January 1689 when their seventh child, Ester, was baptized; Boudinot was in Carolina in 1687 and in New York City the following year; and the Bontecous, who came to Carolina on board the *Margaret* in April 1685, had relocated in New York by 1688.[161] Even Louis Thibou, who trumpeted the advantages of Carolina life in his famed 1683 letter, actually moved in the mid-1680s to New York, where his son Isaac was born, before returning to Charleston sometime before 1696, when he petitioned for naturalization. In 1699 he settled in Antigua, where he died in 1726 after a brief stay in Philadelphia.[162]

In some instances members of Carolina Huguenot families reunited in New York City. This was the case for the Perdriaus from La Rochelle and the Bontecous from nearby Île-de-Ré. In 1695, "considering the great perils and many accidents that may happen during his sea voyage," Louis Perdriau wrote a will in preparation for his move to New York, where he eventually joined his sister Élisabeth.[163] A few years later their brother Étienne left for New York to marry Marguerite, daughter of Pierre and Marguerite Bontecou, who had originally settled in Carolina before relocating in New York City. At about the same time Marguerite (Perdriau) Huger went to New York to attend the christening of Guillaume (William), son of her sister Marie (Perdriau) Moyon, who was godmother of Marie, the sixth child of Pierre and Marguerite Bontecou.[164] These intercolonial movements prove the ability of displaced Huguenots to maintain familial ties, to which they were very much attached, within the diaspora, as long as, of course, they had the financial means to cover the expenses occasioned by these long-distance travels.

Other Huguenots, however, wandered from colony to colony desperately looking for material stability in ways reminiscent of the continental refugees, studied by Michèle Magdelaine, who tragically returned, two or three times on average but more than ten times in some cases, to Frankfurt for additional financial assistance after each unsuccessful relocation.[165] Moyse and Marie (Tauvron) LeBrun, for example, both from Île-de-Ré, settled in Narragansett Bay, Rhode Island, in 1688. When the community disbanded in 1691, they, like most of its members, moved to New York City. In 1694, however, Moyse LeBrun died. In that same year, assisted by the consistory of the French Church, Marie decided to move to Carolina with her French-born son Moyse. There she joined her brother Étienne and petitioned for naturalization in 1696.[166] Thus Marie Tauvron, who must have left France in 1685, arrived in Charleston ten years later, after relocating in two different colonies, enduring the loss of her husband, and traveling more than three thousand miles in North America alone.

The Jouet family offers another instance of Huguenot peregrinations across the Atlantic and along the American eastern seaboard. Daniel and Marie (Courcier) Jouet and their children, Daniel and Pierre, were in London in late 1686 or early 1687 when they received five pounds sterling from the French Committee "to go to Carolina."[167] They moved first to Plymouth however, where their third child, Marie, was born, and then in 1688 to Narragansett Bay, Rhode Island. The following year they relocated to New York City, where Marie gave birth to their fourth child, Ézéchiel. While in New York, the Jouets associated with the Rézeaus, fellow refugees from Île-de-Ré to whom they were related through Marie's sister, Anne Courcier. However, in 1695, after the births of Élisabeth and Anne, they suddenly and surprisingly left for Charleston. The following year they petitioned for naturalization but did not remain in Carolina either. Sometime in the early years of the eighteenth century, the Jouets moved to Elizabethtown, New Jersey, where Daniel died in 1721 and Marie in 1732.[168] Daniel Jouet was a sail maker, and while he probably did not find employment in either Narragansett Bay or Charleston, it is difficult to explain why he did not remain in New York City with the Rézeaus.

Factors as diverse as dissatisfaction with colonial life, personal tragedies, familial regroupings, the search for material stability, and the illusory hope of recovering confiscated property in France all, separately or jointly, motivated these incessant moves. Although these refugees were numerically marginal, their peregrinations, whether forced or voluntary, are somehow symptomatic of the post-Revocation exodus and of the displaced Huguenots' unusual capacity for mobility.

The Carolina Huguenot Migration in a Comparative Atlantic Context

In crossing the Atlantic, Huguenot refugees took on the dual nature of refugees and migrants. From this perspective, it is instructive to examine their immigration to Carolina in a comparative Atlantic context. Four seventeenth-century migratory movements can serve as the basis for this comparison: the pre-Revocation Huguenot migrations to the French Antilles and to Quebec, the Puritan migration to New England, and the English migration to the Chesapeake.

In terms of geographic origins, the Carolina Huguenot migration largely resembled, yet somewhat differed from, the immigration of French Protestants to the Caribbean and to Quebec. The studies of Gérard Lafleur for the French West Indies and of Leslie Choquette and Marc-André Bédard for New France respectively show that 49 and 65 percent of Huguenot emigrants came from the three provinces of Aunis, Saintonge, and Poitou.[169] By emphasizing the role of La Rochelle and its Atlantic trade connections, these figures establish that the recruitment of the Carolina Huguenots largely followed pre-Revocation transatlantic migration patterns. However, the presence of significant numbers of Carolina refugees from areas of France that were not involved in the colonial Atlantic economy illustrates that the post-Revocation Huguenot exodus was a migration caused by unusual circumstances. Thus, for example, whereas Choquette found only one Huguenot from Île-de-France, none from Touraine, and one from Dauphiny, and Lafleur found only two from Île-de-France, three from Touraine, and none from Dauphiny, these provinces respectively represented 3, 7, and 5 percent of the Carolina group.[170] These figures corroborate the fact that although involvement in or exposure to the transatlantic economy exerted a determining influence on the recruitment of the Carolina Huguenots, other factors such as the promotional literature, local persecution, and simply chance also drew French Protestants from areas having little or no contact with the Atlantic world.

The high proportion (79 percent) of migrants from urban areas within the Carolina Huguenots is also found in the Protestant population of New France; Choquette has calculated an urban rate of 86 percent, with three-fourths of that figure hailing from cities of over ten thousand inhabitants.[171] In New France and the West Indies, most Huguenots came from just a few cities, La Rochelle being the most heavily represented. Lafleur found that of the Huguenots settled in the French Islands, 44 percent came from La Rochelle and 17 percent from Dieppe, for a combined representation of 61 percent; and Choquette determined that 50 percent of her sample came from La Rochelle alone.[172] Among the Carolina Huguenots, La Rochelle and Dieppe are also the most represented cities, although with a significantly smaller combined proportion of 18 percent. These high percentages can be explained by the predominantly urban nature of the Huguenot population in early modern France and the greater mobility of town dwellers, who, usually being wealthier and better informed than people from rural communities, could more easily contemplate relocation overseas. This was especially the case for those residing in Atlantic ports. The central role played by La Rochelle within the French Atlantic trade networks before the Revocation explains the heavy Rochelais element in all these migrations. However, the comparatively high proportion of Huguenots within the Carolina group who hailed from villages, 20 percent against 14 percent in New France, is a further sign that the post-Revocation exodus slightly differed from previous Huguenot transatlantic migrations.

Regarding socioeconomic origins, the relative elevated status of the Carolina Huguenots and the high proportion of merchants within the group also characterized the Huguenot migrations to the West Indies and New France. Choquette estimated that close to a tenth of the Protestants in Quebec were nobles, and a 1687 census shows that nearly half of the Huguenots settled in Guadeloupe were *habitants,* the French West Indian term for large landowners. In Quebec a third of the Huguenots were characterized as "bourgeois," most of them being merchants, and in Guadeloupe close to 20 percent of the Protestants were active in the transatlantic trade.[173] These figures match the proportions of nobles and merchants, respectively 12 and 22 percent, found among the Carolina Huguenots. The strong presence of artisans in the Carolina group, about a third, mirrors Choquette's figures but is twice as high as in Guadeloupe, according to a 1671 census.[174] The Carolina migration, however, significantly differs from the Huguenot migrations to the West Indies and New France in the obvious absence of military officers and the quasi-absence of laborers. Most Huguenots serving in Louis XIV's forces who fled at the time of the Revocation joined William's armies and, after the Williamite wars, retired in the British Isles, many of them relocating in the Huguenot community of Portarlington, Ireland.[175] None seems ever to have crossed the Atlantic to settle in North America. As for Huguenot peasants, most immigrated eastward to the German states.

At 14 percent, the percentage of servants among the Carolina Huguenots is almost twice as high as in New France, where, it must be remembered, merchants were theoretically prohibited from importing Protestant servants, and is significantly lower than in Guadeloupe, where it stood at 21 percent.[176] The presence of servants, which is evocative of pre-Revocation Huguenot overseas emigrations, denotes the hybrid nature of the Huguenot migration to Carolina, halfway between a transatlantic migration and *le Refuge.* Indeed, within the diaspora only in North America did Huguenot refugees settle with indentured servants.

This comparison clearly shows that, in terms of geographic and socioeconomic recruitment, the Huguenot immigration to Carolina, all in all, was patterned after pre-Revocation transatlantic migrations. Differences emerge, but they are more of proportions than of nature. Most Carolina refugees also hailed from ports of the Atlantic seaboard, although regional origins were particularly diverse due to the religious dimension of the migration, which led many Huguenots from inland and alpine villages to this unexpected overseas destination. Similarly, as in the West Indies and in New France, the Carolina Huguenot population contained a high percentage of individuals from the upper strata of French society, military officers excepted, and a strong artisanal presence, free and unfree. It is in its familial dimension, however, that the Carolina migration greatly differed from pre-Revocation Huguenot transatlantic migrations. Compared to Choquette's estimated gender ratio of one woman to four men among Protestant migrants to New France, a proportion significantly lower than the one to eight for all migrants, the Carolina gender ratio of 1 to 1.51, or less than one woman to two men, appears much more balanced.[177] This contrast reflects the unusual nature of the Carolina migration, which, despite its undeniable economic component, was nonetheless born out of religious necessity.

A comparison of the Huguenot immigration to Carolina with the English migrations to the Chesapeake and New England in the seventeenth century further highlights its hybrid nature in revealing common characteristics with both. In the Chesapeake, James Horn noted the predominantly urban origin of the settlers (about 60 percent), a feature also found in the Carolina Huguenot group. He also stressed the extreme geographic concentration of these urban migrants, who came from a limited number of cities, namely London, Bristol, and Norwich.[178] Except for a lower proportion of esquires, the occupational profile and socioeconomic stratification of the Carolina Huguenots also resemble those of the free Chesapeake settlers. Horn found that slightly more than a fourth of the latter were merchants and a third were artisans, a tenth of those in textiles. With respectively 22, 30, and 8.5 percent, the Carolina migration offers similar proportions.[179]

The similarities stop there, however, for in the proportion of servants and in the gender as well as familial profiles of the migrants, the Huguenot immigration to Carolina instead mirrors the great Puritan migration. Virginia Anderson found that 14 percent of the migrants who came to New England in the 1630s did so as servants, a figure close to the 17 percent calculated for the Carolina Huguenots. Anderson also determined that nine out of ten New England immigrants settled in family groups and that three out of four came in nuclear family units.[180] Conversely, Horn stressed the role of kinship in the decision to migrate to the Chesapeake but noted that the overwhelming majority of the Chesapeake migrants were single.[181] Although not as high as for the Puritan migration, the proportions of Huguenots who traveled with kin and within nuclear families, respectively 43 and 46 percent, make the Carolina migration much closer to the New England pattern than that of the Chesapeake. Similarly, with 151, the Carolina Huguenot gender ratio is more in line with the New England figure of 132 than with the ratio of 239 calculated by Horn for the free migrants of the Chesapeake.[182]

In short, beyond its own specificities, the Huguenot immigration to Carolina resembles the Chesapeake migration in terms of geographic and social recruitment, but its familial structure and its balanced gender ratio are reminiscent of the Puritan migration to New England. Clearly, though, and somewhat unsurprisingly, in many of its aspects it followed Huguenot pre-Revocation transatlantic migration patterns. Its religious dimension and its suddenness, however, set it apart from earlier migrations to French America and definitely anchor it within the wider post-Revocation Huguenot exodus.

Jacques Le Moyne de Morgues, *Brevis Narratio Eorum Quae in Florida. . .* , plate 6, *Gallorum Praefectus columnam. . .* , in Theodore De Bry, *Great Voyages, America part II*, (Frankfort, 1591). This engraving shows the Port Royal region, where Jean Ribault founded Charlesfort in 1562 and erected a column bearing the arms of France, which can be seen on the small island on the left. Courtesy of Special Collections, College of Charleston Library, Charleston, South Carolina.

Carte Particulière de la Caroline by Nicolas Sanson (*Le Neptune François*, Paris, 1696). This map is a translation of the Thornton-Morden map (ca. 1695). The John Carter Brown Library at Brown University.

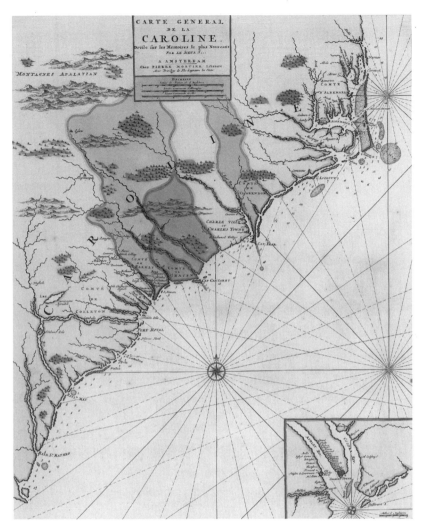

Carte Générale de la Caroline by Nicolas Sanson (*Le Neptune François*, Paris, 1696). This map is based on the Morton-Morden-Lea map (ca. 1685). The John Carter Brown Library at Brown University.

NOUVELLE
RELATION
de la
CAROLINE
PAR

Un Gentil-homme François arrivé,
depuis deux mois, de ce nou-
veau pais.

Où il parle de la route qu'il faut tenir
pour y aller le plus sûrement, &
de l'état où il a trouvé cette
Nouvelle contrée.

A LA HAYE.
Chez MEYNDERT UYTWEFF
Marchand Libraire de Meurant
dans le Gortftraet.

Front cover of *Nouvelle Relation de la Caroline par un Gentilhomme François* (The Hague, 1686). The John Carter Brown Library at Brown University.

Hanover House. This plantation was built by Paul de St. Julien ca. 1716. Threatened with demolition, it was moved from its original location in St. John's Parish, Berkeley County, to Clemson University in 1941. On one chimney is inscribed *"Peu à peu"* in reference to the French proverb *Peu à peu* [or *petit à petit*] *l'oiseau fait son nid* meaning "Little by little the bird builds its nest." Photograph courtesy of Historic American Building Survey, Library of Congress.

Middleburg Plantation, Berkeley County, South Carolina. The nucleus of this plantation, named after the capital of the Dutch province of Zeeland, was built by Huguenot Benjamin Simons in 1697 along the East Branch of the Cooper River. Photograph courtesy of Ray Timmons.

Church of St. James Goose Creek, Berkeley County, South Carolina. St. James, Goose Creek was one of the ten original Anglican (Episcopalian) parishes founded by the Act of Establishment of 1706. Francis LeJau served this congregation from 1706 to 1717. The church was completed around 1714. *Charleston, South Carolina, 1883.* Courtesy of Special Collections, College of Charleston Library, South Carolina.

Church of St. James Santee, Charleston County, South Carolina. St. James, Santee, then located in Craven County, was one of the original ten Anglican (Episcopalian) parishes founded by the Act of Establishment of 1706. The church shown on the photograph was built in 1768. Photograph courtesy of Gene Waddell.

Inset from *Carte de la Louisiane et du Cours du Mississippi Dressée sur un grand nombre de Mémoires* [Map of Louisiana and the Course of the Mississippi Drawn from a large Number of Reports] (1718) by Guillaume De L'Isle (1675–1726). This map was meant to advance the French cause in North America against Spanish and British interests by exaggerating recent, ancient, and imaginary French territorial claims. On the inset one can read "Caroline ainsi nommée en l'honneur de Charles 9 par les François qui la découvrirent, en prirent possession et s'y établirent" [Carolina thus named by the French who discovered it, claimed it and settled it] and "CharlesTown *nommé par les François* Charlesfort" [Charleston named by the French Charlesfort]. Near Santé (Santee) one can also read "Bourg des François Refugiez." Courtesy of Special Collections, College of Charleston Library, Charleston, South Carolina.

Hampton Plantation, St. James Santee, Charleston County, South Carolina. This plantation was originally the home of the Horry family. The core of the house dates from ca. 1735, but its present exterior dates primarily from ca. 1790 (with wings and portico added and the center enlarged). Photograph courtesy of Historic American Building Survey, Library of Congress.

Charleston Huguenot or "French" Church, Charleston, South Carolina. The Charleston Huguenot congregation was founded in the early 1680s and a first church was built by 1687. The present building, the fifth on this site, was designed by Edward Brickell White and erected in 1845. Photograph courtesy of Historic American Building Survey, Library of Congress.

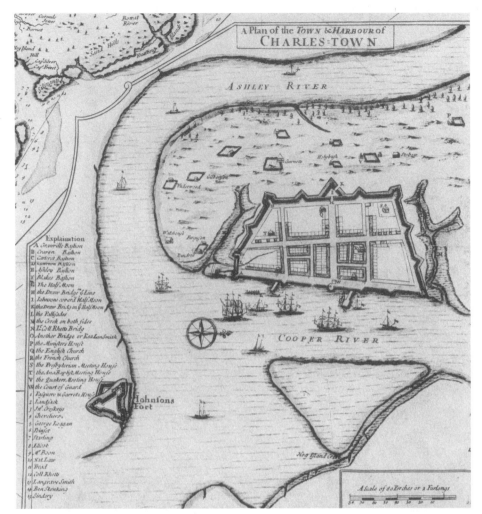

A Plan of the Town and Harbour of Charles Town, inset from *A Compleat Description of the Province of Carolina in 3 parts . . .* (1711) by Edward Crisp. The inset represents Charles Town with its walls and shows the location of the "French" [Huguenot] Church, designated as Q. in the legend. Courtesy of Special Collections, College of Charleston Library, Charleston, South Carolina.

The Joseph Manigault House, Charleston, South Carolina (1803). Designed by architect Gabriel Manigault for his brother Joseph, the Manigault House is a beautiful example of Adams-style or Federal architecture. The Manigaults came from La Rochelle. Courtesy of the Historic American Building Survey, Library of Congress.

Pompion [pronounced "pumpkin"] Hill Chapel, Berkeley County, South Carolina (1763). Located on the former site of a small cypress church a stone's throw from Middleburg Plantation, this chapel was built with bricks supplied by Huguenot Zachariah Villepontoux and served as a chapel of ease for parishioners of St. Thomas and St. Denis. Photograph taken in 1940. Courtesy of the Historic American Building Survey, Library of Congress.

—————

Chapter 5

The Founding Era

Carolina Huguenot Religious Life before 1700

If ethnic and religious groups are to sustain themselves, they must do so as purely voluntary associations. This means that they are more at risk from the indifference of their own members than from the intolerance of the others.

Michael Walzer, *On Toleration* (1997)

God gave me the Blessing of coming out of France, and Escaping the Cruel Persecution carried on there against the Protestants and to express my Thanksgiving for so great a Blessing, I promise, please God, to observe the Anniversary of that by a Fast.

Étienne Mazyck, Bible records (fall 1685)

Reflections on a Thorny Issue

Anglican conformity, or the fact that most Huguenots chose to become members of the Church of England instead of remaining Calvinists, is often perceived as the most striking feature of the Huguenots' settlement in proprietary South Carolina. The main phases of this episode are well known. The French first founded Calvinist congregations in Charleston, Santee, Orange Quarter, Goose Creek, and later Wantoot, but when the Church of England was established in 1706, the rural communities disintegrated or joined the Carolina Anglican parish network while the Charleston congregation, the only one actually able to do so, opted for Nonconformity. That year Santee became St. James Santee and the Orange Quarter became St. Denis; Wantoot was absorbed into St. John's Berkeley and Goose Creek into St. James Goose Creek. In the following decades Charleston Huguenots individually drifted to St. Philip's, the city's only Anglican parish until 1751, while, except for a brief period in the mid-1710s, rural Huguenots gradually adopted more thoroughly Anglican practices and lost the use of French as a liturgical language. Finally, by midcentury, Calvinism had ceased to be a distinctive trait of the refugees and of their descendants. These events are well-known, but the context, reasons, meaning, and pace with which this transformation occurred need further examination in the light of the Huguenot experience in France, England, and other North American colonies.

Conformity must not be confused with conversion since the Church of England, although episcopalian in character and in polity, was in essence a Protestant church, that is, in the eyes of the Huguenots, one born of the Reformation. Conformity must also be studied as a religious *and* political issue with a socioeconomic dimension and not merely as a question of religion. Considering the early Carolina political context, the adoption of Anglicanism was the quasi-inevitable religious counterpart of the Huguenots' political ascendancy, but it also revealed deep socioeconomic divisions within the refugee community.[1] Conformity also needs to be approached in a comparative context. This phenomenon was not unique to South Carolina but occurred—albeit at a different pace—within all the refugee communities dispersed throughout the Anglo-American world. The roots of Carolina Anglican conformity are buried in Restoration England and, to a lesser extent, in France. Furthermore, this religious shift, seemingly swift in its occurrence and radical in its character, was actually the result of a gradual process with gains, compromises, and temporary setbacks. This process reached its completion over a relatively long period of time, some forty years, and met with significant resistance. Anglican conformity also poses a problem of interpretation in the larger issue of the integration of the Huguenots into early Carolina society. Was it the result of ethno-religious disintegration due to an unusual lack of group cohesiveness or the inevitable consequence of a successful adaptation to an inescapable New World religious environment?

Robert M. Kingdon, who published two articles on the issue of Huguenot conformity in British North America, identified six reasons that led the refugees to abandon their Calvinism for the Church of England: financial security, socioeconomic promotion, political ambition, gratitude, Erastianism (that is, the strong lay influence within the Church of England in the colonies), and the belief in the flexibility of the ecclesiology of a true Christian church.[2] This interpretation is insightful yet incomplete.

The difficulty and the cost of recruiting and maintaining French-speaking Calvinist pastors forced rural Huguenot communities to seek Anglican assistance. Had the London Threadneedle Street Church been more attentive to their needs, these isolated congregations would most likely have remained independent, at least through the middle of the eighteenth century. Yet, when the Santee community, for example, sought to become an Anglican parish *before* the 1706 Church Act was passed by the provincial assembly, Santee had a church and a pastor and was in no apparent financial or spiritual distress.

It is also true that conformity reflected a social cleavage within the Huguenot group as the mercantile and landed elite saw it as a means to acquire a higher status within Anglo-American Carolina society. Yet, this does not explain why the Charleston Huguenots, the wealthiest and most Anglicized refugees in the colony, opted for Nonconformity, at least collectively. The aspiration to play a role in local politics was certainly a factor, but even in South Carolina, let alone in colonies such as Massachusetts and New York, siding with the Anglican faction was not necessarily, at least in the early 1700s, the surest means to exert political dominance.

Some Huguenots, especially among the elite, most likely felt gratitude toward the Church of England, notably its episcopal hierarchy, which had been instrumental in providing them with financial assistance during their stay in England. But even to these Huguenots, conformity meant much more. The Church of England offered them a venue in which they could best express the deep sense of monarchistic allegiance that they all shared and which they could no longer feel toward Louis XIV. Conformity provided them with invaluable compensation for the post-Revocation loss of their legitimate monarch.

In the colonies a strong lay influence, coupled with the absence of a residing bishop, made the Church of England as little episcopalian as possible and most likely facilitated conformity. Yet this Huguenot attraction to Low Church ecclesiastical flexibility seemingly contradicts the fact that, in the case of the pastoral leadership especially, it was precisely the need for an episcopal structure that led them into the Anglican fold. Additionally, the apparent indifference with which Huguenot refugees regarded religious institutions seems actually to have been the expression of a certain religious pragmatism rather than complete indifference. Conformity was, at least in South Carolina, essentially a practical response to new challenges brought about by the dispersion and the transatlantic migration. The sudden loss of traditional ecclesiastical structures, which turned out to be difficult to reconstruct in the New World, led the Huguenots literally to seek an environment in which they could best live—albeit somewhat secretly or at least internally—their Calvinism. As odd and surprising as it may sound, this is precisely what some Huguenots hoped to achieve within the colonial Church of England. This observation in turn leads to the puzzling question of why these refugees did not attempt to merge with one of the Carolina dissenting churches whose polity was more in conformity with their Calvinist beliefs. The answer probably lies contrapuntally in the reasons that made the Church of England so attractive to them. In other words, the Anglicans had more to offer, at least in the eyes of most refugees, than did the Congregationalists or the Presbyterians.

Other factors more specifically related to the context of early Carolina, such as the activism of the Society for the Propagation of the Gospel (SPG), the personality of the early Huguenot pastors, the geographic and spiritual isolation of the rural congregations, the dynamics within and between the Huguenot settlements, and the colony's political balance, also came into play. All things considered, the key to understanding the complex and contradictory issue of Huguenot Anglican conformity is to remember that, as diverse as they were, the refugees followed different paths to the Church of England. What appealed to some appalled others and vice versa. Therefore, beyond a necessary and enlightening contextualization, it is in its individual and idiosyncratic dimension that conformity can best be approached.

Huguenot Religious Life in Pre-Revocation France

French Reformed churches are Protestant churches of Calvinist inspiration with a synodical (that is, presbyterian) polity.[3] The two founding documents of French Protestantism are the *Confession de Foi* (Confession of Faith) and the *Discipline des Églises réformées de France* (Discipline of the French Reformed Churches), both drafted and adopted in 1559 at the underground national synod held in Paris.[4] The *Confession* contains the fundamental beliefs and principles of the Huguenot faith, whereas the *Discipline* defines the organizational structure of the French Reformed churches from the congregation to the national synod, the mission of their institutional members, and the rules of conduct of their followers.[5]

The Huguenot Confession of Faith (*Confessio Gallicana*), which served as a model for the Scottish Confession of 1560 (*Scotica*) and the Dutch Confession of 1561 (*Belgica*), was inspired by but not identical to Calvin's *Institution of the Christian Religion,* which was first published in French in 1541.[6] This document, divided into forty articles, comprises fundamental Reformed and Calvinist tenets such as the preeminence of the Bible (*sola scriptura*) and the word of God (sermon), justification or salvation by faith alone (*sola fide*), double and symmetrical predestination (the concept of election), the two sacraments (baptism and Communion), and the priesthood of all believers. It therefore unequivocally refutes basic Catholic practices and beliefs such as processions; pilgrimages; the five other sacraments (confirmation, marriage, penitence, ordination, and the last rites), which the New Rochelle—and previously Charleston—minister Pierre Stouppe, not without a touch of irony, dubbed "les cinq prétendus sacrements";[7] the intercession of saints; purgatory; the cult of images; apostolic succession; and papal legitimacy.[8]

The *Discipline,* which is divided into 275 articles grouped in fourteen chapters in its 1666 version, was originally inspired by Calvin's *Ordonnances Ecclésiastiques,* issued in Geneva in 1541. It created a hybrid ecclesiastical structure, technically known in French as *presbytéro-synodal,* halfway between congregationalism, which gives complete autonomy to the congregation, and Presbyterianism, which emphasizes synodical hierarchy.[9]

The local church, or *église,* is at the center of Huguenot religious life. In 1660 there were nearly seven hundred congregations varying greatly in nature (urban, rural, northern, southern, wealthy, poor, for example) and in size, with populations ranging from fewer than a hundred to a few thousand. The Church of La Rochelle, from which many Carolina Huguenots hailed, boasted a membership of nearly five thousand people, and the church in Nîmes, home of Jean Aunant, numbered more than ten thousand. Conversely, the Tours congregation, home of the Bacot and Royer families, was less than a thousand strong. Vitré, where the Ravenels, St. Juliens, and DuBourdieus came from, had a Huguenot population of under two hundred.[10]

Each of these congregations was run by a board called a consistory (*consistoire* or *compagnie*). Presided over by a pastor, the consistory, that "quintessential Calvinistic institution," as Glenn Sunshine notes, was in theory composed of the apostolic number of twelve elders (*anciens*). Some churches were large enough also to have deacons (*diacres*), who were specifically in charge of poor relief.[11] With one-third of them renewed through co-optation (appointment) every two or three years at Easter, the elders played an essential role in the daily life of the congregation.[12] They maintained the church building and land (which belonged to the consistory); administered the funds of the congregation; submitted requests to the regional synod and enforced its decisions; paid the state and (Catholic) church taxes; collected the members' subscriptions; posted marriage banns; set the time for church services; kept the church records; paid and accommodated the pastor; hired the church personnel (the cantor [*chantre*], the reader [*lecteur*], and the sexton [*concierge*]); assisted the poor; and, most important, exerted moral supervision over the congregation's members.[13]

This last function gave the elders tremendous responsibilities since the consistory literally played the role of a court of morality. Elders were supposed to report Sabbath breakers of all sorts as well as Huguenots who did not attend service, drank at the local tavern, played cards, danced, blasphemed, behaved violently, dressed without modesty, or, more seriously, broke the Ten Commandments.[14] Offenders were heard by the consistory in front of which they had to confess their deviant behavior and make amends, sometimes in front of the entire congregation. Often consistories temporarily suspended offenders from the Lord's Supper by refusing to give them a *méreau,* the token that communicants had to show the elders before receiving Communion. In some extreme and rare cases, such as apostasy, offenders were excommunicated from the church, sometimes permanently. The former sentence was called *suspension* and the latter *excommunication.*[15] This distinction, as Raymond Mentzer explains, corresponded to the medieval church's differentiation between minor and major excommunication.[16] Consistories also played an essential role in preserving social harmony in the community through the settlement of marital disputes and conflicts between parishioners and, in some instances, by hearing civil cases before they reached royal and seignorial courts.[17]

Although the appointment of new elders had to be approved by the congregation, renewal by co-optation and the high level of literacy that their functions required led consistory members to be disproportionately from the nobility and the bourgeoisie, especially in the seventeenth century. In the Languedoc Church of Saint-Jean-du-Gard, nearly 70 percent of the ninety-eight elders appointed between 1663 and 1685 were nobles, merchants, or professionals.[18] In Poitou nearly all seventeenth-century church consistories counted two nobles. In Vitré half the elders belonged to the wealthiest and most prominent families, including the Ravenels, and in Nantes consistorial appointments were almost exclusively held by merchants.[19]

Along with the consistory, the pastor was the other central element of the congregation. Although a significant proportion of pastors were trained in Geneva and Leiden, most Huguenot ministers studied in the five French Protestant académies of Saumur, Sedan, Montauban, Nîmes, and Dié. Interestingly, however, two of the early Charleston pastors, Élie Prioleau and Paul L'Escot, were not trained in France but in Geneva.[20] Prospective pastors pursued a demanding curriculum that included four years of philosophy and metaphysics followed by three to four years of theology, Hebrew, and Greek, with most classes conducted in Latin.[21] Graduates, called *proposants,* were then examined by the synods of their provinces of origin before being appointed to churches. The proposant was asked to read a sermon, to comment on biblical passages in Greek and Hebrew, and to answer questions in philosophy. If successful, he then had to conduct services before his future congregation on three successive Sundays, without being authorized to administer Communion or celebrate marriages. If the congregation showed satisfaction, usually by remaining silent, the proposant was eventually inducted by the elders in front of the parishioners and bore the title M.D.St.E. (*Ministre du Saint Évangile* / Minister of the Holy Gospel). The name of Pierre Robert, Santee's first minister, for example, bears these initials in the 1697 Carolina naturalization list.[22] Newly appointed pastors, who were in their early twenties, were not supposed to change congregations and thus remained for decades officiating in the same churches.[23] Samuel Prioleau, the father of South Carolina Huguenot Élie Prioleau ministered the Pons congregation for thirty-two years until his death in 1683.[24] Pastors were usually men of comfortable means born in pastoral dynasties. As Jaques Fontaine put it, "I had been dedicated to the holy ministry before I was conceived."[25] Unsurprisingly, the familial backgrounds and environments of Charleston's first ministers were pastoral. Élie Prioleau's father, Samuel; grandfather Élizée; and maternal uncle Élie Merlat as well as Florent-Philippe Trouillart's father and brother, both named Pierre, were all pastors.[26]

Ministers, who were lodged for free and whose taxes were paid by the congregations but who could not charge for performing ceremonies, received on average an annual income ranging from three hundred (forty pounds sterling) to nine hundred livres (seventy pounds sterling).[27] In Vitré, for example, home of several Carolina Huguenots, the pastor's salary was five hundred livres (thirty-eight pounds sterling).[28] Until the Peace of Alès (1629), the crown financially assisted Huguenot congregations as stipulated in the Edict of Nantes, but when royal funds became scarce, consistories had to rely increasingly on the subscriptions, called *cotisations* or "*cottizes,*" of the members, who were also subject to the Catholic tithe (*dîme*).[29] As the seventeenth century progressed, smaller churches, which suffered from a decline in membership, were often short of revenue, and the nonpayment of arrears led to conflicts between congregations and their pastors.[30]

The minister's foremost task was to write and read inspiring, elaborate, and edifying sermons. Preaching, sometimes dubbed "the third sacrament," was the focal point of the French Reformed service.[31] Huguenot sermons, which were always in French and lasted an average of ninety minutes each, followed a strict format divided into four sections: introduction or exordium (*exorde*), commentary of biblical verses (*explication*), practical lessons (*application*), and conclusion or peroration (*péroraison*).[32] Pastors almost exclusively based their sermons on the Bible, usually the 1588 Geneva edition, and Clément Marot and Theodore de Beza's 1561–62 French translation of the Psalms, and they rarely quoted from ecclesiastical authors.[33] Seventeenth-century French Reformed sermons centered on themes such as salvation (election, predestination), religion in daily life (faith, prayers, fear of God), penitence (afflictions, fasting), and Jesus' ministry (Jesus' sacrifice, nativity).[34] Ministers preached every Sunday, generally twice, and once during the week, on Wednesdays or Thursdays. They also administered Communion four times during the year (Easter, Whit Sunday, Christmas, and early in the fall) on two or three consecutive Sundays to include all the members of the congregation, performed baptisms, and celebrated marriages.[35]

Baptism was not regarded in the Huguenot discipline as a necessary condition for salvation in cases of death in infancy. A newborn, even if sick, therefore was not systematically baptized immediately after birth, as in the Catholic Church, but instead on the following Sunday.[36] Children were baptized after the main service by the pastor, who followed a standard procedure detailed in the discipline.[37] Although not indispensable, godparents, who had to be at least fourteen years old, were present at the ceremony. In Catholic France, Huguenots stood out for choosing Old Testament names for their children, especially boys, although these tended to be less common in the seventeenth century. In pre-Revocation Poitou they represented about 15 percent of the names, which corresponded to the national trend. As a rule, Old Testament names were more prevalent in northern than southern France and in communities located in predominantly Catholic regions for which name-giving patterns were ways to assert their Huguenot identity. For the same reasons, Old Testament names became even less common but more meaningful in post-Revocation France.[38] Although not regarded as a sacrament, marriages were also celebrated on Sundays, following formal betrothals and the publication of the banns during three consecutive weeks prior to the ceremony.[39] Conversely, the discipline prohibited funeral services and Huguenots had to be buried with modesty and simplicity. In typical fashion, the Carolina refugee Pierre Bertrand requested a burial "without any display or expense whatsoever" and Arnaud Bruneau de La Chabocière, although an écuyer, "with the least ceremony and the utmost simplicity."[40] Pastors sometimes, especially in the seventeenth century, accompanied the corteges to the cemeteries, but prayers were explicitly intended for the living only.[41]

At the request of the provincial or national synods, consistories and pastors could also order days of fasting. The objective was to alleviate collective anxiety caused by bad weather conditions, crop failures, epidemics, or waves of persecution. During those days work was prohibited and the members of the congregation had to attend three services centered on long and detailed sermons, pray together intensely and with humility, and fast until the last service was over.[42] In addition to conducting public worship and performing ceremonies, pastors were supposed to catechize children and adults once a week before Communion, using Calvin's 1541 catechism, and visit the sick and the old.[43] Fontaine explains that his father, pastor at Vaux-sur-Mer, near Royan, Saintonge, "visited each family in his congregation twice a year, poor as well as rich, in order to know their spiritual state . . . never fail[ing] to visit the sick and afflicted."[44]

Although attendance at church services is of primary importance, French Protestantism also stresses private worship, both personal (*culte personnel*) and familial (*culte domestique*). Huguenots were supposed to live their faith by reading and meditating on sermons, which were available in published collections, chapters from the Bible, and diverse books designed to prepare them for Communion and death. They also recited morning and evening prayers and the Apostle's Creed, said Grace before (*benedicite*) and after (*grâces*) meals, and sang psalms.[45] Psalm singing at church, work, and home; in the streets; and even on the battlefield was also an essential and distinctive aspect of Huguenot religious life in Catholic France, at least until it became increasingly restricted and eventually banned through a series of royal arrêts in the early 1660s. Following Calvin, Huguenots fervently believed in the spiritual dimension of individual and communal singing, through which they expressed their faith in immediacy with God.[46] Psalters, which contained a list directing the reader to the most appropriate psalm for each occasion, were available in a multitude of formats, sizes, editions, and prices from Huguenot booksellers.[47]

Although the Calvinist Reformation removed the sacred aura from the church building, Huguenot congregational life nonetheless centered around the church or *temple*.[48] The latter term, which referred to the biblical Temple of Jerusalem, was applied to Huguenot churches to distinguish them from *églises,* which became reserved for Catholic houses of worship.[49] Never in the shape of a cross, temples were rectangular, octagonal, or circular with cut-off corners. Each edifice was usually topped with a bell, sometimes a clock, and always built with modesty and simplicity.[50] Surrounded by a short wall, the glebe included the presbytery, called *consistoire* like the board of elders, where the consistory met in cold winter days and which housed the library (when the congregation was rich enough to own one), the sexton's house, the cemetery, a well, and a small park.[51] The inside of the temple, which never housed an organ, was sober with plain whitewashed walls and no images or statues and only the Decalogue as decoration. The pulpit, along with a table for Communion services, the cantor's lectern, and the elders' pews, was centrally placed at the far end of the church in a slightly elevated and strictly delimited area called *parquet.*[52] Rows of pews were arranged, sometimes in the shape of an amphitheater, on each side of an aisle, with women and men usually sitting separately and nobles and officials, all wearing headdresses, placed in the front. Larger temples, usually fitted with galleries, such as those of Charenton (where the Parisian Huguenot community worshipped), La Rochelle, and Dieppe, could seat from three thousand to five thousand people.[53]

While the discipline explicitly stipulated that each church was equal to the others, it nonetheless provided for a three-tiered hierarchy of appellate assemblies whose decisions *had* to be implemented by the congregations.[54] At the lower level stood the *colloque* (or *classes*), which grouped from five to twenty neighboring churches, depending on the density of the local Huguenot population and the size of the province, and to which each church had to send its minister (one of them if they were served by several) and an elder. Colloques, which were supposed to meet at least twice a year, set the geographical limits of the parishes, supervised ministers and elders, and settled disputes arising between two churches, a pastor and his congregation (these being typically of a financial nature), and parishioners and their consistories.[55]

At the next level, provincial synods, which represented from one to eight colloques, met annually, or every two years in regions where Protestantism was numerically and structurally weaker, and always in the presence of a royal commissaire. After the conquest of Béarn in 1620, Huguenot France was divided into sixteen synodical provinces. The unequal distribution of Protestants across the kingdom inevitably led to great disparities between these entities. Synodical provinces such as Saintonge-Aunis-Angoumois (with 93,500 Huguenots), Poitou (with 78,000), and Dauphiny (with 77,500) dwarfed Brittany and Provence, which had much smaller Protestant populations (3,500 and 8,000, respectively).[56] Regional synods, to which each church was expected to send the (or a) pastor and two elders, judged on appeal disputes that had been heard by the colloques, examined and appointed ministers, planned days of fasting, and took decisions regarding colleges and the académie (if there was one in the province) and the enforcement of the discipline.[57] Fontaine gives the example of a provincial synod that removed a minister from a church that had failed to pay him for five years, forcing the congregation to live without a minister for a year.[58] Because national synods met less and less frequently, especially after the 1620s, provincial synods truly became the backbone of Huguenot institutional life.

National synods, to which each synodical province was to send two ministers and two elders, in theory were to be held annually until 1598 and then every three years, but they actually met infrequently and only on royal permission until banned by the monarchy after 1659.[59] They essentially served as the highest appellate assembly for a variety of disputes and took paramount decisions regarding theology and ecclesiastical practices that were to be enforced in all synodical provinces.[60] In 1644, for example, delegates of the national synod reprimanded churches in the La Rochelle area for displaying too much independence, which they perceived as a sign of Congregationalist deviance that could threaten the stability of the French Reformed churches.[61] More fundamentally, the Alès national synod of 1620 adopted the canons promulgated at the Dutch national synod held at Dort in 1618–19. The Dort position reaffirmed Calvinist orthodoxy regarding predestination and rejected the belief, known as Arminianism after the late sixteenth-century Dutch theologian Jacobus Arminius, that grace could be lost by God's elect.[62] Despite the 1620 Alès synodical decision, however, an Arminian current developed within the French Reformed churches. This current was centered at the Saumur académie, where Moyse Amyrault (1596–1664), one of the most Arminian of Huguenot theologians, taught. Successive national synods therefore had to condemn pro-Arminian teachings and publications repeatedly.[63]

The repressive royal policy carried out from the 1660s to the early 1680s and the Revocation asphyxiated Huguenot collective religious life by annihilating its ecclesiastical structure, and the dispersal forced the refugees to re-create their church institutions in a foreign environment. In countries and cities where previous Walloon and Huguenot migrations had occurred, such as the Netherlands, England, Geneva, and Frankfurt, refugees of the 1680s found Francophone Calvinist ecclesiastical structures to welcome them. In other locations, such as Brandenburg, Ireland, South Africa, and British North America, the Huguenots, however, had to organize their churches ex nihilo. The capacity to reconstruct an institutionalized Calvinist church life, as identical as possible to the one they had enjoyed in pre-Revocation France, turned out to be the indispensable initial condition to the Huguenots' long-term religious survival in South Carolina.

Foundation and Early History of the Lowcountry Huguenot Churches

Although individual Huguenots settled throughout the Carolina lowcountry in the proprietary period, most congregated in four distinct original communities: Charleston, Orange Quarter, and Goose Creek, all in Berkeley County; and Santee, in Craven County. Except for the tiny Goose Creek Church, which quickly collapsed, these Carolina Huguenot congregations, to which must be added Wantoot, a post-1690 offshoot of Santee from which originated the Anglican parish of St. John's Berkeley, stood the test of time.[64] Santee, Orange Quarter, and Wantoot remained active Calvinist communities at least until 1706 and Charleston, albeit intermittently, through most of the eighteenth century. Unfortunately, records are so scarce that not much is known about the time or the circumstances of the foundations of these early Carolina Huguenot churches nor about their early functioning. The few extant documents, however, offer precious glimpses into what the refugees' church organization must have been during what may be called the pre-Anglican period of Carolina Huguenot religious life. They indicate that the latter was undeniably patterned after pre-Revocation French Protestantism. Although their migration to South Carolina was unquestionably motivated by religious *and* economic incentives, the Huguenots endeavored to found Calvinist churches once they were in the colony. In the 1680s and 1690s Anglican conformity was a remote, almost unthinkable, alternative. During these years the Huguenots founded what was undoubtedly the best-structured church on the Carolina stage. The relatively sudden

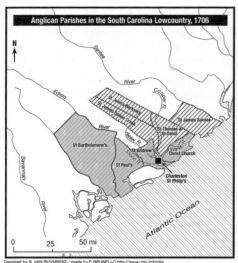

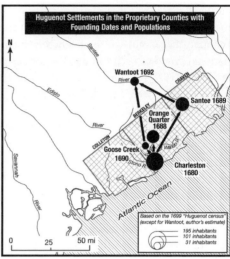

disintegration of this seemingly dynamic spiritual life, however, coupled with the simultaneous ascension of the Church of England, put an early end to this French Calvinist
experiment in colonial America.

The Genesis of the Charleston Huguenot Church

In 1699, with 195 refugees, or nearly 45 percent of the total Carolina Huguenot population, the Charleston French Church was by far the largest Huguenot congregation in the
lowcountry.[65] Despite its historical and demographic significance, the circumstances of
its foundation and its early history are shrouded in mystery. Incomplete records tell us
little about the building of the first temple or the founding of the congregation.[66]

In November 1684 Michael Loving, former servant of John and Affra Coming, con-
veyed town lot number 65, which had been granted to him in 1681, to Arthur
Middleton.[67] Three years later the same lot was sold for sixteen pounds sterling by Mary
Izard, Middleton's remarried widow, to a James Nicholls "for & on ye behalf of ye
Comonalty of the French Church in Charlestown," with the refugees Andrew (André)
Foucault, Jean-Adrien LeSerrurier, and J[acob] Guérard appearing among the witnesses.[68] A few months earlier, however, in December 1686, Jean-François Gignilliat and
Pastor Stephen (Estienne) Dusout received a warrant for "two Lotts in Charles Town
which are now deserted & comonly known by ye numbers of 92 & 93 . . . for ye building
of a Church in behalf of ye french Protestants of this Province."[69] The grant correspon-
ding to this warrant, however, was not issued until November 1701 to Henry LeNoble
and Pierre Buretel, who then represented the French congregation.[70] If the timing of
these acquisitions can be explained by the arrival in Charleston of the *Margaret* in April
1685, with the largest recorded number of Huguenot settlers on board, and possibly
another ship in 1686 or 1687, several questions surrounding the transactions need to be
elucidated. Who was this James Nicholls? Why did the French congregation almost

simultaneously acquire two locations for their church? Where and when was the first temple erected? Was James Nicholls an English settler who served as an intermediary between the Izards and the Charleston Huguenots, or is James Nicholls an Anglicized transcription of Jacques Nicholas (Nicolas)?

Although many Huguenots already owned land, the presence of an English settler, albeit odd, might be explained by the refugees' fear of having the transaction voided because of their foreign status. None of them had then been naturalized in the colony. This being said, it makes more sense to have a Huguenot take possession of the lots in the name of the French congregation. The fact that this Nicholls or Nicholas did not sign the deed removes an essential clue to his identification since Jacques Nicholas, a merchant from Saintonge, usually appeared in the records with his nickname Petitbois.[71] Nicholas had a house built in Charleston in April 1687 and witnessed a transaction between Noé Royer and Robert Skelton in March 1688, and he was also one of the witnesses to the Izard conveyance of lot 65 to the Huguenots. He could well have bought it for the congregation.[72] The question remains open, but the fact that no James Nicholls has been identified among early Carolina settlers gives credence to the Nicholas hypothesis.[73]

The question of why the Huguenots purchased a lot after receiving a warrant for two others is equally intriguing. Did the consistory have two locations in mind and disagree on which one to build a church? Were they unsure of getting a grant pursuant of their December 1686 warrant and therefore decided to purchase a lot themselves? These questions cannot be answered with certainty, but the fact that the grant for lots 92/93 was not issued until 1701, or five years after the warrant, and the Huguenots' decision to switch locations after a few years make these hypotheses equally plausible.

Records, approached chronologically, show that these lots, 65 and 92/93, correspond to two successive locations for the Charleston French Church. A first church building was most likely constructed soon after the Huguenots received the warrant for lots 92/93, as implied by a clause in François Macaire's December 1687 will stipulating that the testator be buried in the "churchyard of those of the [French] reformed Religion of this City."[74] The 1692 law, "An Act for the Better observance of the Lord's Day, commonly called Sunday," which attempted to arbitrarily regulate the hours of Huguenot services, collaterally evidences the existence of a French house of worship in Charleston by the early 1690s.[75] The list of town lot grants further confirms the existence of a cemetery on lot 91, adjacent to lots 92/93, and indicates that in March 1694 Antoine Boureau, then one of the elders, acquired lots 103/104, said in the grant to be located "south french church."[76] The following year Isaac and Marianne (LeSerrurier) Mazyck recorded in their Bible that their one-year-old daughter, Marianne, was interred "den le simetiere de lesglises françoises de Charleston" (in the cemetery of the Charleston French Church).[77] These references clearly establish that the Huguenots built a first house of worship on lots 92/93 between December 1686, when they received the warrant for the land, and June 1692, when the above-mentioned act was voted. The presence of a churchyard without a church building seems so odd and unlikely that it is reasonable to think that a church edifice had actually been constructed on this site before December 1687 when Macaire drew his will in fellow refugee Alexandre Pepin's house. The Huguenots, whose presence in Charleston had significantly increased with the arrival of the *Margaret* in

April 1685, would therefore have had a full year to build a temple. This was enough time, especially since, as Henry A. M. Smith wrote about the first Carolina Anglican church, this first Huguenot religious edifice was in all likelihood "a humble structure of logs in the true original colonial style."[78]

Sometime after 1695, possibly in 1696, however, the Huguenots chose to build a new church on lot 65, which they had originally acquired from the Izard widow back in May 1687.[79] This second church was also a wooden building, and as Pastor Paul L'Escot informs us in a 1701 letter, it was leveled by a hurricane in the summer of 1700 and replaced with a more durable brick structure in 1701 or 1702.[80] The switch to a more central location was probably motivated by the building of the fortifications, lot 65 being within the town walls, and by the fact that the new site was closer to the Cooper River at a time when roads were nonexistent and most settlers traveled along the waterways.[81]

In sum, it can safely be asserted that the Charleston Huguenots built a first church on lots 92/93 between December 1686 and December 1687 but then moved to lot 65 in 1696 and constructed another house of worship there.[82] The question remains as to why they bothered to file a grant for lots 92/93 in 1701 since they already had a church building in another location within the city. Perhaps the answer is that the Charleston Huguenot consistory simply formally acquired land as an asset for the community, as they would have done back in France.

Although a first temple was not built in Charleston until 1687, a Huguenot église (that is, congregation) was founded undoubtedly long before, most likely as early as 1680 when the first refugees landed on the peninsula.[83] Archival evidence of Huguenot congregational life in Charleston in the 1680s and 1690s is scanty at best but is enough to warrant the existence of a church following the French Calvinist model. On October 26, 1679, a few weeks before the planned departure of the *Richmond,* the promoter Jacob Guérard went before the consistory of the London Threadneedle Street Church explaining that "he was about to leave for Carolina with several families" and that his intention was to "found a church thither." Guérard consequently hoped that the consistory would "recommend him a pastor" and "assist the future congregation with his salary for a while." Although the Threadneedle Street Church elders "prayed God that He blessed [Guérard's] endeavour" and "assured him that they would be very content to be able to assist him," they deemed that, "considering the [financial?] state of their church they could do or promise nothing to that effect."[84] Curiously, however, judging from the *Richmond* first passenger list of October 15, 1679, which features a "Forestier, minister," Guérard had already recruited a pastor before being received by the London church consistory.[85] Did Guérard and Petit wish to have a pastor on each of the two ships that were supposed to take the group to Carolina? This is not inconceivable as pastoral presence was deemed essential to alleviate the passengers' collective fear of the oceanic unknown. Or did they simply want two ministers for a hoped-to-be large Charleston congregation? Forestier may have been the student in theology from Béziers, Languedoc, who repented his two-year-old apostasy before the Threadneedle Street Church consistory in September 1679. He does not, however, seem to have served the Charleston congregation if he ever crossed the Atlantic.[86] The difficulty that the *Richmond* promoters experienced when recruiting a pastor should not appear surprising as there were few ministers among the refugees before the intensification of the persecution in the early 1680s and the Revocation. Before then they tended to stay among their beleaguered parishioners to help them cope with adversity until the congregations were eventually disbanded.

Consequently, as Guérard probably feared, the Charleston congregation remained without pastoral leadership for two years from the spring of 1680, when the *Richmond* landed in Carolina, to the fall of 1682, when Laurentius Van den Bosch arrived in Charleston. Although uncomfortable, this ministerial void was certainly not an insurmountable obstacle for Calvinists who hailed from an increasingly hostile Catholic environment. In France small rural congregations in predominantly Catholic regions made do with episodic service from pastors from larger churches, and other congregations were deprived of pastoral guidance due to the post-1660 legislation. These congregations survived without a pastor at least until the Revocation and in some cases beyond. During these two years without ministerial guidance, the Charleston Huguenot Church was most likely informally organized. The congregation probably met in the open or in somebody's house, and whoever had some reliable knowledge of the scriptures performed services using a Bible, a psalter, and perhaps a book of sermons.

In his September 1683 letter, Louis Thibou informed his correspondent that his Carolina-born son Jacob was "présenté au baptême" by the captain of a French warship.[87] The published abstract of Jacob's 1741 will reveals that he was born on February 12, 1683, and baptized less than a month later, on March 10, by Joseph Harrison, "minister of the Gospell," with "Captn Gardarat and Mrs Susanna Varin, God father and God Mother."[88] Nothing is known about this Harrison, who was probably a Dissenting minister, since Atkin Williamson and Phineas Rogers are the only Anglican clergymen known to be in Carolina by 1683, the former arriving in the colony in April 1679 and the latter in October 1682.[89] It is puzzling, to say the least, that Thibou had Harrison baptize his son since the Charleston Huguenot Church was then ministered by Van den Bosch. Was it because the latter had received the Anglican ordination or because the congregation was then involved in a financial dispute with him? Did Van den Bosch charge for baptismal ceremonies contrary to the requirements of the Huguenot discipline? Was the church divided over whether or not to retain Van den Bosch, and was Thibou among his opponents? It is equally intriguing that Thibou chose a visiting sea captain of Louis XIV's navy as godfather to his son instead of a member of the community, such as, for example, Jacques Varin, Suzanne's husband, whom he mentions in his letter.[90] As for the officer, he may have been a Huguenot, which was entirely possible before the Revocation; a new convert; or even, although less likely, a moderate Catholic able to transcend French religious boundaries. Beyond its confusing context, Jacob Thibou's baptism significantly reveals that the Charleston Huguenot Church coped with pastoral difficulties by punctually hiring a minister from an English dissenting church.

With the arrival of the pastors Florent-Philippe Trouillart on board the *Margaret* in 1685 and Élie Prioleau two years later, the Charleston Huguenot Church became a durable feature on the Carolina religious scene. The fact that it was served by two pastors, as an urban church would be back in France, suggests that it was, at least in the late 1680s and early 1690s, a fairly large congregation. The act of 1692, which attempted to impose strict hours for Huguenot worship and which thereby showed that the size of the

French Church there was regarded as threatening by other Charleston denominations, incidentally reveals that the congregation functioned as it would in France, with morning and afternoon services every Sunday.[91] A letter of grievances addressed to the Lords Proprietors by the Huguenots as a result of this adversary act is known to historians only through the subsequent proprietary instructions to the Grand Council and the proprietors' answer to the French, but it shows that they rightly considered the law as a frontal attack on their religious privileges. The episode indicates that the Charleston Huguenot Church catered to refugees living up the Cooper River since the consistory complained specifically that the new law would prevent these parishioners from attending services due to the unpredictable tides. As the proprietors explained to the Carolina authorities, "[to] begin their Divine Worshipp at the Same time that the English doe is Inconvenient to them [the French] in Regard that Severall of their Congregation Liveing out of the Towne are forced to Come and Goe by water, And for ye Conveniency of such they begin their Divine Worshipp Earlyer or Later as the tide serves."[92]

A close look at the Huguenots to whom the proprietary missive was addressed and who, by inference, can be identified as the authors of the letter of complaints, evidences the existence of a typically French Calvinist consistory.[93] The list of addressees appearing at the bottom of the document shows "Mr Trouillard Minister" followed by "Mr. Buretell Ancien, Mr. Jacques [Le]Serrurier Ancien, Mr [B]oureau Ancien, Mr Vervant, Mr De Lisle Cramahé & Mr Dugué."[94] As he would have in France, Trouillart, being the (main?) pastor of the congregation, had precedence over the other members of the consistory simply because he presided over it. Two of the elders, Pierre Buretel of La Rochelle and Jacques LeSerrurier of Saint-Quentin, were well-off Charleston merchants. The third, Antoine Boureau of Lusinan, Poitou, was an equally successful artisan (gunsmith) who acquired two lots adjacent to the French Church building in 1694. Pierre Buretel was also one of the two Huguenots who represented the congregation when the church was granted lots 92/93 in 1701. It is not clear whether Jacques Goulart de Vervant, Alexandre Thésée Chastaigner, and Jacques Dugué, to whom the letter was also addressed but whose names are not followed by the title of *ancien,* were church elders or simply representing the congregation.[95] At any rate, their presence undoubtedly added weight and prestige to the consistory since Vervant and Chasteigner, who each owned more than three thousand acres, were Carolina Lords of the Manor; Vervant also bore the title of baronet, and Dugué was a well-connected Charleston merchant whose daughter married into the Wragg family.[96] This snapshot of the Charleston congregation in the early 1690s unmistakably shows that the church was controlled by the Huguenot mercantile and landed elite, as it would have been in a French seaport town of similar size; all but Boureau, who literally played the role of the token artisan for the sake of social representativeness, were referred to as esquires in the colony's records. The letter also shows that with three to five members, depending on the status of Vervant, Chasteigner, and Dugué, the Charleston consistory was of a decent size for a small overseas refugee congregation. This congregational characteristic must be interpreted as an unmistakable sign of spiritual and institutional vitality.

Two bequests, for the poor and the pastor, specifically made to the Charleston church in the few extant pre-1700 wills also evidence early Huguenot congregational life. In his

1693 testament Pierre Perdriau, merchant from La Rochelle, gave to "Mr. Trouillard, Minister of the Holy Gospel . . . the sum of eight pounds sterling" and to the poor of "L'Eglise françoise de Charlestown the sum of five pounds sterling to be paid after [his] death into the hands of the elders of the said church." In 1695 Louis Perdriau, Pierre's cousin, bequeathed four pounds sterling to "l'esglise de Charlestowne."[97] There must have been comparatively little Huguenot poverty in Charleston in the 1690s, but these donations suggest that one of the elders assumed the function of deacon in handling the funds and identifying needy members of the church. They also highlight the role of the congregation as the center of Huguenot communal life.

The Charleston church remained the largest in terms of membership, the most vigorously Calvinist in its outlook, and the most solidly founded Huguenot congregation in South Carolina throughout the proprietary period. Not all the refugees settled in Charleston, however, and as they spread through the northern parts of the lowcountry they founded four other churches, two of which, Santee and Orange Quarter, also became significant centers of Huguenot spiritual life.

The Origins of the Rural Churches
Santee, Orange Quarter, Goose Creek, and Wantoot

Sometimes referred to as "French" Santee to distinguish it from "English" Santee, which was founded subsequently farther upriver, the Huguenot settlement of the lower Santee long remained the largest lowcountry French Protestant community outside of Charleston. The origin of the name Santee is reminiscent of the chicken and egg story. Did it originate in the French word *santé,* meaning "health" and first applied to the High Hills of Santee, the sandhills overlooking the Wateree River and presumably a relatively healthy place, or was it derived from *Zantee,* an Amerindian word meaning "river" and given to the Santee River by the local natives?[98] The fact that Santee was often spelled *santé* or *santée* in English and French documents, as if a settlement inhabited by French refugees had to bear a Gallic name, is deceiving and inconclusive. The native word *Zantee* in its European derivation, *Santee,* was most likely applied to the river and the area before it was settled by Huguenots and was probably pronounced and spelled *Santé* by the French. Then this usage spread due to the overwhelming presence of refugees in the region before the 1720s.

Santee was located in Craven County, the northernmost of the three counties founded in 1682 by proprietary order. The earliest documented grant made to a "Huguenot" for land on the "south side of [the] Santee" River was issued in January 1689 to the Swiss Jean-François Gignilliat.[99] The timing of this Huguenot relocation and the choice of an area north of Charleston were far from coincidental. They are intimately related to the demise of Stuart Town, the Scottish community established in the Port Royal area late in 1684, and to the failure of the Scots to convince the Huguenots to settle among them and form a sort of Calvinist bulwark against Spain's Catholic Florida.

In October 1686, two months after the Spanish had "plundered [their] houses, burned down to the ground the whole town, destroyed [their] plantations, burned [their] fences, killed [their] hogs and Catle" during a most destructive raid, the Scottish leaders William Dunlop and Lord Cardross "endeavoured to persuade the French protestants who came hither this last year [1685] to setle with [them]." Although the Spaniards informed the Scots that "the first Attempt was chiefely for Information and discovery and that the next [would] be for [their] utter ruine and destruction," a scouting party composed of "some of the [French] gentry" was supposed to come soon to Port Royal to see "if they please[d] the country."[100] Dunlop, who was then "endeavouring to resetle port-Royall," apparently succeeded in his negotiations with the Huguenots—unless he was overly confident— since in November 1686 he wrote that "he [was] in expectation that all the French in this Country [would] generally setle with us" and that the Scots were "upon terms with them."[101] Dunlop had in mind the large contingent of Huguenots who arrived in Charleston in April 1685 and who were probably in Charleston waiting for a place to relocate. The French knew of Port Royal Bay, so named by Ribault back in 1562 and her-alded by the Huguenot explorer as "one of the greatest and fayrest havens of the worlde," and some among the Carolina Huguenots may actually have read the explorer's won-derful and Edenic description of the area.[102]

It remains surprising, however, that the Huguenot party agreed to visit Port Royal while cognizant of the Spanish raid, which tragically echoed the 1565 Matanzas Mas-sacres during which hundreds of Ribault's men were put to the sword by the Spaniards, that "cruel and inveterate Enemy," as Dunlop called them. Perhaps the reason is that Port Royal, a place of Calvinist martyrdom par excellence, was nonetheless attractive to the French and the Scots for historical and economic reasons. Since the early days of the proprietary period, Port Royal had been heralded as the area best suited for settlement along the Carolina coast. Praised by Sanford and Hilton in the 1660s, a century after Rib-ault, Port Royal was where the proprietors had originally hoped to found Charleston.[103] The Port Royal area was also reputed to be an excellent region for wine making and silk production due to the omnipresence of wild mulberry trees. Ribault and Laudonnière had written about it, and the Scots perpetuated this illusion of economic productiveness. In his correspondence Dunlop did not fail to enthusiastically describe the "Mulberries (the leafe whereof is the food of the silk worm and whose fruit is excellent for tast and will make good wine) [that] grow wild in the woods."[104] At a time when the newly arrived Huguenots were planning and expected to make wine and silk for the benefit of the Carolina economy and the proprietors, Port Royal appeared as a natural location for their settlement. The second Spanish raid, however, which occurred in December 1686, put a definitive halt to these projects.

In 1687 the Huguenots, whose numbers had increased due to new arrivals, resumed their search for an area where they could relocate. The Santee River, the Spanish Río Jordan "whereof so muche ha[d] byn spoken" and which Ribault and Laudonnière tried to locate in 1562, also carried a mythical aura, although significantly less than Port Royal did, in Carolina pre-English history.[105] The Santee basin had long been associated with the fabled Chicora, Ayllón's "New Andalucia," whose beauty, agricultural potential, and mineral resources Spanish and Italian chroniclers had fervently extolled in the sixteenth century.[106] The Santee area also offered the Huguenots a location far removed from the Spanish threat without being too far from Charleston. Gignilliat, in a letter to his brother, informed him that "there was from [his] plantation five leagues to the head of the Cooper River from which Charleston could be reached in two tides."[107]

Starting with the Hugers, who had a son baptized there in March 1688, and Gignilliat, who obtained land in early 1689, the French relocated south of the Santee, where they founded a Calvinist enclave such as the Scots had envisioned in the Port Royal area.[108] Settling along the Santee River was certainly a wise move on the part of the Huguenots, to whom the tragic fate of Stuart Town had taught that wherever they settled they would have to fend for themselves in case of a Spanish or Indian raid. In due time, though, this move would have paramount consequences in the politico-religious history of early Carolina. It is reasonable to speculate that a prosperous joint Franco-Scottish Calvinist settlement south of Charleston likely would have weakened the Anglican faction and might have led the Huguenots in different religious and political directions.

In his 1690 letter Gignilliat mentioned that seventeen families were established in South Santee.[109] In 1696 the Santee sublist within the *Liste des François et Suisses,* the "Liste des habitants de Santee," enumerated 171 refugees (87 adults and 84 children) grouped in fifty families.[110] Three years later, in the 1699 census, the Santee community was 111 strong and represented 25 percent of the lowcountry Huguenot population.[111] When John Lawson visited Santee in 1701, he noted the presence of seventy families, but it is unlikely that these were all French.[112] Applying the adult/child ratio of 3.4/1, found in the 1696 naturalization list, to Gignilliat's estimate yields a Santee Huguenot population of 58 in 1690. Considering that the 1696 Santee sublist estimate is probably too high since it also listed Huguenots who were actually settled in Orange Quarter—for example, the Bochets—and others who had a plantation in Santee but whose main residence was on the peninsula—such as Alexandre Thésée Chastaigner, who figured among the Charleston church's elders in 1693—the Santee population, which probably reached a peak in the late 1690s, never exceeded 150 in the proprietary period.[113]

Although no extant records evidence the existence of a congregation or a church in Santee before 1700, it is more than likely that the Huguenots, being too far removed from Charleston to regularly attend services there, quickly formed a congregation and worshipped together at somebody's house or outside until they had the means to build a chapel. This was a situation not unlike Samuel Thomas's experience when, as the first SPG missionary sent to Carolina in 1702, he had to serve St. John's Berkeley. Before an Anglican church was constructed, he "officiated . . . in some Planters house or in the summer under some green tree in some airy place made convenient for Minister and people."[114] The presence of the Swiss pastor Pierre Robert, from Basel, on the 1696 list confirms the existence of an église.[115] It is not known exactly when Robert arrived in the colony and settled in Santee, but he was probably there early on. In 1701 Lawson met a group of Santee Huguenots "coming from their Church." Although Lawson is not explicit in his use of the term "church," it seems that he likely meant church building and not service or he would have simply said "coming from church."[116] Thus it is reasonable to conjecture that a Huguenot church, probably a humble log structure, was erected in Santee sometime in the 1690s.

Located east of "the eastern branch of the T of the Cooper river" and bounded on the southwest by the Cooper River, on the southeast by the Wando River, and to the north by the Craven County line, the Orange Quarter settlement was the third-largest Huguenot community in the lowcountry.[117] The name is derived from William, Prince of Orange-Nassau, stadtholder of the Netherlands since 1672 and king of England since 1689, whose house had acquired the Principality of Orange, located in southern France sixteen miles north of Avignon, in the 1530s.[118] Known to the Huguenots as Guillaume d'Orange, William was Louis XIV's main political rival on the European stage. He was also his personal enemy and, in the 1680s and 1690s, was regarded as the champion of the Protestant cause and the Huguenots' most loyal ally. Countless Huguenot officers and regulars chose to fight in his armies at the time of the Revocation. They fought the French, notably in Ireland where William III's forces, which included three refugee regiments, defeated James II and his French allies in 1690 at the Battle of the Boyne.[119] It is moving to see that, in this remote corner of the Carolina "wilderness," displaced Huguenots faithfully paid homage to William of Orange and named their community in his honor. In doing so they also expressed their loyalty to the English monarchy since William, a foreigner like them, became king of England at about the same time Orange Quarter was settled.

Although the first Huguenot who took up land in Orange Quarter in 1685, Pierre Fouré, was a *Richmond* passenger, no records indicate that the Petit-Guérard contingent collectively settled on the eastern branch of the Cooper River.[120] Not even Fouré seems actually to have relocated in the area since he soon transferred his grant to Pierre de St. Julien in December 1686.[121] Like Santee, Orange Quarter was most likely settled in the late 1680s and early 1690s, probably between 1688 and 1692, by Huguenots who arrived in the colony from 1685 to 1687.[122]

The Orange Quarter community seems always to have been a small but far from negligible settlement of kin-related Huguenots with similar occupational backgrounds. Available figures, however, greatly differ as to its exact size. The *Liste des François et Suisses* enumerated 17 adults, or about 60 individuals (with the *Liste*'s adult/children ratio), but the 1699 census recorded 101 refugees, or 23 percent of the Carolina Huguenot population, living in Orange Quarter. This is quite a significant discrepancy that can be explained either by an incomplete surviving Orange Quarter 1696 sublist or by the inconsistent recording of whoever was in charge of registering Huguenots on the naturalization lists. At any rate, the Orange Quarter community must have been 80 or so strong in the late 1690s, which makes it slightly smaller than the Santee settlement. The 1696–97 naturalization documents (the *Liste* and the act) show that, at the time, most of the Orange Quarter Huguenots were related to the Poitevin family and nearly all of them were textile artisans.[123] For this reason the area was also commonly known as "Poitwin Quarter," a name that was still in use in the early decades of the eighteenth century as related by Francis LeJau.[124]

As in Santee, Orange Quarter Huguenots worshipped on somebody's farm or in the open air until enough funds were gathered for the building of a church. In his June 1687 will, Cézar Mozé bequeathed thirty-seven pounds sterling to the "congregation of the French Protestants refugees in this country of Carolina to be used for the construction of a church or place of assembly." The temple was to be built at the place "most conveniently near and in the vicinity" of the plantation in which Mozé and Nicolas Mayrant were "jointly interested [and which was] situated on the Eastern Branch of the T of the Cooper River."[125] Although this hoped-for church building was clearly to be located in

Orange Quarter, Mozé gave the sum to the "French Protestant Church" without specifying which congregation. He did so simply because, at the time, there was only one
organized Huguenot congregation in the lowcountry and the Orange Quarter church
was regarded as its annexe. Mozé's wish was to have a temple near his plantation that
would be administered by the Charleston consistory and served by its pastor so that the
Orange Quarter Huguenots would not have to ride to Charleston every Sunday. In this
ecclesiastical configuration, the Charleston église was to have two temples, a situation far
from uncommon in France. The timing of Mozé's bequest also corresponds to the year
when the Charleston French Church was in the process of acquiring a town lot for another
temple, this time in the city. Mozé's will confirms that by 1687 the Charleston Huguenot
congregation was showing unmistakable signs of material prosperity and spiritual vitality
and looking for places to build houses of worship. The then newly founded community of
Orange Quarter, which was too small to bear the cost of a pastor, was perceived as part
of the Charleston congregation and not as a separate church.[126] This situation lasted well
into the eighteenth century since successive Charleston pastors, whether Trouillart,
Prioleau, L'Escot, or Stouppe, were all supposed to cater to the Orange Quarter community. Thus, the rubric "Liste des noms des François qui se recueille[nt] en l'Églize du
Cartié d'Orange" (list of the names of the French who worship at the Orange Quarter
Church), which heads the Orange Quarter naturalization sublist, is deceiving as it seems
to imply that there was a full-fledged congregation in the area instead of an annexe,
which was not the case. It is uncertain, however, if and when Mozé's bequest was actually used to build a church in Orange Quarter. The Huguenot letter of grievances
addressed to the Lords Proprietors following the act of 1692 suggests that no church
building had by then been erected on the eastern branch of the Cooper River since the
"commuting" parishioners, so to speak, mentioned in the letter probably canoed down
the river from Orange Quarter to Charleston. In the absence of records, it can only be
conjectured that the Orange Quarter community had its temple built, like Santee, sometime before 1700, but this remains an educated guess.

The Huguenot settlement of Goose Creek remained in an embryonic state and never
really developed into a full-fledged distinct French community. No Goose Creek sublist
was included in the *Liste des François et Suisses,* but the 1699 census gave a figure of thirty-
one refugees, or no more than six to eight families, for the "French Church of Goes Creek,"
and the 1704 report by Samuel Thomas mentioned five Huguenot families living in Goose
Creek.[127] In his 1695 will, Antoine Prudhomme bequeathed "a cow with a heifer calf following her, and another heifer about two years old" to "L'Eglise françoise qui s[']assem-
ble sur Gouscrick."[128] The verb *s'assemble* is not specific enough to attest to the existence
of a church or a congregation in Goose Creek at that time since the Huguenots could
simply meet in somebody's house or outside. A church building must have been constructed, however, at some point, as indicated by a 1791 map drawn by the surveyor
Joseph Purcell, which bore the inscription "remains of a french church," on a tract
granted to Abraham Fleury in 1696.[129] Considering the limited number of families and
the complete lack of sources, the Goose Creek Church must have been small and must
also have functioned as an annexe to the Charleston French Church until it dispersed
early in the eighteenth century. In the late 1680s and in the 1690s the community was

probably served, at best once a week, by Trouillart, one of the two Charleston pastors, who acquired land in Goose Creek sometime before 1698.[130]

Starting in 1693, a handful of Huguenots from Santee, along with English colonists, settled an area situated northwest of the western branch of the Cooper River known as Wantoot or Pooshee. This was one of the three original settlements in St. John's Berkeley.[131] This Huguenot frontier community must have remained small since it was not included in the *Liste des François et Suisses* or even mentioned in the 1699 census. It is therefore difficult to ascertain its size. The list of heads of families who took up land in Wantoot before 1704, which was compiled by historian George Terry, includes seven Huguenots, four of them—René Ravenel, Louis and Pierre de St. Julien, and Samuel DuBourdieu—being part of the original Vitré group that left Brittany in 1686.[132] Provided that these Huguenots were living in Wantoot and did not just own land there for speculative purposes, eight families represent a population of about thirty. To these must be added the four families, or about fifteen people, settled in Comingtee, another settlement located in St. John's Berkeley, where the Cooper River divides between its eastern and western branches.[133] This estimate makes the St. John's Berkeley Huguenot community slightly bigger than the Goose Creek settlement. Its absence from the 1699 census, however, is likely due to the fact that it did not constitute a self-contained community until the arrival of Trouillart in 1706, as well as because of its remote and dual location and the fact that most, if not all, of these families already owned land in one of the four original lowcountry Huguenot settlements.

Nothing is known of the religious life of the Wantoot settlers before the arrival of Reverend Trouillart from Charleston. It can be assumed that in the absence of a pastor they worshipped at home, together or separately, using a Bible and a psalter. A few years after Trouillart settled in the area, they built a church, about which nothing is known except that its construction preceded the building of the first Anglican church in the parish. Robert Maule, first SPG missionary in St. John's, who arrived in 1707, borrowed the church from the French for his services.[134]

The Founding Fathers
The First Carolina Huguenot Pastors

If the difficulty of hiring French Calvinist ministers turned out to be one of the principal factors that eventually weakened the lowcountry Huguenot congregations and, except for Charleston, led them to the path of Anglican conformity, conversely in the 1680s and 1690s the availability of pastors was a strength of the Carolina refugee community. Whereas the Church of England counted no permanent ministers in the colony before the appointment of Samuel Marshall to St. Philip's in 1696, Atkin Williamson being in Charleston since the early 1680s but without having ever formally or durably held a ministry, Carolina Huguenot churches could boast the full-time concurrent presence of three pastors, Trouillart, Prioleau, and Robert, before 1690.[135]

The expulsion of all the Huguenot ministers who refused to convert under article 4 of the Edict of Revocation led some 680 of them to leave France.[136] Because many settled in England, there was an unusually high pastoral reservoir available for the newly founded North American churches. A shortage of pastors would seriously impede Huguenot ecclesiastical survival in the next generation mostly due to the closing of all Huguenot académies in 1685, but ministers were plentiful in *le Refuge* before 1700, particularly in the small overseas communities. In Carolina the Huguenot pastor/individual ratio was 1/120 (3 ministers for 360 refugees) in 1690, while there were two clerks (Atkin Williamson and Phineas Rogers) for over 1,500 Anglicans. Even compared to pre-Revocation France, where there were 870 pastors for a total Huguenot population of over 700,000 people, or a proportion of one minister for 800 individuals, the lowcountry ratio was unusually high. This strong pastoral presence placed the Carolina refugees in an ideal context, at least from the perspective of ecclesiastical leadership, to transplant and maintain their Calvinism.

Without counting Pierre Forestier, who may never have come to Carolina although he was registered on the *Richmond* departure list, four, perhaps five if we include Estienne Dusout, pastors—Laurentius Van den Bosch (or Laurent DuBois), Florent-Philippe Trouillart, Élie Prioleau, and Pierre Robert—tended at one time or another to the spiritual needs of the Carolina Huguenots before 1700. At a time when rules of precedence were all prevailing, the presence of Prioleau and Trouillart as numbers one and two in the 1696 naturalization list, just ahead of the merchants and esquires, confirms the position of leadership that they occupied within the lowcountry Huguenot community.[137]

Charleston's first documented pastor, Van den Bosch or Bosk, was actually a Walloon.[138] He arrived in Carolina sometime in 1682 after having been somewhat enigmatically ordained by the bishop of London *and* sent overseas by the Nonconformist Threadneedle Street Church about a week after his ordination with two pounds sterling and "a quarto edition of a Geneva Bible."[139] The early date of his appointment, three years before the Revocation and the consequent expulsion of Huguenot ministers from France, accounts for the fact that the Threadneedle Street consistory, which held quasi-synodical control over the North American Huguenot churches, was in no position to be demanding in selecting a minister to serve overseas. There was then still a severe ministerial shortage. It remains puzzling, however, as to why the London consistory sent an Anglican-ordained Walloon pastor to a Huguenot Calvinist church. Nothing is known of Van den Bosch's short ministry except that it was marked by deep animosity between him and the congregation. The rift, at least officially, was caused by a financial dispute over the payment of his salary. This is what transpires from a letter that Van den Bosch wrote to the bishop of London soon after his relocation in Boston in 1685.[140] His difficult character, what Baird called his "haughty and stubborn demeanor," however, later led him to hop from church to church in New England and New York and to settle eventually in Maryland. His conformity to the Church of England most likely undermined his Charleston ministry.[141] Louis Thibou's choice of the English clerk Joseph Harrison as pastor for the baptism of his son Jacob in 1683, in lieu of the appointed Huguenot minister, probably testifies to the confrontational climate that reigned within the Charleston congregation while Van den Bosch was serving there.

The Charleston French Church did not remain pastorless for long. Florent-Philippe Trouillart arrived on board the *Margaret* in April 1685, probably soon after Van den Bosch had left the colony.[142] Times had changed. The intense anti-Protestant persecution, which paved the way for the Revocation, had thrown many ministers whose temples had been razed and congregations disbanded onto the roads of northern Europe. In the mid-1680s there was truly a surplus of Huguenot pastors in *le Refuge,* particularly in the Netherlands and in England. The difficulty of finding pastoral appointments, especially for the younger pastors, inevitably made the remote Charleston position, if not attractive, at least tempting. Florent (or Laurent)-Philippe Trouillart was the son of Geneva-trained Pierre Trouillart, professor of theology at the Sedan académie and pastor at Guînes, where he catered to the Calais Huguenot congregation.[143] At the time of his departure from France in March 1685, he had been serving the congregation of the town of Oisemont, some seventy-five miles south of Calais, since 1670.[144] Whereas his father Pierre and his brother Pierre II fled to the Netherlands, as most pastors officiating in northern France did, Florent-Philippe opted instead for England, perhaps after following his family to the Netherlands and remaining there briefly.[145] Florent-Philippe did not stay long in England since he must have arrived in London in March, a few weeks, perhaps days, before the sailing of the *Margaret.* Did he envision settling in the New World while still in France? Was he unable to find a pastoral position in the Low Countries? These questions cannot be answered, but his short stay in England may indicate that he had heard about the Charleston position while in the Netherlands, or even in France, and applied for it immediately. Since no record of his appearance before the consistory of the Threadneedle Street Church has survived, it is entirely possible that Trouillart was recruited with the help of proprietary agents in England or the Netherlands or by a member of the Charleston Huguenot community, a merchant for example, while on a business trip in London or on his way to Carolina. Until the arrival of Prioleau, Trouillart acted as the main Charleston minister and thereby played a crucial role in the formative years of the congregation. Nonetheless, he seems, rather unexpectedly although not inexplicably, to have kept himself somewhat in Prioleau's shadow.

Although it cannot be documented, genealogists have Élie Prioleau arriving in Carolina in 1687, which is likely since he appears in the June 1686–August 1687 rolls of the London Comité Français and was in Santee to baptize Daniel Huger Jr. in March 1688.[146] Prioleau's ministry, which lasted from his arrival in 1687 to his death in 1699, stands prominently in the Charleston Huguenot historical landscape. Traditional accounts, while totally ignoring Van den Bosch and, more importantly, Trouillart, make Prioleau the first minister and founder of the Charleston Huguenot church and a heroic pastoral shepherd who led his forsaken Huguenot flock from Pons, Saintonge, to the lowcountry in a most biblical fashion.[147] This Prioleau-Pons epic, a Pilgrim-like tale in which Scrooby becomes Pons, constitutes a fascinating case of invented tradition when memory drifts away from historical reality and biased accounts completely blur the picture. More than a century ago Baird, who relied more on archival evidence than local traditions, was not deceived by the Pons emigration story and remained rightfully skeptical of its occurrence.[148] Baird was correct. The Pons story is totally undocumented. No Huguenot, not even Prioleau, registered in the 1696–97 naturalization list mentions being from Pons, and Pons does not appear in any Carolina Huguenot archival material.[149] The fact that refugees from Pons were listed in English denization rolls along with Prioleau has been cited as the crucial documentary proof supporting the Pons tradition, but it actually constitutes no evidence since a common presence on a naturalization list does not mean that the refugees were naturalized together or, even less, that the naturalization oath was taken the day the list was recorded.[150]

The Pons story has not been so well perpetuated innocently, out of lack of experience in archival research, however, but was gradually and skillfully elaborated by nineteenth-century mythmakers with several intentions in mind. First, the arrival of Prioleau in the lowcountry coincides with the purchase of lot 65, which has been perceived by most nineteenth-century chroniclers as the founding event of the history of the Charleston church. Both occurrences collided in the chroniclers' undocumented accounts to make Prioleau the founder of the church. Second, while Van den Bosch fell into oblivion, perhaps because of behavior deemed inappropriate by Puritan-minded nineteenth-century Huguenot chroniclers or because of his Anglican conformity, Trouillart was assigned a secondary role because he could not claim the same prestigious (that is, noble) lineage as Prioleau and, perhaps more important, because he left no Carolina descendants. According to some historians, Prioleau was an indirect descendant of a Venetian doge.[151] As George Howe, a nineteenth-century historian of the South Carolina Presbyterian Church, succinctly puts it, Prioleau "left behind him numerous descendants in South Carolina who cherish his memory and emulate his virtues."[152] This genealogical posterity guaranteed Prioleau historical visibility in the lowcountry. Third, back in France in the early 1680s Prioleau had been the victim of documented cases of Catholic persecution, which nineteenth-century antipapist Huguenot hagiographers could use to back their description of Prioleau as a Calvinist heroic figure.[153] In sum, the Pons legend makes the Charleston French Church an offshoot, and therefore the ecclesiastical and spiritual heir, of a Huguenot congregation in France, giving the Carolina Huguenot migration a stamp of authenticity while enhancing Prioleau's role almost to biblical proportions at the expense of Trouillart's. It is true that Trouillart stepped to the side when Prioleau arrived in Charleston, but the Pons story turned this simple historical fact into a one-man show without trying to explain Trouillart's role. Reality was obviously both less romantic and more complex.

In his 1690 will, quoted in Howe's *History of the Presbyterian Church in South Carolina,* Prioleau styled himself "minister of the holy Gospel in the French Church of Charlestown."[154] It seems, however, that both he and Trouillart alternatively served the Charleston, Orange Quarter, and, on a less regular basis, Goose Creek congregations. The Simons family Bible records, one of the few sources that documents early lowcountry Huguenot ecclesiastical life, indicate that one of Benjamin I's sons, Pierre, was baptized "in Charlestown . . . in the French Church by Mr. Trouillart, Minister" in July 1693 and two others, Samuel and François, by "Mr. Prioleau, Minister in Orange Quarter," in 1696 and 1697, respectively.[155] Also, in his will Prioleau instructed his wife and executrix to "give immediately after [his] death five pounds sterling to the church to whose service [he] shall be most ordinarily attached at the end of [his] days; and if there are two which [he] serve[s] with equal assiduity . . . to give each of the said churches two pounds and a half sterling."[156] This testamentary instruction implies that in 1690 Prioleau had and could again serve two churches while regarding himself as Charleston's main pastor. Prioleau's preeminence can be explained by the fact that the two Charleston ministers could not be equal; one necessarily functioned as the first pastor, following the norms of

Huguenot congregational life. The problem is that other available sources only partially substantiate Prioleau's claim. Whoever recorded French and Swiss names on the naturalization list scrupulously followed rules of precedence in listing pastors, esquires, and merchants before the other refugees. The fact that he (or they) registered Prioleau first was therefore not coincidental and confirms Prioleau's preeminence within the low-country Huguenot community as the first pastor of the largest congregation. However, the Latin Ravenel–St. Julien marriage certificate, issued in October 1687, mentions Trouillart as "ecclesiae ref. gal. carolopolitensis minister," although, of course, Prioleau may not have settled in the colony by that date.[157] Then the 1693 proprietary missive sent to the Charleston French Church in the wake of the passing of the 1692 act was addressed to Trouillart, presumably as the chair of the consistory, and the elders while Prioleau was not mentioned.[158] That same year Pierre Perdriau's testamentary bequest for the minister of the Charleston French Church was addressed to Trouillart.[159] Was this because, following the Simons Bible records, Prioleau was then officiating in Orange Quarter, or had Trouillart temporarily become the main Charleston minister?

Clearly Trouillart played an instrumental, and presumably more significant, role than Prioleau did in shaping the early Charleston French Church. He arrived in the low-country first and survived Prioleau by thirteen years, although he left Charleston for Orange Quarter in 1700 after his colleague's death. He also had a pastoral pedigree, with a father teaching theology at the Sedan académie, at least equal to Prioleau's. The naturalization list, however, evidences that Trouillart deferred to his colleague, letting him appear as the main Charleston minister and even as the pastoral leader of the entire low-country Huguenot community. Was it a sign of respect for Prioleau's assumed prestigious lineage by a man possibly younger and of more modest family background? Did Prioleau have a more imposing personality? Was Prioleau preferred by the congregation? These questions cannot be answered from extant sources. One can only speculate that both pastors first agreed to serve alternately the Charleston, Goose Creek, and Orange Quarter congregations while Prioleau was given a more prominent position in Charleston by a deferential Trouillart. Sensing his health declining in the early 1690s, Prioleau may have opted to officiate in the more modest Cooper River Church, leaving Trouillart in charge of the larger Charleston congregation, while keeping his rank within the Huguenot community at large.

Little is known about the Santee Carolina Huguenot pastor Pierre Robert before 1700. Born in 1656 in St. Imier, a small town in the Swiss Jura, Robert first studied in Basel, center of the Zinglian reform, where he matriculated in 1674. He became a minister in 1682, but it is not known which académie he attended.[160] As with all the Swiss who followed the Huguenots to America, emigration was an individual or familial decision and not the result of persecution. It is therefore impossible to ascertain why the Roberts—Pierre, his wife, Jeanne Bayer, and their children, Jeanne and Pierre—left Basel for the Carolina lowcountry. Did Robert have difficulty finding a pastoral position in Switzerland? Did he meet Huguenots passing through Basel on their way to England and befriend them? Was Robert fascinated by the American "wilderness"? Was it simply an economically motivated decision? Robert immigrated to Carolina sometime between 1688 and 1690 and soon after settled in Santee.[161] The fact that when Robert arrived in the lowcountry Trouillart and Prioleau were already serving the churches of Charleston and Orange Quarter may explain why Robert settled in Santee. His decision may also have been influenced by fellow Swiss émigré Gignilliat, who was one of the first Santee settlers and who was instrumental in recruiting another Swiss pastor to succeed Robert in the 1710s. A Santee-Swiss connection is corroborated by the fact that all the Swiss registered in the naturalization list lived in the northern settlement.[162] Because Robert appears in no pre-1700 record, apart from the naturalization list, his relationship with his community and his ties to the two Charleston pastors remain unknown. It is likely that, considering the distance that separated Santee from Charleston and the lack of roads in the lowcountry at the time, Robert rarely, if ever, visited Charleston and at best maintained an episodic correspondence with Trouillart and Prioleau. The Santee community played a peripheral role in early lowcountry Huguenot religious history because of its geographic isolation. Robert's role, despite Santee's demographic significance, was probably similar. The large urban church of Charleston and its two annexes, Goose Creek and Orange Quarter, were undoubtedly the epicenter of Huguenot spiritual life.

Prioleau's death in 1699 abruptly changed the course of events in the religious history of the Carolina Huguenots. While waiting for Prioleau's replacement, Trouillart, although still relatively young, decided against remaining in Charleston and, in what looks like a sort of preretirement, chose to move first to Orange Quarter and then to Wantoot. Trouillart's undocumented motivations have never been explained. Why did he choose to leave Charleston so suddenly? What did Prioleau's death change for him? Trouillart, who had acquired land in Goose Creek by 1698, may have planned to move away from Charleston before Prioleau died because he sensed, or even faced, emerging dissension within the Charleston congregation over conformity to the Church of England and preferred to leave his successor, Paul L'Escot, to settle this difficult issue. Trouillart's departure from Charleston in 1700 and from Orange Quarter in 1706, the year the Church of England was established in South Carolina, and his replacement by a more mundane and Anglican-leaning pastor undoubtedly left the two congregations, Charleston and Orange Quarter, in uncertain hands. Within a year Charleston had lost two ministers who had endured the royal persecutions of the 1670s and early 1680s. Prioleau was not the heroic figure that the Pons legend portrays, but he and Trouillart, as opposed to Robert, who was Swiss and therefore had not lived through the ordeal of pre-Revocation France, were true Huguenot pastors and, like the better-known Fontaine in England, were steadfast in their Calvinist beliefs. The termination of their dual ministry, followed by the arrival of the first missionaries of the newly founded Society for the Propagation of the Gospel (SPG), undeniably marked the end of an era, the Calvinist chapter of Carolina Huguenot spiritual life.

Chapter 6

PROTESTANT MAJORITY

The Carolina Huguenots and the Church of England

Un dieu, Un Roi.
> Tombstone epitaph of Henry Bounetheau (1797–1877)
> Charleston Huguenot Church cemetery

I have affection and esteem for the Divine Service that is practiced in the Church of England, however, I would not want to condemn all those who have not conformed, I leave this judgment to God.
> Élie Neau to SPG (December 20, 1704)

The Church of England in America at the Turn of the Eighteenth Century
A Minority Church on the Offensive

In the early 1700s the Church of England was a minority church in British North America in terms of numbers and influence. It ranked second to Congregationalism with 111 parishes for 146 churches and, like its rival, was unevenly distributed since 93 of these Anglican parishes were located in the Chesapeake.[1] The Church of England was the official or established church in Virginia only. In New England, where Congregationalism reigned, it held the unusual position of a dissenting church, and in the mid-Atlantic colonies it had to compete on equal footing with several other denominations, being ambiguously established in only four New York counties.[2]

Although the Church of England never quite became the dominating colonial church that metropolitan bishops and churchmen envisioned, it nonetheless experienced major growth in the first decades of the eighteenth century due to a more focused policy. While Congregationalism was still leading in terms of churches, by 1750 the Church of England could boast 289 parishes, or more than a twofold increase since 1700, spread more equally from Massachusetts to Georgia, with the Chesapeake accounting for one-half instead of three-fourths of the total number.[3] It was by then established in three southern colonies (Virginia, Maryland, and South Carolina) and firmly rooted in the mid-Atlantic region, whereas Congregationalism was still almost exclusively limited to New England.

The roots of the Anglican resurgence in North America are to be found in post-1689 England. The 1688–89 Revolution indefinitely removed the feeble but much hyped Catholic menace in securing a Protestant royal succession. The 1689 Toleration Act, which sanctioned religious pluralism while guaranteeing Anglicans first-class citizenship through the still-in-force Test Acts, gave the Church of England a new role in English society. As John Spurr noted, "the Glorious Revolution's religious settlement reduced the Church of England from the *national* to merely the *established* church."[4] While it had been defeated and was more divided than ever, this "Church in danger" was revitalized through a new sense of mission. Freed from its unrealistic goal of coerced comprehension, it developed an ambitious program that focused instead on social, religious, and pastoral reforms and overseas expansion. As two historians recently summed it up, "unable to coerce, [it] now had to persuade."[5] In other words, all the energy vainly spent on attempting to become the national church was, in the 1690s, most usefully redirected toward self-reassessment and an aggressive colonial policy.

Traversed by the philanthropic and humanitarian currents that swept England in the 1690s and early 1700s as a result of what has been called "the Moral Revolution of 1688," the Church of England found new ways of exerting its influence. Led by dedicated bishops such as Henry Compton, Edward Stillingfleet, White Kennet, and Gilbert Burnet, it launched social reforms by sponsoring Societies for the Reformation of Manners (SRM), combated illiteracy by opening charity schools, and revitalized its evangelical mission by founding "religious societies" for Bible reading. All these efforts were accompanied by structural reforms within the church's parishes and dioceses aimed at improving clerical performance and gearing it toward a voluntary, more practical, and less ostentatious piety.[6] This policy culminated with the foundation of two highly influential voluntary societies, the Society for Promoting Christian Knowledge (SPCK) in 1698 and the Society for the Propagation of the Gospel in Foreign Parts (SPG) in 1701. Both were significant actors in the Huguenot-Anglican drama that unfolded in Carolina and in Europe in the early decades of the eighteenth century.[7]

At least until the 1730s the SPG was a formidable weapon in the competition for territory and souls in the colonies. Although initially founded as a missionary society, the SPG's objectives, as stated in the first-anniversary sermon pronounced by Richard Willis, dean of Lincoln in 1702, were "in the first place to settle the State of Religion as well as may be among our *own People* . . . and then to proceed in the best Methods [it] can towards *Conversion* of the *Natives*."[8] In addition to appointing eighty missionaries between 1701 and 1725, the society supplied the distant and isolated overseas parishes with money and, jointly with the SPCK, books and Bibles and provided essential spiritual supervision.[9] In its effort to lure settlers into the Anglican fold, the SPG was particularly efficient with regard to foreign Protestants, especially Huguenots.[10] The society led rural Huguenot congregations along the path of conformity by using its financial resources and political acumen to send French Books of Common Prayer and Bibles, appoint French-speaking missionaries to these communities, and financially help conformist pastors already in their posts.[11]

This aggressive post-1700 policy, which Jon Butler has called "the Anglican renaissance," dramatically changed the course of the religious history of early South Carolina and of its Huguenot population.[12] It successfully sponsored the establishment of the Church of England in 1706 and led two of the three Huguenot congregations, Orange Quarter and Santee, to conform. Nowhere else in North America, except perhaps in New York, did the Church of England obtain swifter and greater results than on the Carolina stage.

Big Bang in Eden
The Carolina Church Acts of 1704 and 1706 and Huguenot Support

While undeniably related to the context of a reinvigorated Church of England, its establishment in South Carolina is rooted in the bitter factional politics that had, except for brief peaceful intervals, plagued the colony since its inception. Different and complexly intertwined issues had pitted various groups and personalities against one another, namely the control of the trade with native populations, illegal interaction with Caribbean pirates, the rejection of the Fundamental Constitutions, the naturalization of foreigners (that is, Huguenots), the payment of the land rents, the defense of the colony against French and Spanish attacks, and the degree of primacy to grant to the Church of England. These rivalries were essentially fueled by the desire of each faction and its leaders to control local economic leverages and ascertain a certain measure of political ascendancy in order to satisfy narrow, short-term objectives.

Needless to say, this political action occurred in a fluid environment. Actors changed as early settlers died or left while others arrived in the colony. Although Carolina political life was inevitably conditioned by the North American and metropolitan contexts, issues alternately came to the foreground and receded primarily depending on who controlled power at any given time and, to a certain extent, on the remote influence of the proprietors. At the turn of the century, in the midst of military campaigns against Spanish Florida, and following the death of Governor Joseph Blake in 1700 and the accession of John Carteret, Lord Granville, to the head of the proprietors as lord palatine in 1701, the question of whether or not to establish the Church of England gradually became central both in the colony and among the proprietorship.[13]

Although the three 1669 versions of the Fundamental Constitutions contained no articles providing for the eventual establishment of a church, the 1670 revised version instructed the Carolina council that in due time they should "take care for the building of Churches and the public Maintenance of Divines, to be employed in the Exercise of Religion according to the Church of England . . . the only true and Orthodox, and the National Religion of all the King's Dominions."[14] In 1682, as part of their promotional campaign designed to attract English Dissenters, Scottish Covenanters, and Huguenots, the proprietors revised the constitutions to accommodate these prospective settlers. While the Church of England "alone [was] allowed to receive public maintenance by grant of Parliament," it was no longer referred to as "the only true and Orthodox" church but called "the Religion of the Government of England." Proprietors also exempted Nonconformists from being taxed for its support while each "Congregation of Christians, not of the communion of the Church of Rome, [had] the power to lay a tax on its own members."[15] In the last version of the Fundamental Constitutions, drafted in 1698, however, a renewed proprietorship favored the establishment of the Church of England, again referred to as "the only true and Orthodox [church]," in their colony. While they granted members of other denominations some measure of toleration, they nonetheless removed the August 1682 exemption clause.[16] Although these versions were never implemented, they reveal the evolution of proprietary intentions concerning religious life in the colony.[17] These intentions inevitably influenced Carolina politics through the proprietors' clients or whoever had something to gain by pushing forward their agenda. The Carolina stage would be set for an attempt to establish the Church of England once the right men were in place in the early 1700s.

The disputed gubernatorial election following the death of Governor Joseph Blake in autumn 1700 left an Anglican, Joseph Moore, in the driver's seat until Sir Nathaniel Johnson replaced him as the proprietary appointee in March 1703. Control of the Indian trade and the financing of his military campaign in northeastern Florida dominated Moore's term. Although religion was peripheral to Carolina political life during that period, the fact that Moore's opponents were Dissenters gave a religious flavor to this power struggle. When Moore returned from Florida in December 1702 with an invoice exceeding the funds appropriated by the council by four thousand pounds sterling, the opposition agreed to have the council authorize the colony to pay its creditors with bills of credit. Taking advantage of Moore's financial distress, however, the governor's opponents also introduced three bills regulating assembly elections, the Indian trade, and the naturalization of foreign settlers, that is, Huguenots. Moore stalled for time while attempting to convince the council to issue bills of credit. Soon after, however, Commons House political bickering led to street riots. Peace eventually returned to Carolina when Sir Nathaniel Johnson, ill at the time of his appointment in June 1702, took office in March 1703.[18]

Johnson shared Moore's martial ambitions and concerns about Carolina safety, but unlike his predecessor, he was determined to use the issue of religious establishment to defeat his enemies and serve his own interests. In what Sirmans called "a well-planned coup," Johnson summoned the assembly for an emergency meeting in May 1704 and, while most Colleton County Dissenters were on their way to Charleston, he convinced its members to vote a sort of Carolina Test Act, which potentially excluded all Nonconformists from the Commons House.[19] In October, Johnson successfully requested the assembly to vote a new naturalization law for the Huguenots. The following month the Commons House passed an act establishing the Church of England.[20]

Far from being defenseless, the Carolina Dissenters took their case to London. In an attempt to have both laws disallowed by higher authority after the proprietors refused to repeal them, they hired Daniel Defoe. The Englishman composed a pamphlet, *Party-Tyranny, or an Occasional Bill in Miniature; as Now Practiced in Carolina, Humbly Offered to the Consideration of Both Houses of Parliament,* in the hope that the "[Dissenters'] injuries might, in a legal manner, be redress'd and repair'd."[21] At a time when Parliament was divided over the issue of "occasional conformity," which controversially allowed Nonconformists to take Anglican Communion occasionally so as to be eligible for political offices, Defoe's pamphlet found a most receptive audience.[22] Although Granville managed to have a counterpamphlet published in Johnson's defense, the Dissenters won their case.[23] In March 1706 the crown asked the Carolina proprietors to repeal the exclusion and church acts. Consequently, while Johnson's faction had managed to weather the Dissenting storm back in Carolina, news of the proprietary decision forced them to repeal both acts in November nonetheless. They complied but quickly voted a new church act, this time with the Dissenters being represented in the assembly, before the end of 1706. The Church of England had become the established church in South Carolina.

In essence the 1704 and 1706 Church Acts were identical. They established the Church of England and lay the foundations of a parish-based religious, administrative, and political life that, refined by subsequent laws through the proprietary period, was to endure until the end of the eighteenth century. South Carolina was divided into ten parishes. Each of them was administered by a seven-member board, the equivalent of an English "select" vestry, elected yearly at Easter by the parishioners. Vestries appointed a clerk, a register, and a sexton; elected two churchwardens; and chose the parish minister, who received an annual salary from the assembly paid for by import and export taxes. Both laws created a colonywide lay commission whose main duties were to supervise the implementation of the acts; the construction of new churches, six of which were to be erected after 1706; and the management of the newly appropriated funds. Apart from a broader inclusion of the Carolina French element into this Anglican establishment with the creation of Huguenot parishes and the appointment of a higher number of French commissioners, the main difference between the 1704 and 1706 acts lies in the power of the commission.[24]

The 1704 act originally provided for a twenty-member legislative commission endowed, in a quasi-Calvinist synodical fashion, with the extraordinary power to remove pastors "upon the request and at the desire of any nine of the parishioners" and after hearing "the complaints against such rector or minister [and] allowing him reasonable time to make his defence." Allegedly inspired by the justifiable desire to offer settlers a "remedy . . . in case any immoral or imprudent clergyman should happen to be appointed" in a parish, the inclusion of this highly controversial clause was also more prosaically motivated by the feud that had been opposing the Charleston minister, the nonjuror Edward Marston, to Governor Johnson and some Anglican members of the assembly.[25] Somewhat ironically, this clause, which smacked of Presbyterianism, is what eventually condemned the act in the eyes of the secular and religious authorities in England. The bishop of London and the SPG, along with Defoe, who dubbed the commission "a little High Commission Court to Govern the Clergy," and the agents of the Carolina Dissenters dispatched to London, successfully lobbied Parliament and the crown for its repeal.[26] The 1706 act maintained the commission but wisely curtailed its influence to a supervisory and uniquely administrative role while increasing its membership to twenty-four. This second commission was also somewhat less partisan with the absence of influential Anglicans such as James Moore and Job Howes, who both died in 1706, and the inclusion of more Colleton County residents and Huguenots.[27]

The Huguenot political influence and motivations and the role they played in the turbulent years from 1702 to 1706 will be discussed in detail in the following chapter. It can be said, however, that extant sources all concur in showing that the Huguenots were instrumental in helping Johnson and his supporters establish the Church of England. The presence of Huguenots, of whom several were related, in the seventh and eight assemblies, which voted the two acts, and in the 1704 and 1706 commissions evidences prior conformity to the Church of England and flagrant political support for Johnson's dual strategy of exclusion and establishment.[28] It remains to be seen, though, who these Huguenots were and to what extent they were representative of the French community at large. Perhaps more significant is the petition addressed to the assembly sometime before April 1706 from the Santee Huguenots, who "pray[ed] that a Parish might be erected among them."[29] This initiative shows that the French and Swiss of Craven County, who were "extreamly desireous to be united to the Body of the royall Church of England," volunteered to have their church conform under the 1704 act without questioning the validity or opportuneness of the Exclusion Act.[30]

Jacques LeSerrurier, also known as James Smith, sat in the notorious seventh assembly, which enacted the 1704 Exclusion and Church Acts, and he was also the sole Huguenot appointed to the all powerful and highly controversial commission.[31] Naturalized in England, Jacques arrived in Carolina in 1699, seven years after his parents, Jacques Sr. and Élisabeth Léger. Jacques Jr., a merchant, obtained a one-thousand-acre warrant in 1701 and had become a Berkeley County justice of the peace by 1703.[32] Accused of having "cheated the Scots' Company of a considerable Sum of Money, and with his Keeper [Nathaniel Johnson] made his Escape from London hither" by Lady Blake, the late Governor Blake's widow, in a letter addressed to the proprietors in 1704, LeSerrurier seems to have stood among Johnson's close allies.[33] His vote for the 1704 disputed legislation, which made him the target of Lady Blake's vitriolic accusation, tilted the balance twelve against eleven toward exclusion and establishment. LeSerrurier, however, did not represent the entire Carolina Huguenot community, whose opinion on conformity he obviously did not seek. This is corroborated by the absence of any reference concerning the Huguenots in the 1704 Church Act. Johnson may have needed LeSerrurier's vote and tacit Huguenot support to pass the 1704 Exclusion and Church Acts, but the fact that the assembly did not even think of including Santee and Orange Quarter in the projected parish network confirms that the act was essentially a Charleston affair and, most significantly, reveals that Huguenot conformity was not an issue.

The eighth assembly counted two Huguenots, John-Abraham Motte and Louis Pasquereau, in its ranks, to whom Henry LeNoble, then a member of the council, must be added.[34] A late arrival, Motte was unfamiliar with the political struggles that had divided the settlers since the 1680s and, like LeSerrurier, was quite unrepresentative of the Carolina Huguenot community. He fled France with his parents at a young age and grew up in the Netherlands before being appointed consul in Dublin, where his son Jacob was born. From Dublin he left for Antigua and eventually settled in South Carolina, as agent to the planter James Perry, sometime in 1705, bringing along slaves and capital.[35] Recorded as a communicant at St. Philip's in the year of his death (1711) by the commissary Gideon Johnston, he had likely already conformed to the Church of England before settling in Carolina.[36] His vote in favor of the church act and his presence on the 1706 commission did not constitute a pivotal moment in his integration into Carolina Anglo-Anglican world society.

Although he also left France while still a child, Louis Pasquereau, born in 1674, followed a biographical itinerary more typical of a Huguenot refugee. Hailing from Tours, he settled in Carolina with his parents and was naturalized in 1697, along with the rest of the French and Swiss then present in the colony. By 1705 Pasquereau, who served as "Governor [Joseph Blake]'s Clark," owned a house in Charleston and land in Berkeley County, sat in the South Carolina Assembly, and was a captain in the colonial militia.[37] Pasquereau well embodies the generation of Huguenots who were too young to have understood the context and meaning of their escape from France and who settled in Carolina early enough to become full-fledged members of the host society by the early eighteenth century. By the time he was confronted with the issue of conformity, he was a middle-aged man who had spent twenty-six years away from France. As in the case of Motte, however, his presence in the post–Exclusion Act assembly indicates that he had already conformed to the Church of England.

Three other Huguenots, Henry LeNoble, René Ravenel, and Philippe Gendron, also sat on the 1706 lay commission. LeNoble's profile resembles that of LeSerrurier, who was his brother-in-law, and of Motte. Not much is known about his pre-Carolina past except that he was from Paris, which he left before the Revocation, most likely as a child. Once in England he was denizened in 1682 and naturalized in 1685. In the colony by 1690, he was granted a lot in Charleston in 1694. He did not apply for Carolina naturalization in 1697, which means that he was already well integrated by that time. He was a justice of the peace in Berkeley County and was sitting in the council as Anthony, Lord Ashley's deputy when the assembly voted the 1706 Church Act, which he cosigned along with the 1704 act.[38] Five years earlier, however, LeNoble had been one of the Huguenots representing the Charleston French congregation when the grant for lots 92 and 93 was issued. This is an instance of the dual denominational affiliation, as Butler calls it, that characterized well-integrated and, in the case of LeNoble, politically high-ranking Charleston Huguenots throughout the first half of the eighteenth century.[39]

The other two Huguenot commissioners, René Ravenel and Philippe Gendron (Louis Pasquereau's stepfather), offer a somewhat different case. Born in the 1650s, they left France as adults well aware of what fleeing entailed, settled in Santee where they soon constituted a sort of local gentry, and applied for naturalization in 1697.[40] Unlike LeSerrurier and LeNoble, these Huguenots, as Craven County settlers, stood outside the circle of acrimonious Charleston politics. They were not members of the assembly, although Ravenel had once been elected to it in 1692, and probably pushed for conformity in initiating the 1706 Santee petition in a move somewhat independent from the Anglican-Dissenter rivalry.[41] Consequently they sat on the commission only as representatives from St. James Santee.

Notwithstanding this last observation, a striking feature of this small group of Huguenot conformists was their elite status, politically and socioeconomically, and the fact that several among them were closely related. All these refugees possessed some political experience at the colonial and local levels, owned town lots and/or large country estates, and were well integrated into Carolina Anglo-American society. While two of them, Motte and LeSerrurier, were brothers-in law, LeNoble's daughter Susanne was married to Ravenel's son René-Louis, and Phillipe Gendron was Louis Pasquereau's stepfather. Although not as partisan as LeSerrurier, and perhaps LeNoble, they nonetheless formed a close-knit ensemble of Huguenot officials whose political and socioeconomic interests lay in supporting Governor Johnson's side. While principally motivated by personal interests, in giving the Anglicans a decisive push, they obtained a new naturalization law in 1704 and a generous church act in 1706 with potential benefit for the entire Carolina Huguenot community.

The Church Act of 1706 and Its Huguenot Clauses

While the 1704 Church Act was silent on the question of Huguenot conformity, its successor generously granted the French important linguistic, territorial, and liturgical privileges. Partly occasioned by the Santee April petition, which reminded the assembly of the Huguenot presence in the colony outside of Charleston, and by Johnson's renewed need for French political support, the change was principally a consequence of the desire of the governor and his supporters to have a broad-based new Establishment Act in contrast to the highly partisan act of 1704. At any rate, this politically inspired generosity is much more revealing of the Huguenots' determination to conform to the Church of England and their participation in its establishment than of the 1704 Naturalization Act and LeSerrurier's vote.

In addition to appointing four Huguenots to the 1706 commission, the assembly created two French parishes, St. Denis and St. James Santee, and, aware that most of their parishioners were "born in the kingdom of France and [had] not the advantage to understand the English tongue," provided them with a legal framework within which to have Anglican services in French.[42] While the Goose Creek community was implicitly absorbed into St. James Goose Creek, most likely because of its small and dwindling population, Orange Quarter was made into some sort of French-speaking subparish. It was distinctively named St. Denis in honor of the patron saint of France. Incidentally, this name would not have appealed particularly to the Huguenots, who as Calvinists did not worship saints, but from an Anglican perspective it made the parish unmistakably recognizable as a French enclave.[43]

St. Denis was meant to be a temporary parish uniquely defined, as Butler points out, in linguistic instead of geographic terms.[44] According to the act of 1708, which complemented that of 1706 by defining all the parishes territorially—a measure that surprisingly had been overlooked—the existence of St. Denis, which was "lying in the midst of the bounds [of St. Thomas] and designed at the present only for the use of the French Settlement," depended only on the parishioners' need to have "the divine service . . . in the French language." Presumably, once all settlers were able to attend services in English the church was to become "a chappel of ease to . . . St. Thomas."[45] Whereas the rector of St. James Santee was to receive the same annual salary as his English colleagues, the pastor of St. Denis was to be paid fifty, instead of one hundred, Carolina pounds.[46] Whether it was due to the small size of the congregation or the second-class status of the parish, this lower salary undoubtedly made the St. Denis cure unattractive and, in the long term, created an additional hurdle in the already difficult recruitment of French-speaking pastors.[47]

In addition to creating two parishes for the refugees, the 1706 act defined the conditions of French Anglican worship in specific terms that testify to the assemblymen's surprisingly intimate knowledge of Huguenot conformist religious life in the British Isles. According to article 22, the Huguenots were to use "the translation of the said book of common prayers, &c. which was translated into the said French tongue by Dr. John Durell, by the express command and order of his late Majesty King Charles Second, for the use of his Majesty's Chapel of the Savoy and his Islands of Jersey and Guernsey."[48] Carolina lawmakers had in mind the London Huguenot Church of the Savoy, the west-end conformist rival of the east-end Threadneedle Street congregation. The Church of the Savoy was founded in 1661, much later than its Nonconformist counterpart, and worship was conducted following the usage prevalent in the Channel Islands. John or Jean Durel, who had once been the chaplain of Sir George Carteret, lieutenant governor of Jersey and one of the eight original Carolina proprietors, was its first pastor. Durel was a well-connected royalist Jerseyan who fled the island when it was taken over by parliamentary forces in 1651. He received Anglican ordination while in exile in Paris and, following the restoration of the Stuarts, was commissioned to revise the 1616 French translation of the Book of Common Prayer in accordance with the 1662 English edition.[49] Leaving nothing to chance, the Carolina Assembly made sure that the lowcountry Huguenots would be using a liturgy in conformity, so to speak, with what the crown and the episcopal hierarchy prescribed.

Huguenot Conformity to the Church of England
The Transitional Phase (1706–1730s)

On the face of things, the definitive establishment of the Church of England in 1706 created a new world for the Carolina Huguenots. Santee became the parish of St. James Santee; Orange Quarter was included in the St. Thomas parish as St. Denis; the Goose Creek community was absorbed into St. James Goose Creek and Wantoot into St. John's Berkeley, while the Charleston church remained Calvinist. After 1706 the majority of Carolina Huguenots worshipped and lived within Anglican religious and political structures. Beneath this Anglican veneer, though, sources shed light on a complex reality. The refugees settled in Santee opted for passive resistance in adapting, when not altogether ignoring, Anglican practices to their Calvinist traditions, while those of St. Denis violently rejected conformity in the mid-1710s and again in the 1720s. Meanwhile in Charleston, beyond a Calvinist zeal *de façade,* Huguenots actually first flirted with and then eventually drifted into the Church of England. Clearly, the issue of Carolina Huguenots' acceptance or refusal to conform to the Church of England cannot be circumscribed by the casting of a few votes by a high-profile group.

While 1706 undeniably marked the beginning of a new era in the religious history of the lowcountry Huguenots, conformity obviously went through a transitional period. Most refugees had by then lived and worshipped in Carolina as Calvinists for more than twenty years and assuredly did not become Anglicans overnight. The foundations of Huguenot-Anglican religious life were therefore not erected on a tabula rasa but instead on existing Calvinist congregational structures. This structural superposition solidified gradually over a period of at least two decades until the original immigrants and their descendants became in their religious practices almost indistinguishable from other Carolina Anglican parishioners.

However, no matter how adaptable Carolina Anglican usages would turn out to be, in 1706, as in 1685, the Huguenots were forced to make a less painful yet equally consequential choice: conform or remain Calvinists. Outside of Charleston, where Huguenots could and did join St. Philip's individually, the choice had to be collective. Did the members of the Orange Quarter and Santee congregations meet and vote over conformity, as they did in New Rochelle, New York, in 1709, or, in the case of Santee, did the consistory make the decision and then explain it to their parishioners?[50] This question cannot be answered for lack of available records, but both the fact that the Santee petition was submitted nearly two years after the 1704 Church Act and the turbulence that severely shook St. Denis in the 1720s suggest, as should be expected, the existence of debates and factions over conformity. Once the decision was made, however, as the dissident St. Denis parishioners would soon learn at their expense, a point of no return had been reached.

As spiritual leaders of their congregations, pastors bore the greatest responsibility in adapting their preaching to the standards of the Church of England (and not vice versa), in enforcing the requirements of the Anglican liturgy, and in introducing their parishioners to the Book of Common Prayer. They probably also had to convince those in their congregations who were skeptical of the benefits of joining the Church of England. Needless to say, this theoretically perfect transition did not occur in South Carolina. Santee, St. Denis, and St. John's Berkeley all went through crises of varying seriousness until the Huguenots and their descendants finally became full-fledged members of the Church of England.

The Hidden Side of Conformity
Huguenot Practical Adaptation of Anglican Practices in Santee

In Santee, Pierre Robert, officiating as a Calvinist minister, married Margaret, Daniel Huger's daughter, to Élie Horry the year the first church act was voted and remained in that post after 1706 without having been properly ordained by a bishop.[51] Such procedure, even if Robert had been agreeable to it, would have implied a costly, long, and dangerous voyage to England. It would have left the congregation without a minister for a long while and also brought the risk of no return. Robert, who had been ordained by his pastoral colleagues in Basel in a Calvinist fashion before coming to Carolina, thus became rector of St. James Santee without any training in Anglican rituals. The 1706 petition and the church act therefore entailed no ritual changes whatsoever for the Santee congregation, at least as long as Robert was in that post.

Robert officially terminated his tenure in early 1710 at age fifty-four, four years after the church act vote, after marrying Daniel Huger Jr. to Élisabeth Gendron on January 25. Robert presumably left the post because of declining health but possibly because of Anglican pressure.[52] However, when Jacques Gignilliat, who had been appointed to succeed him in 1709, arrived in St. James, not only was Robert "still alive" but, to his successor's consternation, he also "kept his books & pretend[ed] to Christian all those that [would] be presented to him."[53] Robert thus maintained a Calvinist alternative to Huguenots not quite ready yet for conformity. This awkward situation was to last until Robert's death in 1715.[54]

The act of 1706 recommended the use of the official French translation of the Book of Common Prayer, but the assembly did not provide the Huguenot congregations with copies. Unsurprisingly, Gignilliat reported in 1710 that the Santee parishioners "never had the Common Prayer [Book] before, neither [had they] heard [of it]," and that it "look[ed] so strange to them."[55] Robert had apparently neglected to acquaint his newly conformed flock with the Anglican liturgy. To convince the Santee parishioners to use it, Gignilliat therefore had to argue for its Protestant authenticity in claiming that it "derive[d] from the Primitive Church."[56]

Jacques François Bénédict Gignilliat, whose cousin Jean-François was presumably instrumental in convincing him to apply for the Santee cure, arrived in Carolina in the spring of 1710 as an SPG missionary.[57] Soon the Swiss pastor complained about the 1706 law, "an Act of Parliament very strange" according to which "no minister can be entitled until elected & received by the people but people can't elect him before [receiving] orders of the Commissioners Before this election." Commissary Gideon Johnston, the bishop of London's representative in Charleston and unofficial head of the Carolina Anglican clergy, also denounced this "inconvenience" to the SPG and stressed the difficulty and the cost of summoning the necessary legal quorum of eleven commissioners, who "must Sign an Order for leave for the parishioners to Elect," since they "live scatter'd up and down the province."[58]

By July 1710 Gignilliat had been duly elected to his parish.[59] However, he was not to remain long in Santee. In April 1711 Francis LeJau, an SPG missionary of Huguenot descent posted to St. James Goose Creek since 1706, informed his superiors that Gignilliat altered "his Condition" in marrying fifty-eight-year-old Mary (Postel) Boisseau, "a rich French widow" with "a Considerable fortune, valued at 4,000£." Following this union, Gignilliat "forsook his French Parish without acquainting the Commissioners" and settled in his newly acquired Goose Creek estate.[60] There, as LeJau reports, he was "unwilling to do any more the duty of a Clergyman" and "made himself a person of Great business and projects [becoming] a parishioner and sometimes a hearer of [his]."[61] As if suddenly leaving his parish vacant, a serious breach of ecclesiastical rules, were not enough, Gignilliat before long also started to neglect his wife, "forcing the poor Woman out of doors [and] deny[ing] her necessary food and Cloathing."[62] While Gignilliat's unorthodox behavior justifiably enraged Commissary Johnston, who thought that he "had very much Exposed himselfe by his unkindness to his rich and decrepit wife," LeJau tried "to tell him as a Brother what [he thought] but [was] afraid of the Success."[63] Beyond his denunciation of Gignilliat's conduct, "which gives offence to all honest men, and brings reflections upon the weak and Malicious & upon our Calling," LeJau, with Christian compassion, particularly feared that "Lawyers [would] blow up the fire [and] that they must go to Law and be ruined" through a divorce. Acting as some sort of marriage counselor in a pre-psychology era, the Goose Creek pastor did "the duty of a friend both to him and his wife" in letting "both of them know abt. Xtmas they ought not to present themselves to the Lords Table before they are reconciled."[64]

While the rebellious Gignilliat privately "acknowledged noe Superiour here [in Carolina]," he nonetheless wrote to the SPG in an attempt to justify his pastoral desertion.[65] Along with "presenting [their] Illustrious Lords with an imperfect exposition of the Catechism of the Church of England, which [he] wrote for the benefit of the French people of this Province," Gignilliat explained that he had left his "Parish unprovided to follow [his] spouse, which [sic] was not willing to leave her little Estate to follow [him]." Far from renouncing his pastoral duty, he also claimed that "thô [he] had no church at present, [he] should not nevertheless forsake [his] ministry, and did design to go and Preach in the Parishes of [his] neighbourhood that were vacant of ministers."[66] Gignilliat, who according to LeJau "talks and writes the finest things yt. can be," seems to have put on a show for his distant and, he hoped, little-informed London superiors. Ostracized since spring 1712 by the Carolina Anglican clergy, who did not "approve his leaving his Parish, or his Inhuman usage to his wife," by February 1713, eighteen months after the wedding, Gignilliat had "sold all his wife's Estate in order to Carry what he [could] to Europe." The Swiss pastor was soon reported in Charleston waiting "for an opportunity of going off very Speedily," LeJau supposed, "for London."[67]

Soon after Gignilliat married the Boisseau widow and left St. James Santee, LeJau warned the SPG that considering "the Peoples Disposition [he] durst not give any encouragement for a minister to come to French Santée."[68] LeJau was right. In autumn 1711 the disappointed and presumably angry Santee parishioners decided to find a successor to Gignilliat through their own channels without asking the SPG or the bishop of London for assistance.[69] Most opportunely, Claude Philippe de Richebourg, a distant cousin of Carolina Huguenot Isaac Porcher, left his Virginia conformist congregation of Manakintown that same year. Richebourg's departure apparently followed irreparable disputes with his vestry, who, among other things, accused him of having crossed out acts from the church records without notifying them.[70] Although the deeper causes of these quarrels are unknown, in light of his subsequent behavior in Carolina, Richebourg most likely alienated most of his parishioners. After a brief stay in Trent, North Carolina, in the midst of the Tuscarora Wars, Richebourg sailed to South Carolina on a sloop that was captured and held by privateers, "who plundered what they could in 3 hours they were in possession" until they left "upon the Appearing of one of our Men of Warr."[71] Richebourg, accompanied by a few refugees, safely settled in Santee in August 1712.

Richebourg's arrival in Carolina happened to coincide with the death of Florent-Philippe Trouillart, who had since 1706 served the small Huguenot congregation living in St. John's Berkeley.[72] Therefore, as Commissary Johnston later reported, "being known to some [St. John's] French parishioners, [who] entreated [him] to preach and administer the Sacrament of the Lords Supper to them in their own Language, as being most easy and familiar to them," Richebourg agreed, two months after Trouillart's death, to attend to their spiritual needs "as often as he coud be well absent from his Parish." Robert Maule, the Irish SPG missionary serving at St. John's Berkeley, being "a worthy good Man," consented "provided every thing was done as it should be according to the [Church of England's] Canons and Rubrick," which Richebourg reportedly promised. Before long, however, Maule was informed, "both by Eye and Earwitnesses," that Richebourg had "basely and treacherously broke [his word], and wholly made use of the Geneva way."[73]

The disciplinarian Johnston, who had just been dealing with Gignilliat's "unfair and uncanonical proceedings," decided to confront Richebourg and put an end to his practices because, as LeJau deplored, "that Mungrell sort of Clergy does a great deal of hurt, and greatly foment the differences, and widen the Breaches, between [the] Church and the French."[74] At a general meeting of the Carolina Anglican clergy, Richebourg, presumably after being lectured by Johnston and despite some early "dodging and shuffling," did confess enough of the charge to make him "very criminal" and solemnly promised "he woud do so no more." Perhaps as Johnston expected, Richebourg "broke thro' all those engagements" and "behave[d] himself very ill in worthy Mr. Maules Parish, notwithstanding his Promises to [Johnston] and to the whole Clergy to the contrary."[75]

Richebourg most likely behaved in a similar fashion in Santee because, as LeJau wisely stated, "he that is a Calvinist in another Mans Parish will not stick much at being one in his own."[76] Ten years after the act of establishment, in all practical purposes the Huguenots of St. James Santee and St. John's Berkeley had not yet conformed to the Church of England.

In addition to arousing Johnston's ire for his Calvinist infringements, Richebourg was also facing opposition in his own parish. In a letter addressed to the commissary in December 1712, six months after the arrival of Richebourg, LeJau reported factious and violent behaviors in Santee. According to LeJau's source, the parish was wracked by "divisions and Quarrels" and "Swords were drawn at the Church door after divine Service." Although LeJau optimistically believed that "[his] brother had no share in all those affairs," in light of his previous altercations with the Manakintown vestry, Richebourg was most likely involved in these bitter disputes.[77]

In 1714 and 1718 the Santee Huguenot community was shaken by two related court cases. Richebourg was central to one of them and most likely involved in the other. In March 1714 Charles Ducros de La Bastie and his wife, Hélène, filed a suit for libel in the court of common plea against Barthélemy Gaillard for "falsly, Scandallously, & Malliciously" saying that "[Hélène] was a whore and the whore of Mr. de Richbourg, Minister of Santy and that the whore had four bastards." As their lawyer, George Rodd, explained to the court, Hélène de La Bastie, "Chast & honest Subject of our Soveraign Lady the Queen [Anne] . . . [who] hath been accounted, known, talked & reputed without Stain or Scandall of Whoredom Adultery or fornication or any other hurtfull fault or Notorious Crime," had been "greavously wounded in her fame, name, Creditt and reputation" by Gaillard's accusations. She was constrained to sue Gaillard for redress lest she should be "in great danger of loosing [sic] the Company and Society of her said husband and also to be divorced from him and to fall into extream Infamy and Scandal of being a notorious whore and harlott."[78] The La Basties decided to sue Gaillard for five hundred Carolina pounds (seventy pounds sterling). This was quite a hefty sum considering that the annual salary of an Anglican minister, such as Richebourg, was one hundred Carolina pounds.

Gaillard's allegations against Hélène and the pastor Richebourg may have been totally unfounded. Having been in Santee for barely eighteen months when Gaillard pronounced his accusations in November 1713, Richebourg had certainly not sired the "four bastards" and may have had no illegitimate relationship with La Bastie's wife. His being mentioned in the case, however, was not coincidental. In 1718 the same Barthélemy Gaillard brought a suit against Isaac LeGrand in the court of chancery. The case concerned the fraudulent sale of land at the expense of the vestry and the congregation that had occurred in 1712 and 1713, in the early years of Richebourg's ministry. In March 1712 Alexandre Thésée Chastaigner, "Indebted in Very Greate and Considerable sumes of money . . . Farr Exceeding The Value of his personall Estate," died after dictating a noncupative will to Henry LeNoble and Pierre de St. Julien. In June the assembly authorized his widow, Élisabeth Buretel, Ralph Izard, LeNoble, and St. Julien to sell Chasteigner's lands to pay his debts. At that time the Santee vestry instructed one of its members, Isaac LeGrand Jr., to purchase "as Cheap a Rate as He Could" the three tracts of land, which constituted Chastaigner's estate, collectively known as Dassen. The vestry also wished to acquire the house that Chastaigner had built to be used as a presbytery for the minister of said parish and his successors. They gave LeGrand two hundred Carolina pounds to that effect, instructing him to "returne the Overplus."[79]

However, "Evilly Intending to Cheat and Defraud The Inhabitants of the said Parrish," LeGrand "combin[ed] And Confederat[ed]" with the late LeNoble, who incidentally was then a member of the South Carolina Assembly, to purchase only two of three tracts, or eleven hundred instead of twelve hundred acres, for 200 Carolina pounds, whereas LeNoble had estimated Chasteigner's entire estate at 150 pounds.[80] Allegedly, LeNoble was to keep 50 pounds for his silence. The fraud seemed difficult to detect, for how could the vestry doubt the "Integrity and Honesty" of one of their members and how could they precisely know if they acquired eleven hundred or twelve hundred acres without having the estate surveyed? In November 1713, the same year that Gaillard uttered the accusations against his wife, Charles de La Bastie, who owned land next to Dassen, sold three hundred acres to a Philip Dawes. Included in this transaction were the one hundred acres that LeGrand had acquired illegally and which he presumably wanted to rid himself of quickly, perhaps because Gaillard had already been informed of the fraud by one of the "Confederates."[81] LeGrand and La Bastie were most likely to share the profits of the sale of the La Bastie estate that was assuredly made more attractive with the addition of LeGrand's one hundred acres. Once he had collected enough evidence and safely five years after La Bastie's plaint of libel had been "abated by the death of one of the Plaintiffs," Gaillard, as a churchwarden and a parishioner, decided to bring a class action suit against LeGrand "on behalf of himself and the inhabitants of the parish of St. James, Santee."[82]

When he first learned about LeGrand and La Bastie's illicit dealings in November 1713, Gaillard reacted by libeling La Bastie's wife and Richebourg. Was the pastor an accomplice of LeGrand's, LeNoble's, and La Bastie's? Did he simply know about the transactions and choose not to reveal anything, or did he condone it? In light of the tension that preceded Richebourg's departure from Manakintown, it is safe to assume that the pastor was probably not completely innocent. Available sources do not reveal, however, the extent to which he was implicated in the case. It can only be surmised that Richebourg knew of something and did not inform the vestry, which justifiably enraged Gaillard. Gaillard's reaction was to stain the honor of La Bastie, his wife, and Richebourg in a joint accusation of adultery and bastardy.

Conflicts within Huguenot congregations, either between the pastor and the consistory or between groups of parishioners, were so common in France that they should come as no surprise in the divisive postconformity Carolina context. Whereas in France similar feuds would most likely have been solved by the local presbytery (colloque), which would have reprimanded Richebourg, while the consistory would have temporarily suspended LeGrand from Communion, in the absence of such institutions the case was brought to civil justice. The legal outcome of the *Gaillard v. LeGrand* litigation, however, is not known. It may be surmised, though, that the Santee vestry obtained a decree in its favor, especially since Gaillard was then justice of the peace for Craven County and as such drew the writ of subpoena that was addressed to LeGrand.[83]

What makes Richebourg's ministry quite puzzling, however, is his "playing fast and loose with the Canons and Rubrick [of the Church of England]," as Johnston put it, since, being an Anglican convert from Catholicism, known in England as proselytes, he had not been trained in a Calvinist academy.[84] Why would a former Catholic priest conduct services following the "Geneva way" in a conformist parish? Richebourg must have been under pressure from parishioners who rejected Anglican worship despite having officially joined the Church of England. Conformity appears to have been for them an institutional rather than spiritual move, with a decisive political dimension, resulting from practical considerations.

From Passive to Active Resistance
The Case of St. Denis

The parish of St. Denis, with a social makeup significantly different from that of Santee, experienced two tumultuous decades following the passage of the 1706 Church Act. The dissension over conformity that can only be glimpsed in Santee raged there with such intensity that some parishioners came openly and categorically to reject Anglican worship and their conformist minister, creating thereby a pastoral vacuum that prepared the ground for prophetizing. Only in the late 1720s did St. Denis fully become an Anglican parish. It remained so until it was dissolved into St. Thomas in 1758. In contrast to St. James Santee, where three ministers served from 1706 to 1720, the St. Denis cure was held by Jean LaPierre during these twenty eventful years, except for a brief period in the mid-1710s when he preached at Santee.

Born in LaSalle, Languedoc, in 1681, LaPierre belonged to the post-Revocation generation. Moving to the British Isles at an early age, he was educated at Trinity College, from which he graduated in 1706. Following Trouillart's departure for St. John's Berkeley in 1706, LaPierre arrived in St. Denis in 1708 after being ordained and licensed by Bishop Compton.[85] The fact that he was not in the colony as an SPG missionary turned out to be a major source of financial stress for him and his family since it prevented them from receiving steady monetary assistance from that society.[86]

Although LaPierre's Carolina ministry eventually became a tale of conflicts, reprimands, rejection, and financial distress, it started under most favorable auspices. Two 1708 letters addressed by Huguenot Josias Dupré to his son Jacques, then in London, explained how LaPierre came to Carolina completely destitute, how he was warmly welcomed and materially assisted by his parishioners, and how he gained their trust and admiration through his edifying sermons and polite manners. According to Dupré, LaPierre, his blind wife, and "their little girl," after a four-month voyage, arrived in such a pitiful state of indigence, without sheets, spare clothes, or household items, that the parishioners prepared for them a small house, gave them ten pounds sterling, and purchased linens, blankets, and utensils for them in Charleston. They also provided the LaPierres with "corn, rice, bread, meat, poultry, butter and other provisions and refreshments" as well as "a slave woman to serve them."[87] This cornucopian welcome reflected the generosity of French parishioners happy and relieved to have one of their own preach among them.

Apparently they were not disappointed by their minister's sermons, which "surpassed their hopes," as LaPierre revealed himself to be "a good theologian," expounding on biblical texts "methodically and in a charming manner with his expressions, his voice, and hands" so that "the entire assembly was extremely edified."[88] Within a few weeks LaPierre had won "the heart and affection of his church," and his parishioners were so eager "to bring him what is necessary to life [that soon] he was agreeably overwhelmed with an abundance of goods." In no time LaPierre was "admired by the English as much as by the French" and was heralded as "the most skilful preacher in the French language who ever came to this land of Carolina." This reputation is supported by Thomas Hasell, pastor at St. Thomas and formerly a fellow student of LaPierre's at "l'académie de Dublin," who remembered him as "the most recommendable of all the students for his good behaviour having never been censured."[89]

The honeymoon period of LaPierre's ministry, however, did not last long and was the prelude to more than a decade of bitter conflict. In October 1711, three years after his appointment to the St. Denis cure, LaPierre, while visiting with his compatriot and coreligionist LeJau, informed him that he was "very poor, and unkindly us'd by his people that are mean persons and growing Intollerably ambitious" and that he was "desirous to remove to one of [the] vacant Parishes where he may have more confort."[90] LaPierre and his parishioners apparently came to irreconcilable differences when, through a letter written in April or May 1713, the St. Denis community informed their minister that they "no longer acknowledge[d] [him] as [their] pastor" and encouraged him "to transfer [himself] to another flock." The authors of the letter, who described themselves as "named officers in [the] church" (that is, vestrymen), mentioned a previous missive, written in November 1712, in which they warned LaPierre "not to ask anything of [them] concerning changing the posture of the body in the reception of the Lord's Supper if [he] chose to perform the offices of this ministry among [them]." Apparently LaPierre refused "to comply to [their] request," and the parishioners became angered by the minister's attempts to persuade them to change their behavior.[91] As LaPierre explained to the SPG a few years later, the St. Denis Huguenots had manifestly "altered their first mind of Conforming themselves to the Church of England" and, in a most extraordinary fashion, fired their conformist pastor.[92]

According to Johnston's report, the rebellious parishioners of St. Denis contended that "Sir Nathaniel Johnson faithfully promised them" permission "to receive Communion in the Geneva Posture" when they petitioned to become an Anglican parish and had him "write to the Late Bishop [Compton] for an Episcopal Minister." They also claimed that "the late Bishop allowed the French Episcopal Ministers in all parts of his Diocese in England, to use the English or Geneva Liturgy indifferently according as their People woud have it." As expected, Johnston did not believe that Sir Nathaniel had made such a promise and was skeptical although incognizant of what was being tolerated in London.[93]

At this juncture the punctilious and rigid commissary not only refused to assist his colleague LaPierre but, probably exasperated by the disruptive behaviors of Gignilliat and Richebourg, also turned his anger against the French pastor. Johnston, who thought it "ill luck that Sir Nathaniel Johnson died before this story was trumpt up," believed that it was LaPierre's responsibility to inform the late governor of his parishioners' claim, as he "often visit[ed] him and converse[d] with him." The commissary also accused LaPierre of being "the original cause of all this trouble" and of having "greatly inflamed and exasperated the minds of his People [by] his warm and indiscreet temper." Johnston explained that the St. Denis parishioners considered LaPierre "a Man of No Principle" and blamed him for "double dealing and prevaricating in matter of religion." In short, LaPierre brought adversity upon himself in trying to be conciliatory and please all his parishioners by "taking liberty as to the Rites and ceremonies of [the] Church [of England] . . . without the least force and constraint on their side" instead of being firm and steadfast in following orthodox liturgical practices.[94]

Johnston, who had an ax to grind about Carolina clergymen, English or French, who adapted Anglican rituals, took the side of the rebellious flock and wondered with them why, since "LaPierre began his ministry . . . after the Geneva manner," it should be "unlawful for him now to continue in that practice." Johnston, who thought that LaPierre's heart "was not with [the Church of England], but at Geneva or Elsewhere," was convinced of LaPierre's guilt. In a final burst of authoritarianism and an expression of arbitrary justice, he formally disciplined the French pastor and "threatened him with the total loss and forfeiture of both his Cure and his salary."[95]

Clearly, the quickest way out of the crisis would have been for Johnston to support LaPierre openly while reprimanding him in private. Instead, by blaming the French minister and siding with his factious flock, the commissary not only further undermined LaPierre's legitimacy among them but also, somewhat ironically, considerably weakened the local Anglican establishment in the eyes of its Huguenot opponents. Apart from its unjustified intransigence and blatant lack of objectivity, Johnston's reaction also reflects a total ignorance of—or disregard for—the situation that Huguenot conformist pastors had to face in Carolina. The French ministers, assigned to newly and imperfectly conformed Huguenot-Anglican parishes, were often caught between (no pun on LaPierre's surname intended) a rock and a hard place. Faced with divided and unruly parishioners and at the mercy of vestrymen who were not as thoroughly Anglicanized as their position within the parish structure required, they also had to answer to their superiors within the Church of England hierarchy. As opposed to LeJau, who officiated in an almost exclusively English parish, they *had* to be flexible and conciliatory to hope to remain in their posts while pledging an infallible loyalty to their adoptive church. LaPierre may have been guilty of liturgical concessions, but, as was Richebourg in Santee, he was most likely under pressure from some, perhaps most, of his parishioners and vestrymen on whose subscriptions, it bears emphasizing, he relied to complement his meager salary.

Although the authors of the April/May 1713 letter claimed to act "jointly and in conformity" in the name of the entire congregation, they most likely represented a radical faction influential or loud enough to sway the rest of the parishioners. In his retrospective account of the events, LaPierre also implied a much more violent and much less rational rejection of Anglican worship than the authors of the outrageous yet civil letter would have posterity believe. LaPierre seems actually to have been faced with a grassroots rebellion against Anglican order led by artisans inspired by a millenarian group. The agitators were not just concerned about whether they should take Communion standing, sitting, or kneeling, as Johnston would have it, but expressed fanatic views that could potentially disrupt any kind of orderly religious life, Anglican or Calvinist.

In an August 1714 missive addressed to Claude Grotête de La Mothe, the influential conformist pastor at the London Savoy Church and a member of the SPCK and SPG, LaPierre denounced two ringleaders: an anonymous multilingual stonecutter and a "Maître Bochet."[96] These "two pestilensious fellows" were apparently followers of the so-called "French Prophets," a millenarian group whose founders were from the Cévennes and who attempted to spread spiritual havoc within the Huguenot London community until they were uncompromisingly repudiated by the consistory of the Threadneedle Street Church in 1707.[97] The stonecutter, who cannot be identified, "translated a few sentences from German into French" taken from a book written by, as LaPierre put it, the "*faux prophètes de Londres*" and "*Maître Bochet,*" who must be Nicolas since his brother Abel had died by 1712, "unleashed in a furious way against Anglican ministers."[98]

These two ringleaders and their followers held Antinomian- and Sabbatarian-inspired seditious views.[99] According to LaPierre, they "spread the following tenets that in general men must not be oby'd, that Scriptures of both testaments are but a Dead letter, [and] that ye Jewish Sabbath ought to be kept instead of the Lord's Day."[100] LaPierre attempted to take "all possible methods to prevent and Suppress their Heresy, by preaching against Them as well as calling them before ye Magistrates," but "all this prov'd uneffectual." Determined to defeat the "Sect [that] first crept amongst [his flock] by ye religious observation of the Jewish Sabbath," LaPierre, "having in [Carolina] no Book upon this Subject," composed a pamphlet entitled *The Vindication of ye Christian Sabbath.* This document has not survived and it is not known whether anyone ever read it, but it obviously had no influence whatsoever on the course of events. By the time LaPierre wrote it, St. Denis had temporarily ceased to exist and had become once again a Calvinist congregation under its original name of Orange Quarter.[101]

Secession in the Lowcountry
St. Denis Goes Calvinistic

Sometime in 1716 the St. Denis parishioners, in an extraordinarily bold fashion, opted to secede from the network of Carolina Anglican parishes.[102] Little is known, however, about the four years or so when the Orange Quarter community regained its institutional independence. It can be surmised that a new Calvinist consistory was formed and that the congregation assembled in the former St. Denis church, which the seditious Huguenots most likely considered theirs since it had been, as the minister of St. Thomas explained, "built by their own Contributions about the same time with the parish church."[103]

Back in 1713, soon after asking LaPierre to release his cure, the Orange Quarter Huguenots had "sent their best Orators with a letter from the whole Body" to the Nonconformist Charleston pastor Paul L'Escot "requiring to be admitted to communicate with him." L'Escot, who had by then befriended Commissary Johnston and who had revealed unmistakable—albeit slightly veiled—signs of conformity in his correspondence to various prelates in England, flatly refused to admit them to his congregation, let alone ride a few dozen miles to officiate in their church. L'Escot, who believed "his Conscience much better inform'd than theirs," felt that "not Conscience but Malice or at best groundless Prejudice, made them quarrell at so good a Church."[104]

As during the early years of the Carolina Huguenot settlement with Prioleau and Trouillart, the Orange Quarter community was hoping to become again the Cooper River annexe of the Charleston French Church. L'Escot's refusal was a clear and painful sign that times had changed and, ironically, constituted a blatant Anglican victory, which no doubt Johnston must have considered his. This vividly demonstrated to the Orange Quarter settlers, although they would fail to understand it then, that a point of no return had been reached in 1706. The church act had caused a permanent fracture in the Carolina Huguenot religious history. Secession was not a time machine that would allow dissatisfied and quarrelsome conformist Huguenots to go back to their earlier Calvinist lives.

Following L'Escot's refusal, the Orange Quarter Huguenots remained without a minister until fall 1716, when the Nonconformist Threadneedle Street Church favorably answered their request for a Calvinist pastor. In a letter addressed to the leaders of "l'Eglise Françoise dans le Quartier d'Orange a Caroline," the London consistory informed them that "M. de Malacare [Pierre de St. Julien]," who had "handed [them] the letter . . . concerning a new minister," had "acquainted them with Mr. Stoupan [Stouppe]" and that they "had him preach in [their] church." Pierre Stouppe must have passed the pulpit test since the consistory, acknowledging the "excellent certificates of his acceptance to the ministry, his orthodoxy, [and] his good behaviour," approved of "the choice of Mr. de Malacare" and wholeheartedly recommended him to the Carolina congregation. The London elders did mention, however, that the newly appointed minister did "not yet master the French language well enough" but thought that "not only [could] he remedy this flaw and in little time, but [that] he also spoke intelligibly enough to make himself understand and to edify the souls which only seek salvation and the Glory of God." The consistory members ended their letter with a much welcomed note of encouragement to their correspondents, praying that "He never lets [them] in need of this spiritual and celestial pasture for which [they] long in such an edifying manner."[105]

Pierre de St. Julien was an affluent merchant who by 1715 owned over seven thousand acres of land in the two parishes of St. John's Berkeley and St. James Santee.[106] The fact that he served as an agent of the Orange Quarter community and recommended a pastor to the London consistory while on a business trip overseas reveals the existence of close ties within the lowcountry Huguenot community that transcended social and religious boundaries. In their rebellion against Anglican order, the Orange Quarter settlers, who were mostly impoverished artisans, successfully sought the assistance of a wealthy and presumably conformist Huguenot who did not even own land in St. Denis.

The information on Stouppe's life before his coming to South Carolina is sketchy, and his identity remains somewhat speculative. Born in Switzerland in 1690 and educated at the Geneva academy, Pierre was probably the son of the Swiss pastor Jean-Baptiste Stouppe, Cromwell's messenger to the Valdensians, who officiated at Threadneedle Street in the 1650s and who died on the battlefield in 1692. One wonders, however, why the London consistory failed to mention his father's ministry in their church. It is equally puzzling that Stouppe, presumably the son of a French-speaking Swiss pastor, would not be fluent in French. This may mean that Pierre was raised in England and that French had become to him a second language only spoken at home.[107]

At any rate, Stouppe, who was probably in Carolina by 1717, did not officiate long in Orange Quarter. In December 1720 LaPierre, who had replaced the late Richebourg in Santee by April 1719, triumphantly wrote the SPG that "the French of ye Parish of St. Dennis . . . Called for a new minister according to the french discipline with whom likewise the[y] disagreed insomuch that now they are altogether destitute."[108] The specific reasons leading to Stouppe's departure from Orange Quarter are not documented. It is safe to assume, however, that the impoverished and quarrelsome nature of the Orange Quarter community, coupled with L'Escot's return to England in 1719, which freed the wealthier and more prestigious Charleston cure, persuaded an ambitious Stouppe to move on.

A Prophet, a Virgin, and a Hog
The Dutartre Insurrection

About a year after his return, an overoptimistic and possibly deceived LaPierre assured the SPG that "God was pleased to Succeed [his] endeavours and to bring [his parishioners] again into the bosom of [the] Church."[109] In fact, as LaPierre recognized at the beginning of the same letter, St. Denis was still very much divided over the issue of conformity as was New Rochelle, where a significant number of Huguenots refused conformity and lived a marginalized religious life thereby creating a religious split that Élie Neau dramatically called "le Schisme de Nouvelle rochelle."[110] Observing the religious fracture at St. Denis, Thomas Hasel, rector of St. Thomas, reported in September 1720, a few months after Stouppe's departure, that "part of the people at Orange Quarter [are] conformists and part Use Calvin Liturgy and Discipline."[111]

Anglican order had been officially restored along with LaPierre out of necessity and without the assent of the entire community. But in fact there was still considerable spiritual fluidity and, worse, there were pockets of deinstitutionalized religion within the parish. All that was needed was a spark to set the parish ablaze.

Sometime in 1722 or 1723, "a certain strolling Moravian, Dutch or Swiss Enthusiast, named Christian George" preached and handed out religious pamphlets to the St. Denis parishioners.[112] The Dutartres, "a Family . . . always in low Circumstances in Life, but of honest Repute," turned out to be particularly sensitive to the Moravian's message. "With their Heads filled with many wild and fantastic Notions . . . in a Year or two's Time, they began to *withdraw* or *separate* from public Worship . . . and to conceit that they were the *alone* Family upon Earth who had the true Knowledge and Worship of God."[113]

Soon Pierre Rembert, the husband of Pierre Dutartre's eldest daughter, believed that "God had expressly revealed to him" his intention of destroying "*Mankind a Second Time from off the Face of the Earth, all but that one Family, whom he would preserve as he did Noah's.*" Inspired by what he perceived as his divine mission, Rembert enthusiastically shared an apocalyptic and cryptic vision with his father-in-law. The newly revealed Orange Quarter prophet explained that God had advised him "*to Put away the Woman*" he had for a wife because "*when* [God] *has destroyed this Wicked Generation* . . . [God would] *raise up her first Husband from the Dead* [to be] *Man and Wife as before.*" Rembert was therefore divinely instructed to "*take to Wife her Youngest Sister* [Judith Dutartre] *who is a virgin, so shall that chosen Family be restored entire, and the Holy Seed be preserved pure and undefiled in it.*" As expected, "the old Man the Father was staggered at so strange a Message," but "the Prophet assured him that God would give him a Sign." According to Pierre Rembert, "on their going to the next Plantation, the first living Creature they should See there, should be . . . a Horse . . . or a Hog."[114]

Rembert's prophecy came true, which is not in itself surprising since both creatures were then common sights in rural South Carolina without the need for divine intervention. Probably awed by the sign and the accuracy of Rembert's prophecy, while flattered to be among God's chosen, Pierre Dutartre, in an ultimately patriarchal fashion, obliged his son-in-law by taking "his Youngest Daughter by the Hand [and giving] her to the Prophet to Wife." Commissary Alexander Garden, Johnston's successor, went on to explain that Pierre Rembert "went in unto her and lay with her without any further Ceremony, pursuant to his Revelation [and] possessed . . . with a Conceit of their own Holiness, and of the Impurity and Wickedness of others," and the Dutartres "continued in open and notorious Adultery and Incest."

At some point, however, the Dutartres fatally crossed the line separating religious enthusiasm and ill morality from civil disobedience. In a vein of Antinomianism reminiscent of the Bochet rebellion, they decided to "give no Obedience to the civil Magistrate, nor to any of the Laws and Ordinances of Men." They objected to "the Law for repairing the Highway" and, finding an opportune use for Moravian pacifist teachings, also "refused to comply . . . with the Militia Law (on Pretence that God had revealed to them not to bear Arms)." As expected, the Dutartres raised considerable concern among South Carolina's local civil authorities, who lost no time in issuing "Warrants for levying the Penalties of those Laws upon them." Meanwhile, "the Prophets Revelation Wife [Judith Dutartre] proving with Child," she was subpoenaed to the Court of General Sessions for Bastardy.[115]

The rest of the affair is a violent tale of gun battles, murders, executions, and fantasized resurrections. Barricaded in their house, the Dutartres shot dead Pierre Simons, the justice of the peace who had come to arraign them, and "a woman of the adverse party [Anne Dutartre LeSad]." After they were ultimately placed under arrest, the court decided not to try Judith, whereas Pierre Dutartre, Pierre Rembert, and a Michael Boinneau, all confident that God would "raise them up from the Dead on the third Day," were convicted and executed.[116] Dutartre's younger sons, Daniel and Jean, "Lad's of about Eighteen or Twenty Years of Age," were "Tried and Condemned [but] after finding no Resurrection of the others from the Dead, as they expected, became sensible of their Delusion, at least professed themselves so, and were pardoned." However, one of them (Garden does not specify who) was tried again and executed after he "relapsed into the same Snare, and Murdered an Innocent Person, without any previous Quarrel or Provocation, and for no other Reason as he acknowledged, but that God had revealed it to him."[117]

This "Tragical Scene of Enthusiasm, immediate Revelations and Strong Impulses," as Garden succinctly described it, was, apart from its extreme violence, reminiscent of the earlier Bochet episode that shook the same parish. Except for the refusal to bear arms, Pierre Rembert seemed to have been inspired more by the messages and behaviors of the London French Prophets than by Moravian literature proper.[118] The St. Denis enthusiasts' violent, gory, and apocalyptic message based on the premise of an angry and revengeful God, their anticlericalism, and their claim to read signs denote a clear influence from the French Prophets.[119] Pamphlets defending and incriminating the London enthusiasts were actually circulating in the parish, and the Dutartre, Rembert, and Bochet families necessarily knew each other.[120] Beyond Pierre Rembert's swindling skills and Pierre Dutartre's naïveté, the affair was a sequel to the St. Denis rebellion against LaPierre and the unfortunate consequence of spiritual instability and ministerial vacuum stemming from successive ecclesiological volte-face. When LaPierre answered Bishop Gibson's 1724 queries about his parish, he stated that out of the thirty-four French families residing in St. Denis, eighteen were "in dispute with church." In other words, nearly twenty years after Orange Quarter joined the Church of England and became St. Denis, and in the midst of the "Dutartre affair," a majority of the Huguenots were still rejecting conformity.[121]

It remains to be explained, however, why St. Denis experienced a "sc[h]ismatical Separation," as LaPierre put it, and spiritual convulsions, whereas St. James Santee did not.[122] Poverty is certainly a significant factor. Contrary to Santee and like Orange Quarter earlier, St. Denis was never a land of large estates owned by affluent and influential esquires. The great majority of the Cooper River Huguenots, such as the Bochets and the Dutartres, were weavers of modest means who had to turn to cattle raising and other agricultural pursuits to survive on small tracts of land. Consequently, unlike Santee, there never was a French landed or mercantile elite that could serve as a buffer between the Charleston Anglo-Anglican establishment and the more modest Huguenots.

Furthermore, Orange Quarter, being geographically closer to the province's sources of religious and political power, was also more immediately confronted by Anglicization and Anglicanization forces. While René Ravenel and Philippe Gendron sat on the 1706 lay commission and could smooth Santee's way into the Anglican parochial structure, St. Denis enjoyed no such representation. To be sure, the Anglicanization of Santee experienced setbacks, especially during Richebourg's tenure, but problems there were solved either internally or in a civil court. Santee was no place for religious fanaticism and violent murders. The second-rate treatment as a subparish, with a reduced pastoral salary and no glebe, that St. Denis received from the Anglican establishment may also have created resentment among the settlers, who construed it as condescension and neglect. Additionally, the fact that the Orange Quarter congregation had been an annexe of the Charleston church, which chose not to conform, may at some point have weakened the determination of the St. Denis parishioners to remain within the Church of England. LaPierre, with his wavering commitment to Anglican rituals and, possibly, his impressionable nature, bears some responsibility for failing to contain the inevitable Calvinist aspirations of Huguenots who had recently conformed out of necessity.

In the mid-1720s, at long last, Anglican order was restored in St. Denis, and most Orange Quarter Huguenots accepted conformity to the Church of England.[123] It was not, however, the end of LaPierre's confrontation with the Carolina ecclesiastical authorities. In January 1726 the clergyman wrote to the bishop of London, Edmund Gibson, "appealing to a general arbitration and exposing to ye light [a] slanderous letter." LaPierre was accused by Commissary Garden of "administer[ing] ye holy Sacrament of baptism to a child . . . in a publick form and in a private house" in St. Philip's, Garden's parish, "without either [his] consent or privity . . . [and] contrary to ye express canons and rubricks of ye Church." LaPierre explained to the bishop that when he was in Charleston one day an English settler, "being at variance with his minister [for reasons] unknown to [LaPierre]," asked him to baptize a child while assuring him that "Mr Garden was very willing." LaPierre claimed first to have refused but eventually agreed after the man told him that "it was his wife's earnest desire being a french woman and formerly one of [LaPierre's] hearers," and that "the assistants likewise [were] of ye French nation." Apparently, Garden had never been informed of the couple's plans and reacted to LaPierre's "clandestine piece of intrusion" with contempt, anger, and abuse. In clearly excessive language, the commissary called the French clergyman "a thief and a robber" and regarded his action as that of "an apostate and faithless Traytor." Reminding LaPierre of the "Dutart's [sic] principles," which he hoped "had been quite extinguish'd," Garden emphatically swore that "nothing but death [should] prevent [his] transmiting [the affair] to ye Bishop of London and the honorable Society [SPG] with [his] complaints in the strongest terms." While LaPierre favored an internal solution and claimed that "he would have made [Garden] all reasonable satisfaction in a meeting of ye clergy as our former custom was, without any need troubling [His] Lordship," writing to the bishop was his only defense.[124]

Bishop Gibson, who had just succeeded John Robinson in 1723 and was in the process of strengthening his overseas authority, seems neither to have supported the commissary, reprimanded LaPierre, nor taken any action.[125] This incident confirms, in contrast to the distant and paternal bishops, how severe and uncompromising South Carolina commissaries, whether Johnston or Garden, were toward Huguenot conformist ministers who were not as affable nor as dedicated to promoting the Church of England as LeJau was. This ecclesiastical intransigence truly hindered the work of the Francophone Carolina ministers who, contrary to LeJau, officiated in parishes with predominantly Huguenot populations often hesitant—not to say recalcitrant—about conforming fully.

Following his epistolary altercation with Garden, LaPierre was ready to leave South Carolina. Plagued with monetary problems, LaPierre, accompanied by his blind wife and their five young children and with Garden's expected consent, accepted the cure of New Hanover, North Carolina, in 1728.[126]

The Charleston Huguenot Church
Nonconformity and the Mirage of Congregational Independence

Charleston was the only lowcountry Huguenot church that chose not to conform under the act of 1706. Although this decision was, in subsequent centuries, to bring fame to the congregation for being the "only Huguenot Church in America," it is actually misleading. In no way does it mean that the Charleston community did not experience difficulties, as Orange Quarter and Santee did, nor that it long remained a center of Carolina Huguenot spiritual life. In fact, opting to remain Calvinist turned out, in the long term, to take the congregation along an arduous route that eventually led most of its members to the bosom of the Church of England. By the mid-eighteenth century the once thriving congregation had more or less already become an empty memorial church that barely maintained active status in honor of its founders.

In March 1700 the Threadneedle Street Church consistory received a letter from "les françois de Charlestown en Caroline" praying them to recommend "a minister to replace

Mon. Trouillart."[127] Although the Carolina letter must have been sent following Prioleau's death and the London consistory refers elsewhere to "the Church yesteryear served by the late Monsieur Prioleau," once again Trouillart appears to have been *the* Charleston pastor.[128] After a four-month search, Threadneedle Street was relieved to have found a perfect candidate. In their reply to the Charleston French Church, the elders thanked "la providance" for sending them a pastor "such as [they] wished . . . [having] done all his education at Geneva . . . [and being] Orthodox [and] a man of virtue and of probity."[129] Inviting the Charleston Huguenots to "praise God for the present He is giving them," the consistory, acting as a presbytery, further recommended L'Escot unanimously for his "good mores, his good doctrine, and his honest, wise and righteous deportment" after having duly heard him preach twice.[130]

As in the case of Stouppe's appointment to the dissident Orange Quarter congregation, Pierre de St. Julien played the indispensable role of a transatlantic intermediary between the two consistories. At the Threadneedle Street elders' request, "Mon. de Malacare" agreed to pay L'Escot "the thirty pounds sterling promised for his voyage" by the Charleston French Church. St. Julien, however, had to have his arm twisted to oblige both consistories and accepted only on condition that the London elders duly record his financial participation.[131] L'Escot's Charleston ministry had started, as it would finish, with pecuniary issues.

Born in France in 1655, Paul L'Escot left Louis XIV's kingdom in 1672, thirteen years before the Revocation, and settled with his parents in Geneva. As he claimed when he was pondering the opportuneness of a sojourn to Paris in 1698 with his Viennese patron, he was not strictly speaking a Huguenot refugee and "could even pass as a *Genevois*."[132] After completing his pastoral education at the Genevan academy, L'Escot held successive positions as tutor and chaplain to illustrious noble families in the Netherlands, the Rhineland, and Austria for over twenty-five years.[133] Although he would later crave stability, while he was wandering through parts of Europe, L'Escot undoubtedly built himself an impressive network of influential lay and ecclesiastical friends and patrons, on which he would later rely in time of adversity. In living among sophisticated and learned aristocrats, L'Escot also acquired a lifestyle largely above his birth rank, which would painfully make him stand out in the Carolina "wilderness." Yet, at the age of forty-five in 1700, L'Escot, "weary of wandering around the world," most likely wished to secure a stable position and settle down.[134] This is probably why he decided to go to Charleston, which, as time would confirm, was not the correct place for him considering his material needs.

L'Escot's ministry occupies a crucial place in the history of the Charleston Huguenot Church not only because of its relative length—"eighteen years and two months," as L'Escot recorded it—but also because it spanned the key decade during which the congregation resisted conformity.[135] L'Escot's letters also provide an invaluable non-Anglican source for information on Carolina Huguenot religious life that mirrors the better-known LeJau correspondence.

L'Escot, who had been offered a five-year contract with a comfortable annual salary of sixty pounds sterling, arrived in Carolina full of enthusiasm in December 1700 after "a happy navigation of six weeks."[136] Within a few years L'Escot and his wife, Françoise, who both planned "to finish their days" in Carolina, had acquired "a small tract of land" on which they had "a quite beautiful brick house" built and had purchased two slaves.[137] L'Escot, who had a genuinely curious intellect, was fascinated by the exoticism of the lowcountry fauna and flora, the cultural habits of the nearly extinct local native population, and the rusticity of colonial life. Not only did he fill his correspondence with ethnographic and anthropological remarks, but he also wrote a "*Relation ou histoire naturelle*" of Carolina "as methodical, exact and veritable as [he] could draw and in which [he] shared all that 18 years of knowledge and research gave [him]."[138]

In the first years of his ministry, L'Escot was on excellent terms with the congregation. He preached to a relatively large assembly of one hundred people in a newly built brick temple, and in 1703 his salary was raised to seventy pounds sterling a year. In the summer, "due to the excessive heat," L'Escot had one service on Sunday mornings, but in winter he also catechized on Sunday afternoons, "as in Geneva." As Prioleau and Trouillart had before him, the new Charleston pastor also administered Communion four times a year at Orange Quarter. L'Escot had also been asked to visit the Cooper River settlement more often and to cater to the Goose Creek community, but he refused because "his *Eglise* did not consent to it" and because he felt that "he would be too tired and lose too much time taking the tides to go and come back."[139]

Much later, on his return to England and after several years of conflict with his congregation, L'Escot retrospectively complained about being forced to memorize his sermons instead of reading them, but he did not seem to mind at the time or at least did not mention it in the letters written from Charleston.[140] More than a sign of congregational control, forced memorization was likely a way designed by the parishioners to avoid lengthy sermons in a town where an hourglass must have been a rare and dear commodity. Although discourteous and pregnant with potential resentment on the part of the pastor, this time-saving method was successful since L'Escot later remembered having "to cut [his sermons] short and adjust them to memory."[141] Incidentally, this affair confirms that in the French Calvinist tradition, although he presided over the consistory, the pastor worked under the elders' control.

Ironically, although he ministered to the only Huguenot church that chose not to conform, what epitomizes L'Escot's spiritual leanings is his open admiration for the Church of England, which is best expressed through the fervent friendship he entertained with Johnston. The commissary, ever zealous in his efforts to advance the cause of the Anglican Church in Carolina, cajoled L'Escot soon after his arrival in 1708. While Johnston may have sincerely enjoyed L'Escot's fine education, intellectual curiosity, and sophisticated tastes, he nonetheless perceived the Charleston Huguenot congregation as a key component in the colony's religious makeup that he could tilt to the side of the Church of England by winning their minister.

In a fifty-three-page letter written in July 1710, Johnston optimistically reported to the SPG that L'Escot, "a Person of great merit [who] has . . . greatly distinguished himself in favour of the Church of England against the Dissenting Ministers hereabouts," would "most willingly receive Episcopal Ordination." The commissary, who served as L'Escot's tutor in "let[ting] him into a great many things in our Church, to which he was formerly a Stranger," deplored that the French congregation refused to let L'Escot go back to

England to be ordained. Johnston further explained that the Charleston Huguenots "were very well satisfyed as to the sufficience and validity of [L'Escot]'s Ordination, by the french Ministers in London" and that they could not be "without him for so long a time, as a Voyage to S[outh] Britain wou'd require."[142]

Johnston, who had no qualms about pitting the French minister against his congregation and who sensed that an important battle could be won, advised the society to "favour [L'Escot] wth a short Billet for that good Will and Affection he bears to the Church of England." The commissary also recommended that the SPG send "some french Common Prayer Books of the better sort, and a few other ordinary ones, but all with the Singing Psalms," to be distributed among L'Escot's parishioners.

In the same letter Johnston also cleverly used his influence to help the L'Escots solve a family matter dear to them. John Chardin, a member of the SPG, wished to donate thirty pounds sterling to their daughter but refused to have the L'Escots get hold of the sum even though they thought it "their undoubted right to have this Money and the Interest of it hitherto" in order to "turn it to better advantage for the Childs use." The commissary intervened in the hope that "Chardin . . . may be prevail'd upon" while assuring his correspondents that L'Escot "well deserves, any good Office of this kind that the Venble Society can do for him."[143]

The SPG duly followed the commissary's suggestions and, in February 1711, addressed to L'Escot and Trouillart a note in which they thanked them for their "particular kindness" to Johnston and for their "good will and affection to the Church of England." The society, in a bureaucratic fashion, also offered to send their respective congregations "French Common Prayer Books . . . when the Society is better in Cash and a Proper application made to them."[144] While Trouillart unsurprisingly did not respond, L'Escot took the bait and, before long, wrote the venerable society a letter that deserves to be preserved in the annals of pro-Anglican Huguenot literature. Writing with the eloquence of a graduate of the Geneva academy who had mingled within Europe's most aristocratic milieu, L'Escot unveiled his admiration for the Church of England with a fervor and passion worthy of a recent convert. After thanking Johnston for befriending him soon after his arrival in the colony and recommending him to the society, L'Escot conveyed to his correspondents the "respect and Admiration" that his "Conscience and [his] Duty have strongly forced to give to [the] Church since he carefully examined [its] Confession and Service." The Huguenot pastor further acknowledged the Church of England's Christian authenticity in asserting that the "Church is pure and is but conform to the Holy Doctrine of Jesus Christ and his apostles" and to "what the Primitive Christian Church believed and practiced."[145]

Beyond his enthusiasm, however, L'Escot, who probably realized that he was walking an ecclesiastical tightrope in openly praising the Church of England while ministering a Calvinist congregation, hurried to add that his congregants were not ready to conform. Although "the best part of the [congregation] regards the Anglican Church with the respect that she deserves," L'Escot, almost regretfully and apologetically, explained that "they do not wish to conform because of a lingering attachment and respect which they still feel for the Service practiced yesteryear in the Churches of France which they have had so far the freedom to retain." Therefore, L'Escot declined the society's offer to send

Books of Common Prayer since "there might be people among [the congregation] who through a false Zeal guided by ignorance would object to using them, which would perhaps cause trouble and Division in [his] flock." L'Escot obviously knew how much conformity was a potentially divisive issue and did not want to experience LaPierre's ordeal.

Hoping that if he used diplomacy the society would concur with his prudent statement that "the form of the Public Service must be established with the Common and peaceful Consent of all," L'Escot nonetheless remained optimistic about the chances of his congregation conforming to the Church of England. While recognizing that "it was not in his power to change" his church's liturgy and polity, L'Escot foresightedly predicted that "time would bring [conformity]." Then, "when it will please God that it happens," the French pastor assured the society that he "would joyfully go along with the decision." Whereas "he cannot openly declare that it is his desire, he can at least admit without disguise that it would be quite agreeable to him," L'Escot concluded, if his congregation "conform[ed] in the Service of God since they are already entirely conformed in all points of faith."

By separating faith from discipline, incidentally to justify his own awkward stance, L'Escot considerably narrowed the ecclesiastical gap between his Calvinist congregation and the Church of England to make conformity an eminently practical decision and not a weighty matter of doctrine. Behind L'Escot's opportune and personal ecumenism, however, one can detect the manifest influence of his illustrious Swiss mentor, the theologian Jean-Alphonse Turrettini, and of Turrettini's regular correspondents, Jean-Frédéric Ostervald, Samuel Werenfels, and Bénédict Pictet, who all favored a large-scale Anglican-sponsored Protestant union.[146]

At about the time L'Escot was being courted by Johnston and the SPG, the Anglican episcopal hierarchy, having abandoned their hopes of national comprehension, revived a dormant project of creating a union of Protestant churches under the guidance and protection of the Church of England. According to this ambitious plan, Lutheran and Reformed churches, allied with the Church of England, would be able to deprive Catholicism of its alleged and much-disputed status as the "universal church." Although direct negotiations took place between the episcopate and representatives of the Prussian churches, notably Daniel Ernst Jablonsky, chaplain to the king of Prussia, Anglican bishops usually advanced their interests on the diverse continental fronts through epistolary contacts established by the SPCK and, to a lesser extent, the SPG.[147] The most prominent Swiss theologians of the period, including Turrettini, L'Escot's former professor, actively sought the support of Henry Compton and William Wake, to protect them against the omnipresent French Catholic menace.[148]

Beyond this unifying geopolitical consideration, however, the "anti-Roman grand alliance," as Norman Sykes calls it, envisioned by the Anglican authorities and their continental correspondents was particularly difficult to implement considering the wide range of liturgical, doctrinal, and ecclesiastical traditions that had sprung from the Reformation.[149] However, through goodwill and in the face of political contingency—not to say urgency—latitudinarian Anglicans, Lutherans, and mainstream continental Calvinists were ready to find truth, legitimacy, and common ground in one another's doctrines and to negotiate liturgical compromises.[150] This being said, if all Protestants, to various degrees, accepted the right of each church to differ in matters of polity as a result of distinctive historical traditions and in accordance with different political contexts, the concurrent issues of episcopacy and ministerial ordination nonetheless remained a significant hurdle on the way to reunion.

In a series of letters to English bishops, Swiss and Huguenot theologians expressed pro-Anglican theological views with regard to episcopacy. These opinions, which prevailed in Francophone Calvinist circles, approached the concept of episcopal legitimacy from a secular angle in a most conciliatory way. During a much-enjoyed visit to England in the early 1690s, Turrettini, who felt a profound attraction to English intellectual and religious life, assured his Anglican correspondents that "Calvin did not condemn episcopacy." He went on to explain that since episcopacy "was not of divine nature" and because "each church is master of her rites and direction, there are as many reasons to be Presbyterian in Geneva than to be Episcopalian in England [as] in every country the state of the clergy must be in proportion to the civil government."[151] Are we to infer from this statement that episcopacy could be legitimized in the Protestant Rome were it not a republic?[152]

In a similar vein, most Anglican bishops and theologians justified the loss of episcopacy among Reformed churches as the fruit of historical development in the often violent continental context of Catholic and Protestant antagonism at the time of the Reformation.[153] The absence of episcopacy was regarded as a defect in polity excused by the circumstances of the times but, as Sykes points out, did not make the churches of the Continent unchurched.[154] In sum, as Élisabeth Labrousse notes, to most Anglicans continental Calvinism was *non*-episcopalian rather than *anti*-episcopalian.[155]

Regarding the highly controversial episcopal ordination, or rather reordination, made mandatory for foreign ministers—but ironically not for proselytes—by the 1662 Act of Uniformity, Swiss and Huguenot theologians emphasized that it should not be interpreted as an Anglican refutation of the validity of Calvinist ministry but as the product of civil law.[156] The Huguenot pastor La Mothe argued in his controversial 1705 pamphlet on the Anglican efforts at Protestant union, entitled *Correspondance Fraternelle de l'Église Anglicane, avec les Églises Réformées et Étrangères,* that ordination was performed in England "in accordance with civil law." La Mothe went on to explain that although "ministers of foreign churches, with defective governments, are true ministers," when "transported by Providence to a kingdom where they have more liberty" they must "give their ministry *'une plénitude de perfection.'*" Thus, while "it is obvious that the second ordination given in England" does not presume the invalidity of the first, "one supposes . . . that the original ministry is imperfect although one recognizes that it has all the truth and all the essence of the ministry."[157] Similarly, Anglican advocates of the Protestant union justified continental compliance with episcopal reordination on the grounds that "at Geneva it is their common practice . . . whenever they remove a minister from one church to the other, to give him a new and solemn ordination." Therefore, as Joseph Bingham wrote, "if it be lawful at Geneva for a minister to receive a new ordination, because the laws require it: I do not see what can make it unlawful in England to submit to the same thing, in compliance with the law, when men have no other regular way to settle themselves in any cure."[158]

Placed in a transatlantic context, L'Escot's Anglican leanings should therefore not appear as an oddity or a betrayal of the Calvinist faith and traditions but as the reflection of contemporaneous theological and ecclesiastical mutations. In the early eighteenth century Calvinism, in Geneva and elsewhere, had lost its orthodox rigidity and had become amenable to contextual adaptations in terms of liturgy and polity.[159] L'Escot's thoughts on the Protestant authenticity of the Anglican doctrine and his readiness to adopt their formulaic liturgy should not strike us as anomalous but rather seems to have been quite the norm for early eighteenth-century Huguenot pastors. François Guichard, an episcopally ordained minister who served the (still) Nonconformist Charleston Huguenot congregation in the 1730s, to Commissary Garden's dismay, admitted using "one or the other Liturgy as the People were minded & that he thought the matter of no consequence."[160] Even Jaques Fontaine, who eventually refused to conform, "found nothing [he] could not heartily embrace in the [Anglican] Confession of faith, except as to discipline and Episcopacy by divine rights," and he would have been ready "to pass over these difficulties," were it not for the churchmen's "cruel persecution that they exercised against their Calvinist brothers."[161]

Fontaine's resentment was definitely an exception as most Huguenots were little aware of the intricacies of England's domestic politico-religious struggles. As Erskine Clarke puts it, "the bitter divisions that had separated republicans and royalists in Britain were not part of their experience," and "when they looked at the Church of England they saw, after all, a historic Protestant church whose classic documents reflected the influence of Geneva."[162] Furthermore, the Huguenots were not at all in the same position with regard to the Church of England as English and Scottish Dissenters were. They did not perceive it as a source of domination and persecution but of protection. Between the Restoration and the 1689 settlement, while English Dissenters experienced tough times, Huguenots lived virtually unmolested and enjoyed precious religious privileges.[163] In the early eighteenth century, in the same manner as the Swiss and Prussian theologians who were eager to achieve Protestant ecumenism, the Huguenots, especially the pastors, saw the Church of England as a beacon of institutionalized Protestantism in Europe, a church "set up by Providence to be the bulwark of the protestant religion," as Bishop Thomas Sherlock emphatically described it a few decades later.[164] In sum, therefore, "the worthy Mr. Paul L'Escot," as Johnston put it, and his congregation were small prizes in a major chess game played by the Church of England.[165] In the eyes of the bishop of London, of the SPG's eminent board of directors, and of Commissary Johnston, winning the Charleston Huguenot congregation over to the Church of England was part of a much larger endeavor.

Johnston, who even graciously invited L'Escot to perform a marriage ceremony in the prestigious parish of St. Philip's in 1712, might have persuaded the French pastor to conform had it not been for the steadfast determination of the Charleston Huguenots to preserve their Calvinism.[166] By the early 1710s, however, L'Escot's eventual reordination was a foregone conclusion and predictably occurred on his return to England. In the meantime, L'Escot became gradually estranged from his congregation largely, as the pastor later explained, over financial matters. L'Escot, who in 1719 described the Charleston congregation as "the most ungrateful of churches," accused his consistory of not meeting their financial engagements and of having reduced his salary from £70 to £24 in 1716. The fact that the Charleston pastor came to be paid in Carolina pounds, which steadily lost value to the pound sterling while, conversely, the cost of living was continuously increasing, worsened his finances. In 1716 he asked his congregation to help him pay a £50 debt, which "they refused flat."[167] L'Escot, who had to sell his personal library to finance his passage back to England, could legitimately complain and would actually have done so officially had there been a Carolina Huguenot presbytery. It is also true that his purchases of land and slaves, which he estimated at £250, were probably inconsiderate investments.[168]

L'Escot, who lost Johnston, his friend and fellow in erudition, in 1716, the same year he experienced difficulties with his congregation, also mentioned being tormented by a Parisian, "who declared himself [his] enemy," and who "blew a certain black smoke against [him] from Carolina." The conflict, according to the pastor, originated in L'Escot's disapproving of the mysterious Parisian's "extravagant views on religion" and his trying out different denominations including Quakerism "without substance or principle."[169]

Once in England, L'Escot had to answer the accusations of forsaking his congregation without waiting for a successor and of abandoning his wife and his daughter in Carolina. With respect to the former, the pastor first argued that if he had decided to wait he "would have ran the risk of suffering for many more years" due to the scarcity of French Calvinist ministers and the cost of bringing them to the lowcountry. He thus rightly pointed out that "one needs a lot of sterling money to pay for the passage of noncon-formist ministers from Europe to America" and that "one can no longer find [pastors] of this type in England as one must look for them in the Netherlands or elsewhere and find one by chance." L'Escot bitterly added that the infant Carolina Huguenot ecclesiastical structure and excessive influence of the laity within the churches were further obstacles to recruiting ministers. Pastors, he complained, "must be at the discretion of those who give them their subsistence and their bread through voluntary subscriptions [and] treat them with condescension because they depend on them . . . without the possibility of being supported by a synod." In sum, L'Escot sarcastically concluded that "noncon-formist churches in America are not in so good reputation that a single blow of a whis-tle in this country" brings "a flight of ministers from Europe."[170]

With regard to his own situation, L'Escot explained that the Charleston congregation had "set him free three weeks before his departure." Allegedly, they had written to Providence, in the Bahamas, to hire "a Mons. Pajot, a Swiss minister" who had immi-grated there with a group of people from the Palatinate but who remained idle after the loss of his flock. L'Escot claimed to have received letters saying that this "Mr. Pajot had arrived in Carolina very few days after his departure."[171] The absence of church records prevents historians from being certain, but the fact that the Charleston congregation, after L'Escot left, recruited Stouppe seems to indicate that this "Mr. Pajot" never came to the lowcountry.

Regarding the second accusation, definitely of a more personal nature, L'Escot explained that, although his wife "had no more reasons than him to praise Carolina," she chose to remain temporarily in Charleston with their married daughter. L'Escot, who felt that he "deserv[ed] pity rather than reproaches," expected her to join him in England once she managed to sell their house and their two slaves. Although he had been much less definitive in an earlier letter regarding what his wife planned to do, which shows that he was ready to abandon spouse and daughter at the time of his departure, L'Escot turned out to be right.[172] About eighteen months after he left Charleston, in November 1720, his wife had returned to England, "leaving her daughter in Carolina without any hope of seeing her again."[173]

L'Escot's bitterness actually may have been occasioned by the accusations that he had to face once in England since in May 1729 he happily announced to Turrettini that he had left Charleston "honorably and in good friendship with his church" and with a letter of recommendation.[174] In this document, after expressing their satisfaction about L'Escot's sermons and behavior in a formulaic fashion, the Charleston consistory explained that, since L'Escot's engagement had run out, they could not "resist his strong Desire to leave this land for Geneva," where he would "finish his days among his friends."[175] It is therefore unclear whether or not L'Escot fell out with his congregation before his departure. The letter of recommendation and L'Escot's satisfaction could simply reflect the two parties' mutual relief at leaving one another.

L'Escot may have indeed felt homesick and wished to return to Geneva, which he called "ma chère Genève." However, he may well have desired all along to go to Britain and conform to the Church of England while hiding it from the consistory lest they would not, as in 1710, let him go and write the necessary letter of recommendation.[176] His pro-Anglican position, which must have created tension between him and his congregation, although he fails to mention it, may have been one of the reasons, perhaps the principal one, for his departure. Once in England, L'Escot, who wanted to minister "a small congregation in the country for the big London theaters frighten[ed] him," wrote Turrettini, on whose patronage (among others) he relied to obtain a cure, that he specifically wished to settle in "a port where he could peacefully finish a life that had him wander around the old and the new world."[177]

God must have heard L'Escot. In December 1719, immediately after his ordination, the former Charleston pastor was inducted into the Huguenot conformist parish of Dover.[178] There, L'Escot replaced a proselyte from Poitou who returned to France and converted back to Catholicism after obtaining the pardon of the bishop of Poitiers. Five years later, in December 1724, on his return to Dover to bid farewell to his congregation and retrieve his household possessions after having been elected at Wandsworth, near London, L'Escot fell ill and died at age sixty-nine.[179]

Stouppe's decampment from Orange Quarter opportunely offered the Charleston Huguenot Church a chance to get a French-speaking Calvinist pastor without the expense of having to hire one from Europe. Stouppe answered the call and officiated in Charleston from sometime in 1719 until spring 1723, when he left Carolina to be ordained in England before being appointed by the SPG to New Rochelle, New York.[180]

A sermon, the only one extant for the entire proprietary period, which Stouppe read in Charleston on January 24, 1720, and which he took with him to New Rochelle, sheds precious light on Huguenot liturgical practices in Carolina.[181] This sermon is also particularly valuable because it enables us to compare Stouppe's theological views *before* and *after* his conformity since he delivered it again, with only minor additions, to his New Rochelle congregation on May 2, 1725.[182] Organized in a typical French Reformed fashion with three sections and entitled "Sommaire de la Loi," the sermon is eight and one-half pages long, which would have made it difficult to memorize, and according to Paula Carlo's calculations, it was likely to have been read in thirty minutes.[183] It is comparatively shorter than Stouppe's New Rochelle sermons, which corroborates the idiosyncratic demand of the Charleston Huguenots for brief sermons. Additionally, the text is written in beautiful and flawless French, which incidentally contradicts the Threadneedle Street consistory's reserve about Stouppe's linguistic skills.

In terms of content, Stouppe's Charleston sermon essentially offers a discussion of the key roles of faith and works in salvation based on 1 John 3:10, which is also reminiscent of seventeenth-century Huguenot preoccupations and sources.[184] After refuting the belief shared by many that "faith is the only condition upon which salvation is granted to us" and confirming that "God offers His mercy [*miséricorde*] to whom He chooses," Stouppe rhetorically asked why "God [would] prescribe duties to us [without] wanting us to observe them." The minister answered that "while we are not saved through works because of their imperfection, but through faith, [works are] nonetheless necessary to testify to the truth of our faith." Stouppe concluded that "faith without works is dead" (*La foy sans les oeuvres est morte*). The rest of the sermon is an enumeration of the characteristics, namely *justice, charité,* and *amour,* by which a child of God can be identified.[185]

The fact that Stouppe read the same sermon after being ordained in the Church of England most significantly shows that conformity did not in the least alter his theological message.[186] In other words, even as an SPG missionary Stouppe, in his sermons, delivered lessons that were essentially Calvinistic. This confirms how much room conformity left for the Huguenot ministers to remain loyal to their original Reformed beliefs. Once the issue of episcopal ordination was rid of its religious dimension and perceived as a necessary requirement in accordance with civil law, Huguenot conformist pastors could freely, and without any sense of wrongdoing, preach in the French Calvinist tradition while adapting Anglican rituals to the wishes of their parishioners.

Stouppe's departure in 1723 opened a period of spiritual desert and institutional instability from which the Charleston congregation never fully recovered. A 1724–25 exchange of letters between Isaac Mazyck and Benjamin Godin, then in London, reveals how critical the situation had become. While Godin, most likely instructed to find a minister, was unable to accomplish his mission successfully, Mazyck was desperately reporting that the congregation "was going over to the Episcopal Establishment."[187] Mazyck was actually describing a case of individual and temporary rather than institutional and permanent conformity since, in the absence of a minister, an increasing number of members attended services at St. Philip's while the Huguenot Church remained Calvinist.[188]

Providence eventually rescued the drifting Charleston parishioners by helping Threadneedle Street find a minister for their church. Answering a request addressed to them in 1731, the London consistory recommended François Guichard, a pastor trained at the Geneva academy. While accepting the conditions offered by the Charleston Huguenot Church, an annual salary of eighty Carolina pounds and twenty-five pounds for his passage, Guichard shrewdly and prudently requested the possibility of returning to England at the cost of the congregation "if after practicing his ministry among [them] for six years Providence would allow them to separate." Guichard, who remained in

Charleston until his death in 1752, obviously knew that the Charleston congregation was in no position to turn down his demand.[189] In a postscript to their letter, the London consistory informed the Charleston Huguenots that "they forgot to mention to them that Monsieur Guichard had been received by a bishop" but reassured them in adding that "he is nothing of a rigid Anglican since he has already served a church governed by the discipline of France." The Charleston congregation, having once again absolutely no leverage in the negotiations, agreed to hire Guichard and were probably relieved to have secured, they hoped, pastoral guidance for the next few decades.[190]

The Scattered Few
The Huguenots and the Dissenting Churches

When he described the religious makeup of the Carolina lowcountry to his Genevan correspondent, L'Escot made a point of stressing that his congregation "kept their distance from the Presbyterians, and [that] the English placed between them and [the Huguenots] *bien de la différence*."[191] In a similar vein, LeJau, who heard that the authors of "a pamphlet lately printed in London" asserted that "the Number of the Presbiterian Dissentrs comprd with the Members of our Cch [was] 5 to 10," hurried to correct that "they put the french protestants among the presbyterians which is notoriously false."[192] These defensive remarks reflect a Huguenot visceral fear, which was shared by pastors and lay members alike, of being associated with the English Dissenters, especially by the Anglican authorities.

Although this collective stand may appear puzzling and paradoxical for a group that claimed to be authentically Calvinistic and who shared a theological—but not historical—tradition with their Reformed brethren across the English Channel, it can be explained. Marginalized in France by an uncompromising Catholic clergy and a repressive monarchy throughout most of the second half of the seventeenth century, the Huguenot refugees clearly sought Anglican approval in their search for Protestant respectability. Their simplified, static, and distant perception of English religious history made them regard English Dissenters, especially the Congregationalists or Independents, as republican regicides. In 1725 at the age of eighty-one Gabriel Bernon, a prominent New England refugee, expressed this stand in a typical Huguenot fashion by denouncing in unequivocal terms the Dissenters for their responsibility for the English civil war. "The arbitrary power of the Presbyterians under Oliver Cromwell," wrote Bernon, "set England ablaze, the Father against the Mother, the brother against the sister, the mother-in-law against the daughter-in-law and the Independents against the Crown and the Church . . . which seems to me the most Deplorable thing in the world."[193] This position, of course, is ironic since following the execution of Charles I, the Huguenots in France had to become zealous royalists in order to protect themselves against the Catholic accusation of seditious republicanism.[194] Therefore, in a strange way the Huguenots espoused the same Catholic prejudices—which posited, as Élisabeth Labrousse puts it, "a simple equation between Protestantism and revolution"—that had gradually excluded them from French political life.[195]

Huguenot theological isolation also explains why the refugees would have found it quite challenging to ally themselves, politically and religiously, to Presbyterians and

Congregationalists. Since the Synod of Dort, which Louis XIII forbade their delegates to attend, the Huguenots had been virtually cut off from their northern Calvinist brethren. From then on, Huguenot internationalism, the so-called *internationale protestante,* became individual and familial—as in the quintessential case of the merchants—instead of structural.[196] Therefore, at the time of the post-Revocation emigration, the refugees were unable to reestablish institutional contacts with the English Dissenters whom they had learned through ignorance to regard with circumspection and at times even condescension, especially in the case of the Quakers.[197]

These prejudices and misconceptions were obviously transplanted to South Carolina, although, of course, they lost some of their vigor in the process. It is also true that, as all generalizations bear exceptions, not all Carolina Huguenots shared negative opinions of the Dissenters. A few refugees opted not to follow in the footsteps of their ministers and joined some of the lowcountry dissenting congregations, especially the Congregational Church. Yet, contrary to what occurred in New York, where groups of refugees joined the Dutch Reformed Church, in South Carolina this shift to other Calvinist denominations only involved a small number of individuals settled in Charleston.

Henry Péronneau, a wealthy Charleston merchant from La Rochelle, was a member of the Congregational or Circular Church, where he held an important position since he was involved in hiring a new minister in 1724. At his death in 1743 Péronneau bequeathed two hundred Carolina pounds to his new congregation and one hundred pounds sterling to its pastor, and in contrast to many Huguenots who requested to be buried in the French cemetery while worshiping at another church, he wished to be interred at the Circular Church.[198] Péronneau, who had occupied the position of ancien at the Charleston Huguenot Church in the mid-1710s, most likely left the French congregation during the confusion following Stouppe's departure.[199] The silversmith Salomon Legaré, who had joined Cotton Mather's Second Church in 1695 during his stay in New England, became a member of the Charleston Congregationalist Church immediately on his arrival in South Carolina, unlike Péronneau.[200] In the following decades a handful of Huguenot descendants joined a variety of other dissenting denominations, including the Quakers, but this remained largely a marginal phenomenon.[201]

The Huguenots and the Church of England
Another Case of French Paradox?

In his history of Calvinism in South Carolina, Clarke points out that the historiography has overestimated the impact of the Church of England on the religious, social, and cultural history of the colony, thereby "ignoring the presence of a vigorous and lively Reformed community in the low country."[202] While fully concurring with this statement, one has to admit that the Huguenot collective religious behavior was a testimony to the Church of England's aura in Protestant Europe and a victim of its aggressive expansion in South Carolina.

In the 1680s the Huguenots brought across the Atlantic an authentically Calvinistic religious tradition and, at least at the congregational level, successfully transplanted their ecclesiastical organization to the lowcountry. With a relatively high number of ministers, the highest of all denominations, the future looked bright. By the early 1700s, however, the rural Huguenot congregations started to fall irresistibly to "the forces of dissolution," as Clarke puts it, and, in a desperate attempt to survive, paradoxically opted to become Anglican parishes.[203] The Huguenots do not appear to have measured, unless they thought that they had no other choice, the irremediable consequences of their decision. Duped by—or overconfident in—the Erastian characteristic of the Carolina Anglican establishment, the refugees believed that they could integrate their traditional Calvinist polity into an Anglican structure. René Ravenel and Philippe Gendron, both Santee members of the commission set up by the 1706 Church Act, nonetheless referred to themselves as "ancien[s] de l'Eglise françoise de Jamestown" in a note drawn in 1708.[204] This "cultural residue within an English superstructure," as Friedlander calls it, was bound to be eroded by the waves of time.[205] Whether or not they fully appreciated it, in 1706 the Huguenots had, at least institutionally if not individually, reached a point of no return, as the desperate and violent but ultimately pathetic St. Denis rebellion showed.

Whereas no Huguenot-Anglican parish could ever return permanently to Calvinism, the spiritual fluidity characteristic of colonial religious culture allowed Huguenots to transcend denominational lines. Annette Laing's statement that many colonists "sought to satisfy their own consciences and convenience at the expense of denominational loyalty and orthodoxy" is particularly true for the Carolina Huguenots.[206]

The Hunt affair in St. John's Berkeley is a case in point. In 1722 Brian Hunt, a Cambridge graduate of pastoral lineage but without strong patronage connections, was appointed SPG missionary to St. John's.[207] At first the parishioners were enthused about their minister and "thought [themselves] extremely happy." In a letter addressed to the bishop of London in July 1727, however, the vestry, which included Huguenots Daniel Ravenel, Gabriel Marion, Peter de St. Julien, and Thomas Cordes, lamented that their "happiness quickly vanished for no Sooner was [Hunt] inducted [than] he began to Open a Scene which [they] heartily wish [they] could Cast a vail over [and] bury it in Perpetuall silence and Oblivion and not therewith offend [the bishop's] Lordship Ears." Unwilling to give specifics, the vestry accused Hunt of "many Lesser Indecencies, transient Levities and follies" and of indulging in the "Gross & Repeated Vices and Immoralities of Drunkenness, Quarrelling, Defamation, Lying" and of using "Insolent, Abusive, and Scurrilous Language." Judging that Hunt's improprieties had "deeply wounded the Holy Church," the vestrymen decided to "go away from it and join in setting up a Presbyterian Meeting in this Parish where no such thing was Even thought of before."[208] Hunt, who may also have been on the losing side of a power struggle with prominent local families, had his salary suspended by the society for behaving improperly, planning to sell Bibles at a profit to himself and the SPG, and performing lucrative clandestine marriages in different parishes.[209] After spending time in the Charleston jail, the missionary resigned and eventually returned to England to defend his case, which he did successfully.[210]

Although filled with resentment and paranoia, the accusatory letters that Hunt wrote in his defense shed light on the superficial and pragmatic nature of many Huguenots' conformity to the Church of England. Hunt first described Carolina as "a factious country . . . [where] there's no King" and where "every man tak[es] ye liberty of doing what's right in his own eyes as to religion." Calling the Huguenots "French occasionalists,"

Hunt then explained that "the French Protestants . . . generally frequenting the Church of England . . . [are] Presbyterian, occasional conformists by principle." He specifically accused these "bigotted French Calvinists" of "crying down Godfathers & Mothers, despising Churching & denying Bishops." Concluding his diatribe with a lesson in French religious history, Hunt asserted that "ye French Protestants casting off Bishops was ye hindrance of France Becoming Protestant long since, particularly in ye reign of their K Henry the 4th."[211] Hunt's accusations contrapuntally highlight one of the core reasons why the Huguenots joined the Church of England: to avoid accusations of sedition and republicanism.[212] More broadly, this affair also shows how easily conformist Huguenots could switch back to Calvinism and how they shrewdly used the threat of doing so to gain leverage in their negotiations with the bishop of London.[213]

Religious and probate sources also attest to the existence of multiple, most often dual, denominational affiliation among the refugees throughout the eighteenth century, especially in Charleston where there was a concentration of churches. Although it increased with time as the Huguenot congregations weakened, this practice was not exclusively subsequent to the passage of the church act. As seen in the previous chapter, the Thibou family had one of their sons baptized by a dissenting pastor in 1683. Daniel Horry and Élisabeth Garnier as well as Isaac Mazyck and Marianne LeSerrurier were respectively married in 1692 and 1693 by the Anglican minister Atkin Williamson.[214] At both times, however, there was a minister officiating at the Charleston Huguenot Church. Benjamin Godin and Benjamin de La Conseillère were both on the provincial Anglican commission when they, with La Conseillère serving as an ancien, signed L'Escot's letter of recommendation. Pierre Manigault had L'Escot baptize his children at the Huguenot Church while he purchased a pew at St. Philip's. Between 1720 and 1730, when the Charleston Huguenot Church had no minister, five Huguenots who attended St. Philip's requested to be buried in the Charleston French Church cemetery as a sign of a curious postmortem attachment to their Calvinist roots.[215] Testamentary bequests of prominent Charleston Huguenots constitute another source that shows their multiple church membership. Péronneau gave two hundred pounds sterling to the Congregational church and also donated one hundred pounds sterling to the French congregation, and the surgeon Jean Thomas, who opened his will by introducing himself as a resident of "Charles Town in the Parish of St. Philip's," nonetheless bequeathed an annual stipend of five pounds sterling to the minister of the Huguenot Church "so long as there be one."[216] Huguenots away from Charleston also showed signs of religious eclecticism in using the services of various ministers—conformists or Nonconformists, French or English—according to, it seems, whoever was in the area. Between 1693 and 1715 Benjamin and Marie Simons had twelve children baptized in churches and plantations by seven different ministers. Three were French Calvinist (F-P. Trouillart, É. Prioleau, and P. L'Escot), one was a conformist (J. LaPierre), and the other three were English SPG missionaries (S. Thomas, T. Hasel, and J. Whitehead).[217]

While their parishioners moved freely back and forth across the thin line of Anglican conformity, probably more out of practical necessity and a certain indifference than a lack of loyalty, Huguenot conformist pastors, such as Richebourg and LaPierre, who crossed the line ended up playing a risky cat-and-mouse game with the commissaries. As we have seen, LaPierre was once threatened with suspension of his salary by Johnston and lectured by Garden on duties of an Anglican clergyman, while Richebourg had to confront in person Johnston's accusations and anger during what must have been a tense meeting of the Carolina clergy. Unsurprisingly, the provincial Anglican authorities, especially Johnston, applied a double standard in their dealings with the Huguenot pastors. In 1713 the Charleston congregation, for an unknown reason, attempted to hire Richebourg's services. While the Santee minister apparently agreed to replace L'Escot, Johnston used his clerical power to forbid "Mr. Richburg to Preach at the French Church in Charlestown, because it is not Episcopal."[218] Yet a few months earlier, he let L'Escot, a Calvinist pastor, perform a marriage in his own church. This is undoubtedly a classic case of the carrot-and-stick policy, with reprimands and threats for LaPierre and Richebourg and compliments and gifts for L'Escot and Trouillart.

Following the passage of the 1706 Church Act, the Carolina Huguenots undeniably showed a wide spectrum of religious sensibilities, which in many ways reflected the centrifugal forces of congregationalism and synodalism inherent to the Reformed churches of seventeenth-century France. The critical mass, however, conformed to the Church of England and remained within its fold. In sum, two sets of reasons explain this behavior. The first comprises factors that are tied to the local Carolina context and are often of a practical nature. It includes the cost and difficulty of recruiting Francophone ministers as the Huguenots never reached what Richard Pointer calls "ecclesiastical self-sufficiency";[219] the absence of Presbyterian ecclesiastical structures, such as presbyteries and synods, which prevented the Huguenots from founding "a denomination-in-exile," as Butler puts it, and gave too much power to the pastoral elite, who abandoned Calvinism to seek Anglican hierarchical support and patronage;[220] the appeal, at least from a Calvinist perspective, of the Low Church nature of the Carolina Anglican settlement, which emphasized lay control of the parishes; the remoteness of the colony from the London Anglican center of power, which, despite commissaries' complaints and reprimands, allowed the Carolina Huguenots to adapt Anglican rituals in multiple ways to fit their Calvinist needs and preferences; the influence of the SPG, which sent Bibles and Books of Common Prayer to the Huguenot-Anglican congregations and provided the conformist pastors with financial gifts and correspondents for those seeking reassurance;[221] the political influence, especially after 1712, that could be exerted at the parish and county level through membership in the vestries; and the social prestige associated with the Church of England as leaving a foreign Calvinist congregation for the established Church, which was an undeniable form of social promotion.

The second group comprises less tangible factors that result from inherited traditions and beliefs brought from France to Carolina and are connected with a distant European context. These include the stigma of republicanism attached since the mid-1640s to the churches of Calvinist obedience by the Anglicans in Britain and the Catholics in France, and with which the Huguenots desperately tried not to be associated; the need of the refugees, especially the elite, to join a national and royal Protestant church after shifting allegiance from Louis XIV to William III; and, most important, the practical theology, coming especially from the Swiss cantons, that emphasized the essential Protestant tenets over the nonessential rituals and structures, and which enabled the Huguenots to attend Anglican services without feeling they had irremedi-ably betrayed their Calvinist traditions.[222]

The Anglicanization of the Carolina Huguenots should be regarded as a process of mutual acculturation since the refugees adapted as much as they adopted Anglican ritu-als. The process was more gradual than the sudden absorption of the rural congregations into the Anglican parish network through the passage of the 1706 Church Act seems to indicate. Nor was it a complete surrender as Anglicanization met significant lay resist-ance, whether passive in the form of ecclesiastical adaptations in Santee or active in the form of secession and violent prophetizing in St. Denis. Furthermore, it needs to be stressed that, in the eyes of the Huguenots and in the context of the violent and uncompromising royal policy in France before the Revocation, conforming to the Church of England had little to do with the painful and alienating process that conversion to Catholicism implied since they remained Protestant.[223]

—⟫-◦-⟪—

Chapter 7

NATURALIZATION AND REPRESENTATION

The Huguenots and Early Carolina Politics

But since people are soe valuable a commodity & [easy naturalization] may be means to invite some & to retain others whom any change has brought hither. It cannot but be for our advantage.

[John Locke], *For a General Naturalization* (1693)

[The petitioners] think it very hard that ye french who are refugees & ought to be Subject to our Laws are permitted to be Law Makers and to serve on Juryes.

Excerpt from a petition addressed to the Grand Council (1695)

The Huguenot decision to join the ranks of the Church of England was not exclusively a religious choice and contained an obvious political dimension. While from an Atlantic perspective it betrayed an undeniable royalist penchant, at the level of Carolina politics it reflected the Huguenots' desire to become full-fledged Carolinians and to play a more decisive role in the shaping of the colony's institutions. By 1704, nearly twenty-five years after the arrival of the *Richmond,* the Huguenots had gained enough familiarity with the complex political forces at play in Charleston to use them to their advantage. The involvement of the refugees in the 1704 and 1706 legislative debates, through which they obtained a second naturalization law, was a clear expression of a newly acquired collective political maturity. In contrast to the 1695–97 years, when the Archdale government granted the French a naturalization law at the expense of their political representation and eligibility, a decade later the Huguenots were able to negotiate the price of their support. Both times, however, naturalization was at the center of their political exclusion and acceptance.

The 1704–6 period was a watershed in Carolina Huguenot political history. First, notwithstanding internal divisions, the refugees had, since their arrival in the colony, systematically followed whatever group promised to naturalize them. After 1704 naturalization suddenly ceased to be an issue altogether. Second, the French decisively took the side of the Church of England faction, alienating the support of Carolina Dissenters for good. Third, the act of establishment, expanded in 1712 and 1717, guaranteed the Huguenots a stable and fair representation in the assembly and better control of local affairs by shifting the center of Carolina's political life from the county to the parish.

In the ensuing years the Huguenot group gradually faded as a political force, and its involvement in Carolina affairs became familial, especially at the parish level; occupational, as in the case of the Charleston merchants; or simply individual. The increasing rate of exogamous marriages, the emergence of a second generation, their full absorption into the colony's socioeconomic fabric, and the decentralization of the political debate led the Huguenots to defend their interest as aliens no longer. Their interests were now issues they shared with their relatives, neighbors, and economic partners. By the end of the proprietary period, the Huguenots had become actors in their own right on the Carolina political stage, and nothing distinguished them from the British settlers except their names and their French origins. The process that Alexander Moore has aptly called "the Huguenots' political naturalization" had reached completion.[1]

Denization and Naturalization
Degrees and Forms of Citizenship in the Anglo-American World

A few years after the accession of James VI of Scotland to the English throne as James I in 1603, a court case opposed a child, Robert Calvin, born in Edinburgh in 1605, to two adults who had allegedly despoiled him. Before this case could be judged, however, jurists needed to decide whether or not Calvin was an English subject since aliens could not sue in matters concerning real estate. Beyond the practical and judicial settlement of what became known as *Calvin's Case,* a decision had to be made regarding the legal status of the *postnati,* Scottish subjects of James VI born after he became James I. In other words, while all concurred that the *antenati* remained aliens, should the *postnati* be considered as English subjects?

The case carried such paramount constitutional repercussions, since jurists had to draw the nature and limits of English citizenship, that it was taken to the Court of Exchequer chamber. There, Sir Edward Coke, attorney general and one of the most influential lawyers of his time, articulated a theory of subjectship based on the medieval concept of allegiance. Concepts of society as the result of consent and contract were gradually emerging, but the definition of citizenship remained rooted in the almost immemorial subject-king relationship.[2]

The immediate consequence of the court's ruling was to make Calvin and all the *postnati* English citizens. More important, however, it set a common law of nationality in defining categories of citizenship and ways to acquire it that would endure until the midnineteenth century. Although there remained significant gray areas that would be elucidated in subsequent judicial and legislative decisions, at the time of the Huguenot immigration one could legally be an alien (enemy or friend), a denizen, or an English subject (natural-born or naturalized). These different statuses implied a variety of rights and restrictions, and an individual could move from one to another category.

Alien enemies were individuals who owed allegiance to sovereigns hostile to the English monarch. The crown enjoyed absolute rights over them, but their status was to be, by definition, temporary since wars were necessarily interrupted by periods of peace.[3] Alien friends owed temporary allegiance to the English prince and were therefore protected by the law. Although they enjoyed many of the rights of English subjects, aliens could not bequeath, inherit, vote, hold office, or own real property in England and were subject to specific customs and corporate duties.

Aliens could join the English community in two ways: through royal denization or parliamentary naturalization. Denization was a sort of intermediate status that partially removed the liabilities attached to aliens by granting its beneficiary only a restricted citizenship. Denizens could hold real property but could not bequeath it to their children born before their denization. They could not inherit either. Unless personally and expressly exempted in the letter of denization, denizens also had to pay customs and corporate duties. Politically, denizens could vote but were ineligible to hold office. Naturalized subjects, however, enjoyed virtually the same civil, economic, and political privileges as natural-born Englishmen until the 1701 Act of Settlement, which was passed to curtail the influence of William III's Dutch followers, banned them from holding civil or military offices. This restriction notwithstanding, naturalization conferred crucial rights, especially in matters of inheritance, simply because its effect was retroactive. Naturalized subjects could bequeath real property to all their children and could themselves inherit.[4] These distinctions were constitutionally rooted in the conflict between royal and parliamentary prerogatives. Denization was more limited because it sprang from the monarch's benevolence whereas naturalization was the expression of the people represented in Parliament.[5]

Unsurprisingly, denization and naturalization resulted from very different procedures. To be denizened, aliens, individually or collectively, simply had to petition the crown. The petition was usually granted without enquiry and the denization registered on the patent rolls. The cost was minimal and was often waived. Conversely, naturalization was acquired through an expensive and cumbersome legislative process. Except between 1709 and 1712, when a general naturalization act was briefly in force, aliens had to submit private bills of naturalization to Parliament.[6] Each needed money, between fifty and seventy pounds sterling, to hire a lawyer to draft the bill and to pay the clerks' and Speaker's fees in the House of Commons and the House of Lords.[7] The act was eventually passed after the bill went through various committees, where names could be added or subtracted, and was read three times in both houses. In addition to the cost and length of the procedure, each petitioner also had to submit a sacrament certificate and ran the risk of losing everything if the parliamentary session was prorogued.[8] In sum, naturalization was reserved for a minority of rich foreign merchants and landowners who could afford to sponsor a private act and who needed its economic guarantees to preserve their assets.

Solicited by diverse parties to make a gesture in favor of the beleaguered Huguenots, Charles II in the July 1681 Declaration of Hampton Court promised to "grant unto every such distressed Protestant who shall come hither for refuge . . . his letters of denization . . . without any charge whatsoever."[9] Through this order the crown established a parallel free denization procedure that would remain in force until 1688. During those seven years over thirty-five hundred aliens, overwhelmingly Huguenots, were endenizened gratis.[10]

Slightly more than one out of five Carolina Huguenots petitioned for denization before crossing the Atlantic. This represents a proportion slightly higher than the one out of six recorded denizations among Huguenots settled in England.[11] Most of these refugees took advantage of Charles II's liberal offer and appeared on the manuscript Carolina naturalization list of 1696 as "*fridénizons*" or "*fridenizés,*" meaning "denizened for free" in a French phonetic transcription.[12] While after 1681 petitioning guaranteed the granting of free denization, few Huguenots managed to leave England with their letters patent. Due to the massive numbers of refugees who applied—over a thousand individuals did so just for 1682, for example—recording delays were extremely long.[13] Therefore, many Huguenots had their denizations registered long after they had actually settled in Carolina.[14] Pierre Poinset [Poincet], who was on board the Carolina-bound *Margaret,* which sailed from England in spring 1685, appeared on the denization records only in July 1694. Jean-François Gignilliat, who had acquired land in Santee by 1689, was officially denizened in June 1694.[15] A handful of Carolina Huguenots obtained parliamentary naturalizations. A comparative sociological profile of the denizened and naturalized refugees confirms that naturalization was the privilege of the wealthiest and most influential among them. If merchants, esquires, surgeons, pastors, artisans, and farmers applied for denization, only merchants and esquires sought and obtained private naturalization acts.[16]

Beyond their formulaic expression, a few extant letters of denization that their beneficiaries had registered by Carolina officials show that the Huguenots were in total knowledge of English legal usage when they secured specific privileges that they needed according to their occupations and goals. Whereas all obtained the right to "Sell & Dispose of Lands, Tenements, and Hereditaments" and access to "all Liberties, Priviledges, and Franchises of Subjects born in this Kingdom," only the merchants requested to pay "Custom and Duties for their Goods and Merchandizes only as Natives Do."[17]

The standard phrase "in this Kingdom or any other of his Majesties Dominions" contained in all letters of denization and private acts of naturalization in theory guaranteed the validity of the Huguenots' newly secured privileges on the other side of the Atlantic. In practice, however, this was not to be the case. Once they were in South Carolina, no distinctions would be made among denizened, naturalized, and alien refugees. All, either individually or collectively, had to find new ways to obtain the necessary economic, juridical, and political rights that would enable them to make the most of their adopted home.

The Proprietors v. the Assembly
The Prerogative of Naturalization in South Carolina

In the colonial context the rules of English naturalization lost much of their rigidity. Ever in need of settlers, colonial authorities, whether legislative, gubernatorial, corporate, or proprietary, approached the issue of citizenship with pragmatism. Legal and procedural differences between denization and naturalization became blurred. Colonial legislatures endenizened and governors naturalized and vice versa, while in some colonies town governments granted virtual citizenship through the right of freemanship. The privileges contained in denization and naturalization documents were often exactly the same. As a rule, however, colonial assemblies gradually controlled naturalization procedures, although the constitutional and legal foundations of this power were tenuous, not to say questionable. At the turn of the eighteenth century, Parliament moved to ban group naturalization, a means used by colonial legislatures to naturalize a large number of aliens indiscriminately, in favor of naturalization by enrollment, which allowed imperial authorities to scrutinize individual applications. Some considerable measure of chaos regarding the territorial validity of colonial naturalizations prevailed until a 1700 order in council explicitly limited these within the bounds of the colonies where they had been issued. Consequently, denizened and naturalized aliens often had to apply anew wherever they moved. Only in 1740 did Parliament pass an act that provided a standardized naturalization procedure specifically for the colonies and whose validity could not be contested anywhere in the empire.[18]

In proprietary South Carolina, where it seems no denizations were issued, the evolution of naturalization procedures fits this broader colonial pattern. In the first decades of the colony's history, distant proprietors adopted a liberal policy founded on a loose construction of their charter. In the 1690s, however, naturalization gradually evolved as the exclusive prerogative of the assembly and, at the Huguenots' expense, became intertwined with highly disputed political issues. It remained a source of conflicts and bargaining as well as a bait to lure the political support of the Huguenots until the 1704 act made naturalization accessible to all present and future resident aliens.

The Carolina charter did not contain any clause regarding potential alien settlers. Probably assuming such settlers would be denizened or naturalized before leaving England, the crown generically declared that all Carolinians would be "Denizens and Lieges . . . of this our Kingdom of England." Legally the settlers still owed "faith, Allegiance, and sovereign dominion" to the English monarch, but for all practical purposes the proprietors, who became "the true and absolute Lords and Proprietaries of the said Province," could claim their allegiance within the bounds of the colony.[19] Construing from the vague and formulaic wording of the charter that they embodied the crown in their territory, the proprietors assumed that they held the right to grant subjectship, at least in Carolina. By definition, aliens were not subjects of the English monarch but of a foreign prince. In immigrating to Carolina, these settlers forsook their original subjectship and, except for the few who were denizened or naturalized in England, were in a sort of intermediate legal state since they were not yet English citizens. Only the proprietors to whom they solely owed allegiance could bring them into the English community by granting them citizenship. The proprietors assumed the right, held in England only by the monarchy and Parliament, to incorporate aliens into the English civil and political community. In other words, the proprietors felt empowered to turn aliens into full-fledged Englishmen by the sole virtue of their settling in Carolina. This loose and questionable construction of the charter remained unchallenged by a negligent and indifferent crown and served as the constitutional basis for the proprietors' naturalization power.

As early as 1665, the year the second Carolina charter was granted, the proprietors chose, however, to delegate this prerogative to an elected colonial assembly. An article of the Concessions and Agreement, which provided the constitutional frame for the embryonic Cape Fear settlement, granted the projected Carolina legislative body the power "to give Unto all strangers . . . a Naturalization." These naturalized settlers would then be "in all respects accounted in the Province and Counties aforesaid as the King's Natural Subjects."[20] In great need of finding volunteers to people the Carolina "wilderness," the proprietors surrendered many of their powers, including naturalization, to a more powerful assembly. This plan of government, which was to last only a few years in Albemarle, was superceded in 1669 by the first version of the Fundamental Constitutions.

The Fundamental Constitutions and Proprietary Naturalization

Drafted with the intention of establishing a government "most agreeable unto the Monarchy" and avoiding the dangers of the "erecting of a numerous Democracy," the conservative Fundamental Constitutions contrasted with the liberal Concessions and Agreement.[21] This new constitutional arrangement created a hierarchical society based on landownership and governmental institutions that considerably diluted the political influence of the freemen by replacing the unicameral elected assembly with a bicameral legislature controlled by the local nobility and the proprietary deputies. Unsurprisingly, this conservative about-face also affected the naturalization procedure, which became an exclusive prerogative of the proprietors. From 1669 to the early 1690s the proprietors were the only authorities allowed to confer citizenship in Carolina.

In the 1669, 1670, and 1682 versions of the Fundamental Constitutions, a clause stipulated that "whatsoever Alien [who] shall . . . Subscribe these Fundamental Constitutions shall be thereby Naturalized."[22] This extraordinary, simple procedure allowed the Carolina foreign settlers the theoretical possibility of becoming naturalized English subjects at no cost. As in the Concessions and Agreement, the proprietors consistently used the word "naturalization." They could not have used this term lightly or generically. The proprietors clearly intended to grant full citizenship free of charge. In other words, they generously offered something impossible to obtain in England.

In the July 1669 version, the clause mentioned the "Allegiance to our Sovereigne Lord the King & Submission & Fidelity to & defence of the Proprietors," thereby implying that the proprietors would naturalize on behalf of the monarch.[23] Constitutionally, however, this "naturalization" was actually the equivalent of a royal denization. When in 1665 they had delegated this prerogative to an elected assembly, the term "naturalization" was more appropriate since the assembly virtually represented all Carolinians, but with the Fundamental Constitutions the proprietors were clearly crossing constitutional boundaries. In the Anglo-American world, only Parliament could naturalize aliens. Nothing was said about the territorial validity of this citizenship, which could lead aliens to assume mistakenly that it carried no restrictions. Was it valid in any other colony or in England? This question did not concern most Huguenots since few would eventually relocate to other colonies, but merchants who would operate ships in the intracolonial and transatlantic trade needed legal answers. Beyond these proprietary silences, no one with political sense could expect this naturalization to be equivalent to one granted by Parliament or even to a royal denization.

Although the Fundamental Constitutions had to be approved by the entire proprietorship before being issued, the liberal naturalization policy that it provided for was manifestly influenced by the political and economic views of its chief designers, Shaftesbury and Locke. As Whigs and advocates of mercantilism, both argued for the general naturalization of Protestant aliens as a way to contribute to the nation's prosperity. Locke, following a Whiggish mercantilist logic, posited in 1693 that "Tis the number of people that make the riches of any country" and that "Naturalization is the safest & easiest way of increasing [the] people."[24] Needless to say, what was true for a country such as England was all the more so for a nascent colony such as Carolina. Locke also developed an innovative voluntaristic and contractual approach to naturalization at sharp variance with Coke's 1608 quasi-medieval definition that emphasized the unalterable character of subjectship allegiance.[25] To Locke, the loyalty of naturalized citizens was not to be questioned, as they would be "perfect Englishmen as those that have been here since William the Conquerers days & came over with him." He added, "For tis hardly to be doubted but that most of even our Ancestors were Forainers."[26] Regarding naturalization policies, as with other political and economic innovations, Carolina, Ashley's "darling," served as some sort of laboratory for Ashley's and Locke's convictions.

Whether the proprietors possessed infallible political acumen or simply followed Ashley's recommendations, by offering full naturalization in return for a mere signature they anticipated and fully met the expectations of the Huguenots. In their 1679 petition, addressed to the king and Parliament a decade after the drafting of the first version of the Fundamental Constitutions, René Petit and Jacob Guérard listed the granting of naturalization as an essential condition to the successful settlement of the Huguenots in the colonies. Remarking that "the English Nation is jealous of her prerogatives and [that] it considers refugees as aliens," if the Huguenots were not naturalized "they would not be able to practice their trades in full Liberty, [which] could maintain Hatred and jealousy."[27] Written at a time when a small but growing influx of French refugees into England led to an extensive parliamentary debate over the pros and cons of a general naturalization act, this petition echoes the many requests for a liberal policy toward the Huguenots that were addressed to the English and Carolina authorities. A few years later a petition drafted by representatives of families from Poitou and Aunis specifically asked the proprietors if "the rights of citizenship [*les droits de naturalité*] are acquired through the purchase of land or if one must go to England to obtain it" and inquired about the naturalization procedure and its cost. The petition further and significantly asked if "a father just needed to be naturalized to have his children, whatever their ages may be, enjoy the rights of citizenship in perpetuity."[28] To be sure, the proprietors answered the call. Regardless of the legal uncertainty concerning the validity of proprietary naturalization, as good salesmen they quickly made its availability known to their prospective French customers through promotional pamphlets.

Description du Pays nommé Caroline, published a few months before the departure of the *Richmond* and most likely written by Petit and/or Guérard, reassuringly mentions twice that foreign Protestants are "granted the rights of citizenship [*les droits de naturalité*] and the same privileges as [His Majesty's] other subjects in the Province."[29] In a contrived question-answer section of the 1685 *Description de la Carolline,* the seventh answer explains that "one is naturalized gratis in Carolina" and assures the reader that "those born there are naturalized in all the places that depend on the sovereignty of the King."[30] Beyond answering the query addressed by the Poitou families, this apparently cryptic statement actually conveys a crucial message regarding the citizenship of the refugees' children. It unequivocally guarantees that Carolina-born Huguenot children, whether or not their parents are naturalized, will be British citizens. Proprietary naturalization therefore, as the term "naturalization" duly indicates, did not offer a limited citizenship similar to the English royal denization but was equivalent to a full parliamentary naturalization. The Carolina naturalization procedure was specifically outlined in *Plan pour former un établissement en Caroline*, which informed readers that "the Fundamental Constitutions explicitly stipulate that Aliens who will sign them . . . will thereby be Naturalized."[31]

Partial lists of settlers who subscribed to the Fundamental Constitutions between 1685 and 1689 show that the Huguenots took advantage of the proprietary offer of naturalization even if it required swearing allegiance to the proprietors and to James II. About a quarter, or more than twice the number that the French actually represented in the colony's population, of the thirty-nine subscribers in the surviving manuscript were refugees, and the proportion reached half for the year 1686.[32] However, does this document reveal any Huguenot political allegiance? Nothing is less certain. Unlike the British settlers for whom naturalization was moot, the Huguenots found their political leanings skewed by the promise of naturalization: proprietary allegiance seemed a small price to pay for the legal right to practice their trades and own, bequeath, and inherit land. The arrangement of the extant document also makes it difficult to determine whether this group of settlers, especially the French, agreed to subscribe to the first July 1669 copy of the Fundamental Constitutions or to the more recent and highly divisive 1682 revised version.[33] The Huguenots may have followed the political flow since most settlers were then opposing Governor Joseph Morton, who had attempted to impose the Fundamental Constitutions on them in autumn 1685, or they could have been divided over the issue.[34] They may also have been indifferent to the political climate and would have signed any version since all offered naturalization in the same terms, no matter which faction was in power. It seems more likely, however, that except for a few individuals the Huguenots, most of whom had just arrived in the colony, were not yet interested in taking sides in the political contentions of early Carolina. Naturalization was their priority.

Several of the 1686–89 Huguenot subscribers had actually already applied for denization before coming to Carolina. They nevertheless took the royal and proprietary oath thinking, with prudence, that, at least in Charleston, a proprietary naturalization was worth more than a royal denization. This was a cautious move since most of these refugees would not have their denization officially recorded by the English bureaucracy until many years—fifteen for one of them—after their arrival in the colony.[35] At any rate, these were not isolated cases as a significant number of Carolina Huguenots were successively denizened in England and naturalized in Carolina. A few even obtained royal denizations and Carolina proprietary and legislative naturalizations.

The Rise of the Carolina Assembly and Legislative Naturalization

In South Carolina the monarchy-parliament constitutional rivalry over the granting of citizenship to aliens mutated into a conflict between the proprietors and the assembly. Once the proprietors created an assembly separate from the original unicameral council and gave it the power to legislate, the issue of naturalization became inextricably entangled in the sometimes petty politics of Carolina. The Huguenots therefore no longer had the possibility of remaining alien bystanders seeking only naturalization. Nor could they make separate deals with the distant proprietors. They had to commit. As seen in the previous chapter, a striking feature of their history in the colony turns out to be their Anglican sympathy. However, in the same way that their conformity to the Church of England was unpredictable and unforeseen in the early years of their settlement, their pro-Anglican political leaning was not a foregone conclusion. The involvement of the Huguenots in the colony's often fratricidal politics, as with any other group of settlers, followed the ebb and flow of issues such as the control of the Indian trade, the payment of quitrents, the acceptance or refusal of the Fundamental Constitutions, and the establishment of the Church of England. Two characteristics remained constant, however. First, rather than basing their political allegiance on some preconceived and expected religious and political alignment, the Huguenots went with whichever faction had the most to offer them, namely, naturalization. Second, like any other Carolina political group, they were internally divided into various continually changing subgroups arranged along social, geographic, political, personal, and kinship lines. In other words, they deliberately sided with those, Huguenot or not, who shared their interests. Charleston and Craven Huguenots, merchants and artisans, and different families may or may not have sought the same political allies. There were even times when some Huguenots chose to take the side of one English faction without consulting the rest of the group. Never, except perhaps during the 1695–97 crisis when Carolina Francophobia reached a peak, was there such a thing as a monolithic Huguenot party.

At the beginning of Carolina institutional history, there was no representative assembly. The governor ruled with the assistance of a parliament composed of the Grand Council, the nobility (that is, caciques and landgraves), and an elected assembly. Dubbed by Sirmans "a tricameral assembly," this early parliament spoke in fact with a unicameral voice, that of its main component, the Grand Council.[36] Councillors, who were either proprietary deputies or wealthy and influential—not to say manipulative—settlers elected by the assembly, held all the legislative powers. The Carolina nobility exerted only a consultative role, and the twenty-member assembly elected by the freemen could only ratify or reject laws proposed by the Grand Council.[37] This institutional arrangement reflected the proprietors' aspiration for political stability, best expressed in the elaborate Fundamental Constitutions, through a balanced but not equal representation among their deputies, the nobility, and the freemen. In practice, however, it favored clannish factionalism and electoral corruption. Proprietary deputies and elected councillors were pitted against one another, and the latter manipulated the small pool of voters through threats, promises, and favors. As a group of unscrupulous settlers once boasted, "with a bole of punch [they could] get who they would Chosen of the parliament and afterwards who they would chosen of the grand Councell."[38] Meanwhile, governors, who were powerless without the support of the councillors, often played, when not themselves manipulated, one faction against the other to serve their own interests in complete disregard of the proprietors' instructions and the well-being of the colony and the settlers. In addition, the proprietors, who could and did remove governors and repeal laws, made up another preponderant albeit distant political force that had to be reckoned with. Early Carolina political life was therefore chaotic and crippled by internal strife. Counting multiple terms of office, sixteen governors served between 1670 and 1700. This represents an average of less than two years for each term, one of them lasting a mere three months.[39] It is precisely in reaction to one of the multiple crises poisoning early Carolina political life that the proprietors at last introduced major institutional reforms to bring the colony more stability and a more representative legislative system.

The 1690 Coup and the First Naturalization Law

Unsuccessful in his attempt to have a majority of the Carolina parliament subscribe to the 1682 Fundamental Constitutions, Governor Morton was eventually deemed incapable of bringing political stability to the colony. The unsatisfied proprietors wondered "if [he] was to govern the people or the people [him]."[40] Consequently, following a dual Spanish attack on the southern Carolina frontier that annihilated Stuart Town, Morton was replaced in November 1686 by the Barbadian James Colleton, younger brother of the proprietor Sir Peter Colleton. The new governor did not enjoy much success during his term either. Colleton was manipulated by crafty and shameless opponents who first lured him into introducing a unanimously unpopular bill raising his own salary and later challenged his effort to implement the revised 1682 Fundamental Constitutions by claiming to abide by the unaltered and royal 1665 charter instead of the successively modified proprietary document. When they introduced a so-called "charter bill" to that effect, Colleton opted to prorogue parliament in the midst of political confusion. Unable to impose the 1682 Fundamental Constitutions on the parliament, he sapped his own political base in his attempt to silence his opponents.

The "Glorious Revolution" of 1689 brought news of an upcoming war between France and England. Fearing and anticipating a French attack, Colleton and his unconditional supporters chose to declare martial law. This decision, along with the earlier prorogation of the parliament, exposed Colleton to the accusation of tyranny. This represented a virtually unanswerable attack in an Anglo-American world so attached to the revered although vaguely defined English liberties. The summer 1690 chance arrival from North Carolina of Seth Sothell, an opportunist who had acquired the Clarendon proprietary share in 1677, turned out to be the coup de grâce to Colleton's governorship.[41]

Sothell, who had irreconcilably antagonized most North Carolina settlers during his governorship there, took precedence over Colleton on the basis of a clause in the Fundamental Constitutions that made any proprietor present in the colony the highest ranking official. Oblivious to the fact that he was placed in power by the very faction that had sworn not to abide by the same constitution that legitimized what was actually a coup d'état, Sothell unsurprisingly governed to defend the interests of his supporters. Sothell's Carolina administration represents an early and extreme illustration of the spoils system. Proprietary officials of the former administration were dismissed or jailed, Colleton was banished from the colony, and some of Colleton's supporters were disqualified from holding office. Sothell eventually turned out to be a rogue governor and an unreliable ally. He reserved for his own use two-thirds of the revenues raised through a newly adopted export duty on deerskin, and of the three land grants he signed, two were for himself.[42] Although he encouraged trade with Caribbean pirates to the benefit of himself and his supporters, he quickly alienated his flimsy political base while angering the proprietors. In April 1692 a new governor, Philip Ludwell, who coincidentally had succeeded Sothell previously in North Carolina, was appointed, and all the laws that had been passed during Sothell's short term were repealed by the proprietorship.[43]

South Carolina historians have traditionally inferred that most Huguenots sided with the anti-Colleton/pro-Sothell and allegedly antiproprietary faction led by the famed, although elusive, Goose Creek Men.[44] This opinion is largely based on two partisan sources, namely the correspondence of John Stewart, a Colleton supporter, and a petition addressed to Sothell by his onetime friends, plus the fact that the French obtained a naturalization law from Sothell.[45] Reality seems to have been more complex, and it remains difficult to pigeonhole the Huguenots with one or the other faction.

When Governor Colleton requested popular support to declare martial law early in 1690, he asked John Stewart, a gifted pamphleteer, to write a tract in defense of his policy and of the Fundamental Constitutions. Targeting Dissenters and Huguenots, Stewart explicitly warned his readership that if the constitutions were discarded, as the advocates of the charter bill would have it, "the woeful consequence is apparent to Aliens and dissenters: farewell then Liberty of Conscience [and] Naturalization."[46] The pamphlet was translated into French by Jacques LeBas to reach the widest possible Huguenot audience.[47] Stewart later claimed that 150 settlers signed the petition requesting martial law, among whom were a significant number of Charleston Huguenots. The petition asking Sothell to take over the Carolina governorship, however, later explained that the "French in towne" had been misinformed and duped into believing that martial law "was onely to cause a guard to be kept in Towne."[48] The same petitioners claimed to have gathered the signatures of "four or five hundred of the best people in this Country," many of whom, apparently, were also Huguenot.[49]

Once in power, Governor Sothell's administration quickly passed a naturalization law, thereby emphatically refuting Stewart's statement that Carolina aliens could be naturalized only by subscribing to the Fundamental Constitutions. The proprietors, however, soon repealed the act. Ludwell's government, which succeeded Sothell's, apparently in a spirit of retribution attempted forcefully to regulate the hours of the Huguenots' worship in Charleston while denying the validity of their marriages. It also threatened them with a possible proprietary escheat of their land on the basis of their alien status. With their first naturalization law repealed and their church under attack, the Huguenots must have seen Stewart's 1690 warning as a premonition. Desperate although not resourceless, the politically isolated refugees turned to the proprietors for help. In April 1693 Their Lordships, who "desired things may be Remedied," ordered the Carolina authorities to stop harassing the French, who should "have Equall Justice with English men and Injoy the Same Priviledges."[50] In a letter to the Charleston congregation, the paternal proprietors reassured the Huguenots of their support while giving them a not totally unmerited lecture in political loyalty and realpolitik. While wondering why the Huguenots rejected the Fundamental Constitutions, they first reminded them that "Had the Constitutions been ratifyed in Parliament you [would have] no need of our Assistance now"; then, "Heartily wish[ing] [they] may never feel any inconvenience by hearkening to those who misled [them], and who in the bottom love [them] not," Their Lordships, with a subtle touch of irony, went on to warn the Huguenots that "when [they] have tried all [they] will find the Lords Proprietors themselves the best friends [they] have."[51] No one can blame the proprietors for telling a few political truths to the seemingly disloyal and wavering French settlers. Yet, Carolina politics were definitely more complex and fast-changing than they might have appeared to distant English aristocrats.

What are we to make of all these developments in terms of Huguenot political allegiance? Although it is impossible to determine how representative they were of the community at large, a significant number of Huguenots, as noted earlier, subscribed to the Fundamental Constitutions between 1686 and 1689, presumably in the hope of being naturalized for free. The French had therefore no particular reason to be antiproprietary, if such a faction ever existed, and their political behavior at that point does not warrant any such assumption. Nor could they be personally opposed to James Colleton, whose brother Sir Peter Colleton had been so instrumental in promoting Carolina among Huguenot circles when Shaftesbury's influence declined and who must have been their privileged contact on the proprietorship, judging by his omnipresence in the promotional pamphlets. In fact, when threatened by political exclusion in 1695, the Huguenots appealed to Governor Archdale and Anthony Ashley Cooper and duly evoked James Colleton's protection. They regretfully explained that "Since the death of Sir Peter Colleton [May 1694], the case of affairs" in Carolina had been "much altered concerning the french."[52] Additionally, the interest of the Huguenots was undeniably to favor martial law since they particularly needed to demonstrate their loyalty to their new *patrie* in a time of war against France so as not to be suspected of treason. Political accounts of the crisis tell us that while those living in Berkeley County (Goose Creek and presumably Orange Quarter) and in Craven County did not support Colleton, Huguenots living in Charleston did support him. The dynamics of this opposition has to be surmised. In case of a French assault, Charleston Huguenots may have felt more exposed than those settled inland.[53]

At any rate, Sothell's faction claimed to have gathered more Huguenot supporters than Colleton's. This support was obviously obtained at the price of a naturalization law. This behavior of the French was perhaps foolish or inconsiderate but cannot and should not be interpreted as antiproprietary. The proprietors backed Sothell at first. It is the proprietary about-face, following news about Sothell's dishonest and tyrannical practices, that made supporting him an antiproprietary behavior, but it was not so originally. In 1690 and 1691 the Huguenots were certain to obtain some sort of naturalization, proprietary or legislative, but either way necessarily entailed political commitment. Some, perhaps most, Huguenots followed the majority of settlers and backed Sothell, who, let us not forget, was a proprietor. However, the proprietors, somewhat unpredictably, forsook Sothell and repealed all the laws passed under his administration. The naturalization act was therefore disallowed not in a spirit of hostility or punishment toward the French but simply because it had been passed by a government now deemed illegitimate. In suspending the Fundamental Constitutions when they appointed Ludwell in 1692, however, the proprietors de facto renounced their exclusive prerogative over naturalization and were consequently not, as the 1695–97 events would confirm, opposed to legislative naturalization. Perhaps in a bumbling way or simply by chance the Huguenots anticipated that they could eventually be naturalized only through the Carolina Assembly.[54]

The Sothell crisis represents a turning point in the institutional development of the colony and in the history of the naturalization of the Huguenots. Not only did the proprietors temporarily suspend the highly divisive Fundamental Constitutions that had ironically served to legitimize the 1690 coup, but they also decided to break up the unicameral parliament by separating the assembly from the Grand Council. The Carolina legislature became bicameral with an elected house that came to be called the Commons House of Assembly and a council composed of proprietary deputies. In 1693 the proprietors granted the Commons House of Assembly the right to initiate legislation while the once powerful council devolved into an advisory and ratifying body.[55] With the virtual abandonment of the Fundamental Constitutions and the 1691–93 legislative reforms, proprietary influence definitely slipped into the background as the Huguenots had to enter the game of Carolina politics fully.

Carolina Francophobia and the Huguenot Exclusion Crisis

On August 9, 1692, Governor Ludwell issued writs for the elections of the first session of the newly born Commons House of Assembly.[56] Late in September the twenty house members convened for their first meeting in a private residence. Since the seats were apportioned by county, the Huguenots, who had by then solidly settled Craven County, elected five representatives, or a quarter of the house. This was not an outrageous proportion but a small overrepresentation since the refugees constituted about 15 percent of the colony's white population in the early 1690s. Nevertheless, having French people make up a fourth of a British colonial assembly must have been quite a remarkable situation. What may be regarded simply as an oddity by historians, however, was doomed to erupt into conflicts in the bitter and unstable political context of proprietary Carolina. Beyond the unexpected Gallic flavor the Huguenot members gave to this first Carolina Commons House of Assembly, their presence raised two thorny political issues. First, the refugees were not only French speakers but also still aliens since the 1691 naturalization law had been disallowed and the Fundamental Constitutions had been placed on the back burner while at the same time their English denization status was not recognized. Second, the new institutional arrangement favored the Huguenots by giving them the means to exert a decisive political influence on Carolina affairs. They had until then been politically discreet. In the wake of the Sothell crisis and in the context of King William's War (1689–97), which was propitious to the awakening of Francophobic sentiments, this new situation led to confrontation. The 1692–94 period represents the zenith of Huguenot representation and involvement in Carolina politics as much as the 1695–97 years constitute the nadir of their influence.

Historians have ascribed the anti-Huguenot feelings of the mid-1690s to the Carolina Dissenters and have explained that these feelings paved the way for the 1704–6 Huguenot-Anglican alliance. While resentment over the Sothell crisis probably lingered through the 1690s and the Dissenters of Colleton County may have led the 1695–97 anti-French charge, the phenomenon had in fact a broader political base.[57]

The first salvo of the anti-Huguenot campaign was fired in October 1692, a month after the September election returns conspicuously brought a slate of five Huguenots to the assembly, with the issuing of the "Act for the better Observance of the Lord's Day."

Through this no longer extant law, whose main clauses are indirectly known to us through the proprietary instructions of April 1693, its sponsors not only tried to regulate Huguenot hours of worship in Charleston but, much more important, also denied the legality of their marriages because their pastors were not ordained.[58] It is unlikely that this law was inspired by Dissenters. First, for Nonconformists to require fellow Calvinists to have episcopally ordained ministers is simply against nature no matter how Machiavellian politics sometimes turn out to be. Second, such a move would have been a blatant political mistake since it would have pushed the Huguenots farther along the path of Anglican conformity. Third, as would happen again in 1695, the proprietors, not the Carolina Anglicans, stood for the defense of the Huguenots.[59]

A few years after the Huguenots, with proprietary help, fought back the attack on their religious life, their legal right to trade was challenged under the dubious pretense of enforcing the Navigation Acts. In February 1695 the *Blue Star,* a sloop belonging to denizened New York Huguenots, was seized and her crew convicted by an ad hoc Court of Vice Admiralty.[60] However, on receiving a petition for the issuance of a writ of error (appeal), the council suspended the judgment on the basis of procedural irregularities and "the ambiguity of the verdict." The defense argued that the informant, Pierre-Jacob Guérard, was an "Alien Enemy" and that therefore his deposition was not legally admissible. The council conceded that Guérard "was borne a subject of ye french Kings, Never naturalized nor Denizened," but explained that he had "lived Twenty Yeares under ye protection of ye King of England" and, most important, had been "Comissioned by ye Officers of ye Custome House in London to be his Majesties Collector for Carolina."[61] Revealing that there had been controversy among them regarding the necessity for foreign merchants and sailors to be naturalized in compliance with the Navigation Acts and unwilling "to medle with ye Validity of Denizacon," the members of the council wisely acknowledged the legal uncertainty of the verdict and asked the proprietors for instructions.[62]

The court judgment and the council's unwillingness to rule on the commercial rights of denizened merchants illustrate the legal ambiguities surrounding denization in the colonies.[63] However, without doubting the bona fides of the council's request for proprietary assistance, the suspicious zeal shown by the court most likely reflected a partisan political maneuver meant to threaten Huguenot economic interests. The refugees, whether or not they were naturalized, had been allowed to trade without restrictions since their arrival in the colony.[64] Why should their commercial rights suddenly be suspended? It also seems preposterous that an alien juror would be able to convict a denizened merchant. The court, as well as the council, knew all along that residence in England or in the colonies did not per se equal citizenship.[65] Furthermore, Carolinians had consistently and conspicuously flouted the Navigation Acts, notably through the pirate trade, and it is puzzling that the colony's authorities suddenly decided to comply with long-standing imperial regulations. Additionally, it was audacious, to say the least, "to despise the Kings authority," as the proprietors put it, by challenging the status of royal denization. As expected, the proprietors wisely annulled the court decision. Their Lordships took the affair seriously and clearly perceived that this sort of decision, although aimed at

New Yorkers, could only make matters worse in Carolina in "Incit[ing] ye people to fall upon the french."[66]

In fall 1695 the Quaker John Archdale, who had held a proprietary share on behalf of his minor son since 1678 and who had some experience of North American colonial life, arrived in Charleston as the newly appointed governor.[67] Archdale had been sent to Carolina to promote economic prosperity and political peace and to solve a series of divisive issues, such as the regulations regarding land acquisition, the collection of quitrents, and the construction of walls around Charleston.[68] However, as Alexander Moore points out, the Huguenot question dominated his term.[69] Shortly after his arrival the council presented Archdale with a petition, allegedly signed by a hundred English settlers, requesting "an Assembly of Purely English & Elected onely by English."[70] With this request, which had all the appearance of an ultimatum, anti-Huguenot sentiment had reached a peak and confrontation seemed inevitable.

Well aware that his fellow proprietors would never agree to the disenfranchisement and ineligibility of the Huguenots merely to satisfy the exorbitant demands of an unruly faction, Archdale first refused to yield. In August 1695 the governor and the council informed the proprietors that to avoid a potentially dangerous conflict they had dissolved the assembly while validating the laws it had enacted despite the presence of French assemblymen. In an effort to humor both parties, however, they explained to the proprietors that when Their Lordships instructed Governor Ludwell to have the inhabitants of Craven County elect assemblymen, they mistakenly believed the county "to be inhabited by an intermixter of English and French." The fact that the representatives from Craven were all Huguenots had been, according to the council, "very Dissatisfactory to ye English & the cause of ye Address." The above-mentioned petitioners, who "think it very hard that ye french who are refugees & ought to be Subject to our Laws are permitted to be Law Makers and to serve on Juryes," apparently wished "to Assert their priviledge of English men." The governor and the council also posed a legitimate question in asking the proprietors "to let [them] know the Distinction" they made between "ye Scots who though not Subjects of England are Subjects to ye King of England and the french who are in all respects as Alienes."[71]

At about the same time the Craven Huguenots, represented by Jacques Boyd, addressed to Governor Archdale a plea not to give in to factionalism and wrote to Anthony Ashley Cooper requesting proprietary protection. Both letters reflect a thorough knowledge of the history of the French settlement in Carolina and of English institutional practices. They confirm that the Huguenots were not clueless victims of manipulations but active players in the merciless game of Carolina politics.[72]

After first thanking Governor Archdale for his protection, Boyd stated at the outset of his argument that "the interests of the Lords [were] narrowly bound up with [the Huguenots']." Tracing the history of the French immigration and settlement in the colony since the arrival of the *Richmond* in 1680, Boyd argued that they had come at the solicitation of the Lords Proprietors "as the Lord Bishop of London did for Maryland & Mr Pen for Pensilvania." Once in Carolina, the Huguenots, whom the lords promised the same privileges as "Naturals English," were granted land and given civil and military offices. Boyd also explained that the Huguenots elected representatives to the assembly "by an express order from the Lords, [who] knew very well that all the inhabitants of Craven county Were French." Additionally, he argued, when Governor Ludwell had sent the acts passed under his term, along with a list of the 1692 assembly members, to London for proprietary ratification, nothing was said about the lack of legitimacy of the French assemblymen.[73]

Boyd designated (Robert) Daniel, a former Goose Creek Man and a power-hungry settler of ill reputation, as the sponsor of the anti-Huguenot address.[74] In Boyd's eyes, the "pretended petition [was] a Seditious libell in respect to the King and to the Lords, & Scandalous in respect to the French, which [sic] they compare[d] to the Devil who got in amongst the Sons of God & to Judas who was Intruded amongst the apostles." On the face of things, the petitioners wanted only to exclude the Huguenots from the assembly and the juries, but the French, in this wartime Francophobic climate, feared that they actually risked losing all their privileges and, above all, their land titles.[75] Boyd's letter implied that Daniel and his followers had summoned the Huguenots to appear before the council to defend their position and that Archdale had encouraged them to do so. The Huguenots, however, deeming that "it would not be Wellcoming to enter in any discussion of their priviledges With men that [they] could Sue Criminally," flatly refused. In their eyes, the sponsors of the petition "intended nothing but to be in some manner the masters of the vote" and, most important, "gave their judgments upon things that are above their reach."[76]

With this last argument, Boyd astutely made a parallel between challenging Huguenot rights and proprietary legitimacy. Beyond the privileges of the French, it was the proprietors' prerogative to grant these privileges that was at stake. This right, Boyd explained, could only be challenged before the king because the council is "an Inferior court in Which ye Lords Deputys cannot be judges" and, in this particular case, because "the judges [were] party." The core of the issue, however, as Boyd implicitly argued, was the legitimacy of the exclusive proprietary power to naturalize, which the lords had originally inferred from the colonial charter. Then, adroitly casting his lot with the rest of the non-English settlers, Boyd asked Archdale what would happen to the political rights of the "Scotch, Suissers, [&] Dutch that are included under the name of Strangers" if the petitioners succeeded in revoking Huguenots' privileges.[77]

In his epistolary appeal to Anthony Ashley Cooper, Boyd expounded on the petitioners' threats and further explained how the Huguenot and proprietary causes were entwined. This second letter confirms that the French, who had barely escaped the horrors of pre-Revocation France, deeply feared losing their economic and civil rights once again and had no illusion about the seriousness of the crisis. According to Boyd, the petitioners indiscriminately refused to acknowledge Huguenots' privileges, arguing that they had "no right to possess houses in town or lands in the country" and that they could not "be confirmed in any office whatsoever." Conceding that their political enemies had "suspended their fury" yet "not altered their design" after the arrival of Archdale, the Huguenots, as they did in 1692, again sought proprietary protection in a desperate attempt to preserve their homes and livelihoods. Judging that Archdale was unwilling rather than simply unable to rebuke the petitioners' unjustified threats, Boyd did not hesitate to ask the proprietors to assert their authority above that of the council, the assembly, and the governor.[78]

Boyd explained that the Huguenots' enemies contested the proprietors' right to naturalize on the grounds that "naturalization could only be made by the parliament of England." However, Boyd, in a lesson in colonial legal history, argued that "the province appartaining not to the crown but belonging to the King, the Lords who were invested of his power could make [the French] free denizions, as the King doth by his governors in the other colonys of America." While Archdale, according to Boyd, sided with the petitioners in asserting that the "charter [did] not grant that power to the Lords," the Huguenots rhetorically asked Anthony Ashley Cooper "to examine if [they] had the power to make [them] freedenizens."[79]

Boyd's letters confirm that the proprietary prerogative to naturalize aliens was rooted in the colonial charter and that it had long been a bone of contention between some of the settlers and the proprietors. They also show that the Huguenots were well aware of the difference between a royal denization and a parliamentary naturalization. Unlike the proprietors, who took over the right to naturalize on shaky legal grounds, the French reasonably asked for a (free) proprietary *denization*. However, it was too late. The Huguenots, or at least a majority of them, had accepted, and had possibly sought or even negotiated, a naturalization act following Sothell's 1691 coup. By 1695 they could not decently request that the proprietors step in once again and naturalize or denizen them. For all practical purposes, naturalization had become a prerogative of the Carolina legislative.

Naturalization without Representation
The Give and Take of Politics

As Boyd intimated in his letter to Anthony Ashley Cooper, Archdale quickly yielded to popular pressure. In October 1695 he opted to issue election writs only to Berkeley and Colleton counties while personally requesting that the Huguenots temporarily abstain from voting "for their own safeties and the preservation of the publick peace."[80] In his October 19 letter addressed to "Pierre Buretel, LeSerrurier, LaSalle, & others," Archdale, while sympathizing with the Huguenots on account of his having suffered religious persecution and banishment "out of his native soil," argued that forbearing voting would not jeopardize their franchise in the future. Archdale also assured them that going against "the present humor of ye people" would compromise their hope of legislative or proprietary naturalization.[81]

While the governor and the council still cautiously asked the proprietors "to let them Know what does in Law quallifie an Alien borne for Electing or being Elected," they had by then shifted their argumentation to firmer grounds. Based on earlier proprietary instructions granting the governor the power to regulate legislative elections, Archdale excluded Craven County because "there being not above Thirty Inhabitants & those all french."[82] The new seat apportionment, however, could potentially result in a deadlock since each county had ten seats. Consequently, when Archdale called new elections in November, Berkeley, merged with Craven, had twenty seats and Colleton was given ten.[83]

As expected, the proprietors, who still "hoped to find the good effects of Carolina becoming a place of refuge from arbitrary government in other parts," did not support the governor and the council in their effort to infringe on the Huguenots' privileges with an implicit challenge to the proprietors' power to grant them.[84] The proprietors did not buy Archdale's argument that proprietary instructions regarding the conduct of elections allowed him to exclude Craven County from the assembly; nor did they concur in disenfranchising Craven Huguenots simply because the county was thinly settled. The proprietors, and the Carolina authorities, well knew that in early modern England legislative representation was not based on population. As they had once reminded Carolinians a decade earlier, at a time when Berkeley inhabitants opposed an even county representation, "not having an equall number of Inhabitants is no good reason why it should not Choose an equall number of members of Parliament . . . those things always going by the place & not the proportion of people."[85] However, if in Carolina population was to be the basis of representation, with much common sense the proprietors suggested an increase in the number of representatives from Berkeley County, since it was more densely populated, while keeping a separate Craven representation. The proprietors did not mention it explicitly but probably thought that this arrangement would also dilute the French element in the assembly. In the meantime, the assembly elected in November 1695 had to be dissolved.[86] In June 1696 Their Lordships ostentatiously and authoritatively reiterated their position in reminding Carolinians that "ye Rights of Craven County must be continued which we cannot in honour depart from."[87] Despite this late show of force and as always since the beginning of the colonization of Carolina, the proprietors were to be as powerless as they were distant.

In August 1696 Archdale answered Their Lordships that political peace had been restored in Carolina, where "we have now no Contending Different factions or Interests in the Government." Nothing apparently could be done about the French who "Seeme Dissatisfied and uneasy that they have not all the priviledges and franchises of an Englishman." Unable to contest the validity of proprietary power to grant Huguenots economic privileges, the governor reassured his fellow proprietors that the refugees "have and Enjoy all [privileges] except voting for and being Elected members of Assembly."[88] Having no qualms about dramatizing the situation, Archdale justified the restriction on the grounds that maintaining Huguenot franchise and eligibility would have pitted English and French settlers against one another "in a Sort of Civill warr the Consequence of which could not probably have been Less then the Dispeopling of this Colony."[89]

Then, in a fine chess move, Archdale counteracted the proprietors' objection about denying Craven County separate legislative representation by citing proprietary instructions that stipulated that no county could be represented in the assembly if it did not have a population of forty freeholders.[90] Judging by the 1696 *Liste des François et Suisses* and the 1699 Huguenot lowcountry census, it is doubtful that Craven County, which had a total population approaching 150, did not meet the freeholder requirements for representation, but neither the governor nor the council seems to have bothered to check.[91]

Unsure of how the proprietors would react to their unilateral curtailing of Huguenot privileges, the governor and the council ended the letter on a conciliatory note while defending their position. Hoping that Their Lordships would not think they had disobeyed their instructions and hypocritically emphasizing that every Carolina official was a friend of the Huguenots, they asked the proprietors to let them know what privileges they wanted to grant the French but to specify "from what powers they bee Derived from."[92]

Archdale and the council won their case by acting as though it were a fait accompli. Satisfied with the council's promise to have the assembly enact a naturalization law as soon as possible and relieved that, in the meantime, Archdale had managed to negotiate a compromise on the issues that opposed them to the settlers, the proprietors acquiesced in denying Craven County separate representation, but only on the basis of insufficient population. Nothing was said about how extensive the naturalization law should be, but the proprietors certainly did not favor Huguenot ineligibility and disenfranchisement. These two questions, which topped the council's agenda, would be the objects of another round of argumentation.

In order to appease the proprietors and the Huguenots while sweetening the pill of political exclusion, Archdale and the council promised a naturalization law, but it would be enacted on their terms. As in the case of the Fundamental Constitutions, Carolina officials and whoever led the anti-Huguenot attack would not be satisfied with a victorious battle against the proprietors but intended to win the war. Archdale left the colony in October 1696. His successor Joseph Blake, another Dissenter, would mastermind the council's strategy.

The same month that Archdale returned to England, Governor Blake wrote the proprietors to reiterate his intention to naturalize the Huguenots while foreseeing difficulties in reaching agreement on the exact contents of the law. Blake, however, perhaps a bit prematurely, acknowledged that the planned naturalization act would qualify the French "to vote for and bee members of Assembly." With legitimate relief, the governor announced to Their Lordships that the French had agreed to formally petition for naturalization and, until the enacting of the law, to stay out of Carolina politics.[93]

Although merging Craven and Berkeley counties guaranteed that the assembly would never again be one-third French, the council, despite its conciliatory rhetoric, aimed at total political exclusion. In December, Blake skillfully justified that no election writs had yet been issued to the Huguenots of Craven County because the 1696 Navigation Act opportunely required that "all Places of Trust in the Courts of Laws, or what relates to the Treasury of the [colonies]" be given only to natural-born subjects.[94] Stalling for time, the council further explained to the proprietors that a group of Huguenot leaders refused to petition for naturalization and take the required oath of allegiance. Apparently convinced that "the war betweene the Crowns of England and France canot End but with the Restauration of all the french Protestants to their Native Kingdom and Estates," these "french gentlemen" expected "to returne home to France to their Estates there in Som Short Time."[95] While the upcoming Peace of Ryswick (September 1697) undoubtedly raised fantasies among some Huguenot refugees, mainly in Europe, about the willingness and capacity of the victorious members of the League of Augsburg to force Louis XIV to restore the Edict of Nantes, it is highly unlikely that "the Leading men of the french" in Carolina planned to go back to France. After more than ten years in the colony, the Huguenot elite had heavily invested in land and slaves and aspired to a more complete role in Carolina politics, not a return to the exclusive Catholic France of Louis XIV. Return may have been contemplated by a handful of Huguenots, but it could not possibly have influenced the whole group, especially since at about the same time the quasi-exhaustive *Liste des François et Suisses* was being compiled. The council's claim was obviously an exaggeration meant to confuse the proprietors and gain time. At this juncture the Huguenots were at the mercy of Carolina officials. They could neither vote nor be elected because they were aliens, and only the assembly, with the approval of the governor and the council, could remove these disqualifications with an act of naturalization whose contents Carolinians would define regardless of the proprietary position.[96]

The die was cast. During the legislative elections of January 1696, Jacques LeSade and Jonas Bonhost were denied their votes by Sheriff Robert Gibbes on the grounds that they were "natural born subjects of the French king" and could show neither letters of naturalization nor denization. The two Huguenots claimed that they had lived in South Carolina for several years and "never before had been denied to vote for members of Assembly," but they argued to no avail.[97] At that point the council was apparently ready at least to let denizened Huguenots vote, probably because they were uncomfortable with contesting the validity of royal denization. The following month Jean Thomas petitioned the assembly for a private act of naturalization for a five-pound fee.[98] This individual initiative illustrates that in early 1696 the Huguenots were still unsure of obtaining a collective naturalization law and that they must have been divided on a plan of action to follow.

In March 1696 Governor Archdale and the assembly received "The Humble Petition of Noah Royer, Jr., Jonas Bonhost, and Peter Poinsett on behalf of the rest who hath hereto Subscribed with wives and children." The thirty petitioners, in rhetoric reminiscent of Boyd's letters, reminded the assembly that they had been encouraged to settle in Carolina and promised land by the proprietors. "Inhabitants [in the colony] of many years" and having "borne armes & been obedient to all commands millitary and civill and in all matters [having] behaved as Subjects borne," the Huguenots deserved to be naturalized. At the end of the petition the subscribers further requested the Carolina authorities to consider that, bearing in mind the ongoing Anglo-French military conflict, "in case of an Invasion or being taken prisoner, [they] cannot Expect Quarters from the Subjects of the french King."[99] This argument emphasizes the inescapable fact that in these uncertain war times the Huguenots were still legally French since Carolinians had formally recognized neither English denization and naturalization nor proprietary naturalization. As French subjects who had fled the kingdom of His Very Christian Majesty, they were in real danger of being taken prisoners and sentenced to serve on Louis XIV's galleys. This had happened to New York merchant Élie Neau in 1692 and many others.[100] In a last request the petitioners asked the governor and the assembly to see that the act would include a clause securing "the titles of their lands already taken up & bought to them, their heirs & Assigns for Ever."[101] Probably sensing that these privileges would not be granted to them and because they did not constitute priorities, the petitioners, who were all Charleston Huguenots, did not mention anything about franchise and eligibility.

This petition was submitted too late to be considered by the assembly, which ended its session on March 17. Nothing was done, however, in the 1696 fall session. It may be surmised that the Carolina authorities requested that the Huguenots gather a more exhaustive and perhaps more detailed list of heads of family wishing to be naturalized, which would include those who had settled outside of Charleston. In all likelihood this demand was also a maneuver to stall for time. The assembly needed a few months to reflect on how to legally grant the refugees a naturalization law and simultaneously bar them, especially those living in Craven County, from the Commons House of Assembly without provoking the ire of the Huguenots and of the proprietors. In October 1696 the governor and the council reported to the proprietors that the French were preparing a (new) petition.[102] This is when the *Liste des François et Suisses Refugiez en Caroline qui souhaittent d'être naturalisés Anglois* was compiled by a Huguenot committee.[103]

When the assembly met in February 1697 they pledged "to Think of Secureing to all Aliens their Estates and Give them an Act Such Encouragement as Shall be Thought Convenient" in the hope of "Better strengthening and uniteing ye Inhabitants of this Province." Within a month a bill for "Makeing Aliens free of this part of This Province and for Granting Liberty of Conscience To all Protestants" was passed.[104] In March the governor and the council proceeded to inform the proprietors that the assembly had successfully passed two related laws: a naturalization act and an election act guaranteeing Huguenot ineligibility.[105] Soon afterward Their Lordships conceded that they had made a mistake in requesting that Craven County be represented separately in the assembly since "there being . . . allmost as many to be Elected as there [are] Electors in that County."[106] A year later the proprietors ratified the 1697 Naturalization Act without a word about Huguenot franchise and eligibility.[107]

This was no less than a *victoire totale* for the colony's authorities and whoever wished to curtail French influence in Carolina politics. The Huguenots had been naturalized by the assembly, not by the proprietors. Legislative naturalization had become the rule, and the naturalization clause was accordingly removed from the 1698 version of the nearly defunct Fundamental Constitutions.[108] While it seems that the French could vote since no decision had formally been made regarding their disenfranchisement, the disputed 1702 elections would show that the Huguenots would have to fight to retain this right. If Huguenot ineligibility turned out to be loosely and ineffectively enforced in practice, eligibility nonetheless remained the privilege of an exclusive group of happy few who were either born or naturalized in England and who enjoyed kin and socioeconomic connections of some sort to English settlers.

Beyond the question of Huguenot franchise and eligibility, however, the proprietors failed to see that the merging of Berkeley and Craven counties, the 1697 electoral law, and the 1692 disqualification of Jacques LeBas actually illustrated the desire and the ability of the South Carolina Assembly to control its membership. This crucial process culminated with the 1717 electoral law, which replaced the proprietary county constituencies with an assembly-sponsored parish apportionment.[109]

The 1697 Act of Naturalization was the consensual outcome of a bitter decade of political turmoil during which the refugees played every card they had. In the small and faction-ridden world of proprietary Carolina politics, the Huguenots paradoxically fell victim to wartime Francophobic discrimination while obtaining the naturalization they had sought since their settlement in the colony. This complex period of Carolina Huguenot history (1689–97), however, cannot be satisfactorily explained uniquely in terms of religious, political, or even county alignments.[110]

There is no doubt that whoever wanted to curtail Huguenot legislative representation had a point. While there were more than forty freeholders in Craven County in 1692, with six members the Huguenots were proportionately overrepresented in the assembly. No matter how fluent in English and how familiar with English political life these men may have been, this situation was understandably uncomfortable for British Carolinians. Additionally, the council was right to raise the issue of the eligibility of aliens in the Anglo-American world. In 1692 the refugees, following Coke's legal distinctions, were aliens. They still owed a *ligeantia naturalis* to a not only foreign but also Catholic sovereign against whom, to make matters worse, England was currently at war. At this juncture the Huguenots may have made a political mistake in sitting in the assembly while they were not technically naturalized. They had truly put the cart before the horse. Although they had acquired land, voted, and occupied civil and militia positions from the time of their migration, it was probably politically naive of them to think that time alone would secure them the religious, political, and economic privileges they had enjoyed through proprietary generosity and local political indifference. In 1695 the Huguenots probably felt betrayed by their fellow Carolinians, but their premigration experiences in France should have taught them that any privilege could suddenly become precarious.

It does not seem, however, that only the Dissenters were against the Huguenots. It is true that the judge Stephen Bull and the attorney general Edmund Bellinger, involved in the conviction of the *Blue Star,* were Nonconformists, but the informant at the origin of the case was a Huguenot. Equally true is that Archdale and Blake were Dissenters, but in his epistolary appeal to Archdale, Boyd named Robert Daniel, a Goose Creek Man, as the Huguenots' worst enemy. Additionally, no Berkeley Anglican stood up to defend the rights of the French in 1692 and in 1695 when their church life and political rights, respectively, were threatened.

In the fluid and treacherous context of Carolina proprietary politics, the refugees successively alienated various factions under Colleton's and Sothell's administrations. By 1695 they had become the scapegoats for the colony's problems, and Archdale effectively capitalized on this situation. It is only later, probably after Blake's death in 1700, and perhaps as a result of the merging of Craven and Berkeley counties in the assembly that the Huguenots sealed a long-lasting alliance with the Anglicans. The 1689–97 period blatantly demonstrated to the Huguenots that they desperately needed political allies other than the distant proprietors. The so-called Berkeley-Craven / Huguenot-Anglican alliance that would emerge after Blake's death in 1700 seems to have been an alliance as much of necessity as of political and religious affinities.

While helping to explain why Huguenots and Anglicans experienced a decisive rapprochement in the early 1700s, county alignments nonetheless obscure internal divisions among the refugees. It is clear that Craven County Huguenots never represented the interest of the entire group. In fact, in January 1696, in the midst of the "exclusion crisis," the Charleston Huguenot Henry LeNoble sat in the assembly in complete indifference to the ineligibility of the Craven French. During the entire period, whether under Colleton's, Sothell's, Archdale's, or Blake's administrations, Charleston and Santee Huguenots did not side with the same factions. Naturalization benefited all the French, but the fact that the first petition was signed only by Charleston Huguenots means that the French still did not speak with one voice. Perhaps at that point the Craven Huguenots, who were to lose their block representation in the final deal, were unwilling to accept it while those in Charleston expected always to have at least one assemblyman even with the new seat apportionment.

Between 1689 and 1697 Carolinians lived in the midst of what John Stewart called "a french papisticall Warr."[111] In other words, from the time a few Huguenots controversially subscribed to the Fundamental Constitutions on Colleton's invitation until they obtained a naturalization act that allowed them to vote while being declared ineligible, South Carolina was exposed to French raids.[112] In fact, when Carolina authorities were debating the extent of the planned naturalization law in the winter of 1696–97, they received alarming reports warning them that a French fleet had been ordered "to take or Burne Charles Town" the following spring.[113] There is no doubt that the Huguenots, although Protestants, were the victims of an exacerbated wartime Francophobia that transcended religious and political boundaries. By the same token, as the war continued through the 1690s it became more and more urgent for the refugees to shed their alien enemy status through naturalization. Unsurprisingly, just seven months after the enactment of the naturalization law, the governor and the council, with joy and relief, confirmed to the proprietors that they had received notification that the war had ended and pledged to "strictly observe the Articles of Peace between ye two Crowns."[114]

Although contemporary wartime Francophobia certainly helps to explain the intensity of the anti-French sentiment prevalent in Carolina in the 1690s, one cannot help wondering why the Huguenots aroused so much hatred. In fifteen years their presence seems to have angered the colonists to a point of no return and, if we are to believe Archdale, nothing short of disenfranchisement and ineligibility could appease their opponents, while their alleged "friends" remained quite discreet, to say the least. Were the Huguenots particularly economically successful? Were they too numerous, thereby creating an all too visible alien minority? Did they successively alienate all Carolina factions by their somewhat erratic political behavior? Although the "civil war" reportedly feared by Governor Archdale was undoubtedly a remote possibility, the threat of having Huguenot land titles challenged, as happened in Rhode Island in the early 1690s, was real.[115] More than political representation, a somewhat accessory privilege for people who had lived in absolutist France, it is ultimately the preservation of their estates and the freedom to practice their trades that motivated the Huguenots to agree to naturalization on the council's and the assembly's terms.

Archdale is remembered by historians as an efficient governor and a fine politician who succeeded in bringing political peace and economic prosperity to Carolina through a unique flair for compromises. It is clear, though, that Huguenots' political rights were sacrificed to restore harmony among settlers and between Carolinians and the proprietors. However, beyond the short-term relief that the so-called Archdale laws may have brought to Their Lordships, the 1695–97 crisis constitutes another proprietary political defeat. In reneging on the promises they made to the Huguenots in the early 1680s and failing to stand up resolutely for the refugees' rights, the proprietors let the Carolina government naturalize the Huguenots. This concession may seem minor within the perspective of early South Carolina history, but it actually heralds the eventual proprietary failure in imposing the last version of the Fundamental Constitutions in 1698.[116] In yielding their exclusive prerogative to naturalize, the proprietors made the assembly the principal source of political power in the colony. As for the Huguenots, they did not lose as much as it might appear nor as much as the proprietors did. The refugees obtained a first and relatively generous naturalization law and were not statutorily disenfranchised. In time, especially following the establishment of a parish-based seat apportionment, the Huguenots would once again sit in the assembly, although never again in the proportions of 1692. There was a time of exclusion, but there would be one for readmission.

South Carolina Naturalization Laws

The Huguenots obtained three naturalization laws between 1691 and 1704.[117] These laws differed in the naturalization processes they provided and in the privileges they granted. The differences reflect the political contexts surrounding their enactment. The 1691 act was a political gift from Sothell's faction to their Huguenot supporters. As such it offered generous conditions to the French. A long preamble drafted in a style reminiscent of Boyd's letters first reminded Carolinians that the Huguenots had been encouraged by the proprietors and the monarchy to settle in the colony and that they had lawfully acquired land, occupied military and civil posts, and freely practiced commercial and artisanal occupations. In short, the act was legalizing a de facto condition. Consequently, the council made the French and Swiss Protestants "as free to all intents and purposes . . . as if they . . . had been and were borne within that part of this province," provided that they registered within six months and paid a small fee of seven pence. This was no less than a Carolina general naturalization law. The generous terms of the act are easily explained. Sothell's supporters were then competing with political opponents, among whom there were other Huguenots, who favored implementing the Fundamental Constitutions, and consequently had to offer the refugees as much as the proprietors had. Although this law was repealed, it showed the Huguenots how much they could obtain for their political support by carefully negotiating, provided, of course, that they backed the right horse.[118]

The Commons House of Assembly passed the 1697 law in a radically different context. While adversarial factions had vied for Huguenot support in 1690, Carolinians were now determined to solve the issues that divided them and set them against the proprietors without trying to win the French in the colony. The 1697 act was a concession made to the proprietors and, to use one of Archdale's favorite arguments, to public peace. The refugees had little or no influence in the wording and contents of the law. A short preamble explained that religious persecution and the fertility of the colony—that is, not the proprietors or His Majesty—had encouraged aliens to settle in Carolina. In principle the law offered them "the rights, privileges, powers and immunities" of English subjects but explicitly mentioned only property rights. Nothing was said regarding commercial and occupational privileges, and contrary to what Archdale had promised them in his 1695 October letter, another law denied them eligibility.[119] In addition the act restrictively applied to a list of sixty Huguenots and four Jews with a three-month window for anyone who had not yet petitioned the assembly.[120] Naturalized aliens were required to take an oath of allegiance to William III. In all likelihood, Huguenots happily complied to this condition, which was in accordance with the prevalent European practices that equated citizenship with subjectship. A final paragraph, which may have been included in response to a specific Huguenot request to avoid an attack on their church similar to that of 1692, guaranteed all Protestants "the full, free and undisturbed liberty of their consciences" and "the exercise of their worship . . . without any . . . molestation or hindrance."[121]

The 1704 act was passed by an Anglican-dominated assembly that had just attempted to exclude Dissenters from its ranks and establish the Church of England in the colony with the help or at least the political neutrality of the Huguenots. The act was a general naturalization law that applied retroactively to all aliens who had not been naturalized in 1697 and prospectively to all who "shall hereafter come into this part of the Province."[122] Each applicant simply had to pledge allegiance to Queen Anne, take an antipopery oath, and pay a registration fee of "one royal."[123] The provisions of this act, however, were not particularly generous but were in line with the previous naturalization law. The act confirmed the Huguenots' property and legal rights and statutorily secured their enfranchisement but reiterated their ineligibility.[124] This important restriction, which, contrary to what occurred in 1697, was included in the naturalization act at a time when the Huguenots had ostensibly sided with the dominating faction, shows the limit of their political influence.[125]

All things considered, Carolina naturalization laws were in keeping with legislation passed in other colonies. Local in scope and designed to encourage further immigration, they offered significantly more than alien Protestant settlers could reasonably expect to obtain in England and at a considerably lower cost. Unsurprisingly, the right to purchase, sell, own, bequeath, and inherit land held a prominent and explicit place in all colonial naturalization acts. Commercial and occupational rights were, however, often left implicit. Naturalized aliens were usually, implicitly or explicitly, allowed to vote but were ineligible in Connecticut, New Jersey, Maryland, Georgia, and, of course, South Carolina. The obligation to take an oath of allegiance to the ruling monarch and one against the pope, which is not to be confused with the more exacting sacramental test, was also common. In sum, Governor Blake, despite the fact that it served his political interests, was right to contend in 1697 that the Huguenots had obtained a naturalization act "as ample as [the council] could prevail with the Commons," in contrast with the chimerical and extravagant proprietary promises of free and full naturalization.[126]

Each of the three naturalization laws resulted from negotiations, not to say horse dealing, that involved the Huguenots (or part of the group) to varying degrees. In turn these negotiations reflect an undeniable Huguenot willingness and capacity to participate actively in the political life of the colony. Except perhaps in the early years of their settlement when they went through a necessary phase of adaptation, the refugees never were idle bystanders or hapless victims of Machiavellian manipulations. During the entire proprietary period and within the bounds of the law, the Huguenots voted, made use of the courts, sat and debated bills in the assembly, and occupied military and civil positions at the county and province levels.

Huguenot Electoral Behavior and Political Representation

The simple fact that their political opponents adamantly, not to say vehemently, wished to exclude them from the colony's political life is evidence that the Huguenots voted and did so in numbers large enough to be perceived by some as a threat. Since no voter lists have survived, it is difficult to determine who among them exercised their right of suffrage and whom they elected. A few extant documents offer only precious snapshots on lowcountry Huguenot electoral behavior.

The first record of Huguenot voting is the May 1696 deposition by Isaac Caillabœuf reporting that during the previous January, Robert Gibbes, sheriff of Berkeley County, had refused to register the votes of Jacques LeSade and Jonas Bonhost for failing to show naturalization or denization papers. Identified as "gentleman" and wheelwright respectively, LeSade and Bonhost lived in Charleston. That same year Bonhost was one of the prime movers behind the March 1696 petition, thereby showing his undeniable interest in Carolina politics and even activism in the defense of Huguenots' rights. The fact that LeSade and Bonhost claimed that "never before had they been denied to vote for members of Assembly" confirms that some refugees consistently voted.[127]

Characterized as "an especially wild affair" by Sirmans, the disputed elections of March 1702, following the controversial appointment of Governor James Moore by a divided council, led to an investigation at the initiative of a Dissenter-controlled assembly.[128] Accusing Moore of having rigged the elections in allowing "Strangers, Servants, Aliens . . . Malatoes, and Negroes" to vote, the Nonconformist assemblymen summoned forty-one illegal voters in April.[129] Locked in a power struggle with the governor, who attempted to put an end to this investigation by proroguing the assembly, the Dissenters reacted by expanding the list to eighty-three settlers a month later. All in all, twenty-seven identified Huguenots were summoned before the assembly for having voted without first "Registering Their Certificates [of naturalization] in the Secretaries office of this Province" in accordance with the 1697 act.[130] Although partisan in spirit, most likely unfounded, and ultimately dropped, this investigation ironically provides the historian with a unique slice of the lowcountry Huguenot electorate.[131] The socioeconomic and regional profiles of the listed refugees reveal that voting was not circumscribed to a social group or a particular settlement. Among the fifteen whose occupations are known, eleven were of modest economic means (five farmers, three weavers, and three small artisans) and four were of higher social status (two silversmiths, one apothecary, and one merchant). Among the twelve whose places of residence have been determined, six lived in Orange Quarter, three in Charleston, and three in Santee.[132] This list of allegedly illegal voters confirms the fact that Huguenots by and large were interested and participated in the political life of the colony no matter how fluent in English and how familiar with English institutions they may or may not have been.

Lowcountry Huguenots undeniably voted, but for whom? It can be reasonably assumed that they voted for Huguenot candidates, but this was not always and everywhere possible, especially after the 1697 legislative reforms. Once again records are

scarce, but existing assembly lists and reports of electoral connivance and alleged manipulations involving Anglicans and Huguenots provide a few clues. The membership of
the first recorded assembly (September 1692–June 1694) includes six Huguenots. All six
were wealthy landowners, five of them claiming the title *écuyer* or *sieur,* and represented
Craven County.[133] If Huguenots of all economic conditions voted, their candidates expectedly were men of wealth and status. Having no candidates of their own, Charleston and
Orange Quarter Huguenots must have elected one of the seven Englishmen representing
Berkeley County, showing thereby no ethnic political exclusiveness.

As expected, Huguenot representation in the assembly was altered following the
Archdale and Blake 1695–97 reforms. Six refugees had been elected in 1692 alone, but
only four sat in the nine assemblies that met between 1695 and 1708.[134] The second (1695),
fourth (1698–99), fifth (1700–1702), and ninth (1707) assemblies included no
Huguenots.[135] To make it worse, while Huguenot representation declined, the total number of assemblymen rose from twenty to thirty in 1695, further diluting their political
influence. The profile of the elected Huguenots also considerably changed. Santee écuyers from Brittany and Aunis who had left France in their late twenties and early thirties
were succeeded by thoroughly Anglicized Charleston merchants, such as Jacques LeSerrurier-Smith and John-Abraham Motte, who had spent most of their lives safely outside
Louis XIV's kingdom and had presumably been naturalized in England. Between 1708
and 1717 there were most often three, and at least two, Huguenots per assembly representing Berkeley-Craven. Yet, if Huguenot legislative representation became more regular, the fact is that it remained controlled by a handful of repeatedly elected Charleston
merchants.[136] This dual planter/merchant and Santee/Charleston shift was undeniably an
important impact of the 1695 exclusion crisis.[137] Only after 1717, when electoral reforms
switched from a county-based to a parish-based seat apportionment, did Santee regain
the distinct representation that it had lost in 1695, but by then most Huguenot assemblymen were Carolina natives.[138]

Sectarian ethnic voting was never the rule in proprietary Carolina since voters indifferently elected French and English candidates. In 1692 the Berkeley Huguenot vote
undoubtedly helped elect the seven English representatives of the county, and Craven
Huguenots voted for Englishmen after 1695. In the wake of the January 1706 elections,
a Dissenter explained that the Anglicans had won the Huguenots "by putting a French
man naturalized into their List." Notwithstanding this partisan accusation, this was basic
electoral strategy on the part of the Berkeley Anglicans. It also shows that the Huguenots
had enough leverage to get one of their own on the ballot.[139] .

The following year, locked in a power struggle over the regulation of the Indian
trade, Governor Nathaniel Johnson, who had just succeeded in establishing the Church
of England in the province, dissolved the house. This was to no avail as the next assembly turned out to be controlled by Governor Johnson's opponents, who were in majority, although not exclusively, Dissenters.[140] In this post-church-act climate, the spring 1707
elections must have been rather heated. Once again a few Huguenots were at the center of a legislative investigation. In early June, Peter Mailhet was summoned to the house
to answer the charge of electoral manipulation following the incriminatory deposition
of Joseph Marbœuf, Thomas Lynch, and Antoine Bonneau. Mailhet was accused of

circulating a letter in Orange Quarter asking his fellow Huguenots "to come down to Vote . . . for the Governor was oblig'd to disolve the last Assembly because they were goeing to take away our privileges not only of Voteing but also of Inheriting" and warning them that "the Gentlemen Presbitarians would bring Tyranny upon us as Paraoh did upon the Children of Israel." Mailhet added that "the true lists of who to vote for to oblige the Governor and the rest of the French" was available at his home. He further instructed Antoine Poitevin, the Huguenot to whom the letter was addressed, to share it with his neighbors and "have it read to [his] Church to the Congregation."[141]

When Mailhet came before the assembly, he denied writing such a letter and contemptuously declared that "if he had, he Should not deliver it." The house voted to prosecute Mailhet, who was accordingly held in custody. The assembly was worried enough by this affair that it issued an official declaration "to Quiet and Appease ye minds of ye french Inhabitants." The house assured the Huguenots that they "never had ye Least Thoughts or Design of Depriveing [them] of any Right They have hitherto enjoyed in This Province" and pledged that they "Would rather . . . do their utmost To Confirm & Strengthen Their Intrest & Inheritance to Them." By the end of the month Mailhet was freed.[142]

Mailhet had served as messenger of the house in the seventh (1703–5) and eighth (1706–7) assemblies and had been once reprimanded by the house for letting the landgrave Thomas Smith escape while under his custody.[143] As messenger he was privy to house debates and bills and could very well have been Johnson's messenger, so to speak, in Huguenot circles.[144] Although it is doubtful that Mailhet's letter had any impact on the spring 1707 elections, his attempt to sway the Huguenot vote in Orange Quarter confirms the central roles played by kin and religious networks in this rural lowcountry community. The Poitevin family members, who were related to many Huguenots of the area, were, along with the pastor, the central figures of St. Denis and as such were well placed to influence their neighbors.

Assuredly, seventeenth-century French people, in contrast to the English, were not accustomed to nationwide electoral consultation on a regular basis.[145] They nonetheless were actively engaged in governmental affairs at the municipal, village, and parish levels. Therefore, no matter what their Carolina enemies may have claimed, the Huguenots were not passive, voiceless, and politically immature subjects of an absolutist king. In fact, there is no doubt that the Craven écuyers and Charleston merchants who were elected to the assembly, which they may have compared to a French provincial parlement, had significant premigration experience in local and provincial politics. Armed with this political background, Carolina Huguenots, as long as they were allowed to, actively participated in provincial lawmaking. Jack Greene's quantitative study of the members of the Carolina Assembly by rank, based on the importance of the committees they sat on, shows that, out of the seven Huguenots he identified for the proprietary period, four were ranked "first assemblymen" at least once and two were never ranked as "second assemblymen."[146]

As early as 1692 Alexandre T. Chastaigner, René Ravenel, and Jean Boyd were together appointed to ad hoc committees to draft various laws ranging from the peripheral "Act for the Making and Mending of Highways and Paths, and for the cutting of

Creeks and Water-courses" to the more central "Act for Ascertaining Public Officer Fees."[147] There was thus a time in proprietary Carolina when English laws were written by Frenchmen without it causing any political tumult. Whenever Huguenots sat in the assembly they were active lawmakers. Even in 1696, 1702, and 1707 when Carolina Francophobia peaked, French assemblymen Henry LeNoble, Jacques LeSerrurier-Smith, Louis Pasquereau, and John-Abraham Motte were appointed to ad hoc and permanent committees to prepare bills.[148] After 1695, however, no law would ever be drafted by a committee composed solely of Huguenots. This was, of course, not just as a result of the 1695–97 crisis but also corresponded to an inevitable evolution. With time and the passing of a new generation, the Carolina French no longer acted and were no longer perceived as representatives of an alien group but were considered full-fledged Carolinians.

Although, as Butler wrote, "the rivulets of early American prejudice ran swift not deep" and the Huguenots, when elected, always took part in the provincial legislative process, the 1695–97 exclusion crisis shifted the focus of the leading French from provincial to local affairs.[149] Once the Huguenots lost their collective representation in the assembly, they turned to running the counties and, after 1706, the parishes in which they had settled, thereby fading as a collective force in provincewide politics. The political crisis of the mid-1690s and the consequent necessity for the Huguenots to find another avenue of power appears therefore to have been as instrumental as their growing affection toward the Church of England in their decision to join ranks with Carolina Anglicans. Five of the seven Huguenots elected to the 1692 assembly held local offices in the following decades. Although as early as 1692 Henry Auguste Chastaigner was appointed sheriff and Paul Bruneau served as justice of the peace of Craven County, Huguenot control of county and parish offices, whether elective or appointive, clearly intensified after 1695.[150] Craven County, a Huguenot stronghold par excellence, even looked like a French *bailliage,* with a Huguenot justice of the peace swearing in another Huguenot sheriff and with official documents being registered in French.[151] This is the time when a few families, such as the St. Juliens, the Ravenels, the LeBas, and the LeGrands, started taking control of local offices, thereby founding influential office-holding dynasties.[152] The involvement of the Huguenot "responsible gentry," to use Richard Waterhouse's phrase, in local government assuredly reflected the more general development of the local administration as a sign of increasingly sophisticated, and more harmonious, Carolina politics resulting from the growth of the colony and the fact that Carolina gentility did not neglect to serve.[153] This trend, however, was undeniably more pronounced in the case of the Huguenots, who did not have much choice but to delve into local affairs if they wanted to play any sort of political role in Carolina after 1695.

After the well-being of their Calvinist congregations, naturalization was the single most important issue in the eyes of the Huguenots, and as such guided their political behavior until 1697. Once naturalized in Carolina, the refugees were legally admitted into the colony's society and were guaranteed the essential rights to hold, bequeath, and inherit real estate and to practice their occupations. Political participation, which was at first perceived as a means to obtain naturalization, turned out to be a secondary issue whose sacrifice the Huguenots reluctantly agreed to in the face of tremendous hostility. The 1695–97 crisis is undoubtedly mirrored by the 1704–6 establishment victory as, for the Huguenots, the former represents exclusion and the latter acceptance. In both instances, however, the Huguenots had to give away two privileges: political participation and religious independence. Of course, in 1695–97 the Huguenots were blackmailed into relinquishing their eligibility in exchange for naturalization, whereas in 1704 they willingly abandoned Calvinism to embrace the Church of England. Yet, these two Carolina historical moments are related as the Huguenots vividly remembered the Archdale years when the time came to side for or against the establishment of the Church of England. This does not mean, as it has often been written, that the Huguenots backed the Carolina Anglicans in 1704 in a spirit of revenge against the Dissenters, although a few individuals may have done so. Huguenot political exclusion was the result of a consensus that crossed political and religious boundaries and solved, at least for a while, most issues that divided the colonists and opposed them to the proprietors. Therefore, the Dissenters alone cannot be blamed. Nonetheless, the 1695–97 years taught the Huguenots a lesson. In order to be fully accepted they had to become Englishmen or Carolinian and not just by formally and somewhat artificially changing citizenship through naturalization. Abandoning French Calvinism for the *English church,* as the Church of England was known among the Huguenots, was a spectacular way to prove their loyalty to England, embodied by the monarchy, and to show irrefutably their willingness to become Carolinian.

Chapter 8

LAND, TRADE, AND SLAVES

From Rags to Riches in Colonial South Carolina

[A planter] is at home a little lord. He orders his troop of negroes like a king.
Pastor Paul L'Escot (March 1, 1703)

Beyond its overoptimism and its exaggerations meant to attract more refugees to Carolina, the letter Louis Thibou wrote in 1683 from his "plantation on the river Ashley" to the godfather to one of his sons, Gabriel Bontefoy, in London, perfectly describes early Huguenot economic life in the colony. Thibou first mentioned the fertile Carolina land and how easy it was to acquire and clear. He went on to describe his crops of corn, peas, melons, and potatoes and his attempt at making wine. He bragged about his fat chickens; his cows that gave him a lot of milk and a calf every year, at no cost since they grazed freely in the woods; and his pigs, which only needed to be given "a little corn every evening to make them come back home." Thibou also shared his hope of purchasing "a couple of negroes" and hiring a maid, and he explained to his likely envious and intrigued correspondent that for a small fee he could have an Indian hunter bring him as much game and venison as his family could eat. He did not fail, either, to mention the Indian trade, which "brings [the English] a great quantity of deer skins and furs," and the abundance of fish in the lowcountry rivers. Thibou concluded his letter with a reference to a fellow Carolina Huguenot who "has made at least 30 pounds of silk this year" and a description of various building materials abundantly available in the lowcountry.[1]

Huguenots' economic life in proprietary Carolina can be roughly divided into three phases. In the 1680s, as documented by Thibou's letter, the Huguenots first attempted to make silk and wine, as the Lords Proprietors had hoped, while engaging in subsistence farming with a variety of crops and, especially in Santee, practicing a marginal trade with the local natives. A decade later, however, the French stopped pursuing the proprietary dreams of sericulture and viticulture and, like their English fellow colonists, went into cattle ranching to accumulate enough capital to purchase slaves and acquire more land. At the turn of the eighteenth century the wealthiest among them had successfully experimented with rice cultivation and enjoyed an economic prosperity that would have been quite difficult if not impossible to achieve back in France. Huguenots who could not afford the expenses inherent in establishing a lucrative rice plantation or who did not own land favorably located for such endeavor stuck to ranching and grain farming, selling their crops locally and to Charleston merchants.

Meanwhile, Huguenot merchants and artisans who chose to acquire town lots in lieu of land in the 1680s continued to practice their premigratory occupations. In the early 1690s the former carried on a small trade in provisions and wood with the Caribbean and the northern mainland colonies, while the latter enjoyed real success due to the scarcity of skilled artisans in early Charleston. Once the merchants acquired enough capital and experience in Anglo-American commercial ways and their trading rights were guaranteed by naturalization laws, they engaged in transatlantic trade with Huguenot and non-Huguenot partners in Charleston and London. In the early years of the eighteenth century, younger Huguenot merchants with extensive contacts in England and in the Caribbean arrived in Carolina. After a few years in Charleston as factors of English companies, which were sometimes Huguenot-owned, they decided to settle for good in the colony. They formed, often in partnership, successful mercantile firms dealing in a variety of trades across the Atlantic while supplying Carolina Indian traders with highly coveted manufactured goods. Over time many of the most financially successful Charleston Huguenot merchants and artisans eventually acquired land away from the town and engaged in cattle ranching and rice culture while purchasing many slaves.

Carolina Gold
The Insatiable Drive for Land

It is true that the possibility of acquiring land, in and outside Charleston, at little or no cost greatly appealed to all Huguenots whether they had left handsome seigneuries or modest farms in France or had never owned real estate. In this respect, beyond their status as persecuted refugees, the Huguenots were similar to all other migrants to early America. Land was their Carolina gold. To make their colony as attractive as possible the proprietors capitalized on this thirst for land by providing a wide variety of offers to fit the needs and means of all refugees, from the modest servant to the wealthy noble. Following various proprietary reforms, Carolina land could be acquired in four ways: head-right grants, outright land sales, manorial grants, and proprietary gifts. In the early decades of the settlement of Carolina, the proprietors faced a dilemma nearly impossible to resolve. They had to be generous enough to draw as many settlers as possible in a particularly competitive post-Restoration colonial America and also use land gifts as a way to reward aristocrats who had agreed to settle the colony and in order to build a local political network. However, giving too much land away would inevitably lead to an excessive dispersion of the settlers, which, in the eyes of the proprietors, was to be avoided since it would make the colony harder to control and hamper its orderly economic development. In an effort to conciliate their own aspirations and those of the colonists, over the years the proprietors, while still being comparatively liberal, reduced the amount of land obtainable through the head-right system, encouraged settlers to occupy the land as compactly as possible, organized the colony into counties with the hope of having a town founded in each, and attempted to control the distribution, size, and location of land gifts more efficiently. Despite these efforts, however, the settlement of Carolina followed its own dynamics quasi-independently from the proprietors' wishes.

Although the colonists, and for that matter the proprietors too, frequently flouted them, the precise, though often amended, instructions for the taking up of land established a standard warrant-plat-grant procedure that remained in place throughout the propri-etary period. In theory, once in Carolina the settler was to petition the governor and the council for a legal patent. He received a warrant containing instructions for the surveyor to prepare a map or plat indicating the location and boundaries of the property. The set-tler then had ninety days to take the "return of survey" to the secretary of the province to acquire a sealed grant, which became official once it was signed by the governor and the council and recorded by the register of the province.[2]

According to the terminology of the time, the Carolina proprietors, as was the rule in early America except in New England, held and granted their land "in free and common socage," or fee simple. This type of tenure implied the payment of an annual rent or quitrent by the grantee, which, as the historian Alan Watson explains, represented "a monetary commutation of feudal obligations" that the tenant owed to the lord of the manor.[3] In a desire to capitalize on their immense land resources and in need of recover-ing their initial investments, the proprietors justifiably expected to raise revenues through the collection of quitrents and, after 1682, the sale of estates. Stripped of its archaic feudal flavor, the quitrent was simply a property tax. It was levied only on land acquired through the head-right system until the mid-1690s, when the proprietors also decided to tax land that had been purchased. At a rate of one penny per acre in the case of a head-right grant and one shilling per one hundred acres for a purchase, this requirement was far from being unreasonable, especially for French settlers used to pay-ing multiple taxes and tolls. As Thibou explained to his correspondent, except for the "one *sou* [penny] per year [owed] to the owner of the land," prospective Carolina Huguenots would not "have to pay any taxes here or money for the high roads nor chim-ney taxes, for nothing of that sort is charged in this country."[4]

Despite elaborate plans, detailed instructions, and rigid regulations, the granting of Carolina land did not run as smoothly as the proprietors had hoped. Many settlers never completed the warrant-plat-grant process because they either left the colony, died, or chose to hold land only on the basis of a warrant or a survey to avoid paying the quitrent. Additionally, groups of settlers vied with each other and the proprietors to control the distribution of land as a means to reward friends and allies. Political infight-ing over the control of the parliament and the governorship, especially in the 1680s, fur-ther disrupted the granting process. The grantee's right to choose where he wanted to settle also per se limited proprietary influence over the geographic distribution of the colonists. In fact, as Linda Pett-Conklin remarks in her cadastral survey of colonial South Carolina, foremost among the factors that determined the evolution of the land occupation pattern was "the ability of settlers to choose the sites of their landholdings."[5] Also, quitrents remained a major source of complaint for the settlers and frustration for the proprietors until a compromise was eventually reached under Governor Archdale in 1695–96, as we have seen, at the expense of the Huguenot political representation in the assembly. Beyond these dysfunctions, however, the proprietors were successful in satisfy-ing the Carolinians' quasi-boundless appetite for land.

The vast majority of colonists obtained land through the head-right system, which rewarded them for choosing to brave the high seas to settle in Carolina with their fami-lies, servants, and, if they came from the Caribbean, slaves. The number of acres allotted varied over time and according to the civil status, sex, and age of the recipient. In an effort to entice the first settlers and because they ran greater risks than their followers did, before 1671 the proprietors "generously" offered each free colonist and each male servant 150 acres, and 100 acres for each woman servant and manservant under the age of sixteen. Each manservant at the end of his indenture also was eligible for 100 acres. Under the pretense that large land grants were not conducive to founding compact settlements, the proprietors reduced head rights in 1679 to 70 acres for free settlers and male servants and 50 for female servants and male servants under sixteen. In 1682 land grant criteria were slightly altered and allotments were further reduced to 50 acres for all free immigrants over sixteen, all male servants, and marriageable women servants. Each servant was eligible for 40 acres at the expiration of his or her service.[6]

Frustrated with the difficulty in levying quitrents and looking for ways to have more cash available, in the early 1680s the proprietors started to sell Carolina land at the rate of a shilling per acre or twenty-five pounds sterling for five hundred acres. This was quite a comparatively competitive price, even for North America, since in the seventeenth century land was sold at ten shillings an acre in Virginia and was fourteen times more expensive in New England.[7] Until 1695 settlers who acquired land under this system owed only nominal rent, generally an ear of Indian corn each, and only if requested. Then, as part of the legislation passed under Governor Archdale, the proprietors levied a rent of one shilling per acre but in compensation considerably lowered the price of land to twenty pounds sterling for one thousand acres.[8] The proprietors undoubtedly preferred to sell land in London to avoid delays in payment and have the money available in England, but the purchase could also be made in Charleston. Proprietary instructions, however, made clear that only a tenth of the revenues raised through land sales could remain in Carolina to cover various administrative expenses. Alan Watson estimated that land sales and quitrent returns may have amounted to five hundred pounds sterling a year, but even if the proprietors managed to bring in some long-needed cash by selling acres of Carolina "wilderness," all in all land sales remained marginal simply because few settlers had capital available before or on arriving in the colony.

Eager to implement a social model that would guarantee the emergence of an orderly society and empowered through the royal charter to found a Carolina hereditary nobility as long as "titles and honours be not the same as . . . [in the] Kingdom of England," the proprietors early on designed an elaborate idealized land division.[9] The lowcountry was to be divided into three counties of 480,000 acres each containing eight seigniories and eight baronies of 12,000 acres each and four precincts in turn subdivided into six colonies of 12,000 acres each. Each proprietor was to hold a seigniory; the provincial nobility, namely the landgraves and the caciques, held four and two baronies, respectively; while the rest of the settlers shared a precinct. The proprietors also provided for a sort of lower nobility made up of relatively influential settlers, called lords of the manor, who owned estates ranging from 3,000 to 12,000 acres.[10] Baronies and manors were usually proprietary land grants, with a reduced quitrent of one penny per acre, but settlers could purchase manors, which a few did.[11] While all landgraves, caciques, and manorial lords held indivisible estates, transmittable only through primogeniture, and enjoyed judicial privileges on their land, only the first two were members of the council with the proprietary deputies, while the lords of the manor sat in the assembly with the rest of the settlers. Although this intricate and idealized manorial system, reminiscent of early seignorial Maryland, was never implemented in full and did not stand the test of time, there was a period when Carolina had a true nobility with immense estates and extravagant quasi-feudal privileges. The proprietors also rewarded settlers who encouraged further immigration, introduced new crops to the lowcountry, or promised to establish a town with extensive land gifts. These estates ranged from a few hundred to thousands of acres (the Scots, for example, obtained an entire county), were often rent free, and could even be endowed with manorial privileges.[12] Proprietary land gifts included the payment of a small quitrent of ten shillings per 1,000 acres, as shown in the 3,000-acre grant to Jacques Boyd.[13]

Unsurprisingly, the proprietors used land as promotional bait, and the authors of French pamphlets published in the 1680s were quick to give their readers detailed information on how to acquire real estate in faraway Carolina. They all advertised a fifty-acre land grant for each head of family; an additional fifty acres for each son, male servant over sixteen, marriageable daughter, and female servant; and forty acres for children and servants under sixteen. Grantees could bequeath land to their heirs "in perpetuity" and, two years after obtaining their grants, owed the proprietors an annual rent of a shilling per acre, or "*un sol par Acre*." A servant who had completed his term was eligible for a fifty-acre grant with the same conditions. Huguenots who so desired and who had the necessary cash also could purchase a thousand acres for £50 with a nominal rent of "*un grain de poivre*" (peppercorn), due only if asked by the proprietors. To cater to the Huguenot nobility in exile, the promoters also mentioned the sale of estates of three thousand acres for £150 with the title of seigneur and judicial privileges, and grants of twenty-four thousand acres, which corresponded to two baronies according to the hierarchical land distribution detailed in the Fundamental Constitutions, for £1,200. These extensive grants carried with them the title of cacique, advertised in the pamphlets as the equivalent of count or baron in England; a seat in the colony's upper house; and judicial privileges.[14] The Huguenots thus left the British Isles with a good knowledge of what awaited them in terms of landholding, and records show that they acted as informed settlers.

Keeping in mind that means to acquire land were obviously not mutually exclusive, since settlers could claim their head-right dues or receive proprietary gifts and still buy more land, curiously a majority of Huguenots, unlike the British, acquired land through purchase. Out of 108 identified first-generation refugees for whom warrants are extant, 55 bought their land, 43 obtained it through the head-right system, and 10 received it as a gift.[15]

If the fact that most refugees purchased their land can be explained by their fear of escheat for nonpayment of the quitrent, this implicitly denotes that they either left France with money or acquired enough of it soon after they settled in the lowcountry. Purchasing land was also a means to acquire more of it since the number of acres was not limited by proprietary regulations. As Samuel Wilson pragmatically explained in his *Account of the Province of Carolina,* purchasing land was a perfect option for settlers who wished "to secure to themselves good large convenient tracts" but "desired not to be cumber'd with paying a Rent" and "without being forced to bring thither a great number of servants at one time."[16] About a third of the Huguenots who bought land did so in

London directly from the proprietors. A handful of them were écuyers, such as Jacques Martel Goulart de Vervant; the Chastaigner brothers, Henry Auguste and Alexandre Thésée; and Jacques LeBas, all of whom likely left large estates behind in France. The amount of land they acquired, the conditions of payment, and the offers they received from the proprietors varied tremendously. Once again, Goulart de Vervant stands out as the wealthiest and most ambitious of all Huguenot refugees of the period. In December 1686, with bills of exchange, he paid the proprietors the amazing sum of £600 for twelve thousand acres or a barony and three thousand more at the advantageous price of £75 for a total of fifteen thousand acres.[17] The Chastaigners bought a thousand acres for £50 in September 1686 and were given two thousand extra acres by the proprietors in order to form a manor for which they had to remit annually an £8 quitrent.[18] Jacques LeBas bought a three-thousand-acre manor for £150 in September 1685 but could pay only £90 and promised to give the proprietors the remainder of the sum before Christmas "here in London," as they duly noted in their records. Apparently LeBas was never able to come up with the remaining £60, and in December 1689, four years later, he successfully requested from the proprietors to merge the fifteen hundred acres he had bought from the landgrave Joseph West for £120 with what he had purchased in London to form a manor. LeBas's intention was most likely to use the land he had bought in Carolina to create a manor with a nominal rent, which would spare him the cost of an annual quitrent of £6.[19]

The other "London purchasers" acquired smaller amounts ranging from 100 to 950 acres. Most of them were merchants, such as Jacques Boyd, Jacques Dugué, Isaac Fleury, and Jacques Nicolas; but there was also an artisan, Nicolas de Longuemare, and a pastor, Élie Prioleau, among them. Prioleau was a special case since he was already in Charleston when he had another refugee, Daniel Du Thais, buy the land for him in London.[20] Except for Prioleau, all of them purchased their land between April 1685, six months before the Revocation, and July 1687. These refugees undoubtedly planned their settlement in Carolina while in London, or perhaps back in France, and were well informed about proprietary land policies either by having read promotional pamphlets or by having visited the Carolina Coffee House. Notwithstanding that the amount of land between the smallest and the largest of these purchases varied tenfold, exclusive of Vervant's atypical purchase, they bought an average of 570 acres and all purchased at least 100 acres—twice the acreage allowed per free immigrant through the head-right system.

These refugees constitute a small minority as the overwhelming majority of Huguenots obtained land, whether by purchase or head right, once in the colony. A close reading of the land records (warrants and grants), however, reveals an unexpected trend. Most Huguenots did not rush to claim their head-right dues soon after arriving in the colony but waited a few years and bought much larger amounts of land. One can understand why they needed to wait in order to raise enough capital to purchase as much land as possible and why they would prefer owning land without rent to avoid a possible escheat, but why not claim land through head right and buy more later? Perhaps the answer lies in the fact that after 1682, when most Huguenots settled in Carolina, the proprietors moved the date for a first quitrent payment from 1689 to two years after a grant was sealed; since many Huguenots were single on arriving in the lowcountry, perhaps many did not think it was possible to clear their land and establish a farm quickly enough, under those circumstances, to afford to pay their rent. There were, of course, ways to evade proprietary regulations by settling permanently on a warrant or a plat without bothering to go through the entire procedure or by taking advantage of local political confusion to simply refuse to pay any rent. However, the Huguenots, as aliens, were in a potentially precarious situation, at least until the 1697 Naturalization Law was passed by the assembly. Instead of tempting fate by squatting on land they held only on the basis of a warrant or by challenging distant proprietors, whenever possible, they preferred to own land rent free, and their caution is understandable.[21]

Seen chronologically, land acquisition patterns show that before 1695 all Huguenots acquired land through the head-right system, between 1696 and 1700 the proportions of those using that system and those buying land evened out, and after 1700, more refugees purchased their land. In the early years of the migration, the absence of financial resources forced the Huguenots to take up their head-right dues even if they ran the risk of failing to pay the quitrent, but with time those who had raised the necessary capital opted to buy instead. At the turn of the eighteenth century most recent arrivals came from other colonies in the Caribbean and North America and had enough money to acquire land through purchase. Huguenots who used the head-right system obtained an average of 190 acres each, less than half the average amount (420 acres) of those who bought land. This statistic corroborates the fact that refugees who could afford land preferred to buy it in order to acquire larger tracts. Only three Huguenots, Jacob Guérard, Thomas Bellamy, and René Rézeau, took up head-right warrants of over 400 acres each. However, all three came to the lowcountry with their spouses, and in addition Guérard had six servants, Bellamy had eight slaves, and Rézeau had five children over sixteen and a marriageable female servant.[22] In one case a Huguenot, Abraham Fleury de La Plaine, who had already obtained 350 acres for himself and four servants, claimed another 140 acres based on the head rights of Henry Blanchart and James Phillips, who had come to the colony in 1680 and were therefore by law entitled to 70 acres each. Nothing else is known about James Phillips, but it is unclear why Henry Blanchart, whose continuous presence in Carolina until July 1684 is documented and who had by 1690 bought and sold land, chose to transfer his rights to La Plaine unless he was in need of cash and was not yet ready or interested in establishing a farm.[23] Clearly though, and notwithstanding this type of arrangement, if they wanted to acquire several hundred acres, refugees had to wait to have enough funds to do so since most of them arrived in the colony either unmarried or with a spouse and young children, making them eligible for only a hundred acres through the head-right system.

Land records, however, also show that even Huguenots who took up head-right warrants waited several years to do so, especially after 1685. Statistically, the *Richmond* passengers, who landed in Charleston in 1680, waited an average of two and one-half years before getting any land, and those of the *Margaret,* who arrived in 1685, waited an average of ten years. Daniel Huger and Isaac Caillabœuf, for example, arrived on the *Margaret* but petitioned for a first warrant only in 1694.[24] Even if some of them bought land from other settlers in the meantime, one wonders why each did not take up a warrant of fifty acres soon after arrival. Historians can only speculate as to what the reasons for this time lag may have been beyond individual situations, but this strongly suggests that Huguenots applied for their head-right dues only when they felt they were ready.

The possibility of acquiring manorial estates either as proprietary gifts or through purchase greatly appealed to the Huguenots, who held half of the manors created in the colony.[25] This is a proportionately high number since the Huguenots never represented more than 15 percent of the lowcountry population. These refugees, to whom must be added the Swiss Jean-François Gignilliat and the Walloon Jean d'Arsent, Sieur de Wernhaut, turned out to be the happy beneficiaries of the proprietors' generosity. All but two, Goulart de Vervant and Jacques LeBas, did not have to pay a farthing for their manorial estates. Manors were granted to Huguenots who had brought settlers to the colony, who contributed to the development of the colony's economy, or, in the case of Gignilliat and D'Arsent, whose prosperity in the colony was thought by the proprietors to "Incourage more of [their] nation[s] to become settlers in [the] Province."[26] Jacob Guérard received four thousand acres in December 1679 for his role in promoting the passage of the *Richmond*.[27] Arnaud and Paul Bruneau and Josias Marvilleau were granted three thousand acres each in January 1686 in return for their plans to invest in the construction of a sawmill and to import five servants and two Dutch carpenters.[28] Jacques Boyd received a three-thousand-acre manor with a "quit rent of ten shillings per thousand acres yearly" in December 1694 "for having been very Instrumentall in ye Settl[e]ment of ye French Protestants in Carolina, [having] transacted their Affairs here and been at great Charges in endeavouring ye establishment of a Vintage."[29]

In the pamphlet *Plan pour former un établissement en Caroline,* published in The Hague in 1686, the proprietors even tried to entice twelve Huguenot gentilshommes to jointly acquire twenty-four thousand acres, or the equivalent of two baronies, for twelve thousand pounds sterling by offering three thousand extra acres for free and by promising that one of the investors would become a lord.[30] In the wake of the publication of this pamphlet, a handwritten memoir entitled "Mémoires des Grâces que les S[eigneurs] Proprietaires accordent à un de mes amis" [Memoirs of the Privileges That the Lord Proprietors Granted to One of My Friends] mentions the effective creation of an association of eight Huguenots (including the supposed friend) who purchased the twenty-four thousand acres. The author also conveyed the proprietary promise that a new purchaser would be made a cacique as a sign of encouragement to the *"nation Française"* and so as to enable the Huguenots to be represented in the *"grand conseil."* This gentleman, however, would have to be a rich man with the necessary *"qualitez."*[31] Beyond the fact that the elaborate *Plan* was a house of cards and notwithstanding the proprietors' real intention to attract settlers of means to the lowcountry, their generosity had its limits. No Huguenot cacique ever sat in the council, and even Goulart de Vervant, whom St. Julien Childs conjectured to be the only Huguenot to buy a share of the twenty-four-thousand-acre estate advertised in *Plan* and who eventually acquired fifteen thousand acres, was never made a cacique. The proprietors contained Huguenot seignorial aspirations to the status of lords of the manor. They did not mean to deceive Huguenot gentilshommes as they were probably personally not opposed to having foreign caciques as long as they poured money into the Carolina venture. This restriction was most likely part of a political strategy to avoid further conflict with the British settlers. This was a wise decision considering the tumult that the French presence caused at times in the early history of the colony. One can imagine the adverse reactions of some of the prominent settlers if the proprietors had ennobled aliens.

Town and Country
Huguenot Settlement Patterns in the Carolina Lowcountry

The Carolina proprietors, like their French and Spanish counterparts, were adamant about having settlers establish towns instead of fanning out in unorganized fashion throughout the colony. In this respect, they did not hide their admiration for New England land policies, which they held up as a model. They saw the Virginia way, so to speak, as a flawed pattern not to be followed. When in 1697 John Locke, then sitting on the Board of Trade as an outside expert, was asked to write a sort of audit on Virginia, under the rubric "The country ill peopled," he clearly deplored that "No Care was taken in the beginning to seat that Country in Townships as in New England . . . by which means they are deprived of the great Company of Citizens and Tradesmen that are in other Countrys."[32]

In the early years of the colonization the proprietors attempted to force settlers to follow their guidelines and accordingly issued instructions regarding the foundation of towns. In April 1671 Ashley Cooper reminded Governor William Sayle that "there is none [instructions] of more consequence than the security and thriving of our settlement than that of planting in townes," and he told his successor Sir John Yeamans that "the Planting of People in Townes . . . [is] the Chief thing that hath given New England soe much the advantage over Virginia and advanced that Plantation in so short a time to the height it is now."[33] In the 1670s and 1680s the proprietors, whose objective was to have "one Town in each Collony," granted vast expanses of land, sometimes specifically to religious and ethnic groups, on the condition that towns be founded on the sites.[34] In 1671 a James Town was to be established by settlers from New York, and in 1676 the proprietors promised a group of Quakers twelve thousand acres with the instruction to build a town of thirty houses within five years.[35] Neither of these plans materialized, but with the foundation of Stuart Town by the Scots in 1684 the proprietary urban policy met with some success. Unfortunately for the Scottish settlers and the proprietors, two successive Spanish raids devastated the town two years later.

As with other specific groups of immigrants, the proprietors wanted the Huguenots to found towns in the lowcountry. Probably as a condition for successful negotiations, in their 1679 petition Jacob Guérard and René Petit promised Their Lordships that "the said foreign Protestants will settle together . . . in the place that will be assigned for them."[36] Notwithstanding the promoters' eagerness to please the proprietors, the *Richmond* passengers chose instead to remain in Charleston or dispersed randomly in Berkeley County. In the mid-1680s, however, the proprietors renewed their efforts to have the Huguenots found compact settlements. In April 1686 they shared with Governor Joseph Morton their desire that "such French who come to Carolina & have not Bought land of us And are only to have what we allow for persons imported Be settled together in Villages."[37] The following summer *Plan pour former un établissement en Caroline* was published in the Netherlands. Beyond the ambitious sale of twenty-four thousand acres, this pamphlet was actually nothing but a proprietary attempt to have wealthy French Protestants invest in the foundation of a town, or as the author puts it, "une espèce de petit hameau" (a sort of small hamlet).[38] The previously mentioned memoir echoed *Plan* by explaining to interested Huguenots that three thousand acres located in the middle of the twenty-four-thousand-acre grant would be reserved for the construction of houses "next to one another in the manner of a town or village." In reference to French administrative divisions, the author called the projected town "la ville de bailliage ou de sénéchaussée," with a court and a church, which would be the "principale église du Sinode des François." Additionally, the proprietors promised the inhabitants of the town that they would enjoy specific representation in the parliament.[39] Nothing came out of this project, but a Huguenot town was indeed founded in Santee, perhaps even twice, and survived for a while before vanishing altogether in the Carolina "wilderness."

In October 1687 Joachim Gaillard received a land warrant in "the Jamestown precinct," and twelve years later Isaac Dejean acquired "200 Acres of Land, being part of that Land formerly Laid out for a Town at Santee."[40] These mentions indicate that a town was at least planned if not actually founded in Craven County in the early or mid-1680s. By 1699, however, it was already regarded as something of the past. Like a phoenix, though, Jamestown on Santee rose again when in September 1705 René Ravenel, Barthélemy Gaillard, and Henry Bruneau bought from the proprietors 360 acres for £7.40 Carolina money (£5 sterling) to establish a town for themselves and "the rest of the inhabitants of Santee."[41] These three plus Jean Guibal and Pierre Robert Jr., the son of the Swiss minister, were then appointed town commissioners. Most fortunately, the extant French bill of sale for one lot, that of Nicolas LeNud, and a map with the numbered lots, also in French, which was made when the abandoned site was sold to Jean Gaillard in 1716, shed precious light on this failed urban experiment.[42] The town site was bordered by the Santee River and clockwise by the lands of Jacques Boyd, Jean Gaillard, and Philippe Gendron. The map shows a thin margin along the river with the locations of the church, the cemetery, and the common. Below appear four rows of lots of unequal size. There is a first row of eighteen one-acre lots facing the river, another of six three-acre lots, and two of six (twelve total) six-acre lots. For obvious reasons, sizes and prices decreased as lots were located farther away from the river. LeNud purchased a six-acre lot, number 29, on July 4, 1706, for £3 Carolina money. Considering that the thirty-six lots represented less than half the site and that lots closer to the river than LeNud's were sold for 40 shillings for the smallest and probably 50 shillings (or £2.5) for the largest, the commissioners intended to sell the entire town site for a minimum of £70 Carolina money, or nearly ten times the price they originally paid for it. Clearly, they were not acting solely for the good of the community. Lots were held forever rent free, but buyers had to maintain the streets bordering them. Apparently the town was settled in earnest, at least on paper, since twenty-seven lots were sold to twenty Huguenots in 1706 and Jamestown was officially mentioned in the 1706 Church Act.[43] Among these purchasers were familiar Santee names such as Philippe Gendron, Paul Bruneau, Charles Ducros de La Bastie, Jean Gaillard, Alexandre Thésée Chastaigner, Isaac Dubosc, André Rembert, and, of course, all the commissioners. Jamestown, however, did not survive long and may have been abandoned as early as 1709. In 1716 the entire site was sold to Jean Gaillard, brother of one of the commissioners, who by this purchase gained access to the river.[44] Among the reasons that may explain this failure are the location of the site, exposed to freshets from the Santee River and too far upriver to become a port for Craven County, and the population of the county, which then was probably too small to sustain the development of a town. In fact, Georgetown, which became Charleston's rival port town in northern South Carolina, was founded in the mid-1730s when the area became much more heavily populated and the need for a town was more acute.[45]

No Huguenot town would ever thrive in the Carolina lowcountry, but until the 1730s Charleston had a significant French flavor. Charleston was first founded in 1670 further up the Ashley River and moved to its present peninsular location, known as Oyster or White Point and to the French simply as *la Pointe,* in 1680 exactly when the arrival of the *Richmond* launched the Huguenot immigration to Carolina.[46] The governor and the council began to grant lots in earnest roughly following a grid pattern given by the proprietors and known as the "Grand Modell," and the town quickly developed within an eighty-acre space bordered by present-day Meeting (west), Beaufain (north), and Water (south) streets and the Cooper River (east).[47] The proprietors specifically instructed the council to grant a lot on the condition that a house be erected within two years and recommended that houses be "30 foot long and 16 foot broad & two stories high." In March 1681 they celebrated the fact that "there was already upwards of 20 houses built at Charles Towne on ye Oyster poynt and yt 10 more were building." A year later a promotional pamphlet claimed that "about a hundred Houses" had been built on the site, and in 1690 the Swiss Jean-François Gignilliat estimated that "there were about 300 houses" in Charleston.[48] From the time of its foundation, space was at a premium in Charleston primarily because settlers wanted to have access to the waterfront and be within the projected walls.[49] Consequently, and also because half-acre lots gave grantees enough space to build their own houses and subdivide the rest in half or quarter lots with the intent of selling or renting them, houses were erected rather compactly and in rows.[50]

L'Escot noted on his arrival in Charleston in 1700 that houses were almost exclusively built of cedar wood and boasted that his floor and fireplace were made of Carolina cedar, which he claimed was woodworm free and had a pleasant smell.[51] Fourteen years later, however, the L'Escot family, who had saved "300 pièces du pays" (£300 Carolina money, or £200 sterling) thanks to Mrs. L'Escot's home management skills, left their first house, presumably provided for by the community and made of wood, to purchase a lot or part of a lot where they had "a quite pretty and convenient brick house" built.[52] Although a growing number of brick edifices were erected in Charleston, especially after 1700, the local availability of wood and, as Gene Waddell points out, the strong presence of carpenters over bricklayers (a ratio of eight to one by 1700) reinforced the tendency to prefer wood to brick as the primary construction material.[53] As this building frenzy suggests, the Charleston population grew at a steady rate throughout the proprietary period, increasing from eight hundred people in 1690 to nearly three thousand in 1720, and soon became the fourth-largest city in British North America after Philadelphia, New York, and Boston.[54]

The Grand Council created 337 lots that were, for the most part, granted between 1680 and 1698.[55] The granting moved at an uneven pace since for unknown reasons 54 lots were granted between 1679 and 1685, only 22 between 1686 and 1693, and no fewer than 195 in the 1694–95 span. Although political instability caused by continual bickering and the successive changes of governors and administrations likely disrupted the overall granting process, it remains puzzling as to why lots were granted in such an erratic manner. Twenty-two Huguenots acquired a total of 56 Charleston lots, which represents an average of 2.5, with individual grants ranging from 1 to 9 lots, and all but 1 were granted between October 1692 and February 1695.[56] Since the grantees arrived in Carolina during different periods, one wonders why these "Huguenot grants" were made only between these two dates. Perhaps they had to wait for a favorable political and administrative context, or, since many acquired more than 1, these refugees may have actually purchased their town lots and consequently had to wait to raise enough capital. This speculation leads to other unanswered questions regarding the granting process. Did settlers choose whether to take up land outside Charleston or town lots? If not, who decided, through what process, and according to what criteria? Since records do not contain any clues, it can only be surmised that a settler could probably choose to have a town lot instead of, or in exchange for, his fifty acres and had to make it known to the governor and the council. Availability, luck, timing, and political influence probably contributed to the successful completion of the granting process.[57]

One-third (six of eighteen) of the Huguenots who were granted town lots before 1696 did not acquire land in the country and opted to have only half an acre each *en ville*. Remarkably, they waited an average of five years before receiving their grants. During this time they most likely lived with relatives in or outside Charleston or rented houses in town, as advised in a promotional pamphlet, or any who brought with him a tent could camp anywhere for free, as was recommended by another.[58] Settlers could also lease lots from grantees. Gabriel Ribouteau leased "one parcel of land in Charleston" from Richard Tradd in February 1694 and committed himself to building "one new tenement or dwelling house . . . fifteen foot in breath, one story high containing nine foot in said story and in length thirty foot . . . & a chimney." Ribouteau also agreed to pay a rent of "two Capons" to be remitted "at the feast of the nativity of our Saviour Christ."[59]

Most Charleston Huguenots, however, took up land also in Santee or up the Cooper River, usually before but sometimes after acquiring town lots. Daniel Huger and Isaac Caillabœuf, who had "imported" into the colony respectively six and five people, "at [their] proper cost & charge," each took up 300 acres in 1694 and a year later bought a town lot, presumably after selling their land.[60] In some cases Huguenots waited over a decade before relocating in Charleston. Louis Thibou, who arrived in 1680 on the *Richmond,* bought a town lot in 1697 although he had received a warrant for 210 acres in 1683.[61] Two widows, Anne Vignau and Marie Fougeraut, bought town lots respectively in 1688 and 1691, presumably to avoid having to clear acres of land themselves and for reasons of safety.[62] Conversely, the gunsmith Antoine Boureau first received a town lot in 1694 and then successively acquired 220 acres in 1695 and 316 acres in 1698.[63]

As was the case with land outside Charleston, there was a considerable amount of buying and selling of town lots between Huguenots, and these lots inevitably became a source of speculation. Since, as expected, lots increased in value as Charleston grew bigger, they were often divided into halves, quarters, or even eighths before being sold.

Anybody with patience and a shrewd business sense could easily make a significant amount of money. In May 1698 the shipwright Humphrey Torquett sold to Pierre de St. Julien half a town lot for the hefty sum of £30 sterling whereas he had paid only £35 for the entire lot in February 1697 when he acquired it from Jacob Guérard. Whether or not potential profits were as attractive as this, trade in town lots among Huguenots remained brisk business in Charleston in the 1690s. Antoine Boureau sold Isaac Caillabeuf a quarter of lot 103 in June 1694 for £10 Carolina money and the other three-quarters to Louis Thibou in July 1695 for £30. In June and July 1697 Salomon Legaré bought both shares from Thibou and Caillabeuf for £30 and £13.10 respectively.[64]

In terms of location, the original Huguenot grantees acquired contiguous lots and whenever possible settled near one another, thereby implying that the granting process included some element of choice. By 1695, when most "Huguenot lots" had been granted, the majority of the refugees had congregated along Broad Street making it already a sort of Huguenot street. Antoine Boureau, Jacques Dugué, Jonas Bonhost, Pierre Couillandeau, Jacques Potel, and Paul Pépin all acquired one or two lots each on Broad west of present-day Meeting Street, while Pierre LeChevalier and Jacques de Bourdeaux had lots across the street from Boureau, Dugué, and Bonhost and Noé Seré lived behind Pépin. South of Broad Street on present-day King Street, Dugué and Bonhost also owned lots across the street from the first (pre-1695) Charleston French Church and its adjacent graveyard. A few Huguenots also owned entire blocks. De Bourdeaux and LeChevalier had lots along two rows between Broad and present-day Queen streets, and Daniel Huger acquired five contiguous lots east of Meeting and north of Broad. Although these refugees enjoyed the reassuring proximity of one another, these lots were not the best located since they were farther away from the Cooper River and were no longer near the church after its move to its present location on Church Street (lot 65), where Noé Royer Sr. and Pierre Buretel lived. In the same years the construction of the walls along Meeting Street placed the part of Broad Street where the Huguenots had settled outside the town limits, strictly speaking. Huguenots who did not live in this early "French Quarter" almost always settled in pairs acquiring adjacent lots. Gignilliat was Henry LeNoble's neighbor. Jacques Lardant lived next to James LaRoche. Suzanne Varin, Isaac Caillabœuf, Antoine Bonneau, and Marie Fougeraut were all in the same area.[65]

Throughout the proprietary period the Huguenots constituted between one-eighth and one-fifth of the Charleston population. The twenty-two original grantees and their families must have statistically represented about a hundred people within a total population estimated at eight hundred in 1690. A decade later the French community had grown to nearly two hundred within a city population of twelve hundred, and in 1722 a petition drawn against the possible incorporation of Charleston by the assembly claimed that the Huguenots represented "almost one fifth of the Inhabitants," or three hundred people within a white population numbering about fifteen hundred.[66] From the start, Charleston Huguenots were, as might be expected, nearly all merchants and artisans hailing from cities and market towns in France. Of the twenty-eight heads of family settled in Charleston before 1700 for whom the occupations and geographic origins are known, fifteen were artisans, ten were merchants, and fifteen came from cities of more than ten thousand people, such as La Rochelle, Dieppe, Grenoble, Orléans, Poitiers, and Tours, and smaller towns such as Saint-Lô, Normandy; La Tremblade and Saint-Jean d'Angély, Saintonge; and Loudun, Poitou.[67] Huguenot artisans worked in the building and maritime trades since carpenters, joiners, blacksmiths, coopers, and shipwrights were in great demand in Charleston at a time when housing was scarce and commerce was expanding. The goldsmiths Nicolas de Longuemare and Salomon Legaré had to reside in the town to cater to the wealthy. Although trade remained relatively embryonic until the 1720s, the Charleston Huguenot community always had a significant mercantile element, which was reinforced in the early 1700s with the arrival of a younger generation of refugees, such as Benjamin Godin, Benjamin de La Conseillère, Thomas Satur, and the Motte brothers, John-Abraham and Isaac. Inevitably, as the port grew so did the wealth and the religious and political influence, within and outside the Huguenot community, of these merchants.

Although some Huguenots, especially after 1700, had enough money to maintain plantations in Santee or Goose Creek and residences in Charleston, most of them, like their British counterparts, had to choose between living in town or in the country.[68] Warrants and grants taken up by the Huguenots blatantly show that the land of Carolina, as promotional pamphlets had promised them, turned out to be an El Dorado. The Huguenots collectively acquired warrants for 100,138 acres, or an average of 735 per individual, between 1680 and 1711 and grants worth 113,868 acres, or an average of 973 per person, from 1689 to 1718.[69] These averages are higher than those for the Carolina settlers at large. In her study of total land warrants and grants acquired from 1670 to 1722, Meaghan Duff calculated an average of 355 acres (warrants) and 539 acres (grants), or almost 400 fewer acres than for the Huguenots. This difference can be explained by the relative wealth of many Huguenots, the high number of manorial lords within the group, and perhaps proprietary generosity toward the French.[70] As in the case of all Carolina settlers, the Huguenots obtained a higher average of land through grants than through warrants and this in about the same proportion (roughly 200–240 acres), but they obtained a much higher total acreage through grants than the British settlers did.[71] The fact that they were aliens and the uncertainty of Carolina politics, which could threaten the rights they acquired with the 1697 naturalization law, probably led them to feel particularly vulnerable to escheat and therefore eager to secure legal grants instead of settling permanently on land held simply on the basis of warrants. As expected, these global statistics hide wide disparities. Daniel Huger, Pierre de St. Julien, Jacques Boyd, and Barthélemy Gaillard acquired several thousand acres each, while Nicholas LeNud, Daniel LeGendre, Abraham Dupont, and Daniel Sénécheau received grants totaling only one hundred or two hundred acres and Daniel Jaudon obtained only fifty acres, or the bare minimum available through the head-right system. Beyond these inevitable discrepancies, however, it remains undeniable that nearly all Huguenots, including the pastors, acquired enough land to establish prosperous farms provided that the grantees had the necessary patience, energy, and capital to clear and improve those properties.[72] The 1694 inventory of Arnaud Bruneau, one of the few that listed the amount and value of clear and uncleared land, offers a rare illustration of the importance of improving the land and how long the process took. Nine years after the Bruneaus received a manor from the proprietors, only seven hundred acres, or less than a fourth, had been cleared. In terms of monetary value, these seven hundred acres were estimated to be worth seventy-four pounds and the other twenty-three hundred acres were appraised at eighty pounds, which represents a threefold difference.[73]

The principle of indiscriminate location adopted from the start by the proprietors in their land-granting policies was one of the foremost factors that shaped the settling of the lowcountry. Settlers' preferences evolved through time based on the prevalent notions regarding the healthfulness of the environment and the economic activities they were pursuing or planned to pursue at the time when they acquired land. In the seventeenth century the colonists avoided swamps and marshes regarded as wasteland and reputed to be unhealthful and looked for pastureland for cattle and wooded areas with extensive timber resources for naval stores.[74] This perception completely changed in the early decades of the eighteenth century when rice developed as a profitable crop and swamps were perceived as highly desirable locations. Throughout the proprietary period and beyond, however, settlers preferred to have private access to navigable bodies of water, especially in the early years of the colonization when roads were nonexistent. As Gignilliat described to his brother in Switzerland in 1690, colonists "always prefer to settle near rivers, brooks, and creeks as much for the convenience of [having access] to water as for the good soil."[75] Proprietary regulations limited river frontage to one-fifth of the depth of a grant, but a settler could increase his access to a waterway by selecting a site along, say, a river bend or simply by buying more land.[76] Notwithstanding these preferences, which the Huguenots obviously shared with the other settlers, extant warrants that mention the county where the land was specifically allocated show that the refugees did not overwhelmingly settle in Craven but rather in equal numbers in both Craven and Berkeley counties.[77] This tendency corroborates the fact that, although obviously they were more comfortable in the company of fellow refugees, the Huguenots generally did not seek to settle in French enclaves away from the rest of the settlers.

Adjusting to the Colonial Economy
From Proprietary Pipe Dreams to Lowcountry Reality

Huguenot economic life in the Carolina lowcountry followed relatively simple lines. Those who acquired land outside of Charleston, after unsuccessfully attempting to grow wine grapes and make silk, wisely and pragmatically switched to cattle ranching and, for a few of them, deerskin trading. At the turn of the eighteenth century, Huguenots who had raised enough capital to invest in large numbers of African slaves and buy land near swamps and rivers went into rice culture.[78] The artisans and merchants who acquired town lots continued to practice their premigration occupations, sometimes with considerable success. Eventually nearly all, however, acquired slaves, whether African or Native Americans.

The Huguenot migration to proprietary South Carolina, from an economic perspective, was rooted in the mercantilist dreams and ambitions of a handful of English aristocrats and the nascent Board of Trade and Plantations. Although the Carolina proprietorship was acutely aware of the religious context that led thousands of Huguenots to leave France and used it to their advantage, helping many of them to relocate across the

Atlantic was no gesture of philanthropy. The proprietors unmistakably had a strong economic interest in having the French successfully settle in the lowcountry. Jacob Guérard and René Petit purposefully struck this proprietary chord in emphasizing, throughout the negotiations preceding the departure of the *Richmond,* that they planned to take with them to Carolina "protestant familys skilled in ye Manufactures of Silkes, Oyles, [and] Wines."[79] Although their claim to be sending Huguenots specifically knowledgeable in the making of silk, wine, and olive oil to the lowcountry was an exaggeration, or perhaps an illusory objective, Guérard and Petit kept their word and carried silk cocoons on board the *Richmond.* Unfortunately, as Thomas Ashe reported in 1682, "the [silkworm] Eggs which they [the Huguenots] brought with them hatch'd at Sea, before we could reach the Land, the Worms for want of Provision were untimely lost and destroyed."[80] It would take more to discourage the Huguenots and the proprietors, though. Scattered references in the early records show that at least until the mid-1690s the refugees consistently pursued the proprietary fantasy of an agricultural Carolina fashioned in the image of a Mediterranean province.

Although Thomas Amy claimed that James Colleton "brought an Olive Stick . . . cut off at both Ends to Carolina, which put into the Ground, grew and prospered exceedingly" and hoped that "if the Olive be well improved, there may be expected from thence perhaps as good Oyl as any the World yields," the production of olive oil remained a source of speculation—or if it occurred must have been minimal at best—and it never became a Carolina staple.[81] In 1690 Gignilliat wished that olive trees could be planted for they "assuredly grow well," and Nicolas de Longuemare mentioned in his account book the sale of "a bottle of olive oil" in January 1708, but it may not have been produced in the colony.[82] Proprietors and Huguenots alike originally placed great hopes in making wine from Carolina's wild grapevines, but that soon turned out impracticable because, as Thibou reported, they "produce too much wood and [bear] too heavy a growth of leaf which hinders the fruit from ripening" and also because, Gignilliat observed, its grapes were "small . . . and full of pits."[83] The Huguenots persevered, though, and were rewarded in their endeavors by the proprietors, as attested by the eight-hundred-acre and one-thousand-acre tracts François de Rousserye and Jacques Boyd respectively received for their efforts toward "ye establishment of a Vintage" in 1683 and 1694.[84] It is doubtful, however, that the Carolina French ever made enough wine to carry on any significant trade, which must have disappointed Thibou, who, as a vintner, thought "he could quickly do good business in this country because wine is so dear."[85]

Although silk production remained marginal at best in the economic development of the lowcountry, French and British settlers alike not only placed great hope in it but also did make silk and even exported some.[86] Three years after the arrival of the *Richmond,* Thibou wrote his correspondent to tell the wife of a friend that her brother had produced "thirty pounds of silk"; and Gignilliat observed in 1690 that he was not making any silk that year for he was waiting for the mulberry trees that he had recently planted on his plantation "to grow bigger."[87] Although the proprietors judged "very acceptable" the sample of silk that they received from Charleston in 1699 and a decade later the council claimed to have commercially exported some, the Carolina silk trade, which seemed to have been particularly active at the turn of the eighteenth century, was carried out essentially within the colony.[88] Within the Huguenot community Nicolas de Longue-mare, judging from his account book, must have occupied a central place as the most prominent French silk dealer. In 1708 he recorded ordering unworked and homespun silk, two handkerchiefs, and a nightcap from "Monsieur [Pierre] DuTartre," selling silk-worm eggs to "Master [Benjamin] Simons," buying three bushels at fifteen shillings each from "Madame Poulain" [?], and selling half an ounce "de soye" to Josias DuPré.[89] This situation is not as surprising as it may at first seem since as a Charleston goldsmith De Longuemare had the necessary clientele and capital to carry on such a trade and to serve as an intermediary between his fellow Huguenot weavers and Carolinians who could afford silk handkerchiefs. Apart from the fact that the lowcountry does not have a Mediterranean soil or climate, the manufacture of silk could not develop simply because, at least as far as the Huguenots were concerned, only Jean Aunant from Nîmes in Languedoc, Pierre Bacot from Tours, and possibly Pierre Dutartre from Beauce had any recognized expertise in silk making.[90] Most Huguenot textile artisans—Antoine Poitevin, Salomon Brémar, and Daniel Trézévant among them—were wool and hemp weavers from northern France.[91]

In attempting to make wine, silk, and perhaps even olive oil, the Huguenots fully par-ticipated in what may be called the experimental stage of South Carolina agricultural history, during which settlers attempted to grow a variety of crops in their desperate search for a source of lucrative exports.[92] As Gignilliat explained from his newly estab-lished plantation where he had planted vines and mulberry trees and where he was growing cotton, rice, indigo, wheat, corn, and various vegetables while raising cattle, pigs, and poultry, settlers "every year successfully try something that may make the coun-try rich."[93] Gignilliat's and De Longuemare's agricultural, artisanal, and commercial ver-satility, which echoes Daniel Axtell's, who apart from his plantation owned a sawmill, a tannery, and a tar kiln, was probably shared by the most enterprising settlers.[94] This being said, however, early Carolina economic prosperity rested on three principal eco-nomic activities: livestock raising, the Indian trade, and rice.

With great common sense the Huguenots, although eager to try out wine and silk making in the lowcountry, did not cross the Atlantic to pursue proprietary pipe dreams but to follow whatever economic activity would guarantee their material well-being and prosperity. In the 1680s and 1690s they mainly engaged in livestock raising, which required little expertise and only a minimal investment since cattle and pigs were rel-atively cheap in the lowcountry, while engaging in a marginal trade with local natives.[95] At the turn of the eighteenth century the wealthiest among them jumped on the rice bandwagon and achieved, for most of them, a prosperity unattainable in France. In the process the most successful Huguenots shed their status of modest farmers to don that of rich planters.

At the turn of the eighteenth century, the proprietors expressed their disappointment at having "graziers" instead of "planters" in Carolina.[96] Livestock raising had become the leading agricultural pursuit in the lowcountry by then and remained so until it was supplanted by rice planting in the early 1710s. Livestock raising in early proprietary Carolina resembled the cattle ranching practiced in the American West in the 1880s more than anything to which European farmers were accustomed. Cattle and pigs grazed freely on the savannas and in the forests where, due to the mild climate, they foraged for food throughout the year at virtually no cost to the settlers, "an Ox" consequently being "raised at almost as little expense in Carolina, as a hen is in England."[97] As opposed to what was done in Europe, animals did not need to be butchered annually, and Carolinians soon owned and tended literally dozens of heads of cattle and pigs with a minimal workforce.[98] Thibou explained to his probably intrigued London correspondent that "cattle only feed in the woods, on the plains or on the savannas, the bulls, the cows and the rest of the cattle feed themselves perfectly well at no cost whatever" and consequently since it costs "no more to feed a lot than a few . . . you feed them by the thousands in the woods." To anticipate a possible skeptical remark, he added that "one has only to keep the calves in the house to bring all the cows back every evening" while admitting that "the only trouble . . . is to milk them."[99] Although in the early years of the colonization cattle and pigs were raised to supply the local population with meat, soon an increasingly significant provisions trade with the Caribbean developed. With time, profits raised from that trade would enable settlers to acquire more and better-located land and purchase slaves.

Regardless of their original occupations, many Huguenots bought and sold cattle and pigs. In January 1687 the merchant Alard Belin bought a dozen cows and hogs for fifty-two pounds sterling, and in August 1698 the gunsmith Antoine Boureau sold "107 heads of neat cattle, fifty-five swines old and young and one horse colt about two years old" to an English settler for the comfortable sum of eighty-four pounds sterling.[100] Most Huguenot inventories probated between 1690 and 1720 list heads of cattle. Herds, however, did not reach the proportions advertised in the pamphlets, the largest of them, that of the appropriately named apothecary Joseph Marbœuf, consisting of forty-two heads.[101] When in 1690 Gignilliat owned only thirty-four cows, "besides thirty pigs," he nonetheless celebrated the fact that his herd had grown significantly since he last wrote his brother in Switzerland.[102]

Since cattle and hogs were grazing freely in the wild, to avoid disputes between owners and potential theft the council, as early as 1683, required settlers to have them, along with their horses, marked on the ears and branded on the buttocks.[103] The nuisance caused by roaming stray cattle was taken seriously by the assembly, which in the mid-1690s passed an act for the destroying of unmarked cattle and regularly licensed hunters to kill unmarked wandering cows.[104] Extant records show that of the 189 marks registered between 1695 and 1717, 28, or about 1 in 6, were by Huguenots of various occupations (including pastors) from Santee, Orange Quarter, and even Charleston, thereby confirming their collective involvement in the cattle industry.[105] Most of the marks were simply the owners' initials, such as "P.R" for Pierre Robert or "D.H." for Daniel Huger, but some Huguenots also had fleurs-de-lis marked on their animals' ears or, like Isaac Mazyck, branded "upon ye Right Buttock."[106] Even when the marks were simply of their initials, some Huguenots designed them in an artistic manner. Antoine Boureau had the base of the A of his first name joined sideways to the base of the B; Peter Manigault had the P attached horizontally to the base of an upside-down M; and Isaac Mazyck had the I placed in between the branches of the M. Stock marks were thus not simply identifiable initials but real signatures.

Like the French in Louisiana and New France or the Dutch in New Netherland, the Carolinians quickly established commercial relations with the natives, at first with small neighboring groups such as the Sewees, Santees, and Westoes, and later with larger tribes of the interior such as the Creeks, Cherokees, and Choctaws. Settlers exchanged blankets, belts, hats, mirrors, tools, alcohol, weapons, and ammunition for furs, oils, horses, and most important, deerskins and slaves.[107] As can be expected, the control of this lucrative Indian trade, as it was generically known, was soon a source of conflict between the proprietors and prominent settlers, including their own officials. The proprietors actively encouraged this commerce but attempted to impose a proprietary monopoly while being opposed to the traffic in slaves. Later, with the waning of proprietary influence on Carolina affairs, the organization and regulation of this increasingly essential trade remained a bone of contention between the Carolina authorities and individual traders until the successful establishment in 1707 of the legislative-inspired Board of Indian Commissioners, whose role was to expand the trade geographically and quantitatively while regulating competition and preventing cruelty on the part of some traders.[108] Despite these internal struggles, the Indian trade flourished and deerskins remained the colony's leading export until the trade suffered a major setback in 1715 with the Yamassee War and when rice emerged as the Carolina staple.[109] If in the early years of the settlement almost any settler could be involved in the Indian trade by bartering with local natives, as it developed into a major economic activity the trade gradually became more specialized. It thereby fell under the control of Charleston merchants who had access to manufactured goods and of a few individuals, referred to as master traders, who were familiar with the Indian country and had the means to purchase large quantities of the necessary goods and to finance long and far-reaching expeditions.[110]

Huguenot involvement in the Indian trade followed these trends. At first, individual settlers traded locally and on a small scale with the natives regardless of proprietary wishes and regulations. In his 1683 letter Thibou evoked the natives "who bring [the English] a great quantity of deer skins and furs" and, hoping to carry on trade with them, wanted fellow refugees to come from England and bring him "some brandy, white and blue linen and bits of cloth for the Indians."[111] In Santee, where they were settled away from Charleston and among several native groups, the Huguenots traded with them. The English naturalist John Lawson observed, during his 1700 visit, that "Many of the French follow a trade with the Indians, living very conveniently for that interest."[112] However, as the trade grew in volume and value and spread to the Appalachians and even beyond, Huguenot involvement, except for a handful of enterprising planters from Santee, became largely limited to a few Charleston artisans who occasionally worked for the commission and to prominent merchants who supplied large-scale traders through the board, of which several refugees were also members.[113] The visit of a Cherokee delegation with porters in Charleston in 1716 was an opportunity for Huguenot merchants to strike deals. Isaac Mazyck sold the commissioners £120 worth of goods destined for the "Cherikee Indians," with "1 Gun given to a Charikee King (by the Hands of the Governour) for ten Skins and Slaves, and [received] a Gratuity for his Trouble in coming down with the Burdeners [porters]." The commission also bought "31½ Yards of blue Duffields" for about £23 from Elias Foissin to be used for "the Payment of the Charikee burdeners" and £9.7 worth of kettles from Elisha Prioleau, son of the late Charleston pastor, also to be sent to "the Charikees."[114]

In the aftermath of the Yamassee War, three Huguenot planters had extensive dealings with the commission: Barthélemy Gaillard, who opened a factory at Santee; and Pierre de St. Julien Jr. and René-Louis Ravenel, whose plantations were used as way stations for the Catawba trade. In July 1716 Gaillard, who was by then captain of the local militia, "informed the board, that some of the Wineau [Winyah] Indians were seated at Santee, and have been found beneficial to that Part of the Province, for their Safety, by keeping the Negroes there in Awe" and "proposed the Settling [of] a small Factory there, to engage those Indians . . . and further offered to manage that Trade, gratis."[115] The commission was interested in Gaillard's proposal because the "Northward Trade" along the coast was served only by a factory at Winyah Bay and it seemed convenient to open another along the way.[116] In October the board sent Gaillard "sundry Goods amounting to £35:07:9" to be sold "to the aforesaid Wineau Indians only, for the sole Use of the Publick" and detailed instructions on how to deal with the Indians and operate the factory. Along with listing the official rates for "white drest Deer Skins . . . raw buck Skins . . . raw Doe and other light Skins . . . [and] Bever and other Furs," the commission warned Gaillard "not, on any Pretence whatsoever, to credit or trust any Indian" or "deal with any Indian or Indians whatsoever, on [his] own private Account, or the Account of any other Person" and instructed him "to give [them] speedy information" if he discovered "any Frauds committed or intended" against the board. Additionally, Gaillard was told "to be of friendly and peaceable Behaviour towards the Indians" and to endeavor "by all Means possible to prevent any Abuses being offered to them."[117] Between November 1716 and September 1717 Gaillard delivered 224 "raw Deer Skins" to the commission for a value of about fifty-six pounds sterling.[118] However, Gaillard soon suffered from unfair competition by settlers who "slighted the Act" and did not recognize his state monopoly of the local trade. He immediately informed the board that "he suspected some fraudulent and clandestine Dealings with the Wineau Indians at Santé." Gaillard even mentioned that "one Mr. Royer [Noé Royer Jr.], a Tanner at Santé," had bought skins from "a White man" but refused to release his identity. Gaillard was in a difficult situation since his competitors purchased the best merchandise—that is, dressed skins—at a better rate than the commission allowed him to offer. Consequently, only once was he able to bring dressed skins back to Charleston, although unfortunately they were "wetted with salt Water and much damnified in the Voyage."[119] Gaillard nonetheless successfully requested that "a general Warrant of Seizure may be reposed in him" to seize skins illegally bought, although his request to the commission for "an Abatement on the Prices of the Goods" was refused.[120] Considering that it acted within the context of a state monopoly, the board was understandably adamant about setting the official rates of exchange in the Indian trade and preferred giving its agents the legal means to enforce this monopoly rather than adjust to the fluctuations of an illegal market. The Santee factory eventually closed after the death of Gaillard in early 1719 without having been a real commercial success.[121]

Pierre de St. Julien and René-Louis Ravenel, the second son of Daniel Ravenel, regularly provided food and accommodation to traders and burdeners involved in the

Catawba and Cherokee trades while occasionally allowing the commission to use their plantations as entrepôts.[122] This arrangement could be burdensome at times—for example, in November 1717 St. Julien had to accommodate "160 Indian Burdeners" at his plantation at Wantoot—but apart from the fact that the commission well compensated these two Huguenots for their expenses, it allowed them to profit from the trade on the side.[123] In August 1713 St. Julien was accused by traders of having retained "three Cherokee women" as slaves, which he probably held to sell at a later date; and in November 1717 the same St. Julien sold the board ten guns for over sixty-seven pounds Carolina money.[124] The commission eventually, in July 1718, rewarded St. Julien for his services by offering him a seat as a commissioner "to oversee and direct the Business of the Northern Factories." The Huguenot accepted but only on the condition of not having to attend meetings regularly on account of his living away from Charleston, to which the board consented. This appointment was, however, of short duration since St. Julien died the following year.[125]

Scattered references in the records show that some Huguenots were also involved in the growing of rice, the making of tar, and in the lumber industry. Before it became king and dominated the lowcountry economy in the eighteenth century, rice, which was first grown for home consumption, was one of the many crops early settlers experimented with in their search for a staple. It is only following the fortuitous introduction of a new variety, possibly from Madagascar, in the mid-1690s and the improvement of growing techniques in the first half of the eighteenth century, which led settlers from upland to inland swamp and eventually to tidal culture, that rice became the leading export, even surpassing deerskins.[126] In his 1690 letter Gignilliat wrote that he had "sawn an acre of rice" for his own consumption and mentioned the difficulty of husking the grain, having to do it manually with a pestle since there was then no milling machinery in the lowcountry.[127] Although Gignilliat mentioned that rice "grows perfectly," he devoted only a few lines of his letter to it, expounding instead on his corn, wheat, and cattle.[128] In the settlers' early quest for more efficient milling techniques Peter-Jacob Guérard, son of the *Richmond* promoter Jacob Guérard, stands out for receiving a two-year patent for "a Pendulum Engine, which doth much better, and in less time and labour, huske rice, than any other [that] theretofore hath been used within the Province." Although the assembly noted that Guérard's invention had been "brought to perfection," it seems unlikely that this machine, whose exact design and operation are still objects of speculation among agricultural historians, was ever successfully commercialized.[129] Following a wider lowcountry economic trend, as rice culture expanded in the 1710s and 1720s some Carolina Huguenots became more dependent on it. In a 1716 letter to his son, the merchant-turned-planter Isaac Mazyck complained about the heavy summer rain that would jeopardize his rice and wheat crops, and Jacques LeGrand's 1725 inventory lists 817 bushels of rice and four hand-operated rice mills.[130]

The immense economic potential of the Carolina pine forests, real and imagined, did not escape the settlers who quickly looked for ways to capitalize on it. As early as February 1686 the gentilshommes Arnaud Bruneau de La Chabocière; his son Paul Bruneau, Sieur de Rivedoux; and the aptly named Josias Marvilleau de La Forêt Montpensier met in London and "entered into partnership for ye Construction of a Mill to Saw Timber whether it bee a Wind Mill or Water Mill" and then left for the low-country with "five men Servts & . . . two Dutch Carpenters" whom they agreed "to maintain & feed in comon."[131] These plans were slightly altered, perhaps due to renegotiations, since in his 1709 will Paul Bruneau mentioned the partners' intention to build a sawmill and a forge and their coming to Carolina with a blacksmith and a carpenter.[132] Although the two artisans and Josias Marvilleau died soon after arriving in the lowcountry, the Bruneaus managed to carry out part of the agreement. Arnaud's 1695 inventory mentioned the forge, but its wording implied that the sawmill was not yet built. However, the thirty-eight saws, the worn carpentry tools, and the "150 new iron bars" listed suggest that the Bruneaus were quite active in the lumber and iron business.[133] In the early eighteenth century the Carolina forest industry also included the production of naval stores. Although references in the records are scarce, Huguenots most likely were also involved in the production of pitch and tar. In 1719 Pierre Royer, son of Noé and Madeleine (Saulnier) Royer, purchased 247 acres that were paid for in part with slaves and four hundred barrels of tar, while André Deveaux was sentenced by the Court of Common Pleas for failing to deliver eight hundred barrels of tar to Samuel Eveleigh and Charles Hill.[134]

After a period of agricultural experimentation, which for them primarily included but was not limited to olive oil, wine, and silk, the Huguenots who acquired land outside Charleston followed the routes that led Carolina to material prosperity. By the end of the proprietary period, they were no longer the agents of the proprietary dreams of a colony thriving on the export of Mediterranean products but were successfully pursuing their own economic interests. In the meantime, Charleston Huguenot merchants, along with their British counterparts with whom they sometimes entered into partnership, set the foundations of the colony's various trades.

The Lowcountry Huguenot Merchants and the Atlantic Economy

In the early 1680s, when Charleston was but a small frontier outpost, the authors of French and English promotional pamphlets nonetheless extolled its commercial potential. Ever adept at the hyperbole, Wilson in his *Account of the Province of Carolina* claimed that in November 1680, "There rode at one time, sixteen sail of Vessels, some of which were upwards of two hundred tons, that came from diverse parts of the Kings Kingdom to trade."[135] Thibou echoed this optimism in assuring his London correspondent, "Those who want to come to Carolina could not fail to have opportunities because so many ships arrive from England, Barbados, New England, etc. . . . the country becoming a great traffic centre."[136] In addition, French promotional pamphlets informed Huguenots that trade was tax free for "anyone who come and settle in Carolina," thereby implying that alien merchants were not subjected to specific customs duty, unlike in Britain, and that no "Company in England" had any monopoly on "le Commerce de la Caroline."[137] In fact, in *Questions et Responses faites au sujet de la Caroline,* "Mr. Colleton," in what looked like an attempt to flout the Navigation Acts, is said to intend to travel to New Biscaye (Mexico) "to discreetly [*sans bruit*] establish a trade with the Spanish," so as to enable them to buy European goods through Carolina, which was deemed a great potential source of profits and apparently an easy thing to accomplish since "from Carolina to

Vera Cruz there are only 400 leagues."[138] Even without indulging in such commercial fantasies, promoters and settlers in unison emphasized the "considerable profits," as the author of *Nouvelle Relation de la Caroline* put it, made in the trade with Europe.[139] In 1703 Paul L'Escot explained that due to the high cost of European goods in Carolina, notably articles of clothing, merchants charged a 100 percent markup and that when items were particularly rare, profits rose to "3 or 400 percent." When, unable to contain his curiosity, L'Escot asked merchants why things cost so much, their answer was, "the risks of sea voyages, etc."[140]

Even if trade in early Carolina was a lucrative business, contrary to what pamphlets claimed and settlers believed, it grew slowly in volume and value until 1720, when rice and later indigo exports made Charleston a premier North American port.[141] As had been the case demographically and culturally, commercially South Carolina's early existence was heavily dependent on the Caribbean islands, especially Barbados, a status that Peter Wood captured particularly well when he coined the phrase "the colony of a colony."[142] Except for a small, although rapidly growing, volume of deerskins exported to England, Carolina's oceanic trade was geared toward supplying West Indian islands with provisions (especially meat), timber products, and native slaves in exchange for sugar, bills of exchange, European goods, and African slaves.[143] To a question concerning potential trade with neighboring colonies, the author of *Questions et Responses faites au sujet de la Caroline* did not mention Virginia but wrote that lowcountry settlers "traded with the Islands, principally with Barbados and Jamaica in beef and salt pork for sugar, indigo, cochineal, and beautiful piastres worth in Carolina as much as *écus de France*."[144] Although essential to the colony's early development, not to say survival, this trade was nonetheless small in scope since it occupied only about a dozen ships in the mid-1680s and was not destined to grow for structural reasons and also because it was partly carried on with pirates.[145] Carolina's future commercial prosperity lay in the establishment of a large-scale transatlantic trade with England and within the legal bounds set by the Navigation Acts. This trade fully developed only at the end of the proprietary period when rice exports soared from 10,000 to 6.5 million pounds between 1698 and 1720, pitch and tar exports peaked at nearly sixty thousand barrels in 1725, and deerskin exports continued to be substantial.[146] As trade expanded in volume, scale, and value, the profile of the Charleston merchants evolved as they became more specialized, wealthier, and more influential.

From the beginning of the Huguenot migration, merchants had represented a numerically significant occupational subgroup.[147] However, this community showed great internal disparities based on the individuals' geographic origins, their degrees of specialization, and most important, their capacity to transfer capital to the lowcountry and preserve at least part of their premigratory mercantile network in order to engage in trade immediately on their arrival in the colony. After 1705, or a quarter-century after the landing of the *Richmond* passengers, the Charleston Huguenot merchant community became more homogeneous and professional as a younger generation of refugees, with money and contacts, arrived in the colony. These were no longer displaced Huguenots trying to reestablish former trade connections or establish new ones in an unknown environment but experienced merchants or factors drawn to Carolina by its expanding trade.

Except for Pierre Buretel, who acquired only a town lot, the Huguenot merchants of the 1680s and 1690s were actually planter-merchants who kept livestock and grew a variety of crops on their plantations while carrying on a little trade from Charleston and, occasionally, with local natives. Thibou, who entertained dreams of wine trade on his plantation "sur la Rivière d'Ashly" and of profits from an illusory Indian trade and who purchased a town lot in 1695, probably to be in a better location for his commercial activities, stands as a perfect illustration of this group. Thibou was a vintner from central France who before the migration had specialized in the wine trade between the Sancerre region and Paris and therefore had no experience or contact in the Atlantic trade. When he arrived in Carolina, Thibou literally had to start from scratch, being "not worth a farthing" on his arrival, and using his business skills he attempted to profit from the commercial opportunities associated with the foundation of a colony.[148] Other planter-merchants, significantly many of whom came from western France, were not as desperate as Thibou and were able to be active in the Atlantic or colonial trade with contacts in London, New York, or the Caribbean. Cézar Mozé, who jointly owned a plantation with his fellow merchant Nicolas Mayrant, awaited a shipment of goods from London while on his deathbed in early summer 1687.[149] Pierre Perdriau, his cousin Louis, and Elie Boudinot had relatives and partners in New York City with whom they traded from Charleston until Boudinot settled there in the mid-1690s, likely because of the northern city's better commercial prospects.[150] Josias Dupré, barely three years after his arrival in the colony, was already consigning a motley shipment of fancy articles of clothing, shoes, rings, powder, horns, and bayonets, which he necessarily had imported from Europe, for a merchant in Antigua.[151]

Dupré's unusually sophisticated shipment and more generally the ease and rapidity with which a few Huguenot merchants were able to engage in long distance trade raise the issue of the successful transfer of capital from France to Carolina through England. Historians of the Huguenot migration and of proprietary Carolina have often assumed that many refugees immigrated with money, but I agree with Norris Nash, who wrote that this is somewhat speculative since it has never been documented and that the time lag between the arrival of most merchants and their first recorded shipments would indicate the need to raise capital in the colony through agriculture before engaging in any mercantile activity proper.[152] With the exceptions of Pierre Buretel, Josias Dupré, the Perdriaus, and perhaps a handful of others, most Huguenot merchants had to try their hands at various occupations before being able to engage in oceanic trade. Noteworthy examples are Jean Guérard, who first occupied himself as a weaver and a planter before eventually founding a trading house in Charleston with his Huguenot partners, and Pierre Manigault, who first, in 1687, acquired a few hundred acres in the country where he raised cattle and then, in 1701, after selling his estate at a comfortable profit, moved to Charleston where he worked as a cooper and where he later founded and operated distilleries until he successfully established himself as a wine merchant in the late 1710s.[153] Most of these early planter-merchants, such as Isaac Mazyck and Jacques Boyd, did not own ships, even after the 1697 Naturalization Act was passed by the assembly, but jointly invested in parts of a ship, hold, or cargo.[154]

In the first two decades of the eighteenth century a new wave of Huguenot merchants, such as Benjamin Godin, Benjamin de La Conseillère, John-Abraham and Isaac Motte, Jacob Satur, and Benjamin D'Harriette, arrived in the colony from the British Isles, the Caribbean, and New York. They differed from their predecessors in several significant ways. First, they were usually somewhat—or, at times, considerably as was the case with Benjamin de La Conseillère, who was born in 1684—younger.[155] Fleeing France with their parents, they did not experience the Revocation and flight as adults. They grew up in the British Isles and were consequently thoroughly Anglicized before coming to Carolina. They were drawn to the lowcountry by its nascent prosperity, and many of them, such as Thomas Satur, originally settled in Charleston as factors of English-based companies.[156] Second, although they usually joined the Huguenot Church and some of them, for example Godin and La Conseillère, were even elected elders, their migration had no religious dimension. Third, either having inherited a mercantile, and often Huguenot kin-based, network from their fathers or having built one after the migration, these relatively specialized merchants had numerous contacts in the Americas and western Europe, and they took full advantage of the booming Carolina Atlantic trades. D'Harriette, originally from La Rochelle, had familial business ties in New York, Saint Kitts, and Bordeaux and was related to the Belins, the Boudinots, and the Perdriaus.[157] Fourth, they were not merchant-planters but "aspiring-to-be-planter-" merchants since their ultimate goal, once settled in the lowcountry, was to establish thriving rice plantations.[158] A case in point is Benjamin Godin, of rich mercantile familial background from Rouen (the Godin-Beuzelin family), who carried on a highly profitable transatlantic trade using his cousins in London as contacts, was active in the Indian trade, owned ships, loaned money, and eventually retired on his plantation in Goose Creek—which was worked by over a hundred slaves—while still maintaining a residence in Charleston.[159] Although Huguenot merchants by and large also worked with English partners and married into English families, these younger merchants often entered into partnerships with sons or grandsons of earlier refugees from the same provinces in France. Soon after their arrival in Charleston, Benjamin Godin and Benjamin de La Conseillère, both from Normandy, in 1711 became partners with their fellow Norman refugee John Guérard, son of Jacob Guérard of *Richmond* fame, in John Guerard & Company, which exported deerskins and slaves (Native American and African) and imported dry goods from London. The Godin-Guérard partnership transcended economic interests and perpetuated regional affinities since following his first wife's death in 1744, John Guérard married Marianne Godin, daughter of Benjamin and Marianne (Mazyck) Godin, and they even named one of their sons Godin.[160]

Many of these Huguenot merchants, including the wealthiest and most successful of them, especially after the 1710s, engaged in the Indian and African slave trades. Considering that from an economic and cultural perspective, South Carolina history, perhaps more than any other British mainland colony, was intertwined with the issue of slavery from the time of its foundation, the fact that the Huguenots one way or another participated in this tragedy should come as no surprise. Once safely out of France and assured that they could continue to live as Calvinists, or simply as Protestants, they came to

Carolina to settle plantations, maintain shops, or found trading companies and, if possible, become prosperous. If this prosperity involved owning other human beings, so be it.

Refugees with Slaves, or the Huguenots and the Curse of Slavery

It can be stated unequivocally that nearly all Huguenots aspired to be slave owners, and most became such. In fact, some Huguenot migrants came to the lowcountry with their slaves. In March 1693 Benjamin Marion landed in Charleston with his family, his servants, and "rose a negro woman"; and in July 1695 Henry LeNoble arrived with "his wife Katharine & five negros," and Gabriel Manigault with "one negro man by name Sambo."[161] To put it simply and bluntly, slavery was not a religious or moral issue for the vast majority of Huguenots.[162] Even Élie Neau's exemplary work among New York City slaves, which stands out as unique among the Huguenot lay and pastoral community in North America, was the result of his deep soul searching caused by the immense loneliness he felt and the harsh treatment he endured in Louis XIV's galleys.[163] Similarly, Francis LeJau, who "designed with God's blessing to have a day in the week for the Instruction of poor Indians and Negroes," reached out to the natives and the black slaves from sincere personal compassion partly based on his previous experience in the Caribbean and his perception of his role as a Christian missionary in a slave society.[164] Neither Neau nor LeJau, however, came to challenge the institution of slavery, cautiously limiting themselves to deploring the brutality and callousness of some masters and recommending overall better treatment of slaves.[165] The two Frenchmen's Christianizing efforts were nonetheless praiseworthy, all the more so since they were carried out despite undeniable and widespread criticism and even hostility, but they were essentially individual initiatives.[166] In no way did they reflect the general Huguenot outlook, whether lay or pastoral, on slavery, especially since LeJau and Neau Christianized natives and black slaves respectively as a missionary and a catechist for the Church of England.

In proprietary South Carolina, Huguenot pastors owned slaves. Soon after his arrival in Charleston, L'Escot wrote his former Genevan professor that he planned to "buy a negro woman [*négresse*] as soon as he could afford it," since "one can only be helped in this land by this sort of people or rather animals," and that he had indeed purchased not one but two female slaves within two years.[167] Likewise, when he retired to St. John's Berkeley in 1703, Florent-Philippe Trouillart did not fail to buy slaves for his plantation.[168] In doing so, Huguenot pastors acted like their Anglican counterparts whose cures each included the so-called "parish slaves," usually a male slave and a female slave.[169] French Calvinism, institutionally, had never opposed slavery. Although the national synod that met in Alençon, Normandy, in 1637 sadly deplored that "the very inhumane custom of traffiquing in slaves and selling them in public markets has slowly crept among merchants," in reference to the growing number of Huguenot Rochelais merchants involved in the slave trade, they still formally declared that "Men have the right to buy and keep Slaves, [which] is not condemned by the word of God." The same synod, following an Augustinian approach, only recommended that slaves not be placed "in the hands of those that are cruel but sold to good-natured [*débonnaires*] Christians."[170] In other words, slavery was accepted, perhaps as a necessary economic evil, as long as masters treated their slaves "humanely." This official position echoed that of LeJau, who observed that lowcountry slaves "were well used . . . , better than in the Islands," and of L'Escot, who not only felt no compassion for them but also reckoned that "slaves would be fools to leave their masters" for " they are well fed, and their condition is a hundred times happier than peasants in France."[171] In their eyes, therefore, there was no need to challenge a socioeconomic system that appeared to be in keeping with the order of things. This Huguenot collective acceptance of slavery should not strike us as odd, even for people who could be held as galley slaves in their country, since it was shared by all major Protestant groups, including the Quakers.[172] Antislavery pamphlets, such as the 1688 Germantown petition, were rare before the mid-eighteenth century.[173]

As early as 1669 the Carolina proprietors, hoping to draw as many planters as possible from the Caribbean, especially Barbados, provided a legal framework for the development of slavery in the Fundamental Constitutions and offered extra acres to settlers who arrived with slaves in their head-right regulations.[174] Article 101 of the 1669 version of the Fundamental Constitutions clearly stipulated that "Every Freeman of Carolina shall have absolute Authority over his Negro Slaves, of what opinion or Religion soever."[175] Authors of French promotional pamphlets systematically mentioned the possibility of purchasing slaves, gave their prices—between twenty and twenty-five pounds sterling—and in some cases, based on the increasingly widespread view that Africans were well-suited to the semitropical climate of the lowcountry, explained that "Negroes by reason of the Mildness of the Winter thrive and stand much better, than in any of the more Northern Colonys, and require less Clothes, which is a great Charge saved."[176] Describing the difference between Indian slaves and African slaves to prospective settlers, the author of *Suite de la Description de la Carolline* explained that "Indians do not work for the Europeans, but hunt and fish for them."[177] In his much-publicized letter Thibou also wrote about these hunters, claiming that "an Indian will provide a family of 30 with enough game and venison, as much as they can eat, all year round."[178] Although Indians may occasionally have been hired for their hunting and fishing skills in the early years of the colonization, South Carolinians enslaved a comparatively large number of them, and while many were exported to the West Indies, the Chesapeake, and the northern colonies, most remained and worked on plantations along with African slaves.[179] In 1708, when the number of Indian slaves rose to fourteen hundred, they represented a quarter of the entire enslaved labor force.[180]

Following the distinction made by Ira Berlin between societies with slaves, in which slavery as one form of bound labor among several was "marginal to the central productive process," and slave societies, in which "slavery stood at the center of economic production," South Carolina was the former for a brief period and had become the latter before 1705.[181] At first settlers relied on indentured servants as the primary source of a bound workforce. Then, for a variety of reasons, such as the rise of wages in England, the high cost of the transatlantic voyage, the lack of regular trade between Charleston and London, and the bad reputation of the lowcountry climate, servants became harder to obtain while demand steadily grew as the local economy expanded.[182] Therefore, in the early years of the eighteenth century Carolina planters turned to slaves, Indian first and then black—first from the West Indies and then from Africa—thereby completing a process described by Russell Menard as "the Africanization of the Lowcountry labor force."[183] African slaves were deemed resistant to the epidemiological environment of the lowcountry; many of them were familiar with rice cultivation, which made them extraordinarily valuable in the eyes of planters; and, of course, they were bound in perpetuity.[184] The high initial cost of a black slave, a major impediment to the early development of slavery, was removed when African slaves became comparatively cheaper as English slavers gained an increasing share of the trade and when Carolina planters grew wealthier. Slave imports then literally exploded. While only 206 black slaves had been imported into South Carolina prior to 1710, annual imports averaged 275 in the 1710s, nearly 900 in the 1720s, and over 2,000 in the 1740s.[185] Consequently, while a Swiss settler reported in 1737 that Carolina looked "more like a Negro country than like a country settled by white people" and black slaves statistically exceeded white colonists only from 1708, as early as 1703 L'Escot wrote his correspondent that "our Negroes are in greater number than the whites."[186] In 1720 the number of blacks in the total South Carolina population had reached an extraordinary 70 percent, a proportion unequaled by any other mainland colony at any period of their histories.[187] Through the eighteenth century the importance of Charleston as a slave port never ceased to grow. Historians estimate that over 40 percent of the slaves who were shipped to the British mainland colonies from 1700 to 1775 came through Charleston, a fact that led Peter Wood to call Sullivan's Island, where slaves were quarantined, "the Ellis Island of black Americans."[188]

Except for the handful of previously mentioned refugees who arrived in Carolina with slaves, the vast majority of the Huguenots had had little or no contact with slavery before the migration. Those who hailed from La Rochelle, the second-largest French slave port after Nantes, might have seen a slave ship in the harbor or might have had a relative active in the slave trade but had never thought they would someday own a slave.[189] The wealthiest among them knew, however, that they would need some sort of workforce to clear and till the vast expanses of land they purchased. Although they had read about the possibility of buying African slaves once in Carolina, because of the low supply and high cost, and perhaps their unfamiliarity with a then ill-defined slavery, they, like Jacob Guérard and the Bruneaus, opted to cross the Atlantic with their servants. As soon as they had enough capital, though, the Huguenots, including successful former servants, bought slaves, Indian and African, and after 1700 more and more Huguenots owned more and more slaves.[190]

A statistical survey of extant Huguenot wills and inventories from 1680 to 1730 confirms these general trends. The three inventories and eight wills available before 1700 mention seven slaves for two servants.[191] For the period 1700–1730, the ten inventories and twenty-five testaments list or contain a reference to 152 slaves, 9 of whom were Indian, or an average per refugee twice as high as that for the seventeenth century.[192] For the period 1736–45 Jon Butler has found that the few surviving first-generation Huguenots and their descendants owned an average of 25 slaves.[193] Although, as these statistics show, Huguenots acquired mostly black slaves, a few of them also purchased Indians. In 1690 Gignilliat, after the successive losses of his first wife and his daughter, deplored the death of his "Indian female slave, fat and strong [*grosse et vigoureuse*]," and in 1692 Daniel Huger unsuccessfully petitioned the Grand Council for help in retrieving his Indian slave named Betty who had run away and was "detained by the Yemassees."[194] Later in the eighteenth century, in her will, Marie de Longuemare manumitted her Indian slave Maria and Maria's two children, Charles and Elizabeth, for whose education she set aside money, and Abraham Fleury de La Plaine bequeathed his Indian slave Diana and her three mustee children to his brother Isaac specifying that she must be freed two years after the birth of her fifth child "as he had promised her."[195] Notwithstanding these individual, and unfortunately rare, examples of human generosity, slave ownership, the ultimate sign of wealth in colonial South Carolina, is but a sad testimony of many Huguenots' eventual prosperity in their adopted home.[196]

Huguenot Economic Success in South Carolina
Mirage or Miracle?

In different ways and with different intentions, Hirsch and Butler nonetheless both emphasized the collective economic success of the Huguenots in colonial South Carolina. Hirsch, in Weberian fashion, described these thrifty and industrious Calvinists as "Frenchmen of remarkable economic ability" and interpreted their prosperity, which led to the coining of the phrase "rich as a Huguenot," as evidence of their extraordinary capacity to confront adversity and adapt to the harsh environment of early Carolina.[197] Conversely, Butler used "their remarkable material success," tragically embodied by their exponential acquisition of slaves, to stress the economic and secular dimensions of the migration, which somewhat set Carolina Huguenots apart from their fellow refugees elsewhere in the colonies and in Europe.[198] While most of the Huguenots, and the few Swiss who accompanied them to the lowcountry, undeniably achieved material prosperity difficult to equal in Europe or elsewhere in British America, how does their prosperity compare to that of other Carolina settlers? In other words, were the first-generation Huguenots *that* successful?

To gauge the material gains achieved by the Huguenots in Carolina comparatively considering the relative paucity of extant records for the seventeenth century and the skewed representativeness of these documents, which advantage the wealthy, three parameters can be used: the number of acres acquired, the number of slaves owned, and the total value of estates as indicated in extant postmortem inventories (table 7). By the end of the proprietary period the Huguenots had been granted an average of 973 acres per individual. This figure is significantly higher than the 540 acres calculated by Duff

TABLE 7.   *Comparative economic success of the South Carolina Huguenots, 1686–1730*

	Huguenots	**All Settlers**
Acres granted (by individual)	973	540 (Duff) 760 (Coclanis)
Number of slaves owned (by household)		
(1686–1700)	2.3	2.6 (1678–98) (Menard)
Idem (1710–30)	8	9.6 (1722–26)
Movable wealth (by individual)	£259	£204 (1678–98)
Idem (1710–30)	£352	£357 (1722–26)

and the 760 acres found by Coclanis.[199] Several reasons account for these differences. The Huguenots constituted a small group of people who were not escaping economic failure in their home but conversely came to Carolina with capital and/or skills. Additionally, there were a few individuals who acquired manors either by purchase, gift, or both. Another reason is that, as alien settlers, they were probably bent on securing as much wealth as possible in its least volatile form, namely real estate. The eleven first-generation Huguenot inventories available for the proprietary period, three of which were recorded in the seventeenth century, list a total of 94 slaves. Although they are too few to be representative of the entire community, they nonetheless show that the refugees owned an average of 2.3 slaves per household and averaged £259 sterling in movable wealth for the seventeenth century and 8 slaves and £352 for the period 1710–30. In his study of South Carolina probate inventories, Russell Menard obtained the respective figures of 2.6 and £204 for the period 1678–98 and 9.6 and £357 for the 1722–26 span.[200] For all it is worth, this comparison shows that the first-generation Huguenots did well as transplanted foreign settlers who had to leave most of what they owned behind in France, but does not make their material success particularly spectacular in regard to what the British settlers achieved under the same conditions. The Huguenots undoubtedly reached a level of wealth that the vast majority of them could not possibly have achieved in France, and for this reason migrating to South Carolina, provided one did not die of disease, was a wise economic decision. Away from the New Babylon, most of them found in this subtropical Eden a land of true opportunity for themselves and their descendants.

EPILOGUE

Beyond the Myth—The Legacy of the South Carolina Huguenots

The site of Charlesfort; the towns of Port Royal and Ravenel; Ribault Road in Beaufort; Horry County; Prioleau, Gendron, and Legare streets in Charleston; Gervais Street in Columbia; the Manigault House; the Charleston Huguenot Church; Hanover House in Clemson; the Middleburg and Hampton plantations; Revolutionary War hero Francis Marion; the saying "rich as a Huguenot"; and the dessert known as the Huguenot torte are some of the many testimonies to the indelible mark the Huguenot refugees have left on the history, toponymy, architectural scene, and cultural landscape of the lowcountry and the state of South Carolina.[1] Beyond the myth, this is an undeniable fact. Although the Huguenots did not "make South Carolina"—nor America for that matter, as their descendants regularly trumpeted in the nineteenth century—or exert an overwhelming influence on the history of the state, as Hirsch would have it, it is clear that no other non-British group of settlers has enjoyed this visibility. When one remembers that probably fewer than a thousand of them immigrated to South Carolina from 1680 to 1775 and fewer than five hundred between 1680 and 1700, the heroic age of the migration, and that the large majority of them arrived in Charleston as penniless foreigners, from a historical and anthropological perspective this is quite a remarkable phenomenon.

How and why did this happen? Why is this influence more visible and heralded in Charleston than in, say, New York and Virginia, where at least as many and perhaps more Huguenot refugees settled? Why is the Huguenot immigration celebrated as *the* French immigration to the lowcountry when so many more Saint Domingue refugees settled there in the 1790s? Ever since I first visited Charleston I have pondered these questions. After more than a decade of research and writing on the subject, I still do not have definitive answers, only possible explanations. One is that the Huguenots settled in America, as Butler puts it, at "extraordinarily auspicious times" when British North America was at the outset of a long-term phase of dramatic demographic, territorial, and economic expansion.[2] There is no doubt that the refugees who remained and survived, with a little luck and business sense, could take advantage of this growth, which merchants and planters did in South Carolina, New York, and New England. In South Carolina, a colony founded a mere ten years before the arrival of the first Huguenots and with a white population that did not exceed eight hundred people in 1680 when the *Richmond* sailed up the Ashley River, the demographic, economic, and even cultural impact of several hundred refugees on a total population that eventually grew but remained nonetheless comparatively small was bound to have an effect.[3] In fact, there was a time in Charleston when French could commonly be heard in the streets and when South Carolina laws were not only voted on but also drafted by Frenchmen. Given these circumstances, since the mid-nineteenth century Huguenot descendants have been quick to elevate their ancestors to the sacrosanct status of founders. The overlapping rolls of the

Society of the First Families of South Carolina, whose members must document that their ancestors were present in the lowcountry before 1700—not an easy task for a colony founded in 1670—and the Huguenot Society of South Carolina amplify and give credence to this claim, remembering also that the *Richmond* arrived not only with Huguenots on board but also carried the (founding) proprietary order to relocate Charleston on its current peninsular site.

Considering that it is unlikely anyone will ever be able to determine specifically who founded what in proprietary South Carolina, the fact is that a large majority of Huguenots were indeed in the colony before 1700, and even before 1690. Beyond the impact that the Huguenots collectively may or may not have had on the development of South Carolina, this early presence clearly allowed certain families to build extensive dynasties with deep roots in the lowcountry. It bears repeating, however, that these dynasties were rarely exclusively Huguenot since most early Carolina gentry families, French and British, intermarried with the goal of consolidating their estates and strengthening their local elite status, and with little thought to preserving any type of ethnic cohesion. Additionally, different Huguenot families gained prominence during successive periods of South Carolina history, thereby often drawing considerable local attention to themselves and their ancestors at the expense of other lines that had become extinct but whose founders had held a higher status at the time of the migration. There are several examples of this. Chroniclers of the history of the Charleston Huguenot Church and local Huguenot memory have nearly forgotten Florent-Philippe Trouillart simply because the Prioleau family has survived—whereas the Trouillart family did not—and various of its representatives have held positions of prestige in the lowcountry since the 1700s. Similarly, in the late eighteenth century the Laurens and the Manigault families were prominent, and the nineteenth century saw the rise of the Ravenels, but in the 1680s the LeSerrurier, LeGrand, LeBas, and Motte families and especially the now forgotten Goulart de Vervant enjoyed much more wealth and influence. In fact, Vervant and Peter Du Moulin III were undeniably the most prestigious Huguenots who ever set foot on Carolina soil, but—surprisingly?—both returned to England.

If this early arrival had a major impact on the history of South Carolina, it is also because Charleston never became a major port of entry for European immigrants. Sullivan's Island, as Peter Wood stresses, was an Ellis Island only for African Americans.[4] Unlike the situation in New York, where Huguenot refugees were more numerous in the 1680s though proportionately less visible, in Charleston the Huguenots were not lost among millions of other immigrants from elsewhere in Europe and from Asia who came over the centuries. Therefore, if Charleston was one of the most populous cities in British North America after Philadelphia, New York, Boston, and Newport in the eighteenth century, the fact that it grew at a much slower pace than its northern rivals after the Revolution helped early Charleston families to maintain their local influence. Ironically, though, when it comes to typical South Carolina Huguenot names such as Manigault, Ravenel, Mazyck, and Gaillard, it should be mentioned for those who are not familiar with the lowcountry that in a situation reminiscent of Edward Ball's nationwide best-seller, *Slaves in the Family,* many people who bear them are African American.[5]

The Huguenot migration to South Carolina also fits a certain perception of the history of the United States, which purports that America was a "promised land" for persecuted Protestants and which we could call "the Puritan paradigm." Following this narrow and simplistic reading of early American history, the Huguenots, as beleaguered Calvinists in a Catholic land, in crossing the Atlantic in a semblance of a biblical exodus embodied the archetypical image of Protestant refugees seeking freedom of religion in America. In the process the Huguenots become French Puritans, a sort of French chosen people who left an absolutist regime. In this scheme the Manigaults, Ravenels, Marions, Hugers, and Prioleaus were the French pilgrim fathers, and the *Richmond* was no less than a Huguenot *Mayflower.*[6] Claiming to have ancestors who came to America to live their Calvinism freely *like the Puritans* undeniably bestows considerable prestige on Huguenot descendants, and one can certainly understand that in the nineteenth century, when the WASP model had a firm grip on the American culture and psyche, they trumpeted this claim. At the time this was a legitimate way for descendants of a non-British group of early immigrants to gain acceptance.[7]

The founding of Charlesfort on Parris Island in the 1560s, Sancé's plans to ship Huguenot salters from La Rochelle to Heath's "Carolana" in the 1620s, the immigration of the 1680s, and the settlement of New Bordeaux in the 1760s give the illusion of continuous intentional Huguenot involvement in the history of South Carolina, which has made enthusiastic chroniclers claim that "South Carolina was the home of the Huguenots." The lowcountry was undoubtedly the eventual home of over a thousand refugees over nearly a century, but these successive historical episodes belonged to different eras and were unrelated. Jean-Louis Gibert and his "New Bordeaux group" actually originally petitioned British authorities for land along the Ohio River, not the Savannah. Only a simplistic causative reading of history buttresses the idea that Huguenots always chose to settle in South Carolina to follow previous migratory waves. Claiming that the Huguenots and South Carolina enjoyed a *relation spéciale,* however, has certainly made Huguenot descendants feel a particular sense of belonging in their cherished state.

The strength of Huguenot memory in South Carolina, perhaps unparalleled in the rest of the United States, undoubtedly owes much to the state's Huguenot Society. At the instigation of New York Huguenot descendants who had organized their society two years before, it was founded in 1885, the year of the bicentennial of the Revocation of the Edict of Nantes and the publication of Baird's thorough study of the Huguenot settlement in early America. The two-thousand-member-strong Huguenot Society of South Carolina has ever since played a vital role in constructing and preserving this memory. Since its foundation, the society has continuously published an annual journal, *Transactions,* which although of uneven editorial quality over the years has, especially early on, published original documents of true historical and genealogical value and, more recently, informative articles that have highlighted lesser-known aspects of the history of the Huguenots and their descendants in South Carolina. The society, often in conjunction with other local institutions, has also done much work to preserve the particularly rich Huguenot architectural heritage in Charleston and throughout the lowcountry.

Beyond the embellishment of local memory, what are we to make of the Huguenot immigration to colonial South Carolina as a historical phenomenon? In the proprietary era approximately five hundred refugees settled in the lowcountry within a short period of time, most of them arriving between 1680 and 1690. This represented a large number in proportion to the colony's white population but remains statistically insignificant in comparison with other destinations within the Refuge and other immigrant groups who came to South Carolina. Even if only French immigrants are considered, the number of the nearly forgotten Saint Domingue refugees may have been ten times that of the Huguenots.[8] The Huguenots were mostly merchants and artisans, a characteristic that mirrored the socioeconomic profile of the Huguenot population in France and early modern transatlantic migrations, but a significant proportion of the refugees were members of the French lower nobility. However, they were not all noble and rich, as local memory would have it. Actually, it was quite the contrary as most of them were penniless and many requested financial assistance from the crown and the Church of England or indentured themselves in order to pay for their transatlantic passage.

Within the context of South Carolina history, a close study of the Huguenot migration reveals that most of the early proprietors were not fumbling aristocrats obsessed with imagined profits of fantastic proportions but rather colonial entrepreneurs who created specific policies to achieve reasonable objectives. They wanted Huguenots to come and settle the lowcountry and did what was necessary to draw as many of them as possible, considering the short span of time during which Carolina was in the limelight of English expansion and refugees were available for overseas settlement. Once in the colony, the Huguenots attempted to acquire the economic and legal means to put down roots and prosper. They did so quickly but not *that* quickly, since in terms of integration speed is a relative notion. It took seventeen years for the Huguenots to obtain a naturalization law, and many were still landless by the end of the seventeenth century. As for their much-proclaimed and much-debated religious integration, it is notable that if most Huguenots opted to join the ranks of the Church of England by 1706, they had nonetheless before 1690 founded four Calvinist *églises* and *annexes* in the lowcountry served by three Swiss and French Reformed pastors. The structures of this Calvinist life crumbled, but this does not in the least mean that the refugees suddenly stopped being Calvinists. Remnants of their French Reformed beliefs and usages endured through the 1740s.

Overall, the Huguenot experience in colonial South Carolina and in British North America at large fits the immigration history paradigm. As Russell Menard wrote in an essay on immigration in early America, integrating into a dominant multiethnic and multicultural creole society rather than remaining separate was the norm, not the exception.[9] The Huguenots settled in New England, New York, Virginia, and South Carolina not to preserve their once-threatened religious and cultural ways in isolated French enclaves, but to live fully and to participate in the formation of New World societies. Their experience was quintessentially American.

APPENDIX

Huguenot Refugees in Proprietary South Carolina (1680–1718)

This table presents a list of 395 Huguenots and Swiss who immigrated to—but did not necessarily settle permanently in—South Carolina between 1680, the year the *Richmond* sailed to Charleston, and 1718. This list, which covers the entire proprietary period, is meant to be as inclusive as possible by including the refugees we might call *les oubliés de la migration* (the forgotten of the migration), who comprise those about whom we know nothing except that they were in South Carolina at some point between 1680 and 1718. Consequently, the number of refugees listed in this table is higher than the number of migrants used to compute the statistics in chapter 4 (see chapter 4, note 5).

(a) Regarding women refugees, they are listed under their maiden names if known, and if not, the married names appear in brackets. [?] means that only the first name of the refugee, a servant, appears in the records.

(b) *Gentilshommes* were refugees who had the title of *écuyers* in France and who became large landowners in the lowcountry to be distinguished from merchants and surgeons who appear under the inflated title of esquires in the colonial records. At that time the term "planter" referred to modest farmers, the gentilshommes being planters in the modern sense of the word (see chapter 4, note 86).

(c) For the refugees whose dates of arrival in the colony are unknown, especially those who first appeared in the records at the time of the naturalization procedure of 1696–97, it can probably be assumed that they were in the colony long before but that this early presence in South Carolina is undocumented. In some cases the dates of arrival shown in the column are educated guesses based on information gathered in the records, such as the number of children born in Carolina at the time the 1696 naturalization list was compiled. A question mark indicates that the refugee's presence in the colony is documented only by a will. While obviously s/he had been in the colony for some time before this, no other date can be inferred through cross-referencing.

(d) If a year appears alone, it corresponds to when the refugee died in the colony. The mention "between . . . and . . ." means that the refugee died sometime between January 1 of the first year and December 31 of the second year and that a date of death can only be inferred from an index of no longer extant wills and inventories (see Charles H. Lesser, *South Carolina Begins: The Records of a Proprietary Colony,* [Columbia: South Carolina Department of Archives and History, 1995], 307). If it is a two-year span, "or" is used instead of "between." If it is known that the refugee died in another colony or in Europe, this is indicated.

Name of Refugee	Town and/or Province of Origin	Occupation or Status	Date of Birth	Date of Arrival or First Date in SC Records	Date of Death	Date of Departure from SC and/or Destination
Allaire, Catherine				1692		
Antoine, Michel		Indentured servant		1687		
Archambaud, Jeanne				1718		
Ardouin, Madelaine	Gémoset, Saintonge			1694		
Arriné, Anne				1696		
Aunant, Jean	Nîmes, Languedoc	Silk-throwster		1696	1716	
Avou [or Avaul], Daniel				?	1718	
Bacot, Pierre, Jr.	Tours, Touraine		1671	1685		
Bacot, Pierre, Sr.	Tours, Touraine		1638	1685	Between 1710 and 1712	
Balluet, Ester Madeleine				1694	Before 1712	
Baluet, Judith.				1694		
Baton, Isaac	Picardy	Weaver		1680		
Baudoin, Georges	Tours, Touraine			1695	1695	
Bayer, Jeanne	Basel, Switzerland			1690		
Beauchamp, John		Merchant		1710	1717	
Belin, Alard	La Rochelle, Aunis	Merchant		1687		
Belin, James	La Rochelle, Aunis	Merchant		1704		
Bellamy, Thomas		Hat maker		1685	1725	
Benoit, Jean	Sussay, Poitou			1685	Before 1703	
Berchaud, Jeanne	La Rochelle, Aunis			1692		
Bérou, Gabrielle	Ormey, Beauce			1685		
Berteaud, Jean	Saint-Lô, Normandy			1696		
Berterand, Pierre	Île-de-Ré, Aunis		1668	1692	1692	
Bertomeau, Sara	Île-de-Ré, Aunis		1645	1690		
Bilbeau, James		Planter		1709	1735	
Billon, Marye	La Rochelle, Aunis			1690		
Bisset, Élye	Saint-Jean d'Angély, Saintonge	Shammy-dresser		1691	Between 1708 and 1711	

Blanchard, François		Planter		1693		
Blanchard, Henry				1680		
Bochet, Abel	Nanteuil-les-Meaux, Brie	Planter		1696	Between 1708 and 1711	
Bochet, Nicolas	Nanteuil-les-Meaux, Brie	Planter		1692	Between 1716 and 1719	
Boisgard, Mathurin	Marennes, Saintonge	Planter		1715	1732	
Boisseau, Jean	Paris			1689	1710	
Bonhoste, Jonas		Wheelwright		1692	1699 or 1700	
Bonneau, Antoine	La Rochelle, Aunis	Cooper	1647	1685	1699	New Rochelle, New York
Bonneau, Louis				1685		
Bonneau, Marie	La Rochelle, Aunis			1685	1699	
Bonnel, Daniel				1696	Before 1699	
Bonnet, François		Indentured servant		1687	After 1708	
Bonnin, Arnaud	Île-de-Ré, Aunis	Merchant		1698	1709	Before 1689 (New York City)
[Bontecoul], Marie				1685		
Bontecou, Pierre	Île-de-Ré, Aunis			1685		Before 1689 (New York City)
Boudinot, Elie	Marans, Aunis	Merchant		1687	1702 (died New York City)	Left Carolina in 1688
Bouquet, Suzanne	Saint-Nazaire, Saintonge		1674	1702		
Bourdelle, Jacob				1694		
Boureau, Antoine	Lusinain, Poitou	Gunsmith	1642	1686	Before 1704	
Boyd, Gabriel	Guyenne	Merchant		1686		
Boyd, Jacques	Guyenne	Merchant		1686		
Boyd, Jean	Guyenne	Merchant		1704		
Brabant, Daniel		Surgeon		1686		
Brau, Jeanne				1680		
Brémar, Salomon	Ansême, Picardy	Indentured servant/Weaver		1688	1721	
Bressan, Anne	Pont-en-Royan, Dauphiny					
Breton, Jean				1709		

Name of Refugee	Town and/or Province of Origin	Occupation or Status	Date of Birth	Date of Arrival or First Date in SC Records	Date of Death	Date of Departure from SC and/or Destination
Brigaud, Moyse	Seuvet, Poitou			1687		
Broussard, Jeanne				1691		
Brugnet, Marie	Dieppe, Normandy			1688		
Bruneau, Arnaud, Sieur de la Chabossière	La Rochelle, Aunis	Gentilhomme	1609	1686		
Bruneau, Henri	La Rochelle, Aunis	Gentilhomme	1679	1686	1717	
Bruneau, Paul, Sieur de Rivedoux	La Rochelle, Aunis	Gentilhomme		1686	1711	
Buretel, Élisabeth	La Rochelle, Aunis	Merchant	1673	1687	Before 1708	
Buretel, Pierre	La Rochelle, Aunis			1687	1702	
Burgeaud, Jeanne	Île-de-Ré, Aunis			1687		
Cadeau, Pierre				1704		
Caillabeuf, Isaac	Sainte-Soline, Poitou	Merchant		1685	1699	
Carion, Moïse	Faugère, Languedoc	Joiner		1696		
Carlié, Adam				1686		New York City
Carrière, Jean	Normandy	Indentured servant/Cooper		1680		
Carron, Claude	Tours, Touraine	Planter		1695		
Carteau, Jean				1701		
Challiou, Catherine	Lyon, Lyonnais					
Chardon, Madeleine	Tours, Touraine		1657	1690		
Charron, Benoît		Indentured servant		1687		
Chastaigner, Alexandre Thésée, Sieur de L'Isle	La Rochelle, Aunis	Gentilhomme		1686		
Chastaigner, Henry Auguste, Sieur de Cramahé	La Rochelle, Aunis	Gentilhomme		1686		
Chauvin, Isaac		Joiner		1714	1735	

Name	Origin	Occupation				
Cheriny, Claude	La Roche Posay, Touraine		1661	1687	1726	
Chintrié [or Chintrier], Élisabeth					1727	
Collin, Pierre	Île-de-Ré, Aunis	Merchant		1695	1699 or 1700	
Cordes, Antoine	Mazamet, Languedoc	Surgeon		1690	1712	
Cordes, James	Languedoc	Planter		1705	1718	
[Cordes] Jeanne				?	1715	
Cothonneau, Jérémie	La Rochelle, Aunis	Cooper	1645	1690		
Couillandeau, Pierre	LaTremblade, Saintonge	Blacksmith		1688		
Couillandeau, Suzanne	LaTremblade, Saintonge		1663	1688		
Courage, François		Planter		1709	1725	
Courcier, Marie	Île-de-Ré, Aunis			1695	1732 (died in New Jersey)	1687 (New York City)
Coursier, Anne	Île-de-Ré, Aunis			1685		
Couturier, Daniel				1709		
D'Amberbaut, Elizabeth	Amsterdam, The Netherlands		1656	1685		
D'Harriette, Benjamin	La Rochelle, Aunis	Merchant	1676	After 1703	1756	
De Bordeaux, Marguerite	Grenoble, Dauphiny			1686		
De Bourdeaux, Jacques	Grenoble, Dauphiny	Smith	1630	1686	1699	
De Farcy, Jean	Vitré, Brittany			1690		England, then Virginia
[De Farcy] Marguerite	Vitré, Brittany			1690		England, then Virginia
De France, Isaac				1699		
De la Brosse Marbœuf, Joseph	Vieillevigne, Brittany	Apothecary		1687	1713	
De la Tour, François	Saintonge	Mariner		1700		
De Liesseline, Jean		Planter		1725		
De Longuemare, Nicolas, Jr.	Dieppe, Normandy	Silversmith		1685	1712	
De Longuemare, Nicolas, Sr.	Forêt de Lyone, Normandy	Silversmith		1685	1699	
De Richebourg, Claude Philippe		Pastor		1711	1719	

Name of Refugee	Town and/or Province of Origin	Occupation or Status	Date of Birth	Date of Arrival or First Date in SC Records	Date of Death	Date of Departure from SC and/or Destination
De Roussery, François	Montpellier, Languedoc	Vintner		1680		
De St. Julien, Charlotte	Vitré, Brittany		1668	1686		
De St. Julien, Louis	Vitré, Brittany	Gentilhomme		1686	1719	
De St. Julien, Pierre, Jr.	Vitré, Brittany	Gentilhomme	1669	1686		
De St. Julien, Pierre, Sr., Sieur de Malacare	Vitré, Brittany	Gentilhomme	1635	1686	1705 (died in Dublin)	
Dehays, Suzanne	Magny, Brie			1692		
DeJean, Isaac				1699	Between 1703 and 1706	
Delauné, Jean				1716	1727 (died in England)	
Delorme, Marie		Indentured servant		1680		
Deveau, André				1694		
Dieu, Élisabeth	Caen, Normandy			1687		
Donnedieu, Jean				1702	Between 1702 and 1705	
Doucet, Jean				1696		
Douxsaint, Paul		Merchant		1714	1742	
Du Bloys, Catherine	La Rochelle, Aunis			1685		
[Du Moulin], Marie				1684		
Du Moulin, Pierre				1684		
Dubois, Jean				1702	1724	
DuBosc, Jacques	Saint-Ambroix, Languedoc	Merchant		1696	1706	
Dubosc, Isaac	Dieppe, Normandy		1665	1690		
DuBosc, Marie				1696		
DuBourdieu, Samuel	Vitré, Brittany	Gentilhomme	1650	1686	Between 1706 and 1709	
Dubreuil, Jean		Joiner		1710	Between 1717 and 1719	

Name	Place of origin	Occupation			
Ducros de La Bastie, Charles					1704
Dugué, Élisabeth	Bésance, Berry	Shipwright		1685	
Dugué, Isaac	Bésance, Berry			1685	1696
Dugué, Jacques, Jr.	Bézance, Berry	Merchant		1686	1696
Dugué, Jacques, Sr.	Bézance, Berry			1685	
Dugué, Judith	Bézance, Berry			1685	
Dugué, Marie	Bésance, Berry	Shipwright		1685	
Dugué, Pierre	Bésance, Berry			1685	1734
Dumay, Étienne				1727	Between 1716 and 1718
Dupont, Abraham	Normandy	Brazier		1695	In England by 1699
Dupré, Cornelius		Planter		1686	
Dupré, Jacques				1686	
Dupré, Josias, Jr.		Shipwright		1686	
Dupré, Josias, Sr.		Merchant		1686	Between 1711 and 1714
Dupré, Marie Ester				1693	1737
Dupré, Marthe				1686	
Dupuy, André		Merchant	1654	1718	1722
Durouzeau, Michel				1711	
Durouzeaux, Daniel	Saint-Jean d'Angély, Saintonge	Shammy-dresser		1693	1700
Dusoul, Étienne	Rennes, Brittany	Pastor		1686	
Dutan, Elizabeth				1685	
Dutarque, Louis	Picardy	Weaver		1696	
Dutartre, Pierre	Châteaudun, Beauce	Weaver		1685	1748
Fanton, Élisabeth	Île-de-Ré, Aunis			1685	
Fanton, Rachel	Île-de-Ré, Aunis			1685	
Faucheraud, Charles	Soubise, Saintonge	Gunsmith	1645	1683	Before 1691
Faucheraud, Élisabeth	Port-aux-Barques, Saintonge			1683	
Faucheraud, Sarah				1685	1699

Name of Refugee	Town and/or Province of Origin	Occupation or Status	Date of Birth	Date of Arrival or First Date in SC Records	Date of Death	Date of Departure from SC and/or Destination
Filleux, Pierre		Cooper	1655	1700	1741	
Fleury, Isaac	Tours, Touraine			1685		
Fleury, Madeleine	Tours, Touraine		1638	1685		
Fleury, Marianne	Paris					
Fleury de la Plaine, Abraham	Tours, Touraine		1642	1680	Before 1715	
Foissin, Élie				1700		
Forger, Jean				1694		
Formé, Isaac		Indentured servant	1674	1685		
Forteresse, Marie		Indentured servant		1680		
Foucault, André	LaTremblade, Saintonge			1684		
Fougeraut, Marie	Paris, Île-de-France			1688		
Fouré, Pierre		Planter		1680		
[France], Alamazett				1685		
France, Arnaud	Île-de-Ré, Aunis			1685	ca. 1688	
Franchomme, Charles		Merchant	1645	1685	1723 (died in England)	
Fromaget, Charles	Châtellereault, Poitou	Planter/Weaver		1680		
Fromaget, Étienne	Tours, Touraine	Weaver		1687		
Gaillard, Barthélemy	Montpellier, Languedoc	Druggist	1666	1687	1718	
Gaillard, Jean	Montpellier, Languedoc	Merchant	1668	1687	1716	
Gaillard, Joachim	Montpellier, Languedoc	Merchant	1625	1687		
Gaillard, Pierre	Montpellier, Languedoc			1687	1710	
Gaillard, Pierre	Cherneux, Poitou	Stonecutter		1685	1710	
Gallopin, Jacques	Laigle, Normandy	Saddler		1685		
Garillion, Madeleine	Grenoble, Dauphiny			1687		
Garillond [or Garillan], Madelaine	Grenoble, Dauphiny			1686		
Garnier, Daniel	Île-de-Ré, Aunis	Merchant		1685	1708	

(Date of Departure from SC and/or Destination: France, Arnaud — 1692 (New York City))

Name	Origin	Occupation				
Garnier, Élisabeth	Île-de-Ré, Aunis			1692		
Gendron, Jean	Marans, Aunis	Merchant		1690		
Gendron, Philippe	Marans, Aunis	Cooper		1690		
Gignilliat, Jacques François Bénédict	Switzerland	Pastor		1710		1713 (England)
Gignilliat, Jean-François	Vevey, Switzerland	*Gentilhomme*	1652	1685	1699	
Girard, Pierre	Poitiers, Poitou	Merchant		1690	Between 1706 and 1709	
Girardeau, Jean	Tallemont, Poitou		1663	1696	1721	
Giton, Judith	La Voulte, Vivarais			1685		
Gobard, Anne					Before 1718	
Godin, Benjamin	Le Havre, Normandy	Merchant		1707	1748	
Gourdain, Louis	Concourt, Artois	Planter		1696	1716	
Guérard, Isaac	Normandy			1680		
Guérard, Jacob	Dieppe, Normandy			1680	1703	
Guérard, Jean (John)	Normandy	Weaver		1680	1714	
Guérard, Joseph	Normandy			1680		
Guérard, Pierre Jacob	Normandy	Silversmith		1680	1711 or 1712	
Guéri, Pierre	Seuvet, Poitou			1691	1730	
Guérin, François	Saint-Nazaire, Saintonge	Laborer		1691	Between 1710 and 1712	
Guérin, Mathurin	Saint-Nazaire, Saintonge	Gardener		1691	1722	
Guérin, Pierre	Saint-Nazaire, Saintonge			1710		
Guérin, Thomas				1709		
Guérin, Vincent		Planter		1703		
Guerrian, François	Saint-Nazaire, Saintonge			1696		
Guibal, Jean	Saint-André de Val, Languedoc			1696		
Guillard, Anne		Indentured servant		1685		
Héraud, Jean	Île d'Oléron, Saintonge		1670	1696	1699	
Horry, Daniel				1692	Before 1696	
Horry, Élye	Charenton, Île-de-France			1696		
Horry, Suzanne	Neuchâtel, Switzerland			1680	1736	

Name of Refugee	Town and/or Province of Origin	Occupation or Status	Date of Birth	Date of Arrival or First Date in SC Records	Date of Death	Date of Departure from SC and/or Destination
Huger, Daniel	Loudun, Poitou	Merchant	1651	1685	1711	
Isambert, Marie				1685	1699	
Jay, Auguste	La Rochelle, Aunis	Merchant	1665	1685		1686 (New York City)
Jodon, Daniel	Île-de-Ré, Aunis		1683	1690	1739	
Jodon, Ester	Île-de-Ré, Aunis			1690	1698	
Jouet, Daniel	Île-de-Ré, Aunis	Sail maker	1672	1695	1721 (died in New Jersey)	
Juin, Élisabeth	Cherveux, Poitou			1696	Between 1715 and 1719	
Juin, Georges	Cherneux, Poitou	Planter		1694		
Juin, Louis		Planter		1696		
Juin, René		Planter		1696		
La Salle, Pierre	Bordeaux, Guyenne	Merchant		1690	1699	
Laffeleine, Anne		Indentured servant		1680		
Lansac, Louis		Merchant		1704	1716	
LaPierre, Jean	Lasalle, Languedoc	Pastor	1679	1708	1755	
Lapôtre David, Jacob		Merchant		1702	Between 1710 and 1712	1728 (North Carolina)
Lardan, Jacques	Dieppe, Normandy	Joiner		1693	1698	
LaRiche, Suzanne	London		1677	1680		
LaRoche, James		Planter		1694	1721	
Laumonié [or Laumonier], Jacques [Laumonié (or Laumonier)], Marie	Poitou			1708	Between 1711 and 1714	
Laurans [Laurens], André	La Rochelle, Aunis			1716		
Laurans [Laurens], Charles		Saddler		1716		1719 (Philadelphia)
Laurans [Laurens], John Samuel	New York	Saddler	1696	1716		
LeBas, Jacques	Caen, Normandy	*Gentilhomme*		1686		

Name	Origin	Occupation				
Lebert, Jean	Redon, Brittany	Merchant		1692	1725	
LeBrasseur, François	Rennes, Brittany	Merchant		1710		
Lecert, Ester				1696		
LeChevalier, Pierre	Saint-Lô, Normandy	Joiner		1692	1712	
Leclair, Élisabeth						
Legaré, Salomon	Lyon, Lyonnais	Silversmith	1673	1697	1760	
LeGendre, Daniel	Rouen, Normandy			1693	1703	
Léger, Élisabeth	Saint-Quentin, Picardy			1692	1725 (died in London)	
Léger, Pierre		Planter		1709	1722	
LeGrand, Isaac, Sieur D'Arneville	Caen, Normandy	*Gentilhomme*		1687	1706	
LeGrand, Jacques, Sieur de Lomboy	Normandy	*Gentilhomme*		1702	1725	
LeJau, François	Angers, Anjou	Pastor		1706	1718	
LeJay, Isaac	Tours, Touraine			1685		
LeMotteux, Judith	Normandy			1686		
LeMotteux, Marguerite	Rouen, Normandy			1685		England
LeMoyne, Jacques				1686	Between 1692 and 1700	
Lenecal, Jean		Indentured servant		1685		
LeNoble, Henry	Paris, Île-de-France			1690	Between 1716 and 1719	
LeNoir, Isaac				1687		Left by 1696 (New York City)
LeNud, Nicolas	Dieppe, Normandy			1696	1709	
Lerous, Louis				1710		
LeSade, Jacques	Normandy			1685	1703	
LeSade, Pierre	Normandy	Planter		1689	1716	
LeSerrurier, Damaris E.	Saint-Quentin, Picardy			1692	1736	
LeSerrurier, Jacques, Jr.	Saint-Quentin, Picardy	Merchant		1699		
LeSerrurier, Jacques, Sr.	Saint-Quentin, Picardy	Merchant	1635	1692	1708 (died in London)	

Name of Refugee	Town and/or Province of Origin	Occupation or Status	Date of Birth	Date of Arrival or First Date in SC Records	Date of Death	Date of Departure from SC and/or Destination
LeSerrurier, Jean-Adrien				1684		1687 (London)
LeSerrurier, Marianne	Saint-Quentin, Picardy		1675	1692	1732	
LeSerrurier, Suzanne	Saint-Quentin, Picardy		1668	1692		
Lesesne, Isaac		Cooper	1674	1706	1736	
LeSueur, Abraham	Harfleur, Normandy	Joiner		1696		
LeSueur, James				1696		
LeSueur, Marie				1718		
Lutellier [or Tellier], James		Indendured servant		1685		
Macaire, François	Pont-en-Royan, Dauphiny	Merchant		1687	1687	
Mailhet, Pierre				1703	Between 1708 and 1711	
Manigault, Gabriel	La Rochelle, Aunis	Merchant		1695		
Manigault, Pierre	La Rochelle, Aunis	Victualler/ Vintner		1695		
Marcher, Charles				1712	1719	
Marcher, Jacques				?	1718	
Marguillier, Jean				1699		
Mariette, Charlotte	Orléans, Orléanais			1680		
Marion, Benjamin	LaChaume, Poitou			1694	1734	
Marquet [or Marquis] Emmanuel				1706		
Marscau, Gabriel	Poitou			1696	Before 1696	
Marscau, Jacques	Chainé, Poitou			1696	1709	
Martel Goulart, Jacques, Sieur de Vervant		*Gentilhomme* (baronet)		1686		1696 (England)
Marvilleau, Josias, Sieur de La Forest Montpensier		*Gentilhomme*		1686	1686	
Maslet, Madeleine	Sète, Languedoc					

Name	Origin	Occupation				
Maulard, Suzanne	Chanseuil, Beauce	Planter		1685		
Mayrant, Nicolas				1686		
Mazyck, [or Mazycque], Isaac	Île-de-Ré, Aunis	Merchant	1661	1686	1736	
Meherenc, Benjamin, Sieur de La Conseillère	Rouen, Normandy	*Gentilhomme*/Merchant	1684	1710		
Memim, Auguste	La Forge Nossay, Poitou	Gunsmith		1696	1709	
Mercier, Jacquine	Tours, Touraine		1649	1686	1709	
Messet, Élisabeth				1696		
Michaud, Abraham	Villedieu d'Aunay, Poitou		1670	1690	1705	
Michaud, Honoré	Tour de Pé, Switzerland			1695	Between 1703 and 1706	
Michaud, Pierre	Villedieu d'Aunay, Poitou			1690		
Monereau, Jean				1710		
Moreau, Marthe				1695		
Moreau, Moyse				1700		
Motte, Isaac		Merchant		1712		
Motte, John Abraham	Dublin	Merchant		1705	1711	
Mounart, Françoise	Chainé, Poitou			1696		
Mounier, Pierre	Île-de-Ré, Aunis			1685		
Mounier, Sara	Île-de-Ré, Aunis			1685		
Mouzon, Louis		Planter		1705	1756	
Mozé, Cézar	La Rochelle, Aunis	Merchant		1686	1687	
Mozé, Jeanne Élisabeth	La Rochelle, Aunis		1668	1687		
Naudin, Louis		Indentured servant		1686		
Nicolas (Nicholas), Jacques	Chalais, Saintonge	Merchant		1685	Before 1708	1705 (England)
Nicolas, Marie	Chaumé, Poitou			1694		
Normand, Philippe	Germain, Poitou	Smith		1696		
Olivier, Pierre		Indentured servant		1680		
Paget, François		Planter		1700		
Paget, John				1700	1731	

Name of Refugee	Town and/or Province of Origin	Occupation or Status	Date of Birth	Date of Arrival or First Date in SC Records	Date of Death	Date of Departure from SC and/or Destination
Paparel, Ester	Boën-en-Forez, Lyonnais			1687		
Pasquereau, Louis, Jr.	Tours, Touraine	Merchant	1674	1690	1711	
Pasquereau, Louis, Sr.	Tours, Touraine	Merchant		1690		
Pasquereau, Pierre	Tours, Touraine	Merchant		1690	1721	
Pécontal, Jean	Cossade, Languedoc			1696		
[Pelé], Gabrielle	Pays de Vaud, Switzerland			1696		
Pelé, Jean Pierre	Pays de Vaud, Switzerland			1696	Before 1718	
Pépin, Alexandre	Grenoble, Dauphiny	Swordcutter		1686	1688	
Pépin, Paul	Grenoble, Dauphiny	Smith		1686	1699	
Perdriau, Étienne	La Rochelle, Aunis	Merchant		1695		1698 (New York City)
Perdriau, Louis	La Rochelle, Aunis	Merchant		1692	1695	
Perdriau, Marguerite	La Rochelle, Aunis			1685	1717	
Perdriau, Pierre	La Rochelle, Aunis	Merchant		1690	1692	
Peronneau, Henry	La Rochelle, Aunis	Merchant	1667	1687	1743	
Pétineau, Jean		Weaver		1693	1722	
Pétineau, Judith				1703		
Petit, Marguerite				1680	Between 1702 and 1706	
Peyre, David				1711	1734	
Picault, Michel				1703		
Piston, Raymond				1695		
Poinset, Catherine				1692		
Poinset [Poincet], Jeanne				1685		
Poinset, Pierre, Jr.	Soubise, Saintonge	Smith		1685	1700	
Poinset, Pierre, Sr.	Soubise, Saintonge	Smith		1685	1699	
Poitevin, Anne	Duplessis Mornay, Beauce			1685		
Poitevin, Antoine	Mainthenon, Beauce	Weaver		1696		
Poitevin, Antoine, Sr.	Orsemont, Beauce	Weaver		1685	Between 1707 and 1709	

Name	Origin	Occupation				
Poitevin, Pierre	Menthenon, Beauce	Planter	1660	1685		
Porcher, Isaac	Saint-Sévère, Berry			1687	1727	
Postel, Marie	Dieppe, Normandy			1689		
Potell, Jean	Dieppe, Normandy			1688		
Prempain, Corneille				1707	Between 1711 and 1715	
Prioleau, Élie	Pons, Saintonge	Pastor	1659	1687	1699	
Prou, Jean	Poitou			1696	Between 1698 and 1700	
[Proul], Jeanne	Poitou			1696		
Prudhomme, Anne				1695		
Prudhomme, Antoine				1695	1696	
Ravenel, René, Sieur de Boisteilleul	Vitré, Brittany	*Gentilhomme*	1656	1686		
Rembert, André	Pont-en-Royan, Dauphiny	Shoemaker		1688		
Rézeau, René	Île-de-Ré, Aunis			1685		1687 (New York City)
Ribouteau, Anne	Poitou			1685		
Ribouteau, Gabriel	LaChaume, Poitou	Cooper		1685	1706	
Rivasson, Jeanne	Bergerac, Guyenne		1658	1702		
Robert, Pierre	Saint-Imier, Switzerland	Pastor		1690	1715	
Robinet, Louise	Aunis			1685		
Roux, Étienne				1710	Between 1715 and 1718	
Royer, Madeleine	Tours, Touraine	Weaver	1663	1687		
Royer, Noé, Jr.	Tours, Touraine	Shoemaker	1639	1685	1698	
Royer, Noé, Sr.				1685	Before 1712	
Ruchonet, Jean-Noé				1722		
Sarrazin, Étienne	Montauban, Languedoc	Merchant		1709	Between 1716 and 1719	
Satur, Jacob		Merchant		1707		
[Satur], Marie				1707		

Name of Refugee	Town and/or Province of Origin	Occupation or Status	Date of Birth	Date of Arrival or First Date in SC Records	Date of Death	Date of Departure from SC and/or Destination
Saulnier, Madeleine	Châtellereault, Poitou			1685		
Sauseau, Jean				1704		
Sauvagot, Marie	Saintonge			1696		
Seneschaud, Daniel	Saint-Maixant, Poitou			1696	1705	
Serré, Noé	Luminie, Brie	Weaver		1680	1700 or 1701	
Sicard, Ambroise			1631	1680		Before 1688 (New York City)
Simmons, Benjamin		Planter		1686	1717	
Soyer, Marie	Dieppe, Normandy			1696	1712	
Tampié, Étienne	Saintonge			1696		
Tauvron, Étienne	Île-de-Ré, Aunis	Cooper		1692	1729	
Tauvron, Marie	Île-de-Ré, Aunis			1694		
Thibaud, Étienne		Cooper		1711		
Thibou, Louis	Orléans, Orléanais	Merchant		1680	1726 (died in Antigua)	
Thomas, Jean	Saint-Jean d'Angély, Saintonge	Surgeon		1692	1710	
Thoury, Louise	Rennes, Brittany	House servant		1687	Before 1694	
Torquet, Jacques	Normandy			1686		
[Torquet], Jeanne				1696		
Torquet, Omphroy (Humphrey)	Normandy	Shipwright		1696	1704	
Torquet, Paul	Normandy	Shipwright		1696	1711	
[Torquet], Sara				1696	1704	
Trapier, Paul	Grenoble, Dauphiny			1710		
Trézévant, Daniel, Jr.	Menthenon, Beauce	Weaver		1685	Before 1706	
Trézévant, Daniel, Sr.	Authon-en-Perche, Beauce	Weaver		1685	1727	
Trouillart, Florent-Philippe	Normandy	Pastor		1685	1712	
Varin, Catherine	Caen, Normandy			1686		
Varin, Jacques	Rouen, Normandy	Merchant		1680	1688	

Name	Origin	Occupation				
Vary [or Varin], Isaac		Indentured servant		1686		
Verdity, Théodore		Planter		1704	1720	
Videau, Pierre	La Rochelle, Aunis	Planter	1662	1687		
Vignaud, Anne	Port-aux-Barques, Saintonge	Planter		1683	Between 1716 and 1719	
Villepontoux, Pierre	Bergerac, Guyenne	Planter (lawyer)	1643	1702	1711	
[?], Antoinette		Indentured servant		1687		London
[?], Françoise		Indentured servant		1687		
[?], Robert		Indentured servant		1680		

NOTES

The following abbreviations are used in the notes.

AN   Archives Nationales, Paris
BN   Bibliothèque Nationale (rue de Richelieu), Paris
BPRO   British Public Record Office (now the National Archives), Kew
BSHPF *Bulletin de la Société de l'Histoire du Protestantisme Français*
FPCL   French Protestant Church Library, London
HSP   *Huguenot Society of Great Britain and Ireland Proceedings*
HSSCT *Huguenot Society of South Carolina Transactions*
SCDAH   South Carolina Department of Archives and History, Columbia
SCHGM *South Carolina Historical and Genealogical Magazine*
SCHM *South Carolina Historical Magazine*

Introduction

1. Although I favor and recommend a strict use of the term Huguenot that includes neither Swiss nor Walloons, for the sake of simplicity in this book Huguenot—unless otherwise specified—refers generically to the French-speaking migrants who came to South Carolina between 1680 and 1740.

2. Unlike these two groups and contrary to what is usually believed, however, the Huguenots were not expelled from France but, conversely, forced to remain and convert to Catholicism. For two recent studies that have used the term "Diaspora" over "Refuge," see Eckart Birnstiel, ed., *La diaspora des huguenots: Les réfugiés protestants de France et leur dispersion dans le monde (XVIe–XVIIIe siècles)* (Paris: Honoré Champion, 2001); Bertrand Van Ruymbeke and Randy J. Sparks, eds., *Memory and Identity: The Huguenots in France and the Atlantic Diaspora* (Columbia: University of South Carolina Press, 2003).

3. Butler's maximum estimate of two thousand Huguenots does not include the five hundred or so refugees who settled in Virginia in 1701 and 1702 and needs therefore to be adjusted accordingly. Although all colonies from New Hampshire to Georgia can probably boast an early presence of Huguenot settlers, significant Huguenot communities were founded only in Massachusetts, New York, Virginia, and South Carolina. See Jon Butler, *The Huguenots in America: A Refugee People in New World Society* (Cambridge, Mass.: Harvard University Press, 1983), 49. For a map of these communities, see Van Ruymbeke and Sparks, *Memory and Identity,* xii.

4. On the late eighteenth-century migration to South Carolina, see Anne C. Gibert, *Pierre Gibert, Esq., the Devoted Huguenot: A History of the French Settlement of New Bordeaux, South Carolina* (n.p.: privately printed, 1976).

5. On this search of the Garden of Eden in the wake of Columbus's voyages, see Jean-Pierre Sanchez, *Mythes et légendes de la conquête de l'Amérique,* 2 vols. (Rennes: Presses Universitaires de Rennes, 1996), 1:93–101; Jean Delumeau, *Une histoire du paradis,* 2 vols. (Paris: Fayard, 1992, 1995), 1:203–27, 2:275–87. For the Huguenot dream of a refuge in a transoceanic Eden, see Paolo Carile, *Huguenots sans frontières: Voyage et écriture à la Renaissance et à l'Âge classique* (Paris: Honoré Champion, 2001), 97–136.

6. "Judith Giton's letter" (undated), Manigault Family Papers, ms. folder 11/275/3, South Carolina Historical Society, Charleston.

7. Quoted in James I. Waring, *A History of Medicine in South Carolina, 1670–1825* (Charleston: South Carolina Medical Association, 1964), 20–21. See also John Duffy, "Yellow Fever in Colonial Charleston," *SCHGM* 52 (1951): 189–97; Duffy, "Eighteenth-Century Carolina Health Conditions," *Journal of Southern History* 18 (1952): 289–302.

8. BPRO, Colonial Office Papers (hereafter CO) 5/1258 (1699). A copy of this census can be found in Alexander S. Salley, ed., *Papers in the British Public Record Office Relating to South Carolina [1663–1710],* 5 vols. (Columbia: Historical Commission of South Carolina, 1928–47), 4:75.

9. This vulnerability is also emphasized by Peter Wood, who noted the sudden disappearance of many French names from the proprietary records. See Peter H. Wood, *Black Majority: Negroes in Colonial South Carolina from 1670 through the Stono Rebellion* (New York: Alfred A. Knopf, 1974), 67. See also St. Julien Childs, who rightly stressed the devastating impact of the unhealthy epidemiological environment in the settlement of Carolina and Huguenot vulnerability to it. Yet, Childs overestimated the number of migrants (2,000) and went too far in saying that Huguenot settlers never reached that number because of deaths and departures caused by malaria. See St. Julien R. Childs, *Malaria and Colonization in the Carolina Low Country, 1526–1696* (Baltimore: Johns Hopkins University Press, 1940), 251.

10. "Will of Paul Bruneau" (November 14, 1709), Miscellaneous Records (Proprietary Series), vol. 1711–14:65, SCDAH.

11. "Will of Pierre Bertrand" (September 8, 1692), Miscellaneous Records (Proprietary Series), vol. 1692–1700:9, SCDAH.

12. H. Roy Merrens and George D. Terry, "Dying in Paradise: Malaria, Mortality, and the Perceptual Environment in Colonial South Carolina," *Journal of Southern History* 4 (1984): 533–50.

13. R. M. Golden, ed., *The Huguenot Connection: The Edict of Nantes, Its Revocation, and Early French Migration to South Carolina* (Boston: Kluwer Academic Publishers, 1988), 141. On this ambivalent representation of life in America that stresses edenic cornucopia and hard work, see Michael Zuckerman, "Identity in British America: Unease in Eden," in *Colonial Identity in the Atlantic World, 1500–1800,* ed. Nicholas Canny and Anthony Pagden (Princeton: Princeton University Press, 1987), 123–27.

14. Charles W. Baird, *History of the Huguenot Migration to America,* 2 vols. (New York: Dodd & Mead, 1885). For a more contextualized and detailed account of Huguenot historiography in the United States since the 1880s, see Bertrand Van Ruymbeke, "Ethnic History and Mystic Chords of Memory: One Hundred and Twenty Years of Huguenot-Walloon Historiography in the United States (1883–2003)," *Bulletin du Centre d'études nord-américaines,* École des hautes études en sciences sociales, 8 (2002): 57–77.

15. Gilbert Chinard, *Les réfugiés huguenots en Amérique* (Paris: Belles-Lettres, 1925).

16. On Hirsch's work and the historiographical context surrounding the publication of his study, see my preface in Arthur H. Hirsch, *The Huguenots of Colonial South Carolina,* Southern Classics Series (1928; reprint, Columbia: University of South Carolina Press, 1999), xix–xxvii.

17. Amy E. Friedlander, "Carolina Huguenots: A Study in Cultural Pluralism in the Low Country, 1679–1768" (Ph.D. diss., Emory University, 1979); Butler, *Huguenots in America.*

18. Butler, *Huguenots in America,* 199–215.

Prologue

"CAROLINE ainsi nommez en l'honneur de Charles 9 par les François qui la découvrirent, en prirent possession et si [s'y] établirent" (Guillaume De L'Isle, *Carte de la Louisiane* [N.p., 1718]).

1. The most recent studies of the Franco-Spanish colonial rivalry in the Southeast and of the sixteenth-century Huguenot colonial enterprises are John T. McGrath, "France in America, 1555–1565: A Reevaluation of the Evidence" (Ph.D. diss., Boston University, 1995), published as *The French in Early Florida: In the Eye of the Hurricane* (Gainesville: University Presses of Florida, 2000); Paul E. Hoffman, *A New Andalucia and a Way to the Orient: The American Southeast during the Sixteenth Century* (Baton Rouge: Louisiana State University Press, 1990); Frank Lestringant, *Le huguenot et le sauvage: La controverse coloniale en France au temps des guerres de religion (1555–1589)* (Paris: Aux Amateurs du Livre-Klincksieck, 1990); Eugene Lyon, *The Enterprise of Florida: Pedro Menéndez de Avilés and the Spanish Conquest of 1565–1568* (Gainesville: University Presses of Florida, 1976). On Admiral Coligny, see Liliane Crété, *Coligny* (Paris: Fayard, 1985); *Actes du Colloque "L'Amiral de Coligny et son temps," Paris, 18–24 Octobre 1972* (Paris: Société de l'Histoire du Protestantisme Français, 1974); Martine Acerra and Guy Martinière, eds., *Coligny, les protestants et la mer* (Paris: Presses Universitaires de Paris–Sorbonne, 1997).

2. Little has been written on Ribault; see nonetheless Jared Sparks, *Life of John Ribault: Comprising an Account of the French to Found a Colony in North America* (Boston: The Library of American Biography, vol. 17, 1836); Paul Bertrand de La Grassière, *Jean Ribault, marin dieppois et lieutenant du roi en Neuve-France, Floride française en 1565* (Paris: La Pensée Universelle, 1971); Jeannette T. Connor, ed., *The Whole and True Discoverye of Terra Florida: Together with a Transcript of an English Version of the British Museum by H. M. Biggar, and a Biography by Jeannette Thurber Connor* (Gainesville: University Presses of Florida, 1927), 3–44; Bertrand Van Ruymbeke, "Ribault, Jean," in *American National Biography,* ed. John A. Garraty and Mark C. Carnes, 24 vols. (New York: Oxford University Press, 1999), 18:401–2.

3. The University of South Carolina archaeologist Chester DePratter recently located the exact location of Charlesfort. See Chester B. DePratter, Stanley South, and James Legg, "The Discovery of Charlesfort (1562–1563)," *HSSCT* 101 (1996): 39–48.

4. Ribault's original account is at the British Library (ms. Sloane 3644, fol. 111–121b). Published transcriptions are available in Henry P. Biggar, ed., "Jean Ribaut's Discoverye of Terra Florida," *English Historical Review* 32 (1917): 253–70; Connor, *Jean Ribaut;* David B. Quinn, ed., *New American World: A Documentary History of North America to 1612,* 5 vols. (New York: Arno Press, 1979), 2:285–94. Ribault's account was published in English in 1563. A recent French translation is available in Suzanne Lussagnet, ed., *Les Français en Amérique pendant la deuxième moitié du XVIe siècle,* vol. 2, *Les Français en Floride* (Paris: Presses Universitaires de France, 1958), 1–6. A French manuscript, which Ribault would have written in his cell at the Tower of London, may have existed at some point but has now been lost.

5. The Spanish report detailing the destruction of Charlesfort can be found in Lucy Wenhold, "Menrique de Rojas' Report on the French Settlement in Florida," *Florida Historical Quarterly* 38 (1959): 55–60; and Charles E. Bennett, *Laudonniere & Fort Caroline: History and Documents* (Gainesville: University Presses of Florida, 1964), 107–24. Like Ribault, Laudonnière wrote an account of his Florida experience; entitled *Histoire Notable de la Floride située ès Indes Occidentales,* it appeared in London in 1686. For recently published transcriptions in French and in English, see Lussagnet, *Les Français en Floride,* 27–200; René Goulaine de Laudonnière, *Three Voyages,* ed. Charles E. Bennett (Gainesville: University Presses of Florida, 1975); Quinn, *New American World,* 2:294–307, 317–60.

6. Hoffman, *New Andalucia,* 223–30; Lyon, *Enterprise of Florida,* 100–130; McGrath, *French in Early Florida,* 134–55; Larry Rowland, Alexander Moore, and George C. Rogers Jr., *History of Beaufort County, South Carolina* (Columbia: University of South Carolina Press, 1996), 1:22–29;

and Larry S. Rowland, *Window on the Atlantic: The Rise and Fall of Santa Elena, South Carolina's Spanish City* (Columbia: South Carolina Department of Archives and History, 1990), 8–15.

7. On Sancé, see Jacques Evesque, "Ridouet de Sancé, famille protestante d'Anjou," *Cahiers du Centre de Généalogie Protestante* 8 (1984): 403–4.

8. BPRO, CO 1/5/24. The letter is also available in Baird, *History,* 1:165.

9. BPRO, CO 1/5/18.

10. Paul E. Kopperman, "Profile of a Failure: The Carolana Project, 1629–1640,"*North Carolina Historical Review* 59 (1982): 6–7; William S. Powell, "Carolana and the Incomparable Roanoke: Explorations and Attempted Settlements, 1629–1663," *North Carolina Historical Review* 51 (1974) 4–5.

11. *Calendar of State Papers, Colonial Series, America and West Indies,* ed. W. Noel Sainsbury and J. W. Fortescue, 40 vols. (1860–1926; Vaduz: Kraus Reprint Ltd, 1964), 1 (1574–1660):109.

12. The conformity to the Church of England clause may have also been intended to exclude Dissenters, especially Puritans. Samuel Vassall, an English merchant of Huguenot descent, and Edward Kingswell managed to send settlers to Carolana in 1633, but due to miscarriage, they eventually reached Virginia, where most of them perished. Contrary to what Hirsch claims, it is highly unlikely that Huguenots were among these colonists. See Hirsch, *Huguenots,* 8.

13. Baird, *History,* 1:i–ii, 57–77; Hirsch, *Huguenots,* 6–9; Chinard, *Réfugiés huguenots,* chap. 1.

14. For an interpretation that conversely emphasizes the Refuge motivation in Coligny's colonization plans, see Frank Lestringant, "Geneva and America in the Renaissance: The Dream of a Huguenot Refuge, 1555–1560," trans. Ann Blair, *Sixteenth-Century Journal* 26 (1995): 285–97.

15. On Coligny's and other sixteenth-century Huguenot colonial entrepreneurs' motivations, see Laurent Vidal and Mickaël Augeron, "Refuges et réseaux? Les dynamiques atlantiques protestantes au XVIe siècle," in *D'un rivage à l'autre: Villes et protestantisme dans l'aire atlantique (XVIe–XVIIe siècles),* ed. Guy Martinière, Didier Poton, and François Souty (Paris: Imprimerie Nationale, 1999), 31–61.

16. Van Ruymbeke, "Ribault, Jean," 401.

17. D. W. Meinig, *The Shaping of America: A Geographical Perspective on 500 Years of History,* vol. 1, *Atlantic America (1492–1800)* (New Haven: Yale University Press, 1986–93), 173.

18. Kopperman, "Profile of a Failure," 19.

19. The siege of La Rochelle lasted from August 1627 to November 1628. Out of the twenty-five thousand original inhabitants, seventeen thousand died and five thousand escaped during the campaign, leaving La Rochelle "a city of ghosts, not people" (comment cited in Mack P. Holt, *The French Wars of Religion, 1562–1629* [Cambridge: Cambridge University Press, 1995], 186).

20. See, for example, the Walloon party who petitioned to settle in Virginia in 1621. This beautiful and unusual document is sometimes referred to as "the round robin petition" because petitioners signed in a circle around an insert containing the text of their petition. The original is at the British Public Record Office, ref. no. MFQ 505. See Baird, *History,* 1:157–65.

21. D. B. Quinn, ed., *The Hakluyt Handbook,* 2 vols. (London: Hakluyt Society, 1974), 2:462.

22. Laudonnière, *Histoire Notable,* 28; Quinn, *Hakluyt Handbook,* 2:472. See also F. M. Rogers, "Hakluyt as a Translator," in ibid., 1:39–40; Loren E. Pennington, "The Origins of English Promotional Literature for America, 1553–1625" (Ph.D. diss., University of Michigan, 1962), chap. 4, pp. 75–81. For a facsimile reprint of the 1587 English edition, see René Laudonnière, *A Notable History Containing Four Voyages Made by Certain French Captains unto Florida* (Larchmont, N.Y.: Henry Stevens, Sons & Stiles, 1964). Incidentally, Hakluyt was also instrumental in the publication of the first French edition of *Histoire Notable.* See Lestringant, *Huguenot et le sauvage,* 163–71.

23. Pennington, "Origins of English," 75.

24. For a brief biographical sketch, see Bertrand Van Ruymbeke "Le Moyne de Morgues, Jacques," in *American National Biography*, ed. Garraty and Carnes, 13:475–76. Le Moyne also wrote an account of his sojourn in Florida entitled *Brevis Narratio Eorum Quae in Florida Americae Provicia Gallis Acciderunt* . . . and published in Theodore De Bry's *Grands Voyages*, pt. 2 (Frankfurt, 1591). Recent editions of Le Moyne's map, sketches, and narratives are: Jean-Paul Duviols and Marc Bouyer, eds., *Voyages en Floride 1562–1567: Textes de Jean Ribaut, René de Laudonnière, Dominique de Gourgues et textes et illustrations de Jacques Le Moyne de Morgues* (1927; reprint, Nanterre, France: Éditions de l'Espace Européen, 1990); Michael Alexander, ed., *Discovering the New World Based on the Works of Theodore De Bry* (New York: Harper & Row Publishers, 1976); Stefan Lorant, ed., *The New World: The First Pictures of America* (1946; New York: Duell, Sloan and Pearce, 1965). On Le Moyne's life and works before and after his Florida experience, see Paul Hulton et al., *The Work of Jacques Le Moyne de Morgues: A Huguenot Artist in France, Florida, and England*, 2 vols. (London: British Museum Publications, 1977).

25. David B. Quinn, *Set Fair for Roanoke: Voyages and Colonies, 1584–1606* (Chapel Hill: University of North Carolina Press, 1985), 183.

26. Laudonnière, *Three Voyages*, 51.

27. Hoffman, *New Andalucia*, 212; Connor, *Jean Ribaut*, 10–11.

28. Kenneth R. Andrews, *Trade, Plunder and Settlement: Maritime Enterprise and the Genesis of the British Empire, 1480–1630* (Cambridge: Cambridge University Press, 1984), 122. Hawkins, who was accompanied by one of the Charlesfort survivors, offered Laudonnière "to take [him] and [his] entire company" to France, but the French captain, "being in doubt as to why [Hawkins] was so liberal in his treatment . . . flatly refused" because he "feared that [Hawkins] might want to do something in Florida in the name of his Queen" (Laudonnière, *Three Voyages*, 142–43).

29. Pennington, "Origins of English," 70–71.

30. As John C. Appleby recently wrote about English colonization in the Atlantic in the 1560s and 1570s, "At this stage . . . the English seemed content to follow in the wake of the French [i.e., Huguenots]" ("War, Politics, and Colonization, 1558–1625," in *The Oxford History of the British Empire*, 5 vols., gen. ed. Wm. Roger Lewis, vol. 1, *The Origins of Empire*, ed. Nicholas P. Canny [New York: Oxford University Press, 1998], 61). In the same vein, the French historian Henri Dubief did not hesitate to see in Walter Raleigh the heir to Coligny ("Gaspard de Coligny et Walter Raleigh: un grand dessein et son échec," *BSHPF* 128 [1982]: 493–504). See also Andrews, *Trade*, 138.

31. Quoted in Meinig, *Shaping of America*, 1:28. In the same decades (1560s and 1570s), privateering constituted an important and efficient aspect of this Anglo-Huguenot Atlantic collaboration. See Andrews, *Trade*, 129; Mickaël Augeron, "Coligny et les Espagnols à travers la course (c. 1500–1572): Une politique maritime au service de la Cause protestante," in *Coligny*, ed. Acerra and Martinière, 155–76.

32. Frank Lestringant, "Une Saint-Barthélemy américaine: L'agonie de la Floride huguenote (septembre–octobre 1565) d'après les sources espagnoles et françaises," *BSHPF* 138 (1992): 459–73; Andrews, *Trade*, 201.

33. Quinn, *Set Fair for Roanoke*, 131–32; Andrews, *Trade*, 201.

34. Hoffman, *New Andalucia*, 300, 305. Ironically, an additional legacy of "Huguenot Florida" on the early English colonization of North America is the idea that transatlantic settlements might serve as havens for persecuted Catholics. See Andrews, *Trade*, 32.

35. For a more detailed account of the influence of "French Florida" on the early history of South Carolina, see Bertrand Van Ruymbeke, "Un refuge avant le refuge? La 'Floride huguenote' et les origines de la Caroline du Sud," in *Coligny,* ed. Acerra and Martinière, 235–45.

36. *A Relation of a Discovery, Lately Made on the Coast of Florida . . . by William Hilton,* in *Early Narratives of Carolina,* Early Narratives Series, ed. Alexander S. Salley (1911; New York: Charles Scribner's Sons, 1967), 41.

37. At Santa Elena, as Port Royal Bay was known to the Spanish, three forts were successively constructed: San Marcos (I) (1566–74), San Felipe (1574–76), and San Marcos (II) (1577–87). See Stanley South, *Archaeology at Santa Elena: Doorway to the Past* (Columbia: University of South Carolina Institute of Archaeology and Anthropology, 1991), 2–3; Rowland et al., *History of Beaufort County,* 1:29–47.

38. *A Relation of a Voyage on the Coast of the Province of Carolina Formerly Called Florida . . . Performed by Robert Sandford,* in *Early Narratives,* ed. Salley, 87. Incidentally, Ribault did not use the name Gironde in his travel account, but the cartographer Jacques Le Moyne did. See Connor, *Jean Ribaut,* 86–90; "Sex alia flumina à Gallis observata" (The French Explore Six Other Rivers), in *Voyages en Floride,* ed. Duviols and Bouyer, 138, plate 4.

39. Already in the 1665 Concessions and Agreement, the proprietors planned for "a Fort, to be Erected and built near Port Royall" (Mattie E. E. Parker, ed., *North Carolina Charters and Constitutions, 1578–1698* [Raleigh: Carolina Charter Tercentenary Commission, 1963], 110; Rowland et al., *History of Beaufort County,* 1:62). Similarly, when John Locke compiled a list of "writers of Carolina," he duly included Laudonnière. Locke owned an English edition of Laudonnière's *Histoire notable* as well as De Bry's *America Grands Voyages.* See Langdon Cheves, ed., *The Shaftesbury Papers and Other Records Relating to Carolina and the First Settlement on Ashley River Prior to the Year 1676* (1897; Charleston, S.C.: Tempus Publishing, 2000), 265; John Harrison and Peter Laslett, *The Library of John Locke* (Oxford: Clarendon Press, 1971), "Locke's Library Catalogue," 96 and 169. In the mid-eighteenth century Governor Glen wrote the Board of Trade that the colony "is generally thought to have its name Carolina from Charles the Ninth of France, in whose reign Admiral Colligny made some settlement here, tho they were soon expelled by the Spaniards." Contrary to this statement, which by itself constitutes further evidence of the legacy of "Huguenot Florida" in the historical awareness of English officials, and what nineteenth-century historians and hagiographers eager to emphasize the impact of the Huguenots on the history of South Carolina claimed, the term "Carolina," however, is not etymologically derived from Charles IX (*Carolus* in Latin), king of France from 1560 to 1574, via Fort Caroline and Charlesfort. Carolina was named after Charles II of England (1660–85). See "Copy of J. Glen, Esq. Gov. of South Carolina to the Queries proposed by the Lords of Trade (1749)," British Library, ms. King's 205, fol. 279. For examples of nineteenth- and twentieth-century assertions of the French etymological origin of Carolina, see Bartholomew R. Carroll, ed., *Historical Collections of South Carolina embracing many rare & valuable Pamphlets & other documents relating to the History of that State from its first Discovery to its Independence in the year 1776* (1836; New York: A.M.S. Reprint, 1973), xxxvii; Hirsch, *Huguenots,* 7; St. Julien R. Childs, "French Origins of Carolina," *HSSCT* 50 (1945): 29.

40. *Description du Pays nommé Caroline* (London, 1679), [1].

41. Citri de La Guette, *Histoire de la conquête de la Floride par les Espagnols sous Ferdinand de Soto* (Paris: Chez Denys Thierry, 1685).

42. This pamphlet is only available in a nineteenth-century translation done by William G. Simms and published in a journal, *Magnolia,* which Simms edited ("Remarks on the New Account of Carolina by a French Gentleman, 1686," [trans. William G. Simms], *Magnolia* 1 [1842]: 226–30).

43. Ibid., 229.

44. Guillaume De L'Isle, *Carte de la Louisiane* (1718); William P. Cumming, *The Southeast in Early Maps* (Chapel Hill: University of North Carolina Press, 1962), plate 47. In 1671 a most eccentric albeit beautiful view of Fort Caroline was published in Amsterdam by the Dutch Arnoldus Montanus (Arnoldus van Bergen) in his *De Nieuwe en onbekende Weereld of beschryving van America.* The figure represents the fort, based on one of Le Moyne's engravings (plate 10), with brick buildings within and outside the fortifications, and several ships anchored in the bay in the midst of a flurry of activity. There is even a Catholic cross on one of the river banks, a most unlikely site in this Huguenot frontier settlement. In his English translation of Montanus's work, John Ogilby, who had somewhat more reliable and accurate information on English America, omitted this view and replaced it with a more recent map of South Carolina while confusing Charles Fort and Fort Caroline. Montanus's view, with the title "Arx Carolina, Charles Fort, sur Floride," was also included in Pieter van der Aa's *La galérie agréable du monde, divisée en LXVI tomes,* published in Leiden in 1733. In describing *Arx Carolina,* Frank Lestringant aptly writes about "une scénographie spectaculaire" and "une vue hyperbolique." See Arnoldus Montanus, *De Nieuwe en onbekende Weereld: of beschryving van America* (Amsterdam: Jacob van Meurs, 1671), "Arx Carolina," between pp. 93 and 94; John Ogilby, *America, being a latest and most accurate description of the New World* (London: printed by the author, 1671), "A New Description of Carolina by the Order of the Lords Proprietors," between pp. 104 and 105 (both copies were consulted at the Bibliothèque Nationale); J. Le Moyne de Morgues, "*Arcis Carolinae delineatio,*" in *Voyages en Floride,* ed. Duviols and Bouyer, 150, plate 10; John W. Reps, *The Making of Urban America: A History of City Planning in the United States* (Princeton: Princeton University Press, 1965), 441, figure 260; Frank Lestringant, *Le livre des îles: Atlas et récits insulaires de la Genèse à Jules Verne* (Geneva: Droz, 2002), 216–17.

1. East of Eden

Epigraphs from Michael Walzer, *On Toleration* (New Haven: Yale University Press, 1997), 52; de Cosnac quoted in Catherine Bergeal and André Durrleman, eds., *Éloge et condamnation de la révocation de l'Édit de Nantes* (Carrières-sous-Poissy, France: La Cause, 1985), 13, 74. Unless noted otherwise, all translations from the French are the author's.

1. Pierre Goubert, *Louis XIV et vingt millions de Français,* rev. ed. (Paris: Fayard, 1991), 27. England had a population of five million people, Spain twelve, and Russia fourteen. See John Lough, ed., *Introduction to Seventeenth-Century France* (New York: David McKay Company, Inc., 1966), xviii–xix.

2. Benoît Garnot, *Les villes en France aux XVIe, XVIIe, XVIIIe siècles* (Paris: Ophrys, 1996), 12.

3. Ibid., 14; Paul Bairoch, Jean Batou, and Pierre Chèvre, *La population des villes européennes / The Population of European Cities* (Geneva: Droz, 1988), 23–31; Philip Benedict, "French Cities from the Sixteenth Century to the Revolution: An Overview," in *Cities and Social Change in Early Modern France,* ed. P. Benedict (London: Unwin Hyman, 1989), 7–68.

4. For a useful guide to the history of French regions, see Jean Sellier, *Atlas historique des provinces et régions de France: Genèse d'un peuple* (Paris: La Découverte, 1997).

5. Anette Smedley-Weil, *Les intendants de Louis XIV* (Paris: Fayard, 1995), 89–91. A useful glossary of French ancien régime administrative terms can be found in James B. Collins, *The State in Early Modern France* (Cambridge: Cambridge University Press, 1995), xix–xxxiv.

6. The number of parlements varied over time, as some were created and others abolished. In 1680 there were twelve of them: Paris, Dijon, Aix-en-Provence, Toulouse, Bordeaux, Rennes, Rouen, Besançon, Grenoble, Pau, Metz, and Trévoux.

7. To be specific, the parlement of Rouen agreed to temporarily register the Edict as early as September 1599 but with a secret list of modifications that it wished to adopt. Only in 1609 did the parlement eventually record the Edict and renounce to modify it. See Olivier Christin, "L'Édit de Nantes: Bilan historiographique," *Revue historique* 301 (1999): 132n29.

8. Alsace was gradually acquired by France between 1648 and 1681 and Roussillon in 1659.

9. Phillipe Barbaud, *Le choc des patois en Nouvelle-France: Essai sur l'histoire de la francisation au Canada* (Sillery: Presses de l'Université du Québec, 1984), 122. See also Sellier, *Atlas,* 19.

10. Robin Briggs, *Early Modern France 1560–1715* (Oxford: Oxford University Press, 1977), 57–59; Michel Nassiet, *La France du second XVIIe siècle* (Paris: Éditions Belin, 1997), 54–55.

11. Pierre Goubert and Daniel Roche, *Les Français et l'Ancien Régime,* 2 vols. (Paris: Armand Colin, 1984), 1:97.

12. Nassiet, *France,* 87.

13. Goubert and Roche, *Français,* 2:51–54.

14. Nassiet, *France,* 91. In 1680, with 40 percent of the market, France was the first supplier of textiles to Spanish America. See Olivier Pétré-Grenouilleau, *Les négoces maritimes français XVIIe–XXe siècle* (Paris: Éditions Belin, 1997), 22.

15. Quoted in John Lough, *France Observed in the Seventeenth Century by British Travellers* (Stockfield, U.K.: Oriel Press, 1985), 32.

16. Quoted in ibid., 87.

17. André Zysberg, "Flotte de commerce," in *Dictionnaire de l'Ancien Régime: Royaume de France XVIIe–XVIIIe siècle,* ed. Lucien Bély (Paris: Presses Universitaires de France, 1996), 560; Robert Mandrou, *Louis XIV en son temps, 1661–1715* (Paris: Presses Universitaires de France, 1973), 126.

18. The Alsatian Lutherans were not affected by the Edict of Nantes or its revocation. On Alsatian Lutheranism, see Bernard Vogler, "En Alsace: Orthodoxie et territorialisme," in Robert Mandrou et al., *Histoire des protestants en France* (Toulouse: Éditions Privat, 1977), 151–87; Vogler, "Les protestants alsaciens et les paix de religion (1555–1648)," in *Coexister dans l'intolérance: L'Édit de Nantes (1598),* ed. Michel Grandjean and Bernard Roussel, special issue, *BSHPF* 144 (1998): 465–69; Vogler, "Louis XIV et les protestants alsaciens de 1680 à 1690," in *La révocation de l'Édit de Nantes et le protestantisme français en 1685,* ed. Roger Zuber and Laurent Theis (Paris: Société de l'Histoire du Protestantisme Français, 1986), 173–86; Vogler, "Louis XIV et les protestants alsaciens," in *De la mort de Colbert à la révocation de l'Édit de Nantes: Un monde nouveau?,* ed. Roger Duchene and Louise Gondard de Donville (Marseille: C. M. R., 1984), 285–91.

19. This was a royal title whose usage became firmly entrenched by the end of the thirteenth century under the reign of Philip (IV) the Fair (1285–1314). See Joseph R. Strayer, "France: The Holy Land, the Chosen People, and the Most Christian King," in *Medieval Statecraft and the Perspectives of History: Essays by Joseph R. Strayer* (Princeton: Princeton University Press, 1971), 300–314. Such honorific religious titles were not exclusive to the French monarchy since the Spanish ruler bore the title of "Most Catholic King" and the Portuguese that of "Most Loyal."

20. Philip Benedict, *The Huguenot Population of France, 1600–1685: The Demographic Fate and Customs of a Religious Minority,* Transactions of the American Philosophical Society, 81, pt. 5 (Philadelphia, 1991), 75–78. With his new estimates, Benedict significantly revised the work of Pastor Samuel Mours, one of the most influential Huguenot demographers. See, for example, his *Essai sommaire de géographie du protestantisme réformé français au XVIIe siècle* (Paris: Librairie Protestante, 1966).

21. The northern provinces are Île-de-France, Champagne, Picardy, Normandy, Brittany, Anjou, Maine, Touraine, Orléanais, Berry, and Burgundy; the southern provinces are Poitou, Aunis, Saintonge, Angoumois, Guyenne, Béarn, Languedoc, Cévennes, Vivarais, Provence, and Dauphiny. See Benedict, *Huguenot Population,* 10.

22. Benedict, *Huguenot Population,* 10.

23. Janine Garrisson, *L'homme protestant* (Paris: Éditions Complexe, 1986), 52.

24. Ibid., 61; Jean Quéniart, *La révocation de l'Édit de Nantes: Protestants et catholiques français de 1598 à 1685* (Paris: Desclée de Brouwer, 1985), 31.

25. Quéniart, *Révocation,* 31. This type of church, authorized by the Edict of Nantes and limited to thirty parishioners for members of the lower nobility, prevailed in northern France where Huguenot density was low.

26. Garrisson, *L'homme protestant,* 63.

27. Élisabeth Labrousse, *Conscience et conviction: Études sur le XVIIe siècle* (Oxford: Universitas, 1996), 71 (quotations); Labrousse, *La révocation de l'Édit de Nantes: Une foi, une loi, un roi?* (1985; Paris: Éditions Payot, 1990), 63–64.

28. "Des Français un peu particuliers," in Labrousse, *Révocation,* 63.

29. On the French Wars of Religion and the religious and political context of the promulgation of the Edict of Nantes, see Bernard Cottret, *1598: L'Édit de Nantes; Pour en finir avec les guerres de religion* (Paris: Librairie Académique Perrin, 1998); Lucienne Hubler, Jean-Daniel Candaux, and Christophe Chalamet, eds., *L'Édit de Nantes revisité: Actes de la journée d'étude de Waldegg (30 octobre 1998)* (Geneva: Droz, 2000); Janine Garrisson, *L'Édit de Nantes: Chronique d'une paix attendue* (Paris: Fayard, 1998); Thierry Wanegffelen, *L'Édit de Nantes: Une histoire européenne de la tolérance du XVIe au XXe siècle* (Paris: Le Livre de Poche, 1998); Guy Saupin, ed., *Tolérance et intolérance de l'Édit de Nantes à nos jours* (Rennes: Presses Universitaires de Rennes, 1998); Grandjean and Roussel, *Coexister dans l'Intolérance;* Holt, *French Wars;* Janet G. Gray, *The French Huguenots: Anatomy of Courage* (Grand Rapids: Baker Book House, 1981); N. M. Sutherland, *The Huguenot Struggle for Recognition* (New Haven: Yale University Press, 1980); George A. Rothrock, *The Huguenots: A Biography of a Minority* (Chicago: Nelson-Hall, 1979); Raymond A. Mentzer, "The French Wars of Religion," in *The Reformation World,* ed. Andrew Pettigree (New York: Routledge, 2000), 323–43; Menna Prestwich, "Calvinism in France, 1555–1629," in *International Calvinism 1541–1715,* ed. M. Prestwich (Oxford: Clarendon Press, 1985), 71–107. On the 1998 commemoration and historiographical interpretations, see Christin, "L'Édit de Nantes," 128–35; Hubert Bost, "Les 400 ans de l'Édit de Nantes: Oubli civique et mémoire historique," in *L'Édit de Nantes revisité,* ed. Hubler et al., 55–77.

30. These specific courts of justice were dependent on the parlements. In 1669 there were five of them: Paris, Rouen, Toulouse, Bordeaux, and Grenoble. In theory, except that of the parlement of Paris, which counted only one Huguenot judge, these courts were to be bipartisan tribunals staffed by an even number of Catholic and Protestant magistrates; hence they were sometimes called *chambres mi-parties,* literally "mixed chambers." See Raymond A. Mentzer, "The Edict of Nantes and Its Institutions," in *Society and Culture in the Huguenot World, 1559–1685,* ed. Raymond A. Mentzer and Andrew Spicer (Cambridge: Cambridge University Press, 2002), 106–13. On the Paris Chambre de l'Édit, see Diane C. Margolf, "Identity, Law, and the Huguenots in Early Modern France," in *Memory and Identity,* ed. Van Ruymbeke and Sparks, 26–44; and Margolf, *Religion and Royal Justice in Early Modern France: The Paris Chambre de l'Édit, 1598–1665* (Kirksville, Mo.: Truman State University Press, 2003).

31. Recent published transcriptions of the Edict of Nantes are available in French in Cottret, *1598,* 361–88; Garrisson, *L'Édit de Nantes,* 171–94; Wanegffelen, *L'Édit de Nantes,* annexe 1:259–72; and in English in Richard L. Goodbar, ed., *The Edict of Nantes: Five Essays and a New Translation* (Bloomington, Minn.: The National Huguenot Society, 1998), 41–68; Golden, *Huguenot Connection,* 86–134. For a summary of the Edict's provisions in English, see Mack P. Holt, "The Memory of All Things Past: Provisions of the Edict of Nantes (1598)," in *Edict of Nantes,* ed. Goodbar, 27–32; Mentzer, "Edict of Nantes," 98–116; and Jean-Paul Willaime, "Nantes, Edict of," in *The Encyclopedia of Protestantism,* 4 vols., ed. Hans J. Hillerbrand (New York: Routledge, 2004), 3:1345–48.

32. For examples of Huguenot-controlled cities where Catholicism had been outlawed, see Philip Benedict, *"Un roi, une loi, deux fois:* Parameters for the History of Catholic-Reformed Coexistence in France, 1555–1685," in *Tolerance and Intolerance in the European Reformation,* ed. Ole P. Grell and Bob Scribner (Cambridge: Cambridge University Press, 1996), 77–78.

33. Holt, *French Wars,* 165.

34. Ibid., 166; N. M. Sutherland, "The Crown, the Huguenots, and the Edict of Nantes," in *Huguenot Connection,* ed. Golden, 34–36.

35. "Ce que le roi *peut* donner, il *peut* aussi bien le reprendre" (Cottret, *1598,* 194).

36. Holt, *French Wars,* 186–87; Sutherland, "Crown," 48.

37. This exclusive council was called Conseil d'État or Conseil d'En-Haut. Between 1661 and 1690 it never contained more than seven ministers at a time. Four *secrétaires d'État,* who each headed a specific department, assisted these ministers. Since 1588 one of them was in charge of Huguenot affairs. Between 1629 and 1700 this department remained in the hands of Louis Phelypeaux, Sieur de La Vrillière (1629–81), and his son Balthazar, marquis de Châteauneuf (1669–1700). Joël Cornette, *Chronique du règne de Louis XIV* (Paris: SEDES, 1997), 84, 95–100; Solange Deyon, "Secrétaire d'État de la Religion Prétendue Réformée," in *Dictionnaire de l'Ancien Régime,* ed. Bély, 1141–42. For a study of the role of the council during the two decades preceding Louis XIV's personal rule in 1661, see Ruth Kleinman, "Changing Interpretations of the Edict of Nantes: The Administrative Aspect, 1643–1661," *French Historical Studies* 10 (1978): 541–71.

38. Louis XIV, *Memoirs for the Instruction of the Dauphin,* trans. and ed., Paul Sonnino (New York: The Free Press, 1970), 56. For a recent French version, see Louis XIV, *Mémoires pour l'instruction du Dauphin,* ed. Pierre Goubert (Paris: Imprimerie Nationale, 1992).

39. Bernard Dompnier, *Le venin de l'hérésie: Image du protestantisme et combat catholique au XVIIe siècle* (Paris: Le Centurion, 1997), 129.

40. A policy which Élisabeth Labrousse calls "the casuistical application of the Edict" (Labrousse, "Calvinism in France, 1598–1685," in *International Calvinism,* ed. Prestwich, 307).

41. *Commissaires* were royal officials holding a temporary commission limiting their jurisdiction and their time in the position (Collins, *State,* xxi). The decree setting up these commissions of inquiry had actually been adopted under Cardinal Mazarin in 1656 but had never been enforced (Labrousse, *Révocation,* 28). Already in 1598 the Edict of Nantes had provided for the creation of bipartisan commissions of implementation (*commissions d'application*) to ensure that the Edict would be implemented in fairness to both parties, but the post-1660 commissions had another agenda. On the 1598 commissions, see Mentzer, "Edict of Nantes," 102–6.

42. In the Huguenot ecclesiastical discipline, the board of elders is called a consistory (*consistoire*).

43. Élie Prioleau graduated from the Geneva Academy in 1673 and succeeded his father at Pons in 1683. Suzanne Stelling-Michaud, ed., *Le livre du recteur de l'Académie de Genève (1559–1878),* 6 vols. (Geneva: Droz, 1959–80), 1:229, 5:244–45.

44. AN, série TT, "Affaires et biens des protestants," folder 262, pièces 906–13.

45. The Huguenots call their congregations *églises* and their church buildings *temples*.

46. Didier Poton and Patrick Cabanel, *Les protestants français du XVIe au XXe siècle* (Paris: Nathan, 1994), 38.

47. Solange Deyon, "La destruction des temples," in *Révocation de l'Édit de Nantes,* ed. Zuber and Theis, 242.

48. John Locke, *Travels in France 1675–1679, as Related in His Journals, Correspondence and Other Papers,* ed. John Lough (Cambridge: Cambridge University Press, 1953), 27–28.

49. Deyon, "Destruction des temples," 245–48; Labrousse, *Révocation,* 112–15.

50. Many of these *arrêts* can be found in Léon Pilatte, ed., *Édits, déclarations et arrests concernans la religion p[rétendue] réformée, 1662–1751* (Paris: Librairie Fischbacher & Cie, 1885).

51. Quoted in Lough, *France,* 254.

52. Bernard Dompnier, "En France," in *Histoire du christianisme: Des origines à nos jours,* gen. ed. J. M. Mayeur, C. and L. Pietri, A. Vauchez, and M. Vénard, vol. 9, *L'âge de raison (1620/30–1750),* ed. M. Venard (Paris: Desclée, 1997), 124.

53. Labrousse, *Révocation,* 121–22; Roger Mettam, "Louis XIV and the Persecution of Huguenots: The Role of the Ministers and Royal Officials," in *Huguenots in Britain and Their French Background, 1550–1800,* ed. Irene Scouloudi (Totowa, N.J.: Barnes & Noble Books, 1987), 209–10.

54. Daniel Ligou, *Le protestantisme en France de 1598 à 1715* (Paris: Sedes, 1968), 218.

55. Arie Theodorius van Deursen, *Professions et métiers interdits: Un aspect de l'histoire de la révocation de l'Édit de Nantes* (Groningen: J. B. Wolters, 1960), 261. *Déclarations* were official compilations and reassertions of previous *arrêts.* Two déclarations were issued regarding the rights of the Huguenots in 1666 and 1669.

56. Locke, *Travels in France,* 15.

57. Ibid., 22–23.

58. Van Deursen, *Professions,* 118.

59. Labrousse, *Révocation,* 128–29.

60. Locke, *Travels in France,* 113.

61. Labrousse, *Révocation,* 122–23.

62. Ibid., 124.

63. Quoted in Lough, *France,* 256.

64. Labrousse, *Révocation,* 124.

65. Ligou, *Protestantisme,* 223. See in the case of Poitou, Keith P. Luria, "Cemeteries, Religious Difference, and the Creation of Cultural Boundaries in Seventeenth-Century French Communities," in *Memory and Identity,* ed. Van Ruymbeke and Sparks, 58–72.

66. Quoted in Lough, *France,* 256.

67. Henry Phillips, *Church and Culture in Seventeenth-Century France* (Cambridge: Cambridge University Press, 1997), 212.

68. Garrisson, *L'homme protestant,* 166.

69. Dompnier, *Venin de l'hérésie,* 31; Jean-Paul Pittion, "Les académies réformées de l'Édit de Nantes à la révocation," in *Révocation de l'Édit de Nantes,* ed. Zuber and Theis, 191. Huguenot *académies* were not called *universités* because they could not legally offer curricula in law and medicine. Jean-Robert Armogathe, *Croire en la liberté: L'Église catholique et la révocation de l'Édit de Nantes* (Paris: O.E.I.L., 1985), 25.

70. Garrisson, *L'homme protestant,* 167; Pittion, "Académies réformées," 190. The five académies, with dates of foundation, were those of Saumur (1598) in the center west, Sedan (1602)

254 Notes to pages 14–15

in the northeast, Nîmes (1562) and Montauban (1598) in the southwest, and Die (1604) in the southeast. The académie of Montpellier, Languedoc (1596), and Orthez, Béarn (1566), were closed in 1617 and 1620, respectively. There was also an académie in the Orange-Nassau principality of Orange (founded in 1573). See Karin Maag, "The Huguenot Academies: Preparing for an Uncertain Future," in *Society and Culture,* ed. Mentzer and Spicer, 139n1, 155–56.

71. Van Deursen, *Professions,* 40.

72. Labrousse, *Révocation,* 129; Van Deursen, *Professions,* 42.

73. Dompnier, *Venin de l'hérésie,* 159.

74. Ligou, *Protestantisme,* 217; Quéniart, *Révocation,* 109.

75. Louis XIV, *Memoirs,* 56.

76. Ibid., 56–57.

77. Dompnier, *Venin de l'hérésie,* 217.

78. Ibid., 199–201. For an illustrative description of this type of missionary endeavor and of the methods used by the Catholic clergy to obtain Huguenot conversions, see Keith P. Luria's essay on the 1617 Capuchin mission in Poitou, "Rituals of Conversion: Catholics and Protestants in Seventeenth-Century Poitou," in *Culture and Identity in Early Modern Europe (1500–1800),* ed. Barbara B. Diefendorf and Carla Hesse (Ann Arbor: University of Michigan Press, 1993), 65–81.

79. Andrew Lossky, *Louis XIV and the French Monarchy* (New Brunswick, N.J.: Rutgers University Press, 1994), 203; Dompnier, *Venin de l'hérésie,* 219.

80. The Catholic clergy assimilated the Huguenots to the fourth-century Christian sectarians known as the Donatists and justified all the means, including physical violence, used to bring them back to Catholicism by quoting Saint Augustine. Letters by Saint Augustine justifying the use of violence against the Donatists and drawing a parallel between them and the Huguenots were published in France in 1685 under the title *Conformité de la conduite de l'Église de France, pour ramener les protestants, avec celle de l'Église d'Afrique pour ramener les Donatistes à l'Église catholique* (Conformity between the Policy of the Church of France to Bring Back the Huguenots and That of the Church of Africa to Bring Back the Donatists to the Catholic Church). See Labrousse, "Calvinism in France, 1598–1685," 306; Labrousse, *Révocation,* 88–90; Dompnier, "En France," 126; Émile G. Léonard, *Histoire générale du protestantisme,* 3 vols. (Paris: Presses Universitaires de France, 1961), 2:369; Barbara de Negroni, *Intolérances: Catholiques et protestants en France, 1560–1787* (Paris: Hachette, 1996), 86–87.

81. Francine Miot-Duclouzeaux, "La révocation de l'Édit de Nantes et les protestants jusqu'à l'Édit de Tolérance (1787) en Aunis et Saintonge" (Ph.D., Écoles des Chartes, 1964), 67.

82. Dompnier, *Venin de l'hérésie,* 222.

83. Quéniart, *Révocation,* 113. The Waldensians or Vaudois, who occupied villages in the Rhône Valley, Provence, and Dauphiny, were members of a Christian sect founded in the late twelfth century by a merchant from Lyon named Pierre Vaudès (Waldo). Although many of them became Calvinists in the second half of the sixteenth century, strictly speaking they were not Huguenots. See Gabriel Audisio, "Vaudois," in *Dictionnaire de l'Ancien Régime,* ed. Bély, 1245–46; Audisio, "Une mutation: Les Vaudois passent à la réforme (1530–1532)," *BSHPF* 126 (1980): 153–65.

84. Lossky, *Louis XIV,* 203–4; Gilles Deregnaucourt and Didier Poton, *La vie religieuse en France aux XVIe, XVIIe, XVIIIe siècles* (Paris: Ophrys, 1994), 153; Léonard, *Histoire,* 2:357–58.

85. Janine Garrisson, *L'Édit de Nantes et sa révocation: Histoire d'une intolérance* (Paris: Éditions du Seuil, 1985), 184–85.

86. "Sa volonté était une loi d'un bout de l'Europe à l'autre" (Voltaire, *Le siècle de Louis XIV,* 2 vols. [1751; repr., Paris: Garnier-Flammarion, 1966], 1:166).

87. Thomas Munck, *Seventeenth-Century Europe: State, Conflict and the Social Order in Europe 1598–1700* (New York: St. Martin's Press, 1990), 374–75.

88. Quéniart, *Révocation,* 117.

89. The term *dragonnade* is derived from the word *dragon,* which referred to a type of seventeenth-century musket and to the soldier who was armed with it.

90. Léonard, *Histoire,* 2:365.

91. The chambre de l'Edit in Paris and the one in Rouen had been abolished in 1669. A decade later it was the turn of those of Toulouse, Bordeaux, and Grenoble. Labrousse, *Révocation,* 153.

92. *Colloques* or *classes* were the biannual meetings of delegates from close-by congregations, from ten to twenty according to the local density of the Huguenot population. After 1657 they could only meet once a year following the meeting of provincial synods. Poton and Cabanel, *Protestants français,* 48–49; Labrousse, *Révocation,* 126, 153.

93. Quéniart, *Révocation,* 119.

94. "Procès-verbal de la démolition du temple de Nanteuil," *BSHPF* 46 (1897): 671–72.

95. Van Deursen, *Professions,* 154–55.

96. Warren C. Scoville, *The Persecution of Huguenots and French Economic Development, 1680–1720* (Berkeley: University of California Press, 1960), 50–51.

97. Van Deursen, *Professions,* 364–65; Scoville, *Persecution of Huguenots,* 49.

98. Sedan closed in 1681, Die in 1684, and Montauban and Saumur in 1685 (Maag, "Huguenot Academies," 155–56).

99. Ligou, *Protestantisme,* 219–22; Garrisson, *L'Édit de Nantes* (1985), 194.

100. Jaques Fontaine, *Memoirs of the Reverend Jaques Fontaine, 1658–1728,* ed. Dianne W. Ressinger (London: The Huguenot Society of Ireland and Great Britain, 1992), 37.

101. AN, série TT, folder 262, pièce 1069.

102. Alexandre Crottet, *Histoire des églises réformées de Pons, Gémozac et Mortagne, en Saintonge, précédée d'une notice sur l'établissement de la réforme dans cette province, l'Aunis et l'Angoumois* (Bordeaux: A. Castillon, 1841), 133–34.

103. On this two-way conversion phenomenon, see Élisabeth Labrousse, "La conversion dans les deux sens," in her *Conscience et conviction,* 96–107.

104. Louis Pérouas, *Le diocèse de La Rochelle de 1648 à 1724: Étude de sociologie pastorale* (Paris: S.E.V.P.E.N, 1964), 305.

105. Dompnier, *Venin de l'hérésie,* 242.

106. Ligou, *Protestantisme,* 221–22; Labrousse, *Révocation,* 153.

107. Labrousse, *Révocation,* 155.

108. Ibid., 157–58.

109. Ligou, *Protestantisme,* 223 (quotation).

110. Labrousse, *Révocation,* 158.

111. Fontaine, *Memoirs,* 113.

112. Ligou, *Protestantisme,* 231. In his study of Huguenot Poitou, Yves Krumenacker, using the term "*pré-dragonnades,*" mentions examples of troops being used to obtain abjurations before the actual *dragonnade* of 1681. See Yves Krumenacker, *Les protestants du Poitou au XVIIIe siècle (1681–1789)* (Paris: Honoré Champion, 1998), 66, 66n17.

113. Ibid., 231; Nassiet, *France,* 65–69.

114. Yves Krumenacker, "Les dragonnades du Poitou: leur écho dans les mémoires," *BSHPF* 131 (1985): 405; Krumenacker, *Protestants du Poitou,* 79.

115. Labrousse, *Révocation,* 160–61; Krumenacker, *Protestants du Poitou,* 84–85.

116. "Judith Giton's letter" (undated, original), Manigault Family Papers, 11/275/3, fol. 1, South Carolina Historical Society, Charleston.

117. Poton and Cabanel, *Protestants français,* 41–42.

118. Fontaine, *Memoirs,* 114.

119. "Ils [les dragons] demandaient des choses impossibles à trouver dans toute la paroisse" (Jean Migault, *Journal de Jean Migault ou malheurs d'une famille protestante du Poitou victime de la révocation de l'Édit de Nantes [1682–1689],* ed. Yves Krumenacker [Paris: Les Éditions de Paris, 1995], 30). For an English translation of this account, see *Jean Migault; or the Trials of a French Protestant Family during the Period of the Revocation of the Edict of Nantes,* trans. and ed. William Anderson (Edinburgh: Johnstone and Hunter, 1852).

120. Locke, *Travels in France,* 229–30.

121. "Monstre moitié prêtre et moitié dragon." The pun is based on the fact that in French the words "dragoon" and "dragon" are the same (quoted in de Negroni, *Intolérances,* 107).

122. Krumenacker, "Dragonnades du Poitou," 411.

123. Labrousse, *Révocation,* 159–60.

124. Although one account mentions two *dragons* and the other four, it is possible that Thomas Bureau's mother was the Niort bookseller's wife Locke met.

125. "Copie d'une lettre escrite par le Sr. Thomas Bureau de Niort en Poitou le 30 aoust 1685 à son frère marchand libraire à Londres," Bodleian Library, Oxford, Rawlinson Papers, C 984, fol. 62–63. A transcription of this letter can be found in C. E. Lart, ed., "Roads of Destiny: The Dragonnades of 1685 from Unpublished Letters and Manuscripts," *HSP* 15 (1933–37): 256–58. The letter does not say if the mother and the daughter eventually abjured, but Thomas (and probably his mother and sister) managed to escape to London where he became a prosperous merchant and early investor in the Bank of England. Incidentally, Thomas Bureau was the maternal granduncle (grandfather's brother) of Peter Faneuil, the Huguenot of Boston fame. See Lart, "Roads of Destiny," 258; and J. F. Bosher, "Huguenot Merchants and the Protestant International in the Seventeenth Century," *William and Mary Quarterly* 52 (1995): 90–91.

126. Poton and Cabanel, *Protestants français,* 42; Léonard, *Histoire,* 1:371.

127. Philippe Joutard, "1685, une fin et une nouvelle chance pour le protestantisme français," in *Le refuge huguenot,* ed. Michèle Magdelaine and Rudolf von Thadden (Paris: Armand Colin, 1985), 18. A longer English version of this essay, entitled "The Revocation of the Edict of Nantes: End or Renewal of French Protestantism," can be found in *International Calvinism,* ed. Prestwich, 339–68.

128. Krumenacker, *Protestants du Poitou,* 82.

129. Miot-Duclouzeaux, "Révocation," 53.

130. Krumenacker, "Les dragonnades du Poitou," 412. For a discussion on the controversial validity of Huguenot conversions in seventeenth-century France and on the political dimension that many of them carried, see Keith P. Luria, "The Politics of Protestant Conversion to Catholicism in Seventeenth-Century France," in *Conversion to Modernities: The Globalization of Christianity,* ed. Peter van der Veer (New York: Routledge, 1996), 23–46.

131. A Manigault also appeared twice before the Threadneedle Street Church consistory in January and February 1686 before being authorized to make his reconnaissance publicly on February 24, 1686. However, his first name was not recorded, making it impossible to know if it was Pierre or Gabriel. See "Livre des Actes du Consistoire, 1679–1692," ms. 7, Archives of the French Protestant Church of London (January 1685 [P. Bertrand]), (September 12, 1686 [B. Marion, J. & M. Baluet, and M. Nicolas]), (January 14, February 17 and 24, 1686 [Manigault]). Needless to say, it was imperative for refugees who planned to relocate in America to do their

reconnaissances before leaving as they could not be assured of finding a Huguenot church with a consistory wherever they settled in the colonies. Some used this argument to convince the London elders to let them do their reconnaissances speedily, as illustrated by the case of one Jean Sénécal from Dieppe, Normandy, whom the consistory expressly let do his reconnaissance because he was leaving the following day "for the Indies." ("On [le consistoire] a résolu de l'admettre en particulier parce qu'il part demain pour aller aux Indes"). Before the Revocation, consistories of churches outside of France requested refugees to present certificates from their churches of origins, called *témoignage*, instead of reconnaissances. Threadneedle Street Church *témoignage* records also contain names of Carolina Huguenots, among them Jean Aunant (September 1681), Isaac Bacot (June 29, 1684), Daniel Huger (October 21, 1681), and Jacques LeSerrurier (October 18, 1682). See William Minet and Suzanne Minet, eds., *Témoignage de l'Église de Threadneedle Street (1669–1789)*, Huguenot Society of London Quarto Publications, vol. 21 (London: Spottiswoods & Co., 1909), 8, 9, 143, 173.

132. Ligou, *Le Protestantisme en France*, 242.

133. Ibid., 243.

134. In addition to the different works cited infra, see the short and clear *synthèse* on the causes of the Revocation: Daniel Ligou, "Pourquoi la révocation de l'Édit de Nantes?," in *Un siècle et demi d'histoire protestante: Théodore de Bèze et les protestants sujets du roi*, ed. Léo Hamon (Paris: Éditions de la Maison des Sciences de l'Homme, 1989), 30–51. A recent historiographical interpretation of the Revocation can be found in Myriam Yardeni, "Un événement pivot: La révocation de l'Édit de Nantes," in *L'État Classique: Regards sur la pensée politique de la France dans le second XVIIe siècle*, ed. Henri Méchoulan and Joël Cornette (Paris: J. Vrin, 1996), 305–15.

135. Transcriptions of the Edict of Fontainebleau can be found in French in Catherine Bergeal and Antoine Durrleman, eds., *Protestantisme et libertés en France au 17e siècle de l'Édit de Nantes à sa révocation 1598–1685* (Carrières-sous-Poissy, France: La Cause, 1985), 143–48; and in English in Golden, *Huguenot Connection*, app. 2:135–39 (quotation, 136). For an analysis of this preamble, see Jean Carbonnier, "Sociologie et psychologie juridiques de l'Édit de Révocation," in *Révocation de l'Édit de Nantes*, ed. Zuber and Theis, 37–41.

136. As Raymond Mentzer aptly points out, "perpetuity was not 'éternité' in the minds of royal jurists and the Catholic faithful" (Mentzer, "Edict of Nantes," 99n6). For an extensive discussion of the contemporary and historiographic misconstruction of the "perpetual and irrevocable" character of the Edict of Nantes, see Mario Turchetti, "Une question mal posée: La qualification de 'perpétuel et irrévocable' appliquée à l'Édit de Nantes (1598)," *BSHPF* 139 (1993): 41–78.

137. Labrousse, *Révocation*, 179.

138. Ibid., 177.

139. Pierre Chaunu, "La décision royale(?): Un système de la révocation," in *Révocation de l'Édit de Nantes*, ed. Zuber and Theis, 19.

140. Emmanuel Le Roy Ladurie, "Glorious Revolution, Shameful Revocation," afterword in Bernard Cottret, *The Huguenots in England: Immigration and Settlement, c. 1550–1700* (Cambridge: Cambridge University Press, 1991), 286.

141. Cottret, *1598*, 318.

142. Joutard, "1685," 18.

143. Maréchal de Vauban, *Mémoire pour le rappel des huguenots*, ed. Philippe Vassaux (1689; repr., Carrières-sous-Poissy, France: La Cause, 1998), 14, 16.

144. Labrousse, *Révocation*, 179.

145. On the Assemblies of the Clergy and the Huguenot question from the Wars of Religion to the Revocation, see Michel Peronnet, "Les assemblées du Clergé de France et la révocation des édits de religion (1560–1685)," *BSHPF* 131 (1985): 453–79.

146. *Avertissement pastoral de l'Église gallicane assemblée à Paris . . . à ceux de la religion préten-due réformée, pour les porter à se convertir et se réconcilier avec l'Église.*

147. Garrisson, *L'Édit de Nantes* (1985), 190–91; Élisabeth Labrousse, "Understanding the Revocation of the Edict of Nantes from the Perspective of the French Court," in *Huguenot Connection,* ed. Golden, 56–57.

148. Quoted in Labrousse, *Révocation,* 163.

149. Munck, *Seventeenth-Century Europe,* 374–76; Golden, *Huguenot Connection,* 18–19; Lossky, *Louis XIV,* 217–19; Ligou, *Protestantisme,* 245–46.

150. On the stormy relation between Louis XIV and Innocent XI, see Lossky, *Louis XIV,* 205–17.

151. Garrisson, *L'Édit de Nantes* (1985), 186–87; Scoville, *Persecution of Huguenots,* 30.

152. Quoted in Scoville, *Persecution of Huguenots,* 33.

153. The expression is from Ligou, *Protestantisme,* 245.

154. René Pillorget and Suzanne Pillorget, *France Baroque, France Classique, 1589–1715,* 2 vols. (Paris: Robert Laffont, 1995), 1:745–47.

155. Emmanuel Le Roy Ladurie, foreword to *Terre d'exil: L'Angleterre et ses réfugiés français et Wallons, 1550–1700,* by Bernard Cottret (Paris: Aubier, 1985), 28. Michel Le Tellier even con-tributed to the writing of the Edict of Fontainebleau.

156. Scoville, *Persecution of Huguenots,* 33.

157. Chaunu, "Décision royale(?)," 14–15; Garrisson, *L'Édit de Nantes* (1985), 187–88. See also Stanis Perez, ed., *Journal de santé de Louis XIV* (Paris: Jérôme Millon, 2004), "Remarques pour l'année 1685," 225–30. Any influence from Mme de Maintenon on the decision to revoke the Edict of Nantes is to be excluded as she did not play a political role before 1690 (Chaunu, "Décision royale[?]," 15).

158. Le Roy Ladurie, "Glorious Revolution," 298.

159. For a comparative study of different religious peace settlements, including the Edict of Nantes, see Olivier Christin, "L'Europe des paix de religion: Semblants et faux-semblants," in *Coexister dans l'intolérance,* ed. Grandjean and Roussel, 489–505.

160. Carbonnier, "Sociologie et psychologie," 53.

161. Chaunu, "Décision royale(?)," 25.

162. Le Roy Ladurie, "Glorious Revolution," 299–301; Bernard Cottret, "Révocation et pro-dromes de la tolérance: Le parallèle des protestants français et des catholiques d'Angleterre," *BSHPF* 126 (1980): 559–66.

163. Carbonnier, "Sociologie et psychologie," 53; Chaunu, "Décision royale(?)," 24.

164. Labrousse, *Révocation,* 182, 185–86.

165. Labrousse, "Calvinism in France, 1598–1685," 311.

166. Élisabeth Labrousse, "Les protestants," in *Histoire de la France religieuse,* gen. ed. Jacques Le Goff and René Rémond, vol. 2, *Du christianisme flamboyant à l'aube des Lumières (xive–xviiie siècles),* ed. François Lebrun (Paris: Seuil, 1988), 478–79.

167. Phillips, *Church and Culture,* 225.

2. The Carolina Proprietors and the Recruitment of Huguenots

Marvell quoted in Warren L. Chernaik, *The Poet's Time: Politics and Religion in the Work of Andrew Marvell* (Cambridge: Cambridge University Press, 1983), 91; second epigraph from Christopher Columbus's "Letter on the Third Voyage," in *Four Voyages to the New World: Letters and Selected Documents*, trans. and ed. R. H. Major, bilingual ed. (New York: Corinth Books, 1961), 136–37.

1. Christopher Hill, *The Century of Revolution 1603–1714* (1961; New York: W. W. Norton & Company, 1966), 155–59, 209–13.

2. On the historiographical debate regarding the significance of the Restoration in British imperial history, see Robert M. Bliss, *Revolution and Empire: English Politics and the American Colonies in the Seventeenth Century* (Manchester: Manchester University Press, 1990), intro.

3. Anthony McFarlane, *The British in the Americas, 1480–1815* (New York: Longman, 1994), 195–97.

4. Michael Kammen, *Empire and Interest: The American Colonies and the Politics of Mercantilism* (Philadelphia: J. B. Lippincott Company, 1970), 22–25; Nuala Zahedieh, "Overseas Expansion and Trade in the Seventeenth Century," in *Oxford History of the British Empire*, ed. Roger, vol. 1, *Origins of Empire*, ed. Canny, 405–6.

5. J. M. Sosin, *English America and the Restoration Monarchy of Charles II: Transatlantic Politics, Commerce, and Kinship* (Lincoln: University of Nebraska Press, 1980), 10–11.

6. K. G. Davies, *The North Atlantic World in the Seventeenth Century* (Minneapolis: University of Minnesota Press, 1974), 313. For a comparative Dutch/English perspective, see Niels Steensgaard, "The Growth and Composition of Long-Distance Trade of England and the Dutch Republic before 1750," in *The Rise of Merchant Empires: Long-Distance Trade in the Early Modern World, 1350–1750*, ed. James D. Tracy (1990; Cambridge: Cambridge University Press, 1995), 102–52 (*Trade with America*, 131–45).

7. Zahedieh, "Overseas Expansion," 399; Geoffrey Holmes, *The Making of a Great Power: Late Stuart and Early Georgian Britain, 1660–1722* (New York: Longman, 1993), 445.

8. Zahedieh, "Overseas Expansion," 407; Davies, *North Atlantic*, 314–15; Holmes, *Making of a Great Power*, 61 (quote).

9. In the field of colonial administration as well as in domestic political history, recent historiography tends to interpret the Restoration no longer as an abrupt change of policy but as an intensification of previous trends. See, for example, Michael J. Braddick, "The English Government, War, Trade, and Settlement, 1625–1688," in *Oxford History of the British Empire*, ed. Roger, vol. 1., *Origins of Empire*, ed. Canny, 298–301.

10. Ian K. Steele, *Politics of Colonial Policy: The Board of Trade in Colonial Administration, 1696–1720* (Oxford: Clarendon Press, 1968), 4–5 (quote, 5); R. C. Simmons, *The American Colonies: From Settlement to Independence* (1976; New York: W. W. Norton & Company, 1981), 54–55; Sosin, *English America*, 39–45.

11. Holmes, *Making of a Great Power*, 103.

12. Robert M. Weir, *Colonial South Carolina: A History* (Millwood, N.Y.: KTO Press, 1983), 49–50; Amy T. Bushnell, *Situado and Sabana: Spain's Support System for the Presidio and Mission Provinces of Florida* (Athens: University of Georgia Press, 1994), 135 (quote). Charles II's two colonial charters to the Carolina proprietors are similar in the essentials. The 1665 charter was issued primarily to meet the legal need to regrant Carolina after claims to the territory by Sir Robert Heath's heirs had been invalidated and to satisfy the proprietors' wish to extend the boundaries of the colony to include all of Albemarle Sound where Virginians had started to settle. See Parker, *North Carolina Charters*, 90; M. Eugene Sirmans, *South Carolina: A Political History, 1663–1763* (Chapel Hill: University of North Carolina Press, 1966), 5; Daniel W. Fagg, "Carolina, 1663–1683: The Founding of a Proprietary" (Ph.D. diss., Emory University, 1970), 84–86.

13. This treaty, called the American Treaty and signed two years after Spain recognized the independence of Portugal due to English pressure, contained a clause asserting that England had the right to "hold and possess forever" all lands it occupied, including Jamaica. J. Leitch Wright Jr., *Anglo-Spanish Rivalry in North America* (Athens: University of Georgia Press, 1971), 52; Wright, "Spanish Reaction to Carolina," *North Carolina Historical Review* 41 (1964): 464–76; Verner W. Crane, *The Southern Frontier, 1670–1732* (Ann Arbor: University of Michigan Press, 1956), 8–9.

14. Holmes, *Making of a Great Power,* App. D:415–21; Fagg, "Carolina, 1663–1683," 7–28; Paul D. Nelson, "Berkeley, William," in *American National Biography,* ed. Garraty and Carnes, 2:650–51; William S. Powell, *The Proprietors of Carolina* (1963; Raleigh, N.C.: State Department of Archives and History, 1968), 12–49. Colleton, the least ranked of the original proprietors, has traditionally been described as the prime mover in this collective enterprise, but Monck's and Clarendon's stature and influence were certainly decisive in obtaining the Carolina grant. See Sirmans, *South Carolina,* 4; Weir, *Colonial South Carolina,* 49. For a nuanced view on Colleton's role, see Charles H. Lesser, *South Carolina Begins: The Records of a Proprietary Colony, 1663–1721* (Columbia: South Carolina Department of Archives and History, 1995), 3–5; Louis H. Roper, *Conceiving Carolina: Proprietors, Planters, and Plots, 1662–1729* (New York: Palgrave, 2004), 15–17.

15. Lesser, *South Carolina Begins,* 2–9, 81n9. 15–17.

16. Wesley F. Craven, *The Southern Colonies in the Seventeenth Century, 1607–1689* (Baton Rouge: Louisiana State University Press, 1949), 322n20.

17. Mark Kishlansky, *A Monarchy Transformed: Britain 1603–1714* (London: Penguin Books Ltd, 1996), 242 (quote); Lesser, *South Carolina Begins,* 2–6; Fagg, "Carolina, 1663–1683," 8–12.

18. Hugh T. Lefler and William S. Powell, *Colonial North Carolina: A History* (New York: Charles Scribner's Sons, 1973), 38–46; Craven, *Southern Colonies,* 330–33; Sosin, *English America,* 125–30.

19. Sirmans, *South Carolina,* 6; Roper, *Conceiving Carolina,* 19–20.

20. On the 1669–70 founding fleet, see Joseph I. Waring, *The First Voyage and Settlement at Charles Town, 1670–1680,* Tricentennial Booklet 4 (Columbia: University of South Carolina Press, 1970), 22–57.

21. Sir Peter Colleton inherited the share of his father, Sir John, in 1668. See J. E. Buchanan, "The Colleton Family and the Early History of South Carolina and Barbados" (Ph.D. thesis, University of Edinburgh, 1989), 91; Lesser, *South Carolina Begins,* 15, 23.

22. Sirmans, *South Carolina,* 7.

23. See infra prologue.

24. Joyce O. Appleby, *Economic Thought and Ideology in Seventeenth-Century England* (Princeton: Princeton University Press, 1978), 40 (quote); John J. McCusker and Russell R. Menard, *The Economy of British America, 1607–1789* (Chapel Hill: University of North Carolina Press, 1985), 35n1; Peter A. Coclanis, *The Shadow of a Dream: Economic Life and Death in the South Carolina Low Country 1670–1920* (Oxford: Oxford University Press, 1989), 15–20; D. C. Coleman, "Mercantilism Revisited," *Historical Journal* 23 (1980): 773–91; Pierre Deyon, "Mercantilisme," in *Dictionnaire de l'Ancien Régime,* ed. Bély, 816–17; Deyon, "Théorie et Pratique du Mercantilisme," in *Histoire économique et sociale du monde,* 6 vols., gen. ed. Pierre Léon, vol. 2, *Les hésitations de la croissance 1580–1740,* ed. Pierre Deyon et al. (Paris: Armand Collin, 1977), 197–218; Jean-Claude Perrot, "Les économistes, les philosophes et la population," in *Histoire de la population française,* vol. 2, *De la Renaissance à 1789,* ed. Jacques Dupâquier (1988; Paris: Presses Universitaires de France, 1995), 499–551. For a comparison between English and French mercantilist policies, see

Roger Dehem, *Histoire de la pensée économique des mercantilistes à Keynes* (Quebec: Les Presses Universitaires de l'Université de Laval, 1984), 13–43.

25. Daniel Statt, *Foreigners and Englishmen: The Controversy over Immigration and Population, 1660–1760* (Newark: University of Delaware Press, 1995), 44.

26. Appleby, *Economic Thought,* 158–59.

27. Kammen, *Empire and Interest,* 4–5.

28. John J. McCusker, "British Mercantilist Policies and the American Colonies," in *The Cambridge Economic History of the United States,* vol. 1, *The Colonial Era,* ed. Stanley L. Engerman and Robert E. Gallman (Cambridge: Cambridge University Press, 1996), 337–62; Sosin, *English America,* 53–56. See also Carole Shammas, "English Commercial Development and American Colonization, 1560–1620," in which Shammas describes what she calls "the commercializing of colonization" in the first half of the seventeenth century (in K. R. Andrews, N. P. Canny, and P. E. H. Hair, eds., *The Westward Enterprise: English Activities in Ireland, the Atlantic, and America, 1480–1650* [Liverpool: Liverpool University Press, 1978], 173).

29. Appleby, *Economic Thought,* 133 (first quote); Statt, *Foreigners and Englishmen,* 48 (second quote).

30. Statt, *Foreigners and Englishmen,* 45.

31. Quoted in ibid., 48.

32. Ibid., 75, 81; Mildred Campbell, "'Of People Either Too Few or Too Many': The Conflict of Opinion on Population and Its Relation to Emigration," in *Conflict in Stuart England: Essays in Honour of Wallace Notestein,* ed. William A. Aiken and Basil D. Henning (1960; London: Archon Books, 1970), 185–86.

33. Robert A. Houston, Cormac O Gráda, Roger Schofield, and Tony Wrigley, "Les îles Britanniques," in *Histoire des populations de l'Europe,* ed. Jean-Pierre Bardet and Jacques Dupâquier (Paris: Fayard, 1997), 1:370.

34. Statt, *Foreigners and Englishmen,* 75.

35. Ibid., 57–58, 70; Caroline Robbins, "A Note on General Naturalization under the Later Stuarts and a Speech in the House of Commons on the Subject in 1664," *Journal of Modern History* 24 (1962): 168–77.

36. Campbell, "Of People," 172–85; Appleby, *Economic Thought,* 135–36.

37. Quoted in Statt, *Foreigners and Englishmen,* 77. This fear of peopling the colonies at the expense of the mother country's demographics was not limited to England but was even prevalent in France, where overseas migration was much smaller. In a letter addressed to Colbert in 1666, Jean Talon, intendant in Quebec, wrote that "it would not be wise to depeople the kingdom to people Canada," to which Colbert assentingly answered that "there are not enough supernumenary in the old France to people the New" (quoted in Peter N. Moogk, "Reluctant Exiles: Emigrants from France in Canada before 1760," *William and Mary Quarterly* 46 [1989]: 468n14). As opposed to England, however, in the second half of the seventeenth century French populationist policies were primarily motivated by military rather than economic considerations (Statt, *Foreigners and Englishmen,* 49–51; Perrot, "Économistes," 502–3).

38. Kishlansky, *Monarchy Transformed,* 251.

39. Ibid., 252.

40. John Miller, *Popery and Politics in England 1660–1688* (Cambridge: Cambridge University Press, 1973), 11; Barry Coward, *The Stuart Age: England, 1603–1714* (London: Longman, 1994), 314–15.

41. Holmes, *Making of a Great Power,* 121. English Catholics were called "recusant" because they "recused" the English nation, its king, and its faith and refused to attend the services of the

Church of England. On the Elizabethan Catholics and the origins of recusancy, see Peter Holmes, *Resistance and Compromise: The Political Thought of the Elizabethan Catholics* (Cambridge: Cambridge University Press, 1982), 81–89.

42.   On the international economic and political context, especially the Franco-Anglo-Dutch rivalry and how it influenced English domestic issues, see J. R. Jones, *Britain and Europe in the Seventeenth Century* (New York: W. W. Norton & Company, 1966), chaps. 4–7.

43.   Steven C. A. Pincus, *Protestantism and Patriotism: Ideologies and the Making of English Foreign Policy, 1650–1668* (Cambridge: Cambridge University Press, 1996), 256–60. See also his "Republicanism, Absolutism and Universal Monarchy: English Popular Sentiment during the Third Dutch War," in *Culture and Society in the Stuart Restoration: Literature, Drama, History,* ed. Gerald Maclean (Cambridge: Cambridge University Press, 1995), 241–66, esp. 252–58; and his "From Butterboxes to Wooden Shoes: The Shift in English Popular Sentiment from Anti-Dutch to Anti-French in the 1670s," *Historical Journal* 38 (1995): 333–61, in which he also argues that it is the fear of France that sharpened English anti-Catholicism and not vice versa.

44.   Quoted in Pincus, *Protestantism and Patriotism,* 433. Marvell's quote, taken from *An Account of the Growth of Popery,* is in Chernaik, *Poet's Time,* 91.

45.   What John Bosher has called "the Franco-Catholic danger" ("The Franco-Catholic Danger, 1660–1715," in John F. Bosher, *Business and Religion in the Age of New France, 1600–1760: Twenty-Two Studies* [Toronto: Canadian Scholars' Press, 1994], 257–90).

46.   Kishlansky, *Monarchy Transformed,* 251.

47.   Ibid., 243.

48.   The quotation is from the text of a parliamentary resolution moved in 1678 (quoted in Holmes, *Making of a Great Power,* 123).

49.   J. R. Jones, *The First Whigs: The Politics of the Exclusion Crisis 1678–1683,* rev. ed. (London: Oxford University Press, 1970), 20–33; Miller, *Popery and Politics,* 169–82.

50.   Andrew Marvell, *An Account of the Growth of Popery and Arbitrary Government in England: More Particularly from the Long* Prorogation, *of* November *1675, Ending the 15th of* February, *1676, till the Last Meeting of* Parliament, *the 16th of* July *1677* (Amsterdam: [s.n.], 1677), 53. On the possible collective authorship of *An Account of the Growth of Popery,* which is compared to a "Shaftesburian pamphlet," and Marvell's Whig leanings and political activism through his satiric prose and poetic work in the 1660s and 1670s, see Chernaik, *Poet's Time,* 63–101.

51.   Shaftesbury's political career can be best followed in Timothy Eustace, "Anthony Ashley Cooper, Earl of Shaftesbury," in *Statesmen and Politicians of the Stuart Age,* ed. Timothy Eustace (New York: St. Martin's Press, 1985), 179–200. For a detailed biography, see K. H. D. Haley, *The First Earl of Shaftesbury* (Oxford: Clarendon Press, 1968). For Shaftesbury's leadership of the Whig Party, see Jones, *First Whigs.*

52.   Pincus, "Republicanism," 255–56 (Pincus's quote, 255); Pincus, "From Butterboxes to Wooden Shoes," 344–51.

53.   Quoted in Richard Ashcraft, *Revolutionary Politics and Locke's Two Treatises of Government* (Princeton: Princeton University Press, 1986), 114. Edward Cooke, another Whig pamphleteer, also claimed that the "advancement of the Protestant religion [and] the welfare of this kingdom doth chiefly depend" on Shaftesbury (Melinda S. Zook, *Radical Whigs and Conspiratorial Politics in Late Stuart England* [University Park: Pennsylvania State University Press, 1999], 82–83). In 1705 Anthony Ashley Cooper, third Earl of Shaftesbury, wrote that his "Grandfather's Aversion & irreconcileable Hatred to Popery, was (as Phanaticisme) confessd by his greatest Enemyes to be his Master-Passion" (Rex A. Barrell, ed., *Anthony Ashley Cooper, Earl of*

Shaftesbury [1671–1713] and "Le Refuge Français"-Correspondence [Lewiston, N.Y.: The Edwin Mellen Press, 1989], 89).

54. Quoted in Haley, *First Earl of Shaftesbury,* 502.

55. Whig propagandists however were not alone in denouncing France's oppressive regime, which is shown by the publication of *Les soupirs de la France esclave qui aspire après la liberté* (Amsterdam, 1689–90), erroneously attributed to the Huguenot exile Pierre Jurieu. See Élisabeth Labrousse, "The Political Ideas of the Huguenot Diaspora (Bayle and Jurieu)," in *Church, State, and Society under the Bourbon Kings,* ed. Richard M. Golden (Lawrence, Kans.: Coronado Press, 1982), 253.

56. Quoted in Pincus, "Republicanism," 259.

57. *Popery and Tyranny: or the Present State of France, in Relation to Its Government, Trade, Manners of the People, and Nature of the Country; As it was sent in a Letter from an English Gentleman Abroad to His Friend in England; Wherein may be seen the Tyranny the Subjects of France are under Being Enslav'd by the Two Greatest Enemies to Reason, as well as to Christian or Human Liberty, I mean Popery and Arbitrary Power* (London, 1679).

58. *True Protestant Mercury,* July 1681. In the April issue, for example, an article described how Catholics burned Huguenot Bibles in Grenoble, Dauphiny.

59. Haley, *First Earl of Shaftesbury,* 227. Hill, quite accurately, pointed out that Shaftesbury "personified the continuity" between Cromwellian and Stuart imperial policies (Hill, *Century of Revolution,* 209).

60. Ashcraft, *Revolutionary Politics,* 115.

61. Quoted in Campbell, "Of People," 190. In the same memorial, Shaftesbury recognized that "the strength and glory of your Majesty and the wealth of your kingdoms depend not so much on anything as in the multitude of your subjects."

62. Statt, *Foreigners and Englishmen,* 78, 99–100.

63. Haley, *First Earl of Shaftesbury,* 227–28; Steele, *Politics,* 4–5; E. E. Rich, "The First Earl of Shaftesbury's Colonial Policy," *Transactions of the Royal Historical Society* 7 (1957): 47–70; Roper, *Conceiving Carolina,* 25–26.

64. Wood, *Black Majority,* 34.

65. Richard S. Dunn, *Sugar and Slaves: The Rise of the Planter Class in the English West Indies, 1624–1713* (Chapel Hill: University of North Carolina Press, 1972), 87 (population estimates); Campbell, "Of People," 190 (quote).

66. Hilary McD Beckles, *A History of Barbados: From Amerindian Settlement to Nation-State* (Cambridge: Cambridge University Press, 1990), 21–27. On early Barbadian immigration to and influence on South Carolina, see Warren Allen and Henry Fraser, *The Barbados-Carolina Connection* (London: Macmillan, 1988); Richard Waterhouse, "England, the Caribbean, and the Settlement of Carolina," *Journal of American Studies* 9 (1975): 259–81; Richard S. Dunn, "The English Sugar Islands and the Founding of South Carolina," *SCHM* 72 (1971): 81–93.

67. Jack P. Greene, "Colonial South Carolina and the Caribbean Connection," in *Colonial America: Essays in Politics and Social Development,* ed. Stanley N. Katz, John N. Murrin, and Douglas Greenberg (1983; New York: McGraw-Hill, 1993), 186; Peter F. Campbell, *Some Early Barbadian History* (St. Michael, Barbados: privately printed, 1993), 148–60. Richard Dunn, for example, estimated that out of the 593 planters who left Barbados in 1679, 96 settled in New England, 62 in Virginia, and 38 in South Carolina (Dunn, *Sugar and Slaves,* 11).

68. Sirmans, *South Carolina,* 35.

69. Converse D. Clowse, *Economic Beginnings in Colonial South Carolina, 1670–1730* (Columbia: University of South Carolina Press, 1971), 69, 73.

70. Weir, *Colonial South Carolina,* 62–65; Sirmans, *South Carolina,* 36, 41–43;

71. Louis H. Roper, "Kings of the Carolina Frontier: New Light on the 'Goose Creek Men,'" paper delivered at the Fifth Omohundro Institute of Early American History and Culture Conference, Austin, Tex., June 1999.

72. Lesser, *South Carolina Begins,* 56.

73. Ibid., 27, 56; Ashcraft, *Revolutionary Politics,* 114n143.

74. [Samuel Wilson], *An Account of the Province of Carolina in America: Together with an Abstract of the Patent, and Several other Necessary and Useful Particulars, to such as have thought of transporting themselves thither* (London: G. Larkin, 1682); also published in *Early Narratives,* ed. Salley, 164–76.

75. R[obert] F[erguson], *The Present State of Carolina with Advice to the Settlers* (London: John Bringhurst, 1682); Ashcraft, *Revolutionary Politics,* 113; Roper, *Carolina Conceived,* 70; Zook, *Radical Whigs,* 94–101; Childs, *Malaria and Colonization,* 199. Ferguson also published a sequel to Marvell's *An Account of the Growth of Popery* (Robert Ferguson, *The Second Part of the Growth of Popery . . . from the Year 1677 unto . . . 1682 by Philo-Veritas* [Cologne: Philiotus (i.e., London), 1682]).

76. Buchanan, "Colleton Family," 162, 175, 179–80; Lesser, *South Carolina Begins,* 56. Shaftesbury, Locke, Ferguson, and the Huguenots Thomas Papillon and John Dubois were all members of what Zook calls "a network of radical Whigs" (Zook, *Radical Whigs,* 1, 195–201).

77. Locke's published letters contain a multitude of references to Huguenot correspondents (E. S. De Beer, ed., *The Correspondence of John Locke,* 8 vols. [Oxford: Clarendon Press, 1976]). Jean LeClerc and Nicolas Thoynard, whom he met in France, and Pierre Coste, translator of Locke's works into French, are some of Locke's best-known Huguenot friends. See Locke, *Travels in France,* xxxviii; Margaret E. Rumbold, *Pierre Coste: Traducteur huguenot* (New York: Peter Lang, 1991). Shaftesbury's grandson Anthony Ashley Cooper, who was tutored by Locke and whom he regarded as a "friend and Foster-Father," still maintained a correspondence with Jean LeClerc and Pierre Coste after Locke's death in 1704 (Barrell, *Anthony Ashley Cooper,* 87 [quote]). Locke's library also contained a large and varied selection of works by Huguenot authors and about Huguenot history. Locke owned, for example, the writings of Pierre Bayle, Pierre Jurieu, Pierre Allix, Moïse Amyraut, Jean Claude, Jean Le Clerc, and Pierre Coste, as well as copies of the Edicts of Nantes and of Fontainebleau (Edict of Revocation) (John Harrison and Peter Laslett, *The Library of John Locke* [Oxford: Clarendon Press, 1971], "Locke's Library Catalogue," 70–72, 82, 109–17, 128, 164, 194).

78. Locke had already sojourned in France in 1672 but very briefly and only stayed in Paris (Locke, *Travels in France,* xv).

79. Locke did so notably in Orange, Nîmes, Montpellier, and Aigues Mortes (Locke, *Travels in France,* 11, 13, 23, 61; Benedict, *Huguenot Population,* 1–3).

80. Shaftesbury had a fruit orchard in his estate of Wimborne St. Giles. Locke and Shaftesbury were both interested in agricultural experimentation and were members of the Royal Society. Additionally, both had investments in the commerce of raw silk. See Lesser, *South Carolina Begins,* 29; Haley, *First Earl of Shaftesbury,* 228.

81. Thus, for example, Locke lists thirteen sorts of olives from the area of Montpellier, nine varieties of plums, and eighteen of pears from the Tours region (John Locke, *Observations upon the Growth and Culture of Vines and Olives: The Production of Raw Silk & the Preservation of Fruits* [London: W. Sandby, 1766], 25 and 56). This book was not published until 1766 in the wake of renewed interest in the production of silk in the American Southeast following the development of the Carolina backcountry and the relatively recent foundation of Georgia. During his travels

Locke also mailed Shaftesbury "boxes of vines of [different] sorts," as he did, for example, in February 1676 while he was staying in Montpellier (Locke, *Travels in France,* 28).

82. Ashcraft, *Revolutionary Politics,* 132–36. This is a strong possibility, or at least was regarded as such by the English government, which decided to keep an eye on Locke while he was in France (ibid., 135).

83. Cheves, *Shaftesbury Papers,* 378.

84. BPRO, CO 5/288/20 (October 28, 1684); Salley, *Papers,* 1 (1663–84):312; De Beer, *Correspondence of John Locke,* 1:485. Moyse Charas (1619–98) wrote several renowned pharmaceutical treatises, one of which, *Pharmacopée royale galénique et chymique,* went through multiple editions in various languages from 1676 to 1717. See John E. Alden, Dennis C. Lanning, et al., eds., *European Americana: A Chronological Guide to Works Printed in Europe Relating to the Americas* (1493–1776), 4 vols. (New Canaan, Conn.: Readex Books for the John Carter Brown Library, 1980–97), 4 (1676–1700):3 (for reference to original first edition). Unsurprisingly, Locke owned several of Charas's books (Harrison and Laslett, *Library of John Locke,* 105).

85. These negotiations, which lasted from March to October 1679, can be easily followed in Salley, *Papers,* 1:62–81; and in the *Calendar of State Papers,* 10 (1677–80):336–428. See also St. Julien R. Childs, "The Petit-Guérard Colony," *SCHGM* 43 (1942): 1–4.

86. Locke returned from France in April 1679, and that same month Shaftesbury was appointed lord president of the Council of Trade and Plantations. See Locke, *Travels in France,* xix; Eustace, "Anthony Ashley," 190–91; Haley, *First Earl of Shaftesbury,* 264. In the sources, Petit is somewhat mysteriously described as "the King's agent at Rouen [Normandy]" and Guérard as "a gentleman of Normandy" (BPRO, CO 1/43/53).

87. Salley, *Papers,* 1:71.

88. *Calendar of State Papers,* 10:351 (n967).

89. Ibid., 364 (n1000).

90. Ibid., 336 (n918); Salley, *Papers,* 1:71.

91. The negotiations provided for the fitting of two ships, but only one of them, the *Richmond,* actually reached South Carolina. For further discussion on the existence and fate of the second ship, see infra page 72.

92. BPRO, CO 1/43/250 (October 17, 1679).

93. *Description du Pays nommé Caroline,* [3]. This pamphlet is undated, but the crossing out of "Aoust" (August) and its replacement by "Septembre" in the Huntington Library copy and by "Septembre ou au commencement d'Octobre" in the British Library copy, regarding the departure date of the ships, indicates that it was published sometime before the month of August, presumably in the spring, to give the promoters enough time to advertise. The John Carter Brown Library (Providence, R.I.) has negative photostats of both originals, (Facsim E 679 D449p).

94. On the secular and religious perceptions of America as an Eden into which the Carolina promotional literature is rooted, see, for example, Jack P. Greene, *The Intellectual Construction of America: Exceptionalism and Identity from 1492 to 1800* (Chapel Hill: University of North Carolina Press, 1993), 68–78; Delumeau, "L'Amérique du Nord, terre de toutes les promesses (XVIIe–XVIIIe siècle)," in *Histoire,* 2:274–87.

95. H. Roy Merrens, "The Physical Environment of Early America: Images and Image Makers in Colonial South Carolina," *Geographical Review* 59 (1969): 530; Merrens and Terry, "Dying in Paradise," 534.

96. Jack P. Greene, *Selling a New World: Two Colonial South Carolina Promotional Pamphlets* (Columbia: University of South Carolina Press, 1989).

97. All the quotes in this paragraph are from *Description du Pays nommé Caroline.*

98. Six rather than seven because it is not known where one of them, *Questions et Responses faites au sujet de la Caroline,* was published since it is only extant in a hand-copy manuscript. The publication of these Carolina French and English promotional pamphlets can be traced in Hope F. Kane, "Abstract of the Thesis 'Colonial Promotion and Promotion Literature of Carolina, 1660–1700'" (Providence, R.I.: Brown University, 1930), 14–23; William S. Powell, "Carolina in the Seventeenth Century: An Annotated Bibliography of Contemporary Publications," *North Carolina Historical Review* 41 (1964): 74–104; Durand Echeverria and Everett C. Wilkie Jr., eds., *The French Image of America: A Chronological and Subject Bibliography of French Books Printed before 1816 Relating to the British North American Colonies and the United States,* 2 vols. (Metuchen, N.J.: Scarecrow Press, 1994), vol. 1. For successive editions of each pamphlet, see Alden et al., *European Americana,* vol. 4 (1676–1700). Two pamphlets only extant in manuscript form, the above-mentioned 1685 *Questions et Responses* and a 1684 translation of Wilson's *Account of the Province of Carolina,* are not listed in these bibliographical works. They are deposited at the Bibliothèque Municipale de La Rochelle (Recueil de documents divers, "Le commerce avec la Caroline, vers 1685," ms. 1909, fols. 51–55) and the Bibliothèque Nationale, Paris (Ms. français, n.a. 5052, fols. 177–80), respectively.

99. The complete title is *Récit de l'Estat présent des célèbres colonies de la Virginie, de Marie-Land, de la Caroline, du nouveau Duché d'York, de Penn-Sylvanie, & de la nouvelle Angleterre, situées dans l'Amérique septentrionale, & qui relèvent de la couronne du Roy de la grand' Bretagne: Tiré fidèle-ment des mémoires des habitants des mêmes colonies, en faveur de ceus, qui auroyent le dessein de s'y transporter pour s'y établir* (Rotterdam: Chez Reinier Leers, 1681).

100. On Rochefort and his works, see Everett C. Wilkie's thorough article "The Authorship and Purpose of the *Histoire naturelle et morale des îles Antilles,* an Early Huguenot Emigration Guide," *Harvard University Library Bulletin* 38 (1991): 27–82. See also Gilbert Chinard, *L'Amérique et le rêve exotique dans la littérature française au XVIIe et au XVIIIe siècle* (Paris: Droz, 1934), 54–58.

101. Wilkie, "Authorship and Purpose," 33.

102. *Récit de l'Estat présent,* 14–15.

103. "Sir Peter Colleton to Locke" (early summer 1671?), in De Beer, *Correspondence of John Locke,* 1:355–56 (n254).

104. It is entirely possible, as St. Julien Childs conjectured, that Rochefort obtained his infor-mation from Shaftesbury or one of his agents in the Netherlands. See Childs, *Malaria and Colonization,* 247. Shaftesbury certainly knew of Rochefort's works since Locke owned several edi-tions of the pastor's *Histoire naturelle* (Harrison and Laslett, *Library of John Locke,* 73, 222).

105. *Description de la Carolline Prés la Floride, ou La Nouvelle Angleterre en l'Amerique . . .* (Geneva: Chez Jacques de Tournes, 1684). The manuscript copy of the other translation is headed "Description de la Carolline imprimée à Londres en 1684," and it can be assumed that the title of the original was the same as the Geneva translation (Ms. français, n.a. 5052, fol. 177, BN).

106. The full title is *Suite de la Description de la Carolline qui contient diverses Lettres et vint & quatre questions et réponses qui ont été faites sur ce sujet, après ce qui en a esté ci-devant publié* (Geneva: Chez Jacques de Tournes, 1685).

107. This manuscript is undated, but a reference to "the Scots who arrived four months ago" (October 1684) most likely indicates that it was written in March 1685 ("Questions et Responses," fol. 53 back). As already mentioned (see supra note 98), it is not known for certain where this pam-phlet was published since it is only extant in manuscript form. However, the fact that this copy is deposited in the La Rochelle Archives strongly suggests that the original was published in London or in a Dutch city and brought over on a merchant ship.

108. *Nouvelle Relation de la Caroline* (The Hague: Chez Meyndert Uytweft, [1686]), 12, 31.

109. *Plan pour former un établissement en Caroline* (The Hague: Chez Meindert Uytwerf, 1686), [3]–[10]. See also Hope F. Kane, "Colonial Promotion and Promotion Literature of Carolina, 1660–1700" (Ph.D. diss., Brown University, 1930), 114–18. The value of the investment is given in *livre tournois,* which was the standard unit of money of account in early modern France and which was worth one-third of an *écu.* According to John McCusker's exchange tables, in the 1680s an *écu,* which was worth 3 *livres,* equaled 54 pence. A pound sterling was therefore worth 13 *livres tournois* (1 pound = 240/55 = 4.3 *écus* = 13 *livres*). This value is confirmed by a marginal note written by the copyist who transcribed the Bibliothèque Nationale copy of the London edition of *Description de la Carolline,* which read, "la livre sterling vaut 13 [livres] tournois." see John J. McCusker, *Money and Exchange in Europe & America, 1600–1775: A Handbook* (Chapel Hill: University of North Carolina Press, 1978), [35], [88], [91]; "Description de la Carolline," fol. 177 back. See also *Instruction Très-Exacte pour ceux qui ont dessein de se transporter en Amerique, Et Principalement Pour Ceux qui sont déjà intéressés dans la Province de Pennsylvanie* ([Amsterdam], 1686), in which the author writes "un[e] Livre sterlin est environ 13: Livres Tournois" (1).

110. *True Protestant Mercury,* no. 186 (October 14–18, 1682), for quote; no. 183 (October 4–7, 1682).

111. *True Protestant Mercury,* no. 186 (October 14–18, 1682).

112. Ibid., no. 126 (March 21, 1681).

113. The opening date of this coffeehouse is undocumented, but historians, following Childs, think it was founded no earlier than in 1682. See Childs, *Malaria and Colonization,* 212n132; Lesser, *South Carolina Begins,* 95–96, 96n80. For a guide to London coffeehouses, see Bryant Lillywhite, *London Coffee Houses: A Reference Book of Coffee Houses of the Seventeenth, Eighteenth and Nineteenth Centuries* (London: George Allen and Unwin Ltd., 1963).

114. *Nouvelle Relation de la Caroline,* 4; "Questions et Responses," fol. 1 front.

115. [Simms], "Remarks on the New Account," 226–30 (quote, 228).

116. Haley, *First Earl of Shaftesbury,* 706n2.

117. Ashcraft, *Revolutionary Politics,* 115n148, 131n18; Cottret, *Huguenots in England,* 211.

118. Miscellaneous Records (Proprietary Series), vol. 1675–95:122, SCDAH. For an overview of several generations of the Du Moulins, see Foster Watson, "Notes & Materials on Religious Refugees in Their Relation to Education in England before the Revocation of the Edict of Nantes," *HSP* 9 (1911): 323–25; Élisabeth Labrousse, "Marie Du Moulin éducatrice," *BSHPF* 139 (1993): 255–68.

119. St. Julien Childs History Papers, ms. box 24/315, folder 2, South Carolina Historical Society, Charleston; *Plan pour former un établissement,* [15].

120. In May 1683 Samuel Wilson received "a Guiney" for "Translating ye constitu[ti]ons into French." This was a translation of the version printed in January 1682 and available at the Carolina Coffee House. See William L. Saunders, coll. and ed., *The Colonial Records of North Carolina,* vol. 1 (1662–1712) (Raleigh, N.C.: P. M. Hale, Printer to the State, 1886), 344; Powell, "Carolina in the Seventeenth Century," 94; Lesser, *South Carolina Begins,* 28.

121. J. A Gruys & C. de Wolf, eds., *Thesaurus 1473–1800: Dutch Printers and Booksellers,* (Nieuwkoop: De Graaf Publishers, 1989), 124; Katherine Swift, "Dutch Penetration of the London Market for Books, c. 1690–1730," in C. Berkvens-Stevelinck et al., *Le magasin de l'univers: The Dutch Republic as the Centre of the European Book Trade* (Leiden: E. J. Brill, 1992), 268–69. These two maps were actually illegal reproductions of French *cartes* drawn by Nicolas Sanson and included in his bestseller *Le Neptune François ou Atlas Nouveau des Cartes Marines* (Paris: Chez Hubert Jaillot, 1696). Incidentally, Sanson's Carolina *cartes* were themselves based on earlier maps published in London. See William P. Cumming, *The Southeast in Early Maps,* new revised and

enlarged edition by Louis de Vorsey Jr. (Chapel Hill: University of North Carolina Press, 1998), 188, map 120, and 189, map 121. On Sanson's work and its multiple plagiaries, see Mireille Pastoureau, "Contrefaçon et plagiat des cartes de géographie et des atlas français de la fin du XVIe au début du XVIIIe siècle," in *Les presses grises: la contrefaçon du livre (XVIe–XIXe siècles),* ed. François Moureau (Paris: Aux Amateurs du Livre, 1988), 275–301 (289–95 for Mortier's plagiaries).

122. Leers, for example, was the purveyor of the States' General Library in the Netherlands and of the Bibliothèque du Roi in France. See Gerald Cerny, *Theology, Politics and Letters at the Crossroads of European Civilization: Jacques Basnage and the Baylean Huguenot Refugees in the Dutch Republic* (Dordrecht: Martinus Nijhoff Publishers, 1987), 88; Cerny, "Jacques Basnage and Pierre Bayle: An Intimate Collaboration in Refugee Literary Circles and in the Affairs of the Republic of Letters, 1685–1706," in *De l'humanisme aux lumières, Bayle et le protestantisme: Mélanges en l'honneur d'Élisabeth Labrousse,* ed. Michèle Magdelaine, Maria-Christina Pitassi, Ruth Whelan, and Antony McKenna (Oxford: Voltaire Foundation, 1996), 497–98; Alden et al., *European Americana,* 4:313; Otto S. Lankhorst, "Reinier Leers Libraire-Imprimeur à Rotterdam (1654–1714) et ses contrefaçons," in *Les Presses Grises,* ed. Moureau, 49–63.

123. Jean-Dominique Mellot and Élisabeth Queval, eds., *Répertoire d'imprimeurs/libraires XVIe–XVIIIe siècle* (Paris: Bibliothèque Nationale de France, 1997), 583; Gruys and de Wolf, *Thesaurus,* 179.

124. John R. Kleinschmidt, *Les imprimeurs et libraires de la République de Genève* (Geneva: A. Julien éditeur, 1948), 102n2.

125. Henri-Jean Martin, "Les relations entre les libraires genevois et la France au XVIIe siècle: Quelques reflexions," in *Cinq siècles d'imprimerie genevoise: Actes du Colloque international sur l'histoire de l'imprimerie et du livre à Genève (April 1978)* (Geneva: Société d'Histoire et d'Archéologie, 1980), 292–93; Laurence Fontaine, *Histoire du colportage en Europe (XVe–XIXe siècle)* (Paris: Albin Michel, 1993), 78–79.

126. "Geographical Index of Printers and Booksellers," in Alden et al., *European Americana,* 1 (1493–1600):277; Alfred Cartier, *Bibliographie des éditions de Tournes, imprimeurs lyonnais,* 2 vols. (1937; reprint, Geneva: Slatkine Reprint, 1970).

127. "Letters to Bishop Compton (1677–1710) and other papers," Rawlinson Ms C 984 fol. 312, Bodleian Library, Oxford. This document is undated but must have been drawn either in 1685 or 1686 when Carolina French pamphlets were penetrating France.

128. "Questions et Responses," fol. 1 back.

129. [Durand de Dauphiné], *Voyages d'un François exilé pour la Religion avec une Description de la Virgine & Marilan dans l'Amérique* (The Hague: the author, 1687), 37–38. For modern French and English editions of this narrative, see Gilbert Chinard, ed., *Un Français en Virginie: Voyages d'un François exilé pour la religion avec une description de la Virgine & Marilan d'après l'édition originale de 1687* (Baltimore: Johns Hopkins University Press, 1932); Chinard, ed., *A Huguenot Exile in Virginia, or Voyages of a Frenchman Exiled for Religion with a Description of Virginia and Maryland* (New York: Press of the Pioneers, 1934).

130. "Letter of Judith Giton," Manigault Family Papers, 11/275/4, fol. 1 back, South Carolina Historical Society, Charleston.

131. This was, for example, the case for René Rézeau, Pierre Bontecou, and Daniel Garnier, all from Île-de-Ré. See Baird, *History,* 1:305n4, 307n4, 309n3.

132. "Mémoire sur La Rochelle" (December 28, 1684), AN, série TT, box 232, folder Aunis, pièces 946–47. Incidentally, the handwritten copy of one of these pamphlets that the intendant sent

to Versailles may very well be the manuscript copy of the 1684 London edition of *Description de la Carolline,* now deposited at the Bibliothèque Nationale, Paris (see supra chap. 2, note 98).

133. A memoir probably drawn by a Huguenot and addressed to Henry Compton, bishop of London, suggested that "to meet fresh incursions [of refugees,] temporary building should be constructed, and that those who could not be so housed should be sent off in groups of twenty or thirty to Carolina" (*Mémoire touchant la manière de recevoir et employer les prosélytes et protestans qui se réfugient en Angleterre,* undated but most likely early or mid-1680s, cited in Edward Carpenter, *The Protestant Bishop: Being the Life of Henry Compton, 1632–1713, Bishop of London* (New York: Longmans, Green and Co, 1956), 341–42.

134. Durand, *Voyages,* 38–39.

135. "Letter of Louis Thibou," back (both references), South Caroliniana Library, Columbia, S.C. An English translation is available in Golden, *Huguenot Connection,* 140–44.

136. *Description de la Carolline,* 53. Morton was governor of Carolina from September 1682 to August 1684 and from October 1685 to November 1686 (Lesser, *South Carolina Begins,* 176–77).

137. *Remarques sur la Nouvelle Relation,* 226–27. Interestingly enough, Locke owned a copy of *Remarques* (Harrison and Laslett, *Library of John Locke,* 101).

138. Ibid., 228–30 (quote, 228).

139. Ibid., 228.

140. Ibid., 229.

141. In fact, in a typical *leyenda negra* fashion, the words "sanguinary" and "treachery" echo the characterization of the Spanish as a "cruell and inveterate Enemy" found in the Scottish report of the invasion sent to the proprietors in September 1686 (J. G. Dunlop and Mabel L. Webber, "Spanish Depredations, 1686," *SCHGM* 30 [1929]: 85). In the same vein, when commenting on Ribaut's death in the hands of the Spaniards, John Ogilby wrote with great imagination, "Ribald being quarter'd, they [the Spanish] fix'd his Limbs upon Poles about the Walls [of Fort Caroline], sending his Head to Sevil [Seville]" (John Ogilby, *America, being a latest and most accurate description of the New World, containing the original of the inhabitants and the remarkable voyages thither, the conquest of the vast empires of Mexico and Peru and other large provinces and territories, with the several European plantations . . .* [London: printed by the author, 1671], 106).

142. Rowland et al., *History of Beaufort County,* 1:74; Lesser, *South Carolina Begins,* 143.

143. Gilbert Chinard, for example, one of the first French chroniclers of the Huguenot migration to North America, originally thought that Durand's account was a fabricated tale, a true adventure story whose description of Virginia had been borrowed from earlier travel publications, and he even doubted Durand's existence. Aside from the novelistic aspect of the narrative, Chinard could not explain how Durand managed to visit parts of the Chesapeake, return to London, and have his book published in The Hague in only nine months. He then reversed his opinion about Durand, however, and decided to edit his *Voyages,* which he nonetheless rightly interpreted as a disguised promotional pamphlet. See Chinard, *Réfugiés huguenots,* 66–75; Chinard, *Français en Virginie,* 7–9. For examples of historians who have taken Durand's narrative at face value, see Baird, *History,* 114–15; Childs, *Malaria and Colonization,* 244–45.

144. Durand, *Voyages,* 129–30.

145. Ibid., 60 (quote).

146. Ibid., 95.

147. Ibid., 133.

148. Chinard identified these patrons as Nicholas Heyward, William Fitzhugh, and the Catholic(!) George Brent, who owned extensive estates in Middlesex and Stafford counties and

specifically wished to recruit Huguenot settlers for their projected Brenton settlement (Chinard, *Français en Virginie,* 27–30). See also Fairfax Harrison, *Landmarks of Old Prince William: A Study of Origins in Northern Virginia* (Berryville, Va.: Chesapeake Book Co., 1964), 186–90; Warren M. Billings, John E. Selby, and Thad W. Tate, *Colonial Virginia: A History* (White Plains, N.Y.: KTO Press, 1986), 119–21. For Fitzhugh's offers to Huguenot settlers, see his May 1686 letter in the *Virginia Magazine of History and Biography* 1 (1893): 408–10.

149. Durand, *Voyages,* 111.

150. In a letter written a week after the Revocation, Penn sympathetically evoked the French Protestants who faced the dragoons, "the King's Inquisitors and Converters," and who were "caught, executed or sent to the Galleys to row" ("Letter to James Harrison" [October 25, 1685], in *The Papers of William Penn,* 5 vols., ed. Mary M. Dunn and Richard S. Dunn [Philadelphia: University of Pennsylvania Press, 1981–87], 3:66). Out of eight Pennsylvania pamphlets published in a foreign language between 1681 and 1686, five were in German, two in French, and one in Dutch (Kane, "Colonial Promotion," 20–22). On the promotion of Pennsylvania, see Hope F. Kane, "Notes on the Early Pennsylvania Promotion Literature," *Pennsylvania Magazine of History and Biography* 63 (1939): 144–68; Richard S. Dunn, "William Penn and the Selling of Pennsylvania, 1681–1685," *Proceedings of the American Philosophical Society* 127 (1983): 322–29.

151. [Benjamin Furly], *Recüeil de Diverses Pièces concernant la Pennsylvanie* (The Hague: Chez Abraham Troyel, 1684); *Instruction Très-Exacte.* A second edition of *Recüeil de Pièces* also appeared in 1692. An English translation of *Recüeil's* first edition is available in *Pennsylvania Magazine of History and Biography* 6 (1882): 312–18. *Instruction Très-Exacte* is a lesser known tract about which the place of publication is conjectural and the publisher unknown (Alden et al., *European Americana,* 4:162).

152. *Recüeil de Diverses Pièces* is a translation of *Beschreibung der America new-erfunden Proving Pensylvanien: Der Inwohner Gesets Arth Sitten und Gebrauch; auch Samlicher Riviren des Landes sonderlich der haupt-stadt Philadelphia* (Description of the Newly Founded Province of Pennsylvania in America: The Law of Its Citizens, Their Customs and Habits; Also of the Entire Region, Especially the Capital, Philadelphia) (Hamburg: H. Heuss, 1684). *Instruction Très-Exacte* is a translation of *Information and Direction to such Persons as are inclined to America, more specially those related to the province of Pensilvania* (London: A. Sowle, [1686]). See Kane, "Colonial Promotion," 138, 171n22; Alden et al., *European Americana,* 4:162.

153. In *England's Present Interest Discovered* (London, 1675), for example, Penn encouraged the recruitment of "Prudent Forreigners" to people the American colonies, "especially at this Time of Day, when our Forreign Islands yearly take off so many necessary inhabitants from us" (44–45). Penn expressed his specific intention to recruit Huguenot wine growers in *Recüeil de Pièces.* "I am of the opinion," he wrote, "that we should have several thousands young vines imported from France with a few skillful wine growers" (97–98).

154. On Penn's sojourn in Saumur and Huguenot influences on his religious beliefs, see René Fillet, "Les relations entre la Touraine et la Pennsylvanie au XVIIe siècle," *Bulletin de la société d'études anglo-américaines des XVIIe et XVIIIe siècles* 37 (1993): 121–40; Kenneth R. Morris, "Theological Sources of William Penn's Concept of Religious Toleration," *Journal of Church and State* 35 (1993): 83–111.

155. Cerny, *Theology, Politics and Letters,* 89; William M. Barber, "Pierre Bayle, Benjamin Furly, and Quakerism," and Cerny, "Jacques Basnage and Pierre Bayle," both in *De l'Humanisme aux Lumières,* ed. Michèle Magdelaine et al., 495–507 and 623–33, respectively; William I. Hull, *Benjamin Furly and Quakerism in Rotterdam* (Swarthmore, Pa.: Swarthmore College, 1941), 86–89.

Other prominent members of The Lantern were Gilbert Burnet, Algernon Sidney, Anthony Ashley Cooper (Shaftesbury's grandson), and John Locke.

156. Alden et al., *European Americana,* 4:203; Gruys and de Wolf, *Thesaurus,* 177.

157. *Recüeil de Pièces,* 33–34.

158. Jean Claude, *Les plaintes des protestants cruellement opprimez dans le royaume de France* (Cologne: P. Marteau, 1686). P[ierre] Marteau in Cologne was a fake publisher's name and address used by Reinier Leers. Claude's pamphlet was published in English under the title *A Short Account of the Complaints and Cruel Persecution of the Protestants in the Kingdom of France* (London: W. Redmayne, 1707). See Cottret, *Huguenots in England,* 205; Solange Deyon, "Les relations de famille et d'affaires de Jean Claude d'après sa correspondance à la veille de la révocation (1683–1685)," *BSHPF* 116 (1970): 159; Lankhorst, "Reinier Leers Libraire-Imprimeur à Rotterdam," in *Les Presses Grises,* ed. Moureau, 57.

159. "Livre des Actes du Consistoire, 1679–1692," ms. 7, Archives of the French Protestant Church of London (February 15, March 29, and April 12 1685). For a recent English abstract of these records, see Robin D. Gwynn, ed., *Minutes of the Consistory of the French Church of London Threadneedle Street 1679–1692,* Quarto Series, vol. 58 (London: Huguenot Society of Great Britain and Ireland (hereafter HSGB&I) Publications, 1994).

160. "Report by Monsr Robert, Agent to the French Ambassador," *HSP* 7 (1901): 161.

161. Durand, *Voyages,* 37.

162. Sally Schwartz, *"A Mixed Multitude": The Struggle for Toleration in Colonial Pennsylvania* (New York: New York University Press, 1987), 21–23. On the few Huguenots who immigrated to Pennsylvania among German Palatines, see Edith W. Birch, "The Huguenot Settlers of Pennsylvania," *Historical Review of Berks County* 6 (1941): 78–82. Needless to say, the author's assertion that Pennsylvania was the colony where most Huguenots settled is incorrect (78). For a similar erroneous statement, see Kane, "Colonial Promotion," 144.

163. Dunn et al., *Papers of William Penn,* 5:287–98. The "First Purchasers" were overwhelmingly British since only 6 of the 531 (out of 589) whose geographic origins have been identified came from continental Europe. See "The Geographical Origins of the 531 First Purchasers of Land in Pennsylvania, 1681–1685," in Dunn, "William Penn and the Selling of Pennsylvania," 326. On Daillé see Butler, *Huguenots in America,* 78–84.

164. Most Huguenots, and especially the clerical leadership, like the majority of people in England, held the Quakers in contempt and were therefore presumably reluctant to settle in a colony founded and, at the time, largely settled by Quakers. An illustration of this negative perception appears in the Threadneedle Street Church registers where the consistory, in September 1689, recorded that the refugee Jean Serré from Saint-Quentin, Picardy, had broken the discipline ("violé la discipline") in marrying a Quaker against his mother's consent. Three months later Serré asked publicly for forgiveness in order to have access to communion again. See "Livre des Actes du Consistoire, 1679–1692," ms. 7, Archives of the French Protestant Church of London (September 29 and December 29, 1689). As Bernard Cottret suggested to me, William Penn's pro-Stuart leanings might have also made the Whiggish Huguenot leadership reluctant to encourage refugees to settle in Pennsylvania.

165. In 1710 South Carolina had a white population under seven thousand, whereas Pennsylvania, founded nearly twenty years later, had one above eighteen thousand (Jack P. Greene, *Pursuits of Happiness: The Social Development of Early Modern British Colonies and the Formation of American Culture* [Chapel Hill: University of North Carolina Press, 1988], 178–79, table 8.1). Penn has traditionally been perceived as a nonpareil promoter, and yet he had only three more pamphlets

published than the Carolina proprietors had (18 and 15, respectively) between 1679 and 1686. See Dunn, "William Penn and the Selling of Pennsylvania," 322; David W. Galenson, "The Settlement and Growth of the Colonies: Population, Labor, and Economic Development," in *Cambridge Economic History of the United States,* vol. 1, *Colonial Era,* ed. Engerman and Gallman, 147–48; Kane, "Abstract," 15–17, 20–22. I have added the French pamphlets unknown to Kane in these totals.

166. Massachusetts and, especially, New York, which attracted significant numbers of Huguenots, being older and consequently better known in continental Europe, did not need to be promoted as did the recently founded Restoration colonies.

167. In 1707 the Carolina proprietors commissioned the Lutheran minister Joshua Kocherthal to write a promotional piece entitled *Ausführlich und umständlicher Bericht von der berühmten Landschafft Carolina in dem Egelländischen America gelegen* (Complete and Detailed Report of the Famed District of Carolina Located in English America) (Frankfurt: G. H. Oerhling, 1707). Ironically, it is this pamphlet, not Penn's, that triggered the first significant transatlantic migration of German Palatines. See Philip L. Otterness, "The Unattained Canaan: The 1709 Palatine Migration and the Formation of German Society in Colonial America" (Ph.D. diss., University of Iowa, 1996), 56–61; Statt, *Foreigners and Englishmen,* 125–29; Alden et al., *European Americana,* 5 (1701–25):117.

168. For published lists of these titles, see supra chap. 2, note 98.

169. Durand, *Voyages,* 50.

170. *Description de la Carolline,* 33; *Suite de la Description de la Carolline,* 16. In Prussia also, Huguenot refugees preferably settled where there was an already established French presence. See François David, "Les colonies des réfugiés protestants français en Brandebourg-Prusse (1685–1809): institutions, géographie et évolution de leur peuplement," *BSHPF* 140 (1994): 115.

171. Rochefort, *Récit de l'Estat présent,* 14. See also supra chap. 2, note 111 for passages about these Huguenot settlers in the *True Protestant Mercury.*

172. "Whatsoever Alien shall, in this Form, before any Precinct Register, Subscribe these Fundamental Constitutions shall be thereby Naturalized," articles 118 (January 1682) and 123 (August 1682) (Parker, *North Carolina Charters,* 206, 231).

173. Thus probably at Furly's request, an article on the naturalization of foreign settlers was included in *Instruction Très-Exacte.* See "Benjamin Furly's Comments on William Penn's *Frame of Government,*" *Pennsylvania Magazine of History and Biography* 19 (1895): 297; Kane, "Colonial Promotion," 130; *Instruction Très-Exacte,* 19.

174. Haley, *First Earl of Shaftesbury,* 675; Zook, *Radical Whigs,* 17–19; Malcolm R. Thorp, "The English Government and the Huguenot Settlement, 1680–1702" (Ph.D. diss., University of Wisconsin, 1972), 55–57. On Papillon, see Irene Scouloudi, "Thomas Papillon, Merchant and Whig, 1623–1702," *HSP* 18 (1947): 49–72. Papillon had also been a member of the 1668 Council of Trade under Shaftesbury's presidency (Haley, *First Earl of Shaftesbury,* 255–56).

175. Cottret, *Huguenots in England,* 218–19; Kishlansky, *Monarchy Transformed,* 260.

176. Cottret, *Huguenots in England,* 219; Scouloudi, "Thomas Papillon," 60; Bosher, "Franco-Catholic Danger," 285.

177. Lesser, *South Carolina Begins,* 42–43.

178. "Questions et Responses," fol. 51 front.

179. *Nouvelle Relation de la Caroline,* 36.

180. *Suite de la Description de la Carolline,* 11.

181. James D. Douglas, *Light in the North: The Story of the Scottish Covenanters* (Grand Rapids: Wm. B. Eerdmans, 1964), 153–67; Ian B. Cowan, *The Scottish Covenanters 1660–1688* (London: Victor Gollancz Ltd, 1976), 120–33. Alluding to these difficult times and paralleling Huguenot

history, George Insh, historian of the Covenanter immigration to the New World, even wrote of "the dragonnades of those troubled days" (George P. Insh, *Scottish Colonial Schemes, 1620–1686* [Glasgow: Maclehose, Jackson & Co., 1922], 208).

182. Cowan, *Scottish Covenanters,* 120–23.

183. Insh, *Scottish Colonial Schemes,* 189.

184. Ibid., 194; Buchanan, "Colleton Family," 179.

185. [John Crawford], *A New and Most Exact Account of the Fertiles [sic] and Famous Colony of Carolina (On the Continent of America)* . . . (Dublin: Nathan Tarrant, 1683); Walter Gibson, *Proposals by Walter Gibson, Merchant in Glasgow, to such persons as are desirous to Transport themselves to America in a ship belonging to him bound for Bermudas, Carolina, New Providence, and the Carrily Islands, and ready to set sail out of the River of Clyd against the 20 February in this instant year, 1684* (Glasgow, 1684); Powell, "Carolina in the Seventeenth Century," 97–99; Kane, "Colonial Promotion," 96–97.

186. On the debate over whether the Stuart Town project was a political cover for the Scottish Whigs, see Insh, *Scottish Colonial Schemes,* 190–93; Roper, *Conceiving Carolina,* 73–76.

187. Linda G. Fryer, "Documents Relating to the Formation of the Carolina Company in Scotland, 1682," *SCHM* 99 (1998): 110–34; Rowland et al., *History of Beaufort County,* 1:68–73.

188. George P. Insh, "Arrival of the Cardross Settlers," *SCHGM* 30 (1929): 72; Rowland et al., *History of Beaufort County,* 1:71.

189. Robin Gwynn's demographic studies have shown that the Huguenot migration to England reached a peak in 1687. See, for example, R. Gwynn, "The Arrival of Huguenot Refugees in England 1680–1705," *HSP* 21 (1969): 370.

190. Durand had purchased Jurieu's *Accomplissement des Prophéties ou la délivrance prochaine de l'Église* (Rotterdam: Chez Abraham Acher, 1686) before leaving for Virginia. Based on an interpretation of the resurrection of the Witnesses following three days and a half in "three years and a half," many believed that persecutions in France would end in 1689. As a Huguenot who fled to the Netherlands explained in a letter written in 1687 and addressed to his relatives in Nîmes, Languedoc, "Many are convinced that in eighty-nine we shall witness the Peace of the Church," based on "the eleventh chapter of the Apoc[alypse]." The author, however, did not believe it. Although admitting that persecutions could cease in 1689, Jurieu, on an elaborate reading and intricate exegesis of the Apocalypse, actually prophesized that 1710 would mark the fall of Babylon and the end of papism exactly 1,260 years after the fall of the Roman Empire in 450–55. See N[athanaël] W[eiss], ed., "Le sort des réfugiés en Hollande, Angleterre et ailleurs d'après une lettre originale et inédite," *BSHPF* 43 (1894): 197 [quote]; Durand, *Voyages,* 125; Pierre Jurieu, *L'accomplissement des Prophéties,* ed. Jean Delumeau (Paris: Imprimerie Nationale, 1994), 159, 148.

191. On this "seasoning passage" and how it was perceived by Calvinists, see David Cressy, "The Vast and Furious Ocean: The Passage to Puritan New England," *New England Quarterly* 57 (1984): 511–32. In the same vain, a 1682 French poem about the missionary voyage of nuns to Martinique mentioned the "fury of the waves" (Philip Boucher, "France 'Discovers' America: The Image of Tropical America in Sixteenth and Seventeenth Century France and Its Impact on Early French Colonialism" [Ph.D. diss., University of Connecticut, 1974], 276). More generally, on the negative perception of the sea in early modern Europe, see Alain Cabantous, *Le ciel dans la mer: Christianisme et civilisation maritime XVIe–XIXe siècle* (Paris: Fayard, 1990), chap. 3, "L'océan redoutable," 85–119; Alain Corbin, *Le territoire du vide: L'Occident et le désir du rivage, 1750–1840* (Paris: Aubier, 1988), chap. 1, "Les racines de la peur et de la répulsion," 11–30.

192. David, "Colonies des réfugiés," 123.

274 Notes to pages 51–53

3. From New Babylon to Eden

Epigraphs from Bishop Burnet, *A Sermon preached before the House of Peers* (November 5, 1689), quoted in Ashcraft, *Revolutionary Politics,* 205; Fontaine, *Memoirs,* 113; Increase Mather, *A Sermon wherein is Shewed that the Church of God is Sometimes a Subject of Great Persecution: Preached on a Publick FAST at Boston in New England; occasioned by the Tidings of a great Persecution Raised against the Protestants in France* (Boston: printed for Samuel Sewall, 1682), 9.

1. In a reflective essay on Huguenot history between the Edict of Fontainebleau (1685) and the Edict of Toleration (1787) published on the occasion of the three hundredth anniversary of the Revocation, the French historian Georges Gusdorf even characterized the Revocation as a genocide in a cultural but also literal sense (G. Gusdorf, "L'Europe protestante au siècle des Lumières," in "Le Protestantisme français en France," special issue, *Dix-huitième Siècle* 17 [1985]: 13–14).

2. From 1685 to 1700 the Académie Française even offered prizes for works celebrating the Edict of Fontainebleau (Geoffrey Adams, *The Huguenots and French Opinion, 1685–1787: The Enlightenment Debate on Toleration* [Waterloo, Ontario: Wilfrid Laurier University Press, 1991], 19–23). For a qualified view of this spontaneous artistic enthusiasm, see Hélène Himelfarb, "Les arts à la rescousse de l'Édit de Fontainebleau? Les paradoxes des Académies royales," in *Révocation de l'Édit de Nantes,* ed. Zuber and Theis, 335–57.

3. Quoted in Bergeal and Durrleman, *Éloge et condamnation,* 20–21.

4. Quoted in Dompnier, *Venin de l'hérésie,* 251.

5. Quoted in Bergeal and Durrleman, *Éloge et condamnation,* 26.

6. Ibid., 30–31. The Jansenists, followers of the bishop of Ypres, Cornelius Jansenius (1585–1638), were Catholic reformers who stressed the sinful nature of man and moral rigorism, which made Catholic polemists assimilate them with the Puritans. Declared heretics by the papacy in 1653, the Jansenists, who were particularly influential within the lay and ecclesiastical French educated elites, were intensely persecuted by the monarchy in the 1670s and 1680s. Often accused of promoting a theology close to Calvinism by their Catholic opponents, they made a point in distancing themselves from the Huguenots. This explains why their leaders praised the Revocation but disapproved of the dragonnades. See Bergeal and Durrleman, *Éloge et condamnation,* 30–31; Monique Cottret, "Jansénisme," in *Dictionnaire de l'Ancien Régime,* ed. Bély, 684–87; Phillips, *Church and Culture,* 189–205; Bernard Cottret, Monique Cottret, and Marie-José Michel, eds., *Jansénisme et puritanisme* (Paris: Nolin, 2002).

7. Munck, *Seventeenth-Century Europe,* 375–76; Garrisson, *L'Édit de Nantes* (1998), 261; Coward, *Stuart Age,* 342–43; Cornette, *Chronique,* 341–42; Nassiet, *France,* 182–86.

8. Pierre Blet, "Les papes et la Révocation," in *Révocation de l'Édit de Nantes,* ed. Zuber and Theis, 263–80.

9. Labrousse, *Révocation,* 180, 180n18.

10. A French transcription and an English translation of the Edict of Fontainebleau can be found in Bergeal and Durrleman, *Protestantisme et libertés,* 43–48; and Golden, *Huguenot Connection,* app. 2:135–39.

11. Golden, *Huguenot Connection,* 136–38.

12. Labrousse, *Révocation,* 185–86.

13. [Pierre Bayle], *Ce que c'est que la France toute catholique sous le règne de Louis Le Grand* (The Hague: Chez Abraham Troyel, 1690); ed. Élisabeth Labrousse (Paris: Librairie Philosophique J. Vrin, 1973).

14. Throughout the eighteenth century the acronym N.C. evolved to mean ironically *non catholique* (Didier Poton, "La monarchie et les protestants en France au XVIIIe siècle," in *Lectures de Voltaire: Le traité sur la tolérance,* ed. Isabelle Brouard-Arends [Rennes: Presses Universitaires de Rennes, 1999], 45).

15. Jean-Jacques Rousseau, *On the Social Contract, or Essay about the Form of the Republic* [first version, commonly called the *Geneva Manuscript*], in *The Collected Writings of Rousseau,* 4 vols., ed. Roger D. Masters and Christopher Kelly (Hanover, N.H.: University Press of New England, 1994), 4:123. For the French version, see J. J. Rousseau, *Du contrat social* (première version, manuscrit de Genève), in *Œuvres complètes,* ed. Bernard Gagnebin (Paris: Gallimard, 1959), 3:343.

16. Labrousse, *Révocation,* 188.

17. Ibid., 189–91; Ligou, *Protestantisme,* 248–49.

18. Quoted in Joutard, "Revocation of the Edict of Nantes," 360.

19. Phillips, *Church and Culture,* 215.

20. Ibid., 216.

21. Labrousse, *Révocation,* 191; Quéniart, *Révocation,* 132; Phillips, *Church and Culture,* 216.

22. Quoted in Joutard, "Revocaton of the Edict of Nantes," 361. See also Jean-Paul Chabrol, *Élie Marion, le vagabond de Dieu (1687–1713): Prophétisme et millénarisme protestants en Europe à l'aube des Lumières* (Aix-en-Provence: Edisud, 1999).

23. Labrousse, *Révocation,* 190.

24. The term *camisard* comes either from *camisade,* meaning night attack, or from *camisa,* the simple white shirt that the rebels wore in contrast to the uniform of the troops (Michel Péronnet, "Camisards," in *Dictionnaire de l'Ancien Régime,* ed. Bély, 199).

25. *Les huguenots, catalogue de l'exposition organisée par les Archives Nationales* (Paris: La Documentation Française, 1985), 132.

26. André Zysberg, *Les galériens: Vies et destins de 60 000 forçats sur les galères de France 1680–1748* (Paris: Seuil, 1987), 102. Scoville mentions 1,447 Huguenot galley slaves for the period 1685–1715 (Scoville, *Persecution of Huguenots,* 79n42). The 1985 anniversary catalog gives an estimate of 1,940 Huguenot galley slaves for the period 1685–1787 (*Huguenots,* 132).

27. Zysberg, *Galériens,* 65, 105. The breakdown of Scoville's estimate of 1,232 Huguenots for whom the date of condemnation is known shows that 704 Huguenots were sentenced to the galleys between 1685 and 1690, or a period of five years, and 428 between 1691 and 1715, or twenty-five years (Scoville, *Persecution of Huguenots,* 79).

28. Scoville, *Persecution of Huguenots,* 107.

29. The story is actually more complicated. The corsairs who captured Neau and his ship were short on men and could not keep their prize. In consequence, Neau suggested to buy his own ship and cargo from them so that it could be sent back to New York (which Neau generically calls Nouvelle-Angleterre in reference and by opposition to New France). Neau remained on board as a security for the actual payment. While in Saint-Malo, however, Neau was recognized as a Huguenot fugitive and tried, to the corsairs' dismay. See *An Account of the Sufferings of the French Protestants, Slaves on Board the French Kings' Galleys: By Elias Neau, One of their Fellow Sufferers; Together with a List of Those who are still on Board the said Galleys* (London: Richard Parker, 1699). Neau's account can also be found in Edward Arber, ed., *The Torments of Protestant Slaves in the French King's Galleys, and in the Dungeons of Marseilles, 1686–1707 A.D* (London: privately printed, 1907), 259–80. On Neau, see Didier Poton and Bertrand Van Ruymbeke, "Élie Neau: 'Galérien pour la foi' (1669–1722)," in *La violence et la mer dans l'espace atlantique XII–XIXe siècle,* ed. Mickaël Augeron and Mathias Tranchant (Rennes: Presses Universitaires de Rennes, 2004),

325–36; Léonard, *Histoire,* 3:61–64; Butler, *Huguenots in America,* 162–66; Jon Butler, "Les 'Hymnes ou cantiques sacrez' d'Élie Neau: un nouveau manuscrit du 'grand mystique des galères,'" *BSHPF* 124 (1978): 417–23; "Élie Neau, de Soubise (1662–1722)," in *Protestants d'Aunis, Saintonge et Angoumois,* ed. Pierre Boismorand, Freddy Bossy, and Denis Vatinel (Paris: Le Croît vif, 1998), 143–53 (reprints of two articles on Neau published in the *BSHPF* in vols. 23 [1874] and 24 [1875]); Sheldon S. Cohen, "Elias Neau, Instructor to New York's Slaves," *New York Historical Society Quarterly* 55 (1971): 6–27. Neau's ordeal also inspired Cotton Mather, who prefaced an early American edition of his account published under the title *[A Present] from a Farr Countrey, [to the] People of New England* (Boston: B. Green & J. Allen for Michael Perry, 1698).

30. Zysberg, *Galériens,* 103.

31. Marie Durand is the best-documented example, and certainly one of the most moving, of a Huguenot woman who was sentenced to prison. Caught with her parents attending an outdoor illicit service, she was imprisoned at the Tour de Constance in Aigues-Mortes, Languedoc, from age nineteen to fifty-seven. See Étienne Gamonnet, ed., *Lettres de Marie Durand (1711–1776): Prisonnière à la Tour de Constance de 1730 à 1768* (1986; Montpellier: Les Presses du Languedoc, 1998).

32. *Huguenots,* 132.

33. Geneviève Reynes, *Couvents de femmes: La vie des religieuses contemplatives dans la France des XVIIe et XVIIIe siècles* (Paris: Fayard, 1987), 226.

34. Garrisson, *L'Édit de Nantes* (1998), 257. One of these institutions was founded in Pons, Saintonge, home of Élie Prioleau. See Miot-Duclouzeaux, "Révocation," 162.

35. Reynes, *Couvents de femmes,* 226–27; Miot-Duclouzeaux, "Révocation," 135.

36. Garrisson, *L'Édit de Nantes* (1998), 258; Léonard, *Histoire,* 3:382.

37. A total of 426 convicts in seven ships, not 1,000 in ten ships as Baird claimed (Baird, *History,* 1:221). The five transport ships, with 411 Huguenots on board, departed from Marseille, where the Mediterranean Sea galley fleet was based. The two merchant ships left La Rochelle and Île-de-Ré with fifteen prisoners. See Gérard Lafleur, *Les Protestants aux Antilles françaises du Vent sous l'Ancien Régime* (Basse-Terre: Société d'Histoire de la Guadeloupe, 1988), 194–96, 202.

38. Lafleur, *Protestants aux Antilles,* 195–96.

39. Ibid., 196.

40. Many of these Huguenot convicts were guides who helped refugees escape from France (ibid., 184–88).

41. Mathieu Lelièvre, ed., *Un déporté pour la foi: quatre lettres* (Paris: Librairie évangélique, 1881), 139. This account was originally published under the title *Quatre relations véritables du Sieur Serres de Montpellier* (Amsterdam: Paul Marret, 1688).

42. Lelièvre, *Déporté pour la foi,* 139.

43. Gérard Lafleur, ed., "Rapport du Gouverneur de la Guadeloupe sur l'arrivée de Nouveaux Convertis déportés dans cette île (1687)," *BSHPF* 27 (1981): 264.

44. Lafleur, *Protestants aux Antilles,* 227–28.

45. Lelièvre, *Déporté pour la foi,* 141.

46. Samuel de Pechels, *Mémoires,* ed. Raoul de Cazenove (Toulouse: Société des Livres Religieux, 1878), 44, 48, 55, 60, 64. See also Robert Garrisson, *Mémoires de Samuel de Pechels, 1685–1692, et documents sur la révocation à Montauban* (Miallet: Musée du Désert, 1936).

47. J. J. Digges La Touche, ed., *Registers of the French Conformed Churches of St. Patrick and St. Mary, Dublin,* Quarto Series, vol. 7 (Lymington, U.K.: HSGB&I Publications, 1893), 120.

48. Ligou, *Protestantisme,* 256; Adams, *Huguenots,* 38–39.

49. Adams, *Huguenots,* 39; Poton, "Monarchie," 50–51.

50. Daniel Ligou and Philippe Joutard, "Les Déserts," in *Histoire des Protestants en France,* ed. Robert Mandrou et al. (Toulouse: Éditions Privat, 1977), 244.

51. The origins of term *refuge* is biblical and refers to a few towns, sort of sanctuaries or havens, where ancient Hebrews could literally take refuge to escape persecution or the law. See Suzanne Hoyez and Andrée Ruffelard, "Les migrations protestantes sous le règne de Louis XIV: Essai sur l'état de la question," 2 vols. (thèse de doctorat, Université Panthéon-Sorbonne, 1978), 1:223–24; Birnstiel, *Diaspora des huguenots,* intro.; Van Ruymbeke and Sparks, *Memory and Identity,* 1–26. In French, English, and Dutch the word *refugee* was first coined at the end of the seventeenth century to designate Huguenot exiles and then became a generic term referring to all individuals escaping political or religious persecutions. See Cottret, *Huguenots in England,* 2; J. Stouten, "Quelques textes littéraires sur la révocation de l'Édit de Nantes: roman ou autobiographie?," in *La révocation de l'Édit de Nantes et les Provinces-Unies: The Revocation of the Edict of Nantes and the Dutch Republic,* ed. J. A. H. Bots and G. H. M. Posthumus Meyjès (Amsterdam: Holland University Press, 1986), 77; Jean-Luc Mathieu, *Migrants et réfugiés* (Paris: Presses Universitaires de France, 1991), 11.

52. Myriam Yardeni, *Le refuge protestant* (Paris: Presses Universitaires de France, 1985), 15–17; Hoyez and Ruffelard, "Migrations protestantes," 1:225–30.

53. Jean-Pierre Poussou, "Mobilité et migrations," in *Histoire de la population française,* ed. Jacques Dupâquier, vol. 2, *De la Renaissance à 1789* (1988; Paris: Presses Universitaires de France, 1995), 130.

54. Walloons were French-speaking Calvinists living in the provinces of the southern Netherlands such as Flanders, Walloon Flanders (Lille), Artois, Brabant, and Hainault. Some or part of these (Artois, Walloon Flanders, and southern Flanders) would later be conquered by France but were under Spanish rule at the time of the Walloon migrations. See Jonathan I. Israel, *The Dutch Republic: Its Rise, Greatness, and Fall, 1477–1806* (1995; Oxford: Clarendon Press, 1998), 36, 782 (maps); Paul Dibon, "Le refuge wallon précurseur du refuge huguenot," *Dix-Septième Siècle* 76–77 (1967): 53–74; H. H. Bolhuis, "La Hollande et les deux refuges," in "Le refuge huguenot," special issue, *BSHPF* 115 (1969): 407–28; Charles Littleton, "Acculturation and the French Church of London, 1600–c. 1640," in *Memory and Identity,* ed. Van Ruymbeke and Sparks, 90–109. Similarly, the majority of the first French-speaking Calvinists who settled or attempted to settle in Virginia and New Netherland in the 1620s were Walloons not Huguenots. See Baird, *History,* 1:148–200, app.:350–54; Michael Kammen, *Colonial New York: A History* (1975; White Plains, N.Y.: KTO Press, 1987), 28–29; Bertrand Van Ruymbeke, "The Walloon and Huguenot Elements in New Netherland and Seventeenth-Century New York: Identity, History, and Memory," in *Revisiting New Netherland: Perspectives on Early Dutch America,* ed. Joyce D. Goodfriend (Leiden: E. J. Brill, 2005), 41–54.

55. Estimates varied enormously, from under 100,000 to 3 million, until the 1960s when Samuel Mours and Warren Scoville first put forward a figure of about 200,000. Despite some variations, the considerable international research that has been done on the Refuge since the mid-1980s, with the three hundredth anniversary of the Revocation, has corroborated this estimate. Lately, though, the historiographical tendency has been to lower this figure to 150–180,000 refugees between 1680 and 1700. See Léonard, *Histoire,* 2:384; Scoville, *Persecution of Huguenots,* 118–21; Robin Gwynn, *Huguenot Heritage: The History and Contribution of the Huguenots in Britain,* 2nd rev. ed. (1985; Brighton: Sussex Academic Press, 2001), 29–30; Hoyez and Ruffelard, "Migrations protestantes," 2:375; Mours, *Essai sommaire de géographie,* 39; Garrisson, *L'Édit de Nantes et sa révocation,* 250; Jean-Pierre Poussou, "Les mouvements migratoires en France et à partir de la

France de la fin du XVe siècle au début du XIXe siècle: Approches pour une synthèse," *Annales de démographie historique* (1970): 56–59; Poussou, "Migrations et mobilité de la population en Europe à l'époque moderne," in *Histoire des populations de l'Europe,* ed. Jean-Pierre Bardet and Jacques Dupâquier, vol. 1, *Des origines aux prémices de la révolution démographique* (Paris: Fayard, 1997), 267; Leslie P. Moch, *Moving Europeans: Migration in Western Europe since 1650* (Bloomington: Indiana University Press, 1992), 28; Labrousse, *Révocation,* 194; Labrousse, "Le refuge huguenot," in "Emigrer, immigrer," special issue, *Le genre humain* 19 (1989): 147.

56. Emigration did not abruptly end in 1700 but continued until the 1760s. In the eighteenth century, however, it was punctual and numerically small. The departure of the Huguenots who, led by pastor Jean-Louis Gibert, founded the town of New Bordeaux in Hillsborough Township in the South Carolina backcountry represents the last significant emigration wave. See Robert L. Merriwether, *The Expansion of South Carolina, 1729–1765* (Kingsport, Tenn.: Southern Publishers, 1940), 252–54; Gibert, *Pierre Gibert;* Myriam Khaoua, "Conception, vie et mort d'un projet colonial à la fin du XVIIIe siècle: Jean-Louis Gibert et le *township* huguenot de New Bordeaux en Caroline du Sud (1752–1783)" (Mémoire de maîtrise, Université de La Rochelle, 1999).

57. Early on during the Revolution, to encourage *le retour des huguenots,* the National Assembly even issued a decree (*Décret concernant les biens des religionnaires fugitifs,* July 10, 1790) allowing descendants of refugees to claim their fugitive ancestors' estates provided they were still being managed by the state. See Eckart Birnstiel, "Le retour des huguenots du Refuge en France," *BSHPF* 135 (1989): 784–87; Yardeni, *Refuge protestant,* 161–68.

58. On the Jews, see Erna Paris, *The End of Days: A Story of Tolerance, Tyranny, and the Expulsion of the Jews from Spain* (Amherst, N.Y.: Prometheus Books, 1995), 237–63; Norman Roth, *Conversos, Inquisition and the Expulsion of the Jews from Spain* (Madison: University of Wisconsin Press, 1995), 271–316. On the Moriscos, see Antonio Domínguez Ortiz and Bernard Vincent, *Historia de los moriscos: Vida y tragedia de una minoría* (1978; Madrid: Alianza Editorial, 1997); Pierre Chaunu, "Minorités et conjoncture: L'expulsion des Moresques en 1609," *Revue Historique* 225 (1961): 81–98.

59. Vauban estimated that by 1689 eighty to one hundred thousand refugees had taken more than thirty million *livres tournois* (£2.3 million) with them and that the exodus had impoverished France's manufactures and ruined the greatest part of France's trade. See Vauban, *Mémoire,* 14–15; Myriam Yardeni, "Naissance et essor d'un mythe: La révocation de l'Édit de Nantes et le déclin économique de la France," *BSHPF* 139 (1993): 79–96.

60. Scoville, *Persecution of Huguenots,* 365–433; Nassiet, *France,* 79–86, 174–77.

61. Fontaine, *Memoirs,* 113–14.

62. Cotton Mather, *Une Grande Voix du Ciel à la France* (Boston: Bernby & Green, 1725), [5] (quote).

63. Scoville, *Persecution of Huguenots,* 321–64; Scoville, "The Huguenots and the Diffusion of Technology," *Journal of Political Economy* 60 (1952): 294–311; Yardeni, "Naissance," 93–95.

64. Twice, through most of 1687 and briefly in 1688, borders were opened and coast guards recalled. Whereas in 1688 it was caused by a misinterpretation of orders, in 1687 the monarchy deliberately let Huguenots escape, curiously thinking that only a few would leave once the restraints on emigration were lifted. See Scoville, *Persecution of Huguenots,* 103–4.

65. Pilatte, *Édits,* 26–29 (August 1669), 119–20 (July 1682), 192–94 (May 1685); Scoville, *Persecution of Huguenots,* 98–101.

66. Pilatte, *Édits,* 248 (November 1685), 286–87 (May 1686), 300–301 (October 1687).

67. Ibid., 281–82 (April 1686).

68. Ibid., 119–20 (*Déclaration* of July 1682); Scoville, *Persecution of Huguenots,* 111–12; Emmanuel Jahan, *La confiscation des biens des religionnaires fugitifs de la révocation de l'Édit de Nantes à la Révolution* (Paris: R. Pichon and R. Durand-Auzias, 1959), 13–14.

69. Pilatte, *Édits,* 302–6 (January 1688), 330–36 (December 1689); Jahan, *Confiscation,* 16–17.

70. Pilatte, *Édits,* 384–86 (February 1699); Jahan, *Confiscation,* 19–21; Scoville, *Persecution of Huguenots,* 111.

71. After 1700, and until the 1787 Edict of Toleration, the fugitives' confiscated estates were managed by an independent administration, *la Régie des biens des religionnaires fugitifs,* specifically created for that purpose (Jahan, *Confiscation,* 29–33, 47–49).

72. AN, série TT, box 236 (Bretagne 1681–85), pièce 933.

73. AN, TT/232/911 (Aunis). For the conversion of *livres tournois* into sterling pounds, see supra chap. 2, note 109.

74. "The Passenger List of the *Margaret,*" *HSSCT* 93 (1988): 34; Ms. Nouvelles Acquisitions Françaises (hereafter NAF) 21334 (Arnoul correspondence), fol. 456, BN.

75. NAF f 21 333, fols. 608/609–13, 640, BN.

76. Ibid., fol. 417.

77. Pilatte, *Édits,* 251–52 (November 1685), 266–67 (January 1686); Scoville, *Persecution of Huguenots,* 114 (July 1686); Jahan, *Confiscation,* 14–17.

78. Pilatte, *Édits,* 379–84 (December 1698); Jahan, *Confiscation,* 18–19.

79. Ms. NAF 21333 (Arnoul correspondence), fol. 97 (February 1686), BN.

80. Based on a privately owned manuscript account, Hirsch mentions that Isaac Mazyck was able to transfer fifteen hundred pounds sterling out of France, which seems an unlikely large sum (Hirsch, *Huguenots,* 232–33). For Josias DuPré, see St. Julien R. Childs, "Exports from Charles Town, 1690," *HSSCT* 54 (1949): 30–31. As Norris Nash aptly points out, however, the fact that most first-generation Carolina Huguenot merchants who arrived in the colony before 1700 did not set up businesses immediately after their arrival but first followed artisanal and agricultural pursuits seems to suggest that they did not emigrate with capital (Norris Nash, "The Huguenot Diaspora and the Development of the Atlantic Economy: Huguenots and the Growth of the South Carolina Economy, 1680–1725," in *Memory and Identity,* ed. Van Ruymbeke and Sparks, 216).

81. Jacques LeBas bought fifteen hundred acres in September 1685, Isaac LeGrand one hundred in August 1686, and Jacques Nicolas two hundred in March 1687. See Alexander S. Salley and R. Nicholas Olsberg, eds., *Warrants for Lands in South Carolina, 1672–1711* (Columbia: University of South Carolina Press, 1973), 405–6, 420, 410; Alexander S. Salley, ed., *Commissions and Instructions from the Lords Proprietors of Carolina to Public Officials of South Carolina, 1685–1715* (Columbia: Historical Commission of South Carolina, 1916), 42–45.

82. Labrousse, *Révocation,* 212.

83. In Brittany and Burgundy, 58 and 59 percent, respectively, of the Huguenot population left compared to 6 and 8 percent in Cévennes and Vivarais (both in Languedoc), respectively (Butler, *Huguenots in America,* p. 23, table 1 [Butler's percentages are based on Samuel Mours's estimates]).

84. Yardeni, *Refuge protestant,* 49–53; Hoyez and Ruffelard, "Migrations protestantes," 2:247–50; Michèle Magdelaine, "Francfort-sur-le-Main: plaque tournante du Refuge," in *Le refuge huguenot,* ed. M. Magdelaine and Rudolf von Thadden (Paris: Armand Colin, 1985), 36–37; M. Magdelaine, "Le Refuge: le rôle de Francfort-sur-le-Main," in *Révocation de l'Édit de Nantes,* ed. Bots and Posthumus Meyjes, 201–6; Scoville, *Persecutions of Huguenots,* 107.

85. AN, TT/236/984 (Bretagne); Jean-Yves Carluer, "Les protestants bretons XVIe–XXe siècles," 4 vols. (thèse de doctorat, Université de Rennes, 1990), 2:553–54.

86. Ms. NAF 21333, fol. 640, BN; J. F. Bosher, "Huguenot Merchants," 84–86.

87. C. E. Lart, ed., "Some Letters from France, 1585–1685," *HSP* 16 (1937): 71–72; Carluer, "Protestants bretons," app. 2:8–12. The De Farcy family was in Carolina at least until 1690 but returned to England to settle eventually in Manakintown, Virginia. See Register of the Province, Conveyance Books, vol. A, 1682–93:380–81, SCDAH; Priscilla H. Cabell, *Turf and Twig: The French Lands,* 2 vols. (Richmond: privately printed, 1988), 1:121.

88. Th. Maillard, "Les routes de l'exil du Poitou vers les îles Normandes et l'Angleterre: Le guide Pierre Michaut," *BSHPF* 49 (1900): 281–91; Hoyez and Ruffelard, "Migrations protestantes," 2:272.

89. "Memoir of Pastor Etienne DuSoul," Bodleian Library, Oxford, Rawlinson ms., C 984, fol. 278–278a.

90. Photocopy of the April 1715 questioning of Marie Thoreau deposited in the Archives du département de la Vienne (Poitiers); M. Philippe Marty, letter to the author, May 22, 1996. Marie's married name was Laummonier or Aummonier, and her son, Jacques, was in Carolina at least in 1708. Jacques's sister, married to Pierre Sauzeau, was also among those arrested that day. See Maillard, "Routes de l'exil," 282; Records of the Register of the Province (Conveyance Series), vol. 1709–12:7, SCDAH; Lesser, *South Carolina Begins,* 315.

91. Maillard, "Routes de l'exil," 288; Carluer, "Protestants bretons," 606. Nationwide, guides could make profits up to 1,500 livres (£115) per escape (Hoyez and Ruffelard, "Migrations protestantes," 2:251).

92. Maillard, "Routes de l'exil," 289.

93. Krunemacker, *Les protestants du Poitou,* 128–29.

94. Fontaine, *Memoirs,* 119–22; Migault, *Journal,* 103–11.

95. Durand, *Voyages,* 47–61.

96. Hoyez and Ruffelard, "Migrations protestantes," 2:277, map, "Les sorties de France."

97. Judith's father was by then deceased. Judith had a married sister who lived in Pont-en-Royans, Dauphiny, and a third brother, whom she mentioned in her letter, stationed with Louis XIV's troops in Lüneburg, Lower Saxony. See "Judith Giton Manigault to Her Brother," Manigault Family Papers, 11/275/3, fol. 1, South Carolina Historical Society, Charleston; Samuel Mours, *Le protestantisme en Vivarais et en Velay: Des origines à nos jours* (Valence: Imprimeries Réunies, 1949), 280. Judith Giton's letter, a classic of South Carolina literature, has been published many times in French and in English. See, for example, Baird, *History,* 2:396–97; Slann L. C. Simmons, trans. and ed., "Early Manigault Records," *HSSCT* 59 (1954): 25–27.

98. Judith's mother, Madeleine, died during the passage, and Pierre died eighteen months after their arrival in Carolina. Only Judith and Louis indentured themselves to pay for the final leg of the voyage, possibly because they were the youngest of the three children. See "Letter of Judith (Giton) Manigault" (original/undated) and "Receipt for Transatlantic Passage" (Pierre Giton) (April 27, 1685), Manigault Family Papers, 11/275/3, fol. 1 and 11/275/5.

99. Judith mentions in her letter a "Mme de Choiseul," who lived near Langres, Burgundy, and from whom they expected some assistance, but the latter having died before their arrival, they were ill-received by her son-in-law, who threatened to turn them in "Letter of Judith (Giton) Manigault (original undated)," Manigault Family Papers, 11/275/3, fol. 1.

100. Jeanne Skalski-Coignard, "Une famille languedocienne en Caroline du Sud: les Gaillard," *Cahiers de Généalogie Protestante* 45 (1994): 9–13; Daniel Ravenel, ed., *Liste des François et Suisses: From an Old Manuscript List of French and Swiss Protestants Settled in Charleston, Santee, and at the Orange Quarter in Carolina Who Desired Naturalization Prepared Probably about 1695–6* (1868; Baltimore: Genealogical Publishing Company, 1990), 56 (#74); Salley, *Papers,* 2:216.

101. This return to France explains why Barthélemy is not on the 1697 Naturalization List. See Ravenel, *Liste,* 56 (#74); Skalski-Coignard, "Une famille languedocienne," 11; "Barthélemy Gaillard, letter of attorney to his brother Jean" (May 22, 1692), Miscellaneous Records (Proprietary series), vol. 1696–1703:218, SCDAH.

102. Thus, for example, a breakdown by *départements* of the geographic origins of 449 Huguenots whose arrival in London was recorded in the *Livre de Témoignages de l'Église de Threadneedle Street* for May 1687 shows that 435 of them came from five Normandy départements (Seine Maritime, Calvados, Eure, Manche, and Orne). Similarly, Cottret's study of the records of the La Patente Church in London for 1688 shows that 25 percent of the refugees hailed from Normandy. See Gwynn, "Arrival of Huguenot Refugees," 371; Cottret, *Huguenots in England,* 186.

103. "A Litteral Translation taken from my Grand father Stephen Mazyck's Registry kept and wrote by himself in an old French Bible by me his Grand Son Peter Hamon in the year 1786," The Huguenot Society of South Carolina Library, Charleston, ms. collection, [2].

104. Michèle Magdelaine, comp., "Printed Listing of Refugees Assisted at the French Reformed Church of Frankfurt-am-Main" (computer printout).

105. "Letter of Judith (Giton) Manigault," Manigault Family Papers, 11/275/3, fol. 1, back.

106. Magdelaine, "Printed Listing"; Ravenel, *Liste,* 61 (#113).

107. In New England also this edict provoked outrage among the Congregationalists. In the above-cited 1682 sermon, Increase Mather denounced "an edict come forth concerning them [the French Protestants], more bloody than what came from the court of Pharaoh: Pharaoh's Edict was to destroy onely the Bodyes of Israelitish Infants: But now there's an Edict that reacheth further: An Edict for the destruction of the Souls of the Children of Protestants. An Edict to make Idolaters of them" (Mather, *Sermon,* [18]).

108. See, for example, *The Humble Petition of the Protestants of France to the French King, to recall his declaration for taking their children from them at the age of seven years* (London: printed by N. T. for Andrew Forrester, 1681); *The Present state of the Protestants in France in three letters: Written by a gentleman at London to his friend in the country . . .* (London: printed for John Holford, 1681); *The horrible persecution of the French Protestants in the province of Poitou truly set forth by a gentleman of great quality . . .* (London: printed for Randolph Taylor, 1681); *A Letter from Rochel France: to Mr. Demeuare, one of the French ministers at the French church in the Savoy, shewing the intolerable persecutions that are there exercised against them* (London: printed for R. Bentley, 1681); *A Strange but true account of the barbarous usage of three young ladies in France for being Protestants: with a relation also of their wonderful escape from thence into England* (London: printed for E. Brooks, 1681).

109. Thorp, "English Government," 62–63. Whereas parliamentary naturalization offered aliens the same rights as natural-born Englishmen, royal denization granted only limited privileges (i.e., contained in the letters patent) to its recipients. For more on this subject, see infra chap. 7.

110. The declaration (July 28, 1681) can be found in Arber, *Torments of Protestant Slaves,* xxviii–xxx (quote, xxviii–ix).

111. [David Primrose], *An Harangue to the King by a Minister of the* French *Church in the Savoy the Nineteenth of* October, *1681* (London: R. Bentley & M. Magnes, 1681), 1–2.

112. Fontaine, *Memoirs,* 123.

113. [René Petit and Jacob Guérard], "Humble proposition faite au Roy et à son Parlement pour donner retraite aux Étrangers protestants et aux prosélites dans ses Colonies de L'Amérique et Surtout en la Caroline," BPRO, CO 1/43/16 and transcribed in Salley, *Papers,* 1:62.

282 Notes to pages 66–67

114. Rounded off amounts for each collection are 1681 (£15,000), 1686 (£43,000), 1688 (£20,000), and 1694 (£12,000) or a total of £90,000 in thirteen years exclusively for the Huguenots. In comparison, the 1699 collect for the Vaudois (Waldensians) and the 1709 brief for the Palatines raised £27,000 and £22,500, respectively. See Roy A. Sundstrom, "Aid and Assimilation: A Study of the Economic Support Given French Protestants in England, 1680–1727" (Ph.D. diss., Kent State, 1972), 35–46; Sugiko Nishikawa, "English Attitudes toward Continental Protestants with Particular Reference to Church Briefs, c. 1680–1740" (Ph.D. thesis, University of London, 1998), 23, 57, 34.

115. Even in New England where initial enthusiasm for the "Huguenot cause" ran high, generosity somewhat faded with time, as a Huguenot settled in Boston realistically described. "The impression that advantages are granted here to the refugees," he wrote in a 1687 letter, "is one that needs to be dispelled. At first, indeed, some supplied were given them, but at present, nothing is to be hoped for in behalf of those who bring nothing" ("Relation d'un protestant français réfugié à Boston," in Baird, *History,* 2:386–87).

116. G. C. Gibbs, "The Reception of the Huguenots in England and the Dutch Republic, 1680–1690," in *From Persecution to Toleration: The Glorious Revolution and Religion in England,* ed. Ole P. Grell, Johnathan I. Israel, and Nicholas Tyacke (Oxford: Clarendon Press, 1991), 291.

117. Malcolm R. Thorp, "The Anti-Huguenot Undercurrent in Late-Seventeenth-Century England," *HSP* 23 (1976): 569–80.

118. Gibbs, "Reception of the Huguenots," 293; Butler, *Huguenots in America,* 33–34; Thorp, "English Government," 40–41.

119. Thorp, "English Government," 29–36; Cottret, *Huguenots in England,* 195–99.

120. Gibbs, "Reception of Huguenots," 293, 291 (first two quotes); Thorp, "English Government," 38–42 (quote, 39). The pejorative term "frog" first referred to the Dutch because most of the coastal Netherlands is under sea level, but it gradually came to mean French because (in some regions of France) frog legs are regarded as a culinary delicacy. The analogy shifted from living like an amphibian to eating one.

121. Thorp, "Anti-Huguenot Undercurrent," 571–74. As Cottret notes about the religious climate of late Stuart England, "the identification of Protestantism with England had two corollaries: every papist was a foreigner and every foreigner was a potential papist" (Cottret, *Huguenots in England,* 203). For a nuanced approach to the nature English Francophobia, which emphasizes its limits due to acknowledged Anglo-Gallic affinities based on a shared "Gothick past," see Colin Kidd, *British Identities before Nationalism: Ethnicity and Nationhood in the Atlantic World, 1600–1800* (Cambridge: Cambridge University Press, 1999), chap. 9, especially "The limits of Francophobia," 233–45.

122. Gwynn, *Huguenot Heritage,* 173; John Miller, *James II: A Study in Kingship* (Hove, U.K.: Wayland Publishers, 1978), 144–45; Thorp, "English Government," 132–40.

123. Thorp, "English Government," 127–29; Gwynn, *Huguenot Heritage,* 170–71.

124. Sundstrom, "Aid and Assimilation," 41–42.

125. Nishikawa, "English Attitudes," 29–34 (quote).

126. Robin D. Gwynn, "James II in the Light of His Treatment of Huguenot Refugees in England, 1685–1686," *HSP* 23 (1980): 212–25; Miller, *James II,* 144–45; Cottret, *Huguenots in England,* 204–7; Thorp, "English Government," 111–16.

127. Over the years these collections were replaced by more regular and systematic sources of funds: a king's weekly grant of one hundred pounds sterling from April 1695 to March 1697; a parliamentary (civil list) annual grant of fifteen thousand pounds sterling, called the Royal Bounty, from 1696 to 1702; various grants under Queen Anne and the Hanoverians from 1702 to 1803; and

parliamentary grants from 1804 until the last "Huguenot" pensioner died in 1876. These were also complemented by occasional donations. See Raymond Smith, comp., *Records of the Royal Bounty and Connected Funds, the Burn Donation, and the Savoy Church in the Huguenot Library, University College, London,* Quarto Series, vol. 51 (London: HSGB&I Publications, 1974), 1; Sundstrom, "Aid and Assimilation," iv. This system of financial assistance for exiled Huguenots was not specific to England but was organized throughout northern Europe, especially in the main urban refugee centers such as Amsterdam, Frankfort, and Geneva.

128. Briefs were issued for a variety of reasons. Most were intended to help congregations in Britain to cope with fires and natural disasters and for church repairs. Others raised funds to redeem captives and to compensate for losses at sea from pirates, usually French, and to assist continental Protestants, such as the Waldensians, Huguenots, Orangeois (Protestants from the Principality of Orange in southern France), Palatines, and other groups from central and oriental Europe, who were all victims of persecution at some point. Out of the ninety-three briefs issued from 1680 to 1690, nearly 70 percent were intended for congregations damaged by fire and 7.5 percent for foreign Protestants. In the second half of the seventeenth century, briefs were so common that Samuel Pepys thought that their frequency discouraged donation. "To church," he wrote on June 30, 1661, "where we observe the trade of briefs is come now up to so constant a course every Sunday, that we resolve to give no more to them" (Nishikawa, "English Attitudes," 5, 15 [quote], 68, figure 3).

129. Whereas in 1681 Charles II had mentioned "the great hardships and persecutions" endured by Huguenots "forced to abandon their native abodes . . . in haste and confusion," in 1686 James II made no reference to conditions in France, simply acknowledging that public acts of charity were "the highest prerogative, and most desirable advantage of kings" (quoted in Gwynn, *Huguenot Heritage,* 170).

130. The account of the 1681 collection, for example, was first closed in September 1683 when the brief expired but was soon reopened until May 1689 when the last donation was recorded. See A. P. Hands and Irene Scouloudi, eds., *French Protestant Refugees Relieved through the Threadneedle Street Church, London 1681–1687,* Quarto Series, vol. 49 (London: HSGB&I Publications, 1971), 6.

131. Thorp, "English Government," 94–103; Sundstrom, "Aid and Assimilation," 33–36; Raymond Smith, "Financial Aid to French Protestant Refugees 1681–1727: Briefs and the Royal Bounty," *HSP* 23 (1973): 248–56. Most of the funds were handled by the London churches. For the 1681 collection, for example, the Threadneedle Street and Savoy churches received nearly fifty-eight hundred and forty-three hundred pounds sterling, respectively, or a total of slightly over ten thousand of the fifteen thousand pounds sterling raised. See Sundstrom, "Aid and Assimilation," 37–38; Nishikawa, "English Attitudes," 23. The seven commissioners for the 1681 brief were William Sancroft, archbishop of Canterbury; Henry Compton, bishop of London; Edward Stillingfleet, dean of St. Paul's; Sir Patience Ward, lord mayor of London; Thomas Papillon and John Dubois, the London Whig sheriffs of Huguenot descent who had won the turbulent 1682 elections; and the philanthropist Thomas Firmin. See Irene Scouloudi, "L'aide apportée aux réfugiés protestants français par l'Église de Threadneedle Street, l'Église de Londres, 1681–1687," *BSHPF* 115 (1969): 434; Hands and Scouloudi, *French Protestant Refugees,* 8n1.

132. This number even rose to seventy-four when the 1686 brief was renewed in 1688 (Sundstrom, "Aid and Assimilation," 56–57).

133. Evidently these different committees evolved through time. While the commissioners were operative until 1831, an English committee called Comité de Messieurs les Commissaires Anglais took over the task of supervising the French Committee from 1705 to 1771. From that year to 1802 the French Committee acted under the supervision of three or more directors of the

Bank of England before being eventually placed under the direction of the treasury. In 1696 the French Committee was divided into Lay and Ecclesiastical Committees in charge of distributing the funds to the laity and the clergy, respectively. These two committees were in existence until 1876. See Smith, *Records of the Royal Bounty,* 2.

134. Thorp, "English Government," 107–11.

135. Sundstrom, "Aid and Assimilation," 132–48; Cottret, *Huguenots in England,* 222–23.

136. Sundstrom, "Aid and Assimilation," 161–65.

137. Pastors seemed to have been the target of many complaints, judging by a 1687 letter from a refugee who explained that in England "[ministers] are supported by the collections, but generously and in preference to all the others" ("grassement et préférablement à tous les autres") (N[athanaël] W[eiss], ed., "Le sort des réfugiés en Hollande, Angleterre et ailleurs," *BSHPF* 34 [1885]: 192).

138. Huguenot Society of Great Britain and Ireland Library, London (hereafter HSGB&I Library), "Bounty Papers," ms. 1, "Index of names of all the persons who received assistance from the brief (*collecte*) of 1686 as recorded in the three registers of resolutions (*délibérations*) of the [French] Committee covering the period 4 June 1686–28 August 1687," fol. 133 (Pirou), ms. 2, "Accounts of £2645.3.9 Sterlings Payd in part of the £3115.10 allowed by ye Lords Commiss[ione]rs to Severall french Conformed Protestants ye 4th May 1687," fol. 2 (Prioleau). These registers, which contain the records of the distribution of part of the monies collected under James II's 1686 brief but not of the funds allocated by the crown through William III's Royal Bounty, are nonetheless inaccurately known under the generic terms "Bounty Papers" or "Bounty Records." See Smith, *Records of the Royal Bounty,* 12–13.

139. Margaret M. Escott, "Profiles of Relief: Royal Bounty Grants to Huguenot Refugees, 1686–1709," *HSP* 25 (1991): 263–64, 273; Hands and Scouloudi, *French Protestant Refugees,* 11–13.

140. HSGB&I Library, "Bounty Papers," ms. 2, fol. 2 front and back (Horry); ms. 2, fol. 1 back, fol. 4 (Perdriau).

141. Hands and Scouloudi, *French Protestant Refugees,* 86–87.

142. HSGB&I Library, "Bounty Papers," ms. 1 (1686–87), ms. 2 (1686–88); French Protestant Church Library, London (hereafter FPCL), Records of the French Church, ms. 64, "Register of poor refugees assisted by the Church of London and the Church of the Savoy acting in common, August 1685–Dec. 1686." See also Raymond Smith, comp., *The Archives of the French Protestant Church of London,* Quarto Series, vol. 50 (London: HSGB&I Publications, 1972). Occasional references to Huguenots receiving financial aid to settle in British North America or in the "West Indies," which often meant North America, can also be found in the Corporation of London Record Office, Guildhall Library, London, "Collections for the French Protestant Refugees," ms. 346 (1681–85) and ms. 347 (1686–90) (vouchers).

143. These are found in FPCL, ms. 63, "Account book in ledger form of receipts from the Chamber of London and disbursements for the relief of named refugees, and for surgeons, apothecaries, clothes, beds, etc., 5 August 1681–1684."

144. The presence of the Earl of Craven, one of the Carolina proprietors, on the Commissioners Committee appointed for the 1688 brief may also have been a factor, although most Huguenots were already in the colony by then (Smith, *Records of the Royal Bounty,* 15).

145. HSGB&I Library, "Bounty Papers," ms. 1, fol. 160; Howard S. F. Randolph, ed., "The Census of 1698 for Mamaroneck, Morrisania, and New Rochelle, Westchester County, New York," *New York Genealogical and Biographical Record* 59 (1928): 107.

146. HSGB&I Library, "Bounty Papers," ms. 1, fol. 26.

147. Conversely, a few Huguenots who originally intended to immigrate to another colony actually settled in the lowcountry, such as Daniel Huger "and other Poor French Protestants," who were given fifteen pounds sterling to go to "Pensilvania att or about the month [of] June 1685." (Corporation of London Record Office, Guildhall Library, London, "Collections for the French Protestant Refugees," ms. 347, no. 1; Gwynn, *Minutes,* 143n1).

148. If the children are included, the average goes down to six pounds sterling. These figures must be interpreted as high estimates because in several cases recipients did not specify how many people were to leave with them. Furthermore, it is important to remember that we are dealing with grants and that it is impossible to verify whether or not the refugees actually received these sums of money, although it is likely that they did. See HSGB&I Library, "Bounty Papers," mss. 1, 2; *Nouvelle Relation de la Caroline,* 4; *Suite de la Description de la Carolline,* 17.

149. HSGB&I Library, "Bounty Papers," ms. 1, fol. 89 (St. Julien); ms. 1, fol. 89 (Jouet).

150. HSGB&I Library, "Bounty Papers," ms. 1, fol. 88 (Joly); ms. 1, fol. 168 (Thoury); ms. 1, fol. 1 (Bondet); ms. 2, fol. 2 (Prioleau). Daniel Bondet settled in Oxford, Massachusetts, instead of Charleston, as he had apparently informed the committee (Butler, *Huguenots in America,* 63).

151. Butler, *Huguenots in America,* 53; Escott, "Profiles of Relief," 273.

152. Thorp, "English Government," 192–96. On Manakintown, see Cabell, *Turf and Twig;* R. A. Brock, ed., *Documents Chiefly Unpublished Relating to the Huguenot Emigration to Virginia and to the Settlement at Manakin-Town* (1886; Baltimore: Clearfield Company Reprints and Remainders, 1979); James L. Bugg, "The French Huguenot Frontier Settlement of Manakintown," *Virginia Magazine of History and Biography* 61 (1953): 360–94; Leslie Tobias, "Manakintown: The Development and Demise of a French Protestant Refugee Community in Colonial Virginia, 1700–1750" (master's thesis, College of William and Mary, 1982).

4. The South Carolina Huguenots

Epigraph from "Letter of February 1685" (no. 3), *Suite de la Description de la Carolline,* 8.

1. The existence of these passenger lists is not just coincidental since it is due to specific contemporary circumstances prevailing at the time of their compiling. The list of the *Richmond* was duly recorded and filed in the Admiralty Papers because the *Richmond* was an HMS frigate and her voyage was financed by the crown. The *Margaret* left England after the Monmouth Rebellion at a time when ship captains were required to report the names of their passengers. As for the *Loyal Jamaica,* it is not strictly speaking a passenger list that is extant but a list of passengers who disembarked in Charleston and for whom Carolina settlers posted bond. For the *Richmond,* see BPRO, Admiralty Papers 1/5139, Orders in Council, 1679–88, fol. 162; E. H. Fairbrother, comp., "Foreign Protestants for Carolina in 1679," *HSP* 10 (1912): 187–89; Martha B. Burns, "The Richmond," *HSSCT* 85 (1980): 43–49; Childs, "Petit-Guérard Colony," 1–17, 88–97. For the *Margaret,* see BPRO, State Papers 44/336, 163; "The Passenger List of the *Margaret,*" *HSSCT* 93 (1988): 32–34; Lesser, *South Carolina Begins,* 78. For the *Loyal Jamaica,* see Alexander S. Salley, ed., *Journal of the Grand Council of South Carolina, August 25, 1671–June 24, 1680* (Columbia: Historical Commission of South Carolina, 1907), 61; Alexander S. Salley, ed., *Journal of the Grand Council of South Carolina, April 11, 1692–September 26, 1692* (Columbia: Historical Commission of South Carolina, 1907), 16–19; Lesser, *South Carolina Begins,* 219n102.

2. This document is sometimes referred to as the St. Julien List because the original manuscript was found "in a parcel of old papers which belonged to Henry de St. Julien . . . the youngest son of [the refugee] Pierre de St. Julien." While the original is no longer extant, this list has been

published many times in different forms since 1822. I am using the 1990 reprint of the 1868 edition. See Ravenel, *Liste,* 7, 41 (quote).

3.   Their absence from the 1696 naturalization list could be due to their unwillingness to be naturalized, their unawareness of the existence of the *Liste,* or simply the fact that parts of the original *Liste* may be missing.

4.   The Naturalization Act is in Thomas Cooper and David J. McCord, eds., *The Statutes at Large of South Carolina,* 10 vols. (Columbia: A. S. Johnston, 1836–41), 2:131–32. The original is no longer extant, but a contemporary copy can be found in the John Archdale Papers, Library of Congress, microfilm copy, fols. 140–42, SCDAH.

5.   The year 1680 marks the beginning of the migration with the arrival of the *Richmond,* and 1712 is the year when the last group of Huguenots, who came from Manakintown, Virginia, settled in the colony. The figure of 347 corresponds to the number of adult refugees who *migrated* to South Carolina and does not differentiate between the Huguenots who stayed and those who left. For a description of the methods used to identify Huguenots in the proprietary records, see Bertrand Van Ruymbeke, "L'émigration huguenote en Caroline du Sud sous le régime des Seigneurs Propriétaires: Étude d'une communauté du Refuge dans une province britannique d'Amérique du Nord, 1680–1720," 2 vols. (thèse de doctorat, La Sorbonne-Nouvelle, 1995), 1:283–90. The total of 347 adult refugees represents more than two and a half times the number included in Friedlander's list (136), almost exclusively based on the 1696–97 naturalization records (Friedlander, "Carolina Huguenots," 86–88, 322–25).

6.   This last method was not used indifferently but on a case by case basis and exclusive of the Huguenots who first appeared in the records at the occasion of the 1696–97 naturalization procedure. If a Huguenot first surfaced in the records before 1693, one can assume that this date corresponds to his arrival in the colony with a statistically insignificant margin of error since we know ships with Huguenots on board arrived in 1680, 1685 (perhaps two), and 1692 and possibly in 1686 and 1687. If the first date in the records is between 1693 and 1700, and if it is known through a cross reference that the refugee came via another North American colony or the Caribbean, one can safely assume that the date corresponds to their arrival in the colony. Finally, for the period 1700–1712 dates of land warrants can be safely interpreted as dates of arrival since there is little chance that these Huguenots would have lived in the province fifteen to twenty years without appearing in the colony's remarkably complete records at least once.

7.   T[homas] A[my], *Carolina, or a Description of the Present State of That Country* (London: W. C., 1682), in *Early Narratives,* ed. Salley, 143. For the identification of T. A. as Thomas Amy, " a London druggist, probably related to the Colletons," see Childs, *Malaria and Colonization,* 189n40.

8.   "[Jacques] Boyd to Governor Archdale" (Santee, September 2, 1695), John Archdale Papers, Library of Congress, microfilm copy, fol. 100, SCDAH.

9.   In a hagiographic attempt to prove that the Huguenots were among the founders of South Carolina, Hirsch unconvincingly tried to turn early settlers, such as Richard Deyos, Richard Battin, and George Prideaux, who were in Carolina by 1672, or even William Argent, who came "in the first fleet" in 1670, into French Protestants on the sole basis of a French-sounding or French-spelled last name. As already pointed out by Alexander S. Salley in his review of Hirsch's book, these colonists were undoubtedly English. See Hirsch, *Huguenots,* 8–10; Alexander S. Salley, "The Huguenots of Colonial South Carolina," *Columbia State,* March 18, 1928, reprinted in *HSSCT* 93 (1988): 51–59 (esp. 52–53). The same error and the same names are found in Weiss's 1854 *History of the French Protestant Refugees,* which Hirsch used. See M. Charles Weiss, *History*

of the French Protestant Refugees from the Revocation of the Edict of Nantes to Our Own Days, 2 vols., trans. Henry W. Herbert (New York: Stringer & Townsend, 1854), 2:332–33.

10. The *Richmond* documents contain two lists, one dated October 15, 1679, and the other November 8, 1679. The first names eighteen heads of families, thirteen of whom appear in the second list and ten of these in the Carolina records. Fifteen other names, either wives and servants unnamed in the list or other Huguenots who must have sailed on the *Richmond* in lieu of those who withdrew between October and November 1679, could be found through cross referencing with the land warrants and the *Liste des François et Suisses.* This gives a total of twenty-five adults. See BPRO, Admiralty Papers 1/5139, Orders in Council, 1679–88, fol. 162; Childs, "Petit-Guérard Colony," 95–97; Salley and Olsberg, *Warrants for Lands,* 245, 321; Ravenel, *Liste,* 49, 52.

11. Contrary to Childs's calculations based on the first list of prospective passengers, I think that Thomas Amy meant forty-five people not adults. See Childs, "Petit-Guérard Colony," 95.

12. Childs, "Petit-Guérard Colony," 92–94; Salley and Olsberg, *Warrants for Lands,* 336–37.

13. There is a Margaret Petit named in the *Liste des François et Suisses* but as the mother of Nicolas and Abel Bochet; nothing indicates that she ever came to Carolina (Ravenel, *Liste,* 59, 60 [#98, #99]).

14. The passenger list of the *Margaret,* like that of the *Richmond,* is a departure, not an arrival, document and must therefore also be used with caution. I have identified forty-nine passengers who appear in the Carolina records, but this figure could be raised to fifty-five by including others who may have been Huguenots but whose names were anglicized beyond recognition by the clerk, Huguenots who were listed but do not seem to have ever been in Carolina either because they did not actually embark or because they died during the voyage, and others who arrived in Charleston but moved on to another colony soon after. The list was registered on July 15. Provided that the ship left that day or soon after, she must have arrived in Charleston six to eight weeks later. A pink (*pinque* in French) was a relatively small ship "with a flat deck whose raised stern was round." In his published memoirs the Huguenot Samuel de Pechels, who was transported to the Caribbean on a pink, wrote about "l'abominable pinque" (BPRO, State Papers 44/336, 163; "Passenger List of the *Margaret,*" 31–33; de Pechels, *Mémoires,* 48n1 [first quote], 55 [second quote]).

15. BPRO, Privy Council 2/71, 99. I am grateful to Thomas O. Lawton for informing me of the existence of this reference.

16. Hirsch, *Huguenots,* 13.

17. Hirsch's figure of six hundred, however, is totally unrealistic (ibid). A nineteenth-century author, unfortunately without citing it, quoted a 1686 source alluding to a group of Huguenot refugees in the Netherlands making preparations to reach England where they had chartered a ship to sail to Carolina. It is possible that these Huguenots joined with others in England and reached Carolina in 1686 or 1687. See G. P. Disosway, "The Huguenots in America," in Samuel Smiles, *The Huguenots: Their Settlements, Churches, and Industries in England and Ireland with an Appendix Relating to the Huguenots in America* (1868; Baltimore: Genealogical Publishing Co., 1972), 435.

18. "Letter of Ester Dubourdieu, Wife of Louis Fleury, to her Brother Dubourdieu at Vitré" (London, July 6, 1687), in Lart, "Some Letters from France," 68.

19. Salley, *Journal of the Grand Council,* 61; Salley, *Journal of the Grand Council, 1692,* 16–19; Lesser, *South Carolina Begins,* 219n102. Although less significant historiographically, this list is more reliable as a source since it is an arrival document.

20. Contrary to Childs, however, I do not believe that Pierre and Marie Du Moulin, who were in Carolina in 1682, were part of the *Richmond* expedition. Du Moulin's high status and connections

were well above Guérard's and Petit's, and his presence would have had to have been recorded. I think that this couple came on an English ship. See Childs, "Petit-Guérard Colony," 93–94.

21. This figure rises to 151 if we include the six Huguenots who show up in the records in 1688 and 1689 and who may have arrived in the colony during that period.

22. "Papier du consistoire pour l'année 1687 [1687–91]," Narragansett Church Register, Huguenot Society of America Library, New York, ms. 1687 [p. 3]; for a published translation, see L. Effingham de Forest, trans. and ed., "Records of the French Church at Narragansett," *New York Genealogical and Biographical Record* 70 (1939): 236–41, 359–65, and 71 (1940): 51–61; Baird, *History,* 1:309n2; Ravenel, *Liste,* 50 (#43). Another example is Salomon Legaré, who arrived in South Carolina in 1696 or 1697 and whose parents had settled in Massachusetts by 1687. In a letter written in 1687, a refugee, settled in New England, mentioned Legaré, "un marchand orphèvre françois," who owned a house on the coast with ten and half acres twelve miles south of Boston. See Baird, *History,* 2:204; "Relation d'un protestant français réfugié à Boston," in Baird, *History,* 2:app:392; Winifred L. Holman, "Legaré Notes," *American Genealogist* 25 (1949): 8–11; E. Milby Burton, *South Carolina Silversmiths 1690–1860* (1942; rev. by Warren Ripley, Charleston: Contributions from the Charleston Museum, 1991), 57–58; Records of the Register of the Province (Conveyance Series), book D, 1696–1703, pp. 201, 203, SCDAH.

23. Van Ruymbeke, "L'émigration huguenote," 1:308–11; Virginia Gourdin, "Madeleine Chardon, of Tours, Touraine and Her Family," *HSSCT* 91 (1986): 101n173, 104n210; R. C. Nash, "Huguenot Merchants and the Development of the Atlantic Economy," in *Memory and Identity,* ed. Van Ruymbeke and Sparks, 213.

24. The adult-to-child ratio in the *Liste* is 0.85 (182 adults for 156 children). Not all the *Liste* could be used for determining this ratio as section three (Orange Quarter) does not list the children. Therefore the number of adults used in this calculation is smaller than the number of adults mentioned in the *Liste* by 18 (182 instead of 200). Unfortunately, this method has two problems. First, it takes the 1696 adult-to-child ratio as a set parameter, whereas it necessarily evolved through time. Second, it does not differentiate between the children born in Carolina after the migration and those born overseas. After 1700 this method of calculation becomes even less reliable because of the emergence of the second-generation refugees, i.e., those who were children in the 1680s, who start to form families.

25. The original reads, "environ 400 François" ("Lettre au Marquis de Seigneulay" [June 14, 1687], ms. NAF, Arnoul 21334, fol. 194, BN).

26. The original reads, "une centaine de François" ("Questions et Responses faites au sujet de la Caroline" fols. 51–55, 54 back).

27. Ravenel, *Liste;* BPRO, CO 5/1258 (1699). The 1699 census can also be found in Salley, *Papers,* 4 (1698–1700):75.

28. For estimates of the South Carolina white population, see Coclanis, *Shadow of a Dream,* 64.

29. Because we are dealing with small numbers, statistics can be deceiving. Thus, for example, seven of the nine refugees who hailed from Berry and who represent 4 percent of the Carolina Huguenots for whom we know the province of origin, are members of the same family: Jacques, Jacques (Jr.), Isaac, Pierre, Marie, Élisabeth, and Judith Dugué (Ravenel, *Liste,* 46–47 (#15, #16), 52 (#57).

30. The breakdown by province is Aunis (fifty-five refugees / 23 percent), Poitou (twenty-eight/11 percent), Normandy (twenty-six/10.7 percent), Saintonge (twenty-six/10.7 percent), and Brittany (eleven/4.5 percent). See also Bertrand Van Ruymbeke, "The Huguenots of Proprietary South Carolina: Patterns of Migration and Integration," in *Money, Trade, and Power: The Evolution of Colonial South Carolina's Plantation Society,* ed. Jack P. Greene, Rosemary Brana-Shute, and Randy J. Sparks (Columbia: University of South Carolina Press, 2001), 29–32.

31. Quoted in Marcel Delafosse, ed., *Histoire de La Rochelle* (Toulouse: Éditions Privat, 1985), 163.

32. John G. Clark, *La Rochelle and the Atlantic Economy during the Eighteenth Century* (Baltimore: Johns Hopkins University Press, 1981), 26, 27; Jean Delumeau, "Le commerce extérieur français au XVIIe siècle," *XVIIème Siècle* 70 (1966): 94–95.

33. Delafosse, *Histoire de La Rochelle,* 167; Clark, *La Rochelle,* 26–27. Ships numbering 273 left La Rochelle for the West Indies, Africa, and Canada between 1670 and 1679, and 411 left in the following decade (Pétré-Grenouilleau, *Négoces maritimes français,* 31). La Rochelle also actively traded with Quebec, Boston, and New York (Bosher, "Huguenot Merchants," 80–83).

34. Migault, *Journal,* 37.

35. The exact percentages are Dauphiny (4.9 percent), Languedoc (5.5 percent), and Guyenne (5.2 percent).

36. The term "urban" here has to be understood only in contrast to rural.

37. In early modern France a city (*une grande* or *très grande* [thirty thousand plus] *ville*) had more than ten thousand inhabitants, a town (*ville moyenne*) between five thousand and ten thousand, and a market town (*une petite ville*) between two thousand and five thousand. Although population is only one of the criteria that differentiated a city or a town from a village (along with the presence of ramparts, military and/or financial autonomy, the location of a court or a see, and the economic structure), this is the factor that has been used here for statistical purposes. See Garnot, *Villes en France,* 7–9, 12–14; Jean Meyer and Jean-Pierre Poussou, *Études sur les villes francaises: Milieu du XVIIe siècle à la veille de la révolution française* (Paris: SEDES, 1995), 102–9; Bairoch et al., *Population,* 23–31, 289–90; Philip Benedict, "French Cities from the Sixteenth Century to the Revolution: An Overview," in *Cities and Social Change in Early Modern France,* ed. Philip Benedict (London: Unwin Hyman, 1989), 24–25; Philippe Hercule under the direction of J.P. Bardet, G. Arbellot, and B. Lepetit, *Charente-Maritime,* Paroisses et communes de France (Paris: Éditions du Centre National de la Recherche Scientifique, 1985), 317, 389, 468, 493, 590; Benedict, *Huguenot Population,* 9n6, 34, 55; Philip Benedict, "La population réformée française de 1600 à 1685," *Annales E.S.C.* (1987): 1440–42.

38. Yardeni, *Refuge protestant,* 11.

39. On the foundation, decline, and ethnic makeup of Purrysburgh, see Arlin M. Migliazzo, "Ethnic Diversity on the Southern Frontier: A Social History of Purrysburgh, South Carolina, 1732–1792" (Ph.D. diss., Washington State University, 1982); Albert B. Faust, "Swiss Emigration to the American Colonies in the Eighteenth Century," *American Historical Review* 22 (1916–17): 21–44.

40. It is estimated that forty-five thousand Huguenots passed through Switzerland between 1680 and 1700 (Marie-Jeanne Ducommin and Dominique Quadroni, *Le refuge protestant dans le Pays de Vaud (Fin XVIIe–début XVIIIe s.): Aspects d'une migration* (Geneva: Droz, 1991), 13.

41. Ibid., 17–21.

42. Ravenel, *Liste,* 52 (#56), 62 (#117), 59 (#90), 54 (#63).

43. Van Ruymbeke, "Huguenots of Proprietary South Carolina," 32–37. Huguenot pastors are studied in the following chapter. A Huguenot lawyer, Pierre Villepontoux, who migrated to South Carolina via New Rochelle, New York, at the turn of the eighteenth century, never practiced law in Carolina, where he appears in the records as a "planter." See Baird, *History,* 2:141n1; Records of the Court of Common Pleas, Judgment Rolls, box 2, case no. 713, SCDAH.

44. Historians of late seventeenth-century France distinguish three strata within the nobility: the *ducs et pairs de France,* who were few and who, most of the time, were related to the monarch;

the members of the *noblesse seconde,* who occupied high administrative and military positions; and the *gentilshommes,* who controlled much smaller revenues, lived on their estates, and exerted little influence beyond their communities. See Jean-Marie Constant, *La société française aux XVIe–XVIIe–XVIIIe siècles* (Paris: Ophrys, 1994), 29–31; Arlette Jouanna, "Noblesse, noblesses," in *Dictionnaire de l'Ancien Régime,* ed. Bély, 87–93. For a study of the evolution of the different *marques de noblesse* in early modern France, which emphasized birth at the expense of military valor at the turn of the seventeenth century, see Ellery Schalk, *From Valor to Pedigree: Ideas of Nobility in France in the Sixteenth and Seventeenth Centuries* (Princeton: Princeton University Press, 1986), particularly chap. 7.

45. In proprietary Carolina, as in other colonies, the term "esquire" was often improperly used, not to say usurped, by settlers, usually merchants and doctors, whose overseas material success and the lack of a *nobilitas major* promoted them socially. In France, conversely, the term *écuyer* was universally recognized as a sign of nobility (Jouanna, "Noblesses, noblesse," 888). It is entirely possible, as some genealogies have claimed, that a few merchants or even artisans may have actually had roots in the lower nobility. The key, though, was the ability to be recognized as an esquire by the proprietors' agents in London and/or by Carolina officials as well as by the other Huguenots through money, lifestyle, education, titles, flair, and/or luck.

46. "Will of Paul Bruneau" (November 14, 1714), Miscellaneous Records (Proprietary Series), vol. 1711–19:65, SCDAH; Marcel Delafosse, *Petite histoire de l'Île de Ré* (La Rochelle: Quartier Latin, 1977), 43.

47. M. Delavaud, "La révocation et ses suites dans la Saintonge et l'Aunis," *BSHPF* 30 (1881): 166n1; Gourdin, "Madeleine Chardon," 101n172; Baird, *History,* 1:283–84.

48. Henry E. Ravenel, *Ravenel Records* (Dunwoody, Ga.: the author, 1971), 18, 19–20, 24–26; Carluer, "Protestants bretons," 521. After 1666, on Colbert's initiative, the French monarchy periodically led investigations, called *Recherche* or *Réformation de Noblesse,* to check on the exact status and extraction of the nobles (Jouanna, "Noblesse, noblesses," 890–91).

49. Miscellaneous Records (Proprietary Series), vol. 1682–90:335, SCDAH. In France, the title of *chevalier* was above that of *écuyer.*

50. Marthe-Fabrice abjured in 1688, and the Goulart children, Jacques-Alphée (b. 1681) and Henry (b. 1684), were raised in the Catholic religion. See Eugène Haag and Émile Haag, *La France protestante ou vies des protestants français qui se sont fait un nom dans l'histoire,* 10 vols. (1846–58; Geneva: Slatkine Reprints, 1966), 5:328–29; St. Julien R. Childs, "A Huguenot Marquess in South Carolina, 1686–1696" (typescript), St. Julien R. Childs Papers, 24/315/6, South Carolina Historical Society, Charleston.

51. Goulart de Vervant left the colony in 1696, presumably for England. It is not known whether he was able to eventually reunite with his wife and children. See Miscellaneous Records (Proprietary Series), vols. 1675–95/1703–9:317–18, SCDAH.

52. See, for example, *Plan pour former un établissement,* 1; *Nouvelle Relation de la Caroline,* 16–17; *Description de la Carolline,* 22.

53. Salley and Olsberg, *Warrants for Lands;* Salley, *Papers,* vols. 1 (1663–84) and 2 (1684–90).

54. Childs, "Exports from Charles Town, 1690," 30–34.

55. Maurice A. Crouse, "The Manigault Family of South Carolina, 1685–1783" (Ph.D. diss., Northwestern University, 1964), 5–15.

56. Will of Jean Guérard (June 20, 1714), Miscellaneous Records (Proprietary Series), vol. 1711–19:46–49, SCDAH; Cooper and McCord, *Statutes at Large,* 2:132; R. C. Nash, "Trade and Business in Eighteenth-Century South Carolina: The Career of John Guerard, Merchant and Planter," *SCHM* 96 (1995): 8–9.

57. Benjamin Meherenc de La Conseillère was baptized in September 1684 in Quévilly, Normandy (author's correspondence with Michèle Magdelaine [December 16, 1996]); Benjamin Godin was born in Le Havre in 1674 (author's correspondence with Pastor Denis Vatinel [July 1995]).

58. Nash, "Huguenot Merchants," 217–18.

59. Records of the Register of the Province (Conveyance Series), book F, 1707–11, p. 31, SCDAH; Miscellaneous Records (Proprietary Series), vol. 1711–19:46–49, SCDAH.

60. This is an estimate made from his will dated December 26, 1747 (CWA Transcripts, vol. 6, 1747–52, 85–88; Butler, *Huguenots in America,* 122). For the conversion of the Carolina pounds into sterling pounds, see McCusker, *Money and Exchange,* 223.

61. The other port towns are Saint-Martin-de-Ré (three), Bordeaux (three), Dieppe (one), and Le Havre (one).

62. Pérouas, *Diocèse de La Rochelle,* 137. Clark's study also shows that in 1685, the year of the Revocation, fourteen of the sixteen wealthiest La Rochelle merchant families were Huguenot (Clark, *La Rochelle,* 45).

63. Bosher, "Huguenot Merchants," 82–85; John F. Bosher, *Men and Ships in the Canada Trade, 1660–1760* (Ottawa: Park Services, 1992), 93. The same can be said of the Boyds, who were from Bordeaux (ibid, 93).

64. *Suite de la Description,* 16; *Plan pour former un établissement,* 6.

65. Cooper and McCord, *Statutes at Large,* 2:132; Ravenel, *Liste,* 47 (#20), 48 (#26), 51 (#45, #49), 53 (#60), 62 (#118).

66. Records of the Surveyor General, Charleston Town Lots, 1678–98/1717–56, 34b, 35b, SCDAH; Alexander S. Salley, ed., *Journals of the Commons House of Assembly of South Carolina for 1702* (Columbia: Historical Commission of South Carolina, 1932), 36.

67. Cooper and McCord, *Statutes at Large,* 2:132; Ravenel, *Liste,* 62–63.

68. A dresser finishes leather after tanning, and the word "shammy," which comes from the French *chamois* (mountain goat), referred to the deer hide.

69. Samuel G. Stoney, ed., "Nicholas de Longuemare: Huguenot Goldsmith and Silk Dealer in Colonial South Carolina," *HSSCT* 55 (1950): 63–65.

70. "Inventory of Jean Pétineau" (November 21, 1722), Miscellaneous Records (Proprietary Series), vol. 1722–24:21–23, SCDAH.

71. Cooper and McCord, *Statutes at Large,* 2:132; Nash, "Trade and Business," 8–9.

72. Miscellaneous Records (Proprietary Series), vol. 1727–29:84, SCDAH; Gourdin, "Madeleine Chardon," 85.

73. Daniel Jouet wrote his will in June 1711, but it was probated only in October 1721. See Cooper and McCords, *Statutes at Large,* 2:132; Ravenel, *Liste,* 49 (#34); William Nelson, ed., *Documents Relating to the Colonial History of the State of New Jersey,* vol. 23, *Calendar of New Jersey Wills,* vol. 1 (1670–1730) (Paterson, N.J.: The Press Printing and Publishing Co., 1901), 269.

74. Cooper and McCord, *Statutes at Large,* 2:132; Records of the Register of the Province (Conveyance Series), book D, 1696–1703, p. 203, SCDAH; Burton, *South Carolina Silversmiths,* 31, 44, 57. Although he is registered as a goldsmith in the 1697 Act of Naturalization, in the absence of other records, it is possible to say, as Burton speculated, that Pierre-Jacob Guérard never practiced his trade in Carolina, at least commercially.

75. Ravenel, *Liste,* 61 (#110, #111); "Passenger List of the *Margaret,*" 34.

76. Alexander S. Salley, ed., *Journal of the Commons House of Assembly for 1707–1708* (Columbia: Historical Commission of South Carolina, 1941), 20; Burton, *South Carolina Silversmiths,* 31. Longuemare's original ledger is deposited at the Charleston Museum but cannot

be consulted due to its being too brittle (Charleston Museum Archives, acquisition #1953.37). For a published version, see Stoney, "Nicholas de Longuemare," 43–69; Alexander S. Salley, ed., *Journal of the Commons House of Assembly for 1707* (Columbia: Historical Commission of South Carolina, 1940), 14–15.

77. These were Isaac Porcher, Jean Thomas, Joseph de La Brosse Marbeuf, Antoine Cordes, Jean Delauné, and Daniel Brabant.

78. Frank J. Klingberg, ed., *Carolina Chronicle: The Papers of Commissary Gideon Johnston, 1707–1716* (Berkeley: University of California Press, 1946), 41 (July 5, 1710). As Childs wrote, "Distinctions between physicians, surgeons, and apothecaries . . . received scant recognition in South Carolina. Popular usage granted to all the courtesy title of 'doctor'" (Childs, *Malaria and Colonization,* 254).

79. As Johnston complained in the same July 5, 1710, letter, "There is little help to be had from any of the Doctors of this place . . . the best of them, having originally been no more than barbers" (ibid., 55).

80. Miscellaneous Records (Proprietary Series), vol. 1692–1700 (June 22, 1695):227, SCDAH.

81. Waring, *History of Medicine,* 14–16.

82. Records of the Register of the Province (Conveyance Series), vol. 1696–1703:52–53, SCDAH; Miscellaneous Records (Proprietary Series), vol. 1694–1705:293–96, SCDAH; Miscellaneous Records (Proprietary Series), vol. 1709–25:7 (reverse back volume), SCDAH. For a published transcription of some of the cattle marks, see Alexander S. Salley, ed., "Stock Marks Recorded in South Carolina, 1695–1721," *SCHGM* 13 (1912): 126–31, 224–28. See also Lesser, *South Carolina Begins,* 425, 448n32.

83. Miscellaneous Records (Proprietary Series), vol. 1711–19:26 (A. Cordes), SCDAH; Colonial Grants (Copy Series), vol. 38:351, 433, 521; vol. 39:62, 63, 76, 459 (I. Porcher), SCDAH.

84. Probably because there were only four Huguenot apothecaries in Vieillevigne, Marbœuf's flight was duly recorded by the local officials. See AN, TT 236 (Bretagne, 1681–85), fol. 984; Carluer, "Protestants bretons," 553–54; Miscellaneous Records (Proprietary Series), vol. 1711–17:95, SCDAH; Miscellaneous Records (Proprietary Series), vol. 1709–25:4 (reverse back volume), SCDAH.

85. Salley, *Journal of the Grand Council,* 49; Waring, *History of Medicine,* 15.

86. Rhys Isaac similarly observed that in eighteenth-century Virginia the term "planter," contrary to its nineteenth-century and contemporary acceptance, "meant a person who lived by growing crops, but was not entitled to be accorded the dignity of a gentleman. "Planters "were thus men who bent their backs and hardened their hands in the fields" (R. Isaac, *The Transformation of Virginia, 1740–1790* [New York: W. W. Norton & Company, 1988], 16n).

87. Aubrey Land describes a similar situation in seventeenth-century Maryland, where the first "planters" owned "no more than a few acres—five, or ten at most" (Aubrey C. Land," The Planters of Colonial Maryland," *Maryland Historical Magazine* 67 [1972]: 112).

88. Cooper and McCord, *Statutes at Large,* 2:132; Salley and Olsberg, *Warrants for Lands,* ix–xvi; Robert K. Ackerman, *South Carolina Colonial Land Policies* (Columbia: University of South Carolina Press, 1977), 24.

89. Salley and Olsberg, *Warrants for Lands,* 245.

90. Hirsch briefly touches on the subject but does not differentiate between servants and apprentices. Butler only mentions them in passing. Only Friedlander includes them in her study, although underestimating their number at 5 percent of the migrants. See Hirsch, *Huguenots,* 179–80; Butler, *Huguenots in America,* 101; Friedlander, "Carolina Huguenots," 94.

91. Duplicates were avoided by comparing the masters' names. None of the masters of the twenty-five identified servants were Louis Thibou, Abraham de La Plaine, or Paul Bruneau, the three Huguenots who arrived with unidentified servants.

92. "Passenger List of the *Margaret*," 33–34.

93. The trades of those who died before the expiration of their terms and those who left the colony once freed cannot therefore be known.

94. Cooper and McCord, *Statutes at Large*, 2:132. The occupation of Gabriel Ribouleau is mentioned in the Records of the Register of the Province (Conveyance Series), vol. 1696–1703:13, SCDAH. As for Charles Fromaget, his being listed in the Act of Naturalization as a planter gives little indication about his original occupation.

95. "The Will of François Macaire," in Lothrop Withington, ed., "South Carolina Gleanings in England," *SCHGM* 5 (1904): 225; "The Will of Cézar Mozé," Miscellaneous Records (Proprietary Series), vol. 1675–95:283, SCDAH; "Agreement between the Bruneaux and Josias Marvilleau," Miscellaneous Records (Proprietary Series), vol. 1675–95:157, SCDAH.

96. References to female servants in the sources are scarce, but one can be found in the promotional pamphlet *Plan pour former un établissement,* in which the author mentions the need to import "des servantes pour le ménage" (maids for housekeeping) along with indentured laborers (*Plan pour former un établissement,* 8).

97. Ravenel, *Liste,* 52 (#54), 65 (#136), 46 (#13). This figure is a minimum since it is possible, even likely, that several other female servants "vanished" from the records once they married and adopted their husbands' names.

98. "Lettre au Marquis de Seigneulay" (June 14, 1687), ms. NAF, Arnoul 21334, fol. 194, BN.

99. Salley and Olsberg, *Warrants for Lands,* 245, 434.

100. The other two were a gunsmith (Antoine Boureau) and a pastor (Florent-Philippe Trouillart).

101. The French colonial historian Gabriel Debien has shown that most servants imported to French America in the seventeenth century came from these western provinces, especially Poitou (Gabriel Debien, "L'émigration poitevine vers l'Amérique au XVIIe siècle," *Notes d'Histoire Coloniale* 26 [1952]: 1–31).

102. The known exception is Benjamin Marion, whose servant Marie Nicolas was from his hometown of La Chaume, a small community in coastal Poitou. See Ravenel, *Liste,* 66 (#136); Salley and Olsberg, *Warrants for Lands,* 442. It is of course possible, although most likely not the rule, that others among the servants for whom the geographic origins are not known were also recruited locally.

103. David Cressy, *Coming Over: Migration and Communication between England and New England in the Seventeenth Century* (Cambridge: Cambridge University Press, 1987), 57–59; Sharon V. Salinger, *"To Serve Well and Faithfully": Labor and Indentured Servants in Pennsylvania, 1682–1800* (Cambridge: Cambridge University Press, 1987), 25–27. In the French promotional pamphlets the terms *valets* or *valets à gages* (literally "wage servants") are used to refer to indentured servants. (*Description de la Carolline,* 21; *Nouvelle Relation de la Caroline,* 53–54; *Plan pour former un établissement,* 7).

104. Withington, "South Carolina Gleanings," 225.

105. "Passenger List of the *Margaret*," 34; William J. C. Moens, ed., *The Registers of the French Church, Threadneedle Street London,* Quarto Series, vol. 13 (Lymington, U.K.: HSGB&I Publications, 1899), 2:223.

106. HSGB&I Library, "Bounty Papers," ms. 1, fol. 132.

107. "Letter of Louis Thibou"; Salley and Olsberg, *Warrants for Lands,* 352.

108. Ravenel, *Liste,* 52 (#54), 61–62 (#114); Salley and Olsberg, *Warrants for Lands,* 442.

109. HSGB&I Library, "Bounty Papers," ms. 1, fol. 132.

110. Salley and Olsberg, *Warrants for Lands,* 577, 601, 610, 632, 642, 653.

111. "Memoir of Pastor Etienne DuSoul," Bodleian Library, Oxford, Rawlinson ms. C 984, fol. 278; HSGB&I Library, "Bounty Papers," ms. 1, fol. 168; Ravenel, *Liste,* 52–53 (#57).

112. Withington, "South Carolina Gleanings," 225; Miscellaneous Records (Proprietary Series), vol. 1675–95:283, SCDAH; Cressy, *Coming Over,* 61. Hence the expression *valets à gages* used in *Plan pour former un établissement* (see supra chap. 4, note 103).

113. Withington, "South Carolina Gleanings," 225.

114. Moens, *Registers of the French Church,* 2:223; Salley and Olsberg, *Warrants for Lands,* 434.

115. "Passenger List of the *Margaret,*" 34; Alfred V. Wittmeyer, ed., *Registers of the Births, Marriages, and Deaths of the "Église Françoise à la Nouvelle York" from 1688 to 1804,* Collections of the Huguenot Society of America, vol. 1 (New York: Publications of the Huguenot Society of America, 1886), 11; Baird, *History,* 1:307n4; Salley and Olsberg, *Warrants for Lands,* 446.

116. Withington, "South Carolina Gleanings," 225–26.

117. "Letter of February 1685" (n. 3), *Suite de la Description,* 8.

118. Lorri Glover, *All Our Relations: Blood Ties and Emotional Bonds among the Early South Carolina Gentry* (Baltimore: Johns Hopkins University Press, 2000), 2.

119. Forty-nine of those who settled in South Carolina with a sibling came with a brother, thirteen with a sister, and seven with both. See Van Ruymbeke, "L'émigration huguenote," 1:342.

120. Ravenel, *Liste,* 47 (#17), 56 (#75, #76, #77), 57 (#83, #84), 58 (#87, #88), 59 (#97); Cooper and McCord, *Statutes at Large,* 1:132.

121. "Judith Giton's Receipt of Transatlantic Passage," Manigault Family Papers, 11/275/1, South Carolina Historical Society, Charleston; Ravenel, *Liste,* 54 (#67, #68), 56 (#79, #80).

122. Ravenel, *Liste,* 46 (#15), 47 (#16), 52 (#57); Gourdin, "Madeleine Chardon," 84–85nn99, 100; Henry H. A. Smith, "Wraggs of South Carolina and Some Connected Families," *SCHGM* 19 (1918): 123.

123. Childs, "Petit-Guérard Colony," 9–10; "Passenger List of the *Margaret,*" 32–34.

124. "Passenger List of the *Margaret,*" 34; Moens, *Registers of the French Church,* 2:174–76; Gourdin, "Madeleine Chardon," 79–80; author's correspondence with Pastor Denis Vatinel, July 1995. In February, March, and May 1687 Madeleine Guérard from Fécamp, Anne Godin from Le Havre, and Pierre and Anne LeSade did their "reconnaissance" at Threadneedle Street Church ("Livre des Actes du Consistoire, 1679–1692," ms. 7, Archives of the French Protestant Church of London [February 20, March 5, and May 15, 1687]).

125. HSGB&I Library, "Bounty Papers," ms. 1, fol. 89; Ravenel, *Ravenel Records,* 19–20; Carluer, "Protestants bretons," 521–25, 638; Lart, "Some Letters from France," 64; author's correspondence with Jean-Luc Tulot, February 1998.

126. Ravenel, *Liste,* 62–64; Salley and Olsberg, *Warrants for Lands,* 394–95; Cooper and McCord, *Statutes at Large,* 1:132; Gourdin, "Madeleine Chardon," 76–78. Pierre Poitevin had probably also been a weaver back in France.

127. Four entries (Alard Belain [#150], Louis Picar [unnumbered], "Made. Bacot" [130], and Jean Doucet [#154]) that mention names but contain no demographic information were not retained for the cohort study (Ravenel, *Liste,* 64, 68).

128. Unsurprisingly, since this document is a naturalization list, all the marriages were ethnically endogamous as all the registered individuals were French or Swiss. A survey of the complete database, however, confirms this trend. Only four of the total number of Huguenots whose spouses have been identified had married outside the group.

129. René Ravenel was born in September 1656 and Charlotte de St. Julien in May 1668. The wedding took place in 1687. See Ravenel, *Ravenel Records,* 19–20; author's correspondence with Jean-Luc Tulot, January 1998.

130. Huguenots born in or after 1670, who were fifteen years old or younger at the time of the Revocation, were not included.

131. Ages at migration are elusive data to compile since they combine two variables, dates of birth and dates of arrival in Carolina.

132. Sources for these statistics are Jean-Luc Tulot, "Français et Suisses réfugiés en Caroline du Sud qui souhaitent être naturalisés anglais en 1696," *Cahiers du Centre de Généalogie Protestante* 70 (2000): 102–11; and author's research files.

133. This census was compiled in 1698, or ten years after the foundation of New Rochelle. Ten years were thus subtracted from the census age average of forty-two. This method of calculation, of course, takes for granted that they all migrated at the same time, which may not have been the case. See Randolph, "Census of 1698," 105–7; Butler, *Huguenots in America,* 146.

134. Ravenel, *Liste,* 54 (#67, #68), 45 (#5, #6), 51 (#44), 54 (#63).

135. Tulot, "Français et Suisses," 105, 110; Skalski-Coignard, "Les Gaillard de Caroline du Sud," 11n1.

136. To determine the places of marriages of all the couples, widows and widowers who had lost their spouses once in Carolina were included. In the case of the couples formed in the colony, only those with both spouses alive in 1696 were retained. Hence a difference of five couples.

137. Ravenel, *Liste,* 47 (#17), 53 (#58), 57 (#84), 65–66 (#136); Gourdin, "Madeleine Chardon," 93, 100n121, 102n205.

138. Ravenel, *Liste,* 44 (#2), 48 (#26), 52 (#54, #56), 54 (#63); Gourdin, "Madeleine Chardon," 104n213.

139. Although Huguenots who lived in predominantly Catholic regions often had to look for Calvinist spouses in a distant parish to avoid what was called *un mariage mixte,* most French Protestants, like their Catholic countrymen, married locally.

140. In a donation dated July 3, 1716, de Rousserye mentioned a daughter, Élisabeth, born in 1703, thus indicating that he married between 1699 and 1702. See Ravenel, *Liste,* 46 (#11); Childs, "Petit-Guérard Colony," 7; Colonial Grants (Copy Series), vol. 38 (1675–1705):409, SCDAH; Miscellaneous Records (Proprietary Series), vol. 1714–17:375, SCDAH.

141. Ravenel, *Liste,* 50 (#39); Gourdin, "Madeleine Chardon," 81n71.

142. Ravenel, *Liste,* 48 (#29, #30), 50 (#37).

143. Ibid., 58–59 (#89).

144. See page 83 for a discussion of a similar marriage.

145. Ravenel, *Liste,* 50 (#38), 63 (#123). Bourdeaux, not to be confused with the port city of Bordeaux, was a small Huguenot community in Dauphiny (J.B., "Histoire des églises réformées de la vallée de Bourdeaux en Dauphiné," *BSHPF* 26 [1877]: 431).

146. Robert Cohen and Myriam Yardeni, eds., "Un Suisse en Caroline du Sud à la fin du XVIIe siècle," *BSHPF* 137 (1987): 66.

147. "Marriage contract between Jacques Dugué and Samuel DuBourdieu" (September 10, 1690), Miscellaneous Records (Proprietary Series), vol. 1682–90:380–81, SCDAH.

148. Ravenel, *Ravenel Records,* 133, 142–43.

149. Ibid., 20. The marriage certificate of Isaac Mazyck and Marianne LeSerrurier was accidentally filed in the land warrants (Salley and Olsberg, *Warrants for Lands,* 631).

150. Ravenel, *Ravenel Records,* 142–43; Smith, "Wraggs of South Carolina," 123.

151. "Marriage Contract between Daniel Huger and Philippe Gendron, January 7, 1710," Miscellaneous Records (Proprietary Series), vol. 1714–17:173–77, SCDAH.

152. "Will of Élisabeth Léger" (July 1, 1725) and "Will of Jacques LeSerrurier" (October 4, 1706), in Withington, "South Carolina Gleanings," *SCHGM* 4 (1903): 294–95, and 7 (1906): 147–48, respectively; Henry B. Hoff, "The Le Serrurier Family," *HSSCT* 82 (1977): 75–77.

153. Ravenel, *Liste,* 45 (#5).

154. Digges LaTouche, *Registers of the French Conformed Churches,* 212.

155. Miscellaneous Records (Proprietary Series), vol. 1675–95:282, SCDAH; Wittmeyer, *Registers of the Births,* 1.

156. Records of the Register of the Province (Conveyance Series), vol. E, 1705–9:47, SCDAH; Lesser, *South Carolina Begins,* 367.

157. See supra chap. 4, note 51.

158. "Will of Arnaud Bruneau" (December 30, 1692), Miscellaneous Records (Proprietary Series), vol. 1692–1700:172–73, SCDAH; "Will of Henry Bruneau" (dated November 14, 1709; recorded on April 10, 1717), Miscellaneous Records (Proprietary Series), vol. 1711–19:64–65, SCDAH.

159. See pages 63–64.

160. For Boudinot, see note 161 below. I. LeNoir was in Carolina in 1687 and in New York City before 1696 (Miscellaneous Records [Proprietary Series], vol. 1675–95:282, SCDAH; Wittmeyer, *Registers of the Births,* 60).

161. Salley and Olsberg, *Warrants for Lands,* 394; Wittmeyer, *Registers of the Births,* 2; "Passenger List of the *Margaret,*" 34; Joyce D. Goodfriend, *Before the Melting Pot: Society and Culture in Colonial New York City 1664–1730* (Princeton: Princeton University Press, 1992), 85.

162. Wittmeyer, *Registers of the Births,* 74; Ravenel, *Liste,* 49 (#35); Vere L. Oliver, *The History of the Island of Antigua, One of the Leeward Caribbees in the West Indies, from the First Settlement in 1635 to the Present Time* (London: Mitchell and Hughes, 1899), 123–24.

163. "Will of Louis Perdriau" (undated but recorded in January 1695), Miscellaneous Records (Proprietary Series), vol. 1692–1700:182, SCDAH.

164. Wittmeyer, *Registers of the Births,* 10, 48; Ravenel, *Liste,* 45 (#8).

165. Magdelaine, "Francfort-sur-le-Main," 43.

166. Effingham de Forest, "Records of the French Church at Narragansett," 51; Ravenel, *Liste,* 50 (#43); Butler, *Huguenots in America,* 60–63; Baird, *History,* 1:309n2.

167. HSGB&I Library, "Bounty Papers," ms. 1, fol. 89.

168. Wittmeyer, *Registers of the Births,* 5; Ravenel, *Liste,* 49 (#34); Nelson, *Documents,* 1:269; Baird, *History,* 1:306n3; Joanne C. Moore, "Some History and Genealogy of the Jouett Family," *Huguenot* 32 (1985–87): 301–2.

169. Poitou is excluded for Choquette. See Lafleur, *Protestants aux Antilles,* 38; Leslie Choquette, *Frenchmen into Peasants: Modernity and Tradition in the Peopling of French Canada* (Cambridge, Mass.: Harvard University Press, 1997), 133–34; Marc-André Bédard, "Les protestants en Nouvelle-France," *Cahiers d'Histoire de la Société Historique de Québec* 31 (1978): 43.

170. Choquette, *Frenchmen into Peasants,* 134. Bédard's figures differ slightly as he found five Huguenots from Île-de-France, one from Touraine, and none from Dauphiny. See Bédard, "Protestants en Nouvelle-France," 43; Lafleur, *Protestants aux Antilles,* 38.

171. Choquette, *Frenchmen into Peasants,* 134.

172. Ibid.; Lafleur, *Protestants aux Antilles,* 41–42.

173. Choquette, *Frenchmen into Peasants,* 135; "Les chefs de famille protestants à la Guadeloupe suivant le recensement de 1687," in Lucien-René Abénon, "Les protestants de la Guadeloupe

et la communauté réformée de Capesterre sous l'Ancien Régime," *Bulletin de la Société d'Histoire de la Guadeloupe* 32 (1977): 57–59 (see also Abénon's comments, 32–34). Although most individuals listed in this census are Huguenots, Protestants of Dutch and French origins are mixed.

174. Choquette, *Frenchmen into Peasants,* 135; Lafleur, *Protestants aux Antilles,* 82.

175. John S. Powell, *Huguenots, Planters, Portarlington* (York, U.K.: Frenchchurch Press, 1994), 52–54.

176. Choquette, *Frenchmen into Peasants,* 135; Lafleur, *Protestants aux Antilles,* 85.

177. Choquette, *Frenchmen into Peasants,* 135.

178. James Horn, *Adapting to a New World: English Society in the Seventeenth-Century Chesapeake* (Chapel Hill: University of North Carolina Press, 1994), 39; Horn, "'To Parts beyond the Seas': Free Emigration to the Chesapeake in the Seventeenth Century," in *"To Make America": European Emigration in the Early Modern Period,* ed. Ida Altman and James Horn (Berkeley: University of California Press, 1991), 97–99.

179. Horn, "To Parts beyond the Seas," 91–97.

180. Virginia D. Anderson, *New England's Generation: The Great Migration and the Formation of Society and Culture in the Seventeenth Century* (Cambridge: Cambridge University Press, 1991), 20–24.

181. Horn, "To Parts beyond the Seas," 101, 109–11.

182. Ibid., 101; Anderson, *New England's Generation,* 223.

5. The Founding Era

The first epigraph is from Walzer, *On Toleration,* 31. Étienne (Stephen) was Isaac Mazyck's brother; they both fled Île-de-Ré for Rotterdam in the fall of 1685 ("A Litteral Translation taken from my Grand father Stephen Mazyck's Registry kept and wrote by himself in an old French Bible by me his Grand Son Peter Hamon in the year 1786," The Huguenot Society of South Carolina Library, Charleston, ms. collection, [2]).

1. Although the term "Anglicanism" was coined only in the early nineteenth century, it can still be used to refer to the Church of England for earlier periods. On this debate, see J. Robert Wright, "Anglicanism, *Ecclesia Anglicana,* and Anglican: An Essay on Terminology," in *The Study of Anglicanism,* 2nd rev. ed., ed. Stephen Sykes, John Booty, and Jonathan Knight (London: SPCK/Fortress Press, 1998), 477–83.

2. Robert M. Kingdon, "Why Did the Huguenot Refugees in the American Colonies Become Episcopalians?," *Historical Magazine of the Protestant Episcopal Church* 49 (1980): 317–35; "Pourquoi les réfugiés huguenots aux colonies américaines sont-ils devenus épiscopaliens?," in "Le refuge huguenot," special issue, *BSHPF* 115 (1969): 487–509.

3. For an excellent overview of the Huguenots' historical and theological traditions in comparison to those of the Presbyterians and the Congregationalists and in the perspective of their migration to the lowcountry, see Erskine Clarke, *Our Southern Zion: A History of Calvinism in the South Carolina Low Country, 1690–1990* (Tuscaloosa: University of Alabama Press, 1996), 9–23.

4. The Confession of Faith is known as the *Confession de La Rochelle* because it was officially (i.e., openly) adopted at the 1571 national synod of La Rochelle, a year before the Saint-Bartholomew's Day Massacre.

5. For the French and Parisian contexts surrounding the drafting of these two documents, see Denis Crouzet, *La genèse de la réforme française, 1520–1560* (Paris: SEDES, 1996); Glenn S. Sunshine, *Reforming French Protestantism: The Development of Huguenot Ecclesiastical Institutions, 1557–1572* (Kirksville, Mo.: Truman State University Press, 2003); Mark Greengrass, *The French Reformation* (Oxford: Basil Blackwell, 1987); Barbara B. Diefendorf, *Beneath the Cross: Catholics*

and Huguenots in Sixteenth-Century Paris (Oxford: Oxford University Press, 1991); Raymond A. Mentzer, "The French Wars of Religion," in *The Reformation World,* ed. Andrew Pettigree (New York: Routledge, 2000), 323–43; Prestwich, "Calvinism in France, 1555–1629," 71–87. The two documents overlap since the *Confession* also contains a few articles regarding the structures of the congregation.

6. John Bossy, *Christianity in the West 1400–1700* (Oxford: Oxford University Press, 1985), 115–52; Olivier Millet, "Les Églises réformées," in *Histoire du Christianisme,* vol. 8, *Le temps des confessions (1530–1620)* (Paris: Desclée de Brouwer, 1992), 95–99; Johannes van den Berg, "Le protestantisme réformé en Europe au XVIe et au XVIIe siècles," in *L'Europe protestante aux XVIe et XVIIe siècles,* ed. John Miller (Paris: Belin, 1997), 193–208; Jean Delumeau, *Le péché et la peur: La culpabilisation en Occident XIIIe–XVIIIe siècles* (Paris: Fayard, 1983), "En pays protestant," 550–623. On Calvin's influence on French Reformed churches, see Harro M. Höpfl, "Calvin et le calvinisme," in *L'Europe protestante,* ed. Miller, 93–115; Bernard Cottret, *Histoire de la réforme protestante XVIe–XVIIIe siècle* (Paris: Perrin, 2001), chap. 6; Bernard Cottret, *Calvin: A Biography* (Grand Rapids: Eerdsman, 2000), 247–60; Robert M. Kingdon, *Geneva and the Consolidation of the French Protestant Movement 1564–1572* (Geneva: Droz, 1967), 37–42; Glenn S. Sunshine, "Reformed Theology and the Origins of Synodical Polity: Calvin, Beza, and the Gallican Confession," in *Later Calvinism: International Perspectives,* ed. W. Fred Graham (Kirksville: Northeast Missouri State University, 1994), 141–58. In his study of emerging Huguenot religious institutions, Sunshine convincingly argues that although influenced by Geneva (Calvin) and Strasbourg (Bucer), French Protestantism had its own originality due to the specific context in which French Reformed churches developed (Sunshine, *Reforming French Protestantism,* 3–5 , 167–70).

7. Quoted in Paula W. Carlo, "'Playing Fast and Loose with the Canons and Rubrick': French Anglicanism in Colonial New Rochelle, New York," *Journal of the Canadian Church Historical Society* 44 (2002): 48, 48n31. The irony would not have been missed by French Catholic clergymen, who insisted on having French Protestantism called *la réligion prétendue réformée.* I fully agree with Paula Carlo on this point.

8. Jacques Pannier, *Les origines de la Confesssion de foi et la Discipline des Églises réformées de France: Étude historique* (Paris: Librairie Félix Alcan, 1936), 119–31 (abstract in French, 128–31); Jean-Robert Armogathe, "Quelques réflexions sur la Confession de foi de La Rochelle," *BSHPF* 117 (1971): 201–13; Thierry Wanegffelen, "Réforme, réformations, protestantisme," in *L'Europe protestante,* ed. Miller, 31–52; André Gounelle, *Protestantisme* (Paris: Éditions Publisud, 1992), 63–69; Janine Garrisson, *Les protestants au XVIe siècle* (Paris: Fayard, 1988), 186–91; Léonard, *Histoire,* 2:101–3. Recent French transcription and English translation of the Paris/La Rochelle Confession can be found in Olivier Fatio, ed., *Confessions et catéchismes de la foi réformée* (Geneva: Labor et Fides, 1986); and Arthur C. Cochrane, ed., *Reformed Confessions of the 16th Century* (Philadelphia: Westminster Press, 1966), respectively.

9. A complete version of the *Discipline,* with successive synodical additions, can be found in François Méjan, ed., *Discipline de l'Église Réformée de France* (Paris: Éditions "Je sers," 1947), 190–299. See also Isaac d'Huisseau, *La discipline des Églises réformées de France ou l'ordre selon lequel elles sont conduites et gouvernées* (1653; Saumur: Chez Isaac Desbordes, 1666).

10. Benedict, *Huguenot Population,* 35, 55; Louis Pérouas, "Sur la démographie rochelaise," *Annales E.S.C.* 16 (1961): 1137; Delafosse, *Histoire de La Rochelle,* 201; Brigitte Maillard, "Religion et démographie: Les protestants de Tours au XVIIe siècle," *Annales de Bretagne et des Pays de l'Ouest* 104 (1983): 544–45.

11. Deacons also visited the sick, taught catechism at home, and performed minor liturgical duties. Most often, though, and increasingly in the seventeenth century, consistories did not have

separate deacons as some elders took over that function. See Sunshine, *Reforming French Protestantism*, 106–19, 138–41. In practice the number of elders varied greatly from under five to over twenty in proportion to the size of the congregation. In Poitou, for example, consistories had an average of eight to eleven members, but that of the urban church of Niort comprised eighteen elders. See Solange Bertheau, "Le consistoire dans les églises réformées du moyen Poitou au XVIIe siècle," *BSHPF* 116 (1970): 341–42.

12. Paul de Félice, *Les protestants d'autrefois: Vie intérieure des églises, moeurs et usages*, 4 vols. (Paris: Librairie Fischbacher, 1896–1902), 3:12–27; Sunshine, *Reforming French Protestantism*, 130–37.

13. Méjan, *Discipline de l'Église*, chaps. 3, 4, 5, 223–40; Élisabeth Labrousse, "Les protestants sous le régime de la tolérance," in *Histoire de la France religieuse*, ed. Le Goff and Rémond, 2:449–52; Labrousse, "Calvinism in France, 1598–1685," 285–93; Daniel Ligou, "La peau de chagrin (1598–1685)," in *Histoire des protestants*, ed. Mandrou et al., 127–29; Michel-Edmond Richard, *La vie des protestants français de l'Édit de Nantes à la Révolution (1598–1789)* (1966; Paris: Les Éditions de Paris, 1994), 21–24; Bertheau, "Consistoire," 513–49.

14. In a study of extant consistory records for ten rural and urban congregations encompassing 531 sentences between 1561 and 1604, Raymond Mentzer identified four main reasons for excommunications (temporary or definitive) from the Lord's Supper: disputes and quarrels (22 percent of cases); adultery and fornication (18 percent); dancing (12 percent); and contact with "Popery" (12 percent). See Raymond A. Mentzer, "Marking the Taboo: Excommunication in French Reformed Churches," in *Sin and the Calvinists: Morals Control and the Consistory in the Reformed Tradition*, ed. R. Mentzer (Kirksville: Northeast Missouri State University, 1994), 100, 105–9. See also Mentzer's statistical study of the Nîmes consistory records for the years 1561–63 and 1578–83 in "*Disciplina nervus ecclesiae*: The Calvinist Reform of Morals at Nîmes," *Sixteenth Century Journal* 18 (1987): 89–115.

15. Richard, *Vie des protestants*, 50–56; Garrisson, *L'Édit de Nantes et sa révocation*, 33–35; Deregnaucourt and Poton, *Vie religieuse*, 70; Marc Venard and Bernard Vogler, "Les formes collectives de la vie religieuse," in *Histoire du Christianisme*, 8:964–67. On the *méreau*, see Charles Delormeau, *Les méreaux de Communion des Églises protestantes de France et du Refuge* (Mialet: Le Mas Soubeyran, 1983); Bertrand Van Ruymbeke, "Méreaux," *HSSCT* 98 (1993): 50–52.

16. In the aforementioned study (see supra note 14), Mentzer found that "suspension" occurred in 97 percent and "excommunication" in only 4 percent of the cases (Mentzer, "Marking the Taboo," 102–5).

17. Didier Poton, "Le consistoire protestant au XVIIe siècle: un tribunal des mœurs?," in *Ordre moral et délinquance de l'Antiquité au XXe siècle*, ed. Benoît Garnot (Dijon: Publications de l'Université de Bourgogne, 1994), 411–17.

18. Didier Poton, "Le consistoire de l'église réformée de Saint-Jean-du-Gard au XVIIe siècle: élection et composition sociale (1605–1685)," in *Sociétés et idéologies des Temps modernes: Hommage à Arlette Jouanna*, ed. J. Fouilleron, G. Le Thiec, and H. Michel (Montpellier: Presses Universitaires de Montpellier, 1996), 247–57.

19. Bertheau, "Consistoire," 346–47; Carluer, "Protestants bretons," 511; N[athaniel]. W[eiss], "Le temple de Vitré au XVIIe siècle," *BSHPF* 50 (1901): 197–201.

20. Stelling-Michaud, *Livre du recteur*, 5:244–45, 4:323; Calvin L. Traylor, "Pierre Trouillart: Three Generations of Huguenot Ministers; A Chronology of Various Events over One Hundred Years, 1600–1700," unpag. typescript, Trouillart File, HSGB&I Library; Alexandre Crottet, "Recherches historiques sur la famille Prioleau (1859)" (undated typescript from a manuscript account written by Crottet in 1859), South Carolina Huguenot Society Library, 5–6; H. Frost

Prioleau, "The Ancestors of Horry Frost Prioleau" (computer printout, November 1997), 10–11; FPCL, Records of the French Church, ms. 135, "Copies of Letters, 1697–1754" (September 30, 1700). Pierre Robert received his preliminary college education at the University of Basel, Switzerland. It is unknown, however, in which *académie* he was trained as a minister. See Thomas O. Lawton Jr., "A Tribute to Pasteur Pierre Robert in the 300th Anniversary Year of his Ordination to the Ministry," *HSSCT* 87 (1982): 3. The genealogist Calvin Traylor has Florent-Philippe graduating from the Geneva academy in 1668, but he confuses him with his father, Pierre (Stelling-Michaud, *Livre du recteur,* 6:76). Although undocumented, Trouillart possibly studied at Sedan where his father taught.

21. Pittion, "Académies réformées"; Ligou, *Protestantisme,* 162–65; Roger Chartier, Dominique Julia, and Marie-Madeleine Compère, *L'éducation en France du XVIe au XVIIIe siècle* (Paris: SEDES, 1976), 159–66. For a study of a specific académie, see André Roux, "L'académie de Die, en Dauphiné (1604–1684)," in *La Réforme et l'éducation,* ed. Jean Boisset (Toulouse: Éditions Privat, 1974), 101–23.

22. De Félice, *Protestants d'autrefois,* 2:1–10. The initial *F* could precede the *M* for *Fidèle* (faithful). See Richard, *Vie des protestants,* 48; Ravenel, *Liste,* 56 (#78).

23. Méjan, *Discipline de l'Église,* 190–97; Françoise Chevalier, *Prêcher sous l'Édit de Nantes: La prédication réformée au XVIIe siècle en France* (Geneva: Labor et Fides, 1994), 39–41.

24. Crottet, *Histoire des églises,* 129.

25. Fontaine, *Memoirs,* 75.

26. Samuel was pastor at Pons, Élizée at Jonzac, and Élie Merlat at Saintes, all located in Saintonge. Pierre Trouillart I and II both ministered at Guisnes, near Calais in northern France. See Crottet, *Histoire des églises,* 121–22; William Minet and William C. Waller, eds., *Transcripts of the Registers of the Protestant Church at Guisnes from 1668 to 1685,* Quarto Series, vol. 3 (Lymington, U.K.: HSGB&I Publications, 1891), vi, 165.

27. Labrousse, "Protestants sous le régime," 452; De Félice, *Protestants d'autrefois,* 2:228–43.

28. Carluer, "Protestants bretons," 511.

29. Labrousse, "Protestants sous le régime," 452; Richard, *Vie des protestants,* 23–24.

30. For an example of a Huguenot congregation facing increasing financial difficulties in the seventeenth century, see Didier Poton, "Les finances des églises réformées du "Moyen-Poitou" au XVIIe siècle: l'exemple de Niort (1629–1684)," in *Entre idéal et réalité,* ed. M. Aubrun, G. Audisio, B. Dompnier, and A. Gueslin (Clermont-Ferrand, France: Publications de l'Institut d'Études du Massif Central, 1993), 135–45.

31. Labrousse, "Protestants sous le régime," 455.

32. Chevalier, *Prêcher sous l'Édit de Nantes,* 47, 52–61; Peter Bayley, *French Pulpit Oratory 1598–1650* (Cambridge: Cambridge University Press, 1980), 100–21. Sermons, especially those pronounced on special occasions, such as Easter, Christmas, or on a day of fast, could last even longer. To curtail the pastors' propensity to elaborate at length, an hourglass was placed on the pulpit of some churches (De Félice, *Protestants d'autrefois,* 1:35–36).

33. Diefendorf, *Beneath the Cross,* 136–44; Crouzet, *Genèse de la réforme,* 391–98; Chevalier, *Prêcher sous l'Édit de Nantes,* 69–72; Jean-Robert Armogathe, *Le Grand Siècle et la Bible* (Paris: Beauchesne, 1989), 325–34; R. A. Sayce, "The Huguenot Bible," *HSP* 20 (1973): 224–34.

34. Chevalier, *Prêcher sous l'Édit de Nantes,* 251.

35. Méjan, *Discipline de l'Église,* 278; Richard, *Vie des protestants,* 33. The fall communion was usually on the first Sunday in September. This periodization was adopted at the Paris National Synod of 1565. See Marianne Carbonnier-Burkard, "Le temps de la Cène chez les réformés français (milieu du XVIe–début du XVIIe siècle)," in *Édifier ou instruire? Les avatars de la liturgie*

réformée du XVIe au XVIIe siècle, ed. Maria-Christina Pitassi (Paris: Honoré Champion, 2000), 57–73.

36. This usage, incidentally, turned out to be crucial in France during the years leading to the Revocation and at the time of the diaspora when pastors were not always available locally (Méjan, *Discipline de l'Église,* 262–63; Venard and Vogler, "Formes collectives," 947). In some northern areas where Huguenot churches were located deep in Catholic country, immediate baptism was tolerated, if performed by a minister, to avoid a rudimentary baptism by a priest or a Catholic midwife (Labrousse, "Protestants sous le régime," 456–57).

37. Méjan, *Discipline des Église,* 267–74.

38. Krumenacker, *Protestants du Poitou,* 422–24.

39. Méjan, *Discipline des Église,* 278–87.

40. Miscellaneous Records (Proprietary Series), vol. 1692–1700:9 (P. Berterand), 172–73 (A. Bruneau), SCDAH. For transcriptions and English translations, see Robert Wilson, trans. and ed., "Wills of South Carolina Huguenots," *HSSCT* 10 (1903): 35–41.

41. Méjan, *Discipline des Église,* 260–61; Labrousse, "Protestants sous le régime," 456; Richard, *Vie des protestants,* 37–39.

42. Méjan, *Discipline de l'Église,* 259; Chevalier, *Prêcher sous l'Édit de Nantes,* 27–29; Ligou, *Protestantisme,* 137. Fasts could also, although this was exceptional, be used to celebrate a grand occasion, as shown by the quotation from Étienne Mazyck placed at the beginning of this chapter. Étienne, Isaac's brother, decided to fast to commemorate his 1685 escape out of France.

43. The exact title of Calvin's catechism is *Le catéchisme de l'Eglise de Genève: c'est-à-dire, le Formulaire d'instruire les enfants en la chrestienté: faict en manière de dialogue, ou le Ministre interroge, et l'enfant respond* (Olivier Millet, "Rendre raison de la foi: Le Catéchisme de Calvin [1542]," in *Aux origines du catéchisme en France,* ed. P. Colin, E. Germain, J. Joncheray, and M. Venard [Paris: Desclée, 1988], 188–207). A recent transcription of the earliest extant French edition (1545) can be found in Fatio, *Confessions et catéchismes,* 25–110.

44. Fontaine, *Memoirs,* 36.

45. As Calvin wrote, "Each particular family must be a small particular church" (*Chaque famille particulière doit être une petite église particulière*), quoted in Garrisson, *Protestants,* 37; De Félice, *Protestants d'autrefois,* 1:83–88; Chevalier, *Prêcher sous l'Édit de Nantes,* 31–34.

46. As Diefendorf points out, however, "Huguenots' affinity for the Psalms was [not just] theological, but it was also emotional and aesthetic" (Barbara B. Diefendorf, "The Huguenot Psalter and the Faith of French Protestants in the Sixteenth Century," in *Culture and Identity,* ed. Diefendorf and Hesse, 42).

47. Crouzet, *Genèse de la réforme,* 391–94; Diefendorf, *Beneath the Cross,* 136–41.

48. Venard and Vogler, "Formes collectives," 932–33; Jean Delumeau and Thierry Wanegffelen, *Naissance et affirmation de la Réforme* (Paris: Presses Universitaires de France, 1997), 108–11.

49. For the Huguenots, the term *église* meant congregation.

50. Huguenot *temples* were also generally built without steeples (De Félice, *Protestants d'autrefois,* 1:3).

51. Ibid., 1:6–9, 14–18.

52. Ibid., 1:32–34.

53. Venard and Vogler, "Formes collectives," 934–36; Richard, *Vie des protestants,* 29–32; Labrousse, "Protestants sous le régime," 455. For a brief analysis of Huguenot temples, particularly that of Charenton, in the context of Reformation experimental church architecture, see James

F. White, *Protestant Worship and Church Architecture: Theological and Historical Considerations* (Oxford: Oxford University Press, 1964), 90–93.

54. "Nulle église ne pourra prétendre primauté ni domination sur l'autre" (No church can claim primacy or domination over the other), but "L'autorité des Colloques est soumise à celle des Synodes provinciaux, comme celle des consistoires aux Colloques" (*Colloques* are under the authority of provincial synods as consistories are under that of colloques) and "L'autorité des Synodes provinciaux est soumise à celle des Synodes nationaux" (Provincial synods are under the authority of national synods) (Méjan, *Discipline des Église*, 241, 245, 250).

55. Ibid., 244–45; Richard, *Vie des protestants*, 25–26; Poton and Cabanel, *Protestants français*, 48–50; Solange Deyon, *Du loyalisme au refus: Les protestants français et leur député général entre la fronde et la révocation* (Villeneuve-D'Ascq: Presses Universitaires de Lille, 1976), 76–80; Sunshine, *Reforming French Protestantism*, 64–74.

56. Méjan, *Discipline des Église*, 250; Ligou, "La peau de chagrin," 122–25, 130; Benedict, *Huguenot Population*, 10; Mours, *Essai sommaire de géographie*, 7–39.

57. Méjan, *Discipline des Église*, 245–51; Richard, *Vie des protestants*, 26–27; Labrousse, "Protestants sous le régime," 450–51.

58. Fontaine, *Memoirs*, 74.

59. Méjan, *Discipline des Églises*, 252–56; Richard, *Vie des protestants*, 27. National synods met twenty-nine times from 1559 to 1659 and only four times after 1626 (Charenton, Alençon, Charenton, and Loudin). Charenton, being in the outskirts of Paris, was twice imposed by the crown as the location of the national synod to allow for better royal supervision. The successive national synods, with their minutes, can be followed in two useful although incomplete contemporaneous lists: John Quick, *Synodicon in Gallia reformata, or, The Acts, Decisions, Decrees, and Canons of Those Famous National Councils of the Reformed Churches in France* (London: printed for T. Parkhurst and J. Robinson, 1692); Jean Aymon, *Tous les synodes nationaux des Églises réformées de France auxquels on a joint des Mandemens royaux et plusieurs lettres politiques,* 2 vols. (The Hague: Chez Charles Delo, 1710). For critiques of these two compilations, see Bernard Roussel and Solange Deyon, "Pour un nouvel 'Aymon': Les premiers Synodes nationaux des Églises réformées en France (1559–1567)," *BSHPF* 139 (1993): 545–95; Sunshine, *Reforming French Protestantism*, 5–9.

60. Until the meeting of the Synod of Alès in 1620, national synods regularly revised the Confession of Faith. On these changes and the larger issue of perpetual reformation, see Brian G. Armstrong, "*Semper Reformanda:* The Case of the French Reformed Church, 1559–1620," in *Later Calvinism*, ed. Graham, 119–40.

61. Ligou, *Protestantisme*, 128–29.

62. The Synod of Dort was originally a Dutch affair, but the presence of Calvinist theologians from England, the German Calvinist principalities, and the Swiss cantons and cities, including Geneva, gave it an international dimension. The 1617 Huguenot national synod, held in Vitré, elected four delegates to represent them in Dort, but Louis XIII refused to let them attend the Dutch synod. See Ligou, *Protestantisme*, 141–47; Millet, "Églises réformées," 114–16; Delumeau and Wanegffelen, *Naissance et affirmation*, 249–56; Richard A. Muller, "God, Predestination, and the Integrity of the Created Order: A Note on Patterns in Arminius' Theology," in *Later Calvinism*, ed. Graham, 431–46; Nicholas Tyacke, *Anti-Calvinists: The Rise of English Arminianism c. 1590–1640* (Oxford: Clarendon Press, 1987), 87–105. Jakob Hermanszoon (1560–1609), also known as Jacobus Arminius and after whom Arminianism was named, was a professor of theology at the University of Leiden. See Delumeau and Wanegffelen, *Naissance et affirmation*, 250.

63. Ligou, *Protestantisme*, 147–56; Labrousse, "Protestants sous le régime," 469–71.

64. Wantoot is what Hirsch identified as the St. John's Berkeley settlement. St. Stephen's, which Hirsch listed as another lowcountry Huguenot settlement, was split off from St. James Santee later in the 1730s (Hirsch, *Huguenots,* 26–27).

65. BPRO, CO 5/1258 (1699). A copy of this census can be found in Salley, *Papers,* 4 (1698–1700):75.

66. Part of the church register and consistory records were burned during the 1740 Charleston fire, and the rest, along with the communion service, was lost after having been removed to a safe in the Merchants' Bank in Cheraw, S.C., during the Civil War. It remains unknown whether these precious records and artifacts fell "into the hands of the enemy," were stolen, or were simply lost, but a list of the items contained in the safe was published in a footnote to the below-cited article published in the 1885 Charleston yearbook, "in the hope that [it] may aid in the restoration of this invaluable property." See Daniel Ravenel, "Historical Sketch of the Huguenot Congregations of South Carolina," *HSSCT* 7 (1900): 15–16 (quote, 16); [Charles S. Vedder, Gen. Wilmot G. De Saussure, and Daniel Ravenel], "Incorporated as 'The French Protestant Church,' Founded A.D. 1681–2, Charleston, S.C.," in *Year Book—Charleston, S. C., 1885* (Charleston, S.C.: News and Courier Book Presses, 1886), 309n*.

67. Agnes L. Baldwin, *First Settlers of South Carolina, 1670–1700* (Easley, S.C.: Southern Historical Press, 1985), 58, 148; Lesser, *South Carolina Begins,* 196n6, 332–33. See Smith's passage on the "'myth' of Michael Loving," who was "made" a Huguenot by nineteenth-century authors eager to establish the Huguenots' precedence in organizing a Christian church in the Carolina lowcountry. See also [Vedder et al.], "Incorporated as 'The French Protestant Church,'" 302–3; Henry A. M. Smith, "The Orange Quarter and the First French Settlers in South Carolina," *SCHGM* 18 (1917): 118–20.

68. Records of the Register of the Province (Conveyance Series), book E, 1705–9, 250–52, SCDAH. Jean-Adrien LeSerurrier did not remain in South Carolina and was back in London by November 1687. André Foucault, who witnessed Alexandre Pépin's will in May 1687 and also appeared as a witness to a transaction between Robert and Elizabeth Layton and Alard Belin in January 1687, left the colony for New York sometime before 1692 when he witnessed a marriage at the Église Françoise. See Records of the Register of the Province (Conveyance Series), vol. A, 1682–93:256, 289, SCDAH; Caroline T. Moore and Agatha A. Simmons, comp. and ed., *Abstracts of the Wills of the State of South Carolina* (Charlotte, N.C.: The Observer Printing House, 1960), 10–11; Wittmeyer, *Registers of the Births,* 19.

69. Records of the Register of the Province (Conveyances Series), book E, 1705–9, 252, SCDAH. Étienne Dusout was the former pastor of Rennes who accompanied the Ravenels, Dubourdieus, and St. Juliens to Charleston. He is also identified as a merchant in other records, in a way reminiscent of Jaques Fontaine, but it is uncertain whether he served the Charleston Huguenot congregation along with Florent-Philippe Trouillart, who had arrived in 1685. If he did, it must have been for a brief period of time, perhaps before an untimely death, and it has not been recorded. See "Letter of Ester Dubourdieu, Wife of Louis Fleury, to Her Brother Dubourdieu at Vitré" (London, July 6, 1687), in Lart, "Some Letters from France," 68; Gourdin, "Madeleine Chardon," 103n207; Bodleian Library, Oxford, Rawlinson ms., C 982, fol. 278–278a.

70. Records of the Register of the Province (Conveyances Series), book E, 1705–9, p. 252–53, SCDAH. Interestingly, all these transactions were registered on the same day, May 17, 1707, by Peter Guérard, Register of the Province, only a year after the passing of the 1706 Church Act, which established the Church of England in South Carolina. Was it pure coincidence or was it meant to ascertain the historical foundations of the Charleston Huguenot Church, which refused to conform to the Church of England?

71. "Jacques Nicholas, dit petit Bois," in Ravenel, *Liste,* 65 (#133). The presence of Petitbois is not systematic, however, as attested by a reference to a 1688 act on which Nicholas is recorded as simply James Nicholas (Records of the Register of the Province [Conveyance Series], book A, 1682–93, 310, SCDAH).

72. This is what Friedlander thinks (Friedlander, "Carolina Huguenots," 218–19). See also Caroline T. Moore, comp. and ed., *Abstracts of Records of the Secretary of the Province of South Carolina 1692–1721* (Columbia: R. L. Bryan Company, 1978), 191; Register of the Province (Conveyance Series), book A, 1682–90, 310, SCDAH. On Nicholas's departure from Carolina in 1705, see supra page 92.

73. No James Nicholls is mentioned in Baldwin's list of Carolina first settlers or in Lesser's decedent index (Baldwin, *First Settlers,* 172–73; Lesser, *South Carolina Begins,* 367).

74. Worthington, "South Carolina Gleanings," 225.

75. This act, which is no longer extant, is listed in Cooper and McCord, *Statutes at Large,* 2:85, and its vote is mentioned in Salley, *Journals of the Grand Council, 1692,* 44.

76. Certificates of Admeasurement for Charles Town Lots, 1675–98, 1717, 1743–46, Records of the Surveyor General's Office, 24b, SCDAH; "Letter from the Proprietors to the Charleston French Consistory" (April 12, 1693), BPRO, CO 5/288; Salley, *Papers,* 3 (1691–97):103–4.

77. Mazyck Bible, Huguenot Society of South Carolina Library, Charleston.

78. Smith, "Orange Quarter," 120. Without getting involved in a pointless and passé controversy over which religious group "built the first church" in Charleston, the Huguenots were undoubtedly among the first, which is not surprising considering that many of them had been in the colony since 1680 and most arrived between 1685 and 1687. On this controversy, which was apparently raging in the early 1900s, see ibid.

79. Quoting from various Charleston deeds of sale drawn in 1696 and 1697, Dalcho wrote that Church Street ran "parallel with Cooper river, from Ashley to the French church," thus implying that the second Huguenot church had by then been built on lot no. 65 (Frederick Dalcho, *An Historical Account of the Protestant Episcopal Church in South Carolina* [1820; Charleston: Arno Press Inc, Tricentennial Edition, 1970], 21).

80. In April 1701 L'Escot explained that they were about to start construction, so it is reasonable to think that the new brick church was completed either at the end of 1701 or sometime in 1702 ("Letter from Paul L'Escot to Jean-Alphonse Turretini" [April 6, 1701], [copied excerpts], Archives Tronchin 81, fol. 195, Bibliothèque Publique et Universitaire de Genève [hereafter BPU]). The hurricane of 1700, known as the "Rising Sun" hurricane after the name of a Scottish ship that was severely damaged while anchored in the Charleston harbor, actually hit the lowcountry in mid-September (David M. Ludlum, *Early American Hurricanes 1492–1870* [Boston: American Meteorological Society, 1963], 42).

81. Gourdin, "Madeleine Chardon," 103n207; Ravenel, "Historical Sketch," 50. Lot no. 65 is located at the southeastern corner of Queen and Church streets where the present-day Huguenot church stands. Designed by Edward Brickell White (1806–82), a well-known Charleston architect and West Point graduate, this house of worship was constructed in 1845 as the first example of gothic revival architecture in the city. Gothic revival, also known as the ecclesiological style, originated from the Cambridge Camden Society (later Ecclesiological Society), founded in 1836 by a group of Cambridge students dedicated to restoring and preserving medieval buildings, especially churches, in the British Isles and "in the Colonies." Eminently Anglican, or Episcopalian, this architectural school, which spread to the United States in the 1840s through the New York Ecclesiological Society, believed that the function of a building should be expressed in its appearance and that "Gothick is the only Christian architecture" and therefore a style more appropriate

to churches than the then-popular classic revival style. See Kenneth Severens, *Charleston Antebellum Architecture and Civic Destiny* (Knoxville: University of Tennessee Press, 1988), 126–31; Mary M. Jacoby, ed., *The Churches of Charleston and the Lowcountry* (Columbia: University of South Carolina Press, 1994), 9–11; Phoebe B. Stanton, *The Gothic Revival & American Church Architecture: An Episode in Taste 1840–1856* (Baltimore: Johns Hopkins University Press, 1968), 3–29; White, *Protestant Worship*, 131–37 (quote, 132); Beatrice St. Julien Ravenel, *Architects of Charleston* (1945; Columbia: University of South Carolina Press, 1992), 183–202; Jonathan H. Poston, *The Buildings of Charleston: A Guide to the City's Architecture* (Columbia: University of South Carolina Press, 1997), 85–86; Marguerite C. Steedman, *A Short History of the Huguenot Church of Charleston, South Carolina* (Charleston: The Nelson Printing Corporation, 1983), 3–6. L'Escot's letter of 1701, unknown to previous historians, evidences that this is the fourth Huguenot church on its current site (1696, 1701, 1796, and 1845) and the fifth in Charleston ("Letter from Paul L'Escot to Jean-Alphonse Turretini" [April 6, 1701], [copied excerpts], Archives Tronchin 81, fol. 195, BPU).

82. Since it was common, not to say the norm, for settlers to build edifices on land held only on the basis of a warrant before receiving a formal grant, I disagree with Smith when he writes that no French church was built in Charleston "until after 1701," when the Huguenots received a grant for lots 92/93. I agree with him, though, when he writes that no church could have been constructed on lot no. 65 (M. Loving's) as early as 1681. See Smith, "Orange Quarter," 119.

83. The date 1681 is engraved on the fourth step of the current Huguenot church, probably based on the once widely held belief that a church building was erected there.

84. FPCL, ms. 7, "Livre des Actes du Consistoire, 1679–1692" (October 26, 1679).

85. Two passenger lists were compiled before the departure of the *Richmond,* one on October 15 and the other on November 8, 1679. See BPRO, Admiralty Papers 1/5139, Orders in Council, 1679–88, fol. 162; E. H. Fairbrother, comp., "Foreign Protestants for Carolina in 1679," *HSP* 10 (1912): 187–89.

86. At first glance, it seems unlikely that this Henri Forestier was the *Richmond* pastor since he was not yet a minister and because the London church elders would certainly have mentioned his existence to Guérard. Yet, it is entirely possible that Guérard and Petit, out of desperation, recruited him without consulting the consistory and that, being presumably of a young age, Forestier accepted to try his luck in faraway Carolina. St. Julien Childs, who did not know of the Threadneedle Street Church records, conjectured instead that the *Richmond* minister was Louis Forestier, a pastor refugeed in Holland in 1679. See FPCL, ms. 7, "Livre des Actes du Consistoire, 1679–1692" (September 28, 1679); Childs, "Petit-Guérard Colony," 8.

87. "Letter of Louis Thibou" (September 20, 1683), fol. 2, South Caroliniana Library, Columbia, S.C.

88. "Pedigree of Thibou," in Vere L. Oliver, *The History of the Island of Antigua, One of the Leeward Caribbees in the West Indies, from the First Settlement in 1635 to the Present Time* (London: Mitchell and Hughes, 1899), 124. Many thanks to Henry B. Hoff for showing me this source.

89. The presence of only two Anglican pastors in the lowcountry in the early 1680s is confirmed by a 1708 letter that Thomas Smith addressed to the Society for the Propagation of the Gospel in Foreign Parts (hereafter SPG) in which he wrote that when he arrived in Charleston in 1683, Phineas Rogers, also known as "Rogers the Elder," and Atkin Williamson were the "two ministers professing to be of the Church of England" ("Thomas Smith to Robert Stevens" [January 14, 1708], SPG records, Lambeth Palace Library, London, vol. 16 [South Carolina], fol. 193). See also Salley and Olsberg, *Warrants for Lands,* 202, 218, 389; Baldwin, *First Settlers,* 115; S. Charles Bolton, *Southern Anglicanism: The Church of England in Colonial South Carolina* (Westport,

Conn.: Greenwood Press, 1982), 19; Alexander S. Salley, ed., "A Letter by the Second Landgrave Smith," *SCHGM* 33 (1931): 62n2. The generic term "clerk," of course, could also refer to an Anglican priest.

90. Perhaps this was due to the French Calvinist usage of not choosing husbands and wives as godfathers and godmothers.

91. See supra chap. 5, note 75 for references to this act.

92. "Proprietors to Council" (April 10, 1693), in Alexander S. Salley, ed., *Journal of the Commons House of Assembly, January–September 1693* (Columbia: Historical Commission of South Carolina, 1907), 31. Incidentally, rowing to church must have been a familiar scene for F. L. Trouillart since his father's parishioners came to his church at Guisnes from Calais by boat.

93. Additionally, Élie Prioleau took six pastoral exhortations, written by his father Samuel in the mid-1670s, with him to Carolina; three of them concerned the reception of elders and deacons (Prioleau Papers, French Huguenots, ms. 1677, South Caroliniana Library, Columbia, S.C.). See also Yates Snowden, ed., "A Huguenot Exhortation, 1677," *HSSCT* 26 (1921): 34–38.

94. "Proprietors to French Church Consistory" (April 12, 1693), BPRO, CO 5/288 (1682–98).

95. The letter simply mentions "Mr De Lisle Cramahé." Since Alexandre Thésée bore the title of Sieur de L'Isle and Henry Auguste that of Sieur de Cramahé, it is difficult to determine which brother it was. This is an educated guess, but since the title De L'Isle appears first it may have been Alexandre Thésée.

96. On Vervant and Chasteigner, see pages 77–78; Henry A. M. Smith, "Wraggs of South Carolina," *SCHGM* 19 (1918): 123.

97. "Will of Pierre Perdriau" (November 26, 1692) and "Will of Louis Perdriau" (drawn date unknown but probated on January 10, 1695), Miscellaneous Records (Proprietary Series), vol. 1692–1700:18 and 182, respectively, SCDAH. English translations are available in *HSSCT* 10 (1903): 43–44, 46–47.

98. Weir, *Colonial South Carolina,* 38; Henry Savage Jr., *River of the Carolinas: The Santee* (New York: Rinehart & Company, 1956), 20. Santee is also the name of lowcountry natives living in the region.

99. Joachim Gaillard received a warrant for land in the Santee area in 1685 but settled there later. Anne Bridges and Roy Williams have January 1688 for Gignilliat's grant, but records were kept in old style. This dating is corroborated by the land memorials, which show that Gignilliat had his land surveyed in February 1689. The Hugers were also living in Santee as early as 1688. See Colonial Land Grants (Copy Series), vol. 38 (1675–1705):101, SCDAH; Records of the Auditor General, Memorials (Copy Series), vol. 2, part 1, 211–12; Anne Baker Leland Bridges and Roy Williams III, *St. James, Santee, Plantation Parish: History and Records, 1685–1925* (Spartanburg, S.C.: The Reprint Company, Publishers, 1997), 14; Wm. H. Huger, comp., "Paper Describing the First Generations of the Huger Family in South Carolina," *HSSCT* 4 (1897): 13.

100. "William Dunlop to Sir James Montgomerie, tenth Baronet of Skelmorlie" (October 21, 1686), Scottish Record Office, GD.3/E2/114, photocopies at SCDAH; Lesser, *South Carolina Begins,* 146. I am indebted to Charles Lesser for leading me to these unpublished letters. See J. G. Dunlop and Mabel L. Webber, eds., "Spanish Depredations, 1686," *SCHGM* 30 (1929): 86; Paul E. Hoffman, *Florida's Frontiers* (Bloomington: Indiana University Press, 2002), 156–59.

101. "William Dunlop to Sir James Montgomerie" (November 21, 1686), copy, SCDAH.

102. Jean Ribault, *Whole and True,* ed. Biggar, 267. The fact that as late as 1698 a group of refugees petitioned the proprietors in hopes of settling at Port Royal is a further testimony to the fame of this Carolina site in Huguenot circles. See infra chap. 7, note 84.

103. Weir, *Colonial South Carolina,* 51–52, 58–59; Crane, *Southern Frontier,* 5–9.

104. "William Dunlop to Sir James Montgomerie, tenth Baronet of Skelmorlie" (November 21, 1686), copy, SCDAH.

105. Ribault, *Whole and True Discoverye,* ed. Biggar, 268; Hoffman, *New Andalucia,* 209–12.

106. Paul E. Hoffman, "The Chicora Legend and Franco-Spanish Rivalry in *La Florida,*" *Florida Historical Quarterly* 62 (1984): 419–38; Hoffman, *New Andalucia,* 8–21.

107. Cohen and Yardeni, "Un Suisse en Caroline du Sud," 70.

108. Huger, "Paper Describing the Huger Family," 13; Colonial Land Grants (Copy Series), vol. 38:101, SCDAH.

109. Cohen and Yardeni, "Un Suisse en Caroline du Sud," 70.

110. "Liste des habitants de Santee," in Ravenel, *Liste,* 53 (#61), 62 (#119).

111. "Census of March 1699," BPRO, CO 5/1258 (1699).

112. John Lawson, *A New Voyage to Carolina,* ed. Hugh T. Lefler (Chapel Hill: University of North Carolina Press, 1967), [19].

113. Lawson's estimate of 70 families would represent over 200 Huguenots, which would be twice as many individuals as in the census compiled ten months before. Lawson's approximate figure is either much too high or includes English settlers. If we speculate that the proportion of Huguenots among these 70 families was two-thirds, or 46, families, it would represent a community of about 150 individuals, which constitutes a figure more in accordance with other sources. The population of St. James Santee seems to have grown slowly since in 1724 Reverend Albert Pouderous estimated it at "two hundred parishioners all french living together" ("Present State of St. James, Santee, by Albert Pouderous, French minister" [January 20, 1724], SPG records, Lambeth Palace Library, London, B4:135).

114. Samuel Thomas, "An Account of the Church in South Carolina, 1702–1706," ed. Albert S. Thomas, *Historical Magazine of the Protestant Episcopal Church* 23 (1954): 240.

115. Ravenel, *Liste,* 56 (#78).

116. Lawson, *New Voyage,* [20]; Suzanne Cameron Linder, *Anglican Churches in Colonial South Carolina: Their History and Architecture* (Charleston, S.C.: Wyrick & Company, 2000), 51.

117. "The T of the Cooper river" was the standard phrase used in wills, warrants, grants, and transactions to describe the spot where the Cooper River forks into two tributaries flowing west and east. For examples of this use, see Colonial Land Grants (Copy Series), vol. 38:81, 347, 379, 385, SCDAH.

118. Smith, "Orange Quarter," 116–17; Israel, *Dutch Republic,* 37, 802–3; René Moulinas, "Orange (principauté d')," in *Dictionnaire de l'Ancien Régime,* ed. Bély, 930–31. Huguenots from Languedoc, Dauphiny, and Provence regularly took refuge in Orange before it was seized by Louis XIV in 1702, but no Carolina Huguenots hailed from there. Orange Quarter was thus most likely named after William and not the principality of Orange. Although the settlement also became known as French Quarter because it was settled by Huguenots, its original name was unambiguously Orange Quarter or *le Cartié [Quartier] d'Orange.*

119. A meaningful anecdote in Jaques Fontaine's memoirs tells about "a French Captain, also a refugee, [who] had come [to England] with the Prince [of Orange]" and whom Fontaine recognized as a former neighbor of his before they "embraced each other with the affection of brothers" (Fontaine, *Memoirs,* 141). No figures exist for ordinary soldiers, but historians estimate the number of officers who served in the British army in the Williamite wars at nearly eight hundred (Gwynn, *Huguenot Heritage,* 188).

120. Fairbrother, "Foreign Protestants," 188.

121. Henry E. Ravenel, *Ravenel Records* (Dunwoody, Ga.: the author, 1971), 20; Smith, "Orange Quarter," 111–15; Childs, "Petit-Guérard Colony," 8–9. I here disagree with Childs and

follow Smith in thinking that the settlement of Orange Quarter by the *Richmond* passengers is a tradition that is not corroborated by the records.

122. The earliest recorded grant in Orange Quarter is Nicolas de Longuemare's, which was issued in March 1694 and whose warrant was dated March 1689. Longuemare's land was situated on the "Northwest of the Eastern branch of the T of the Cooper River" (Colonial Land Grants [Copy Series], vol. 38:81, SCDAH). Smith made a complete list of the warrants and grants obtained by Huguenots known to have lived in Orange Quarter to determine when the Huguenots started to relocate there. This effort turned out to be inconclusive because all except Longuemare's were issued between 1696 and 1711, long after the refugees had actually settled in the area. See Smith, "Orange Quarter," 114–15.

123. See supra pages 86–87 (and notes).

124. Frank J. Klingberg, ed., *The Carolina Chronicle of Dr. Francis Le Jau 1706–1717* (Berkeley: University of California Press, 1956), 39.

125. "Will of Cézar Mozé" (drawn June 20, 1687; probated July 7, 1687), Miscellaneous Records (Proprietary Series), vol. 1675–95:282, SCDAH.

126. The question whether Mozé's bequeath was for the Orange Quarter or Charleston congregation is therefore a moot point. On this debate, see Smith, "Orange Quarter," 117; Thomas W. Bacot, "Orange Quarter (St. Denis)," *HSSCT* 23 (1917): 41–43.

127. "Census of March 1699," BPRO, CO 5/1258 (1699); Thomas, "Account of the Church," 239. Four of these families were Fleury (Abraham and his brother Isaac), Boisseau (Jean and his wife Marie [Postel]), Postel (Jean), and Porcher (Isaac). Isaac Fleury, Jean Boisseau, Marie [Postel] Boisseau, and Isaac Porcher bear nearly consecutive entry numbers (102, 104, 105, and 107, respectively) in the *Liste des François et Suisses,* which confirms that they lived in the same community. See Henry A. M. Smith, "Goose Creek," *SCHGM* 29 (1928): 174–87; Smith, "The French Huguenot Church of the Parish of St. James, Goose Creek," *HSSCT* 16 (1909): 42–46.

128. "Will of Antoine Prudhomme" (July 20, 1695), Miscellaneous Records (Proprietary Series), vol. 1692–1700:227, SCDAH.

129. Smith, "French Huguenot Church," 42; Smith, "Goose Creek," 265.

130. Smith, "French Huguenot Church," 44.

131. George D. Terry, "'Champaign Country': A Social History of an Eighteenth Century Lowcountry Parish in South Carolina, St. John's, Berkeley County" (Ph.D. diss., University of South Carolina, 1981), 52–55. The other two nuclei were Wampee, founded by New England Anabaptists, and Comingtee, settled by English, Irish, West Indian, and a few Huguenot families. The name Comingtee is derived from John Coming, a very early Carolina settler, and the T-shaped intersection of two branches of the Cooper River. This land was later bequeathed to Elias Ball (Edward Ball, *Slaves in the Family* [N.Y.: Penguin,1989], 27, 39–41).

132. The other three were Jean Dubois, Paul Trapier, and Reverend Trouillart (Terry, "Champaign Country," 54, table 2; Colonial Land Grants [Copy Series], vol. 38:410, 420, 437, 448, 465, 473, 484–85, 496, SCDAH).

133. The Comingtee Huguenots were Jacob Guérard, Alexandre Thésée Chasteigner, Jacques LeBas, and Théodore Verdity (Terry, "Champaign Country," 58–59, table 3).

134. Terry, "Champaign Country," 55–56. Hirsch placed this "small wooden church . . . a little east of what is now Simpson's Basin, on the Santee Canal" (Hirsch, *Huguenots,* 79; Linder, *Anglican Churches,* 57).

135. Philip G. Clarke Jr., comp., *Anglicanism in South Carolina, 1660–1976: A Chronological History of Dates and Events in the Church of England and the Episcopal Church in South Carolina* (Easley, S.C.: Southern Historical Press, 1976), 3; Linder, *Anglican Churches,* 7.

136. This is some 680 out of the 870 officiating in France (Hans Bots, "Les pasteurs français au Refuge des Provinces-Unies: un groupe socio-professionnel tout particulier, 1680–1710," in *La vie intellectuelle aux Refuges protestants,* ed. Jens Häseler and Antony McKenna [Paris: Honoré Champion, 1999], 9).

137. Ravenel, *Liste,* 44.

138. Van den Bosh's Walloon origin is evidenced by his Dutch name and the fact that his record of ordination mentions "Flandriae natione" (the Flemish nation) (Percival Merritt, "The French Protestant Church in Boston," *Publications of the Colonial Society of Massachusetts* 26 [1926]: 324n1).

139. "Laurent van den Bosk to Henry Compton," BPRO, CO 1/58 (1685); FPCL, Records of the French Church, ms. 7, "Livre des Actes, 1679–1692" (August 9, 1682).

140. "Van den Bosk to Compton," BPRO, CO 1/58 (1685).

141. After he left Charleston, Van den Bosch successively officiated in the Huguenot churches of Boston, New York City, and New Paltz, where he never failed to arouse anger and frustration among his parishioners. In Boston he was charged "to have baptized whores and married couples without first posted banns." In the 1690s, however, Van den Bosch officiated at North Sassafras Parish, Cecil County, Maryland, where he drew a map of the lower Mississippi valley based on information gathered from "a French Indian," whom Greg Waselkov conjectures could be "a Moingwena Illinois that could have joined (by marriage for instance) the Shawnee band at Starved Rock before their move to Maryland." This map, which Van den Bosch apparently drew for Governor Francis Nicholson, is deemed by historians as one of the most accurate for the period. I am grateful to Jon Butler for mentioning the existence of this map to me. See Kingdon, "Why Did the Huguenot Refugees Become Episcopalians," 323; Butler, *Huguenots in America,* 64–65; Baird, *History,* 2:224; Gregory A. Waselkov, "Indian Maps of the Colonial Southeast," in *Powhatan's Mantle: Indians in the Colonial Southeast,* ed. Peter H. Wood, Gregory A. Waselkov, and M. Thomas Hatley (Lincoln: University of Nebraska Press, 1989), 293–95, fig. 1, 309–13, fig. 9; W. P. Cumming et al., *The Exploration of North America, 1630–1776* (New York: G. P. Putnam's Sons, 1974), figure 226.

142. "Passenger List of the *Margaret,*" 34.

143. Robert Hovenden, ed., *The Registers of the Walloon or Strangers Church in Canterbury,* Quarto Series, vol. 5 (Lymington, U.K.: HSGB&I Publications, 1891), 540; Traylor, "Pierre Trouillart"; Haag and Haag, *La France protestante,* 9:429; Ravenel, *Liste,* 44 (#2), 67–68 (#149); Butler, *Huguenots in America,* 239n40.

144. Minet and Waller, *Transcripts,* 165; Mours, "Les pasteurs à la révocation," 81.

145. Florent-Philippe's brother Pierre (1646–1701) was officiating in Guînes, where he either assisted or succeeded to his father, before his departure in 1685. By April 1686 he had obtained a ministerial position at Cadzand, Zeeland, but he soon left for Canterbury, where he preached his first sermon in May 1687. In 1699 Pierre returned to Middleburg, Zeeland, where he served as a third pastor. Butler is right to observe that, contrary to what Baird wrote, the Pierre Trouillart of Canterbury was not Florent-Philippe's father but his brother. Trouillart's father, recorded as "défunct" (deceased) in the 1696–97 Carolina naturalization list, died in the early 1690s. See Hovenden, *Registers,* 316; Traylor, "Pierre Trouillart"; Hans Bots, comp., "Liste des pasteurs et proposants réfugiés dans les Provinces-Unies," in *La vie intellectuelle,* 38 and 65; Baird, *History,* 2:98n2; Butler, *Huguenots in America,* 239n40; Ch.-L. Frossard, ed., "Liste des pasteurs des églises réformées de France et présents au synode wallon de Rotterdam en 1686," *BSHPF* 7 (1858): 428.

146. "Historical Sketch of the Prioleau Family in Europe and America" (reprint from *HSSCT* 6 [1899], *HSSCT* 71 [1966]: 88); Gourdin, "Madeleine Chardon," 98n212; Huger, "Paper Describing the Huger Family," 13.

147. Examples of such accounts can be found in Hirsch: "The Charles Town Church was an extension, or perhaps better, a transferred reëstablishment of the French Protestant Church of Pons, France. . . . Hands ruthless in the destruction of visible buildings were unable to destroy the church organization. It reasserted its life on American soil" (Hirsch, *Huguenots*, 51); and in Steedman: "In April, 1686, [the Pons] congregation received notice that their church . . . must be demolished. Weeping, the Huguenots watched the wreckers work, while M. Prioleau preached his last sermon. Then they separated, to reassemble secretly and plan their flight. Many of the congregation joined their pastor in Charles Town" (Steedman, *Short History of the Huguenot Church*, 3). Steedman took the anecdote of Prioleau pronouncing a sermon before a weeping congregation from Baird, who, in turn, took it from Crottet (Baird, *History*, 2:43; Crottet, *Histoire des églises*, 138–39). Crottet does not cite any sources to document this anecdote. This story is hardly credible because it would have been extremely dangerous, in fact nearly impossible, for Prioleau to remain in France until April 1686. Following article 4 of the Edict of Fontainebleau, issued October 25, 1685, all pastors had two weeks to leave France or convert and ran the risk of being executed if they did not comply. It is therefore hard to imagine Prioleau, who was well known in the Pons area and who had already been the object of court proceedings, remaining in Saintonge without the Catholic and royal authorities knowing of his presence.

148. "It has been stated that Prioleau brought with him from Pons a considerable part of his congregation to Charleston. I find little to confirm this statement" (Baird, *History*, 2:45n2).

149. Daniel Ravenel, who transcribed the *Liste des François et Suisses* in the 1860s, left a blank in Prioleau's entry where the place of origin should appear. No doubt he would have recognized the name of Pons had it been in the original, unless, of course, the place name was also left out in that document.

150. This is the denization list of April 9, 1687 (William A. Shaw, ed., *Letters of Denization and Acts of Naturalization for Aliens in England and Ireland 1603–1700*, Quarto Series, vol. 18 [Lymington, U.K.: HSGB&I Publications, 1911], 182–88). For a discussion on naturalization and denization, a sort of incomplete citizenship granted to foreign settlers by royal patent, and their respective records, see infra chap. 7. In a recent article the genealogist Ray Timmons compared the parish records of Pons and the April 9 denization list and, as expected, found no evidence of any congregational transfer (Ray E. Timmons, "The Huguenot Church Register of Pons France: Possible Denization and Migration to Charles Town," *Carolina Herald and Newsletter* 32, no. 1 [2004]: 5–11).

151. Élie Prioleau has a disputed genealogy. Crottet wrote that he descended from Antonio Prioli or Priuli, a Venetian, possibly related to a doge, who settled in France, converted to Calvinism, and became the Duke of Rohan's chaplain. Once in France, the family would have changed their name from Prioli to Prioleau, according to Crottet, to avoid the inappropriate joke *pris au lit* (caught in bed), which the Italian name evokes when pronounced in French. Along with this argumentation, it can be added that the suffix *eau*, being typical of surnames from the La Rochelle area, where the Prioleaus lived at the time of the Revocation, would have granted further French authenticity to the name. The Haag brothers, however, conjectured that the Prioleau family, of neither bourgeois nor noble background, originated from the obscure Languedoc town of Saussignac, situated near Bergerac. Needless to say, the more prestigious and romantic "Venetian-Dogean" origins took precedence over the years. See Crottet, "Recherches historiques sur la famille Prioleau," 1; "Historical Sketch of the Prioleau Family," 81–84; Haag and Haag, *La*

France protestante, 8:331–33. See also Edward Gallaudet, "The Family of Priuli, Also Called Prioli, Priolo, Prioleau," *Huguenot Society of America Proceedings* 2 (1896): 299–321. Gallaudet, who believed in the Priuli-Prioleau connection, nonetheless spoke of "genealogical blunder" when referring to the Prioleaus claiming direct descendance from a Venetian doge (ibid., 300).

152. George Howe, *History of the Presbyterian Church in South Carolina,* 2 vols. (Columbia, S.C.: Duffie & Chapman, 1870), 1:111.

153. The influence of the pastor Alexandre Crottet and of his work on the nineteenth-century Carolina Huguenot chroniclers who sought to enhance Prioleau's role in early Charleston Huguenot history cannot be underestimated. A descendant of Huguenot refugees who fled to the Swiss cantons, Crottet wrote a history of three Saintonge Huguenot churches—Pons, Gémozac, and Mortagne-sur-Gironde—while serving as minister at Pons in the 1830s. This monograph is significant historiographically because Crottet wrote long before Jules Michelet rehabilitated Huguenot history in France in the 1860s, and it is valuable because Crottet had access to many no longer available manuscript sources, which he meticulously transcribed. It became a basic source for American historians interested in the Pons congregation and Prioleau. The influence was mutual, however, since Carolina chroniclers, among them Daniel Ravenel, "a lineal descendant of Elias Prioleau," in turn filled Crottet in on Prioleau's Charleston years. Although the exact circumstances of the transaction are still unknown, the Crottet papers, which contain a mine of information and have been used by contemporary Huguenot demographic historians, and part of his library were "cédés" (donated?) to the Charleston Library Society in the 1850s. These papers, though, are irrelevant to the history of the Charleston Huguenot church because Crottet, overly eager to please his American correspondents, systematically and hastily turned members of the Pons congregation into Carolina Huguenots solely on the basis of homonymous family names without cross-referencing sources. See Crottet, *Histoire des églises;* "Recueil de Manuscrits sur les Églises Réformées de France réunis par les soins de Mr. Alexandre Crottet, ancien Pasteur des Églises Réformées de Pons, Gémozac et Mortagne en Saintonge et actuellement premier Pasteur de l'Église d'Yverdon, Canton de Vaud, en Suisse, accompagné de notes explicatives," Crottet Collection ms., 3 vols., Charleston Library Society, 1:folders 16, 14, 17, 18; Edward D. Seeber, *Choix de pièces huguenotes* (Bloomington: Indiana University Publications, 1942) (Seeber's work is only marginally useful to historians since Seeber was mostly interested in Crottet's papers from a literary perspective); Hilda Kenner, "Births, Baptisms and Marriages in the Records of the Reformed Church of Mortagne-sur-Gironde, 1613–1668, from the Crottet Papers in Charleston, South Carolina," *HSSCT* 106 (2002): 42–104; "Crottet," in Haag and Haag, *La France protestante,* 4:921–23; Van Ruymbeke, "L'émigration huguenote," 1:380–85; Howe, *History of the Presbyterian Church,* 1:108.

154. Howe, *History of the Presbyterian Church,* 1:110. Prioleau's will is no longer extant.

155. A. S. Salley, ed., "Some Early Simons Records," in *South Carolina Genealogies: Articles from the South Carolina Historical (and Genealogical) Magazine,* 5 vols., comp. Margaret H. Cannon (Spartanburg, S.C.: Reprint Co., 1983), 4:223.

156. Howe, *History of the Presbyterian Church,* 1:110–11.

157. Ravenel, *Ravenel Records,* 19.

158. See supra page 110.

159. See supra page 111.

160. Lawton, "Tribute to Pasteur Pierre Robert," 1–13; Lawton, "Pasteur Pierre Robert's Swiss Ancestry," *HSSCT* 90 (1985): 68–71; Annie E. Miller, *Our Family Circle* (Marietta, Ga.: Continental Book Company, 1957), 187–91.

161. In March 1688 Prioleau went to Santee to baptize Daniel and Marguerite (Perdriau) Huger's twelfth son, Daniel; this indicates that Robert was not yet in Santee (Huger, "Paper Describing the Huger Family," 13).

162. Jean-Pierre and Gabrielle Pelé, Honoré Michaud, Pierre and Jeanne Robert, and Jean-François Gignilliat (all the Carolina Swiss except Suzanne Horry, Jacques Varin's widow) settled in Santee (Ravenel, *Liste,* 52 [#56], 54 [#63], 59 [#90], 62 [#117]).

6. Protestant Majority

Epigraphs from Slann L. C. Simmons, "Recorded Burials in the Huguenot Churchyard of Charleston," *HSSCT* 57 (1952): 34; "Élie Neau to SPG Treasurer" (December 20, 1704), SPG Papers, vol. 13, New York (1700–1706), Lambeth Palace Library, London, fol. 102.

1. They numbered seventy-nine in Virginia and twenty-two in Maryland. See Edwin S. Gaustad and Philip L. Barlow, *New Historical Atlas of Religion in America* (New York: Oxford University Press, 2001), 7, figure 1.8; John F. Woolverton, *Colonial Anglicanism in North America* (Detroit: Wayne State University Press, 1984), 28.

2. The 1693 New York Ministry Act provided for public support of a church in New York, Westchester, Queens, and Richmond counties without actually naming it. It was the swift and biased interpretation of the law by the politically influential Anglican minority that led to the establishment of the Church of England. See Kammen, *Colonial New York,* 136–37, 220–21.

3. Woolverton, *Colonial Anglicanism,* 28; Gaustad and Barlow, *New Historical Atlas,* 17, figure 1.16.

4. John Spurr, *The Restoration Church of England, 1646–1689* (New Haven: Yale University Press, 1991), 104.

5. John Walsh and Stephen Taylor, "Introduction: The Church and Anglicanism in the 'Long' Eighteenth Century," in *The Church of England c. 1689–c. 1833: From Toleration to Tractarianism,* ed. John Walsh, Colin Haydon, and Stephen Taylor (Cambridge: Cambridge University Press, 1994), 16.

6. Jon Butler, *Awash in a Sea of Faith: Christianizing the American People* (Cambridge, Mass.: Harvard University Press, 1990), 32–34; Jeremy Gregory, "The Eighteenth-Century Reformation: The Pastoral Task of Anglican Clergy after 1689," and John Spurr, "The Church, the Societies and the Moral Revolution of 1688," in *Church of England,* ed. Walsh et al., 67–85, 127–42, respectively.

7. On the foundation of the SPCK and the post-1689 English religious context, see Craig Rose, "The Origins and Ideals of the SPCK 1699–1716," in *Church of England,* ed. Haydon and Taylor, 172–90. While the SPCK was active both at home and overseas, the work of the SPG, as the terms "Foreign Parts" suggest, was exclusively limited to the colonies.

8. Cited in Charles F. Pascoe, *Classified Digest of the Records of the Society of the Gospel in Foreign Parts, 1701–1892* (London: Society's Office, 1895), 7. The evolution of the SPG's policies and objectives can be conveniently followed through the anniversary sermons. Edgar L. Pennington, "The S. P. G. Anniversary Sermons 1702–1783," *Historical Magazine of the Protestant Episcopal Church* 20 (1951): 10–43.

9. John K. Nelson, "Anglican Missions in America, 1701–1725: A Study of the Society for the Propagation of the Gospel in Foreign Parts" (Ph.D. diss., Northwestern University, 1962), 43. Over the course of the century, the SPCK shipped one hundred libraries of more than one hundred volumes each and the SPG appointed 329 missionaries to British North America (John F.

Woolverton, "Anglicanism," in *Encyclopedia of the North American Colonies,* 4 vols., ed. Jacob E. Cooke [New York: Charles Scribner's Sons, 1993], 3:568–70).

10. On the SPG and the Huguenots, see William A. Bultmann, "The SPG and the French Huguenots in Colonial America," *Historical Magazine of the Protestant Episcopal Church* 20 (1951): 156–72; Anne P. Diffendal, "The Society for the Propagation of the Gospel in Foreign Parts and the Assimilation of Foreign Protestants in British North America" (Ph.D. diss., University of Nebraska, 1974), 114–32.

11. Although undeniably important, this role should not be overestimated in the case of the South Carolina Huguenots since of the pastors who served at St. James Santee and at St. Denis only Jacques Gignilliat was an SPG missionary. As for Francis LeJau, whose correspondence is an invaluable source of information on early Carolina society and about whom much has been written, he played a marginal role in keeping the Huguenots within the fold of the Anglican Church since he officiated in the almost exclusively English parish of St. James Goose Creek. See Charles Bolton, "South Carolina and the Reverend Doctor Francis Le Jau: Southern Society and the Conscience of an Anglican Missionary," *Historical Magazine of the Protestant Episcopal Church* 40 (1971): 63–79; Arthur H. Hirsch, "Reverend Francis LeJau, First Rector of St. James Church, Goose Creek S. C.," *HSSCT* 34 (1929): 25–43.

12. Butler, *Awash in a Sea of Faith,* 100.

13. Sirmans, *South Carolina,* 76–81; Roper, *Conceiving Carolina,* 128–31.

14. Parker, *North Carolina Charters,* 181, article 96.

15. The article stipulated "public maintenance is to arise out of lands or rents assigned voluntarily, contributions, or such other ways whereby no man shall be chargeable to pay out of his particular Estate that is not conformable to the church aforesaid" (ibid., 227, article 101). Two revised versions were drafted in January and August 1682. The exemption clause is to be found only in the latter.

16. Ibid., 238, article 26.

17. A proprietary policy characterized by, as James L. Underwood writes, "vacillation between broad tolerance to all settlers and unflinching preference for the Church of England" (James L. Underwood, "The Dawn of Religious Freedom in South Carolina: The Journey from Limited Tolerance to Constitutional Right," *South Carolina Law Review* 54 [2002]: 124).

18. John A. Moore, "Royalizing South Carolina: The Revolution of 1719 and the Evolution of Early South Carolina Government" (Ph.D. diss., University of South Carolina, 1991), 217–31; Sirmans, *South Carolina,* 81–86; John W. Brinsfield, *Religion and Politics in Colonial South Carolina* (Easley, S.C.: Southern Historical Press, 1983), 16–26; Roper, *Conceiving Carolina,* 128.

19. Two Test Acts, which must not be confused with the Corporation Act (1661) that required all municipal and borough officials to take communion "according to the rites of the Church of England," were voted in 1673 and 1678. The first, which was directed primarily against Catholics rather than Dissenters, imposed the Anglican sacramental test on holders of civil and military offices under the crown and, most important in the comparative context of the Carolina Exclusion Act, did not apply to members of Parliament. The second, which applied to M.P.'s, did not, however, require conformity to the Church of England. See Michael R. Watts, *The Dissenters: From the Reformation to the French Revolution* (Oxford: Clarendon Press, 1978), 223, 251–52.

20. Sidney C. Bolton, "The Anglican Church of Colonial South Carolina, 1704–1754: A Study in Americanization" (Ph.D. diss., University of Wisconsin, 1973), 37–43; Moore, "Royalizing South Carolina," 233–39; Roper, *Conceiving Carolina,* 128–29.

21. Daniel Defoe, *Party-Tyranny, or an Occasional Bill in Miniature; as Now Practiced in Carolina: Humbly Offered to the Consideration of Both Houses of Parliament* [London, 1705], in *Early Narratives,* ed. Salley, 224–64 (quote, 264).

22. In the first decade of the eighteenth century, occasional conformity bitterly divided Whigs and Tories, Dissenters and Churchmen, and Low and High Church Anglicans. Opponents to this practice, which they branded as an "abominable hypocrisy," unsuccessfully attempted to pass a law against it in Parliament on three occasions before 1705 (1702, 1703, and 1704). See Holmes, *Making of a Great Power,* 354–55, 362–63 (quote, 354); John Flaningam, "The Occasional Conformity Controversy: Ideology and Party Politics, 1697–1711," *Journal of British Studies* 17 (1977): 38–62. Defoe personally objected to occasional conformity on moral grounds and simply because of its inherent contradiction. In a 1697 tract entitled *An Enquiry into the Occasional Conformity of Dissenters,* he asserted, "Nothing can be lawful and unlawful at the same time, if it be unlawful for me to Dissent, I ought to Conform; but if it be lawful for me to Conform, I must dissent" (quoted in Flaningam, "Occasional Conformity Controversy," 44).

23. *An Account of the Fair and Impartial Proceedings of the Lords Proprietors, Governor and Council of the Colony of South Carolina, in Answer to the Untrue Suggestions contained in the Petition of Jos. Boon and others, and of a Paper Intituled The Case of the Church of England in Carolina* (London, 1706).

24. "An Act for the Establishment of Religious Worship in this Province, according to the Church of England, and for the erecting of Churches for the Publick Worship of God, and also for the Maintenance of Ministers and the building [of] convenient Houses for them," in Cooper and McCord, *Statutes at Large,* 2:236–46 (no. 225) (Act of 1704), 2:282–95 (no. 256) (Act of 1706).

25. Bolton, "Anglican Church," 39–41; Underwood, "Dawn of Religious Freedom," 127–34. Only a gubernatorial veto power exclusively granted to Johnson for the duration of his term could stop the removal procedure (Cooper and McCord, *Statutes at Large,* 241, article 15). Roper even goes as far as saying that "the [1704] Act's chief purpose was to keep the clergy, notably the Reverend Edward Marston, in check rather than to promote the Church of England" (Roper, *Conceiving Carolina,* 130).

26. Defoe, *Party-Tyranny,* 263.

27. "Decedent Index to South Carolina," in Lesser, *South Carolina Begins,* 365, 353.

28. The assembly numbers vary depending on whether or not the week-long session of November 1695 is regarded as the second assembly or part of the first. I followed the lead of the *Biographical Directory of the South Carolina House of Representatives,* which, based on the fact that a new slate of representatives appears in the records of this meeting, call it the second assembly (Walter B. Edgar, gen. ed., *Biographical Directory of the South Carolina House of Representatives,* 5 vols. [Columbia: University of South Carolina Press, 1974–84], 1:22n1). For a different numbering, see Charles E. Lee and Ruth S. Green, "A Guide to Commons House Journals, 1692–1721," *SCHGM* 68 (1967): 87.

29. This petition is no longer extant and is only known through the "Act to Erect the French Settlement on Santee into a Parish," which was drafted by Ralph Izard and Louis Pasquereau and voted by the assembly in response. See Cooper and McCord, *Statutes at Large,* 2:268–69 (quote, 268); Alexander S. Salley, ed., *Journal of the Commons House of Assembly of South Carolina, March 6–April 9, 1706* (Columbia: Historical Commission of South Carolina, 1937), 41.

30. "Representation of the Inhabitants of St. James, Santee in South Carolina to Generall Nicholson inclosed in his letter of 6 November 1721," SPG ms. Letterbooks (East Ardsley: Micro Methods Limited, 1964), A, 15, 60. In a December 1716 letter addressed to the SPG, Thomas Hasel, the missionary appointed to the parish of St. Thomas, mentioned that the Orange Quarter

congregation "made an application to ye Assembly of the Province to be made into a Parish and to have some Publick Allowance for a Minister." However, this Orange Quarter petition, unlike Santee's, was not recorded in the assembly journals and did not lead to the vote of an act, which incidentally corroborates Santee's respectability and influence. See "Hasel to SPG" (December 27, 1716), ibid., B, 4, 36; Alexander S. Salley, ed., *Journal of the Commons House, March 6–April 9, 1706 and November 20, 1706–February 8, 1707* (Columbia: Historical Commission of South Carolina, 1939); Smith, "Orange Quarter," 120–21.

31. Edgar, *Biographical Directory,* 1:27.

32. Shaw, *Letters of Denization 1603–1700,* 170; Salley and Olsberg, *Warrants for Lands,* 599; Miscellaneous Records (Proprietary Series), vol. 1704–9:23, SCDAH; Records of the Register of the Province (Conveyance Series), book E, 1705–8, p. 142, SCDAH; Edgar, *Biographical Directory,* 2:403; Henry B. Hoff, "The Le Serrurier Family," *HSSCT* 16 (1977): 75–77.

33. The "Scots' Company" referred to in this document is the joint-stock company that promoted the failed Scottish settlement at Darien in Central America. Lady Blake's accusation is corroborated by the fact that LeSerrurier was officially charged for embezzling one thousand pounds sterling. This accusation, to which he preferred not to answer, most likely prompted his departure for Carolina. See "Letter of Lady Blake, Widow of the late Governor to the Lords Proprietors, 16 May 1704," printed in Defoe, *Party-Tyranny,* 250–52 (251, ed. note 1); Edgar, *Biographical Directory,* 2:403.

34. Edgar, *Biographical Directory,* 1:28.

35. Myrta J. Huston, "Early Generations of the Motte Family of South Carolina," *HSSCT* 12 (1951): 57–58; Edgar, *Biographical Directory,* 2:481–82.

36. Frank J. Klingberg, ed., "Commissary Johnston's *Notitias Parochialis,*" *SCHGM* 48 (1947): 31.

37. Ravenel, *Liste,* 51 (#48); Salley and Olsberg, *Warrants for Lands,* 652; Gourdin, "Madeleine Chardon," 73, 98; Edgar, *Biographical Directory,* 2:510–11; Lesser, *South Carolina Begins,* 180, 221n111.

38. Anthony, Lord Ashley, was Ashley Cooper's grandson. See Miscellaneous Records (Proprietary Series), vol. 1675–95:426–27, SCDAH; Colonial Land Grants (Copies Series), vol. 38:175, SCDAH; Shaw, *Letters of Denization 1603–1700,* 159, 172; Salley, *Commissions,* 109; Cooper and McCord, *Statutes at Large,* 2:246, 294; Edgar, *Biographical Directory,* 2:401–2.

39. Butler, *Huguenots in America,* 138.

40. Ravenel, *Liste,* 54 (#70) [P. Gendron], 57 (#82) [R. Ravenel].

41. Edgar, *Biographical Directory,* 1:21.

42. Cooper and McCord, *Statutes at Large,* 2:282–94, articles 3, 4, 5, 22 (quote), 23.

43. St. Denis is also a town, situated north of Paris, and French monarchs have traditionally been interred there since King Dagobert (c. 630). St. Denis could possibly refer to a battle in the Wars of Religion, but I agree with Henry Smith, who thinks it unlikely that the parish was named after a relatively insignificant military encounter (Smith, "Orange Quarter," 122–23).

44. Butler, *Huguenots in America,* 115.

45. "An Additional Act to an Act entitled An Act for the Establishment of Religious Worship in this Province according to the Church of England . . . ," in Cooper and McCord, *Statutes at Large,* 2:329, art. 2.

46. Ibid., 2:287.

47. All parish rectors were to receive an annual salary of 100 Carolina pounds a year (about £15) except that of St. Philip's (150). It is unclear whether the Santee Huguenots managed to have a salary at par with the other rural parishes because of their April petition, which requested "the

same allowance as other ministers," the political influence of their representatives, Ravenel and Gendron, or simply because St. James Santee was regarded as a parish in its own right as opposed to St. Denis. See Salley, *Journal of the Commons House of Assembly, March 6–April 9, 1706,* 41; Cooper and McCord, *Statutes at Large,* 2:286.

48. Cooper and McCord, *Statutes at Large,* 2:288.

49. D. N. Griffiths, "The French Translations of the English Book of Common Prayer," *HSP* 23 (1971–76), no. 2 (1972): 93–98; Gwynn, *Huguenot Heritage,* 122–24. The 1616 French edition had been the work of Pierre de Laune, pastor of the Walloon Church in Norwich. On Delaune, see Charles Littleton, "Acculturation and the French Church of London, 1600–circa 1640," in *Memory and Identity,* ed. Van Ruymbeke and Sparks, 97–100.

50. For New Rochelle's 1709 vote over conformity, see Paula W. Carlo, "The Huguenots of Colonial New Paltz and New Rochelle: A Social and Religious History" (Ph.D. diss., City University of New York, 2001), 309–10.

51. Huger, "Paper Describing the Huger Family," 13.

52. Ibid. As early as March 1709, however, members of the Santee vestry contacted the Charleston pastor Paul L'Escot—although himself a Calvinist—to find a conformist minister for their parish presumably through his extensive European connections. Following this request, L'Escot wrote Mr. Bonet, the King of Prussia's resident in England, "beseeching [him] to take some pains in this matter and to imploy [his] friends therein likewise" while extolling Santee as "one of the most agreable parts of this province" with "good fruit, good victuals, plenty of wild fowl and excellent fish" ("Extract of a letter from Mr. Escot, Minister of the French Church at Charles Town in South Carolina of the 24 March 1709, to the Honorable Mr. Bonet the King of Prussia's Resident in England," SPG records, vol. 16 [South Carolina, 1702–10], Lambeth Palace Library, London, fol. 244).

53. "James Gignilliat to SPG" (May 28, 1710), SPG ms. Letterbooks, vol. 1, 1702–12, A, 5, 119.

54. Hirsch and Friedlander have Robert die in 1710, a few months after Gignilliat's appointment, but genealogists and his descendants think that he died in 1715. None cites an exact source. A 1730 remission of debt involving third-generation Roberts and an entry for a will in the 1716–19 bundle index confirm 1715 as Robert's date of death. See Hirsch, *Huguenots,* 61; Friedlander, "Carolina Huguenots," 201; Miller, *Our Family Circle,* 188; Lawton, "A Tribute to Pasteur Pierre Robert," 7; Lesser, *South Carolina Begins,* "Decedent index," 377.

55. "James Gignilliat to SPG" (May 28, 1710), SPG ms. Letterbooks, vol. 1, 1702–12, A, 5, 119.

56. Ibid.

57. Jacques's father was first cousin to Jean-François Gignilliat. He was licensed by the bishop of London in November 1709. See Samuel G. Stoney, ed., "Eighteenth-Century Affidavit to Prove the Descent of the Gignilliat Family," *HSSCT* 13 (1959): 36; John Clement, comp., "Clergymen Licensed Overseas by the Bishops of London, 1696–1710 and 1715–1716," *Historical Magazine of the Protestant Episcopal Church* 16 (1947): 326. Gignilliat and Thomas Hasel, an SPG missionary appointed to the parish of St. Thomas, were on board the same Carolina-bound ship in March 1710, hoping to be in Charleston within six weeks ("Hasel to SPG" [March 2, 1710], SPG ms. Letterbooks, A, 5, 97).

58. "Gignilliat to SPG" (May 28, 1710), A, 5, 119; Klingberg, *Carolina Chronicle: Papers of Gideon Johnston,* 60 (July 5, 1710). Since bishops of London lived so far from their American diocese, starting with Henry Compton they appointed representatives or commissaries to the colonies. South Carolina had three commissaries during the colonial period: Gideon Johnston (1708–16), William T. Bull (1717–23), and Alexander Garden (1728–53) (Bolton, *Southern Anglicanism,* 38, 41–42, 29–36). See also Alison G. Olson, "The Commissaries of the Bishop of London in Colonial

Politics," in *Anglo-American Political Relations, 1675–1775,* ed. A. G. Olson and Richard M. Brown (New Brunswick: Rutgers University Press, 1970), 109–24; Woolverton, *Colonial Anglicanism,* 84–85.

59. Klingberg, *Carolina Chronicle of Le Jau,* 82 (July 14, 1710).

60. On Boisseau's residence in Goose Creek, see infra chap. 5, note 127. Marie Postel, originally from Dieppe, Normandy, first married Laurens [first name unknown] before 1689, then Jean Boisseau before 1697 (Stoney, "Eighteenth-Century Affidavit," 38). Marie's age is indicated in an unpublished letter by LeJau dated May 2, 1711 (SPG Papers, Lambeth Palace Library, London, vol. 17, fol. 42).

61. Klingberg, *Carolina Chronicle of Le Jau,* 93 (July 10, 1711), 98 (September 5, 1711), 106 (January 10, 1712); Records of the Register of the Province (Conveyance Series), book K, 1731–33, pp. 159–64, SCDAH.

62. Klingberg, *Carolina Chronicle of Le Jau,* 106 (January 10, 1712).

63. Ibid.; Klingberg, *Carolina Chronicle: Papers of Gideon Johnston,* 101 (November 16, 1711).

64. Klingberg, *Carolina Chronicle of Le Jau,* 107.

65. Ibid.

66. "Gignilliat to SPG" (July 15, 1711), SPG ms. Letterbooks, A, 5, 105.

67. Klingberg, *Carolina Chronicle of Le Jau,* 106 (January 10, 1712), 115 (May 27, 1712), 127, 128 (February 23, 1713).

68. "LeJau to SPG" (May 2, 1711), Lambeth Palace Library, London, vol. 17, fol. 42.

69. "Since the writing of the above [September 19, 1711]," wrote Nicholas Trott to the SPG in a postscript, "I'm Informed by Mr. Commissary Johnston that the French Gent. at Santee have Sent for a French Minister to Virginia, and therefore yr Honble Society need not Send any one for that place" ("Trott to SPG," SPG ms. Letterbooks, A, 7, 5).

70. *Vestry Book of King William Parish, Virginia, 1707–1750* (Midlothian: Manakin Episcopal Church, 1966; reprinted, Midlothian: The Huguenot Society of the Founders of Manakin in the Colony of Virginia, 1988), 426–29 (pagination based on the 1905–6 publication in the *Virginia Magazine of History and Biography*). See also Baird, *History,* 2:105; Bridges and Williams, *St. James, Santee, Plantation Parish,* 13.

71. Klingberg, *Carolina Chronicle of Le Jau,* 118 (August 19, 1712).

72. Trouillart, who wrote his will in March 1712, had died by November when his executors settled his estate (Records of the Register of the Province (Conveyance Series), book H, 1711–15, 205–7, SCDAH; Terry, "Champaign Country," 55–56). According to a royal bounty roll of funds granted to "the widows & orphans of Ancient Ministers," Trouillart's sixty-six-year-old widow, Anne, whom he presumably married after the death of his first wife, Madeleine Maslet, who appeared in the *Liste des François et Suisses,* was back in England by 1717. Anne Trouillart, next to whose name a French clerk wrote "Son Mary est mort à la Caroline servant une Église" (Her husband died in Carolina serving a church), was given sixteen pounds sterling. See "The Royal Bounty," *HSP* 1 (1886): 326; Ravenel, *Liste,* 44 (#2).

73. [Commissary Gideon Johnston,] "Representation of ecclesiastical affairs in South Carolina, 1713," Bodleian Library, Oxford, Rawlinson ms., C. 943. An abridged, edited, and footnoted version of this report can be found in Amy Friedlander, ed., "Commissary Johnston's Report, 1713," *SCHM* 83 (1982): 259–71 (quote, 263); and a full version in Hirsch, *Huguenots,* 297–309. Unfortunately, Johnston's report, which he wrote while in England, and LeJau's correspondence, both Anglican biased, are the only sources available on Richebourg's controversial ministry.

74. LeJau's opinion is quoted in a letter addressed to Johnston by his Huguenot wife, the famed Carolina pastelist Henrietta de Beaulieu, while her husband was in England (Friedlander, "Commissary Johnston's Report," 263–64).

75. Ibid., 264. The first quote is from Johnston, and the second is from LeJau.

76. Ibid., 265.

77. "LeJau to Johnston" (December 20, 1712), SPG ms. Letterbooks, A, 8, 504–5; Klingberg, *Carolina Chronicle of Le Jau,* 126.

78. Records of the Court of Common Pleas, Judgment Rolls, box 5 (1714–15), 1714, case #301, SCDAH.

79. "Bartholomew Gaillard, Church Warden, on Behalf of Himself and the Inhabitants of the Parish of St. James Santee v. Isaac Legrand Dunnerville," in Anne King Gregorie, ed., *Records of the Court of Chancery of South Carolina, 1671–1779* (Washington, D..C: The American Historical Association, 1950), 240–43.

80. Gregorie, *Records of the Court of Chancery,* 242; Edgar, *Biographical Directory,* 1:36.

81. Records of the Register of the Province (Conveyance Series), book H, 1711–15, 371–73, SCDAH; Gregorie, *Records of the Court of Chancery,* 242–43.

82. Gregorie, *Records of the Court of Chancery,* 241; Records of the Court of Common Pleas, Judgment Rolls, box 5 (1714–15), 1714, case #301, SCDAH.

83. Gregorie, *Records of the Court of Chancery,* 244–45. The gap between the time the illicit sale occurred and when the case was brought to justice is likely due to the Yamassee War (1715–16), during which Santee was being threatened by Indian raids and Richebourg's home used as a makeshift fort ("Richebourg to Society" [February 12, 1716], SPG ms. Letterbooks, A, 11, 141–42).

84. Friedlander, "Commissary Johnston's Report," 260. In his list of the clergy of South Carolina, the same Johnston indicated about Richebourg: "Rector of St. James's Santee, formerly a Roman" (quoted in Hirsch, *Huguenots,* 291). Albert Pouderous, Richebourg's successor, who officiated at Santee from 1720 until his death in 1731, also happened to be a proselyte ("William Tredwell Bull's memorial on the present state of the church and clergy in South Carolina" [August 10, 1723], Fulham Papers, Lambeth Palace Library, London, vol. 9, South Carolina [1703–33], fol. 119). When Pouderous died, the Santee vestry was understandably weary of these Catholic priests turned Anglicans, especially since as early as 1709, when asking L'Escot to find them a minister, they had already made clear (in L'Escot's words) that they "would not have a proselyte from Popery, nor a monck stript of his habit" ("Extract of a letter from Mr. Escot, Minister of the French Church at Charles Town in South Carolina of the 24 March 1709," SPG records, Lambeth Palace Library, London, Minutes, vol. 2 [1709–11], [October 17, 1709], fol. 64 back). Therefore, following Pouderous's death, they wrote the bishop of London again, "humbly praying [his] Grace if Possible not to send [them] any [minister] that hath been of Roman Catholick Church they being very apt to have Some Erroneous Doctrine which they do not conceal in these remote Part with all ye Care they do in England" ("St. James, Santee vestry to Bishop of London" [March 27, 1731], SPG records, Lambeth Palace Library, London, Fulham ms. S.C. n. 92).

85. This was in 1708, not 1711 as Clute and Friedlander wrote. See Clement, "Clergymen Licensed Overseas," 325; Robert F. Clute, ed., *The Annals and Parish Register of St. Thomas and St. Denis Parish, in South Carolina, from 1680 to 1884* (Charleston, S.C.: Walker, Evans & Cogswell, 1884), 21; Friedlander, "Carolina Huguenots," 211.

86. A. S. Salley, ed., "Some Early Simons Records," in *South Carolina Genealogies,* comp. Cannon, 4:143; Mollie C. Parker, "The Reverend John La Pierre, A. B.," *HSSCT* 85 (1980): 56; Rawlinson Collection, Bodleian Library, Oxford, ms. B375, fol. 150; "LaPierre to Bishop of London" (April 8, 1725), SPG ms. Letterbooks (Fulham, S.C., n. 6).

87. "Josias Dupré to Jacques Dupré" (in French) (August 27, 1708), SPG ms. Papers, Correspondence, vol. 16 (South Carolina, 1702–6), Lambeth Palace Library, London, fol. 218.

88. Ibid.

89. "Josias Dupré to Jacques Dupré" (in French) (September 15, [1708]), SPG ms. Papers, Correspondence, vol. 16 (South Carolina, 1702–6), Lambeth Palace Library, London, fol. 218 back, 219.

90. Klingberg, *Carolina Chronicle of Le Jau,* 97, "LeJau to Secretary" (September 5, 1711).

91. The November 1712 letter is no longer extant. As for that of April/May 1713, it is known through a Latin translation done by Paul L'Escot, minister of the Charleston French Church, to the attention of Commissary Johnston, who included it in extenso in his 1713 ecclesiastical report. For an English version, see Friedlander, "Commissary Johnston's Report," 269n13.

92. "LaPierre to Secretary" (December 1, 1720), SPG ms. Letterbooks, A, 15, 41.

93. Friedlander, "Commissary Johnston's Report," 265–66.

94. Ibid., 266–68. Sir Nathaniel Johnson died on July 1, 1712, or five months before LaPierre received his first epistolary warning from the St. Denis parishioners (Klingberg, *Carolina Chronicle of Le Jau,* 119).

95. Friedlander, "Commissary Johnston's Report," 265–68.

96. "John LaPierre to Rev. C. G. de la Mothe" (August 13, 1714), ms. Aufrère Papers, vol. 6 (1652–1756), HSGB&I Library, London, fol. 20; also published in Winifred Turner, ed., *The Aufrere Papers,* HSGB&I Publications, Quarto Series, vol. 40 (Frome, U.K.: printed by Butler & Tanner Ltd., 1940), 211–12.

97. The term "French Prophets" refers to either the original group of four enthusiasts (Durand Fage, Jean Cavalier de Sauve, Jean Allut, and Élie Marion) who arrived in London from the Cévennes in 1706 or to a millenarist sect that developed after 1713 and throughout the eighteenth century and which comprised a growing number of British followers of these Camisard prophets. However, as Jean-Paul Chabrol underscores, in its second meaning the contemporary term "French Prophets" is historically inappropriate since most members of the group were neither French nor prophets ("LaPierre to Society" [February 15, 1716], SPG ms. Letterbooks, A, 11, 142–44). The most thorough studies of the London Prophets are Chabrol, *Élie Marion;* Hillel Schwartz, *The French Prophets: The History of a Millenarian Group in Eighteenth-Century England* (Berkeley: University of California Press, 1980); Schwartz, *Knaves, Fools, Madmen, and That Subtile Effluvium: A Study of the Opposition to the French Prophets in England, 1706–1710* (Gainesville: University Presses of Florida, 1978). A transcript of the official condemnation of the prophets by the Threadneedle Street Church consistory can be found in Cottret, *Huguenots in England,* document 9, 283.

98. "John LaPierre to Rev. C. G. de la Mothe," 211–12; Lesser, *South Carolina Begins,* "Decedent index," 322. Friedlander wrote that the two troublemakers, so to speak, were "two French ministers who had arrived from London, preaching the doctrines of Pierre Jurieu," but this was not the case (Friedlander, "Carolina Huguenots," 213).

99. Antinomians, religious enthusiasts often dubbed libertines, wished to do away with the law. The most famous case of antinomianism in colonial America is that of Anne Hutchinson in Massachusetts in the late 1630s. Sabbatarians, who appeared in central Europe in the mid-sixteenth century, rejected the Christian Sunday in favor of the Jewish Sabbath (Saturday) and, more generally, sought positive interaction between Christianity and Judaism. It is quite puzzling that a Sabbatarian current shook the small lowcountry Huguenot settlement of Orange Quarter. See Timothy J. Wengert, "Antinomianism," and Daniel Liechty, "Sabbatarianism," in *The Oxford Encyclopedia of the Reformation,* 4 vols., ed. Hans J. Hillerbrand (New York: Oxford University Press, 1996), 1:51–53 and 3:459–60, respectively. See also Daniel Liechty, *Sabbatarianism in the Sixteenth Century: A Page in the History of the Radical Reformation* (Berrien Springs, Mich.: Andrews University Press, 1993).

100. "LaPierre to Society" (February 15, 1716), 144.

101. The Latin translation of the April/May 1713 letter is headed with "Epistola Gallorum Ecclesiae Auriacae in Carolina." The English translation has "Letter of the French of the Church of Auriac in Carolina," and Friedlander footnoted "Auriacae" with a reference to a town named Auriac in Dordogne. This explanation is erroneous as there was no Auriac in South Carolina. "Auriacae" can only be a misspelled transcription of *Aurantium,* the Latin word for "Orange." See Friedlander, "Commissary Johnston's Report," 268–69nn12,13.

102. Pastor Hasel succinctly described this ecclesiastic reversal in 1719 in reporting: "The Orange Quarter make 30 Families formerly Conformists but now Calvinists" ("Hasel to Secretary" [August, 1, 1719], SPG ms. Letterbooks, A, 13, 291).

103. St. Denis being literally a temporary subparish, the Act of 1706 did not provide funds for the building of a church. The construction cost was therefore exclusively borne by the parishioners. See "Hasel to Society" (June 4, 1728), SPG ms. Letterbooks, A, 21, 108; Cooper and McCord, *Statutes at Large,* 2:283.

104. This request is only known through an excerpt from an August 1713 letter sent by Henrietta Johnston to her husband, which the commissary inserted in his 1713 report (Friedlander, "Commissary Johnston's Report," 270).

105. FPCL, Records of the French Church, ms. 135, "Letter of October 28, 1716," Copies of Letters (1697–1754), 32.

106. Colonial Land Grants (Copy Series), vol. 38 (1675–1705):420, 448, 473, 496; vol. 39 (1706–18):33, 168, 223, 535, 537, SCDAH.

107. In his biography, John Jay, who attended Stouppe's parochial school in New Rochelle, New York, noted that the pastor "was a native of Switzerland." Even if his French was hesitant, Stouppe could nonetheless study in Geneva since all classes were conducted in Latin. See Carlo, "Huguenots," 245 (quote), 271–72; Morgan H. Seacord, *Biographical Sketches and Index of Huguenot Settlers of New Rochelle, 1687–1776* (New Rochelle, N.Y.: The Huguenot and Historical Association of New Rochelle, 1941), 48–49; Randolph Vigne, "'Avenge, O Lord Thy Slaughtered Saints' Cromwell's Intervention on Behalf of the Vaudois," *HSP* 24 (1983): 13, 23; Cottret, *Huguenots in England,* 165n26; Élisabeth Labrousse, "Jean-Baptiste Stouppe," in *De l'Humanisme aux Lumières,* ed. Magdelaine et al., 1:38–51.

Stouppe's father even served as a chaplain in Louis XIV's armies when France invaded the Netherlands. In 1673 he published *La Religion des Hollandois,* a pamphlet intended to justify Huguenot involvement in the invasion of a country mostly peopled by Calvinist brethren to "a zealous Huguenot" settled in Bern, Switzerland, who had "pronounced anathema against all those of the Religion who Served the King in the War against the Hollanders" ["un Huguenot zélé . . . qui a prononcé anathème contre tous ceux de la Religion qui Servent le Roy dans la Guerre qu'il fait aux Hollandois"]. Stouppe argues that as only one-third of the Dutch are Calvinists (the others are "Sectarians" and Catholics), the Netherlands are therefore Calvinist "only in name" ["que de nom"], that the religion of the Dutch is their "love of money" ["l'avarice"], that they have massacred Englishmen in the Moluccas, that Louis XIV protects Calvinists in France [i.e., the Edict of Nantes] and in Geneva, and that the Dutch rented out vessels to Louis XIII in his successful—but from a Huguenot perspective devastating—siege of La Rochelle in 1627–28. Beyond its hollandophobic rhetoric, which was also then prevalent in England, the pamphlet shows to what extent the Huguenots still in France devotedly supported their king to whose protection they owed their privileges in the decades before the Revocation of the Edict of Nantes ([J.-B. Stouppe,] *La Religion des Hollandois Représentée en plusieurs lettres écrites par un officier de l'Armée du Roy, à un Pasteur & Professeur en Théologie de Berne* [Paris: Chez François Clousier et Pierre Aubouin, 1673], 1, 95–97, 139, 140, 158–62, 185–86, 190, and 192–94).

108. "LaPierre to Secretary" (April 5, 1719), SPG ms. Letterbooks A, 13, 265; "LaPierre to Secretary" (December 1, 1720), SPG ms. Letterbooks, A, 15, 41. Richebourg's death was reported to Bishop Robinson in a letter dated March 20, 1719 ("William T. Bull to Robinson" [March 20, 1719], Lambeth Palace Library, London, Fulham Papers, vol. 9, South Carolina [1703–34], fol. 86).

109. "LaPierre to Secretary" (October 21, 1721), SPG ms. Letterbooks, A, 15, 61.

110. Carlo, "Huguenots," 309–12; "Élie Neau to Society," SPG Papers, vol. 14, New York (1707–undated), Fulham Palace Library, London, fol. 210a.

111. "Hasel to Secretary" (September 16, 1720), SPG ms. Letterbooks, A, 15, 60.

112. Unfortunately, only two Anglican biased sources describe what has become known as the "Dutartre affair." One is an excerpt from the sermon *Take Heed How Ye Hear,* delivered by Alexander Garden, Johnston's successor as South Carolina commissary, in 1740 and published separately in 1762 under the title *A Brief Account of the Deluded Dutartres.* The other is a short report written by the clergy of South Carolina and addressed to the SPG in 1724. Garden based his Dutartre story on his reminiscences of the case nearly twenty years after the events occurred, when he had served as the chaplain of the convicted Huguenots, and delivered his sermon on the occasion of the revivalist George Whitefield's successful visit to Charleston. Garden's objectives were to condemn religious enthusiasm and thwart Whitefield's impact on South Carolina souls by exposing the Dutartre affair and its violent excesses. The Moravians, also known as the Bohemian or United Brethren, were a pre-Reformation sect, originally from Bohemia, that claimed lineage to John Hus. After they disappeared from the historical scene for a century or so, they reemerged in Saxony in the early eighteenth century. In North America, Moravians settled primarily in Pennsylvania and in North Carolina. Moravians followed a pietistic, enthusiastic, pacifistic, and emotionally intense spirituality marked by a strong belief in providence yet within a structured ecclesiastical environment with a clear hierarchy of church authority. Garden's mention of the Moravian preacher in his sermon served to implicitly denounce the sect's influence on George Whitefield and John Wesley, and beyond them, on early Methodism. See Alexander Garden, *A Brief Account of the Deluded Dutartres* (New Haven, Conn.: James Parker and Company, 1762); "Clergy to Society" (October 1, 1724), SPG ms. Letterbooks, A, 18, 90; David S. Lovejoy, *Religious Enthusiasm in the New World: Heresy to Revolution* (Cambridge, Mass.: Harvard University Press, 1985), 162–68; John R Weinlick, "Moravianism in the American Colonies," in *Continental Pietism and Early American Christianity,* ed. F. Ernest Stoeffler (Grand Rapids: Wm. B. Eerdmans, 1976), 123–63; R. J. W. Evans, "Bohemian Brethren," in *Oxford Encyclopedia of the Reformation,* ed. Hillerbrand, 1:185–86. On the Garden-Whitefield confrontation, see Bolton, "Anglican Church," chap. 6. Butler cites Zachary Grey's *A Serious Address to Lay-Methodists, to Beware of the False Pretences of Their Teachers* (London, 1745), which quoted the Dutartre story from Garden's sermon and similarly used it as a weapon against Methodism (Butler, *Huguenots in America,* 240n51).

113. Garden, *Brief Account,* 5.

114. Ibid., 6. The following quoted material is from this source until otherwise indicated. All the Dutartre and Rembert protagonists of the story can be identified. Pierre Dutartre Sr., described as a seventy-year-old man in the October 1724 clerical report, was a weaver who had been in the colony since 1685. His eldest daughter was Suzanne and his youngest Judith. His two younger sons were Daniel and Jean. Pierre was the son of André Rembert, who came from Dauphiny in the southern Alps. All were longtime Orange Quarter settlers. See "Clergy to Society," 90; Ravenel, *Liste,* 63 (#122), 57 (#81); Gourdin, "Madeleine Chardon," 77–78.

115. Garden, *Brief Account,* 6–7.

116. This Michael Boinneau was possibly of the Bonneau family.

117. Garden, *Brief Account,* 7–8; "Clergy to Society," 90.

118. From 1711 to 1713 Élie Marion, one of the original French Prophets from the Cévennes, traveled through the German states, where his works had been translated. During what Chabrol calls his "odyssée géoprophétique," he came in contact with Moravians, notably their founder Count Zizendorf. It is therefore entirely conceivable that the Remberts and Bochets obtained German translations of pamphlets written by French Prophets from "a strolling Moravian." See Chabrol, *Élie Marion,* 178–83, 207–9.

119. Chabrol, *Élie Marion,* 119–27. Rembert's quasi-incestuous desires similarly echo the behavior of the French Prophets, who were also accused by the Anglican authorities of promiscuity (Lovejoy, *Religious Enthusiasm,* 174).

120. *An Account of the French Prophets and Their Pretended Inspirations* (London, 1708); *Plainte, et censure des calomnieuses accusations publiées par le Sr. Claude Grosteste de la [Mothe]* (London, 1708); Butler, *Huguenots in America,* 117–18. Incidentally, and most interestingly, a 1764 Santee marriage record shows that a John Dutart married a Mary Boinneau, with a Michel Boinneau, widower, and a James and a Judith Rembert as witnesses. The Dutartre, Boinneau, and Rembert families, who most likely faced virtual exclusion from the St. Denis community because of the stigma attached to their violent revolt, were thus still sticking to one another long after the events of the 1720s. See Brent H. Holcomb, comp., *South Carolina Marriages, 1689–1799* (Baltimore: Genealogical Publishing Co., 1980), 71. The Dutartres and Remberts appear in the St. Denis parish records only in the 1800s (Clute, *Annals and Parish Register,* 58, 78).

121. "John LaPierre to Bishop of London," SPG records, Lambeth Palace Library, London, vol. 9, South Carolina (1703–34), fol. 167; Patricia U. Bonomi and Peter R. Eisenstadt, "Church Adherence in the Eighteenth-Century British American Colonies," *William and Mary Quarterly* 39 (1982): 279.

122. "LaPierre to SPG" (October 21, 1721), A, 15, 61.

123. In his 1725 *Notitias Parochialis,* Hasel reported that "most of the French profess themselves of the Church of England," thereby implying that some remained Calvinists and so without minister to officiate among them ("Hasel to Secretary" [January 5, 1725], SPG ms. Letterbooks, A, 19, 54).

124. LaPierre carefully inserted Garden's "slanderous letter" in his missive to the bishop ("LaPierre to Bishop Gibson" [January 1, 1726], Fulham Palace Library, London, Fulham Papers, South Carolina, n. 6). See also Hirsch, *Huguenots,* 321–23.

125. Bolton, "Anglican Church," 228–30.

126. For an account of LaPierre's North Carolina years, see Lillian F. Wood, "The Reverend John LaPierre," *Historical Magazine of the Protestant Episcopal Church* 40 (1971): 414–30. LaPierre, who, contrary to what Hirsch wrote, did not serve the Charleston Church before going to New Hanover, died in 1755. See Hirsch, *Huguenots,* 53; Parker, "Reverend John La Pierre," 57.

127. FPCL, Records of the French Church, ms. 8, "Livres des Actes de 1693 à 1708," fol. 230–31 (May 29, 1700).

128. Ibid. Incidentally, this second consistory entry, dated November 1701, is confusing since L'Escot had been appointed in the summer of 1700. The mention of Trouillart's name may of course be only a matter of chronology since he left Charleston after Prioleau passed away.

129. FPCL, Records of the French Church, ms. 135, "Letter of September 30, 1700," Copies of Letters (1697–1754), 10.

130. Ibid.; "Toutes les voix sont tombées sur Mr. Paul L'Escot" (All the votes were cast in favor of Mr. P. L'Escot) (FPCL, Records of the French Church, ms. 8, "Livres des Actes de 1693 à 1708," fol. 230–31 [July 14, 1700], fol. 242).

131. FPCL, Records of the French Church, ms. 8, "Livres des Actes de 1693 à 1708," fol. 243.

132. "Je ne suis point Refugié . . . même je pourrois passer pour *Genevois*" (Eugène de Budé, ed., *Lettres inédites adressées de 1686 à 1737 à Jean-Alphonse Turrettini, théologien genevois,* 3 vols. [Paris: Librairie de la Suisse française, 1887], 220 [The Hague, March 14, 1698]). Most of what is known of L'Escot in Europe and in Carolina is based on the assiduous correspondence that he kept with Jean-Alphonse Turrettini, his former professor of ecclesiastical history at Geneva. L'Escot was from Nivernais, a duchy in central France whose capital was Nevers and which was sold to Cardinal Mazarin in 1659 (Anne-Marie Chagny-Sève, "Nivernais," in *Dictionnaire de l'Ancien Régime,* ed. Bély, 886–87; Stelling-Michaud, *Livre du recteur,* 4:323).

133. L'Escot and Prioleau were both at the Geneva academy in 1672, but L'Escot, being younger, was just starting his education while Prioleau, who graduated in 1673, was about to complete his (Stelling-Michaud, *Livre du recteur,* 1:229, 4:323, 5:244–45).

134. "L'Escot to Turrettini" (Paris, May 19, 1698), ms. français, 488, fol. 12 back, BPU.

135. "L'Escot to Turrettini" (London, May 25, 1719), ms. français, 488, fol. 17 front, BPU.

136. FPCL, Records of the French Church, ms. 8, "Livres des Actes de 1693 à 1708," fol. 230–31 (May 29, 1700); "L'Escot to Turrettini" (Charleston, April 6, 1701), Archives Tronchin, 81 (copied excerpt), fol. 194 front, BPU.

137. "L'Escot to Turrettini" (London, May 25, 1719), ms. français, 488, fol. 16 front, BPU.

138. Unfortunately, L'Escot's account is no longer extant (ibid., fol. 17 back). For l'Escot's sojourn in Charleston as depicted in his correspondence to Turrettini, see Bertrand Van Ruymbeke, "Paul L'Escot, un ministre genevois à Charles Town (1700–1719)," *Études Francophones* 14 (1999): 147–62.

139. "L'Escot to Turrettini" (Charleston, March 1, 1703), Archives Tronchin, 81 (copied excerpt), fol. 201 front, BPU; "L'Escot to Turrettini" (London, August 10, 1719), ms. français, 488, fol. 18 back, BPU; "L'Escot to Turrettini" (London, October 9, 1719), ms. français, 488, fol. 20 front, BPU.

140. The Huguenot discipline does not give specific instructions on this point, leaving the decision of having pastors deliver sermons with or without notes to the discretion of the congregation. Needless to say, the Charleston Church requirements made L'Escot's work more difficult.

141. "L'Escot to Turrettini" (London, October 9, 1719), ms. français, 488, fol. 20 front and back, BPU.

142. Johnston even confidently reported elsewhere that L'Escot "woud not live a day without Episcopal Ordination, coud he bring his People to it" (Friedlander, "Commissary Johnston's Report," 270).

143. Klingberg, *Carolina Chronicle: Papers of Gideon Johnston,* 42–43, 57–58. For the original, see SPG ms. Letterbooks, A, 5, 158.

144. "Society to L'Escot and Trouillart" (February 20, 1711, in French), SPG Papers, Lambeth Palace Library, London, ms. vol. 17 (South Carolina, 1711–undated), fol. 31.

145. "L'Escot to Society" (September 2, 1711), SPG ms. Letterbooks, A, 7, 3, n.p. The following quoted material is from this same source until otherwise indicated.

146. J-A Turrettini (1671–1737) and B. Pictet (1655–1724) were from Geneva, J-F. Ostervald (1663–1747) from Neuchâtel, and S. Werenfels (1657–1740) from Basel. Turrettini, Ostervald, and Werenfels were collectively known as "le triumvirat théologique de la *Suisse*" (Budé, *Lettres inédites,* 1:374 [quote], 3:227, 408). Incidentally, Samuel Prioleau, son of Élie, in 1767 donated three

books by Ostervald, one of them being an edition of a Genevan Bible, and a treatise on theology by Pictet to the newly formed Charleston Library Society ("Reconstruction of the Foundation Collection of the Charleston Library Society during Its First Twenty Years, 1748–c. 1769," in James Raven, *London Booksellers and American Customers: Transatlantic Literary Community and the Charleston Library Society, 1748–1811* [Columbia: University of South Carolina Press, 2002], 368–69).

147. R. Barry Levis, "The Failure of the Anglican-Prussian Ecumenical Effort of 1710–1714," *Church History* 47 (1978): 381–99; Nishikawa, "English Attitudes," 48–54, 212–14. Jablonsky was also a Moravian bishop (Weinlick, "Moravianism," 130).

148. In the case of Henry Compton, who also was actively helping Huguenot refugees in England, see Carpenter, *Protestant Bishop,* chaps. 17, 18 (321–56).

149. Norman Sykes, *The Church of England and Non-Episcopal Churches in the Sixteenth and Seventeenth Centuries* (London: SPCK, 1948), 4.

150. Ostervald, for example, was ready to accept the Anglican liturgy in Neuchâtel (Nishikawa, "English Attitudes," 239).

151. Maria-Christina Pitassi and Laurence Bergon, "Jean-Alphonse Turrettini, correspondant de l'Europe savante et ecclésiastique au début des Lumières," in *La vie intellectuelle aux Refuges protestants,* ed. Jens Häseler and Antony McKenna (Paris: Honoré Champion, 1999), 157–71; Budé, *Lettres inédites,* 20 (quotes).

152. Further evidence of the aura Anglican bishops enjoyed over most continental Protestants, and particularly displaced Huguenots, is the memoir addressed to the bishop of London in 1709 by Huguenot refugees in Hamburg. Requesting His Lordship to help them solicit assistance from Queen Anne in order to obtain the right to worship publicly in the city instead of having to attend church in a nearby town under the control of the king of Denmark, they mentioned "[his] apostolic zeal venerated by all Protestant churches" ("Leaders of the French reformed Church in Hamburg to the Bishop of London, desiring the queen to obtain for them the free exercise of their religion in Hamburg" [November 15, 1709], BPRO, SP 34/11, fol. 97).

153. An Anglican scholar, Joseph Bingham (1668–1723), rector of the parish of Havant, Hampshire, England, even used the "principles of the Reformed Church of France" to demonstrate the Church of England's Protestant authenticity to Dissenters. Bingham was aware of the novelty and originality of this approach conceding that "the Argument . . . is something singular. There being few that have trod in the same Path before and none that I know of, who have set themselves purposely to examine the *French* synods, with any design to justify the Church of *England* thereby" (Bingham, *The* French *Churches Apology for the Church of England; Or the Objections of Dissenters against the Articles, Homilies, Liturgy, and Canons of the* English *Church, Consider'd, and Answer'd upon the Principles of the Reformed Church of* France [London: Robert Knaplock, 1706], epistle dedicatory).

154. Sykes, *Church of England,* 14–15.

155. Élisabeth Labrousse, "Great Britain as Envisaged by the Huguenots of the Seventeenth Century," in *Huguenots in Britain,* ed. Scouloudi, 148.

156. Gwynn, *Huguenot Heritage,* 124.

157. Quoted in Sykes, *Church of England,* 26. On La Mothe, see "Claude Groteste de la Mothe and the Church of England, 1685 to 1713," *HSP* 20 (1958–64): 89–101.

158. Quoted in Sykes, *Church of England,* 27.

159. This is what J. F. Ostervald called the "reasonable orthodoxy" (Nishikawa, "English Attitudes," 239).

160. "Garden to Bishop of London" (November 8, 1732), SPG ms. Letterbooks (Fulham, SC, n. 31).

161. Fontaine, *Memoirs*, 133.

162. Clarke, *Our Southern Zion*, 41.

163. Cottret, *Huguenots in England*, 158–60.

164. Quoted in Stephen Taylor, "Whigs, Bishops and America: The Politics of Church Reform in Mid-Eighteenth-Century England," *Historical Journal* 36 (1993): 332.

165. "The Present State of the Clergy of South Carolina," in Hirsch, *Huguenots*, 309.

166. L'Escot married Ralph Izard to Madeleine Pasquereau (Klingberg, "Commissary Johnston's *Notitias Parochialis*," 29).

167. "L'Escot to Turrettini" (London, August 10, 1719), ms. français, 488, fol. 18 back, BPU.

168. "L'Escot to Turrettini" (London, May 25, 1719), ms. français, 488, fol. 16 back, BPU.

169. "L'Escot to Turrettini" (London, August 10, 1719), ms. français, 488, fol. 18 back, BPU.

170. Ibid.

171. Ibid., fol. 18 back, 19 front.

172. Ibid. (quote), letters of May and August 1719.

173. "L'Escot to Turrettini" (Dover, November 17, 1720), in Budé, *Lettres inédites*, 2:230. L'Escot's wife died in early fall 1753 after bequeathing their two slaves to their grandchildren. L'Escot's daughter, Françoise (Frances), married one of Pierre Villepontoux's sons, Zacharie. See "Will of Frances L'Escot," in Withington, *South Carolina Gleanings*, 6 (1905):123; William Minet, "The Fourth Foreign Church at Dover, 1685–1731," *HSP* 4 (1891–93): 135n1.

174. "L'Escot to Turrettini" (London, May 25, 1719), ms. français, 488, fol. 17 front, BPU.

175. The letter was signed by eighteen members of the congregation, one of whom, the merchant Benjamin de La Conseillère, bore the title of *ancien* ("L'Escot's Testimonials from Charleston" [March 14, 1719], Bodleian Library, Oxford, Rawlinson ms., B376, fol. 154). An inaccurate transcription of this document can be found in Hirsch, *Huguenots*, 53n21.

176. In fact, once in England, L'Escot does not seem to have asked his numerous Genevan friends to help him get a position in Geneva ("L'Escot to Turrettini" [Dover, November 17, 1720] in Budé, *Lettres inédites*, 2:230).

177. "L'Escot to Turrettini" (London, October 9, 1719), ms. français, 488, fol. 20 front, BPU.

178. "Letter of W. Evans to Bishop Robinson" (December 2, 1719), Bodleian Library, Oxford, Rawlinson ms., B376, fol. 171.

179. Contrary to what Hirsch wrote, L'Escot did not return to Charleston in 1731. See "Dover Actes et Témoignages, 1646–1731," HSGB&I Library, ms., n.p.; Minet, "Fourth Foreign Church," 135, 217; Hirsch, *Huguenots*, 54.

180. In his October 1724 parish questionnaire, Stouppe mentioned leaving Charleston "about 18 months ago" (Lambeth Palace Library, London, Fulham Papers, vol. 41, fol. 108). Published answers to the bishop's questionnaire by parish preceded by an analysis are available in Bonomi and Eisenstadt, "Church Adherence," 245–86.

181. "Sermon of January 24, 1720," ms. sermons by Rev. Pierre Stouppe, Huguenot Church of New Rochelle, Huguenot Society of America Library, New York, [HJ 588], n.p. That the congregation forced L'Escot to memorize his sermons was not conducive to the preservation of the sermons; that Stouppe's sermon survived indicates that he was not subject to the same demands.

182. A complete inventory and an excellent discussion of Stouppe's sermons can be found in Carlo, "Huguenots," 278–97 and 409, table 4. See also Carlo, "'Playing Fast and Loose," 42–50.

183. Carlo, "Huguenots," 278.

184. In her study of seventeenth-century Huguenot sermons, Chevalier found that John was the most quoted section in the Bible and that salvation and faith were among the topics most preached on (Chevalier, *Prêcher sous l'Édit de Nantes*, 232, 251).

185. "Sermon of January 24, 1720," n.p.

186. Jon Butler reached the same conclusion regarding Élie Neau, who completely retained his Calvinist beliefs after conforming to Anglicanism and joining the SPG as a catechist (Butler, "Hymns," 417).

187. These no longer extant letters are mentioned in the nineteenth-century history of the Charleston Church by Daniel Ravenel, who had read them (Daniel Ravenel, "Historical Sketch of the Huguenot Congregations of South Carolina," *HSSCT* 7 [1900]: 59).

188. On the eve of his death in 1736, however, Mazyck feared that "lesglise ne vienne malheureusement à Tomber Par faute de zelle & de piayté & par manque d'avoir la Gloire de Dieu à cœur" (the congregation unhappily finish by falling for lack of zeal, piety, and for not taking the Glory of God to heart) ("Will of Isaac Mazyck" [January 10, 1736], Records of the South Carolina Court of Probate, vol. KK:340–41, SCDAH).

189. In the above-mentioned will, Mazyck instructed his executors to invest seven hundred Carolina pounds, or one hundred pounds sterling, specifying that the interest would be given to the Charleston minister on the condition that he preach "un sermon le Dimanche matin" (a sermon on Sunday morning) and "l'prèsdinée un sermon de Catéchisme" (catechism after supper) and that "le service soit Calviniste Comme de hollande" (service be Calvinistic like in the Netherlands) ("Will of Isaac Mazyck" [January 10, 1736], Records of the South Carolina Court of Probate, vol. KK:340, SCDAH).

190. FPCL, Records of the French Church, ms. 135, "Guichard's appointment letter" (October 10, 1732), Copies of Letters (1697–1754), 39. The Charleston letter is mentioned in Hirsch, *Huguenots,* 59. Sometime after the fire of 1740, the Charleston Huguenot Church adopted J. F. Ostervald's liturgy, entitled *La Liturgie, ou la manière de célébrer le Service Divin, qui est établie dans les Églises de la Principauté de Neufchatel* (Neuchâtel, 1737). The congregation, like several underground Huguenot churches during the same period in France, adopted this well-known 1713 liturgy not because "there were a Considerable number of Swiss among the Emmigrants," as Ravenel surmised, but simply because no Huguenot liturgies were printed in France between the Revocation and the French Revolution. Ostervald's Neufchâtel Liturgy was well-known in the English-speaking world since it was published, along with his Catechism, by the SPCK. See Ravenel, "Historical Sketch," 49; Yves Krumenacker, "La Liturgie, un enjeu dans la renaissance des églises françaises au XVIIIe siècle," in *Édifier ou instruire?,* ed. Pitassi, 114–15; Nishikawa, "English Attitudes," 220.

191. "L'Escot to Turrettini" (Charleston, March 1, 1703), Archives Tronchin, 81, fol. 202 front, BPU.

192. "LeJau to Secretary" (April 12, 1711), Lambeth Palace Library, London, ms. vol. 17 (SPG South Carolina), fol. 37. The April 12, 1711, letter published in Klingberg's *Carolina Chronicle* does not contain this reference (Klingberg, *Carolina Chronicle of Le Jau,* 89). LeJau is most likely referring to Thomas Hairn's *A Letter from South Carolina,* published in London in 1710, in which the author gives a numerical breakdown of Carolina's religious population that has "Presbyterians, including those *French* who retain their own Discipline" counting for 4.5 out of 10 Carolinians.

193. "Gabriel Bernon to Bishop of London" (Providence, May 11, 1725), Fulham Palace Library, London, Section D, Displaced Documents (Rhode Island), fol. 188–89.

194. Geoffrey Adams, "Monarchistes ou républicains?," in "Le protestantisme français en France," special issue, *Dix-huitième Siècle* 17 (1985): 83–86.

195. Labrousse, "Great Britain," 156n21. Defending the French Calvinist discipline against the attack of a councillor who denounced the election of pastors, the Threadneedle Street consistory

claimed that he "did not believe that our government was aristocratic—as it is—but . . . supposed it to be democratic" (quoted in Cottret, *Huguenots in England,* 161).

196. These individual and familial ties were all the more tenuous since, as Labrousse stresses, "in a civilisation so insistent on punctilious formalism, the apparently private character of these communications necessarily weakened their authority" (Labrousse, "Great Britain," 152n1).

197. In typical fashion, when describing the different Charleston meetinghouses, L'Escot wrote that the Quakers only owned "a wretched hut" (*une misérable cabane*) ("L'Escot to Turrettini" [Charleston, March 1, 1703], Archives Tronchin, 81, fol. 202 front, BPU).

198. Mabel L. Webber, ed., "Register of the Independent or Congregational (Circular) Church, 1732–1738," *SCHGM* 12 (1911): 30, 57; Mabel L. Webber, ed., "Inscriptions from the Independent or Congregational (Circular) Church Yard, Charleston, SC," *SCHGM* 29 (1928): 139–40; "Will of Henry Péronneau" (May 3, 1743), Will Book (1740–47), W. P. A. Transcripts, pp. 157–58, Charleston County Library, Charleston, S.C.; Ravenel, *Liste,* 52 (#53).

199. South Carolina Manuscript Acts, 1712–16, n. 57, SCDAH.

200. Butler, *Huguenots in America,* 78; Webber, "Register," 35.

201. Butler, *Huguenots in America,* 138; Clarke, *Our Southern Zion,* 42.

202. Clarke, *Our Southern Zion,* 39.

203. Ibid.

204. Henry A. DeSaussure, "Huguenots on the Santee River," *HSSCT* 14 (1907): 24. The same semantic resistance occurred in King William's Parish, Virginia, where the Huguenots, although assembled from the time of their arrival in 1701 in an Anglican parish, still used the French Reformed term *consistoire* in their vestry book in 1739 (*Vestry Book of King William Parish, Virginia, 1707–1750,* photostat, [ii]).

205. Friedlander, "Carolina Huguenots," 199.

206. Annette S. Laing, "'All Things to All Men': Popular Religious Culture and the Anglican Mission in Colonial America, 1701–1750" (Ph.D. diss., University of California, Riverside, 1995), viii.

207. Annette Laing, "'A Very Immoral and Offensive Man': Religious Culture, Gentility and the Strange Case of Brian Hunt, 1727," *SCHM* 103 (2002): 11nn11,12.

208. Hoping to have Hunt appointed to another parish, the vestrymen attached a letter of recommendation to their missive. The bishop's secretary was not fooled and wrote in the margin: "Testimony granted to him in his favor to get rid of him" ("Vestry of St. John's, Berkeley to Bishop of London" [July 3, 1727], Fulham Palace Library, London, ms. vol. 10 [South Carolina 1703–34], 202–3).

209. Hunt's frustrated aspiration to gentility probably also fueled his bitterness (Laing, "Very Immoral and Offensive Man," 15–16).

210. Bolton, "Anglican Church," 231–37; Terry, "Champaign Country," 319–20.

211. "Hunt to Bishop of London" (December 18, 1727), Fulham Palace Library, London, ms. vol. 10 (South Carolina, 1703–34), n. 204–5; "Hunt to Bishop of London" (February 20, 1728), n. 206–13. The February letter was written from the Charleston jail.

212. At one point in his diatribe, Hunt even referred to Thomas Broughton, "his bitter persecutor," as "a great man here, descend[ing] from one of ye court which murdered K. Charles the first." Broughton, who served as surveyor general from 1706 to 1715 and who became governor in 1735, was apparently siding with the Huguenots to defend common interests in the Indian trade. See "Hunt to Bishop of London" (December 18, 1727), Fulham Palace Library, London, ms. South Carolina, 206–13; Terry, "Champaign Country," 319; Lesser, *South Carolina Begins,* 438–41.

213. In an earlier letter, dated October 26, 1726, Hunt charged the Huguenots to "publickly disown Episcopacy & declare the Church of Scotland [to be] the most pure Church in ye Christian

world." According to these accusations, the French conformists seem to have remained presbyterian at heart. See "Brian Hunt to Society" (October 3, 1726), SPG records, Lambeth Palace Library, London, B, 4, 210.

214. Alexander S. Salley, ed., "The Marriage Bond of Daniel Horry and Elizabeth Garnier," *HSSCT* 32 (1927): 37–38. Salley and Olsberg, *Warrants for Lands,* 631. The fact that Mazyck was married by an Anglican pastor, however, did not keep him, on the eve of his death, from demanding that the Charleston minister conduct services in the Calvinist way to be eligible for the money that he set aside for him in his 1736 will. See supra chap. 6, note 189.

215. Church Commissioner Book, 1717–42, p. 3, SCDAH; Alexander S. Salley Jr., ed., *Register of St. Philip's Parish, Charles Town, South Carolina, 1720–1758* (1904; Columbia: University of South Carolina Press, 1971), 105–27; Ravenel, "Historical Sketch," 59–60; Crouse, "Manigault Family," 12, 17.

216. "Will of Jean Thomas" (July 22, 1710), Miscellaneous Records (Proprietary Series), vol. 1700–1710:163, SCDAH. For Péronneau's will, see supra chap. 6, note 198.

217. Salley, "Some Early Simons Records," 142–43.

218. Friedlander, "Commissary Johnston's Report," 271.

219. A shortage of pastors was far from being an exclusively Huguenot problem as it plagued most churches in British North America, except New England Congregationalism and Virginia Anglicanism. Forty-five of the seventy-five Dutch Reformed pastors who served in New York and New Jersey in the colonial period, for example, were from Europe. With all their académies closed in 1685, the Huguenots did not even have the possibility to hire pastors from France, and consequently their churches in North America were particularly vulnerable. See Richard W. Pointer, *Protestant Pluralism and the New York Experience: A Study of Eighteenth-Century Religious Diversity* (Bloomington: Indiana University Press, 1988), 11, 16.

220. Butler, *Huguenots in America,* 38. Although Huguenot congregations in New England temporarily formed a colloque (presbytery) in the late 1680s, considering that the first Carolina Presbyterian and Congregationalist presbyteries were founded only in the 1720s, one cannot reasonably expect the Huguenots to have organized one in the lowcountry before 1706. See "Papier du consistoire pour l'année 1687 [1687–91]," Narragansett Church Register, Huguenot Society of America Library, New York, ms. 1687 (October 21, 1688), [p. 27]; Clarke, *Our Southern Zion,* 47.

221. In November 1709 LaPierrre received forty copies of Common Prayer books "wel bound in sheeps Leather" and Gignilliat received "a surplice & books" plus fifteen pounds sterling (Lambeth Palace Library, London, ms. SPG Papers, Minutes, vol. 2 [1709–11], fols. 78, 80).

222. On Turrettini's "théologie raisonnable," see Maria-Christina Pitassi, "D'une parole à l'autre: les sermons du théologien genevois Jean-Alphonse Turrettini (1671–1737)," *Annali di storia dell'esegesi* 10 (1993): 71–93. When in 1721 Santee vestrymen Peter Robert, Peter Perdriau, Jacques Guerry, and André Rembert retrospectively mentioned the 1706 petition that led to the formation of their parish, they wrote about "the royall Church of England" ("Representation of the Inhabitants of St. James, Santee, in South Carolina to Generall Nicholson inclosed in his letter [of] 6 Nov. 1721," SPG records, Lambeth Palace Library, London, A, 15, 63–65).

223. For a seminal discussion of Huguenot conformity in the English context, in which many parallels with South Carolina can be drawn, see Cottret, *Huguenots in England,* 158–84.

7. Naturalization and Representation

Epigraphs from Locke's *For a General Naturalization* cited in David Resnick, "John Locke and the Problem of Naturalization," *Review of Politics* 49 (1987): 388; petition quoted in Salley, *Commissions*, 80–81.

1. Moore, "Royalizing South Carolina," 31.

2. James H. Kettner, *The Development of American Citizenship, 1608–1870* (Chapel Hill: University of North Carolina Press, 1975), 7–9; J. Mervyn Jones, *British Nationality Law*, rev. ed. (Oxford: Clarendon Press, 1956), 51–62; Richard Marienstras, *Le proche et le lointain sur Shakespeare, le drame élisabéthain et l'idéologie anglaise aux XVIe et XVIIe siècles* (Paris: Les Éditions de Minuit, 1981), 147–59; Peter Riesenberg, *Citizenship in the Western Tradition: Plato to Rousseau* (Chapel Hill: University of North Carolina Press, 1992), 209–18. Excerpts from Edward Coke's, as well as Francis Bacon's, rulings can be found in Cottret, *Huguenots in England,* 275–76.

3. Coke's ruling also included the category of "perpetual" alien enemies, but it only concerned non-Christians.

4. Kettner, *Development of American Citizenship,* 30–35; Cottret, *Huguenots in England,* 50–54; Daniel Statt, "The Birthright of an Englishman: The Practice of Naturalization and Denization of Immigrants under the Later Stuarts and Early Hanoverians," *HSP* 25 (1989): 61–64.

5. At the same time in France, the monarchy alone naturalized aliens by granting letters of naturalization (*lettres de naturalité*). As an ancien régime French jurist wrote, "Only birth or the Prince's grace can make a Frenchman" and "supplement the defects of nature and repair the vice of origin." Aliens could not hold royal, municipal, or ecclesiastical offices. Although they were entitled to trade and own real estate, they could not bequeath or inherit property either. Once naturalized, they had the same rights as the French except that they had to reside in the kingdom, could only write wills in favor of French-born subjects, and in theory had to be Catholics. See Peter Sahlins, "Fictions of a Catholic France: The Naturalization of Foreigners, 1685–1787," *Representations* 47 (1994): 85–110 (quote, 87); Jean-François Dubost, "Etrangers en France," in *Dictionnaire de l'Ancien Régime,* ed. Bély, 518–22. See also Charlotte C. Wells, *Law and Citizenship in Early Modern France* (Baltimore: Johns Hopkins University Press, 1995); Jean-François Dubost and Peter Sahlins, *Et si on faisait payer les étrangers? Louis XIV, les immigrés et les autres* (Paris: Flammarion, 1999).

6. Nine general naturalization bills were defeated in Parliament from 1664 to 1700 (in 1664, 1667, 1670, 1673, 1680, 1685, 1690, 1693, and 1697). In 1709 a Whig majority managed to pass a general naturalization act that the Tories, back in power in 1711, quickly repealed. The 1709 Act enabled aliens to be naturalized, after taking the oaths of allegiance and supremacy and receiving the sacrament in a Protestant church in England, for the cost of a shilling. This last clause led opponents to the act to accuse its sponsors of reducing "the birthright of an Englishman to the value of 12 pence." See Robbins, "Note on General Naturalization," 168–77; Gwynn, *Huguenot Heritage,* 151–56; Kettner, *Development of American Citizenship,* 69–72; Statt, "Birthright of an Englishman," 71 (quote).

7. In 1673 the cost of a private naturalization act was estimated between £50 and £60 and in 1701 at £63. See Robbins, "Note on General Naturalization," 169n6; Statt, "Birthright of an Englishman," 66.

8. Statt, "Birthright of an Englishman," 66–67.

9. Charles II also promised to recommend Parliament to pass a general naturalization act ("Declaration of Hampton Court" [1681], in Arber, *Torments of Protestant Slaves,* xxviii–ix).

10. In theory, aliens denizened through the 1681 Order in Council were registered in the secretary of state's entry books, while those denizened through the customary procedure appeared on

the patent rolls. Shaw's extensive denization lists, which have been published by the Huguenot Society of Great Britain and Ireland, must be used with caution, however, since many entries were duplicated as officials confused and mixed groups of aliens who were denizened through the new and the old procedures. It can also be safely assumed that all the foreigners denizened between 1681 and 1688 obtained their denization gratis even if many mistakenly appear on the patent rolls. Statt calculated that there were 3,510 actual new denizens out of the 5,659 entries. See Statt, "Birthright of an Englishman," 68–69; Statt, *Foreigners and Englishmen*, 34–37; Shaw, *Letters of Denization 1603–1700*.

11. The exact figure is 73 out 347 Huguenots. For England, Statt calculated that 546 refugees out of the 3,419, or 1 out of 6, who were assisted by the Threadneedle Street Church from 1681 to 1687, petitioned to be denizened (Statt, "Birthright of an Englishman," 71–72).

12. Ravenel, *Liste*, 10.

13. For this reason, historians and genealogists must be careful not to systematically make coincide an actual presence in England with the date of a recorded denization as opposed to a *témoignage* or a *reconnaissance*. Only 11 percent of the refugees for whom we have the dates of arrival in Carolina and of denization were actually denizened before leaving England. Similarly, appearing on a denization list with fellow Huguenots does not mean that the refugees knew each other, petitioned together, and immigrated to Carolina together. See supra chap. 5, in the case of Prioleau and the alleged transfer of the Pons congregation to Charleston.

14. The delay between the securing of a denization letter or naturalization act in England and its recording in South Carolina could be exceedingly long. The examples found show an average of seven years, with an extreme case of twenty-three years.

15. Shaw, *Letters of Denization 1603–1700,* 242 (Poinset), 234 (Gignilliat).

16. Examples of Carolina Huguenots who were naturalized by Parliament are Daniel Ravenel, Jean (John) Boyd, and Paul Pierre LeBas (ibid., 263, 270; W. A. Shaw, ed., *Letters of Denization and Acts of Naturalization for Aliens in England and Ireland, 1701–1800,* Quarto Series, vol. 27 [Manchester: Sherratt and Hughes, 1923], 17; Miscellaneous Records [Proprietary Series], vol. 1711–15:344–45, SCDAH).

17. See, for example, the letters of denization of Jonas Bonhost, Paul Torquet, Isaac Mazyck, and Pierre Perdriau (Miscellaneous Records [Proprietary Series], vol. 1694–1705:164, 1704–9:101, 1694–1705:177, 1711–17:111, respectively, SCDAH). Élie Prioleau is the only nonmerchant who had the clause mentioning custom duties included in his certificate (Ravenel, *Liste,* 69–70). Regarding inheritance privileges, the right to "inheritt and be inheritable and inherited" is only expressly mentioned in private acts of naturalization while left implicit in letters of denization ("An Act for Naturalizing Thomas St. Léger . . . & others," Miscellaneous Records [Proprietary Series], vol. 1711–15:344–45, SCDAH).

18. The 1700 order also prohibited colonial governors from granting letters of denization. See Kettner, *Development of American Citizenship,* 65–105; A. H. Carpenter, "Naturalization in England and the American Colonies," *American Historical Review* 9 (1904): 288–303; Edward A. Hoyt, "Naturalization under the American Colonies: Signs of a New Community," *Political Science Quarterly* 67 (1952): 248–66; Shaw, *Letters of Denization 1701–1800,* xxvi–xxxii.

19. "Charter to the Lords Proprietors of Carolina, June 30, 1665," in Parker, *North Carolina Charters,* 92, 96.

20. "Concessions and Agreement between the Lords Proprietors and Major William Yeamans and Others, January 7, 1665," in Parker, *North Carolina Charters,* 117.

21. "Fundamental Constitutions, version of July 21, 1669," preamble, in Parker, *North Carolina Charters,* 132.

22. This clause is to be found more or less verbatim in the July 1669 (art. 109 [London copy]), March 1670 (art. 118), and January (art. 118) and August (art. 123) 1682 versions in a paragraph either immediately preceding or following the proprietary oath. In the original of the several July 1669 versions, known as the Columbia copy, the procedure is the same but the paragraph (art. 80) is longer, more detailed, and worded differently. This clause is altogether absent from the 1698 version simply because by then the South Carolina Assembly had already voted a naturalization act. See Ruth S. Green, ed., "The South Carolina Archives Copy of the Fundamental Constitutions, July 21, 1669," *SCHM* 71 (1970): 86–100; Parker, *North Carolina Charters,* 132–51, 184, 206, 231. On the different 1669 versions, see Lesser, *South Carolina Begins,* 158; Mattie E. E. Parker, "The First Fundamental Constitutions of Carolina," *SCHM* 71 (1970): 78–85.

23. Green, "South Carolina Archives," art. 80, p. 100. This copy of the first version is not included in Parker, *North Carolina Charters.*

24. Locke is cited in Resnick, "John Locke," 385. *For a General Naturalization,* Locke's short pamphlet, was written in the context of the 1693 debate surrounding the possible adoption of a general naturalization act, which Locke supported. The bill was defeated, like its predecessors.

25. Resnick, "John Locke," 380–82.

26. Locke cited in Resnick, "John Locke," 388.

27. [R. Petit and J. Guérard], "Humble proposition faite au Roy et à son Parlement pour donner retraite aux Étrangers protestans et aux prosélites dans ses Colonies de l'Amérique et surtout en la Caroline" [March 1679], BPRO, CO 1/43/16.

28. [Anon.], "Proposition en Général pour la Caroline" [1685 or 1686], "Letters to Compton, Bishop of London 1677–1710 and Other Papers," Bodleian Library, Oxford, Rawlinson ms. C 984, fol. 312.

29. *Description du Pays nommé Caroline,* [1], [3] (quote).

30. *Description de la Carolline* (Geneva, 1685), 35–36.

31. *Plan pour former un établissement,* [1].

32. The Huguenot subscribers who can be identified (with dates of signing) were J[acques] (possibly I[saac]) Dugué, P[ierre] Bacot, Antoin[e] Poitevin, D[aniel] Trézévant, P[ierre] Dutartre, René Rézeau, I[saac] Fleury, Adam Carlié, [Noé] Royer (the last two signed in October 1686, the first six simply in 1686, possibly also in October), Peter DuMoulin (November 1686), and John-Francis De Gignilliat (January 1688/89). The signature "PHin. Roger," which has been conjectured to be that of Noah Royer (with an *N* in the form of a *PH*), son of the above-mentioned N. Royer, is actually that of Phineas Rogers, an Anglican clerk who came to the colony in 1682. What reads like "Augustin Girrlé" could actually be Abraham Carlié, son of Adam Carlié. See Miscellaneous Records (Proprietary Series), vol. 1692–1700:445–46, SCDAH. For a published transcription, see Alexander S. Salley, "An Interesting and Valuable Old Record," *HSSCT* 21 (1915): 60–61. See also William J. Rivers, *A Sketch of the History of South Carolina* (1856; Spartanburg, S.C.: The Reprint Company, 1972), 334–35; Alexander S. Salley, ed., "A Letter by the Second Landgrave Smith," *SCHGM* 33 (1931): 62n2.

33. The document covers two folios. On the first there are thirteen signatures, including that of Joseph Morton (twice), under the oath. On the second there are twenty-three signatures, eleven (twelve if A. Girrlé [A. Carlié?] is included) by Huguenots on the left margin, and on the right there is an oath with an explicit mention referring to the July 21, 1669, version of the Fundamental Constitutions and under it four signatures including that of Gignilliat. Settlers whose signatures appear on the first folio most likely subscribed to the 1682 version along with the governor, although the paragraph is not a verbatim but rather a simplified copy of the formal oath contained in article 125. It is unclear, however, to which oath the signatures on the left margin of the second

folio refer. See Miscellaneous Records (Proprietary Series), vol. 1692–1700:445–46, SCDAH; Parker, *North Carolina Charters,* 231.

34. The Huguenots may have followed Morton's instructions, but the governor wanted the settlers, particularly the members of the unicameral Parliament, to take an oath to the 1682, not 1669, version of the Fundamental Constitutions. Morton's opponents argued that only the original version had any legitimacy. The Huguenots signed in October and November 1686 when Morton was in power, except Gignilliat, who signed in 1689, over a year after the governor was deposed. Beyond individual positions, this tends to confirm that the Huguenots subscribed to the Fundamental Constitutions regardless of who was in power. Incidentally, Morton had a letter published in the 1685 promotional pamphlet *Description de la Carolline.* The letter is in French and seems to have been addressed to a French friend of Morton's unless it was a translation. See Sirmans, *South Carolina,* 43–44; *Description de la Carolline* (letter of September 1683), 48–55.

35. These were Antoine Poitevin (denizened in 1681), Noé Royer (1685), Jean-François Gignilliat (1694), René Rézeau (1694), and Pierre Bacot (1700) (Shaw, *Letters of Denization 1701–1800,* 152, 173, 234, 244, 312).

36. Sirmans, *South Carolina,* 37.

37. Ibid., 67; Lesser, *South Carolina Begins,* 182.

38. Quoted in Sirmans, *South Carolina,* 38.

39. A useful list of proprietary governors and deputy governors with dates of office can be found in Lesser, *South Carolina Begins,* 176–78. For brief biographical portraits of the governors, see John W. Raimo, *Biographical Directory of American Colonial and Revolutionary Governors 1607–1789* (Westport, Conn.: Meckler Books, 1980).

40. Quoted in Weir, *Colonial South Carolina,* 66.

41. Sirmans, *South Carolina,* 44–49; Weir, *Colonial South Carolina,* 65–67. As historians of proprietary Carolina have noted, the crisis that led to the replacement of Governor Colleton was not a Carolina version of the 1689 English Revolution and was only remotely connected to it. The overthrowing of James II was a pretext more than anything else. Colleton's opponents exploited the Whiggish anti-Jacobite propaganda to accuse the governor of trespassing the "liberties" that they enjoyed as Englishmen and, as Sirmans put it, "to restore power to those who formerly had held it" (49).

42. Sothell's abuses of power led some of his victims to seek redress at the Court of the Grand Council after his demise. In June 1692, for instance, Pierre Poinset, along with other settlers, petitioned against Sothell for "extorting Severall Sums of money from them on pretence of Lycensing them to retail Lyquor." Poinset was granted a compensation of four pounds, ten shillings Carolina money. See Salley, *Journal of the Grand Council, 1692,* 40.

43. Sirmans, *South Carolina,* 50–53.

44. Ibid., 42, 50; Moore, "Royalizing South Carolina," 34–36. On the Goose Creek Men, see chapter 2, notes 70 and 71 and Roper, *Conceiving Carolina,* 51–67.

45. "John Stewart to William Dunlop" (April 27 and June 23, 1690), in "Stewart Letters," *SCHGM* 32 (1931): 1–33; "Petition to Seth Sothell" (May 1691), in Rivers, *Sketch of the History,* 418–30.

46. "John Stewart to William Dunlop" (April 27, 1690), 13.

47. Ibid., 8. The choice of LeBas was not innocent. The Huguenot esquire was a friend of James Colleton as shown by a 1696 power of attorney Colleton signed in favor of "[his] friend" J. LeBas and J. Stewart "to visit [his] plantations once in a quarter to see if overseers attend the management of said honestly according to [his] instructions, to examine the accounts" while Colleton was in the Barbados (Moore, *Records of the Secretary of the Province,* 144).

48. "Petition to Seth Sothell," 423.

49. Ibid., 429. For an analysis of the authorship, contents, and context of this petition, see Roper, *Conceiving Carolina,* 97.

50. The proprietors nonetheless ratified the 1692 "Act for the Better Observance of the Lord's Day," which they were "well pleased with" (Alexander S. Salley, ed., *Journal of the Commons House of Assembly of South Carolina for the Four Sessions of 1693* [Columbia: Historical Commission of South Carolina, 1916], 30–31).

51. "Proprietors to French Church Consistory" (April 12, 1693), BPRO, CO 5/288 (1682–98).

52. "J[acques] Boyd to Governor Archdale," John Archdale Papers, microfilm copy, fols. 100–101, SCDAH; "[Jacques] Boyd to Lord Ashley," John Archdale Papers, fols. 84–85, SCDAH. Sir Peter Colleton died in March 1694. See Buchanan, "Colleton Family," 202; Lesser, *South Carolina Begins,* 44.

53. Perhaps Huguenots in Goose Creek were swayed by the "Goose Creek Men" among whom they had settled.

54. Referring to the Huguenots' seemingly wavering political allegiance, Amy Friedlander wrote that "their first political role was apparently as objects of manipulation" (Friedlander, "Carolina Huguenots," 122). I somewhat disagree with this interpretation. I think that they were divided and that more than being fooled by the faction who controlled Parliament, unsure of which way the wind of political power was blowing, they intelligently moneyed their allegiance for naturalization, whether proprietary or legislative.

55. The landgraves and caciques, representing the politically discreet Carolina nobility, were to sit with the proprietary deputies with a consultative role. See Lesser, *South Carolina Begins,* 182–83; Sirmans, *South Carolina,* 51; Jack P. Greene, *The Quest for Power: The Lower Houses of Assembly in the Southern Royal Colonies, 1689–1776* (Chapel Hill: University of North Carolina Press, 1963), 35–39. On post-Sothell proprietary reforms, see also Roper, *Conceiving Carolina,* 107–13. On the development of representative institutions in South Carolina from the 1660s to the 1790s, see James Haw, "Political Representation in South Carolina, 1669–1794: Evolution of a Lowcountry Tradition," *SCHM* 103 (2002): 106–29.

56. Salley, *Journal of the Grand Council,* 54. Writs of elections had been issued in June 1692 for an assembly, but it was unable to work with the council and quickly disbanded. No records of its deliberations have survived. The September session has therefore been regarded as the first meeting of the newly designed House. See Lesser, *South Carolina Begins,* 183; Edgar, *Biographical Directory,* 1:21.

57. Hirsch, *Huguenots,* 117–18; Sirmans, *South Carolina,* 61; Moore, "Royalizing South Carolina," 35–41.

58. The 1692 act called "An Act for the Better Observance of the Lord's Day, commonly called Sunday" was supposed to regulate Huguenot hours of worship, but like its predecessors, it was essentially designed against Sabbath breakers. See also supra chap. 5, note 75. Salley, *Journal of the Commons House 1693 for the Four Sessions of 1693,* 31. The attack on the legitimacy of their marriages must have been a painful reminder of post-Revocation France, where Huguenot marriages were no longer recognized. In such a context, as Rousseau deplored, "[the Huguenot] sees . . . his wife treated as a concubine and his children as bastards" (Jean-Jacques Rousseau, "Le mariage des protestants," in Rousseau, *Du contrat social;* see supra chap. 3, note 15 for full reference).

59. Although the assembly only formally acquired the right to initiate legislation in 1693, it had nonetheless done so in its first meeting in 1692. As Boyd confirmed in his September 1695 letter to Governor Archdale, the assembly passed the "Act for the better Observance of the Lords' Day" in October 1692. It is intriguing that the Huguenots did not object to it since no opposition

was recorded in the assembly journal or mentioned by Boyd. See Alexander S. Salley, ed., *Journal of the Commons House of Assembly, September 20, 1692–October 15, 1692* (Columbia: Historical Commission of South Carolina, 1907), 27; "J[acques] Boyd to Governor Archdale."

60. The first properly constituted Court of Vice Admiralty in British North America was established in Maryland in 1694. However, in South Carolina the first admiralty case occurred in 1687. Known as the Muschamp case, after George Muschamp, collector of customs, it involved a Scottish ship. Governor Colleton and the council sitting as a Vice Admiralty Court released the ship seized by Muschamp, boldly arguing that the Navigation Acts did not extend to North America. Pressed into action by the Privy Council, however, the proprietors disallowed Governor Colleton's ruling. Until the South Carolina Vice Admiralty Court was formally created in 1697 with Joseph Morton as its first judge, the governor and the council continued to meet as an Admiralty Court on an ad hoc basis. See David R. Owen and Michael C. Tolley, *Courts of Admiralty in Colonial America: The Maryland Experience, 1634–1776* (Durham, N.C.: Carolina Academic Press, 1995), 27–33; Moore, "Royalizing South Carolina," 55–56, 140–48; Edward McCrady, *The History of South Carolina under the Proprietary Government, 1670–1719* (1897; New York: Russell & Russell, 1969), 222, 297.

61. Pierre-Jacob Guérard, who had been in the colony since 1680, was appointed collector of the port of Charleston in October 1694. As an informant, and like the governor, he was entitled to claim a third of the goods carried on the *Blue Star*. Another complaint concerned the fact that one of the jurors (unidentified in the records) was also an alien, but the council argued that he had been naturalized by an act of Parliament in England. See Miscellaneous Records (Proprietary Series), vol. 1694–1705:22, SCDAH; Salley, *Commissions,* 87; Owen and Tolley, *Courts of Admiralty,* 104.

62. Salley, *Commissions,* 87–88.

63. The *Blue Star* affair is far from being an isolated case. Ships belonging to or manned by denizened settlers were regularly seized in the various colonial ports, and court decisions were often appealed in England. There was apparently no uniform ruling on the commercial rights of denizened merchants in the colonies, but the rule of thumb was that the trading privileges of the grantees had to be specified in the denization letter. In 1700 the situation was clarified when an order-in-council ruled that colonial denizations and naturalizations only applied within the colonies where they were granted. It is not known whether the *Blue Star* crew had been denizened in New York or England, but the fact that the proprietors warned the Carolina officials not to challenge royal authority seems to indicate that they had obtained their denization in England (Kettner, *Development of American Citizenship,* 36n29, 95–97).

64. In 1696 a clause in a navigation act being debated in Parliament that would implicitly bar denizens from the colonial trade by reserving it to "Natives of England or Ireland, or such persons as are born in His Majesty's Plantations in Asia, Africa, or America," occasioned a petition by Huguenot merchants "settled in and about London and in the English Plantations in America" for the defense of French Protestants' commercial rights. The petitioners argued that having been "cruelly prosecuted in their Native Country," on the invitation of Charles II and of "several Lords Proprietors," they "sheltered themselves in this kingdom [and in the English Plantations in America]," where "a great many of them were made Free Denisons [denizens]." The refugees, the petitioners went on, "transported themselves and Families [to America] with great Hazards, Troubles and Charges," where "they improved those Colonies . . . particularly Carolina and New York [which] are, for the most, inhabited by them." These French Protestants, the petitioners continued, "having, on all occasions, [showed] their Loyalty, Zeal, and Affection by supporting very chearfully the Charges and Taxes of the Land, and wearing Arms for the Defense of [these Countrys]," should therefore be allowed access to the colonial trade. Besides, they ultimately and

astutely argued, it would be in the interest of England since if Huguenot merchants were excluded by this clause, "they would be reduced to the greatest Extremities, or forced to return back to *England,* where they must starve, or be maintained by the Publick Charity." In other words, such a clause would burden England and defeat the original dual purpose of sending Huguenots across the Atlantic to relieve England, especially London, of poor refugees and develop colonial manufactures. Beyond its interesting argumentation, this petition shows the paramount importance given by Huguenot merchants to their commercial rights and the high degree of coordination reached by refugees settled far apart within the Anglo-American world. See "The Case of the French Protestants Refugees Settled in and about London, and in the English Plantations in America," [London, 1696], Houghton Library, Harvard University.

65. Kettner, *Development of American Citizenship,* 31. The presence of two Huguenots as informant and juror remarkably illustrates the fact that the French were also divided along political lines even when their collective rights as foreign settlers were threatened.

66. Salley, *Commissions,* 87–88; Salley, *Papers,* 3:167–68. Another denizened merchant born in the French Antilles was wrongfully convicted by the Charleston Admiralty Court in 1697 and would later be compensated (Hirsch, *Huguenots,* 123).

67. Lesser, *South Carolina Begins,* 49–50, 109n145; Clarence L. Ver Steeg, *Origins of a Southern Mosaic: Studies of Early Carolina and Georgia* (Athens: University of Georgia Press, 1975), 23; Roper, *Conceiving Carolina,* 115–16.

68. Salley, *Commissions,* 80; Sirmans, *South Carolina,* 62–63.

69. Moore, "Royalizing South Carolina," 40.

70. A similar petition had been presented to Governor Joseph Blake, who served his first term from November 1694 to August 17, 1695. See Salley, *Commissions,* 80; "[Jacques] Boyd to Lord Ashley," John Archdale Papers, microfilm copy, fols. 84–85, SCDAH; Lesser, *South Carolina Begins,* 76, 177.

71. "Governor and Council to Proprietors" (August 20, 1695), in Salley, *Commissions,* 80–81.

72. Jacques, listed as the head of the Boyd family in the *Liste des François et Suisses,* was the oldest of the Boyd sons (Jacques, Jean, and Gabriel). He is in all likelihood the author of the letter, but, unsure of his English, he used "his brothers hand" to write it. The brother in question was Jean [John], who worked in England as a merchant before settling in Carolina and was fluent enough in English to sit in the Carolina assembly in 1692. Needless to say, the two Boyd letters, to Lord Ashley and to Governor Archdale, shed a unique Huguenot light on Carolina proprietary affairs well beyond the 1695 crisis. Contrary to the information given by the *Biographical Directory of the South Carolina House,* the Boyds were Huguenots from Bordeaux and not Englishmen. Boyd is a Scottish name, but many Huguenot merchants in France, such as the Boyds and the Mazycks, had foreign names and origins. See Ravenel, *Liste,* 44–45 (#3); "J[acques] Boyd to Governor Archdale"; Edgar, *Biographical Directory,* 1:21, 2:93; Bosher, *Men and Ships,* 78.

73. "J[acques] Boyd to Governor Archdale."

74. Daniel notoriously opposed Governor Colleton's effort to implement the 1682 Fundamental Constitutions and switched sides later on to become, with Edmund Bellinger, part of the two-member committee appointed by the proprietors to draft the 1698 version of the same constitutions. An example of Daniel's authoritative and fanatical tendencies is found in 1700 when he arbitrarily and illegally imprisoned a group of settlers, among whom were Abraham LeSueur and Pierre Girard, for allegedly not obeying his orders. The House freed these settlers after ruling that Daniel had "abused and breached [their] rights." Daniel eventually served as governor of South Carolina in 1716 and 1717. See Sirmans, *South Carolina,* 76–85, 118–19; Raimo, *Biographical Directory,* 427–28; Roper, *Conceiving Carolina,* 97, 118; Alexander S. Salley, ed., *Journal of the*

Commons House of Assembly, October 30, 1700–November 16, 1700 (Columbia: Historical Commission of South Carolina, 1924), 15, 19–20.

75. This was especially true of Jacques Boyd, who had received a three-thousand-acre grant from the proprietors nine months before in December 1694 (Salley, *Papers,* 3:150).

76. "J[acques] Boyd to Governor Archdale."

77. Ibid.

78. The Huguenots were all the more sensitive to the threat of losing their estates since in France the monarch could escheat aliens' properties through a privilege known as *droit d'aubaine* (an *aubain* being an alien). Although there were many restrictions, the seriousness of the threat was so real that it was a major incentive to seek naturalization, even for those for whom the *droit d'aubaine* was waived on account of their nationality or place of residence (Sahlins, "Fictions of Catholic France," 87–88).

79. To strengthen his case, Boyd duly attached a copy of the petition to his letter to Anthony Ashley Cooper ("J. Boyd to Lord Ashley" [undated], John Archdale Papers, microfilm copy, fols. 84–85, SCDAH).

80. "Governor and Council to Proprietors" (October 2, 1695) and "Governor and Council to Proprietors" (August 28, 1696), in Salley, *Commissions,* 84–85, 94 (quote).

81. "Archdale to Buretel, Serurrier, LaSalle & Others" (October 19, 1695), John Archdale Papers, microfilm copy, fols. 85–87, SCDAH.

82. "Governor and Council to Proprietors" (October 2, 1695), 85.

83. "Robert Gibbes to Proprietors" (December 19, 1695), in Salley, *Commissions,* 90; Moore, "Royalizing South Carolina," 40–41.

84. This quote is from an earlier proprietary letter addressed to Archdale, but in 1698 the proprietors received "Proposalls from a number of French Refugees to . . . Settle upon Port Royall," and their Lordships deplored "ye Unhappy differences between those already Settled there & you [governor and council]," which had "discouraged them to Goe in so usefull a Designe." This 1698 group was most likely the Huguenots whom Daniel Coxe unsuccessfully tried to settle in Louisiana and who eventually founded the settlement of Manakintown, Virginia, in 1701. See "Proprietors to Archdale" (March 27, 1695), in *Calendar of State Papers,* ed. Sainsbury and Fortescue, vol. 14 (1693–96):450; "Proprietors to Blake" (April 11, 1698), in Salley, *Papers,* 4:43 (second quote). On Coxe and his failed attempt to settle Huguenots in Louisiana, see Daniel Coxe, *A Description of the English Province of Carolana by the Spaniards call'd Florida, and by the French La Louisiane* (1722), ed. William S. Coker (Gainesville: University Presses of Florida, 1976); and Bertrand Van Ruymbeke, "'A Dominion of True Believers Not a Republic of Heretics': French Colonial Religious Policy and the Settlement of Early Louisiana (1699–1730)," in *French Colonial Louisiana and the Atlantic World,* ed. Bradley Bond (Baton Rouge: Louisiana State University Press, 2005), 83–94.

85. "Proprietors to Council" (March 13, 1685), in Salley, *Papers,* 2:31–32.

86. "Proprietors to Archdale" (January 29, 1696), in Salley, *Papers,* 3:166–67.

87. "Proprietors to Archdale" (June 17, 1696), in Salley, *Papers,* 3:174–75.

88. Huguenot trade privileges were explicitly confirmed in a subsequent letter ("Governor and Council to Proprietors" [August 28, 1696], in Salley, *Commissions,* 94).

89. "Governor and Council to Proprietors" (August 20, 1696), in Salley, *Commissions,* 92.

90. This quota was apparently based on earlier instructions issued in March 1685. See "Governor and Council to Proprietors" (August 28, 1696), in Salley, *Commissions,* 93; "Proprietors to Council" (March 11, 1685), in Salley, *Papers,* 2:17. The governor and the council had originally

mentioned a quota of thirty freeholders. The increase may be due to a more careful research into earlier proprietary instructions.

91. If we apply the *Liste des François et Suisses* adult/child ratio of 0.85, 150 individuals represent 127 adults. If we suppose that there were at least two adults per family, we have a theoretical number of 63 Huguenot families settled in Craven in 1696.

92. "Governor and Council to Proprietors" (August 28, 1696), in Salley, *Commissions,* 94.

93. "Governor and Council to Proprietors" (October 30, 1696), in Salley, *Commissions,* 96–97.

94. This act, whose exact title is "An Act for Preventing Frauds and Regulating Abuses in the Plantation Trade," was used elsewhere in the colonies to exclude aliens, including Scots, from positions of power, notably in governments and assemblies. These cases of exclusion were based on a loose and abusive interpretation of the term "Places of Trust in the Courts of Law." In South Carolina, Huguenots could be excluded from the council, which also sat as a court, on the basis of this law, but certainly not from the assembly. See Kettner, *Development of American Citizenship,* 45–46, 122–23.

95. "Governor and Council to Proprietors" (December 6, 1696), in Salley, *Commissions,* 99–100.

96. In proprietary South Carolina a bill was sent to the council for approval between each reading.

97. "Deposition of Isaac Caillabeuf" (May 25, 1696), *HSSCT* 5 (1897): 20–21.

98. Records fail to show if this private act was ever passed, but a bill was first read in February 1696. It is entirely possible that this act was read only once and the legislative procedure dropped when Huguenots collectively petitioned for a naturalization law the following March. The presence of Jean Thomas among the sixty Huguenots listed in the 1697 naturalization law would confirm this hypothesis. The fee for a private act was decided on in March 1697. See Alexander S. Salley, ed., *Journal of the Commons House of Assembly, January 30, 1696–March 17, 1696* (Columbia: Historical Commission of South Carolina, 1912), 24, 27; Salley, ed., *Journal of the Commons House of Assembly for the Two Sessions of 1697* (Columbia: Historical Commission of South Carolina, 1913), 12; Cooper and McCord, *Statutes at Large,* 2:131.

99. "The Humble Petition of Noah Royer, Jr., Jonas Bonhost, [and] Peter Poinsett . . .," Miscellaneous Records (Proprietary Series), vol. 1694–1705:83, SCDAH.

100. On E. Neau, see supra page 54, and note 29.

101. "The Humble Petition of Noah Royer, Jr."

102. "Governor and Council to Proprietors" (October 30, 1696), in Salley, *Commissions,* 97.

103. Contrary to what Daniel Ravenel wrote in 1822, the *Liste des François et Suisses* was not compiled in 1695 but later, probably between summer 1696 and spring 1697. Ravenel conjectured that the document had been "prepared or *its materials collected*" before the death of Marianne, daughter of Isaac and Marianne Mazyck, which occurred in September 1695. However, the Mazycks had another daughter also named Marianne (Marie Anne, born in March 1696), as was common in a time when children often did not reach adulthood. This is the Marianne mentioned in the *Liste.* In addition, Marianne Fleury Dugué is listed as Jacques Dugué's widow, and Jacques died in January 1697. Finally, why would Jean Thomas be in the *Liste* while petitioning for a private act of naturalization? The *Liste* was obviously compiled after Thomas submitted his own petition. See Ravenel, *Liste,* 43, 51 (#44); Mazyck Family Bible, back cover, Huguenot Society of South Carolina Library, Charleston; Records of the Register of the Province (Conveyance Series), 1675–95:221–23, SCDAH. The fact that a Huguenot committee compiled the *Liste* is suggested by a reference in the document to a "Comité" (Ravenel, *Liste,* 64).

104. Salley, *Journal of the Commons House 1697,* 5–6, 13.

105. A third act barred Huguenots from serving as jurors in cases regarding customs violation in accordance with the 1696 Navigation Act. The zealous enforcement of this imperial law by the Carolina authorities, however, did not keep Pierre-Jacob Guérard from remaining collector of customs for Charleston until he became register of the province in 1703. See "Governor and Council to Proprietors" (May 13, 1699), in Salley, *Commissions,* 116; Lesser, *South Carolina Begins,* 430.

106. This absurd comment was based on a partisan report addressed to the proprietors by Edmund Bellinger, the same official who had wrongfully prosecuted the Huguenot crew and owners of the *Blue Star* back in February 1695. See "Proprietors to Governor and Council" (April 25, 1697), in Salley, *Papers,* 3 (1691–97):195.

107. "Proprietors to Governor and Council" (April 11, 1698), in Salley, *Papers,* 4:43.

108. Parker, *North Carolina Charters,* 234–40.

109. The 1697 electoral law was the first introduced by the assembly and not the council. For a description of this membership issue within the larger process of colonial legislative autonomy in the southern colonies, see Greene, *Quest for Power,* 169–204.

110. The religious and political alignment approaches have been traditionally argued by historians of proprietary politics, and the county angle has been stressed by Ver Steeg. While all are helpful, these mutually inclusive approaches tend to downplay the fluid nature of proprietary factional politics and to ignore that before being Nonconformists, proprietary, or Craven voters, Huguenots, while being divided, were above all French and perceived as such by their fellow Carolinians. See Moore, "Royalizing South Carolina," 34–37; Sirmans, *South Carolina,* 62, 74; Ver Steeg, *Origins of a Southern Mosaic,* 31–33.

111. "John Stewart to William Dunlop" (April 27 and June 23, 1690), in "Stewart Letters," *SCHGM* 32 (1931): 12. Incidentally, when French *"philibustiers"* from Saint Domingue called at Charleston in 1686 or 1687, according to La Rochelle intendant Arnoul, on the invitation of the Carolina governor, their three ships were held in the harbor and looted. Charlestonians allegedly "wanted to throw themselves onto the French simply because they were Catholic," but the crews were saved through the intervention of "le S[ieu]r. de la Chabossière [Arnaud Bruneau] gentilhomme and refugee" before the "governor sent them back to Saint Domingue after stripping them of their weapons." This incident shows that the buccaneers were under attack not because they were pirates or French (i.e., potential enemies) but because they were Catholic, which must have been reassuring to the Huguenots, and reveals how blurred lines of identity were since Arnaud Bruneau rescued them precisely because they were French without minding their being Catholic. See "Lettre au Marquis de Seigneulay" (June 14, 1687), ms. NAF, Arnoul 21334, fol. 194, BN.

112. This fear had been precisely the reason for Colleton's wish to declare martial law in 1690.

113. "Governor and Council to Proprietors" (December 6, 1696), in Salley, *Commissions,* 100. This French threat endured through the following decade, as shown by a 1705 French report that somewhat optimistically suggested to "détruire les Établissements des Anglais de la Carolline" (wipe out the English settlements in Carolina), in all likelihood a prelude to the 1706 Franco-Spanish assault on Charleston. This combined invasion turned out to be a disaster as, according to English versions of the events, the French and the Spaniards did not expect to find Charleston to be fortified. Incidentally, one French sea captain was named Lewis Pasquereau. This victory was duly celebrated by Carolinians, and when LeJau arrived in Charleston two months later, he found "the Inhabitants rejoycing: they had kept the day before holy for a thanksgiving to Almighty God for being safely delivered from an invasion from the French and Spaniards." See "Proposition d'une entreprise sur la Caroline pour en chasser les Anglais" [1705], ms. n.a.f. 9294 (1870 copy), fols. 114–18, BN; Kenneth R. Jones, "A 'Full and Particular Account' of the Assault on Charleston

in 1706," *SCHM* 83 (1982): 1–11; "LeJau to Secretary, December 2, 1706," in Klingberg, *Carolina Chronicle of Le Jau,* 17; Hoffman, *Florida's Frontiers,* 174–81.

114. "Governor and Council to Proprietors" (March 14, 1698), in Salley, *Commissions,* 103–4. The news reached South Carolina in December 1697. Correspondence between the governor and the proprietors shows that throughout the crisis the Carolina authorities feared a French invasion. This must have undoubtedly been a very uncomfortable situation for all Carolinians but especially for the Huguenots.

115. Butler, *Huguenots in America,* 60–61.

116. On the contents of this new version and how it differed from previous ones, see Roper, *Conceiving Carolina,* 118–20.

117. "An Act for the Better Encouragement of the Settlement of That Part of This Province That Lyes South and West of Cape Feare" (May 1, 1691); "An Act for the Making of Aliens Free of This Part of This Province, and for Granting Liberty of Conscience to All Protestants" (March 10, 1697); and "An Act for the Making Aliens Free of This Part of the Province" (November 4, 1704). A Dissenter-controlled assembly contemplated passing another in February 1703, but after the bill went through a second reading it was dropped following a power shift. The legislative deliberations surrounding its enactment do not mention its contents. However, based on the sponsors of the bills who claimed somewhat defensively that it would offer Huguenots all that "they [could] reasonably expect," it can be surmised that this law would have curtailed Huguenots' rights. See Cooper and McCord, *Statutes at Large,* 2:58–59, 131–33, 251–53; Salley, *Journal of the Commons House 1702,* 42, 49; "The Representation and Address of several of the Members of this present Assembly return'd for Colleton, and other Inhabitants of this Province, whose names are hereunto subscribed," in Rivers, *Sketch of the History,* 457; Moore, "Royalizing South Carolina," 44–45; Sirmans, *South Carolina,* 86.

118. Cooper and McCord, *Statutes at Large,* 2:58–60.

119. The fact that the occupation of each naturalized alien was listed next to his name probably means that the law implicitly offered them economic rights.

120. Although it was specifically designed to advance the interests of Protestants and explicitly referred to "all Christians" in its final religious clause, the act also naturalized Jewish settlers. This should not appear surprising since the Jews, who had been officially readmitted in England in 1655, were better regarded than Catholics in the Anglo-American world. In England, however, as opposed to the colonies, Jews were limited to denization since the sacramental test prevented them from being naturalized by Parliament. The so-called "Jew Bill," briefly in force in England in 1753, removed this impediment by offering Jews parliamentary naturalization. In North America the British naturalization law of 1740 also applied to Jews. See James W. Hagy, *This Happy Land: The Jews of Colonial and Antebellum Charleston* (Tuscaloosa: University of Alabama Press, 1993), 6–7; Kettner, *Development of American Citizenship,* 66–68, 74–76. For the Jewish presence in the early Americas, see Paolo Bernardini and Norman Fiering, eds., *The Jews and the Expansion of Europe to the West, 1450–1800* (New York: Berghan Books, 2001).

121. Cooper and McCord, *Statutes at Large,* 2:131–33. Matching the three lists of aliens compiled in 1696 and 1697 (the February 1696 petition, the *Liste des François et Suisses,* and the 1697 Act of Naturalization list) raises more questions than it answers. Why are all the Huguenots who petitioned in 1696 not listed in the act? Why are a few Huguenots who signed the petition and appeared on the *Liste* also not in the act? Why does the act list not include pastors, esquires, Swiss, and Craven County settlers? Finally, why are seventy Huguenots mentioned in the *Liste* not listed in the act? Since no Craven Huguenots are on the act list, it could be surmised that they refused Archdale's compromise, but why would they appear on the *Liste des François et Suisses?* These

questions cannot be answered. It can only be conjectured that the 1697 act list was hastily drawn and that only Huguenots living in Charleston and Orange Quarter (i.e., Berkeley County), most of them being merchants and artisans, had the time to register for naturalization in Charleston before the act was passed.

122. Since only two naturalization certificates from those not listed in the act itself have survived (Élie Prioleau's and Isaac Mazyck's), it is impossible to know how many Huguenots failed or refused to be naturalized under the 1697 act in the three months following its enactment. One of them is Jacques LeBas, from Santee, the Huguenot who had translated Stewart's pamphlet and whose 1692 election to the assembly had been invalidated. LeBas was eventually naturalized on November 9, 1704 (Miscellaneous Records [Proprietary Series], vol. 1709–25:11, SCDAH). Prioleau's certificate, dated June 3, 1697, is in Ravenel, *Liste,* 70–71; and Mazyck's (same date) is in Miscellaneous Records (Proprietary Series), vol. 1694–1705:178, SCDAH.

123. Edward Hoyt conjectured that two royals equaled thirty shillings (Hoyt, "Naturalization under the American Colonies," 258). Across from one name in the *Liste* appears "donné cinquante chelin" (given fifty shillings), which must have been the cost of registration for a family (it would be much too high for an individual) since the 1697 act mentions no fees. In his introduction, Ravenel also makes reference to a "passer gratis" (go free) next to another name in the original *Liste* but which he did not transcribe (Ravenel, *Liste,* 11, 64 [Made. Bacot] [#130]).

124. When the assembly resolved to have the bill prepared, it explicitly stipulated that the Huguenots "shall not be capable of sitting in the assembly" (John S. Green Transcripts of Commons House Journals (hereafter Green Transcripts), vol. 5 (October 4–November 6, 1704), 254.

125. Cooper and McCord, *Statutes at Large,* 2:251–53.

126. Hoyt, "Naturalization under the American Colonies," 248–66; Carpenter, "Naturalization," 288–303; Kettner, *Development of American Citizenship,* 106–28; "Governor and Council to Proprietors" (March 24, 1697), in Salley, *Commissions,* 102 (quote).

127. "Deposition of Isaac Caillabeuf," 20–21.

128. Sirmans, *South Carolina,* 84.

129. "The Present State of Affairs in Carolina, by John Ash, 1706," in Alexander S. Salley, ed., *Early Narratives of Carolina, 1650–1708* (New York: Barnes & Noble, 1911), 271.

130. Salley, *Journal of the Commons House 1702,* 51 (quote), 53–54, 56–57. Sirmans mentioned "at least twenty-nine French," but I could identify only twenty-seven Huguenots. Since some of the names are anglicized beyond recognition this number is not definite. See Sirmans, *South Carolina,* 84.

131. This argument was specious, to say the least, since most of the summoned refugees were either duly listed in the 1697 act (eleven), appeared in the *Liste des François et Suisses* (four), or arrived in the colony after 1697 (five). The status of the other seven cannot be determined. The investigation was dropped in August 1702 when news of the War of Spanish Succession (Queen Anne's War) reached South Carolina. See Sirmans, *South Carolina,* 84.

132. The farmers were Theodore Verdity, Pierre Poitevin, Pierre Videau, Pierre LeSade, and Mathurin Guérin (gardener); the weavers, Isaac Baton, Pierre Dutartre, and Daniel Trézévant; the small artisans, Abraham Dupont (brazier), Pierre Filleux (cooper), and Abraham LeSueur (joiner); the silversmiths, Nicolas de Longuemare and Salomon Legaré; the apothecary, Joseph Marbeuf; and the merchant, Jacob Lapôtre David. The Huguenots from Orange Quarter were Pierre and Antoine Poitevin, Pierre Dutartre, Daniel Trézévant, Joseph Marbeuf, and Jean Juin; from Charleston, Pierre Cothoneau, Mathurin Guérin, and Salomon Legaré; and from Santee, Nicolas de Longuemare, Pierre Videau, and Benjamin Marion. See Cooper and McCord, *Statutes at Large,* 2:131; Ravenel, *Liste.*

133. These Huguenots were Alexandre T. Chastaigner, Jean Boyd, Paul Bruneau, René Ravenel, Jean Gendron, Jacques LeBas, and Louis de St. Julien. There are seven Huguenots for six seats because LeBas was originally elected but, failing to report to the assembly for a month, was consequently disqualified and replaced by St. Julien, "the Person that had most votes next to Mr. LeBas," in January 1693. It is not inconceivable that LeBas's friendship with Colleton and his previous involvement in Colleton's 1690 attempt to get Huguenot support by translating Stewart's tract into French are the real reasons for his absence and disqualification. See Edgar, *Biographical Directory,* 1:21; Salley, *Journal of the Commons House 1692,* 4, 5, 16; "John Stewart to William Dunlop" (April 27, 1690), 8.

134. These four Huguenots are Jacques LeSerrurier, John-Abraham Motte, Henry LeNoble, and Louis Pasquereau (Edgar, *Biographical Directory,* 1:22–31).

135. In his analysis of assemblymen, Butler found two Huguenots in the second (1695), two in the third (1696–97), one in the fourth (1698–99), and one in the fifth (1700–1702) assemblies, whereas I counted none, one (H. LeNoble), none, and none, respectively. Butler does not mention specific names but probably included delegates whose last names, such as Hext and Bedon, were elsewhere in his book mistakenly identified as French. See table 4, "Huguenots in the South Carolina Assembly, 1691–1776," in Butler, *Huguenots in America,* 128.

136. Henry LeNoble and John-Abraham Motte, for example, were elected four times between 1696 and 1711 and 1706 and 1711, respectively (Butler, *Huguenots in America,* 1:23–37).

137. If all seven Huguenots elected to the 1692–94 assembly were planters, nine of the ten Huguenots elected between 1696 and 1715 were merchants (Edgar, *Biographical Directory,* 1:21–39).

138. This does not mean, however, that Huguenots exclusively represented predominantly French parishes. In the sixteenth assembly (1717), for instance, a few were returned for St. Philip's, St. James Goose Creek, and even St. Helena's. Santee was granted one seat in 1717 and two after 1719, while the membership of the assembly rose to thirty-five in 1720. Mysteriously, nobody was elected in Santee in 1717. St. Denis's representation was merged with St. Thomas for a total of three seats, presumably two for St. Thomas and one for St. Denis. This Huguenot parish, however, never sent a refugee to the assembly. This may be due to the generally modest socioeconomic status of the Orange Quarter Huguenots and the fact that in the late 1710s and early 1720s St. Denis was torn apart by a severe religious crisis. Under the county system Benjamin Simons of St. Denis was elected to the fourteenth assembly (1713–15) but declined to serve. See ibid., 38n5 (B. Simons reference), 41–42, 47.

139. This assembly, whose deliberations were not included in the journal, is only known from an anonymous account (John Alexander Moore, ed., "'A Narrative . . . of an Assembly . . . January the 2d. 1705/6': New Light on Early South Carolina Politics," *SCHM* 85 [1984]: 183).

140. Sirmans, *South Carolina,* 89–91.

141. The letter is not extant since Mailhet never submitted it to the House. Only oral depositions made by St. Denis settlers who heard or read it have been recorded. See Alexander S. Salley, ed., *Journal of the Commons House of Assembly of South Carolina, June 5, 1707–July 19, 1707* (Columbia: Historical Commission of South Carolina, 1940), 12, 23–24.

142. Ibid., 25, 53, 56 (quote).

143. Edgar, *Biographical Directory,* 1:27–28; Green Transcripts, vol. 5 (January 31–February 17, 1705), 308.

144. The messenger served as a link between the governor, the council, and the House. Mailhet also received payment for transcribing acts (Green Transcripts, 5:288).

145. The Estates-General (*Assemblée des États-Généraux*) was the only nationwide assembly remotely comparable to the English Parliament in ancien régime France. However, it only convened in times of crisis and did not between 1614 and 1789.

146. Greene, *Quest for Power,* 475–88.

147. Salley, *Journal of the Commons House 1692,* 8, 15.

148. Salley, *Journal of the Commons House January–March 1696,* 8, 36–37 (LeNoble); Salley, *Journal of the Commons House 1702,* 66 (LeSerrurier-Smith); Alexander S. Salley, ed., *Journal of the Commons House of Assembly, Nov 20, 1706–February 8, 1707* (Columbia: Historical Commission of South Carolina, 1939), 9 (Motte and Pasquereau).

149. Butler, *Huguenots in America,* 202.

150. Salley, *Journal of the Grand Council,* 11.

151. In January 1707 Paul Bruneau sold sixty acres to André Rambert. The memorandum officializing this sale was drafted in French and signed by René Ravenel. See Records of the Register of the Province (Conveyance Series), vol. 1704–9:74–75, SCDAH.

152. Jacques LeBas, who had first been elected to the assembly and then disqualified, was justice of the peace in 1690, and in 1712 so was his son, Paul-Pierre. Jacques LeGrand was highway commissioner in 1705, and his nephew, Isaac, was tax controller in 1719. René Ravenel, assemblyman in 1692, tax controller in 1703, and highway commissioner in 1705 and 1709, was the brother-in-law of Pierre de St. Julien, who sat in the 1692 assembly and then held the office of tax controller in 1703 and 1715. See Miscellaneous Records (Proprietary Series), vol. 1682–90:381, SCDAH; Records of the Register of the Province (Conveyance Series), vol. 1711–15:209 (LeBas), SCDAH; Cooper and McCord, *Statutes at Large,* 2:719, 7:4 (LeGrand); Edgar, *Biographical Directory,* 1:21; Cooper and McCord, *Statutes at Large,* 2:207, 629; 7:4, 12 (Ravenel and St. Julien).

153. Richard Waterhouse, "The Responsible Gentry of South Carolina: A Study in Local Government," in *Town and County: Essays on the Structure of Local Government in the American Colonies,* ed. Bruce C. Daniels (Middletown, Conn.: Wesleyan University Press, 1978), 160.

8. Land, Trade, and Slaves

"[Un planteur] est chez lui un petit seigneur. Il commande à sa troupe de nègres comme un roi" ("L'Escot to Turrettini" [March 1, 1703], Archives Tronchin, ms. 81, fol. 200 back, BPU.

1. "Letter of Louis Thibou" (September 20, 1683), ms. 4289, South Caroliniana Library, Columbia, S.C. An English translation is available in Golden, *Huguenot Connection,* 140–44.

2. Between 1686 and the mid-1690s the proprietors appointed a board of trustees to replace the governor and council in their land-granting function. See Meaghan N. Duff, "Creating a Plantation Province: Proprietary Land Policies and Early Settlement Patterns," in *Money, Trade, and Power,* ed. Greene et al., 4–9; R. Nicholas Olsberg, "Introduction," in Salley and Olsberg, *Warrants for Lands,* ix–xii; Ackerman, *South Carolina Colonial Land Policies,* 20–24; Clowse, *Economic Beginnings,* 47–50. A thorough and very helpful description of the functions of secretary and register of the province and surveyors and their land records can be found in Lesser, *South Carolina Begins,* 420–41.

3. Alan D. Watson, "The Quitrent System in Royal South Carolina," *William and Mary Quarterly* 33 (1976): 182–85 (quote); Watson, "The Quitrent System in Royal South Carolina" (Ph.D. diss., University of South Carolina, 1971), 5–8.

4. "Letter of Louis Thibou," in Golden, *Huguenot Connection,* 143.

5. Linda M. Pett-Conklin, "Cadastral Surveying in Colonial South Carolina: A Historical Geography" (Ph.D. diss., Louisiana State University and Agricultural and Mechanical College, 1986), 171.

6. Ackerman, *South Carolina Colonial Land Policies,* 24.

7. Ibid., 27.

8. Watson, "Quitrent System," 13.

9. "Charter to the Lords Proprietors of Carolina" (June 30, 1665), in Parker, *North Carolina Charters,* 100.

10. "Fundamental Constitutions," in Parker, *North Carolina Charters,* 133–36 (1669), 186–89 (1682).

11. Lesser, *South Carolina Begins,* 414.

12. Ackerman, *South Carolina Colonial Land Policies,* 29–33.

13. "James Boyd's grant" (December 27, 1694) in Salley, *Papers,* 3 (1691–97):150.

14. Quotes are from *Description de la Carolline,* 21–23.

15. This statistic is exclusive of Huguenots who acquired town lots, of second-generation refugees, and of refugees about whom too little is known and only concerns the first land acquisition. See Salley and Olsberg, *Warrants for Lands;* Salley, *Papers,* vols. 2 (1684–90), 3 (1691–97), 4 (1698–1700).

16. [Wilson], *Account of the Province of Carolina,* 14.

17. Salley, *Papers,* 2 (1684–90):172–74.

18. Salley, *Commissions,* 110–11.

19. Ibid., 44–45, 61–62; Lesser, *South Carolina Begins,* 416. LeBas paid £120 instead of £75 for fifteen hundred acres most likely because the land had been, at least partially, already cleared and had therefore much more commercial value.

20. Salley, *Papers,* 2 (1684–90):50, 51, 55, 70, 120, 207, 216, 275.

21. Extant rent rolls for the proprietary period are exceedingly rare. For the seventeenth century, a list combining payments for land purchases and rents compiled under Governor Archdale shows that Jacob Guérard bought five hundred acres for ten pounds, Peter Bacot purchased one hundred acres for two pounds, and Mat Isaac Caillabeuf duly paid his rent (one pound, no land amount recorded) ("Ledger of quit rents collected by J. Archdale in Carolina," [1696], BPRO CO 5/288, 123–25; Salley, *Papers,* 3:223; Roper, *Conceiving Carolina,* 116n406.

22. Warrants records are of unequal quality since some mention the dates of arrival and the number of settlers, while others just indicate the number of acres. As a rule early warrants are relatively detailed. In Rézeau's case, it is an educated guess based on his 1685 warrant of four hundred acres and the 1682 head-right regulations. See Salley and Olsberg, *Warrants for Lands,* 245, 382, 394.

23. Salley and Olsberg, *Warrants for Lands,* 321, 336–37; Miscellaneous Records (Proprietary Series), vol. 1682–90:237, SCDAH; Caroline T. Moore and Agatha A. Simmons, comp. and ed., *Abstracts of the Wills of the State of South Carolina* (Charlotte: The Observer Printing House, 1960), 14 (will of John Godfrey Sr.).

24. Salley and Olsberg, *Warrants for Lands,* 446 (I. Caillabeuf), 464–65 (D. Huger).

25. Most proprietary gifts were manors or parts of manors since only two known Huguenots received gifts without manorial privileges. François de Rousserie was granted eight hundred acres in March 1683 for his effort at developing wine culture in the lowcountry, and Moyse Charas, with whom John Locke stayed while in Paris in 1677, was given three thousand acres for his medical expertise and in return for his hospitality. It is highly unlikely, however, that Charas ever settled in Carolina. See Salley, *Papers,* 1 (1663–84):238, 312.

344 Notes to pages 198–201

26. This is the formulaic statement found in Gignilliat's and D'Arsent's grants with the Swiss and Belgian [i.e., Walloon] nations, respectively, in the proprietors' minds. See Salley, *Commissions,* 40; Salley, *Papers,* 2 (1682–90):168.

27. Contrary to what Friedlander wrote, this grant was for the personal use of Guérard and not the *Richmond* passengers. Presumably on the grantee's request, the proprietors had to write the authorities in Charleston in July 1694 to confirm this rent-free manorial grant to Guérard. The fact that only Guérard is mentioned implicitly corroborates that Petit never came to Carolina. See Friedlander, "Carolina Huguenots," 75; Salley, *Papers,* 3 (1691–97):132.

28. Salley, *Commissions,* 1; Salley, *Papers,* 2:120, 125; Miscellaneous Records (Proprietary Series), vol. 1675–95:157, SCDAH.

29. Salley, *Papers,* 3 (1691–97):150. The wording of the grant alludes to the role of leader that Jacques Boyd seems to have had among the Huguenot community in the mid-1690s, as indicated by his letter of September 1695 to Anthony Ashley Cooper mentioned in chap. 7.

30. *Plan pour former un établissement.*

31. "Mémoires des Grâces que les S[eigneurs] Propriétaires accordent à un de mes amis . . ." (ms. 1909, fol. 56 back, Bibliothèque Municipale de La Rochelle).

32. Michael G. Kammen, ed., "Virginia at the Close of the Seventeenth Century: An Appraisal by James Blair and John Locke," *Virginia Magazine of History and Biography* 74 (1966): 141–42, 155 (quote).

33. "Lord Ashley to Gov. Sayle" (April 1671) and "[Ashley] to Sir John Yeamans" (April 1671), in Cheves, *Shaftesbury Papers,* 311, 315.

34. "Copy of Instructions Annexed to ye Comission for ye Governor & Councell" (July 1669), in Cheves, *Shaftesbury Papers,* 121.

35. Ackerman, *South Carolina Colonial Land Policies,* 29.

36. [Jacob Guérard and René Petit], "Humble proposition faite au Roy et à son Parlement pour donner retraite aux Étrangers protestans et aux prosélites dans ses Colonies de l'Amérique et surtout en la Caroline" [March 1979], BPRO, CO 1/43/16.

37. Salley, *Papers,* 2 (1684–90):134.

38. *Plan pour former un établissement,* [1].

39. "Mémoires des Grâces que les S[eigneurs] Propriétaires," fol. 56 back. In early modern France, a *bailliage* or *sénéchaussée* was a judicial division within a province.

40. Salley, *Papers,* 2 (1684–90):216; Salley and Olsberg, *Warrants for Lands,* 589.

41. "Grant for Jamestown," Memorials, book 4, part 2, p. 402, SCDAH. No exchange rate is available for 1705, but in 1703 and 1707, 150 Carolina pounds were worth £100 sterling (McCusker, *Money and Exchange,* [222]).

42. "Acte de vente d'un lot à Jamestown" (Bill of Sale for a Lot at French Jamestown) (1706) and "Plan de Jamestown" [Map of Jamestown] (1716), Charleston Museum Archives. A transcription and translation of the bill of sale can be found in Samuel Gaillard Stoney, "Jamestown on the Santee River," *HSSCT* 61 (1956): 30–34. The map is in Hirsch, *Huguenots,* 16. On the brief history of Jamestown, see also Henry A. M. Smith, "French James Town," *SCHGM* 9 (1908): 203–21.

43. This list, compiled by Thomas Gaillard from documents no longer extant, is in Smith, "French James Town," 224–25; Cooper and McCord, *Statutes at Large,* 283. A 1705 Craven County grant to Moyse Carion also located the land "north of Jamestown" (Records of the Secretary of the Province, Land Grants, Colonial Series [copies], vol. 38:528, SCDAH).

44. The 1716 map shows the town site located between Jean Gaillard's land and the river.

45. On the founding of Georgetown, see George C. Rogers Jr., *The History of Georgetown County, South Carolina* (Columbia: University of South Carolina Press, 1970), chap. 4.

46. Ravenel, *Liste,* 64.

47. Gene Waddell, *Charleston Architecture, 1670–1860* (Charleston, S.C.: Wyrick and Co., 2003), 1:38–40; Walter J. Fraser Jr., *Charleston! Charleston! The History of a Southern City* (Columbia: University of South Carolina Press, 1989), 7; Coclanis, *Shadow of a Dream,* 5, 179n8; Henry A. M. Smith, "Charleston—The Original Plan and Its Earliest Settlers," *SCHGM* 9 (1910): 12–27; James D. Kornwolf (with the assistance of Georgiana W. Kornwolf), *Architecture and Town Planning in Colonial North America,* 3 vols. (Baltimore and London: Johns Hopkins University Press, 2002), 2:851–58; Reps, *Making of Urban America,* 175–79.

48. "Proprietors to Governor and Council" (March 7, 1681), in Salley, *Papers,* 2 (1684–90):118; [Wilson], *Account of the Province of Carolina,* 7; Cohen and Yardeni, "Un Suisse en Caroline du Sud," 70.

49. Construction of the walls surrounding Charleston started in the mid-1690s and, after much delay, was completed in 1704. The fortifications were eventually removed in 1717 after the Yamassee War. Except for New Amsterdam (New York) earlier in the seventeenth century, Charleston was the only walled town in British North America. In the eyes of European immigrants, the existence of walls gave Charleston the status of town if we are to believe Gignilliat, who in his 1690 letter to his brother described Charleston as "the only town in this land, if we can call it so since it is not enclosed" (*la seule ville de ce pays, même si elle se peut appeler ainsi, car elle n'est point fermée*) (Waddell, *Charleston Architecture,* 1:38; Fraser, *Charleston!,* 16–23; Cohen and Yardeni, "Un Suisse en Caroline du Sud," 70 [quote]).

50. Waddell, *Charleston Architecture,* 1:52–53.

51. "Paul L'Escot to Turrettini" (Charleston, April 6, 1701), Archives Tronchin, 81, fol. 194 back, BPU.

52. "Paul L'Escot to Jean-Alphonse Turrettini" (London, May 25, 1719), ms. français, 488, fol. 16, BPU.

53. Waddell, *Charleston Architecture,* 1:37.

54. Coclanis, *Shadow of a Dream,* 113–14.

55. The original Grand Model is no longer extant, but three copies, two of which date from the seventeenth century, with a list of lots and grantees have survived. Henry Smith published a list of lot owners along with a reproduction of a copy made in 1725 and available at the South Carolina Historical Society, Charleston, but three Huguenots are missing (Nicolas de Longuemare, Antoine Boureau, and Noé Seré). See Charles Town Lot Book, 1678–98, 1717–56, SCDAH; Smith, "Charleston."

56. The exception is Noé Royer Sr., who obtained a first lot as early as March 1687 (Charles Town Lot Book, 1678–98, 1717–56, 22a, SCDAH).

57. Luck was an important factor in determining the location of a town lot at least, provided proprietary instructions stipulating that "freeholders shall draw a lott or chance where his land shall be" were followed (quoted in Pett-Conklin, "Cadastral Surveying," 94).

58. "In Charleston one can find inns for all prices & houses to rent for the price that one wishes to pay" (*Nouvelle Relation de la Caroline,* 11). "One finds accommodation in town houses but the best is to come with tents because one camps where one wishes at no cost and one is no less comfortable than in a house" ("Questions et Responses faites au sujet de la Caroline," ms. 1909, fol. 51 front, Bibliothèque Municipale de La Rochelle). Pierre Manigault was later remembered by his nineteenth-century descendants as taking boarders and lodgers into his Charleston house after his marriage to Judith (Giton) Royer (Crouse, "Manigault Family," 10–11).

59. Records of the Register of the Province (Conveyance Series), vol. D, 1696–1703, p. 13, SCDAH.

60. Salley and Olsberg, *Warrants for Lands,* 446, 464.

61. Records of the Register of the Province (Conveyance Series), vol. D, 1696–1703, p. 202, SCDAH; Salley and Olsberg, *Warrants for Lands,* 352.

62. Anne Vignau, widow of Charles Faucheraud, bought half of lot number 41 for thirty pounds "Carolina money" in 1691, and Marie Brigaud, widow of Moyse Brigaud and Pierre Couillandeau, successively, bought lot number 40 for fourteen pounds sterling in 1688. This does not mean, however, that they became neighbors, as lots with successive numbers were not necessarily contiguous. In this case, for example, lot number 40 was bordered by lots 63 and 72. See Records of the Register of the Province (Conveyances Series), vol. G, 1709–12, p. 151; vol. D, 1696–1703, pp. 142–43, SCDAH.

63. Land Grants, Colonial Series (copies), vol. 38:257, 274, 360, SCDAH.

64. Records of the Register of the Province (Conveyance Series), vol. D, 1696–1703, pp. 199, 201, 202, 203, SCDAH.

65. Locations of the town lots were determined by using the 1725 copy of the Grand Modell (Charles Town Lots Book, SCDAH).

66. "[Carolina Huguenot Census of 1699]," BPRO, CO 5/1258 (1699); Papers of the British Record Office Relating to South Carolina (Sainsbury copies), vol. 10 (1723):82, SCDAH; Coclanis, *Shadow of a Dream,* 114; Waddell, *Charleston Architecture,* 1:40; Bruce T. McCully, ed., "The Charleston Government Act of 1722: A Neglected Document," *SCHM* 83 (1982): 303–19.

67. Twenty-five out of twenty-eight were artisans and merchants, the other three being the pastors Élie Prioleau and Florent-Philippe Trouillart and the surgeon Jean Thomas. See Van Ruymbeke, "L'émigration huguenote," 2:664–65nn376, 377, 378.

68. A study of the published warrants shows that only ten Huguenots, to whom must be added the Swiss J. F. Gignilliat and perhaps Suzanne Horry, widow of Jacques Varin unless she sold her land before acquiring a lot, owned simultaneously (and in theory) a town lot and some land before 1711. The list is Antoine Boureau, Isaac Caillabeuf, Jacques de Bourdeaux, Pierre Girard, Daniel Huger, James LaRoche, Henry LeNoble, Jacques Dugué Sr., Noé Seré, and Jacques Postel. See Salley and Olsberg, *Warrants for Lands.*

69. One cannot expect to carry out a surgical analysis of proprietary land records, not only because they are not complete but also because the registering of land warrants and grants was done amidst considerable confusion and with an undeniable inconsistency. These statistics must therefore be interpreted as rough figures. One hundred and thirty-six identified Huguenots obtained at least one warrant and 117 a grant. Apart from the fact that the list of grantees is exclusive of refugees who each obtained only a town lot since it was drawn to calculate an average acreage, the fact that the second list is shorter is to be expected since for a variety of reasons settlers took up warrants but no grants. If we include the six Huguenots who acquired only town lots (Jonas Bonhost, Pierre Buretel, Nicolas de Longuemare Jr., Pierre LeChevalier, Paul Pépin, and Noé Royer), average acreages go down to 705 (warrants) and 925 (grants). The grant average is higher than for the warrants because grant records run until 1718, when the proprietors instructed Carolina officials to release grants no longer without their explicit permission, whereas no warrants are extant after 1711, and because it is not always possible to determine with certainty when the same grants were registered twice. Therefore, the grand total of land granted to the Huguenots is probably slightly inflated but is exclusive of land acquired through innumerable private transactions.

70. In looking at the 104 one-thousand-acre grants issued between 1670 and 1720, Richard Waterhouse found that Barbadians received 39 of them, English immigrants 35, and the Huguenots 30, or 28 percent. This is a high proportion since the French and Swiss settlers never represented more than 20 percent of the population, and it reflects the fact that they were particularly well treated by the proprietors. See Richard Waterhouse, *A New World Gentry: The Making of a Merchant and Planter Class in South Carolina, 1670–1770* (New York: Garland Publishing, Inc., 1989), 32.

71. Figures for warrants are 1,298,794 acres for 1,641 settlers and for grants 714,839 acres for 580 individuals (Duff, "Creating a Plantation Province," 10).

72. The calling to serve God and a church was not incompatible with acquisitive inclinations, as shown by Florent-Phillipe Trouillart, who received grants for 2,076 acres, and Élie Prioleau, who somewhat more modestly acquired 140 acres (Land Grants, Colonial Series [copies], vol. 38:237, 437, 484, 485; vol. 39:105, SCDAH).

73. "Inventory of Arnaud Bruneau de la Chabocière," Miscellaneous Records (Proprietary Series), vol. 1692–1700:226, SCDAH.

74. As early as 1682, in his promotional pamphlet, Samuel Wilson warned that "Such, who in this Country have seated themselves near great Marshes are subject to Agues" (Wilson, *Account of the Province of Carolina,* in Carroll, *Historical Collections of South Carolina,* 2:26).

75. Cohen and Yardeni, "Un Suisse en Caroline du Sud," 69–70.

76. Pett-Conklin, "Cadastral Surveying," 133–37; Duff, "Creating a Plantation Province," 17.

77. Only after 1697 do warrants contain specific locations more systematically. Out of 165 warrants (exclusive of town lots) delivered to Huguenots with named counties, 59 said Berkeley, 58 Craven, and 4 Colleton. This survey confirms, however, that few Huguenots settled in Dissenter-controlled Colleton County. See Salley and Olsberg, *Warrants for Lands.*

78. In 1710 Thomas Nairne, in his *Letter from South Carolina,* estimated the cost of establishing a rice plantation at one thousand pounds sterling and the necessary number of slaves at between thirty and forty (Jack P. Greene, ed., *Selling a New World: Two Colonial South Carolina Pamphlets* [Columbia: University of South Carolina Press, 1989], 63–65). More generally, on the formidable expenses inherent to setting up a lowcountry plantation, see Russell R. Menard, "Financing the Lowcountry Export Boom: Capital and Growth in Early South Carolina," *William and Mary Quarterly* 51 (1994): 659–67.

79. Salley, *Papers,* 1 (1663–84):69. In the same vein, Peter Colleton instructed Governor Richard Kyrle in 1684 to "give all manner of Incouragement" to one "Mr. Baille, a Frenchman who is skillfull in all those things of Merchandise the Soyle of Carolina is proper" and who "perfectly well understand silke, wine and oyle." Records do not show if this "Frenchman" ever settled in the lowcountry. See Salley, *Papers,* 1:306.

80. Thomas Ashe, "Carolina, or a Description of the Present State of That Country" (London, 1682), in *Early Narratives,* ed. Salley, 143.

81. Ibid., 143–44.

82. Cohen and Yardeni, "Un Suisse en Caroline du Sud," 68; Stoney, "Nicholas de Longuemare," 60. The original is deposited at the Charleston Museum but is too brittle for consultation (acquisition #1953.37, Charleston Museum Archives).

83. "Letter of Louis Thibou," in Golden, *Huguenot Connection,* 140–41; Cohen and Yardeni, "Un Suisse en Caroline du Sud," 68.

84. Salley, *Papers,* 1 (1663–84):238; 3 (1691–97):150 (quote).

85. "Je ferais bien vite de bonnes affaires en ce païs, parce que le vin y est si cher" ("Letter of Louis Thibou" [September 20, 1683], back, South Caroliniana Library, Columbia, S.C.).

86. In 1690 the proprietors even agreed to quitrents in silk (Clowse, *Economic Beginnings,* 78).

87. "Letter of Louis Thibou," back, South Caroliniana Library, Columbia, S.C.; Cohen and Yardeni, "Un Suisse en Caroline du Sud," 70.

88. Salley, *Papers,* 4 (1698–1700):117; 5 (1701–10):204–5.

89. Stoney, "Nicholas de Longuemare," 63–69.

90. Jean Aunant is described as a silk throwster—that is, an artisan who twisted the raw fiber wound from cocoons into threads—in the 1697 Act of Naturalization. See Cooper and McCord, *Statutes at Large,* 2:132; Gourdin, "Madeleine Chardon," 88–89. Interestingly, in 1708 De Longuemare married his fellow refugee from Normandy Marie Soyer, Jean Aunant's widow. [The root of the Soyer family name is the French word for silk, *soie.*] Marie's 1712 will is at the Charleston Museum.

91. Charles Fromaget and Noé Royer Sr. and Jr were also textile artisans from Tours, which was an important silk producing center, but Carolina records do not show if they specifically had any training in silk weaving.

92. The dream of having Huguenots make wine and silk in South Carolina endured through the eighteenth century, as attested by Jean-Louis Gibert's 1763 memorial to the lords of the treasury, which mentioned vines and mulberry trees, and his plan to give each Hillsborough (New Bordeaux) settler acres of vineyards ("Memorial of Pastor Jean-Louis Gibert to the Lords of the Treasury, Read in Council, 6 July, 1763," *HSSCT* 47 [1942]: 15; Gibert, *Pierre Gibert,* 31–33).

93. "Tous les ans l'on fait quelque nouvelle découverte de ce que peut rapporter le pays" (Cohen and Yardeni, "Un Suisse en Caroline du Sud," 69).

94. Alexander Moore, "Daniel Axtell's Account Book and the Economy of Early South Carolina," *SCHM* 95 (1994): 281–301.

95. In "Responses à vingt et quatre Questions touchant la Carolline," a steer is estimated between five and seven pounds sterling, a cow between five and six pounds, a sheep at fifteen shillings, and a pig between twenty and forty shillings (*Suite de la Description de la Carolline,* 13–14 [question 8]).

96. Salley, *Papers,* 5 (1701–10):437–38.

97. This is translated in the French pamphlets as "un Búuf ne revient pas plus à son Maitre, qu'une Poule en Angleterre" ([Wilson], *Account of the Province of Carolina,* 29; "Description de la Carolline," 17–18).

98. The author of *Description de la Carolline* even mentioned herds "of seven or eight hundred heads" See *Description de la Carolline,* 16; John S. Otto, "Livestock-Raising in Early South Carolina, 1670–1700: Prelude to the Rice Plantation Economy," *Agricultural History* 61 (1987): 13–24; Wood, *Black Majority,* 28–34.

99. "Letter of Louis Thibou," in Golden, *Huguenot Connection,* 141. The technique of literally baiting cows back home at night by keeping calves penned in soon appeared in promotional pamphlets across the Atlantic. See, for example, *Nouvelle Relation de la Caroline,* 28–29.

100. Register of the Province (Conveyance Series), vol. A, 1682–93:257, SCDAH; Register of the Province (Conveyance Series), vol. D, 1696–1703:87, SCDAH.

101. "Inventory of Joseph Marbœuf" (1712), Miscellaneous Records (Proprietary Series), vol. 1711–17:95, SCDAH. [*Bœuf* is the French word for a steer.] John Otto listed fourteen seventeenth-century inventories (1680–1700) of cattle raisers with the number of heads of cattle. Only four of them exceeded one hundred heads. This list shows a mean average of seventy-three, for a median size of forty-two. See Otto, "Livestock-Raising," 17.

102. Cohen and Yardeni, "Un Suisse en Caroline du Sud," 67.

103. Cooper and McCord, *Statutes at Large,* 2:v; "The ear marks for cattle & hogs which is a Crop in the left ear & horses branded upon the left shoulder & cattle upon the left buttock," in "A Book for Recordeing of Cattle Markes & others," Miscellaneous Records (Proprietary Series), vol. 1709–25:(back of the volume/unpag.), SCDAH.

104. Cooper and McCord, *Statutes at Large,* 2:106–7; Otto, "Livestock-Raising," 20.

105. Among these Huguenots there were five merchants, three weavers, two shipwrights, a goldsmith, a gunsmith, a surgeon, and a pastor ("A Book for Recordeing of Cattle Markes & others . . . ," Miscellaneous Records [Proprietary Series], vol. 1709–25:[back of the volume/unpag.], SCDAH). These marks, along with the short registration that accompanies them, have been published by Salley, but nothing replaces a look at the original recording to see their—sometimes artistic—designs (Salley, "Stock Marks," 125–31, 224–28).

106. Huguenots with fleurs-de-lis on their cattle were Isaac Mazyck, Francis Paget, Jean Juin, Pierre Dutartre, and Louis Dutarque. Contrary to what Butler inferred, I do not think that fleurs-de-lis branded on cows' buttocks were signs of disrespect toward Louis XIV and the French monarchy but rather marks, so to speak, of the owners' attachment to their French identity (Butler, *Huguenots in America,* 99). In 1703 the surgeon Jean Thomas and Jacques Dubose had the cattle mark with their surnames' initials (T. D.) recorded, implying that they jointly owned cattle ("A Book for Recordeing of Cattle Markes & others," Miscellaneous Records [Proprietary Series], vol. 1709–25:[back of the volume/unpag.], SCDAH).

107. Joel W. Martin, "Southeastern Indians and the English Trade in Skins and Slaves," in *The Forgotten Centuries: Indians and Europeans in the American South, 1521–1704,* ed. Charles Hudson and Carmen C. Tesser (Athens: University of Georgia Press, 1994), 309–13; Eirlys M. Barker, "'Much Blood and Treasure': South Carolina's Indian Traders, 1670–1755" (Ph.D. diss., College of William and Mary, 1993), 65–71; Kathryn E. Holland Braund, *Deerskins & Duffels: The Creek Indian Trade with Anglo-America, 1685–1815* (Lincoln: University of Nebraska Press, 1993), 28–39. For a global survey of Carolina Indian trade in the geopolitical context of various European and Indian nations in the colonial Southeast, see Alan Gallay, *Indian Slavery: The Rise of the English Empire in the American South, 1670–1717* (Cambridge, Mass.: Harvard University Press, 2002).

108. W. L. McDowell Jr., ed., *Journals of the Commissioners of the Indian Trade (September 20, 1710–August 29, 1718)* (Columbia: South Carolina Department of Archives and History, 1955), preface:viii–x; Philip M. Brown, "Early Indian Trade in the Development of South Carolina: Politics, Economics, and Social Mobility during the Proprietary Period, 1670–1719," *SCHM* 76 (1975): 118–23; William R. Snell, "Indian Slavery in Colonial South Carolina, 1671–1795" (Ph.D. diss., University of Alabama, 1972), 68–80; Clowse, *Economic Beginnings,* 162–63; Gallay, *Indian Slavery,* 208–12.

109. For essays on the origins of the Yamassee War, see Richard L. Haan, "The 'Trade Do's Not Flourish as Formerly': The Ecological Origins of the Yamassee War," *Ethnohistory* 28 (1981): 341–58; William L. Ramsey, "'Something Cloudy in Their Looks': The Origins of the Yamassee War Reconsidered," *Journal of American History* 90 (2003): 44–75; Gallay, *Indian Slavery,* 315–27. Whereas traditional interpretations emphasized English traders' misconducts as the primary cause for the war, Ramsey identifies four causes: Anglo-native gender relations, native debts to traders, the changing demands of an expanding market, and most important, the breakdown of diplomacy.

110. Barker, "Much Blood and Treasure," 92–103; Clowse, *Economic Beginnings,* 163–64. For an excellent description of the different people involved in this trade, as well as its internal hierarchy, see Eirlys M. Barker, "Indian Traders, Charles Town and London's Vital Link to the Interior of North America, 1717–1755," in *Money, Trade, and Power,* ed. Greene et al., 141–65.

111. "Letter of Louis Thibou," in Golden, *Huguenot Connection,* 142–43.

112. Lawson, *New Voyage,* 14.

113. The saddler John Laurens received twenty-eight pounds sterling for "fixing and repairing ten Pack-Saddles" in November 1717, and in May 1718 the goldsmith Salomon Legaré was given about nineteen pounds sterling "for stabling horses, and for fodder for them, as also for Hire of a Periaugoe 51 days, in the service of the said Trade." A periauger, from the Spanish *piragua,* an adaptation of a Carib word, was a long and relatively wide dugout canoe designed to transport people and goods along the lowcountry rivers. The French used the equivalent term of *pirogue.* See McDowell, *Journals,* 228, 274; Richard M. Lederer Jr., *Colonial American English, a Glossary* (Essex, Conn.: A Verbatim Book, 1985), 169.

114. McDowell, *Journals,* 70, 83.

115. Ibid., 80.

116. Ibid., preface:ix–x.

117. Ibid., 115–16.

118. The delivery amounts and dates are: fifty-six on November 26, 1716; thirty-nine in December 1716; fifty on May 9 and twenty-five on May 30, 1717; and fifty-four on September 2, 1717 (ibid., 132, 178, 184, 203). The value was calculated on the basis of the commission set price of five shillings for a raw buckskin and must therefore be regarded as a maximum.

119. McDowell, *Journals,* 170.

120. Ibid., 119, 132, 170.

121. Gaillard drew his will on July, 5, 1718, and his widow, Elisabeth (Skrine) Gaillard, appeared before the Court of Common Pleas as "sole executrix of the last will and testament of Bartholomew Gaillard" in March 1719. See Records of the Auditor General, Memorials (Copy Series), vol. 7 (1753–63):432–33, SCDAH; Records of the Court of Common Pleas, Judgment Rolls, box 12, folder F,173A–182A, case number 181A, SCDAH; Lesser, *South Carolina Begins,* 344.

122. Initially, as Barker explained, traders relied on native porters, called burtherners or burdeners, instead of packhorses (Barker, "Much Blood and Treasure," 112–13).

123. On April 11, 1717, St. Julien and Ravenel received eighty-one pounds sterling for "providing provisions to Indians imployed in the Indian Trade"; on June 1, 1717, St. Julien was offered "10 sh. per Bushel of corn . . . for Indian Burdeners"; on March 21, 1718, St. Julien was compensated for furnishing rice to burdeners and for the grazing of packhorses (McDowell, *Journals,* 173, 185, 260, 278).

124. St. Julien argued to the commission that these Indians were Euchees and therefore asked "why the prisoners should not be slaves," but he was nonetheless forced to release them (McDowell, *Journals,* 49, 51, 235).

125. McDowell, *Journals,* 305, 319. Pierre de St. Julien wrote his will on June 6, 1718, and it was probated sometime in 1719 (Miscellaneous Records [Proprietary Series], vol. 1719–21:19–24, SCDAH). St. Julien was not the only Huguenot to sit or to be offered a seat on the commission. Jean Guérard was a commissioner from September 1710 until his death in June 1714, and Benjamin Godin was appointed in Guérard's stead but "refused to take the oath to qualify himself as a commissioner." See McDowell, *Journals,* 3, 58, 59, 60 (quote); Miscellaneous Records (Proprietary Series), vol. 1711–19:49 (J. Guérard's will), SCDAH.

126. James M. Clifton, "The Rice Industry in Colonial America," *Agricultural History* 55 (1981): 266–75; Henry C. Dethloff, *A History of the American Rice Industry, 1685–1985* (College Station: Texas A&M University Press, 1988), 6–9; Judith A. Carney, *Black Rice: The African Origins of Rice Cultivation in the Americas* (Cambridge, Mass.: Harvard University Press, 2001), 78–98,

142–47; Carney, "Rice Milling, Gender and Slave Labour in Colonial South Carolina," *Past and Present* 153 (1996): 111–14; Richard D. Porcher, "Rice Culture in South Carolina: A Brief History, the Role of the Huguenots, and Preservation of Its Legacy," *HSSCT* 92 (1987): 1–7.

127. Rice milling is a particularly delicate and arduous task since the grain must be hulled without being damaged, while in the case of wheat, for example, the grain is reduced to powder (Carney, "Rice Milling," 116–17).

128. Cohen and Yardeni, "Un Suisse en Caroline du Sud," 67, 70.

129. This device could have been simply a pestle attached to the limb of a tree that would swing back after each stroke. Contrary to what Hirsch contended, it is doubtful that the "Guerrard machine . . . revolutionized" rice husking. See Cooper and McCord, *Statutes at Large,* 2:63 (quote); Clifton, "Rice Industry," 272–73; Porcher, "Rice Culture," 10; Hirsch, *Huguenots,* 211.

130. "L'été fort pluvieux fera que la récolte ne sera pas si bonne ni si abondante tems [tant] pour le ris que le blé" ("Letter from Isaac Mazyck to his son Isaac" [July 12, 1716], D. E. H. Smith Papers, 11/389/3, South Carolina Historical Society, Charleston). Pierre Couillandeau's and Jean Pétineau's inventories also list bushels of rice (Miscellaneous Records [Interregnum Series], vol. C, 1722–24:21–23 [P. Couillandeau]; vol. D, 1724–25:56–57 [J. Pétineau]; vol. E, 1726–27:638–39 [J. LeGrand], SCDAH). Jacques LeGrand de Lomboy, who wrote his will in French, was Isaac's brother.

131. Miscellaneous Records (Proprietary Series), vol. 1675–95:157, SCDAH. This agreement has also been published; see Salley, "Documents Concerning Huguenots," 71–72.

132. Marvilleau died sometime before November 9, 1686, when his estate was appraised ("Will of Paul Bruneau" [November 14, 1709], Miscellaneous Records [Proprietary Series], vol. 1711–14:65; vol. 1675–95:152, SCDAH). The blacksmith may have actually been an anchor smith since the original agreement mentioned that the partners were "oblieged to pass an Act of Society with Mr. Charles Fouchereau." Foucheraud, from Port-aux-Barques, Saintonge, was an anchor smith, and his son, Gédéon, a gunsmith (Ravenel, *Liste,* 51 [#45]). Foucheraud was most likely dead by December 1691, when his widow, Anne Vignaud, bought a town lot.

133. "Inventory of Arnaud Bruneau de la Chabocière," Miscellaneous Records (Proprietary Series), vol. 1692–1700:224–25, SCDAH.

134. Records of the Register of the Province (Conveyance Series), vol. 1717–19:323, SCDAH; Records of the Court of Common Pleas, Judgment Rolls, box 13 (1719), folder 44A-52A, case 50A, SCDAH.

135. Wilson, *Account of the Province of Carolina,* in Carroll, *Historical Collections of South Carolina,* 24.

136. "Letter of Louis Thibou," in Golden, *Huguenot Connection,* 144.

137. *Description de la CAROLLINE,* 23–24. This passage is not in Wilson's pamphlet. See *Suite de la Description de la Carolline,* 37.

138. Beyond the improbability of such a trade, this project shows the unrealistic perception of the North American continent still prevalent in the minds of colonial entrepreneurs since Vera Cruz is over forty-five hundred miles away from Charleston ("Questions et Responses faites au sujet de la Caroline," fol. 54 back).

139. *Nouvelle Relation de la Caroline,* 31.

140. " Paul L'Escot to Turrettini" (Charleston, March 1, 1703), Archives Tronchin, 81, fol. 201, BPU (copy in the hands of Louis Tronchin).

141. R. C. Nash, "The Organization of Trade and Finance in the Atlantic Economy: Britain and South Carolina, 1670–1775," in *Money, Trade, and Power,* ed. Greene et al., 75–76.

142. Wood, *Black Majority,* 34.

143. McCusker and Menard, *Economy of British America,* 171.

144. "Questions et Responses faites au sujet de la Caroline," fol.54 back, fol. 55.

145. Stuart O. Stumpf, "The Merchants of Colonial Charleston, 1680–1756" (Ph.D. diss., Michigan State University, 1971), 23–24.

146. Russell R. Menard, "Economic and Social Development of the South," in *Cambridge Economic History of the United States,* vol. 1, *Colonial Era,* ed. Engerman and Gallman, 273–77; McCusker and Menard, *Economy of British America,* 173–80; Marc Egnal, *New World Economies: The Growth of the Thirteen Colonies and Early Canada* (New York: Oxford University Press, 1998), "Lower South," 99–117; R. C. Nash, "South Carolina and the Atlantic Economy in the Late Seventeenth and Eighteenth Centuries," *Economic History Review* 45 (1992): 677–80; Clowse, *Economic Beginnings,* 256–57, table 3; Dethloff, *History of the American Rice Industry,* p. 10, table 1. Coclanis has calculated that the annual mean value (in pounds sterling) of South Carolina exports multiplied fivefold from the 1698–1702 period to the 1718–1722 period and tenfold between 1698–1702 and 1728–1732 (Coclanis, *Shadow of a Dream,* 74, tables 3–9).

147. It needs to be said, though, that refugees sometimes appeared as merchants in the records but were not merchants strictly speaking. A case in point is the minister Étienne Dusout, who despite his pastoral training was recorded as a merchant when he acquired a town lot for the building of Charleston's first French Church in December 1686. This situation is evocative of Pastor Jaques Fontaine, who once in England engaged in an active grain and wine trade with France. Similarly, Gignilliat, who was for all practical purposes a Santee planter, nonetheless labeled himself a merchant in his will. See "Letter from Ester Dubourdieu, Wife of Louis Fleury, to Her Brother Dubourdieu at Vitré," in Lart, "Roads of Destiny," 68; Records of the Register of the Province (Conveyance Series), vol. E., 1705–8:250–53, SCDAH; Gourdin, "Madeleine Chardon," 103n207; Fontaine, *Memoirs,* 123–29. An abstract of J. F. Gignilliat's no-longer-extant will can be found in Richard Yeadon, "The Marion Family," *Southern and Western Magazine and Review* (1845): 281.

148. "Letter of Louis Thibou," front; Yves Guéneau, "Les protestants dans le colloque de Sancerre de 1598 à 1685," *Cahiers d'archéologie et d'histoire du Berry* 30/31 (1972): 84.

149. "Will of Cézar Mozé" (June 20, 1687), Miscellaneous Records (Proprietary Series), vol. 1675–95:282, SCDAH.

150. Pierre also owned an estate in the West Indies (presumably in Saint Thomas) and had contacts in Jamaica. Louis Perdriau, who intended to leave Carolina for New York City to join their cousin Étienne, also had first settled in Carolina, and presumably because of Pierre's recent death, he remarried and died in the lowcountry, where their estates were appraised in January 1693 and January 1695, respectively. See Miscellaneous Records (Proprietary Series), vol. 1692–1700:18, 24–25, 181–82, 213, SCDAH; Alfred V. Wittenmeyer, ed., *Registers of the Births, Marriages, and Deaths of the 'Eglise Françoise à la Nouvelle-York' from 1688 to 1804,* Collections of the Huguenot Society of America, vol. 1 (New York: Huguenot Society of America, 1886), 7, 45–48.

151. Childs, "Exports from Charles Town, 1690," 30–34.

152. R. C. Nash, "Huguenot Merchants and the Development of South Carolina's Slave-Plantation and Atlantic Trading Economy, 1680–1775," in *Memory and Identity,* ed. Van Ruymbeke and Sparks, 216.

153. Cooper and McCord, *Statutes at Large,* 2:132; R. C. Nash, "Trade and Business in Eighteenth-Century South Carolina: The Career of John Guerard, Merchant and Planter," *SCHM* 96 (1995): 6–9; Crouse, "Manigault Family," 4–14.

154. In November 1686 Jacques Boyd and the planter Paul Bruneau received interests on the cargo of the *Endeavour* owned by the Quaker merchant Thomas Bolton, and in August 1711 Isaac

Mazyck purchased one fifth of the *Rebecca and Mary* of which Jacob Satur also owned shares. Before 1697, of course, Huguenots as alien merchants could not own ships. This type of commercial association, meant to be temporary and flexible, was known in France as *société par intéressement* and was particularly prevalent in La Rochelle in the slave trade. See Miscellaneous Records (Proprietary Series), vol. 1675–95:184 (J. Boyd), vol. 1711–17:9 (I. Mazyck), SCDAH; Jean-Michel Deveau, *La traite rochelaise* (Paris: Éditions Karthala, 1990), 25–26.

155. In his excellent study of Charleston Huguenot merchants from the 1680s to the 1760s, R. C. Nash placed in the "first-generation merchants" individuals such as Benjamin Godin or Jacob Satur with Isaac Mazyck or Pierre Buretel. Although these merchants were active during part of the period considered (i.e., 1690–1738), they were not all of the same generation. Pierre Buretel had a child born in France in 1673, whereas Benjamin Godin was born in 1674. As for James Du Poids d'Or (literally "of one's weight in gold"), he was actually the son of Isaac Mazyck but had adopted this unusual and fanciful name probably out of provocation toward Isaac, who refused to recognize him or let him bear his surname. See Nash, "Huguenot Merchants," 213, table 1; Gourdin, "Madeleine Chardon," 102n205; "James Mazyck v. Isaac Mazyck" (January 1718), Records of the Court of Common Pleas, Judgment Rolls, box 12 (1718–19), case 124A, SCDAH.

156. In June 1714 Jacob Satur, along with Samuel and Joseph Wragg, was recorded as being "agent and factor" for John Crowley of London (Moore, *Abstracts of Records,* 281). On the Satur familial background in southwestern France, see Robert Garrisson, "Un pasteur montalbanais au temps du Refuge, Thomas Satur," *BSHPF* 85 (1936): 228–40.

157. Wittenmeyer, *Registers,* 4, 36, 45; Bosher, "Huguenot Merchants," 83–87. These Carolina merchants were well integrated into what John Bosher has aptly described as a mercantile Protestant international in reference to Hebert Lüthy's phrase "l'internationale protestante," which he first used in his work on Huguenot banking networks following the Revocation (H. Lüthy, *La banque protestante en France de la révocation de l'Edit de Nantes à la Révolution,* 2 vols. [Paris, 1959–61]). To complement Bosher's article, see David Ormrod, "The Atlantic Economy and the 'Protestant Capitalist International,' 1651–1775," *Historical Research* 66 (1993): 197–208.

158. As Nash rightly pointed out, in colonial South Carolina as a rule merchants became planters, not vice-versa (Nash, "Organization of Trade," 95–96).

159. "Will of Benjamin Godin" (November 26, 1747), Civil Works Administration typescripts, vol. 1747–52:85–88, South Carolina Room, Charleston County Library, Charleston, S.C.; "Godin, Benjamin," in Edgar, *Biographical Directory,* 2:283–84; Nash, "Huguenot Merchants," 217–18; Stumpf, "Merchants," 74–76.

160. Nash, "Trade and Business," 8–9; Edgar, *Biographical Directory,* 2:296–98.

161. Salley and Olsberg, *Warrants for Lands,* 442, 506, 509. A total of six Huguenots arrived in Carolina with slaves: Timothy Bellamy (eight slaves), François Blanchard (four), Henry LeNoble (five), Gabriel Manigault (one), Benjamin Marion (two), and Étienne Perdriau (one). Three of them (Bellamy, Blanchard, and Perdriau) most likely hailed from the Caribbean, but the others, especially Gabriel Manigault and Benjamin Marion, whose flights from western France are documented, must have bought slaves along the way, presumably in the West Indies.

162. Butler, *Huguenots in America,* 161–68; Goodfriend, *Before the Melting Pot,* 126–32; Cohen, "Elias Neau," 7–27; Poton and Van Ruymbeke, "Élie Neau," 325–26; Frank J. Klingberg, *Anglican Humanitarianism in Colonial New York* (Philadelphia: Church Historical Society, 1940).

163. On the general negative perception of black slaves by the French, see William B. Cohen, *The French Encounter with Africans: White Response to Blacks, 1530–1880* (Bloomington: Indiana University Press, 1980), 13–34.

164. Klingberg, *Carolina Chronicle of Le Jau,* 26; Edgar L. Pennington, "The Reverend Francis Le Jau's Work among Indians and Negro Slaves," *Journal of Southern History* 1 (1935): 442–58.

165. The fact that in the 1760s a clergyman estimated that there were about five hundred black Christians in South Carolina, or barely 1 percent of the slave population, is an acute testimony to the overall failure of the churches regarding the Christianization of the slaves (Philip D. Morgan, *Slave Counterpoint: Black Culture in the Eighteenth-Century Chesapeake and Lowcountry* [Chapel Hill: University of North Carolina Press, 1998], 422).

166. Whether in New York or South Carolina, planters feared that baptizing and educating slaves in the Christian religion would lead them to question their enslavement and eventually rebel. Neau's school was partly blamed for the 1712 slave rebellion in New York City because two of the rebels attended it. Other masters also did not particularly want their slaves to have access to salvation. In South Carolina, LeJau reported that a planter's wife asked him one day, "Is it Possible that any of my slaves could go to Heaven, & must I see them there?," which the missionary thought of as "some strange reasoning." As Winthrop Jordan wrote, "S.P.G. missionaries achieved some success in baptizing Negroes but very little in raising masters' opinions of their slaves." Interestingly, the Carolina proprietors specifically provided a legal framework for the Christianization of slaves in the 1682 version of their Fundamental Constitutions, while conceding, in partly paraphrasing Saint Paul, that "no slave shall thereby be Exempted from that Civil dominion his master has over him, but be in all other things in the same State and condition he was in before." In France Catholic clergymen even argued that slavery was a means to Christianize Africans. See Cohen, "Elias Neau," 21; Klingberg, *Carolina Chronicle of Le Jau,* 102; Wood, *Black Majority,* 133–36; Winthrop D. Jordan, *White over Black: American Attitudes toward the Negro, 1550–1812* (1968; New York: W. W. Norton & Company, 1977), 208; Parker, *North Carolina Charters,* 150 (version of July 21, 1669, article 98); Wayne Glausser, "Three Approaches to Locke and the Slave Trade," *Journal of the History of Ideas* 51 (1990): 203–4; David Brion Davis, *The Problem of Slavery in Western Culture* (Ithaca: Cornell University Press, 1966), 213–18, Cohen, *French Encounter with Africans,* 42–43.

167. "L'Escot to Turrettini" (April 6, 1701), fol. 194 back, fol. 201 front.

168. Miscellaneous Records (Proprietary Series), vol. 1704–9:24, SCDAH.

169. Wood, *Black Majority,* 137.

170. Similarly, Bishop William Fleetwood, in his sermon on the Christianization of slaves, advocated "humane" treatment on the part of masters (Jean Aymon, *Tous les synodes nationaux,* 565; Klingberg, *Chronicle of Le Jau,* 7–8). Augustine expressed the opinion that slaves should be obedient and masters kindly (Lester B. Scherer, *Slavery and the Churches in Early America, 1619–1819* [Grand Rapids: William B. Eerdmans, 1975], 15–17).

171. "Le Jau to Society" (June 30, 1707), in Klingberg, *Carolina Chronicle of Le Jau,* 26; "L'Escot to Turrettini" (March 1, 1703), fol. 201 front.

172. As David Brion Davis put it, "The Quaker commitment to bear collective testimony against slavery came surprisingly late" (David Brion Davis, *The Problem of Slavery in the Age of Revolution, 1770–1823* [Ithaca: Cornell University Press, 1975], 212). See also Scherer, *Slavery,* 29–45; Jordan, *White over Black,* 198–212. On the specific pro- and antislavery positions among the Pennsylvania Quakers, see Jean R. Soderlund, *Quakers and Slavery: A Divided Spirit* (Princeton: Princeton University Press, 1985).

173. Based on the biblical injunction to "do unto others as you would have them do unto you" (Luke 6:31), the 1688 Germantown petition is the earliest known antislavery tract of the Pennsylvania Quakers. Later, in 1710 the Charleston Baptist congregation, which was divided and concerned over the fact that one of them had castrated a captured runaway slave, following a 1712

law, wrote their brethren in England for advice. The answer, in the name of peace and respect of the law, was cautious and conservative. The elders thought that "the Master, Acting according to the Law of your Province, in gelding his Slave, hath not committed any Crime, to give any Offence to Any Member to break Communion with him in the Church" (William G. McLaughlin and Winthrop D. Jordan, "Baptists Face the Barbarities of Slavery in 1710," *Journal of Southern History* 29 [1963]: 501).

174. Robert K. Ackerman, "Colonial Land Policies and the Slave Problem," *Proceedings of the South Carolina Historical Association* (1965): 28–35.

175. Fundamental Constitutions (July 21, 1669), version of March 1, 1670, article 101. This clause appeared verbatim in successive versions except that of August 17, 1682, which nonetheless mentioned slaves in another article. See Parker, *North Carolina Charters,* 151; Wood, *Black Majority,* 16–20. For an interesting historiographical discussion on Locke and slavery, see Glausser, "Three Approaches to Locke," 199–216.

176. This quote, appearing in a verbatim translation in *Description de la Carolline,* is from Wilson's *Account of the Province of Carolina.* In *Questions et Responses faites au sujet de la Caroline,* the author says that "the Climate is very good for them" ("Le climat leur est fort bon"). Prices are twenty pounds sterling in *Description de la Carolline,* between twenty and twenty-five pounds sterling in *Questions et Responses,* and twenty pounds sterling in *Suite de la Description.* See Wilson, *Account of the Province of Carolina,* in Carroll, *Historical Collections,* 2:30–31; *Description de la Carolline,* 10; *Suite de la Description de la Carolline,* 15; "Responses et Questions," fol. 55 front.

177. *Suite de la Description de la Carolline,* 15. In *Description de la CAROLLINE,* it is said that "all settlers of means have an Indian hunter for a pound sterling a year" (14). See also "Questions et Responses faites au sujet de la Caroline," fol. 54 front.

178. "Letter of Louis Thibou," in Golden, *Huguenot Connection,* 141.

179. Gallay gives 24,000–32,200 and 51,000 as low and high estimates of the number of south-eastern native victims of the British slave trade. He also remarks that until 1715 and except for 1714, more Indian slaves were exported out of Charleston than African slaves were imported. See Gallay, *Indian Slavery,* 299 and table 2.

180. William L. Ramsey, "'All & Singular the Slaves': A Demographic Profile of Indian Slavery in Colonial South Carolina," in *Money, Trade, and Power,* ed. Greene et al., 166; Wood, *Black Majority,* 144. An adult Indian slave cost between ten and thirty pounds sterling, or between sixty and two hundred deerskins (Snell, "Indian Slavery," 101, 150–52). See also William L. Ramsey, "A Coat for 'Indian Cuffy': Mapping the Boundary between Freedom and Slavery in Colonial South Carolina," *SCHM* 103 (2002): 48–66.

181. Ira Berlin, *Many Thousands Gone: The First Two Centuries of Slavery in North America* (Cambridge, Mass.: Harvard University Press, 1998), 8–9, 65–71 (quote 8).

182. Statistics blatantly show how comparatively unattractive South Carolina was to servants. David Galenson calculated that out of 20,657 servants who left the British Isles for the colonies in the seventeenth century, only 95 went to South Carolina. Similarly, Russell Menard has calculated that out of the 2,000 who left Bristol between 1683 and 1686, 32 settled in the lowcountry. See David W. Galenson, *White Servitude in Colonial America: An Economic Analysis* (Cambridge, Mass.: Cambridge University Press, 1981), 86; Russell R. Menard, "The Africanization of the Lowcountry Labor Force, 1670–1730," in *Race and Family in the Colonial South,* ed. Winthrop D. Jordan and Sheila L. Skemp (Jackson: University Press of Mississippi, 1987), 88. For a nuanced view on this cost approach, see David Eltis, *The Rise of African Slavery in the Americas* (Cambridge: Cambridge University Press, 2000), 62–84.

183. Menard, "Africanization," 85–87.

184. Wood, *Black Majority*, 59–62; Daniel C. Littlefield, *Rice and Slaves: Ethnicity and the Slave Trade in Colonial South Carolina* (Urbana and Chicago: University of Illinois Press, 1991), 74–114. Beyond rice cultivation, for an overall view on African expertise brought by slaves to the low-country, see Peter H. Wood, "'It Was a Negro Taught Them': A New Look at African Labor in Early South Carolina," *Journal of Asian and African Studies* 9 (1974): 160–79.

185. Menard, "Africanization, 107, table 5; McCusker and Menard, *Economy of British America,* 181; Wood, *Black Majority,* 151, table 3; David Eltis, "The British Transatlantic Slave Trade before 1714: Annual Estimates of Volume and Direction," in *The Lesser Antilles in the Age of European Expansion,* ed. Robert L. Paquette and Stanley L. Engerman (Gainesville: University Presses of Florida, 1996), 182–205; Eltis, "The Volume and Structure of the Transatlantic Slave Trade: A Reassessment," in "New Perspectives on the Transatlantic Slave Trade," special issue, *William and Mary Quarterly* 58 (2001): 17–46; David Richardson, "The British Empire and the Atlantic Slave Trade, 1660–1807," in *Oxford History of the British Empire,* ed. Roger, vol. 2, *The Eighteenth Century,* ed. P. J. Marshall, 440–44, 455–57.

186. Wood, *Black Majority,* 132 (quote), 144, table 1; Peter H. Wood, "The Changing Population of the Colonial South: An Overview by Race and Region, 1685–1790," in *Powhatan's Mantle,* ed. Wood et al., 38, table 1, 46–47; "L'Escot to Turrettini" (March 1, 1703), Archives Tronchin, 81, fol. 201 front, BPU.

187. Peter Kolchin, *American Slavery, 1619–1877* (New York: Hill & Wang, 1993), 240, table 1. Coclanis calculated a different proportion of 65 percent, but both figures are extremely high (Coclanis, *Shadow of a Dream,* 66, table 3.3).

188. Wood, *Black Majority,* xiv.

189. From 1707 to 1793 Nantes carried the largest share of the French slave trade with 43 percent of the expeditions, followed by La Rochelle with 13 percent and Bordeaux and Le Havre with 12 percent each. In the seventeenth century, however, slave ships were only occasionally seen in the La Rochelle harbor. See Deveau, *Traite rochelaise,* 8, 15–17.

190. A good example is Salomon Brémar, a weaver from Picardy who arrived in Charleston in 1680 as one of the servants of Jacob Guérard. During his forty-one years in the lowcountry, Brémar enjoyed a prosperity unequaled among other servants and many of the free Huguenot migrants. Between 1697 and 1709 he acquired 2,310 acres, whereas his freedom dues only included 50 acres, and in 1717 he gave his son and daughter five slaves that he had bought ("quatre négresses et un Nègre qui sont les derniers que j'ay acheté"). See Salley and Olsberg, *Warrants for Lands,* 245 (arrival), 577, 601, 610, 632, 642, 653; Miscellaneous Records (Proprietary Series), vol. 1716–21:120 (quote), SCDAH; Memorials, book 3, 1733–39, p. 59, SCDAH; Lesser, *South Carolina Begins,* 324. For statistics about Huguenot slave ownership beyond our period, see Butler, *Huguenots in America,* 121–22.

191. Extant inventories for proprietary South Carolina are rare. Coclanis found sixty-two of them for the entire period (1670–1721). Consequently, although less useful from a statistical perspective, I have also taken wills into account. See Coclanis, *Shadow of a Dream,* 79. Except for that of Marie De Longuemare (Charleston Museum Archives), René Ravenel (South Carolina Historical Society, Charleston), and François Macaire (ed. Lothrop Withington and published in *SCHGM* 4 [1903]: 225–26), all these inventories and testaments are located in the probate records at the SCDAH. For specific references, see Van Ruymbeke, "L'émigration huguenote," 2:632n255, 634n257, 635n259.

192. No Huguenot inventories have survived for the period 1700–1710. If we only take inventories into account for the period 1710–30, the average number of slaves jumps from 4.5 to 12.

193. Butler, *Huguenots in America,* 122. After 1732 inventories, filed separately, are more numerous and more complete.

194. Cohen and Yardeni, "Un Suisse en Caroline du Sud," 66; Salley, *Journals of the Grand Council, 1692,* 31. Most Huguenots who owned Indian slaves can be traced in Snell's list of owners, gathered essentially from probate records, from 1683 to 1795 (Snell, "Indian Slavery," 185–240). The strong possibility of Indian slaves running away, because they were at least somewhat familiar with the environment, was perceived as an inherent weakness of Indian slavery and was a strong incentive for exporting them to the Caribbean in exchange for black slaves.

195. Mustees, who often appeared in wills and inventories in the early eighteenth century, were slaves born of Indian and black parents. See "Will of Marie de Longuemare" (October 18, 1712), Charleston Museum Archives; "Will of Abraham Fleury de la Plaine" (August 21, 1721), Miscellaneous Records (Proprietary Series), vol. 1721–22:162–66, SCDAH.

196. It bears repeating that the purchase of slaves represented a considerable investment. With an average cost of £25 per slave, Menard estimated that lowcountry planters spent £863,000 sterling in slaves over the period 1706–40. Clearly most settlers, Huguenots and British alike, had to borrow money to set up plantations. Within the Huguenot community, Élisabeth (Chintrier) Buretel, widow of Pierre (d. 1702), literally acted as a bank by offering loans to fellow refugees. Her inventory showed that by 1727, 110 settlers, half of whom had French surnames and more of whom had French ancestry, had borrowed capital from her, presumably to buy land and slaves. See "Inventory of Mrs. Elizabeth Buretel," Miscellaneous Records (Interregnum Series), vol. 1727–29:94–95, SCDAH; Elizabeth M. Pruden, "Investing Widows: Autonomy in a Nascent Capitalist Society," in *Money, Trade, and Power,* ed. Greene et al., 347–48.

197. Hirsch, *Huguenots,* 165–70 (quote, 168) and my introduction, xxxii–xxxv.

198. Butler, *Huguenots in America,* 201–2 (quote, 201). On the larger historiographical contexts surrounding the publications of Hirsch's and Butler's studies, see Van Ruymbeke, "Ethnic History," 69–76.

199. Duff, "Creating a Plantation Province," 10; Coclanis, *Shadow of a Dream,* 69, tables 3–6. Coclanis's estimate is for white wealth holders.

200. Menard, "Economic and Social Development," 278, table 6.5.

Epilogue

1. DePratter et al., "Discovery of Charlesfort," 39–48; Gene Waddell, *Charleston Architecture,* 1:136–38, 278–79; Robert P. Stockton, "French Influence on the Architecture of the Joseph Manigault House: References to an Ancestral Culture?," *HSSCT,* no. 97 (1992): 21–30; Mary M. Jacoby, ed., *The Churches of Charleston and the Lowcountry* (Columbia: University of South Carolina Press, 1994), 9–11; *Hanover House* (pamphlet) (Clemson, S.C.: Clemson University, [1970]). See also Mary B. Wheeler and Genon H. Neblett, *Hidden Glory: The Life and Times of Hampton Plantation, Legend of the South Santee* (Nashville: Rutledge Hill Press, 1983); William P. Baldwin Jr. and Agnes L. Baldwin, *Plantations of the Low Country, South Carolina 1697–1865* (Greensboro, N.C.: Legacy Publications, 1985); Samuel G. Stoney, *Plantations of the Carolina Low Country* (New York: Dover Publications, 1989).

2. Butler, *Huguenots in America,* 200.

3. Coclanis, *Shadow of a Dream,* 64.

4. Wood, *Black Majority,* xiv.

5. Ball, *Slaves in the Family.*

6. For a comparative discussion of the memory of the Huguenot migrations in the United States, in Europe, and in South Africa, see Bertrand Van Ruymbeke, "Minority Survival: The Huguenot Paradigm in France and the Diaspora," in *Memory and Identity,* ed. Van Ruymbeke and Sparks, 13–18.

7. The Puritan dimension is one of two facets of the image of the Huguenot elaborated in the nineteenth century, the other being the Cavalier. See Bertrand Van Ruymbeke, "*Cavalier* et *Puritan:* L'ancêtre huguenot au prisme de l'histoire américaine," in "Diasporas: Histoire et société," special issue, *Généalogies rêvées* 5 (2005): 5–22.

8. Figures are hazy for lack of detailed archival research, but probably as many as five thousand, perhaps even more, Saint Domingue refugees relocated in the lowcountry after the 1791 slave rebellion. For broad estimates, see Winston C. Babb, "French Refugees from Saint-Domingue to the Southern United States: 1791–1810" (Ph.D. diss., University of Virginia, 1954), 370.

9. Russell R. Menard, "Migration, Ethnicity, and the Rise of an Atlantic Economy: The Re-Peopling of British America, 1600–1790," in *A Century of European Migrations, 1830–1930,* ed. Rudolph J. Vecoli and Suzanne M. Sinke (Urbana and Chicago: University of Illinois Press, 1991), 73–74.

Sources and Bibliography

Archival Sources (manuscripts and original accounts and pamphlets)

SOUTH CAROLINA

Charleston Library Society

"Recueil de Manuscrits sur les Églises Réformées de France réunis par les soins de Mr. Alexandre Crottet, ancien Pasteur des Églises Réformées de Pons, Gémozac et Mortagne en Saintonge et actuellement premier Pasteur de l'Eglise d'Yverdon, Canton de Vaud, en Suisse, accompagné de notes explicatives," Crottet Collection ms., 3 volumes

Charleston Museum Archives

"Account Book of Nicholas de Longuemare" (1703–11), ms. 1953 37
"Town Lot, French Jamestown" (July 4, 1706) (not cataloged)
"Will of Marie de Longuemare" (1712) (Longuemare family papers)

Huguenot Society of South Carolina Library, Charleston

Crottet, Alexandre. "Recherches historiques sur la famille Prioleau (1859)" (undated typescript from a manuscript account written by Crottet in 1859)
"A Litteral Translation taken from my Grand father Stephen Mazyck's Registry kept and wrote by himself in an old French Bible by me his Grand Son Peter Hamon in the year 1786"
Mazyck Family Bible (1697)

South Carolina Department of Archives and History, Columbia

Acts of Assembly, 7 boxes (1690–1721)
Archdale, John. Papers. Microfilm from Library of Congress
Catalog of Stock Marks (1695–1721)
Certificates of Admeasurement for Charles Town Lots, 1 volume (1675–98, 1717, 1743–46)
Church Commissioner Book (1717–42)
Colonial Land Grants (Copy Series), 2 volumes (1675–1719)
Journal of the Commons House of Assembly (1840 copies), 6 volumes (1692–1724)
Memorial of Land Titles (1820 copies), 20 volumes (1731–74)
Miscellaneous Records, Interregnum Series, 9 volumes (1721–33)
Miscellaneous Records, Proprietary Series, 12 volumes (1671–1725)
Papers of the British Public Record Office Relating to South Carolina (Sainsbury copies), 7 volumes (1711–27)
Records of the Court of Common Pleas, 18 boxes (1703–23)
Register of the Province, Conveyance Books, 11 volumes (1673–1719)
"William Dunlop to Sir James Montgomerie, tenth Baronet of Skelmorlic" (October 21, 1686) and "William Dunlop to Sir James Montgomerie, tenth Baronet of Skelmorlie" (November 21, 1686), Scottish Record Office, GD.3/E2/114 (photocopies)

South Carolina Historical Society, Charleston

Manigault Family Papers, ms. folder 11/275
St Julien Childs History Papers, ms. box 24/315

South Caroliniana Library, Columbia

"Lettre de Louis Thibou," ms. 4289

Prioleau Papers, French Huguenots, ms. 1677

NEW YORK

Huguenot Society of America Library, New York

"Papier du consistoire pour l'année 1687 [1687–91]," Narragansett Church Register, ms. 1687

Sermons by Rev. Pierre Stouppe, Huguenot Church of New Rochelle (1724–41) ms. HJ 588

RHODE ISLAND

John Carter Brown Library, Providence

Description du Pays nommé Caroline. London, 1679.

[Durand de Dauphiné]. *Voyages d'un François exilé pour la Religion avec une Description de la Virgine & Marilan dans l'Amérique.* The Hague: the author, 1687.

F[erguson], R[obert]. *The Present State of Carolina with Advice to the Settlers.* London: John Bringhurst, 1682.

[Furly, Benjamin]. *Recüeil de Diverses Pièces concernant la Pennsylvanie.* The Hague: Chez Abraham Troyel, 1684.

Mather, Cotton. *[A Present] from a Farr Countrey, [to the] People of New England.* Boston: B. Green & J. Allen for Michael Perry, 1698.

———. *Une Grande Voix du Ciel à la France.* Boston: Bernby & Green, 1725.

Mather, Increase. *A Sermon wherein is Shewed that the Church of God is Sometimes a Subject of Great Persecution: Preached on a Publick FAST at Boston in New England; occasioned by the Tidings of a great Persecution Raised against the Protestants in France.* Boston: Printed for Samuel Sewall, 1682.

Nouvelle Relation de la Caroline. The Hague: Chez Meyndert Uytweft, [1686].

Plan pour former un établissement en Caroline. The Hague: Chez Meindert Uytwerf, 1686.

Rochefort, Charles de. *Récit de l'Estat présent des célèbres colonies de la Virginie, de Marie-Land, de la Caroline, du nouveau Duché d'York, de Penn-Sylvanie, & de la nouvelle Angleterre, situées dans l'Amérique septentrionale, & qui relèvent de la couronne du Roy de la grand' Bretagne. Tiré fidèlement des mémoires des habitants des mêmes colonies, en faveur de ceus, qui auroyent le dessein de s'y transporter pour s'y établir.* Rotterdam: Chez Reinier Leers, 1681.

Sanson, Nicolas. *Carte Générale de la Caroline Dressée sur les Mémoires les plus Nouveaux par le Sieur S[anson].* Amsterdam: Chez Pieter Mortier, 1700 [1696].

———. *Carte Particulière de la Caroline: Dressée sur les Mémoires les plus Nouveaux par le Sieur S[anson].* Amsterdam: Chez Pieter Mortier, 1700 [1696].

———. *Le Neptune François ou Atlas Nouveau des Cartes Marines.* Paris: Chez Hubert Jaillot, 1696.

A Strange but true account of the barbarous usage of three young ladies in France for being Protestants: with a relation also of their wonderful escape from thence into England. London: Printed for E. Brooks, 1681.

[Wilson, Samuel]. *An Account of the Province of Carolina in America: together with an Abstract of the Patent, and Several other Necessary and Useful Particulars, to such as have thought of transporting themselves thither.* London: G. Larkin, 1682.

MICHIGAN

Clements Library, University of Michigan

Description de la Carolline Prés la Floride, ou La Nouvelle Angleterre en l'Amerique. . . . Geneva: Chez Jacques de Tournes, 1684 (microfilm n. 69.3220).

Suite de la Description de la Carolline qui contient diverses Lettres et vint & quatre questions et réponses qui ont été faites sur ce sujet, après ce qui en a esté ci-devant publié. Geneva: Chez Jacques de Tournes, 1685 (microfilm n. 69.3220).

ENGLAND

Bodleian Library, Oxford

Rawlinson Papers, ms. B 376
Rawlinson Papers, mss. C 943, C 984, and C 982

British Library, London

An Account of the French Prophets and Their Pretended Inspirations. London, 1708.

Bingham, Joseph. *The* French *Churches Apology for the Church of England; Or the Objections of Dissenters against the Articles, Homilies, Liturgy, and Canons of the* English *Church, Consider'd, and Answer'd upon the Principles of the Reformed Church of* France. London: Robert Knaplock, 1706.

The Humble Petition of the Protestants of France to the French King, to recall his declaration for taking their children from them at the age of seven years. London: Printed by N. T. for Andrew Forrester, 1681.

Instruction Très-Exacte pour ceux qui ont dessein de se transporter en Amerique, Et Principalement Pour Ceux qui sont déjà intéressés dans la Province de Pennsylvanie. [Amsterdam], 1686.

Locke, John. *Observations upon the Growth and Culture of Vines and Olives: The Production of Raw Silk & the Preservation of Fruits.* London: W. Sandby, 1766.

Marvell, Andrew. *An Account of the Growth of Popery and Arbitrary Government in England: More Particularly from the Long* Prorogation, *of* November *1675, Ending the 15th of* February, *1676, till the Last Meeting of* Parliament, *the 16th of* July *1677.* Amsterdam: [s.n.], 1677.

Plainte, et censure des calomnieuses accusations publiées par le Sr. Claude Grosteste de la [Mothe]. London, 1708.

[Primrose, David]. *An Harangue to the King by a Minister of the* French *Church in the Savoy the Nineteenth of* October, *1681.* London: R. Bentley & M. Magnes, 1681.

La Religion des Hollandois Représentée en plusieurs lettres écrites par un officier de l'Armée du Roy, à un Pasteur & Professeur en Théologie de Berne. Paris: Chez François Clousier et Pierre Aubouin, 1673.

[Stouppe, J.-B.] *La Religion des Hollandois Représentée en plusieurs lettres écrites par un officier de l'Armée du Roy, à un Pasteur & Professeur en Théologie de Berne.* Paris: Chez François Clousier et Pierre Aubouin, 1673.

Corporation of London Record Office, Guildhall Library, London

"Collections for the French Protestant Refugees," ms. 346 (1681–85) and ms. 347 (1686–90) (vouchers)

French Church, Soho Square, London

"Account book in ledger form of receipts from the Chamber of London and disbursements for the relief of named refugees, and for surgeons, apothecaries, clothes, beds, etc., 5 August 1681–1684," ms. 63

"Copies of Letters, 1697–1754," ms. 135

"Livre des Actes du Consistoire, 1679–1692," ms. 7

"Livres des Actes [du Consistoire] de 1693 à 1708," ms. 8

"Register of poor refugees assisted by the Church of London and the Church of the Savoy acting in common, August 1685–Dec. 1686," ms. 64

Lambeth Palace Library, London

Society for the Propagation of the Gospel in Foreign Parts (SPG) Papers
Correspondence
- vol. 13 (New York, 1700–1706)
- vol. 14 (New York, 1707–undated)
- vol. 16 (South Carolina, 1702–6)
- vol. 17 (South Carolina, 1711–undated)
Fulham Papers
- vol. 9 (Carolina, 1703–34)
- vol. 41 (New York)
- Section D, Displaced Documents (Rhode Island)
Minutes
- vol. 1 (1701–8)
- vol. 2 (1709–11)

Library of the Huguenot Society of Great Britain and Ireland, University College, London

Aufrère Papers, ms. vol. 6 (1652–1756)
"Bounty Papers," ms. 1, "Index of names of all the persons who received assistance from the brief (*collecte*) of 1686 as recorded in the three registers of resolutions (*délibérations*) of the [French] Committee covering the period 4 June 1686–28 August 1687"
"Bounty Papers," ms. 2, "Accounts of £2645.3.9 Sterlings Payd in part of the £3115.10 allowed by ye Lords Commiss[ione]rs to Severall french Conformed Protestants ye 4th May 1687"
Traylor, Calvin L. "Pierre Trouillart: Three Generations of Huguenot Ministers; A Chronology of various events over one hundred years, 1600–1700," unpaginated typescript, Trouillart File

The National Archives (formerly British Public Record Office), Kew

"[Carolina Huguenot Census of 1699]," CO 5/1258 (1699)
Entry Books and Minute Books of the Proprietors
Papers of the Privy Council 2/71, fol. 99
"Passenger list of the *Margaret,*" State Papers 44/336, fol. 163
"Passenger lists of the *Richmond,*" Admiralty Papers 1/5139, Orders in Council (1679–88), fol. 162
[Petit, René, and Jacob Guérard]. "Humble proposition faite au Roy et à son Parlement pour donner retraite aux Étrangers protestans et aux prosélites dans ses Colonies de l'Amérique et surtout en la Caroline," [March 1679], British Public Records Office, CO 1/43/16

FRANCE

Archives Nationales, Paris

Série TT, box 232 (Aunis, 1680–85) and box 236 (Bretagne, 1681–85)

Bibliothèque Municipale, La Rochelle

"Mémoire qu'une personne qui est allé [*sic*] à la Caroline écrit à son frère, contenant ce qu'il luy faut pour son ménage" (ms. 1909, fol. 56)
"Mémoires des Grâces que les S[eigneur]s Propiétaires accordent à un de mes amis . . ." (ms. 1909, fol. 56 back)
"Questions et Responses faites au sujet de la Caroline [1685]" (Recueil de documents divers, "Le commerce avec la Caroline, vers 1685," ms. 1909, fols. 51–55)

Bibliothèque Nationale de France, Paris
Département des manuscrits (rue de Richelieu)

"Description de la Caroline imprimée à Londres en 1684" [1684], manuscrits français, nouvelles acquisitions 5052, fols. 177–80

Intendant Arnoul Correspondence, manuscrits, nouvelles acquisitions françaises, 21334

"Lettre au Marquis de Seigneulay" (June 14, 1687), manuscrits, nouvelles acquisitions françaises, Arnoul 21334, fol. 194

"Proposition d'une entreprise sur la Caroline pour en chasser les Anglais" [1705], manuscrits nouvelles acquisitions françaises 9294 (1870 copy), fols. 114–18

Bibliothèque Nationale de France, site François Mitterrand

Montanus, Arnoldus. *De Nieuwe en onbekende Weereld: of beschryving van America en't Zuidland vervaetende d'Oorsprong der Americaenen en Zuidlanders. . . .* Amsterdam: Jacob van Meurs, 1671.

Ogilby, John. *America, being a latest and most accurate description of the New World, containing the original of the inhabitants and the remarkable voyages thither, the conquest of the vast empires of Mexico and Peru and other large provinces and territories, with the several European plantations. . . .* London: Printed by the author, 1671.

SWITZERLAND

Bibliothèque Publique et Universitaire, Geneva

Archives Tronchin 81, fols. 194–204 and ms. Français, 488, fols. 1–20 (Paul L'Escot's letters)

Primary Sources

An Account of the Sufferings of the French Protestants, Slaves on Board the French Kings' Galleys: By Elias Neau, One of their Fellow Sufferers; Together with a List of Those who are still on Board the said Galleys. London: Richard Parker, 1699. In *The Torments of Protestant Slaves in the French King's Galleys, and in the Dungeons of Marseilles, 1686–1707 A.D.,* edited by Edward Arber. London: privately printed, 1907.

Barrell, Rex A., ed. *Anthony Ashley Cooper, Earl of Shaftesbury (1671–1713) and "Le Refuge Français"-Correspondence.* Lewiston, N.Y.: The Edwin Mellen Press, 1989.

[Bayle, Pierre]. *Ce que c'est que la France toute catholique sous le règne de Louis Le Grand.* The Hague: Chez Abraham Troyel, 1690. Ed. Élisabeth Labrousse. Paris: Librairie Philosophique J. Vrin, 1973.

Brock, R. A., ed. *Documents Chiefly Unpublished Relating to the Huguenot Emigration to Virginia and to the Settlement at Manakin-Town.* 1886. Baltimore: Clearfield Company Reprints and Remainders, 1979.

Budé, Eugène de, ed. *Lettres inédites adressées de 1686 à 1737 à Jean-Alphonse Turrettini, théologien genevois.* 3 vols. Paris: Librairie de la Suisse française, 1887.

Calendar of State Papers, Colonial Series, America and West Indies. Ed. W. Noel Sainsbury and J. W. Fortescue, 40 vols. 1860–1926. Vaduz: Kraus Reprint Ltd, 1964, vols. 1 (1574–1660) and 10 (1677–80).

Carroll, Bartholomew R., ed. *Historical Collections of South Carolina embracing many rare & valuable Pamphlets & other documents relating to the History of that State from its first Discovery to its Independence in the year 1776.* 1836. New York: A.M.S. Reprint, 1973.

Cheves, Langdon, ed. *The Shaftesbury Papers and Other Records Relating to Carolina and the First Settlement on Ashley River Prior to the Year 1676.* South Carolina Historical Society Collections, vol. 5, 1897. Charleston, S.C.: Tempus Publishing Inc., 2000 .

Chinard, Gilbert, ed. *Un Français en Virginie: Voyages d'un François exilé pour la religion avec une description de la Virgine & Marilan d'après l'édition originale de 1687.* Baltimore: Johns Hopkins Press, 1932.

———. *A Huguenot Exile in Virginia, or Voyages of a Frenchman Exiled for Religion with a Description of Virginia and Maryland.* New York: Press of the Pioneers, 1934.

Clute, Robert F., ed. *The Annals and Parish Register of St. Thomas and St. Denis Parish, in South Carolina, from 1680 to 1884.* Charleston, S.C.: Walker, Evans & Cogswell, 1884.

Cochrane, Arthur C., ed. *Reformed Confessions of the 16th Century.* Philadelphia: Westminster Press, 1966.

Cohen, Robert, and Myriam Yardeni, eds. "Un Suisse en Caroline du Sud à la fin du XVIIe siècle." *Bulletin de la Société de l'Histoire du Protestantisme Français* 134 (1988): 59–71.

Connor, Jeannette T., ed. *The Whole and True Discoverye of Terra Florida: Together with a Transcript of an English Version of the British Museum by H. M. Biggar, and a Biography by Jeannette Thurber Connor.* Gainesville: University Presses of Florida, 1927.

Cooper, Thomas, and David J. McCord, eds. *The Statutes at Large of South Carolina.* 10 vols. Columbia, S.C.: A. S. Johnston, 1836–41.

Coxe, Daniel. *A Description of the English Province of Carolana by the Spaniards Call'd Florida, and by the French La Louisiane.* 1722. Ed. William S. Coker. Gainesville: University Presses of Florida, 1976.

De Beer, E. S., ed. *The Correspondence of John Locke.* 8 vols. Oxford: The Clarendon Press, 1976.

Defoe, Daniel. *Party-Tyranny, or an Occasional Bill in Miniature; as Now Practiced in Carolina, Humbly offered to the Consideration of Both Houses of Parliament.* [London, 1705]. In *Early Narratives of Carolina,* edited by Alexander S. Salley. New York: Charles Scribner's Sons, 1911.

Digges La Touche, J. J., ed. *Registers of the French Conformed Churches of St. Patrick and St. Mary, Dublin.* Quarto Series, vol. 7. Lymington, U.K.: Huguenot Society of Great Britain and Ireland Publications, 1893.

Dunn, Mary M., and Richard S. Dunn, eds. *The Papers of William Penn.* 5 vols. Philadelphia: University of Pennsylvania Press, 1981–87.

Duviols, Jean-Paul, and Marc Bouyer, eds. *Voyages en Floride 1562–1567: Textes de Jean Ribaut, René de Laudonnière, Dominique de Gourgues et textes et illustrations de Jacques Le Moyne de Morgues.* 1927. Nanterre, France: Éditions de l'Espace Européen, 1990.

Fatio, Olivier, ed. *Confessions et catéchismes de la foi réformée.* Geneva: Labor et Fides, 1986.

Fontaine, Jaques. *Memoirs of the Reverend Jaques Fontaine, 1658–1728.* Ed. Dianne W. Ressinger. London: The Huguenot Society of Great Britain and Ireland, 1992.

Friedlander, Amy, ed. "Commissary Johnston's Report, 1713." *South Carolina Historical Magazine* 83 (1982): 259–71.

Garden, Alexander. *A Brief Account of the Deluded Dutartres.* New Haven, Conn.: James Parker and Company, 1762.

Greene, Jack P., ed. *Selling a New World: Two Colonial South Carolina Pamphlets.* Columbia: University of South Carolina Press, 1989.

Gregorie, Anne King, ed. *Records of the Court of Chancery of South Carolina, 1671–1779.* Washington, D.C.: American Historical Association, 1950.

Gwynn, Robin D., ed. *Minutes of the Consistory of the French Church of London Threadneedle Street, 1679–1692.* Quarto Series, vol. 58. London: Huguenot Society of Great Britain and Ireland Publications, 1994.

Hands, A. P., and Irene Scouloudi, eds. *French Protestant Refugees Relieved through the Threadneedle Street Church, London 1681–1687.* Quarto Series, vol. 49. London: Huguenot Society of Great Britain and Ireland Publications, 1971.

Holcomb, Brent H., comp. *South Carolina Marriages, 1689–1799.* Baltimore: Genealogical Publishing Co., 1980.

Hovenden, Robert, ed. *The Registers of the Walloon or Strangers Church in Canterbury.* Quarto Series, vol. 5. Lymington, U.K.: Huguenot Society of Great Britain and Ireland Publications, 1891.

Jean Migault; or the Trials of a French Protestant Family during the Period of the Revocation of the Edict of Nantes. Trans. and ed. William Anderson. Edinburgh: Johnstone and Hunter, 1852.

Jurieu, Pierre. *L'Accomplissement des Prophéties.* 1686. Ed. Jean Delumeau. Paris: Imprimerie Nationale, 1994.

Kammen, Michael, G., ed. "Virginia at the Close of the Seventeenth Century: An Appraisal by James Blair and John Locke." *Virginia Magazine of History and Biography* 74 (1966): 141–69.

Klingberg, Frank J., ed. *The Carolina Chronicle of Dr. Francis Le Jau, 1706–1717.* Berkeley: University of California Press, 1956.

———. *Carolina Chronicle: The Papers of Commissary Gideon Johnston, 1707–1716.* Berkeley: University of California Press, 1946.

———. "Commissary Johnston's *Notitias Parochialis.*" *South Carolina Historical and Genealogical Magazine* 48 (1947): 26–34.

Lart, C. E., ed. "Roads of Destiny: The Dragonnades of 1685 from Unpublished Letters and Manuscripts." *Huguenot Society of Great Britain and Ireland Proceedings* 15 (1933–37): 50–76.

———. "Some Letters from France, 1585–1685." *Huguenot Society of Great Britain and Ireland Proceedings* 16 (1937): 71–73.

Laudonnière, René Goulaine de. *Histoire Notable de la Floride.* 1585. Reprinted in *Les Français en Amérique pendant la deuxième moitié du XVIe siècle,* vol. 2, *Les Français en Floride,* edited by Suzanne Lussagnet, 27–238. Paris: Presses Universitaires de France, 1958.

Lawson, John. *A New Voyage to Carolina.* Ed. Hugh T. Lefler. Chapel Hill: University of North Carolina Press, 1967.

Locke, John. *Travels in France, 1675–1679, as Related in His Journals, Correspondence and Other Papers.* Ed. John Lough. Cambridge: Cambridge University Press, 1953.

Louis XIV. *Mémoires for the Instruction of the Dauphin.* Trans. and ed. Paul Sonnino. New York: The Free Press, 1970.

———. *Mémoires pour l'instruction du Dauphin.* Ed. Pierre Goubert. Paris: Imprimerie Nationale, 1992.

McDowell, W. L. *Journals of the Commissioners of the Indian Trade (September 20, 1710–August 29, 1718).* Columbia: South Carolina Department of Archives and History, 1955.

Méjan, François, ed. *Discipline de l'Église Réformée de France.* Paris: Éditions "Je sers," 1947.

Migault, Jean. *Journal de Jean Migault ou malheurs d'une famille protestante du Poitou victime de la révocation de l'Édit de Nantes (1682–1689).* Ed. Yves Krumenacker. Paris: Les Éditions de Paris, 1995.

Minet, William, and William C. Waller, eds. *Transcripts of the Registers of the Protestant Church at Guisnes from 1668 to 1685.* Quarto Series, vol. 3. Lymington, U.K.: Huguenot Society of Great Britain and Ireland Publications, 1891.

Moens, William J. C., ed. *The Registers of the French Church, Threadneedle Street, London.* Quarto Series, vol. 9, 13, 16, 23. 4 vols. Lymington, U.K.: Huguenot Society of Great Britain and Ireland Publications, 1896–1916.

Moore, Caroline T., comp. and ed. *Abstracts of Records of the Secretary of the Province of South Carolina 1692–1721.* Columbia, S.C.: R. L. Bryan Company, 1978.

Moore, John Alexander, ed. "'A Narrative . . . of an Assembly . . . January the 2d. 1705/6': New Light on Early South Carolina Politics." *South Carolina Historical Magazine* 85 (1984): 181–86.

Nelson, William, ed. *Calendar of New Jersey Wills, 1670–1730*. Archives of the State of New Jersey, vol. 1. Paterson, N.J.: The Press Printing and Publishing Co., 1901.

Parker, Mattie E. E., ed. *North Carolina Charters and Constitutions, 1578–1698*. Raleigh: Carolina Charter Tercentenary Commission, 1963.

Pechels, Samuel de. *Mémoires*. Ed. Raoul de Cazenove. Toulouse: Société des Livres Religieux, 1878.

Pilatte, Léon, ed. *Édits, déclarations et arrests concernans la religion [prétendue] réformée 1662–1751*. Paris: Librairie Fischbacher & Cie, 1885.

Randolph, Howard S. F., ed. "The Census of 1698 for Mamaroneck, Morrisania, and New Rochelle, Westchester County, New York." *New York Genealogical and Biographical Record* 59 (1928): 103–7.

Ravenel, Daniel, ed. *Liste des François et Suisses: From an Old Manuscript List of French and Swiss Protestants Settled in Charleston, Santee, and at the Orange Quarter in Carolina Who Desired Naturalization Prepared Probably about 1695–6*. 1868. Baltimore: Genealogical Publishing Company, 1990.

Ribault, Jean. "La complète et véridique découverte de la terra Florida." In *Les Français en Amérique pendant la deuxième moitié du XVIe siècle*, vol. 2, *Les Français en Floride*, edited by Suzanne Lussagnet, 1–26. Paris: Presses Universitaires de France, 1958.

Salley, Alexander S., ed. *Commissions and Instructions from the Lords Proprietors of Carolina to Public Officials of South Carolina, 1685–1715*. Columbia: Historical Commission of South Carolina, 1916.

———. "Documents Concerning Huguenots, 1686–1692." *Huguenot Society of South Carolina Transactions* 7 (1922): 71–72.

———. *Early Narratives of Carolina*. New York: Charles Scribner's Sons, 1911.

———. *Journal of the Commons House, March 6–April 9, 1706 and November 20, 1706–February 8, 1707*. Columbia: Historical Commission of South Carolina, 1939.

———. *Journal of the Commons House of Assembly for 1707*. Columbia: Historical Commission of South Carolina, 1940.

———. *Journal of the Commons House of Assembly for 1707–1708*. Columbia: Historical Commission of South Carolina, 1941.

———. *Journal of the Commons House of Assembly for the Two Sessions of 1697*. Columbia: Historical Commission of South Carolina, 1913.

———. *Journal of the Commons House of Assembly, January–September 1693*. Columbia: Historical Commission of South Carolina, 1907.

———. *Journal of the Commons House of Assembly, January 30, 1696–March 17, 1696*. Columbia: Historical Commission of South Carolina, 1912.

———. *Journal of the Commons House of Assembly, October 30, 1700–November 16, 1700*. Columbia: Historical Commission of South Carolina, 1924

———. *Journal of the Commons House of Assembly, September 20, 1692–October 15, 1692*. Columbia: Historical Commission of South Carolina, 1907.

———. *Journal of the Commons House of Assembly, Nov 20, 1706–February 8, 1707*. Columbia: Historical Commission of South Carolina, 1939.

———. *Journal of the Commons House of Assembly of South Carolina for the Four Sessions of 1693*. Columbia: Historical Commission of South Carolina, 1916.

———. *Journal of the Commons House of Assembly of South Carolina, June 5, 1707–July 19, 1707*. Columbia: Historical Commission of South Carolina, 1940.

———. *Journal of the Commons House of Assembly of South Carolina, March 6–April 9, 1706*. Columbia: Historical Commission of South Carolina, 1937.

———. *Journal of the Commons House of Assembly of South Carolina for 1702.* Columbia: Historical Commission of South Carolina, 1932.

———. *Journal of the Grand Council of South Carolina, August 25, 1671–June 24, 1680.* Columbia: Historical Commission of South Carolina, 1907.

———. *Journal of the Grand Council, April 11, 1692–September 26, 1692.* Columbia: Historical Commission of South Carolina, 1907.

———. *Papers in the British Public Record Office Relating to South Carolina [1663–1710].* 5 vols. Columbia: Historical Commission of South Carolina, 1928–47.

———. *Register of St. Philip's Parish, Charles Town, South Carolina, 1720–1758.* 1904. Columbia: University of South Carolina Press, 1971.

———. "Stock Marks Recorded in South Carolina, 1695–1721." *South Carolina Historical and Genealogical Magazine* 13 (1912): 125–31, 224–28.

Salley, Alexander S., and R. Nicholas Olsberg, eds. *Warrants for Lands in South Carolina, 1672–1711.* Columbia: University of South Carolina Press, 1973.

Saunders, William L., coll. and ed. *The Colonial Records of North Carolina.* Vol. 1, 1662–1712. Raleigh: P. M. Hale, Printer to the State, 1886.

Shaw, William A., ed. *Letters of Denization and Acts of Naturalization for Aliens in England and Ireland, 1603–1700.* Quarto Series, vol. 18. Lymington, U.K.: Huguenot Society of Great Britain and Ireland Publications, 1911.

———. ed. *Letters of Denization and Acts of Naturalization for Aliens in England and Ireland, 1701–1800.* Quarto Series, vol. 27. Manchester, U.K.: Sherratt and Hughes, 1923.

Simmons, Slann L. C., trans. and ed. "Early Manigault Records." *Huguenot Society of South Carolina Transactions* 59 (1954): 25–27.

[Simms, William G., trans.] "Remarks on the New Account of Carolina by a French Gentleman, 1686." *Magnolia* 1 (1842): 226–30.

Stelling-Michaud, S., ed. *Le livre du recteur de l'Académie de Genève (1559–1878).* 6 vols. Geneva: Droz, 1959–80.

Stoney, Samuel G., ed. "Nicholas de Longuemare: Huguenot Goldsmith and Silk Dealer in Colonial South Carolina." *Huguenot Society of South Carolina Transactions* 55 (1950): 38–69.

Turner, Winifred, ed. *The Aufrere Papers.* Quarto Series, vol. 40. Frome, U.K.: Printed by Butler & Tanner Ltd., 1940.

Vauban, Maréchal de. *Mémoire pour le rappel des huguenots.* 1689. Reprint, edited by Philipe Vassaux. Carrières-sous-Poissy, France: La Cause, 1998.

Vestry Book of King William Parish, Virginia, 1707–1750. Midlothian, Va.: Manakin Episcopal Church, 1966.

Wittmeyer, Alfred V., ed. *Registers of the Births, Marriages, and Deaths of the "Église Françoise à la Nouvelle York" from 1688 to 1804.* Collections of the Huguenot Society of America, vol.1. New York: Publications of the Huguenot Society of America, 1886.

Secondary Sources

BOOKS

Acerra, Martine, and Guy Martinière, eds. *Coligny, les protestants et la mer.* Paris: Presses Universitaires de Paris-Sorbonne, 1997.

Ackerman, Robert K. *South Carolina Colonial Land Policies.* Columbia: University of South Carolina Press, 1977.

Actes du Colloque "L'Amiral de Coligny et son temps," Paris, 18–24 Octobre 1972. Paris: Société de l'Histoire du Protestantisme Français, 1974.

Adams, Geoffrey. *The Huguenots and French Opinion, 1685–1787: The Enlightenment Debate on Toleration*. Waterloo, Canada: Wilfrid Laurier University Press, 1991.

Alden, John E., Dennis C. Lanning, et al., eds. *European Americana: A Chronological Guide to Works Printed in Europe Relating to the Americas, 1493–1776*. 4 vols. New Canaan, Conn.: Readex Books for the John Carter Brown Library, 1980–97.

Allen, Warren, and Henry Fraser. *The Barbados-Carolina Connection*. London: Macmillan, 1988.

Altman, Ida, and James Horn, eds. *"To Make America": European Emigration in the Early Modern Period*. Berkeley: University of California Press, 1991.

Anderson, Virginia D. *New England's Generation: The Great Migration and the Formation of Society and Culture in the Seventeenth Century*. Cambridge: Cambridge University Press, 1991.

Andrews, Kenneth R. *Trade, Plunder and Settlement: Maritime Enterprise and the Genesis of the British Empire, 1480–1630*. Cambridge: Cambridge University Press, 1984.

Appleby, Joyce O. *Economic Thought and Ideology in Seventeenth-Century England*. Princeton: Princeton University Press, 1978.

Armogathe, Jean-Robert. *Croire en la liberté: L'Église catholique et la révocation de l'Édit de Nantes*. Paris: O.E.I.L, 1985.

———. *Le Grand Siècle et la Bible*. Paris: Beauchesne, 1989.

Arneil, Barbara. *John Locke and America: The Defense of English Colonization*. Oxford: Clarendon Press, 1996.

Ashcraft, Richard. *Revolutionary Politics and Locke's Two Treatises of Government*. Princeton, N.J.: Princeton University Press, 1986.

Baird, Charles W. *History of the Huguenot Emigration to America*. 2 vols. New York: Dodd, Mead and Co, 1885.

Bairoch, Paul, Jean Batou, and Pierre Chèvre. *La population des villes européennes / The Population of European Cities*. Geneva: Droz, 1988.

Baldwin, Agnes L. *First Settlers of South Carolina, 1670–1700*. Easley, S.C.: Southern Historical Press, Inc., 1985.

Barbaud, Philippe. *Le choc des patois en Nouvelle-France: Essai sur l'histoire de la francisation au Canada*. Sillery, Canada: Presses de l'Université du Québec, 1984.

Baseler, Marilyn C. *"Asylum for Mankind": America, 1607–1800*. Ithaca: Cornell University Press, 1998.

Bayley, Peter. *French Pulpit Oratory, 1598–1650*. Cambridge: Cambridge University Press, 1980.

Bély, Lucien, ed. *Dictionnaire de l'Ancien Régime: Royaume de France XVIIe–XVIIIe siècle*. Paris: Presses Universitaires de France, 1996.

Benedict, Philip. *Cities and Social Change in Early Modern France*. London: Unwin Hyman, 1989.

———. *The Huguenot Population of France, 1600–1685: The Demographic Fate and Customs of a Religious Minority*. Transactions of the American Philosophical Society, vol. 81, pt. 5. Philadelphia: American Philosophical Society, 1991.

Bennett, Charles E. *Laudonniere & Fort Caroline: History and Documents*. Gainesville: University Presses of Florida, 1964.

Bergeal, Catherine, and André Durrleman, eds. *Éloge et condamnation de la révocation de l'Édit de Nantes*. Carrières-sous-Poissy, France: La Cause, 1985.

———. *Protestantisme et libertés en France au 17e siècle de l'Édit de Nantes à sa révocation, 1598–1685*. Carrières-sous-Poissy, France: La Cause, 1985.

Berkvens-Stevelinck, C., et al. *Le magasin de l'univers: The Dutch Republic as the Centre of the European Book Trade*. Leiden: E. J. Brill, 1992.

Berlin, Ira. *Many Thousands Gone: The Two Centuries of Slavery in North America*. Cambridge, Mass.: Harvard University Press, 1998.

Bernardini, Paolo, and Norman Fiering, eds. *The Jews and the Expansion of Europe to the West, 1450–1800.* New York: Berghan Books, 2001.

Billings, Warren M., John E. Selby, and Thad W. Tate. *Colonial Virginia: A History.* White Plains, N.Y.: KTO Press, 1986.

Birnstiel, Eckart, ed. *La diaspora des huguenots: Les réfugiés protestants de France et leur dispersion dans le monde (XVIe–XVIIIe siècles).* Paris: Honoré Champion, 2001.

Bliss, Robert M. *Revolution and Empire: English Politics and the American Colonies in the Seventeenth Century.* Manchester: Manchester University Press, 1990.

Boisset, Jean, ed. *La Réforme et l'éducation.* Toulouse: Éditions Privat, 1974.

Bolton, Charles. *Southern Anglicanism: The Church of England in Colonial South Carolina.* Westport, Conn.: Greenwood Press, 1982.

Bosher, John F. *Business and Religion in the Age of New France, 1600–1760: Twenty-two Studies.* Toronto: Canadian Scholars' Press, 1994.

———. *Men and Ships in the Canada Trade, 1660–1760.* Ottawa: Park Services, 1992.

Bossy, John. *Christianity in the West 1400–1700.* Oxford: Oxford University Press, 1985.

Bots, J. A. H., and G. H. M. Posthumus Meyjès, eds. *La révocation de l'Édit de Nantes et les Provinces-Unies: The Revocation of the Edict of Nantes and the Dutch Republic.* Amsterdam: Holland University Press, 1986.

Braund, Kathryn E. Holland. *Deerskins & Duffels: The Creek Indian Trade with Anglo-America, 1685–1815.* Lincoln: University of Nebraska Press, 1993.

Bridges, Anne Baker Leland, and Roy Williams III. *St. James, Santee, Plantation Parish: History and Records, 1685–1925.* Spartanburg, S.C.: The Reprint Company, Publishers, 1997.

Briggs, Robin. *Early Modern France, 1560–1715.* Oxford: Oxford University Press, 1977.

Brinsfield, John W. *Religion and Politics in Colonial South Carolina.* Easley, S.C.: Southern Historical Press, 1983.

Burton, E. Milby. *South Carolina Silversmiths, 1690–1860.* Revised by Warren Ripley. 1942. Charleston, S.C.: Contributions from the Charleston Museum, 1991.

Bushnell, Amy T. *Situado and Sabana: Spain's Support System for the Presidio and Mission Provinces of Florida.* Athens: University of Georgia Press, 1994.

Butler, Jon. *Awash in a Sea of Faith: Christianizing the American People.* Cambridge, Mass.: Harvard University Press, 1990.

———. *Becoming America: The Revolution before 1776.* Cambridge, Mass.: Harvard University Press, 2000.

———. *The Huguenots in America: A Refugee People in New World Society.* Cambridge, Mass.: Harvard University Press, 1983.

Cabantous, Alain. *Le ciel dans la mer: Christianisme et civilisation maritime XVIe–XIXe siècle.* Paris: Fayard, 1990.

Cabell, Priscilla H. *Turf and Twig: The French Lands.* 2 vols. Richmond: privately printed, 1988.

Cannon, Margaret H., comp. *South Carolina Genealogies: Articles from the South Carolina Historical (and Genealogical) Magazine.* 5 vols. Spartanburg, S.C.: Reprint Co., 1983.

Carile, Paolo. *Huguenots sans frontières: Voyage et écriture à la Renaissance et à l'Âge classique.* Paris: Honoré Champion, 2001.

Carlo, Paula W. *Huguenot Refugees in Colonial New York: Becoming American in the Hudson Valley.* Brighton, U.K. and Portland, Ore.: Sussex Academic Press, 2005.

Carney, Judith A. *Black Rice: The African Origins of Rice Cultivation in the Americas.* Cambridge, Mass.: Harvard University Press, 2001.

Carpenter, Edward. *The Protestant Bishop: Being the Life of Henry Compton, 1632–1713, Bishop of London.* New York: Longmans, Green and Co., 1956.

Cartier, Alfred. *Bibliographie des éditions de Tournes, imprimeurs lyonnais.* 2 vols. 1937. Geneva: Slatkine Reprint, 1970.

Cerny, Gerald. *Theology, Politics and Letters at the Crossroads of European Civilization: Jacques Basnage and the Baylean Huguenot Refugees in the Dutch Republic.* Dordrecht: Martinus Nijhoff Publishers, 1987.

Chabrol, Jean-Paul. *Élie Marion, le vagabond de Dieu (1687–1713): Prophétisme et millénarisme protestants en Europe à l'aube des Lumières.* Aix-en-Provence: Edisud, 1999.

Chartier, Roger, Dominique Julia, and Marie-Madeleine Compère. *L'éducation en France du XVIe au XVIIIe siècle.* Paris: SEDES, 1976.

Chernaik, Warren L. *The Poet's Time: Politics and Religion in the Work of Andrew Marvell.* Cambridge: Cambridge University Press, 1983.

Chesnut, David R., and Clyde N. Wilson, eds. *The Meaning of South Carolina History: Essays in Honor of George C. Rogers, Jr.* Columbia: University of South Carolina Press, 1991.

Chevalier, Françoise. *Prêcher sous l'Édit de Nantes: La prédication réformée au XVIIe siècle en France.* Geneva: Labor et Fides, 1994.

Childs, St. Julien R. *Malaria and Colonization in the Carolina Low Country, 1526–1696.* Baltimore: Johns Hopkins University Press, 1940.

Chinard, Gilbert. *L'Amérique et le rêve exotique dans la littérature française au XVIIe et au XVIIIe siècle.* Paris: Droz, 1934.

———. *Les réfugiés huguenots en Amérique.* Paris: Belles-Lettres, 1925.

Choquette, Leslie. *Frenchmen into Peasants: Modernity and Tradition in the Peopling of French Canada.* Cambridge, Mass.: Harvard University Press, 1997.

Clark, John G. *La Rochelle and the Atlantic Economy during the Eighteenth Century.* Baltimore: Johns Hopkins University Press, 1981.

Clarke, Erskine. *Our Southern Zion: A History of Calvinism in the South Carolina Low Country, 1690–1990.* Tuscaloosa: University of Alabama Press, 1996.

Clowse, Converse D. *Economic Beginnings in Colonial South Carolina, 1670–1730.* Columbia: University of South Carolina Press, 1971.

Coclanis, Peter A. *The Shadow of a Dream: Economic Life and Death in the South Carolina Low Country, 1670–1920.* New York: Oxford University Press, 1989.

Cohen, William B. *The French Encounter with Africans: White Response to Blacks, 1530–1880.* Bloomington: Indiana University Press, 1980.

Collins, James B. *The State in Early Modern France.* New York: Cambridge University Press, 1995.

Constant, Jean-Marie. *La société française aux XVIe–XVIIe–XVIIIe siècles.* Paris: Ophrys, 1994.

Cornette, Joël. *Chronique du règne de Louis XIV.* Paris: SEDES, 1997.

Cottret, Bernard. *Calvin: A Biography.* Grand Rapids, Mich.: Wm. B. Eerdsman, 2000.

———. *1598: L'Édit de Nantes; pour en finir avec les guerres de religion.* Paris: Perrin, 1998.

———. *Histoire de la réforme protestante, XVIe–XVIIIe siècle.* Paris: Perrin, 2001.

———. *The Huguenots in England: Immigration and Settlement, c. 1550–1700.* Cambridge: Cambridge University Press, 1991.

———. *Terre d'exil: L'Angleterre et ses réfugiés français et wallons, 1550–1700.* Paris: Aubier, 1985.

Cottret, Bernard, Monique Cottret, and Marie-José Michel, eds. *Jansénisme et puritanisme.* Paris: Nolin, 2002.

Cowan, Ian B. *The Scottish Covenanters, 1660–1688.* London: Victor Gollancz Ltd, 1976.

Coward, Barry. *The Stuart Age: England, 1603–1714.* London: Longman, 1994.

Crane, Verner W. *The Southern Frontier, 1670–1732.* Ann Arbor: University of Michigan Press, 1956.

Craven, Wesley F. *The Southern Colonies in the Seventeenth Century, 1607–1689.* Baton Rouge: Louisiana State University Press, 1949.

Creagh, Ronald. *Nos cousins d'Amérique.* Paris: Éditions Payot, 1988.

Creagh, Ronald, and John P. Clark, eds. *Les Français des États-Unis d'hier à aujourd'hui.* Montpellier: Éditions Espaces 34, 1994.

Cressy, David. *Coming Over: Migration and Communication between England and New England in the Seventeenth Century.* Cambridge: Cambridge University Press, 1987.

Crété, Liliane. *Coligny.* Paris: Fayard, 1985.

Crottet, Alexandre. *Histoire des églises réformées de Pons, Gémozac et Mortagne en Saintonge, précédée d'une notice sur l'établissement de la réforme dans cette province, l'Aunis et l'Angoumois.* Bordeaux: A. Castillon, 1841.

Crouzet, Denis. *La genèse de la réforme française, 1520–1560.* Paris: SEDES, 1996.

Cumming, William P. *The Southeast in Early Maps.* Revised and enlarged by Louis de Vorsey. Chapel Hill: University of North Carolina Press, 1998.

Dalcho, Frederick. *An Historical Account of the Protestant Episcopal Church in South Carolina.* 1820. Tricentennial Edition. Charleston, S.C.: Arno Press, 1970.

Daniels, Bruce C., ed. *Town and County: Essays on the Structure of Local Government in the American Colonies.* Middletown, Conn.: Wesleyan University Press, 1978.

Davies, K. G. *The North Atlantic World in the Seventeenth Century.* Minneapolis: University of Minnesota Press, 1974.

Davis, David Brion. *The Problem of Slavery in the Age of Revolution, 1770–1823.* Ithaca: Cornell University Press, 1975.

———. *The Problem of Slavery in Western Culture.* Ithaca: Cornell University Press, 1966.

Dehem, Roger. *Histoire de la pensée économique des mercantilistes à Keynes.* Québec: Les Presses Universitaires de l'Université de Laval, 1984.

Delafosse, Marcel, ed. *Histoire de La Rochelle.* Toulouse: Éditions Privat, 1985.

———. *Petite histoire de l'Île de Ré.* La Rochelle: Quartier Latin, 1977.

Delumeau, Jean. *Une histoire du paradis.* 2 vols. Paris: Fayard, 1992, 1995.

———. *Le péché et la peur: La culpabilisation en Occident, XIIIe–XVIIIe siècles.* Paris: Fayard, 1983.

Delumeau, Jean, and Thierry Wanegffelen. *Naissance et affirmation de la Réforme.* Paris: Presses Universitaires de France, 1997.

Deregnaucourt, Gilles, and Didier Poton. *La vie religieuse en France aux XVIe, XVIIe, XVIIIe siècles.* Paris: Ophrys, 1994.

Dethloff, Henry C. *A History of the American Rice Industry, 1685–1985.* College Station: Texas A&M University Press, 1988.

Deveau, Jean-Michel. *La traite rochelaise.* Paris: Éditions Karthala, 1990.

Deyon, Pierre, et al. *Les hésitations de la croissance, 1580-1740.* Histoire économique et sociale du monde, vol. 6. Paris: Armand Colin, 1978.

Deyon, Solange. *Du loyalisme au refus: Les protestants français et leur député général entre la fronde et la révocation.* Villeneuve-D'Ascq: Presses Universitaires de Lille, 1976.

Diefendorf, Barbara B. *Beneath the Cross: Catholics and Huguenots in Sixteenth-Century Paris.* Oxford: Oxford University Press, 1991.

Diefendorf, Barbara B., and Carla Hesse, eds. *Culture and Identity in Early Modern Europe (1500–1800).* Ann Arbor: University of Michigan Press, 1993.

Dompnier, Bernard. *Le venin de l'hérésie: Image du protestantisme et combat catholique au XVIIe siècle.* Paris: Le Centurion, 1997.

Douglas, James D. *Light in the North: The Story of the Scottish Covenanters.* Grand Rapids, Mich.: Wm. B. Eerdmans, 1964.

Dubost, Jean-François, and Peter Sahlins. *Et si on faisait payer les étrangers? Louis XIV, les immigrés et les autres.* Paris: Flammarion, 1999.

Duchene, Roger, and Louise Gondard de Donville, eds. *De la mort de Colbert à la révocation de l'Édit de Nantes: Un monde nouveau?* Marseille: C.M.R, 1984.

Ducommin, Marie-Jeanne, and Dominique Quadroni. *Le refuge protestant dans le Pays de Vaud (fin XVIIe–début XVIIIe s.): Aspects d'une migration.* Geneva: Droz, 1991.

Dunn, Richard S. *Sugar and Slaves: The Rise of the Planter Class in the English West Indies, 1624–1713.* Chapel Hill: University of North Carolina Press, 1972.

Dupâquier, Jacques, ed. *Histoire de la population française.* Vol. 2, *De la Renaissance à 1789.* 1988. Paris: Presses Universitaires de France, 1995.

Echeverria, Durand, and Everett C. Wilkie Jr., eds. *The French Image of America: A Chronological and Subject Bibliography of French Books Printed before 1816 Relating to the British North American Colonies and the United States.* 2 vols. Metuchen, N.J.: The Scarecrow Press, 1994.

Edgar, Walter B. *South Carolina. A History.* Columbia: University of South Carolina Press, 1998.

——, gen. ed. *Biographical Directory of the South Carolina House of Representatives.* Vol. 1, *Session Lists 1692/1973* (1974). Ed. J. S. R. Faunt and R. E. Rector with D. K. Bowden; vol. 2, *The Commons House of Assembly 1692–1775* (1974). Ed. W. B. Edgar and N. L. Bailey. Columbia: University of South Carolina Press, 1974–84.

Edgar, Walter B., and N. Louise Bailey, eds. *Directory of the South Carolina House of Representatives.* 5 vols. Columbia: University of South Carolina Press, 1974–77.

Egnal, Marc. *New World Economies: The Growth of the Thirteen Colonies and Early Canada.* New York: Oxford University Press, 1998.

Eltis, David. *The Rise of African Slavery in the Americas.* Cambridge: Cambridge University Press, 2000.

Engerman, Stanley L., and Robert E. Gallman, eds. *The Cambridge Economic History of the United States.* Vol. 1, *The Colonial Era.* Cambridge: Cambridge University Press, 1996.

Félice, Paul de. *Les protestants d'autrefois: Vie intérieure des églises, moeurs et usages.* 4 vols. Paris: Librairie Fischbacher, 1896–1902.

Fontaine, Laurence. *Histoire du colportage en Europe (XVe–XIXe siècle).* Paris: Albin Michel, 1993.

Gallay, Alan. *Indian Slavery: The Rise of the English Empire in the American South, 1670–1717.* Cambridge, Mass.: Harvard University Press, 2002.

Garnot, Benoît. *Les villes en France aux XVIe, XVIIe, XVIIIe siècles.* Paris: Ophrys, 1996.

Garrisson, Janine. *L'Édit de Nantes: Chronique d'une paix attendue.* Paris: Fayard, 1998.

——. *L'Édit de Nantes et sa révocation: Histoire d'une intolérance.* Paris: Éditions du Seuil, 1985.

——. *L'homme protestant.* Paris: Éditions Complexe, 1986.

——. *Les protestants au XVIe siècle.* Paris: Fayard, 1988.

Gaustad, Edwin S., and Philip L. Barlow. *New Historical Atlas of Religion in America.* New York: Oxford University Press, 2001.

Gibert, Anne C. *Pierre Gibert, Esq., the Devoted Huguenot: A History of the French Settlement of New Bordeaux, South Carolina.* N.p.: privately printed, 1976.

Glover, Lorri. *All Our Relations: Blood Ties and Emotional Bonds among the Early South Carolina Gentry.* Baltimore: Johns Hopkins University Press, 2000.

Golden, R. M., ed. *Church, State, and Society under the Bourbon Kings.* Lawrence, Kans.: Coronado Press, 1982.

———. *The Huguenot Connection: The Edict of Nantes, Its Revocation, and Early French Migration to South Carolina.* Boston: Kluwer Academic Publishers, 1988.

Goodbar, Richard L., ed. *The Edict of Nantes: Five Essays and a New Translation.* Bloomington, Minn.: National Huguenot Society, 1998.

Goodfriend, Joyce D. *Before the Melting Pot: Society and Culture in Colonial New York City, 1664–1730.* Princeton: Princeton University Press, 1992.

Goubert, Pierre. *Louis XIV et vingt millions de Français.* 1996. Rev. ed. Paris: Fayard, 1991.

Goubert, Pierre, and Daniel Roche. *Les Français et l'Ancien Régime.* 2 vols. Paris: Armand Colin, 1984.

Gounclle, André. *Protestantisme.* Paris: Éditions Publisud, 1992.

Grassière, Paul Bertrand de la. *Jean Ribault, marin dieppois et lieutenant du roi en Neuve-France, Floride française en 1565.* Paris: La Pensée Universelle, 1971.

Gray, Janet G. *The French Huguenots: Anatomy of Courage.* Grand Rapids, Mich.: Baker Book House, 1981.

Gray, Lewis C. *History of Agriculture in the Southern United States to 1860.* New York: Peter Smith, 1941.

Greene, Jack P. *The Intellectual Construction of America: Exceptionalism and Identity from 1492 to 1800.* Chapel Hill: University of North Carolina Press, 1993.

———. *Pursuits of Happiness: The Social Development of Early Modern British Colonies and the Formation of American Culture.* Chapel Hill: University of North Carolina Press, 1988.

———. *The Quest for Power: The Lower Houses of Assembly in the Southern Royal Colonies, 1689–1776.* Chapel Hill: University of North Carolina Press, 1963.

Greene, Jack P., Rosemary Brana-Shute, and Randy J. Sparks, eds. *Money, Trade and Power: The Evolution of Colonial South Carolina's Plantation Society.* Columbia: University of South Carolina Press, 2001.

Greengrass, Mark. *The French Reformation.* Oxford: Basil Blackwell, 1987.

Grell, Ole P., and Bob Scribner, eds. *Tolerance and Intolerance in the European Reformation.* Cambridge: Cambridge University Press, 1996.

Gruys, J. A., and C. de Wolf, eds. *Thesaurus, 1473–1800: Dutch Printers and Booksellers.* Nieuwkoop: De Graaf Publishers, 1989.

Gwynn, Robin D. *Huguenot Heritage: The History and Contribution of the Huguenots in Britain.* 1985. Rev. ed., Brighton, U.K.: Sussex Academic Press, 2001.

Haag, Eugène, and Émile Haag. *La France protestante ou vies des protestants français qui se sont fait un nom dans l'histoire.* 10 vols. 1846–1858. Geneva: Slatkine Reprints, 1966.

Hagy, James W. *This Happy Land: The Jews of Colonial and Antebellum Charleston.* Tuscaloosa: University of Alabama Press, 1993.

Haley, K. H. D. *The First Earl of Shaftesbury.* Oxford: Clarendon Press, 1968.

Hamon, Léo, ed. *Un siècle et demi d'histoire protestante: Théodore de Bèze et les protestants sujets du roi.* Paris: Éditions de la Maison des Sciences de l'Homme, 1989.

Häseler, Jens, and Antony McKenna, eds. *La vie intellectuelle aux Refuges protestants.* Paris: Honoré Champion, 1999.

Hercule, Philippe, under the direction of J. P. Bardet, G. Arbellot, and B. Lepetit. *Charente-Maritime.* Paroisses et communes de France. Paris: Éditions du Centre National de la Recherche Scientifique, 1985.

Hill, Christopher. *The Century of Revolution, 1603–1714.* 1961. New York: W. W. Norton, 1966.

Hillerbrand, Hans J., gen. ed. *The Oxford Encyclopedia of the Reformation.* 4 vols. Oxford: Oxford University Press, 1996.

Hirsch, Arthur H. *The Huguenots of Colonial South Carolina.* 1928. Columbia: University of South Carolina Press, 1999.

Hoffman, Paul E. *Florida's Frontiers.* Bloomington: Indiana University Press, 2002.

———. *A New Andalucia and a Way to the Orient: The American Southeast during the Sixteenth Century.* Baton Rouge: Louisiana State University Press, 1990.

Holmes, Geoffrey. *The Making of a Great Power: Late Stuart and Early Georgian Britain, 1660–1722.* New York: Longman, 1993.

Holmes, Peter. *Resistance and Compromise: The Political Thought of the Elizabethan Catholics.* Cambridge: Cambridge University Press, 1982.

Holt, Mack P. *The French Wars of Religion, 1562–1629.* Cambridge: Cambridge University Press, 1995.

Horn, James. *Adapting to a New World: English Society in the Seventeenth-Century Chesapeake.* Chapel Hill: University of North Carolina Press, 1994.

Howe, George. *History of the Presbyterian Church in South Carolina.* 2 vols. Columbia, S.C.: Duffie & Chapman, 1870.

Hubler, Lucienne, Jean-Daniel Candaux, and Christophe Chalamet, eds. *L'Édit de Nantes revisité: Actes de la journée d'étude de Waldegg (30 octobre 1998).* Geneva: Droz, 2000.

Hudson, Charles, and Carmen C. Tesser, eds. *The Forgotten Centuries: Indians and Europeans in the American South, 1521–1704.* Athens: University of Georgia Press, 1994.

Les huguenots, catalogue de l'exposition organisée par les Archives Nationales. Paris: La Documentation Française, 1985.

Hull, William I. *Benjamin Furly and Quakerism in Rotterdam.* Swarthmore, Pa.: Swarthmore College, 1941.

Hulton, Paul, et al. *The Work of Jacques Le Moyne de Morgues: A Huguenot Artist in France, Florida, and England.* 2 vols. London: British Museum Publications, 1977.

Insh, George P. *Scottish Colonial Schemes, 1620–1686.* Glasgow: Maclehose, Jackson & Co., 1922.

Israel, Jonathan I. *The Dutch Republic: Its Rise, Greatness, and Fall, 1477–1806.* Oxford: Clarendon Press, 1995.

Jacoby, Mary M., ed. *The Churches of Charleston and the Lowcountry.* Columbia: University of South Carolina Press, 1994.

Jahan, Emmanuel. *La confiscation des biens des religionnaires fugitifs de la révocation de l'Édit de Nantes à la Révolution.* Paris: R. Pichon and R. Durand-Auzias, 1959.

Jones, J. R. *The First Whigs: The Politics of the Exclusion Crisis, 1678–1683.* 1961. Rev. ed. London: Oxford University Press, 1970.

Jordan, Winthrop D. *White over Black: American Attitudes toward the Negro, 1550–1812.* Chapel Hill: University of North Carolina Press, 1968.

Kammen, Michael. *Colonial New York: A History.* White Plains N.Y.: KTO Press, 1975.

———. *Empire and Interest: The American Colonies and the Politics of Mercantilism.* Philadelphia: J. B. Lippincott Company, 1970.

Katz, Stanley N., John N. Murrin, and Douglas Greenberg, eds. *Colonial America: Essays in Politics and Social Development.* New York: McGraw-Hill, 1983.

Kettner, James H. *The Development of American Citizenship, 1608–1870.* Chapel Hill: University of North Carolina Press, 1975.

Kingdon, Robert M. *Geneva and the Consolidation of the French Protestant Movement, 1564–1572.* Geneva: Droz, 1967.

Kishlansky, Mark. *A Monarchy Transformed: Britain, 1603–1714.* London: Penguin Books Ltd, 1996.

Kleinschmidt, John R. *Les imprimeurs et libraires de la République de Genève*. Geneva: A. Julien éditeur, 1948.

Kolchin, Peter. *American Slavery, 1619–1877*. New York: Hill and Wang, 1993.

Kornwolf, James D. (with the assistance of Georgiana W. Kornwolf). *Architecture and Town Planning in Colonial North America*. 3 vols. Baltimore: Johns Hopkins University Press, 2002.

Krumenacker, Yves. *Les protestants du Poitou au XVIIIe siècle (1681–1789)*. Paris: Honoré Champion, 1998.

Labrousse, Élisabeth. *Conscience et conviction: Études sur le XVIIe siècle*. Oxford: Universitas, 1996.

————. *La révocation de l'Édit de Nantes: Une foi, une loi, un roi?* 1985. Paris: Éditions Payot, 1990.

Lafleur, Gérard. *Les Protestants aux Antilles françaises du Vent sous l'Ancien Régime*. Basse-Terre: Société d'Histoire de la Guadeloupe, 1988.

Le Goff, Jacques, and René Rémond, gen. eds. *Histoire de la France religieuse*. Vol. 2, *Du christianisme flamboyant à l'aube des Lumières (XIVe–XVIIIe siècles)*. Ed. François Lebrun. Paris: Seuil, 1988.

Lederer, Richard M., Jr. *Colonial American English, a Glossary*. Essex, Conn.: A Verbatim Book, 1985.

Lefler, Hugh T., and William S. Powell. *Colonial North Carolina: A History*. New York: Charles Scribner's Sons, 1973.

Léonard, Émile G. *Histoire générale du protestantisme*. 3 vols. Paris: Presses Universitaires de France, 1961.

Lesser, Charles H. *South Carolina Begins: The Records of a Proprietary Colony, 1663–1721*. Columbia: South Carolina Department of Archives and History, 1995.

Lestringant, Frank. *L'expérience huguenote au Nouveau Monde (XVIe siècle)*. Geneva: Droz, 1996.

————. *Le huguenot et le sauvage: La controverse coloniale en France au temps des Guerres de Religion (1555–1589)*. Paris: Aux Amateurs du Livre-Klincksieck, 1990.

Lewis, Wm. Roger, gen. ed. *The Oxford History of the British Empire*. Vol. 1, *Origins of Empire: British Overseas Enterprise to the Close of the Seventeenth Century*, ed. Nicholas P. Canny; vol. 2, *The Eighteenth Century*, ed. P. J. Marshall. Oxford: Oxford University Press, 1998.

Liechty, Daniel. *Sabbatarianism in the Sixteenth Century: A Page in the History of the Radical Reformation*. Berrien Springs, Mich.: Andrews University Press, 1993.

Ligou, Daniel. *Le protestantisme en France de 1598 à 1715*. Paris: SEDES, 1968.

Lillywhite, Bryant. *London Coffee Houses: A Reference Book of Coffee Houses of the Seventeenth, Eighteenth, and Nineteenth Centuries*. London: George Allen and Unwin, 1963.

Linder, Suzanne Cameron. *Anglican Churches in Colonial South Carolina: Their History and Architecture*. Charleston, S.C.: Wyrick and Company, 2000.

Littlefield, Daniel C. *Rice and Slaves: Ethnicity and the Slave Trade in Colonial South Carolina*. Urbana and Chicago: University of Illinois Press, 1991.

Lossky, Andrew. *Louis XIV and the French Monarchy*. New Brunswick, N.J.: Rutgers University Press, 1994.

Lough, John. *France Observed in the Seventeenth Century by British Travellers*. Stockfield, U.K.: Oriel Press, 1985.

————, ed. *Introduction to Seventeenth-Century France*. New York: David McKay Company, 1966.

Lovejoy, David S. *Religious Enthusiasm in the New World: Heresy to Revolution*. Cambridge, Mass.: Harvard University Press, 1985.

Ludlum, David M. *Early American Hurricanes, 1492–1870*. Boston: American Meteorological Society, 1963.

Lyon, Eugene. *The Enterprise of Florida: Pedro Menéndez de Avilés and the Spanish Conquest of 1565–1568*. Gainesville: University Presses of Florida, 1976.

Magdelaine, Michèle, and Rudolf von Thadden, eds. *Le refuge huguenot*. Paris: Armand Colin, 1985.

Magdelaine, Michèle, Rudolf von Thadden, Maria-Christina Pitassi, Ruth Whelan, and Antony McKenna, eds. *De l'humanisme aux lumières, Bayle et le protestantisme: Mélanges en l'honneur d'Élisabeth Labrousse.* Oxford: Voltaire Foundation, 1996.

Mandrou, Robert. *Louis XIV en son temps, 1661–1715.* Paris: Presses Universitaires de France, 1973.

Manross, William W. *The Fulham Papers in the Lambeth Palace Library: American Colonial Section Calendar and Indexes.* Oxford: Clarendon Press, 1965.

———. *S.P.G. Papers in the Lambeth Palace Library: Calendar and Indexes.* Oxford: Clarendon Press, 1974.

Marienstras, Richard. *Le proche et le lointain sur Shakespeare, le drame élisabéthain et l'idéologie anglaise aux XVIe et XVIIe siècles.* Paris: Les Éditions de Minuit, 1981.

Martinière, Guy, Didier Poton, and François Souty, eds. *D'un rivage à l'autre: Villes et protestantisme dans l'aire atlantique (XVIe–XVIIe siècles).* Paris: Imprimerie Nationale, 1999.

Mayeur, J. M., C. Petri, L. Pietri, A. Vauchez, and M. Vénard, gen. eds. *Histoire du christianisme: Des origines à nos jours.* Vol. 9, *L'âge de raison (1620/30–1750).* Ed. M. Venard. Paris: Desclée de Brouwer, 1997.

McCrady, Edward. *The History of South Carolina under the Proprietary Government, 1670–1719.* 1897. Reprint, New York: Russell & Russell, 1969.

McCusker, John J. *Money and Exchange in Europe & America, 1600–1775: A Handbook.* Chapel Hill: University of North Carolina Press, 1978.

McCusker, John J., and Russell R. Menard. *The Economy of British America, 1607–1789.* Chapel Hill: University of North Carolina Press, 1985.

McD. Beckles, Hilary. *A History of Barbados: From Amerindian Settlement to Nation-State.* Cambridge: Cambridge University Press, 1990.

McFarlane, Anthony. *The British in the Americas, 1480–1815.* New York: Longman, 1994.

McGrath, John T. *The French in Early Florida: In the Eye of the Hurricane.* Gainesville: University Presses of Florida, 2000.

Méchoulan, Henri, and Joël Cornette, eds. *L'état classique: Regards sur la pensée politique de la France dans le second XVIIe siècle.* Paris: J. Vrin, 1996.

Meinig, D. W. *The Shaping of America: A Geographical Perspective on 500 Years of History.* Vol. 1, *Atlantic America, 1492–1800.* New Haven: Yale University Press, 1986.

Mellot, Jean-Dominique, and Élisabeth Queval, ed. *Répertoire d'imprimeurs/libraires, XVIe–XVIIIe siècle.* Paris: Bibliothèque Nationale de France, 1997.

Mentzer, Raymond A., ed. *Sin and the Calvinists: Morals Control and the Consistory in the Reformed Tradition.* Kirksville, Mo.: Sixteenth Century Journal Publishers, 1994.

Mentzer, Raymond A., and Andrew Spicer, eds. *Society and Culture in the Huguenot World, 1559–1685.* Cambridge: Cambridge University Press, 2002.

Merriwether, Robert L. *The Expansion of South Carolina, 1729–1765.* Kingsport, Tenn.: Southern Publishers, 1940.

Meyer, Jean, and Jean-Pierre Poussou. *Études sur les villes françaises: Milieu du XVIIe siècle à la veille de la Révolution française.* Paris: SEDES, 1995.

Miller, John. *James II: A Study in Kingship.* Hove, U.K.: Wayland Publishers, 1978.

———. *Popery and Politics in England, 1660–1688.* Cambridge: Cambridge University Press, 1973.

———, ed. *L'Europe protestante aux XVIe et XVIIe siècles.* Paris: Belin, 1997.

Moch, Leslie P. *Moving Europeans: Migration in Western Europe since 1650.* Bloomington: Indiana University Press, 1992.

Morgan, Philip D. *Slave Counterpoint: Black Culture in the Eighteenth-Century Chesapeake & Lowcountry.* Chapel Hill: University of North Carolina Press, 1998.

Moureau, François, ed. *Les presses grises: La contrefaçon du livre (XVIe–XIXe siècles)*. Paris: Aux Amateurs du Livre, 1988.

Mours, Samuel. *Essai sommaire de géographie du protestantisme réformé français au XVIIe siècle*. Paris: Librairie Protestante, 1966.

———. *Le protestantisme en Vivarais et en Velay: Des origines à nos jours*. Valence: Imprimeries Réunies, 1949.

Munck, Thomas. *Seventeenth Century Europe: State, Conflict and the Social Order in Europe, 1598–1700*. New York: St. Martin's Press, 1990.

Nassiet, Michel. *La France du second XVIIe siècle*. Paris: Éditions Belin, 1997.

Negroni, Barbara de. *Intolérances: Catholiques et protestants en France, 1560–1787*. Paris: Hachette, 1996.

Otterness, Philip. *Becoming German: The 1709 Palantine Migration to New York*. Ithaca, N.Y.: Cornell University Press, 2004.

Pannier, Jacques. *Les origines de la Confesssion de foi et la Discipline des Églises réformées de France: Étude historique*. Paris: Librairie Félix Alcan, 1936.

Pascoe, Charles F. *Classified Digest of the Records of the Society of the Gospel in Foreign Parts, 1701–1892*. London: Society's Office, 1895.

Peabody, Sue. *"There Are No Slaves in France": The Political Culture of Race and Slavery in the Ancien Régime*. New York: Oxford University Press, 1996.

Pérouas, Louis. *Le diocèse de La Rochelle de 1648 à 1724: Étude de sociologie pastorale*. Paris: S.E.V.P.E.N, 1964.

Pétré-Grenouilleau, Olivier. *Les négoces maritimes français, XVIIe–XXe siècle*. Paris: Éditions Belin, 1997.

Pettigree, Andrew, ed. *The Reformation World*. New York: Routledge, 2000.

Phillips, Henry. *Church and Culture in Seventeenth-Century France*. Cambridge: Cambridge University Press, 1997.

Pillorget, René, and Suzanne Pillorget. *France Baroque, France Classique, 1589–1715*. 2 vols. Paris: Robert Laffont, 1995.

Pincus, Steven C. A. *Protestantism and Patriotism: Ideologies and the Making of English Foreign Policy, 1650–1668*. Cambridge: Cambridge University Press, 1996.

Pitassi, Maria-Christina. *Édifier ou instruire? Les avatars de la liturgie réformée du XVIe au XVIIe siècle,* Paris: Honoré Champion, 2000.

Pointer, Richard W. *Protestant Pluralism and the New York Experience: A Study of Eighteenth-Century Religious Diversity*. Bloomington: Indiana University Press, 1988.

Poton, Didier, and Patrick Cabanel. *Les protestants français du XVIe au XXe siècle*. Paris: Nathan, 1994.

Powell, William S. *The Proprietors of Carolina*. Raleigh, N.C.: State Department of Archives and History, 1963.

Prestwich, Menna, ed. *International Calvinism, 1541–1715*. Oxford: Clarendon Press, 1985.

Quéniart, Jean. *La révocation de l'Édit de Nantes: Protestants et catholiques français de 1598 à 1685*. Paris: Desclée de Brouwer, 1985.

Quinn, David B. *Set Fair for Roanoke: Voyages and Colonies, 1584–1606*. Chapel Hill: University of North Carolina Press, 1985.

Raimo, John W. *Biographical Directory of American Colonial and Revolutionary Governors, 1607–1789*. Westport, Conn.: Meckler Books, 1980.

Raven, James. *London Booksellers and American Customers: Transatlantic Literary Community and the Charleston Library Society, 1748–1811*. Columbia: University of South Carolina Press, 2002.

Ravenel, Henry E. *Ravenel Records*. 1898. Dunwoody, Ga.: N. S. Berg, 1971.

Le refuge huguenot. Special issue, *Bulletin de la Société de l'Histoire du Protestantisme Français* 115 (1969).

Reps, John W. *The Making of Urban America: A History of City Planning in the United States*. Princeton, N.J.: Princeton University Press, 1965.

Richard, Michel-Edmond. *La vie des protestants français de l'Édit de Nantes à la Révolution (1598–1789)*. 1966. Paris: Les Éditions de Paris, 1994.

Riesenberg, Peter. *Citizenship in the Western Tradition: Plato to Rousseau*. Chapel Hill: University of North Carolina Press, 1992.

Rivers, William J. *A Sketch of the History of South Carolina*. 1856. Spartanburg, S.C.: The Reprint Company, 1972.

Roper, Louis H. *Conceiving Carolina: Proprietors, Planters, and Plots, 1662–1729*. New York: Palgrave, 2004.

Rothrock, George A. *The Huguenots: A Biography of a Minority*. Chicago: Nelson-Hall, 1979.

Roussel, Bernard, ed. *Coexister dans l'intolérance: L'Édit de Nantes (1598)*. Special issue, *Bulletin de la Société de l'Histoire du Protestantisme Français* 144 (1998).

Rowland, Larry S. *Window on the Atlantic: The Rise and Fall of Santa Elena, South Carolina's Spanish City*. Columbia: South Carolina Department of Archives and History, 1990.

Rowland, Larry S., Alexander Moore, and George C. Rogers Jr. *The History of Beaufort County, South Carolina*. Vol. 1, *1514–1861*. Columbia: University of South Carolina Press, 1996.

Rumbold, Margaret E. *Pierre Coste: Traducteur huguenot*. New York: Peter Lang, 1991.

Salinger, Sharon V. *"To Serve Well and Faithfully": Labor and Indentured Servants in Pennsylvania, 1682–1800*. Cambridge: Cambridge University Press, 1987.

Sanchez, Jean-Pierre. *Mythes et légendes de la conquête de l'Amérique*. 2 vols. Rennes: Presses Universitaires de Rennes, 1996.

Saupin, Guy, ed. *Tolérance et intolérance de l'Édit de Nantes à nos jours*. Rennes: Presses Universitaires de Rennes, 1998.

Savage, Henry, Jr. *River of the Carolinas: The Santee*. New York: Rinehart & Company, Inc., 1956.

Schalk, Ellery. *From Valor to Pedigree: Ideas of Nobility in France in the Sixteenth and Seventeenth Centuries*. Princeton, N.J.: Princeton University Press, 1986.

Scherer, Lester B. *Slavery and the Churches in Early America, 1619–1819*. Grand Rapids, Mich.: William B. Eerdmans, 1975.

Schwartz, Hillel. *The French Prophets: The History of a Millenarian Group in Eighteenth-Century England*. Berkeley: University of California Press, 1980.

―――. *Knaves, Fools, Madmen, and That Subtile Effluvium: A Study of the Opposition to the French Prophets in England, 1706–1710*. Gainesville: University Presses of Florida, 1978.

Schwartz, Sally. *"A Mixed Multitude": The Struggle for Toleration in Colonial Pennsylvania*. New York: New York University Press, 1987.

Scouloudi, Irene, ed. *Huguenots in Britain and Their French Background, 1550–1800*. Totowa, N.J.: Barnes & Noble Books, 1987.

Scoville, Warren C. *The Persecution of Huguenots and French Economic Development, 1680–1720*. Berkeley: University of California Press, 1960.

Seacord, Morgan H. *Biographical Sketches and Index of Huguenot Settlers of New Rochelle, 1687–1776*. New Rochelle, N.Y.: Huguenot and Historical Association of New Rochelle, 1941.

Sellier, Jean. *Atlas historique des provinces et régions de France: Genèse d'un peuple*. Paris: La Découverte, 1997.

Severens, Kenneth. *Charleston Antebellum Architecture and Civic Destiny*. Knoxville: University of Tennessee Press, 1988.

Simmons, R. C. *The American Colonies: From Settlement to Independence.* New York: W. W. Norton & Company, 1976.

Sirmans, M. Eugene. *South Carolina: A Political History, 1663–1763.* Chapel Hill: University of North Carolina Press, 1966.

Smedley-Weil, Anette. *Les intendants de Louis XIV.* Paris: Fayard, 1995.

Smiles, Samuel. *The Huguenots: Their Settlements, Churches, and Industries in England and Ireland with an Appendix Relating to the Huguenots in America.* 1868. Baltimore: Genealogical Publishing Co., 1972.

Smith, Raymond, comp. *Records of the Royal Bounty and Connected Funds, the Burn Donation, and the Savoy Church in the Huguenot Library, University College, London.* Quarto Series, vol. 51. London: Huguenot Society of Great Britain and Ireland Publications, 1974.

Soderlund, Jean R. *Quakers & Slavery: A Divided Spirit.* Princeton, N.J.: Princeton University Press, 1985.

Sosin, J. M. *English America and the Restoration Monarchy of Charles II: Transatlantic Politics, Commerce, and Kinship.* Lincoln: University of Nebraska Press, 1980.

Sparks, Jared. *Life of John Ribault: Comprising an Account of the French to Found a Colony in North America.* Library of American Biography, vol. 17. Boston: Library of American Biography, 1836.

Spurr, John. *The Restoration Church of England, 1646–1689.* New Haven, Conn.: Yale University Press, 1991.

Stanton, Phoebe B. *The Gothic Revival & American Church Architecture: An Episode in Taste, 1840–1856.* Baltimore: Johns Hopkins University Press, 1968.

Statt, Daniel. *Foreigners and Englishmen: The Controversy over Immigration and Population, 1660–1760.* Newark: University of Delaware Press, 1995.

Steedman, Marguerite C. *A Short History of the Huguenot Church of Charleston, South Carolina.* Charleston, S.C.: Nelson Printing Corporation, 1983.

Steele, Ian K. *Politics of Colonial Policy: The Board of Trade in Colonial Administration, 1696–1720.* Oxford: Clarendon Press, 1968.

Stoeffler, F. Ernest, ed. *Continental Pietism and Early American Christianity.* Grand Rapids, Mich.: Wm. B. Eerdmans, 1976.

Sunshine, Glenn S. *Reforming French Protestantism: The Development of Huguenot Ecclesiastical Institutions, 1557–1572.* Kirksville, Mo.: Truman State University Press, 2003.

Sutherland, N. M. *The Huguenot Struggle for Recognition.* New Haven, Conn.: Yale University Press, 1980.

Sykes, Norman. *The Church of England and Non-Episcopal Churches in the Sixteenth and Seventeenth Centuries.* London: SPCK, 1948.

Sykes, Stephen, John Booty, and Jonathan Knight, eds. *The Study of Anglicanism.* 1988. 2nd rev. ed., London: SPCK/Fortress Press, 1998.

Tolley, Michael C. *Courts of Admiralty in Colonial America: The Maryland Experience, 1634–1776.* Durham, N.C.: Carolina Academic Press, 1995.

Tracy, James D., ed. *The Rise of Merchant Empires: Long-Distance Trade in the Early Modern World, 1350–1750.* Cambridge: Cambridge University Press, 1990.

Tyacke, Nicholas. *Anti-Calvinists: The Rise of English Arminianism, c. 1590–1640.* Oxford: Clarendon Press, 1987.

Van der Veer, Peter, ed. *Conversion to Modernities: The Globalization of Christianity.* New York: Routledge, 1996.

Van Deursen, Arie Theodorius. *Professions et métiers interdits: Un aspect de l'histoire de la révocation de l'Édit de Nantes.* Groningen: J. B. Wolters, 1960.

Van Ruymbeke, Bertrand, and Randy J. Sparks, eds. *Memory and Identity: The Huguenots in France and in the Atlantic Diaspora*. Columbia: University of South Carolina Press, 2003.

Ver Steeg, Clarence L. *Origins of a Southern Mosaic: Studies of Early Carolina and Georgia*. Athens: University of Georgia Press, 1975.

Walsh, John, Colin Haydon, and Stephen Taylor, eds. *The Church of England, c. 1689–c. 1833: From Toleration to Tractarianism*. Cambridge: Cambridge University Press, 1994.

Walzer, Michael. *On Toleration*. New Haven, Conn.: Yale University Press, 1997.

Wanegffelen, Thierry. *L'Édit de Nantes: Une histoire européenne de la tolérance du XVIe au XXe siècle*. Paris: Le Livre de Poche, 1998.

Waring, Joseph I. *A History of Medicine in South Carolina, 1670–1825*. Charleston: South Carolina Medical Association, 1964.

Watts, Michael R. *The Dissenters: From the Reformation to the French Revolution*. Oxford: Clarendon Press, 1978.

Weir, Robert M. *Colonial South Carolina: A History*. Millwood, N.Y.: KTO Press, 1983.

Weiss, M. Charles. *History of the French Protestant Refugees from the Revocation of the Edict of Nantes to Our Own Days*. 2 vols. Trans. Henry W. Herbert. New York: Stringer & Townsend, 1854.

Wells, Charlotte C. *Law and Citizenship in Early Modern France*. Baltimore: Johns Hopkins University Press, 1995.

White, James F. *Protestant Worship and Church Architecture: Theological and Historical Considerations*. Oxford: Oxford University Press, 1964.

Wolf, Philippe, ed. *Histoire des protestants en France*. Toulouse: Éditions Privat, 1977.

Wood, Peter H. *Black Majority: Negroes in Colonial South Carolina from 1670 through the Stono Rebellion*. New York: Alfred A. Knopf, 1974.

Wood, Peter H., Gregory A. Waselkov, and M. Thomas Hatley, eds. *Powhatan's Mantle: Indians in the Colonial Southeast*. Lincoln: University of Nebraska Press, 1989.

Woolverton, John F. *Colonial Anglicanism in North America*. Detroit: Wayne State University Press, 1984.

Wright, J. Leitch, Jr. *Anglo-Spanish Rivalry in North America*. Athens: University of Georgia Press, 1971.

Yardeni, Myriam. *Le refuge huguenot: Assimilation et culture*. Paris: Honoré Champion, 2002.

———. *Le refuge protestant*. Paris: Presses Universitaires de France, 1985.

Zook, Melinda S. *Radical Whigs and Conspiratorial Politics in Late Stuart England*. University Park: Pennsylvania State University Press, 1999.

Zuber, Roger, and Laurent Theis, eds. *La révocation de l'Édit de Nantes et le protestantisme français en 1685*. Paris: Société de l'Histoire du Protestantisme Français, 1986.

Zysberg, André. *Les galériens: Vies et destins de 60 000 forçats sur les galères de France 1680–1748*. Paris: Seuil, 1987.

ARTICLES AND ESSAYS

Ackerman, Robert K. "Colonial Land Policies and the Slave Problem." *Proceedings of the South Carolina Historical Association* (1965): 28–35.

Adamş, Geoffrey. "Monarchistes ou républicains?" Special issue, *Dix-huitième Siècle* 17 (1985): 83–95.

Bédard, Marc-André. "Les protestants en Nouvelle-France." *Cahiers d'Histoire de la Société Historique de Québec* 31 (1978): 1–141.

Birnstiel, Eckart. "Le retour des huguenots du refuge en France." *Bulletin de la Société de l'Histoire du Protestantisme Français* 135 (1989): 765–90.

Bolton, Charles. "South Carolina and the Reverend Doctor Francis Le Jau: Southern Society and the Conscience of an Anglican Missionary." *Historical Magazine of the Protestant Episcopal Church* 40 (1971): 63–79.

Bonomi, Patricia U., and Peter R. Eisenstadt. "Church Adherence in the Eighteenth-Century British American Colonies." *William and Mary Quarterly* 34 (1982): 245–86.

Bosher, John F. "Huguenot Merchants and the Protestant International in the Seventeenth Century." *William and Mary Quarterly,* 3rd series, 52 (1995): 77–102.

Bost, Hubert. "Les 400 ans de l'Édit de Nantes: Oubli civique et mémoire historique." in Hubler et al., eds., *L'Édit de Nantes revisité,* 55–77.

Brown, Philip M. "Early Indian Trade in the Development of South Carolina: Politics, Economics, and Social Mobility during the Proprietary Period, 1670–1719." *South Carolina Historical Magazine* 76 (1975): 118–28.

Bugg, James L. "The French Huguenot Frontier Settlement of Manakintown." *Virginia Magazine of History and Biography* 61 (1953): 360–94.

Bultmann, William A. "The SPG and the French Huguenots in Colonial America." *Historical Magazine of the Protestant Episcopal Church* 20 (1951): 156–72.

Campbell, Mildred. "'Of People Either Too Few or Too Many': The Conflict of Opinion on Population and Its Relation to Emigration." In *Conflict in Stuart England: Essays in Honour of Wallace Notestein,* edited by William A. Aiken and Basil D. Henning, 171–201. 1960. London: Archon Books, 1970.

Carlo, Paula W. "'Playing Fast and Loose with the Canons and Rubrick': French Anglicanism in Colonial New Rochelle, New York." *Journal of the Canadian Church Historical Society* 44 (2002): 35–50.

Carney, Judith. "Rice Milling, Gender and Slave Labour in Colonial South Carolina." *Past and Present* 153 (1996): 108–34.

Carpenter, A. H. "Naturalization in England and the American Colonies." *American Historical Review* 9 (1904): 288–303.

Childs, St. Julien R. "The Petit-Guérard Colony." *South Carolina Historical and Genealogical Magazine* 43 (1942): 1–17, 88–97.

Christin, Olivier. "L'Édit de Nantes: Bilan historiographique." *Revue historique* 301 (1999): 128–35.

Clifton, James M. "The Rice Industry in Colonial America." *Agricultural History* 55 (1981): 265–83.

Cohen, Robert, and Myriam Yardeni, eds. "Un Suisse en Caroline du Sud à la fin du XVIIe siècle." *Bulletin de la Société de l'Histoire du Protestantisme Français* 137 (1987): 66.

Cohen, Sheldon. "Elias Neau, Instructor to New York Slaves." *New-York Historical Society Quarterly* 55 (1971): 7–27.

Coleman, D. C. "Mercantilism Revisited." *Historical Journal* 23 (1980): 773–91.

Cottret, Bernard. "Religious or Secular? The Edict of Nantes, Reformation and State Formation in Late Sixteenth-Century France." In *Toleration and Religious Identity: The Edict of Nantes and Its Implications in France, Britain and Ireland,* edited by R. Whelan and C. Baxter, 107–27. Dublin: Four Courts Press, 2003.

Debien, Gabriel. "L'émigration poitevine vers l'Amérique au XVIIe siècle." *Notes d'Histoire Coloniale* 26 (1952): 1–31.

DePratter, Chester B., Stanley South, and James Legg. "The Discovery of Charlesfort (1562–1563)." *Huguenot Society of South Carolina Transactions* 101 (1996): 39–48.

Dunn, Richard S. "The English Sugar Islands and the Founding of South Carolina." *South Carolina Historical Magazine* 72 (1971): 81–93.

————. "William Penn and the Selling of Pennsylvania, 1681–1685." *Proceedings of the American Philosophical Society* 127 (1983): 322–29.

Eltis, David. "The Volume and Structure of the Transatlantic Slave Trade: A Reassessment." Special issue, *William and Mary Quarterly* 58 (2001): 17–46.

Escott, Margaret M. "Profiles of Relief: Royal Bounty Grants to Huguenot Refugees, 1686–1709." *Huguenot Society of Great Britain and Ireland Proceedings* 25 (1991): 257–78.

Faust, Albert B."Swiss Emigration to the American Colonies in the Eighteenth Century." *American Historical Review* 22 (1916–17): 21–44.

Flaningam, John. "The Occasional Conformity Controversy: Ideology and Party Politics, 1697–1711." *Journal of British Studies* 17 (1977): 38–62.

Glausser, Wayne. "Three Approaches to Locke and the Slave Trade." *Journal of the History of Ideas* 51 (1990): 199–216.

Gourdin, Virginia. "Madeleine Chardon, of Tours, Touraine and Her Family." *Huguenot Society of South Carolina Transactions* 91 (1986): 64–104.

Gusdorf, Georges. "L'Europe protestante au siècle des Lumières." Special issue, *Dix-huitième Siècle* 17 (1985): 13–40.

Gwynn, Robin D. "The Arrival of Huguenot Refugees in England, 1680–1705." *Huguenot Society of Great Britain and Ireland Proceedings* 21 (1969): 366–73.

————. "James II in the Light of His Treatment of Huguenot Refugees in England, 1685–1686." *Huguenot Society of Great Britain and Ireland Proceedings* 23 (1980): 212–25.

Haan, Richard L. "The 'Trade Do's Not Flourish as Formerly': The Ecological Origins of the Yamassee War." *Ethnohistory* 28 (1981): 341–58.

Haw, James. "Political Representation in South Carolina, 1669–1794: Evolution of a Lowcountry Tradition." *South Carolina Historical Magazine* 103 (2002): 106–29.

Hirsch, Arthur H. "French Influence on American Agriculture in the Colonial Period with Special Reference to Southern Provinces." *Agricultural History* 4 (1930): 1–9.

————. "Reverend Francis LeJau, First Rector of St. James Church, Goose Creek S.C." *Huguenot Society of South Carolina Transactions* 34 (1929): 25–43.

Hoffman, Paul E. "The Chicora Legend and Franco-Spanish Rivalry in *La Florida*." *Florida Historical Quarterly* 62 (1984): 419–38.

Hoyt, Edward A. "Naturalization under the American Colonies: Signs of a New Community." *Political Science Quarterly* 67 (1952): 248–66.

Inscoe, John C. "Carolina Slave Names: An Index to Acculturation." *Journal of Southern History* 49 (1983): 527–54.

Kane, Hope F. "Notes on the Early Pennsylvania Promotion Literature." *Pennsylvania Magazine of History and Biography* 63 (1939): 144–68.

Kingdon, Robert M. "Pourquoi les réfugiés huguenots aux colonies américaines sont-ils devenus épiscopaliens?" Special issue, *Bulletin de la Société de l'Histoire du Protestantisme Français,* 115 (1969): 487–509.

————. "Why Did the Huguenot Refugees in the American Colonies Become Episcopalians?" *Historical Magazine of the Protestant Episcopal Church* 49 (1980): 317–35.

Kleinman, Ruth. "Changing Interpretations of the Edict of Nantes: The Administrative Aspect, 1643–1661." *French Historical Studies* 10 (1978): 541–71.

Kopperman, Paul E. "Profile of a Failure: The Carolana Project, 1629–1640." *North Carolina Historical Review* 59 (1982): 1–23.

Laing, Annette. "'A Very Immoral and Offensive Man': Religious Culture, Gentility and the Strange Case of Brian Hunt, 1727." *South Carolina Historical Magazine* 103 (2002): 6–29.

Lestringant, Frank. "Geneva and America in the Renaissance: The Dream of a Huguenot Refuge, 1555–1560." Trans. Ann Blair. *Sixteenth-Century Journal* 26 (1995): 285–97.

Levis, R. Barry. "The Failure of the Anglican-Prussian Ecumenical Effort of 1710–1714." *Church History* 47 (1978): 381–99.

Little, Thomas J. "The South Carolina Slave Laws Reconsidered, 1670–1700." *South Carolina Historical Magazine* 94 (1993): 86–101.

Maillard, Th. "Les routes de l'exil du Poitou vers les îles Normandes et l'Angleterre: Le guide Pierre Michaut." *Bulletin de la Société de l'Histoire du Protestantisme Français* 49 (1900): 281–91.

McLoughlin, William G., and Winthrop D. Jordan, eds. "Baptists Face the Barbarities of Slavery in 1710." *Journal of Southern History* 29 (1963): 495–501.

Mentzer, Raymond A. "*Disciplina nervus ecclesiae:* The Calvinist Reform of Morals at Nîmes." *Sixteenth Century Journal* 18 (1987): 89–115.

Merrens, H. Roy. "The Physical Environment of Early America: Images and Image Makers in Colonial South Carolina." *Geographical Review* 59 (1969): 245–68.

Merrens, H. Roy, and George D. Terry. "Dying in Paradise: Malaria, Mortality, and the Perceptual Environment in Colonial South Carolina." *Journal of Southern History* 4 (1984): 533–50.

Moogk, Peter N. "Reluctant Exiles: Emigrants from France in Canada before 1760." *William and Mary Quarterly* 46 (1989): 463–505.

Moore, John Alexander. "Daniel Axtell's Account Book and the Economy of Early South Carolina." *South Carolina Historical Magazine* 95 (1994): 280–301.

Morgan, Philip D. "Work and Culture: The Task System and the World of Lowcountry Blacks, 1700–1880." In Robert Blair St. George, *Material Life in America, 1600–1860,* 203–29. Boston: Northeastern University Press, 1988.

Morris, Kenneth R. "Theological Sources of William Penn's Concept of Religious Toleration." *Journal of Church and State* 35 (1993): 83–111.

Nash, R. C. "South Carolina and the Atlantic Economy in the Late Seventeenth and Eighteenth Centuries." *Economic History Review* 45 (1992): 677–702.

———. "Trade and Business in Eighteenth-Century South Carolina: The Career of John Guerard, Merchant and Planter." *South Carolina Historical Magazine* 96 (1995): 6–29.

Olson, Alison G. "The Commissaries of the Bishop of London in Colonial Politics." In *Anglo-American Political Relations, 1675–1775,* edited by Alison G. Olson and Richard M. Brown, 109–24. New Brunswick, N.J.: Rutgers University Press, 1970.

Ormrod, David. "The Atlantic Economy and the 'Protestant Capitalist International,' 1651–1775." *Historical Research* 66 (1993): 197–208.

Otto, John S. "Livestock-Raising in Early South Carolina, 1670–1700: Prelude to the Rice Plantation Economy." *Agricultural History* 61 (1987): 13–24.

Parker, Mattie E. E. "The First Fundamental Constitutions of Carolina." *South Carolina Historical Magazine* 71 (1970): 78–85.

Pennington, Edgar L. "The Reverend Francis Le Jau's Work among Indians and Negro Slaves." *Journal of Southern History* 1 (1935): 442–58.

———. "The S.P.G. Anniversary Sermons, 1702–1783." *Historical Magazine of the Protestant Episcopal Church* 20 (1951): 10–43.

Pincus, Steven C. A. "From Butterboxes to Wooden Shoes: The Shift in English Popular Sentiment from Anti-Dutch to Anti-French in the 1670s." *Historical Journal* 38 (1995): 333–61.

———. "Republicanism, Absolutism and Universal Monarchy: English Popular Sentiment during the Third Dutch War." In *Culture and Society in the Stuart Restoration: Literature, Drama, History,* edited by Gerald Maclean, 241–66. Cambridge: Cambridge University Press, 1995.

Pitassi, Maria-Christina. "D'une parole à l'autre: Les sermons du théologien genevois Jean-Alphonse Turrettini (1671–1737)." *Annali di storia dell'esegesi* 10 (1993): 71–93.

Porcher, Richard D. "Rice Culture in South Carolina: A Brief History, the Role of the Huguenots, and Preservation of Its Legacy." *Huguenot Society of South Carolina Transactions* 92 (1987): 1–20.

Poton, Didier. "Le consistoire de l'église réformée de Saint-Jean-du-Gard au XVIIe siècle: Élection et composition sociale (1605–1685)." In *Sociétés et idéologies des Temps modernes: Hommage à Arlette Jouanna,* edited by J. Fouilleron, G. Le Thiec, and H. Michel, 247–57. Montpellier: Presses Universitaires de Montpellier, 1996.

———. "Le consistoire protestant au XVIIe siècle: Un tribunal des mœurs?" In *Ordre moral et délinquance de l'Antiquité au XXe siècle,* edited by Benoît Garnot. Dijon: Publications de l'Université de Bourgogne, 1994.

———. "Les finances des églises réformées du 'Moyen-Poitou' au XVIIe siècle: L'exemple de Niort (1629–1684)." In *Entre idéal et réalité,* edited by M. Aubrun, G. Audisio, B. Dompnier, and A. Gueslin, 135–45. Clermont-Ferrand: Publications de l'Institut d'Études du Massif Central, 1993.

———. "La monarchie et les protestants en France au XVIIIe siècle." In *Lectures de Voltaire: Le traité sur la tolérance,* edited by Isabelle Brouard-Arends. Rennes: Presses Universitaires de Rennes, 1999.

Poton, Didier, and Bertrand Van Ruymbeke. "Élie Neau: 'Galérien pour la foi' (1669–1722)." In *La violence et la mer dans l'espace atlantique, XIIe–XIXe siècle,* edited by Mickaël Augeron and Mathias Tranchant, 325–36. Rennes: Presses Universitaires de Rennes, 2004.

Poussou, Jean-Pierre. "Les mouvements migratoires en France et à partir de la France de la fin du XVe siècle au début du XIXe siècle: Approches pour une synthèse." *Annales de Démographie Historique* (1970): 11–78.

Powell, William S. "Carolina in the Seventeenth Century: An Annotated Bibliography of Contemporary Publications." *North Carolina Historical Review* 41 (1964): 74–104.

———. "Carolina and the Incomparable Roanoke: Explorations and Attempted Settlements, 1620–1663." *North Carolina Historical Review* 51 (1974): 1–21.

Ramsey, William L. "A Coat for 'Indian Cuffy': Mapping the Boundary between Freedom and Slavery in Colonial South Carolina." *South Carolina Historical Magazine* 103 (2002): 48–66.

———. "'Something Cloudy in Their Looks': The Origins of the Yamassee War Reconsidered." *Journal of American History* 90 (2003): 44–75.

Rich, E. E. "The First Earl of Shaftesbury's Colonial Policy." *Transactions of the Royal Historical Society* 7 (1957): 47–70.

Robbins, Caroline. "A Note on General Naturalization under the Later Stuarts and a Speech in the House of Commons on the Subject in 1664." *Journal of Modern History* 24 (1962): 168–77.

Roussel, Bernard, and Solange Deyon. "Pour un nouvel 'Aymon': Les premiers Synodes nationaux des églises réformées en France (1559–1567)." *Bulletin de la Société de l'Histoire du Protestantisme Français* 139 (1993): 545–95.

Sahlins, Peter. "Fictions of a Catholic France: The Naturalization of Foreigners, 1685–1787." *Representations* 47 (1994): 85–110.

Scoville, Warren. "The Huguenots and the Diffusion of Technology." *Journal of Political Economy* 60 (1952): 294–311.

Skalski-Coignard, Jeanne. "Une famille languedocienne en Caroline du Sud: Les Gaillard." *Cahiers de Généalogie Protestante* 45 (1994): 9–13.

Smith, Henry A. M. "The Orange Quarter and the First French Settlers in South Carolina." *South Carolina Historical and Genealogical Magazine* 18 (1917): 101–23.

Smith, Raymond. "Financial Aid to French Protestant Refugees 1681–1727: Briefs and the Royal Bounty." *Huguenot Society of Great Britain and Ireland Proceedings* 23 (1973): 248–56.

Statt, Daniel. "The Birthright of an Englishman: The Practice of Naturalization and Denization of Immigrants under the Later Stuarts and Early Hanoverians." *Huguenot Society of Great Britain and Ireland Proceedings* 25 (1989): 61–74.

Sunshine, Glenn S. "Reformed Theology and the Origins of Synodical Polity: Calvin, Beza, and the Gallican Confession." In *Later Calvinism: International Perspectives,* edited by W. Fred Graham, 141–58. Kirksville: Northeast Missouri State University, 1994.

Taylor, Stephen. "Whigs, Bishops and America: The Politics of Church Reform in Mid-Eighteenth-Century England." *Historical Journal* 36 (1993): 331–36.

Thorp, Malcolm R. "The Anti-Huguenot Undercurrent in Late-Seventeenth-Century England." *Huguenot Society of Great Britain and Ireland Proceedings* 23 (1976): 569–80.

Timmons, Ray E. "The Huguenot Church Register of Pons France: Possible Denization and Migration to Charles Town." *Carolina Herald and Newsletter* 32, no. 1 (2004): 5–11.

Timothy, Eustace. "Anthony Ashley Cooper, Earl of Shaftesbury." In *Statesmen and Politicians of the Stuart Age,* edited by Eustace Timothy, 179–200. New York: St. Martin's Press, 1985.

Tulot, Jean-Luc. "Français et Suisses réfugiés en Caroline du Sud qui souhaitent être naturalisés anglais en 1696." *Cahiers du Centre de Généalogie Protestante* 70 (2000): 102–11.

Underwood, James L. "The Dawn of Religious Freedom in South Carolina: The Journey from Limited Tolerance to Constitutional Right." *South Carolina Law Review* 54 (2002): 111–80.

Van Ruymbeke, Bertrand. "*Cavalier* et *Puritan*. L'ancêtre huguenot au prisme de l'histoire américaine." Special issue, *Généalogies rêvées* 5 (2005): 5–22.

———. "'A Dominion of True Believers Not a Republic of Heretics': French Colonial Religious Policy and the Settlement of Early Louisiana (1699–1730)." In *French Colonial Louisiana and the Atlantic World,* edited by Bradley Bond, 83–94. Baton Rouge: Louisiana State University Press, forthcoming.

———. "Ethnic History and Mystic Chords of Memory: One Hundred and Twenty Years of Huguenot-Walloon Historiography in the United States (1883–2003). "*Bulletin du Centre d'Études Nord-américaines,* École des hautes études en sciences sociales, 8 (2002): 57–77.

———. "The Huguenots of Proprietary South Carolina: Patterns of Migration and Integration." In *Money, Trade, and Power: The Evolution of Colonial South Carolina's Plantation Society,* edited by Jack P. Greene, Rosemary Brana-Shute, and Randy J. Sparks, 26–48. Columbia: University of South Carolina Press, 2001.

———. "Minority Survival: The Huguenot Paradigm in France and in the Diaspora." In *Memory and Identity: The Huguenots in France and the Atlantic Diaspora,* edited by Bertrand Van Ruymbeke and Randy J. Sparks, 1–25. Columbia: University of South Carolina Press, 2003.

———. "Paul L'Escot, un ministre genevois à Charles Town (1700–1719)." *Études Francophones* 15 (1999): 147–62.

———. "Le refuge atlantique: La diaspora huguenote et l'Atlantique anglo-américain." In *D'un rivage à l'autre: Villes et protestantisme dans l'aire atlantique (XVIe–XVIIe siècles),* edited by Guy Martinière, Didier Poton, and François Souty, 195–204. Paris: Imprimerie Nationale, 1999.

———. "Un refuge avant le refuge? La 'Floride huguenote' et les orignes de la Caroline du Sud." In *Coligny, les protestants, et la mer,* edited by Martine Acerra and Guy Martinière, 235–45. Paris: Presses de l'Université de Paris-Sorbonne, 1997.

———. "The Walloon and Huguenot Elements in New Netherland and Seventeeth-Century New York: Identity, History, and Memory." In *Revisitng New Netherland: Perspectives on Early Dutch America,* edited by Joyce D. Goodfriend, 41–54. Leiden: Brill, 2005.

Waterhouse, Richard. "England, the Caribbean, and the Settlement of Carolina." *Journal of American Studies* 9 (1975): 259–81.

Wiecek, William M. "The Statutory Law of Slavery and Race in the Thirteen Mainland Colonies of British America." *William and Mary Quarterly* 34 (1977): 258–80.

Wilkie, Everett C. "The Authorship and Purpose of the *Histoire naturelle et morale des îles Antilles,* an Early Huguenot Emigration Guide." *Harvard University Library Bulletin* 38 (1991): 27–82.

Wood, Lillian F. "The Reverend John LaPierre." *Historical Magazine of the Protestant Episcopal Church* 40 (1971): 414–30.

Wood, Peter H. "'It was a Negro Taught Them,' a New Look at African Labor in Early South Carolina." *Journal of Asian and African Studies* 9 (1974): 160–79.

Wright, J. Leitch, Jr. "Spanish Reaction to Carolina." *North Carolina Historical Review* 41 (1964): 464–76.

Yardeni, Myriam. "Naissance et essor d'un mythe: La révocation de l'Édit de Nantes et le déclin économique de la France." *Bulletin de la Société de l'Histoire du Protestantisme Français* 139 (1993): 79–96.

DISSERTATIONS AND THESES

Bolton, Sidney C. "The Anglican Church of Colonial South Carolina, 1704–1754: A Study in Americanization." Ph.D. diss., University of Wisconsin, 1973.

Boucher, Philip. "France 'Discovers' America: The Image of Tropical America in Sixteenth and Seventeenth Century France and Its Impact on Early French Colonialism." Ph.D. diss., University of Connecticut, 1974.

Buchanan, J. E. "The Colleton Family and the Early History of South Carolina and Barbados." Ph.D. thesis, University of Edinburgh, 1989.

Carlo, Paula W. "The Huguenots of Colonial New Paltz and New Rochelle: A Social and Religious History." Ph.D. diss., City University of New York, 2001.

Carluer, Jean-Yves."Les protestants bretons, XVIe–XXe siècles." Thèse de doctorat, 4 vols., Université de Rennes, 1990.

Crouse, Maurice A. "The Manigault Family of South Carolina, 1685–1783." Ph.D. diss., Northwestern University, 1964.

Diffendal, Anne P. "The Society for the Propagation of the Gospel in Foreign Parts and the Assimilation of Foreign Protestants in British North America." Ph.D. diss., University of Nebraska, 1974.

Fagg, Daniel W. "Carolina, 1663–1683: The Founding of a Proprietary." Ph.D. diss., Emory University, 1970.

Friedlander, Amy E. "Carolina Huguenots: A Study in Cultural Pluralism in the Low Country, 1679–1768." Ph.D. diss., Emory University, 1979.

Hoez, Suzanne, and Andrée Ruffelard. "Les migrations protestantes sous le règne de Louis XIV: Essai sur l'état de la question." Thèse de doctorat, Université Panthéon-Sorbonne, 2 vols., 1978.

Kane, Hope F. "Colonial Promotion and Promotion Literature of Carolina, 1660–1700." Ph.D. diss., Brown University, 1930.

Laing, Annette S. "'All Things to All Men': Popular Religious Culture and the Anglican Mission in Colonial America, 1701–1750." Ph.D. diss., University of California, Riverside, 1995.

McGrath, John T. "France in America, 1555–1565: A Reevaluation of the Evidence." Ph.D. diss., Boston University, 1995.

Migliazzo, Arlin M. "Ethnic Diversity on the Southern Frontier: A Social History of Purrysburgh, South Carolina, 1732–1792." Ph.D. diss., Washington State University, 1982.

Miot-Duclouzeaux, Francine. "La révocation de l'Édit de Nantes et les protestants jusqu'à l'Édit de Tolérance (1787) en Aunis et Saintonge." Thèse de doctorat, Écoles des Chartes, 1964.

Moore, John A. "Royalizing South Carolina: The Revolution of 1719 and the Evolution of Early South Carolina Government." Ph.D. diss., University of South Carolina, 1991.

Nelson, John K. "Anglican Missions in America, 1701–1725: A Study of the Society for the Propagation of the Gospel in Foreign Parts." Ph.D. diss., Northwestern University, 1962.

Nishikawa, Sugiko. "English Attitudes toward Continental Protestants with Particular Reference to Church Briefs, c. 1680–1740." Ph.D. thesis, University of London, 1998.

Pennington, Loren E. "The Origins of English Promotional Literature for America, 1553–1625." Ph.D. diss., University of Michigan, 1962.

Pett-Conklin, Linda M. "Cadastral Surveying in Colonial South Carolina: A Historical Geography." Ph.D. diss., Louisiana State University and Agricultural and Mechanical College, 1986.

Snell, William. "Indian Slavery in Colonial South Carolina, 1671–1795." Ph.D. diss., University of Alabama, 1972.

Sundstrom, Roy A. "Aid and Assimilation: A Study of the Economic Support Given French Protestants in England, 1680–1727." Ph.D. diss., Kent State, 1972.

Terry, George D. "'Champaign Country': A Social History of an Eighteenth Century Lowcountry Parish in South Carolina, St. John's, Berkeley County." Ph.D. diss., University of South Carolina, 1981.

Thorp, Malcolm R. "The English Government and the Huguenot Settlement, 1680–1702." Ph.D. diss., University of Wisconsin, 1972.

Tobias, Leslie. "Manakintown: The Development and Demise of a French Protestant Refugee Community in Colonial Virginia, 1700–1750." Master's thesis, College of William and Mary, 1982.

Van Ruymbeke, Bertrand. "L'émigration huguenote en Caroline du Sud sous le régime des Seigneurs Propriétaires: Étude d'une communauté du Refuge dans une province britannique d'Amérique du Nord, 1680–1720." Thèse de doctorat, 2 vols., La Sorbonne-Nouvelle, 1995.

Watson, Alan D. "The Quitrent System in Royal South Carolina." Ph.D. diss., University of South Carolina, 1971.

Index